THE SOUL OF ADOLESCENCE ALIGNS WITH THE HEART OF DEMOCRACY

Orphans, Rebels and Civic Lovers Unite

ALFRED H. KURLAND

The Soul of Adolescence Aligns with the Heart of Democracy

Orphans, Rebels and Civic Lovers Unite

©2021 Alfred H. Kurland

print ISBN: 978-1-66780-141-4

ebook ISBN: 978-1-66780-142-1

IN REMEMBERANCE

I dedicate this book to those who have passed on. They exemplify the qualities I seek from a co-mentor in my life. Each has exemplified what it takes to provide guidance in life which keeps one aligned with life purpose and for dedication to pursuing the public good.

To my mother, Jane Claire (Johannet-Kurland) who was known to those who loved her as the Empress of Embrace. For those in her life who had been disowned and dispossessed from secure places, she provided sanctuary and support with grace. Jane Claire generously would open the door to our home to those who had been mistreated and lost. Orphans now had a new home.

To my father, John Kurland, who was a storyteller providing counsel to eager listeners with a flavor of humor and insight. John never gave up on his mission of challenging official authority or advocating for progressive causes. John, alongside his wife, Jane Claire, encouraged each of their four children, Alfred, Nicole, Jacquie and Pierre, to develop our own life story, and to live life according to our self-directed counsel. Rebels got to create and relate authentic story.

To Alan Kaplan, who had been my younger brother after my former marriage to Harriet Kaplan. Alan's life was cut short by a fatal childhood disease in 1972. His health made him vulnerable, but his spirit was, and continues as unconquerable. His presence and spirit invokes in those he loved a possession of limitless possibility. Alan lives on in the hearts and dreams of those he left behind. Alan was an artist and musician, who remains forever innocent, and continues to instill in us an eternal belief in better days.

To Paul Joseph Rothman (also known as PJ), a cousin to my siblings and I, who was more like another brother to us. He was always there for each of us and dedicated his life to keeping extended family close. PJ was a co-founder of the Search Alliance in southern California. Doctors and alternative health practitioners had conduced fast-track research in hope of finding treatments and ultimately a cure to AIDS. PJ succumbed to AIDS in early 1994.

To Richard Crenshaw, Jr. (also known as Rick), who served as a counselor and a big brother to those caught up in the perils of street life. Rick, without any reservations, would extend his helping hand to those in need, in pain, and to searchers seeking a new life. Rick would convince them, one moment at a time, to take the tiny steps leading to a life which could be good. Rick passed away during the COVID crisis in 2020.

To my younger brother, Pierre Kurland, who was taken away from his family, friends and co-workers who had adored him. His life ended when struck by a car on a street in San Fernando Valley on September 15, 2019. He left behind his wife, Susan, and three young adult children, Rebecca, Jon, and Jessica. Pierre would ceaselessly provide counsel and support to the family members he loved. He practiced by using the skill of Occam's Razor, taking the short route in solving problems, and with the patience of a saint. He encouraged each of us to extract wisdom through wandering, while at the same time inspiring us to maintain inner peace. Pierre never got to write the book he had dreamed about. This book is dedicated to Pierre as his book.

Acknowledgements

Just as it takes a village to raise a child, it takes an extended family to assist a change agent in community organizing and teen empowerment, as well as with inspiring a new writer. Those listed below, to whom I express gratitude, have given me essential guidance and enriched my life.

Those helping me in my early years of life includes Mr. Paul, a high school teacher from Jamaica High School in the 1960's, who encouraged my imaginative muscle. I also thank my student-organizer peers at Whittier College in the late 1960's – Roi Milton, Chris Paulino, Kent Somerville and John Taitano, who in sum introduced me to the counsel of eastern religious beliefs and to libraries of political liberation. My political science instructor, and advisor, was Peter Wengert, who worked at York College/CUNY in the early 1970s. He guided me in my development of a senior project, in which I had advocated for participatory civics instruction in high schools.

In the 1980s, after I had moved to Washington Heights, Dr. Albert Blumberg, and his executive committee members at the Audubon Reform Democratic Club taught me the techniques of co-joining grassroots work with reform politics, and for creating effective coalitions. Maria Luna and her sister, also in the 1980's, provided crucial support for me in guiding community-based initiatives. They also served on my first Board of Directors for my first neighborhood youth program, Southern Heights: Communities Organized for Public Service. Steve Simon, who had been a staff director and policy advisor for then Councilperson Stan Michels, made sure my youth programs got attention and support. He also co-edited with me my first neighborhood newsletter called the Riverside Heights Monitor. Jessica Brockington was a publisher and editor for the Washington Heights and Bridge Leader in the early 1990's. She published articles written by me which offered critique of flawed political policies and advocated for greater social justice. In the second decade of the 2000's, Robert K. Snyder, a writer and uptown historian, wrote a book titled Crossing Broadway, in which he highlighted the community work of Coach Dave Crenshaw and me. He placed our civic contributions in the larger context of advocacy and community building which has sustained Washington Heights since the 1930's. Ann Beaudry was my unofficial editor, who had been serving on the Board of Trustees for the Petra Foundation. She gave me endless hours of advice and critique with early drafts of this book written between 2009 and 2011. She inspired me to offer more compelling narrative and to provoke a sense of urgency for implementing my proposed policy changes for teen empowerment. I am also deeply indebted to the trustees for the Petra Foundation, and the 99 Petra Foundation Fellow, who provided soul-searching testimony about their commitment to community and insightful social justice storytelling. I also deeply appreciate the support given to me as a developing writer and author from members of the Unitarian-Universalist All Souls Church writers group, led by co-chairs Marilyn Mehr and Tim Kelly.

Teens involved in civic change, and the staff who mentored them in their organizing, have served as role models for me. I mention a few program names here, but I am indebted to teen officers and adult staff who led these projects. These teen leadership projects include the Southern Heights and Uptown Dreamer's Explorer Post #280, the Ivy League's Female Finesse, the Uptown Dreamer's Coaches Who Care, the IN-STEP program and Youth Link program at the Police Athletic League, the High School Congress representatives sponsored by the Future Voters of America, and the Action Civic Clubs promoted by Generation Citizen.

The final success of the Teens on Board campaign would not have been possible without the support of elected officials - Manhattan Borough

President Gale Brewer, City Councilperson Mark Levine, State Senator Lanza, and State Assemblymembers Brian Kavanagh and Nily Rozic.

Closest to me in my personal life is my goddaughter Aida E. Ramos. She has offered me crucial guidance and inspiration for never giving up on one's life purpose. She started, in her early days of schooling, as a special education castoff. After changing her mind about her capabilities and opening her heart to the higher angels in her universe, she changed the course of her life. She recently graduated from the Borough of Manhattan Community College at CUNY with honors. She is now enrolled at Columbia University as a major in sociology and ethnic studies and is pursuing a medical career path. One of her primary lessons for me is about transforming early life trauma into passionate and dedicated energy used for exploring personal truths and social justice.

Testimonials for *The Soul of Adolescence Aligns With the Heart of Democracy*

In my seventeen years as the principal of PS 128M in Washington Heights, I experienced many challenges related to over-crowding, split sessions, and budget constraints. I sought effective afterschool programming which engaged my most vulnerable students. When I opened my doors to Al Kurland, Dave Crenshaw, and the Uptown Dreamers, hundreds of students were coached and involved in art projects, sports, homework help, and much more by teen volunteers from the neighborhood. These teens were caring, involved and responsible for the decisions to implement projects. This afterschool approach provided teens with a framework of ongoing communication and affirmed involvement in the program. Teen volunteers were trusted by adult staff (who also were volunteers) and became instrumental in shaping one of the most effective afterschool programs under my tenure. Many of these teens became advocates against injustice and moved on to become model professionals in our community.

> *Blanca Battino, former principal of PS 128M (Manhattan); RTI Specialist; SEL trainer; and Vice-President for Community Services with Faith, Hope and Charity.*

Living in the southern section of Washington Heights in the nineteen eighties had its positives and its negatives. As a young girl relocating from Liberia, living in the United States was quite a cultural shock. Fortunately for me and my siblings, Al Kurland helped to challenge all that when he built a youth program in Washington Heights. Al helped to shape the minds of young people though various sport programs, allowing us leadership opportunities, and providing us with advocacy trainings. Through his dedication and hard work, beginning in the eighties, and continuing thereafter, moving on with my life was no longer a cultural shock for me. Washington Heights became a great place to live for me.

> **Miriam Payne,** *former volunteer teen leader for the Uptown Dreamers and for the Southern Heights afterschool program. I am also an alumnus of Explorer Post #280, a chartered, co-ed teen leadership program sponsored by the Greater NY Boy Scout Council. I currently hold a master's degree in social work earned at Columbia University.*

Teens have always been the secret weapon of the Uptown Team Dreamers program. One of the prime lessons I learned, while still a Hunter High School student years ago, was the prime importance of figuring out that at my core I was more than what I wore. It took the collaborative efforts of school staff and my fellow students to help me to figure this out. Each teen is like a cloud, what you see on the outside is only a cover for what is on the inside. Any given teen possesses their own source of strength. They can bring on thunder and lightning, or a summer shower to cool us off. Even when encountering a teen's inner storms, a mentor must reach into the cloud, through the turbulence, even through the cold and hail, to find the gold within, and the silver lining. Every young person contributes to constructing a rainbow. If you develop a relationship with a teen while believing all of this, you can find what enriches the character of a teen and assist them in generating a multiplication of social possibilities for the common good. When working from places of authentic partnership, 1 plus 1 adds up not to 2, but equals 11. Every student is a star, and it is up to us, as trusted adults to help them shine.

> **Coach Dave Crenshaw,** *Founder of the Uptown Team Dreamers, community coach and black health specialist.*

Early in my career, I had the honor of working with Al Kurland with the Police Athletic League's IN STEP program. (In School Student Training and Employment Program) My role was to support our youth advisory council and to facilitate the process of planning and hosting a citywide youth forum. During this period, I witnessed the incredible capacity of youth to be brave, to be creative, and to be engaged in their communities. In my experience, teenagers regularly demonstrate leadership, commitment, and vision. With one of our teen leadership initiatives, I took part in a campaign for obtaining the right of fully vetted sixteen- and seventeen-year-olds to serve on New York City Community Boards. As the field of youth development evolves, let us embrace the reality that the voices, action, and dreams of our youth will shape the future.

Marcel Braithwaite, Board member of the New York State Network of Youth Success

Years ago, I was a teen who had been involved with a Police Athletic League program called IN STEP. I took an active part in the campaign for obtaining the right of sixteen-and-seventeen-year-old teens to serve on New York City Community Boards. I had to learn the process of advocacy and organizing, as these were new to me. As teen leaders, we worked with youth development professionals, and with New York City elected officials such as then Councilperson Richie Torres, who was a strong advocate for our campaign. I gained exposure to the world of politics and to the workings of municipal government. I am now serving as a Director for a Police Athletic League center located at the Armory in Washington Heights. I now use the same techniques of empowerment that I learned as a teen. I develop programs that promote sports readiness and mental health for youth enrolled between elementary school through high school.

Ramon Spence, PAL INSTEP alumnus and currently a PAL Center Director

Mr. Kurland is a fervent advocate of the term "youth civic engagement". He has been committed for decades to serving his communities. His service includes having been a lead coordinator for the Teens on Community Boards campaign. Al has also been my civic soul mate in the Youth and Police Building Bridges initiative, which advocates for improved communication and program partnerships with the NYC Police Department's Neighborhood Policing program. A theme of this campaign, as with his book, is that when adolescent leaders are included in the civic problem-solving process, the building of trustworthy relationships with adults creates faith in one's neighborhood by all stakeholders.

Fe Florimon, Chair of the Youth Services and Education Committee for Community Board #12M. Former Manhattan Borough President appointee to the District #6 Community Education Council. Founder of the Youth and Police Building bridges campaign.

Al Kurland is a visionary, but his vision for a stronger democracy and a healthier society is grounded in experience and relationship. His programs are continuously co-created by him and his many collaborators, including teachers young and old, as well as friends. We all stand to learn from his example, and the lessons of his lifetime of work, which is defined by listening to and advocating with and for young people. After joining the teens on community boards campaign, I witnessed his humility, mastery and persistence first -hand. He taught me so much about letting young people lead, about knowing your strengths, and leveraging others in collaborative partnerships. His work is about building stronger programs and fighting for structural reform. This book is an inspiration for all of you who know there must be a better way, from one who has helped to blaze the trail, one courageous conversation at a time.

Sarah Andes, former National Director of Programming for Generation Citizen

Al Kurland has been a champion of youth civic participation in New York City for more than three decades. This book makes a valuable contribution to the Youth Studies literature by recounting historical and current movements to garner political power for and with New York City's youngest citizens. Learning from the hard-won struggle to serve on Community Boards is imperative for a new generation of youth and adults as they fight to lower the voting age, increase participatory budgeting, create the schools they deserve, move us toward restorative justice, and push elected officials to engage in intergenerational youth policymaking. Telling these stories of the past, including our triumphs and missteps, is critical to the evolution of youth movements in our city. I am grateful for this powerful personal narrative and dynamic history of youth movements in our city.

Sarah Zeller-Berkman, Ph.D. Director of Youth Studies at CUNY SPS and Director of the Intergenerational Change Initiative

At times, as an adult, I feel like a small fish in a big pond when dealing with the issue of promoting youth voice and power sharing. I work with youth services staff daily. In observing their methods of promoting youth engagement, I often see them using teens as tokens in the process and reserving decision-making exclusively for adults. In our civic practices with teens, there is a need for a language and cultural shift to change the narrative of hierarchical thinking about the place of young people in civic engagement. This change of course, with both conceptualization and practice demands of us some deep reflection. Authentic power sharing uses a holistic developmental paradigm, provides opportunities for cultivating responsive adult/ adolescent relationships, and promotes joint creation of vital resources for our schools, our communities and municipal governance.

Diane Shirley NY State T-Tap School Age PD Specialist; NY State SACC Credential Advisor and Endorser; NY State School-Age Credential Trainer

Al Kurland has taken on a formidable task: he is asking us adults to stop ignoring the future. We do precisely that when we fail to understand how our biggest debt is incurred when we fail to arm, protect, and train our young people to be prepared for a troubled world that adults have created for them. They will be inheriting the absolute mess we have created with the world's climate, and they will be struggling with the political outcomes of nearsighted, racist decision-making policies that will leave them to cope with a nation and a world that is horribly divided against itself. Al makes it clear; we need to do better. This book will help us to figure it out.

Robert E. Fullilove, Ed.D. Dr. Fullilove is the Associate Dean for Community and Minority Affairs, Professor of Clinical Sociomedical Sciences and Co-Director of the Cities Research Group at Columbia University School of Professional Studies. He is a three-time recipient of the Distinguished Teaching Award from the Mailman School of Public Health and teaches public health courses in six New York State prisons under the Bard College Prison Initiative.

CONTENTS

speak to the role of teen empowerment allies whom I call civic co-mentors. Co-mentors are social justice leaders who guide teens who learn to apply the principles and practices of civic engagement. Co-mentors relate well with teens, as they are empathetic leaders who keep their inner adolescent alive. Readers will also meet civic allies who have been important co-mentors for me, beginning in my youth, and continuing through the course of my leading teen empowerment programs. These co-mentors had a special impact on my developing a teen empowerment portfolio, teaching me about connections to social-emotional and soul-related intelligences. As part of their civic engagement portfolio, co-mentors navigate the congruent relationship between adolescent soul development and the attainment of fully inclusive democratic practice. This part of the book features episodes in which enlightened co-mentors and teens work on establishing beloved community. What results is an evolved set of democratic exercises, which affirm the presence of optimally developed teens who advocate for ecologically responsible and spiritually informed civic and governance practice.

IV. Afterwards

The final chapter of the book profiles promising practices led by teen social justice activists. A few of the movements I discuss are those which are teen-led initiatives in developmental stages, which are also teaching adults about successfully navigating for the needs of the 21st Century. The focus of these teen led groups focus on a wide range of needs, such as addressing issues from food justice to criminal justice. A new generation of teen social justice leaders are arising as we transition from an era of adult only civic leadership and electoral participation to an emergent eco-soulful era supportive of and encouraging teen initiatives through their inclusively welcomed civic participation. Also profiled are recommendations for lowering the voting age to sixteen, which are now on the federal legislative agenda, as well as introduced by New York State and California elected officials.

AUTHOR'S NOTE

A specter is haunting the American version of adultism.[1] Adultism, as defined by practitioners in the teen-enfranchisement movement, contains three elements. The first includes language and institutional practices, which lead to the demeaning of teen identity. The second includes a set of attitudes laying a basis for dismissal of their assets and inherent right to civic participation. The third involves a process of denial, which is the detachment of adults from taking responsibility for the negative outcomes experienced by teens as well as by their whole generation[2]. This book explores these topics in detail.

I have supported teen empowerment for thirty years. My position as an adult civic mentor to teens has allowed me to counsel teens who have participated in projects involving community improvement and municipal policy changes.[3] While many assume that adults are teachers, and youth are students, as I progressed through scores of social justice and community campaigns in which teens became involved, I made both cognitive adjustments and program changes reflective of the following tenets, which I now hold on to dearly:

First, teens have a fundamental right to articulate, advocate for, and address their concerns as equal partners within the sphere of civic life.

Second, adult leaders are crucially important for creating and sustaining rites of passage for the responsibilities of democratic citizenship.

Third, we have a historic imperative to release our old paradigm about the nature of adolescence and to embrace the new understandings that are now emerging. I describe the differences between falsely held assumptions in the past, and new understandings about the nature of adolescence in the forward/backward section of this book. In sum, professional constructs about adolescence have described them in terms of limitation and excess. The former is based upon outdated scientific studies about under-developed frontal lobes in the brain which dispose teens toward poor decision-making. These proposed links to a developing teen's biological and physiological structures are conflated with the socially constructed influences referred to by Dr. Martin Luther King's laments about our cultural and political production of what he describes as the four catastrophes— "institutional promotion of materialism, racism, poverty and militarism."[4] Bill Plotkin, the writer and proponent for cultivating individual wholeness and communal integrity, refers to these dire factors as responsible not for describing the real adolescent, but rather what he calls the "patho-adolescent."[5] Teens learn, through social training, to seek compulsive attachments, to reject others who are different from ourselves based upon biased perceptions, to hoard at the expense of vulnerable people being denied basic necessities, and resorting to excessive forms of violence when addressing unwanted threats. Under the old paradigm, connections between the physiological and behavior are based upon misinterpreted studies, which propose direct links between rapid and unstable hormonal development and behaviors in which they are a danger to themselves and others. The evolving awareness about the essence of adolescence is fully developed in the introduction section of this book. Here I turn to the words of the author and explorer of the mind, Daniel J. Siegel, to describe a composite picture of what he calls the essence of adolescence: "…the essence of adolescence includes an emotional spark (in which a teen strives for) social engagement, novelty-seeking and creative exploration."[6] The third tenet is foundational to the first two, suggesting best practice for adult and teen relationship; put into practice, it means inviting ostracized teens to our decision-making tables, affirming their authentically based identities and stories, and weaving their wisdom and actions into the larger process of deepening universal participation in our great experiment called democracy.

For now, I briefly describe disabling behavioral elements that have traditionally been practiced by adults in their relationships with adolescents. In addition to wishing to outline key elements that have been destructive towards teen civic efficacy, I also list these points in the spirit of simply and subtly suggesting possible best practices for enhancing teen–adult relationships. These elements are outcomes derived through the practice of adultism.

The first element involves adults exercising control over teens rather than engaging in consultation with them. The former practice ranges from imposition of discipline codes in school that warn teens about the dire consequences of even minor infractions, the routine placement of metal detectors at the entrances of schools, and schools escalating resort to suspensions and expulsions—a form of punishment against which students have little remedy.

The second element substitutes the practice of containment in lieu of meaningful conversations with youth who are profiled as being the cause of problem behavior.[7] This is especially true of male students of Black or Latino ancestry, who are sent to special education placement, as well as suspended, in much higher numbers than White students.

For each of these two elements, students have little input into designing either disciplinary codes or challenging special class placements. Conflict resolution and mediation programs do exist, but they encompass a small share of options within the realm of either school or community governance.

Developmental psychologist Alice Miller outlined this cycle of diminished expectations and escalating problematic outcomes in what she called the vicious cycle of contempt. As Ms. Miller explains: "Contempt is a weapon of the weak, and a defense against our (adults') own despised and unwanted feelings. The fountainhead of all contempt, all discrimination, is the conscious, uncontrolled, and secret exercise of power over the child, by the adult, which is tolerated by society."[8] In this book, I describe practices that have negatively impacted individual teen development while causing whole segments of our youth population to receive grossly unfair sentencing from the criminal justice system. Defaming profiles routinely posted by the media have sentenced teens in the court of public opinion. Phrases such as wilding-packs and super-predators created undue apprehension and fear about teens being a threat to society.8

The third element concerns the space where adults profess their concern for teens. Even when punishing the young, adults profess to do so for the teens' own good. The old perceptions, held by adult leaders in municipal agencies and then followed through on with the administration of harsh corrective consequences, identify teens as problems to themselves and others. Educators and researchers have produced volumes of studies postulating that because teens possess raging hormones and deficient brain function, they are innately at risk. More recent work, by writers such as science writers Robert Epstein, former contributing editor to *Scientific American Mind*, and Daniel J. Siegel, clinical professor of psychology at UCLA, have, after reviewing more modern research both in the United States and abroad, debunked the conclusions drawn from older studies.[9]

As had been the case with earlier scientific studies attempting to prove that Blacks and women are inherently inferior to Whites and men, earlier studies about teens confused correlation with cause.[10] Practices and policies put in place to regulate and educate teens conflated social/political/cultural impacts upon teens with an imagined structure of innate teen identity, capacity, and nature. Both scientific studies supporting public policies and adult expectations about teens discounted the impact of cultural, class, and political environments in promoting unwanted behaviors within negatively targeted populations. The later pages of this book take a closer look at all three elements.

I have found the following to be true about the nature of the teen mind: the adolescent mind promotes adolescents' intuitive and spontaneous style of thinking, the openness of their hearts toward those previously unknown to them, as well as for the urgency of idealism in facing problems head-on.

I seek here not to debunk science, but rather to question the mismeasurement of teens. We have done this with what is now recognized prior use of poorly practiced scientific methods which were used to support racist beliefs and policies.[11] Teens have a charged, innate curiosity and an inclusive spirit disposing them to open acceptance of others. When the elements of the teen mind are embraced by adults who serve as allied supporters of their wisdom and talent, what results are positive outcomes for teens and the communities to which they selflessly contribute.[12]

Teens have been positioned in public affairs to keep them perpetually in positions of dependence and endless waiting. In their relationship with adults, it has been grown-ups who have been arbiters wielding absolute authority. This constant condition of subordination resembles what our nation's founders faced at the dawn of our struggle for independence. In his book, *To Begin the World Anew*, Bernard Bailyn writes about rulers' expectations regarding the success of colonists' struggle for independence: "Again and again, they were warned of the folly of defying the received traditions, the sheer unlikelihood that they, obscure people on the outer borders of European civilization, knew better than the established authorities who ruled them, that they could successfully create something freer, and ultimately more enduring than what was then known in the center of metropolitan life."[13]

In this work about empowered teens and universal democratic franchise, readers meet the cunningly self-serving yet idealistic work of teens and their mentors who share vision, and who demonstrate proven work. Creative and constructive, while still positioned at the margins of governance, teen leadership, from Black Lives Matters to the movement called March for our Lives, have initiated great change about how we see problems and generate solutions.

In this book, I share the contributions made by teens, at the municipal level, in the city of New York. My timeline begins with the work of the Uptown Dreamers, who in 1986 transformed a neglected city park into a useable public space. It continues with the Teens on Board Coalition,[14] which successfully changed the New York State Public Officer Law, allowing fully vetted sixteen- and seventeen-year-olds to serve on New York City Community Board in 2014. New York City is subdivided into fifty-nine Community Districts, and Community Boards each have fifty volunteers appointed by elected officials. The value of their work, of which many adults were initially skeptical and dismissive, is self-evident today. My motivation for this book is driven by my belief that the time for welcoming teens to the municipal decision-making table has come. It is here. Now. Today. Teens and adults have a world to win, and nothing to lose but our shame.[15]

I also weave in my narrative the place for adults who have, over the years as well as today, agreed to collaborate with teens as "guides on the side" instead of as "sages on the front of stages." Teen social change activists have twenty-first century allies called "civic co-mentors" who adore their work and join them as equal partners. Co-mentors are, by nature, eccentrics, living outside the box of outworn opinion and misdirected policy. Working side by side with teens, they co-navigate teen rites of civic passage, as well as their rights for passage in journeys of self-discovery[16] and experimental action, and as teammates with civic allies promoting social change.

This story begins with the journey of one co-mentor—namely, me. I had come to be known as Mr. Al in my early days of teen program organizing. As I continue with this narrative, reflecting upon the stages of experience on my path, the evolving story includes the impact that adult co-mentors and I had on each other while I was working on behalf of teen enfranchisement. I have engaged in civic partnership with some of these leaders, and in other cases observed their work on visits to their programs. In my readings and research about programs with which I had no direct contacts, but which have come to be recognized as model youth engagement programs, the written testimonials provided have influenced my approach with civic work and teens. I, therefore, consider these leaders as my co-mentors also.[17] In my universe working with teens, which began in Washington Heights and expanded to New York, civic mentors for teen activists learned to facilitate changes in mindsets and opportunities to ensure fully inclusive participation by teens. Today, ancestral allies, present-day organizers, and fellow co-mentors make up the team that trains young leaders to facilitate our journey into a new era of ecologically astute and soulfully aware collaboration.

Our journey is a marriage between the fierce idealism of the young and the wisdom of elders. In our nation, this work began with suffragists and abolitionists, and continues today with the Dreamers, the Black Lives Matter movement, and tree huggers. Thousands of youth-led groups, working with the non-obtrusive guidance of co-mentors, facilitate creative change, under the radar, and in congruence with the spirit guides of the future.

As you (the reader) make your way through this narrative tale, I hope that my civic adventure becomes clearer. I imagine that this montage, composed of anecdotes, civic relationships, and related research appears at times as mystery. This is how my progress appeared to me on each step along my path, a mixture of certainty and invitations to move on through the unknown. I imagine myself to having been guided by the flickering light of three candles, illuminating the bending possibilities along the course. The first leads the wanderer to safe harbor, the port where authentic purpose is moored from within. The second sheds light on self-created stories, which become further inspired by the validation of kindred souls. The last brightens the space, revealing enough room to celebrate our civic gatherings in the welcome of best friends. Multitudes, grounded and reaching for higher limits, weave a fabric of wonderous change and networks of hope.

INDUCTION

In *The Soul of Adolescence Aligns with the Heart of Democracy*, I write about my journey working for teen enfranchisement, and how I came to understand the congruent relationship between a wholesomely nourished teen soul and integrally practiced democracy. My 30 years of civic education and social justice work with teens served me in my search for staying true to my life purpose. People living on the streets of Washington Heights identify the school of civic education by the name SUNY university, the Street University of New York SUNY. This was a nickname developed by people steeped in trouble who learned the hard lessons of life through a direct encounter with challenging conditions.

My body of work began in December of 1984 in Washington Heights and finished with a citywide advocacy campaign, which successfully procured the placement of sixteen- and seventeen-year-old teens on community boards throughout New York City. Thanks to my grassroots educational experience, I gradually learned the skill sets necessary to assist teens in demanding that their voices be acknowledged. As a civics-learning leader, I guided them in developing a deep connection to their life purpose as well as navigating partnerships with trusted civic allies.

In this chapter that I title Induction, I describe early experiences in my life, in which I could have taken one of two roads. Without my social justice partners, I may have learned to distrust and withdraw from others, and indeed, decide to walk away from my own life purpose. With my community-building and youth leadership experiences, I learned that to walk away from myself is to walk in the dark.[18] During my journey, I aided teens in the discovery of their light. A few of the young I assisted were on the rebound from suicidal ideation; many others found themselves in the throes of loss due to the death of loved ones because of gun violence. Difficult and challenging obstacles helped me to gain cognitive, emotionally centered, soulful muscles. My relationships empowered my sense of determination to work with those whom I embraced, and who embraced me.

Three experiences became proving grounds, contributing to my development as a leader and youth organizer. I describe each of them briefly before delving in them in more detail. These pivotal experiences assisted me in developing an intuitive intelligence, guiding me to turning wounds from enemies into friends, as the saying goes. I came to experience my intuitive intelligence early on as a felt sense, or a buzz. In later years, I learned how to read these cognitions after reflecting upon the past and applying my expanded understanding to my unfolding circumstances. My fears became transformed into a constructive use of energy. As suggested to me by Dr. Stephanie Marango, who has served me as a spiritual mentor, I decided to assert myself with active awareness.[19] Dr. Marango, a medical doctor who incorporates multiple levels of energetic practices into her body of work, and whom I introduce later (in the section titled "Civic Lovers"), has counseled me to establish connection with the intelligence of the brain, the mind, the body, the heart, and the gifts of the universe with which we are all intertwined.

A. Classroom confrontation

The first episode occurred during my high school years in the 1960s. I was in an English class led by a teacher I trusted deeply—at least until that day of classroom confrontation. My belief that wars consist of a series of malpractices[20] came into conflict with hers. My teacher subscribed to a school of historical thought which was embedded in a social construction known as American exceptionalism. This traditional position held, in brief, "my country, right or wrong."[21] I got up in front of the class, reading a piece I had written to alter the story. My selection had pacifist inclinations. The teacher rose in anger to dismiss my work as unworthy. She also castigated my parents as Communists. At the end of the semester, she arbitrarily lowered my grade, which had on average been about 85. The final grade assigned was 70.

Coming out of this humiliating encounter, I proceeded on a path where I found myself challenging adult authority. I became a social change agent, practicing resistance to unfounded beliefs about the status quo. My orientation informed my civic work with teens years later, when I counseled them on resisting stereotypes defining them as agents of wilding misadventures and underdeveloped human beings with immature minds not yet ready to responsibly engage in the world. Being raised in communities under siege by the war on drugs, adolescents, by necessity, had to demand that their viewpoints and talents be recognized.

Today, the squelching of the youth voice and the arbitrary enforcement of censorship remain issues that diminish both the right to express one's individual opinion and the integrity of maintaining free assembly and a free press in our democracy. In 2019, a high school administrator in the Lodi Unified School District in California initially forced the removal of a news article written by a high school student for the student paper. Caitlin Fink had written about her experiences and aspirations to become a porn star, describing her decision, and defending the choices she made getting to her decision. Caitlin's teacher defended her right to publish. She was subsequently threatened with punishment "up to and including dismissal" if she did not cease and desist with her support.

The teacher and students had to obtain legal counsel, while simultaneously securing the support of the larger student community. The school was forced to back down and allow the publishing of the article. In this case, a judgment was made in which free press was supported. However, in cases across the country, arbitrary decisions limiting the right of free expression by teens are exercised by adult authorities and continue to persist. According to the Student Press Law Center, Supreme Court rulings such as Hazelwood "reduced but did not eliminate" First Amendment protections. When censuring a student, a school needs "a legitimate education reason." In the Lodi United School District, the district leadership had failed to provide a valid reason for refusing to publish Caitlin's account.[22] Half a century after my classroom encounter, the subjective use of the burden of proof can still stifle student dissent.

B. Death at my door

The second scenario involved the loss of my roommate, who was murdered— not because of any wrongdoing on her part, but because at one point in her life, when she was still living in Colombia, she had been married to a man in the drug trade. She had fled her native country and moved to America, looking for a new start and a safe place for her children. The news of her untimely death was reported to me by a male detective after he knocked unexpectedly on my apartment door one evening. Although the detective assured me that I had nothing to fear for myself, the boundary line concerning where I was safe, or *if* I was safe, remained unconsciously and emotionally porous. The adolescent quest, in neighborhoods from Washington Heights to East New York, is to escape dangerous and life-limiting intrusions upon the teen lives. Their personal successes are defined by escaping the clutches of gang intimidation and recruitment. Young people also learned to be leery of becoming dependent upon the crutches of disabling adult-led interventions.

The headlines I had read in the local press about unexpected violence entering one's life had suddenly come home. In a single edition of the *Washington Heights and Inwood News* (July 1984), the biweekly police blotter page read as follows: "Guadalupe Diaz, a 54-year-old widow, on arriving home, surprised a burglar in her apartment, and was later found dead. She at first had been raped, and then strangled with an electric cord.... Felix Barbara, at age 30, was found shot dead in the lobby of his building at 630 West 170th Street. A native of Ecuador, he had worked in the operating room at NY Presbyterian Hospital since he was 17 years old."[23] Neither the innocent nor the do-gooder was immune from the sudden intrusion of life-threatening actions in their lives.

The choice I made was between exercising hypervigilance (which has since been documented as common to those who experience trauma), withdrawal, and isolation, or finding allies with common experiences such as mine, who would offer their embrace and support. My communally affirming choice has been shared by those whose lives became defined by moving beyond limitations and embracing the benefits of mutual support. This type of decision-making is aptly described by Robert Snyder, in his biographical and historical work about inspirational change-makers in Washington Heights. As profiled by Mr. Snyder, the heroes of Washington Heights stepped out of their familiar worlds to work in new ways, with new people and unfamiliar communities. As Mr. Snyder continues, "… in actions big and small, they fought for a generous and inclusive right to the city."[24] My allies became my on-the-ground therapists, aiding me in responding with optimism and trust. To name just a few: I include folks like Dave and Jeanne Dubnau, whose work with the Riverside-Edgecombe Neighborhood Association provided tenants with the organizing skills to maintain their right to stay in their own apartments. I learned from the work of Maria A. Luna, a co-founder of the Riverside Neighborhood Security Association, which encourages residents to work in cooperation with police efforts for public safety, and to partner with each other with watchfulness for each person's well-being. I was blessed with the support of Blanca Battino, the principal at PS 128M, which hosted my first youth service program. She worked with community-based initiatives as equal partners in providing service to children and families. Ms. Battino (whom my neighbors and I referred to as the people's principal) made sure that the school space was a safe space in which we could all work hopefully and productively in pursuit of more fruitful lives.

C. Streets on Fire

My third scenario describes the day of the Kiko Garcia riots in Washington Heights.[25] I had been running a track and field practice. Garcia, a known drug dealer, had been fatally shot by a police officer (after Kiko fired the first shots); soon after, riots broke out in the surrounding streets in the southern section of Washington Heights. I had been running my track and field practice in an area of Edgecombe Park we called the Pit, which was situated thirty feet or so below street level. It was not until I ascended the stairs from the park (along with my platoon of young runners) that I found myself in the middle of a mob of angry rioters. Close to the curb, some flipped upside-down parked cars had been set on fire. I was not quite sure whether I was escorting children in my neighborhood, or on a Hollywood action movie set. I made my way safely across Edgecombe Avenue and ushered the children into their buildings. Even given the extreme danger, parents and their friends on the block made it their business to escort me beyond the fire zone so that I could get home safely. It was during this incident that I discovered the spontaneously invoked safety net that people on the block had developed as a drill, and as an obligation towards those they cared about. This lynchpin of social/emotional concern and street smarts would become second nature to me, and it would become part of the living curriculum of my youth services program as well.

Intuitively Instructive Scenarios

A. *Scenario #1: Classroom confrontation. The cultural context. The classroom as community, and the community as classroom—the environmental setting of American education and the nature of public-school classrooms.*

I now elaborate in more depth the context and details about my high school class confrontation. I begin with a few words about the nature of the communities that I as well as my friends and classmates grew up in. Beginning in the 1950s, and continuing into the mid-1960s, young people grew up with sets of assumptions very much conditioned by a society that valued the right to being comfortable in your home and school setting.[26] The pursuit of trivialized possessions—for example, having things for the sake of having them—and valuing a surplus of owned things that were not essential to our lives was supported by the increasing accessibility of bank and credit care borrowing. The more one had constituted evidence of progress up the ladder of success. One example of a family having made it up the ladder of success was hoarding kitchen utensils that were run on electric power, such as can-openers. Devices such as these would do for you what you could otherwise do for yourself, saving effort and minutes in time. Companies producing toys used commercialized design, that is, substitution of play items related to comic book figures and action heroes. Imagination was contextualized within the parameters of heroes and stories defined by the major media. The media, in film and on TV, was saturated with storylines centered on solving crimes on the home front and fighting wars abroad. News accounts were full of warnings about the impending Communist menace; they were also sprinkled with accounts about the rising threat of juvenile delinquency and gangs. Movies like *Blackboard Jungle* and *West Side Story* reinforced the stereotypes. Shows depicting family scenes were always embedded in comic themes and always involved two-parent families, usually living in private homes, always of Caucasian heritage. In both the family shows and the shows, profiling helpers such as doctors, male authority figures always offered the wisest of counsel and practical solutions despite the foibles of emotionally charged women and clueless children. This profile was dominant in shows from *Father Knows Best* to *Ben Casey*.

In our actual lives, elected officials were largely trusted, and teachers were completely entrusted with having both the possession of "true" knowledge *and* the ethics and skill of delivering credible knowledge equitably to all students- as approved by official sources[27] equitably to all students. One example was the promotion of public support for "just" wars, in which the policies of our government, and the actions of our soldiers were justified by the pursuit of the common good in defense against the evil intent of enemies. This assumption, and others (such as our nation being on the brink of invasion by communists if we did not remain hypervigilant) was used to garner citizen support for the war in Vietnam. Government officials and the media obliged public officials in their analysis by simply issuing press releases which repeated policy positions and decisions, word for word, with no critique. The overarching rationale was known at the time as a Domino Theory. According to this reasoning, small nations were being controlled by the larger and unified forces of communism. If one of these nations fell to the communists, then others would inevitably also fall, just as one domino falling knocks down other dominoes adjacent to them. The accuracy and inevitability of this paradigm was challenged by some journalists and writers, such as Pete Hamill, who beginning in 1969 wrote scathing critiques contributing to the lifting of the veil of delusion.

Pete Hamill also used his incisive analysis to expose misconceptions about institutions operating on the domestic scene. High schools with dominant White census tracks had been assumed to have superior rates of graduation and college entrance probabilities for students, but this was questioned in Mr. Hamill's writings, beginning with his article headlined "The White High School."[28] In his article for the *New York Post*, Mr. Hamill shared findings from a Queens College report by the Institute of Community Studies, which showed: Amongst studies based on a cross section of white high school, (high schools with predominantly white populations), three had less than 50 per cent of students graduating with academic diplomas, a virtual prerequisite for gaining entrance to college."[29] As Mr. Hamill's article continues: "…of the 13 schools examined for students reading at least at grade level, only two schools had reached this level when analyzed as a composite of all students; and amongst all schools studied for 9th grade students taking that level of

Regent exam for mathematics, 57 per cent of students taking the exam failed, and for the history Regents, 50 per cent also failed that one."[30]

During my teen years, I became privy to some significant practices of insightful questioning of unsupported educational outcomes after being guided by early-life civic mentors. I learned to make connections between the nature and functioning of classroom environments with community problems, as well as with misdirected governmental practices.[31] Beginning with the urging of my parents, who questioned everything, I was encouraged to take part in civil rights and anti-war demonstrations. I spent virtually every Sunday in the Unitarian Community Church of New York. My Sunday Class teacher, the Reverend Richard D. Leonard, taught me about the perspective of social justice-oriented dissenters such as Michael Harrington. It was Mr. Harrington's book, *The Other America*, that had been attributed to influencing then President John F. Kennedy into more diligently addressing the dire circumstances of people caught in the webs of poverty.[32] Harrington's exposé about the chronically poor brought to light the diminished fortunes of those who lived in the invisible America. These people included miners in Appalachia, farm workers in grape fields, and poor working women attending to the houses and families of the affluent. The representations that I been exposed to and that I had readily adopted were biased by the ethnic and class compositions of the schools I attended and segregated neighborhoods within which I resided. In those days, as is still true today, New York City manages one of the most segregated school districts in the United States. Textbooks and television shows such as *Father Knows Best* reinforced my perceptions that fairness and opportunity were available to all, especially when guided by benevolent White men. Representations depicting a totally fair and equitable society had begun to be questioned by me.[33] Under the guidance of organizations outside of the school system, such as the social justice-oriented Unitarian and American Friends Service Committee initiatives, my educational experience became broadened to include the school of life experiences of those subject to racial injustice and the excesses of military interventionism.

Many of the questionable assumptions embedded in these representations had been the standard fare of history textbooks and lectures delivered by teachers. Trusting in the veracity of the official word, both in the books I was told to memorize and in the words from the mouths of teachers whom I had respected, I had not, up until my fateful classroom encounter, experienced school as being possessed by teachers with biases, nor had I encountered teachers delivering their lessons unfairly. But in an English classroom, in my sophomore year in high school, my world became radically changed.

In high school classrooms across New York City, curricula were designed by outside sources, approved companies adhering to the official story of designated experts. These sources became the exclusive source of historical knowledge whether the curricula were delivered in the form of textbooks or through themes emphasized by specialists working out of the Central Board of Education. My English teacher used a recommended anthology of readings[34] as part of her semester coursework; the coursework had a section focusing on a theme that was popular at the time—that of the theater of war. My teacher proposed that each student choose a short story and use his or her imagination to alter the substance and ending in a way of our own choosing. During my previous time studying in the teacher's class, I had enjoyed her selections, her thought-provoking questions, and her committed interventions in which she focused on helping us develop our writing skills.

The selection I was given to read, from an approved anthology of war-time stories, was a staple for our time. It took place during World War II, on an isolated island in the South Pacific. It involved a scenario in which American soldiers stormed the island and defeated Japanese forces who had previously controlled the island. After a fierce firefight, the American patrol captured and imprisoned the enemy in makeshift jails, keeping the Japanese captive until help could arrive from an Allied battleship. The central theme was typical of a narrative in which suspect enemy soldiers were defeated and American heroes conquered the day. The members of the Asian force were profiled as not to be trusted and devoid of concern for the value of an individual's life when fighting for the greater cause. American soldiers were portrayed as a clean-cut lot of do-good heroes who perform heroically, without human defect.

The student's assignment was to read a selection from the anthology, and then to re-write sections of the stories, including their endings. As a student whose extracurricular activity included attendance at marches protesting our actions during the invasion and bombing of Vietnam, I had already, in real life, developed deep questions and antipathy toward our policy choices, as well as to some of the horrific actions practiced by some soldiers. In my rewrite, I attempted to apply some of my newly found observations and beliefs to the World War II story. In my narrative, I tried to reach for elements of humanity we all have in common, even as we engage each other in fiercely fought adversarial relations.

In the short story I was assigned, the setting for the story took place after an Allied forces victory on a South Pacific island. In my re-write, I introduced a force of nature, a typhoon, which altered the destinies of both American and Japanese soldiers on that island. I wrote that this huge tropical storm overwhelmed the island with searing winds and drenching rain. Most of the island's infrastructure was swept away or destroyed, and the threat to the safety and survival of everyone on the island escalated radically. The American soldiers maintained a strategic advantage, but the Japanese troops were enlisted in actions designed to ensure the survival of all. This included, once the storm had passed, the rebuilding of the island's infrastructure, the procurement of food from newly established sources, and the accounting for of friends and enemies who had been injured. As a synopsis for my re-write, I proposed that under these mutually life-threatening conditions, even a country's enemies had to act in the spirit of cooperation and become friends. As enemies turned temporarily into friends, the Americans and Japanese constructed a mantle of authority ensuring their mutual survival and strategic advantage over the devastating results inflicted by natural forces more destructive than those imposed by man. The expected battleship eventually arrived, picking up American soldiers and adversaries alike. New thoughts popped up for soldiers on both sides—including that of appreciating the fact that even in a theatre of war, with an overwhelming common threat, cooperation ensured universal survival in the end.

After I had approached the teacher's desk to offer my reading of this amendment to the class, albeit with some trepidation as I was not comfortable with oral presentations in general (and especially of one that I knew would be controversial), I sucked it up and delivered my goods. The reaction among several of my classmates was positive—even from those who had previously voiced objections to my anti-war viewpoints about the Vietnam War; the reaction from my English teacher, whom I had previously held in such high esteem, was anything but.

After the applause subsided, my teacher stood from behind her desk, her face flushed red, and her voice already booming with unreserved anger. She shouted out: "This work is terrible; it must have been inspired by communists! I will not give this piece a passing grade, and I am alarmed by the fact that Alfred has created a piece that discredits the value of our war efforts and questions the valor of our troops!" She continued to vent for another minute, perhaps; to me it seemed like hours.

I half-stumbled back to my desk, ashamed, humiliated, and feeling shocked by my teacher's explosive display of contempt for my best efforts. Along the path back to my desk, my classmates gave me visual support, expressed by their sympathetic eye contact. A few classmates whispered congratulations for my creative work. As I passed one student, Ronnie, who through previous discussions I knew was very pro-war—he would often tell me "might is right!"—shook my hand and told me, "Great job!" An unsettled atmosphere overtook the classroom, and unsettling consequences for me were to follow.

At the end of the semester, except for this reading, I had maintained work at the 85 per cent average mark. I received a final grade in English of 70. My parents came to school to protest and speak to the teacher, who would not yield. When my parents complained to the principal, the teacher's response was totally supported.

In the 1950s and 1960s, the authority of the teacher, and the authority of the school system, was not to be challenged. It was absolute. There was no uncertainty in discussions with parents, let alone students, about the questioning of "official knowledge" nor the validity of its system of thought.[35] The fact that I, as a student, and my parents were not given any control over the outcome of this confrontation was business as usual. The value of creating a space and a relationship between teacher and student that engenders creativity and dissent, along with the right to discover meaning, could, on a teacher's whim, and with administrative consent, be tossed away. Protecting authoritarian control and the ideology associated with the American war machine was eye-opening.

The practice that had been put into place here also defied the findings and suggestions of educational specialist Douglas Reeves regarding the vision necessary to become a "learning leader." Mr. Reeves is an education writer and a consultant hired for training of teachers and principals by public school systems around the country. As summarized by Mr. Reeves: [These [suggestions] include learning more from error than from certainty, and that appropriate and insightful monitoring are strongly associated with the improvement of equity, as opposed to compliance drills, which simply reinforce dependencies on external authority.][36] As I progressed along my mentoring path in schools in Washington Heights and across the city, what remained as an intransigent practice was the continuance of authoritarian school governance even up until this day. Three issues which I highlight further on in this narrative are the practices of racialized discrimination in the enforcement of discipline, the construction of the school-to-prison pipeline, and the continual imposition of censorship. After years of using these practices, educational system officials have made these institutional rules a habitual standard operating procedure.

This connection between what I experienced and what I had both observed and heard through testimony by trusted allies would also become a subject of interest to me—a subject I studied through the works of educators, psychologists, and those attending to the value of a spiritual critique of the system. The findings of these groups are summarized by Parker Palmer. Mr. Palmer is a writer on the culture of schools that are welcoming to the souls of both students and teachers. Mr. Palmer describes the assets and attitudes essential for developing the democratic heart:[37] We are all in this together; appreciate the value of others; can hold the creative tensions of life-giving ways; honor a sense of personal voice and agency; and strengthen the capacity to create community.

These propensities for developing inner-sourced and spiritual aptitude became reinforced for me in a book written by two of my mentors, Dr. Stephanie Marango (who I mentioned previously) and Rebecca Gordon. Ms. Marango is a medical doctor and spiritual counselor. Ms. Gordon is a nationally renowned astrologer providing counseling to professionals and business managers. In their co-authored book, *Your Body and the Stars*, they draw correspondences between the energies of celestial objects and the organs of our bodies. One chapter speaks to the role of the heart in supporting assertive skills development: "Shine a light on the heart, which helps you to see, to gain confidence to stand up straight and tall, and helps you to radiate your truth as well as the truths held in our universal house of knowledge."[38]

Alexis de Tocqueville was a sociologically oriented writer from France who came to admire the link between the instinct of Americans to improve lives and the evolution of supportive communities. The findings in his work provide a useful correspondence to teachings such as those promoted by Ms. Marango and Ms. Gordon. As often put forth by Gandhi, a fighter for the independence and empowerment of Indian people, it is crucial to be the change you seek to effect.

Two final points here. The first concerns what happened to me that day—and what has happened to millions of students who have suffered more intensely than I had. In these cases, what resulted was the opening of a psychic wound, a wound that results in emotional injury like experiencing trauma; namely, the separation of our conscious lives from the guidance of our souls.[39] Under these conditions, as I previously referenced, the soul retreats—and without its inner guidance for our aligning with life purpose, we walk away from our higher selves.

Our mission here is not to eliminate the wound, nor to totally cure it, but rather to learn to manage the wound as an unfolding healing experience, in which we rediscover the beauty in ourselves and the complementary magnificence in others. Nelson Mandela was the first Black president of South Africa in the post-Apartheid period. Mr. Mandela was attributed to having stated, in his inaugural presidential address, "Our problem is not in fearing the dark, but rather that of finding our light, shining the light on ourselves, and in turn seeing the light in both our friends as well as in our adversaries."[40] He also counseled the young not to look at themselves as aspiring to be small, but rather modestly practicing people whose positive example might have significant impact on other people. As this book unfolds, readers will be exposed to an anthology of anecdotes about leaders in small communities—leaders whose quiet examples create ripple effects that inspire people who have known them or who even just recently came to learn about them.[41]

My second point is that my English teacher on the day of my reading was merely doing her duty in supporting a cultural narrative common back then, a narrative sustaining the controversial concept critical historians call American exceptionalism. For those seeking to see behind the bylines of approved textbooks and American exceptionalism, we had to learn to research and explore the works of dissenting histories presenting a counternarrative. In his book *Teaching What Really Happened: Avoid the Tyranny of Textbooks*, dissident historian James W. Loewen describes an especially powerful example of the multifarious ways in which American exceptionalism is promoted:[42] "There is a monument in Battery Park, erected in 1926, celebrating the sale of Manhattan by Native Americans to the Dutch.… However, this transaction never really happened.…[T]he headdress depicted in a painting of this same transaction shows natives in headdress never worn by East Coast Indians, only by Plains Indians, and then only starting one hundred years after this transaction.… [W]hat is shown is a transaction involving beads, which were of no value to the tribe inhabiting Manhattan.… [T]hey would typically trade for what they really needed, axes, knives, guns, and metal kettles.… [T]he sale was purportedly made to the Canarsie tribe, a clan that only inhabited Brooklyn.… [I]t was the Weckquaesgeeks who inhabited Lower Manhattan." [43]

Mr. Loewen goes on to speculate that this narrative was created to support the "legitimacy of acquisition." [44] The transfer of land from the hands of tribal leaders to colonists, and later to representatives of the U.S. government, was executed by force and not mutual consent to contracts. These transfers through extortion became established as continual practice, and help to explain how Europeans, and later American officials, stole land and drove populations into near extinction. One of the purposes of my writing this book is to retell the story of community and citizenship from the perspective of community organizers and teen social justice agents who have made a difference. In remembering the civic instruction, I received during my early school years, I recall that those growing up in the 1950s were trained to believe in the infallibility and consistent "just" cause of Americans. As revealed in government records decades later, the North Vietnamese attack in the Gulf of Tonkin, used by our president to justify escalating the conflict in Vietnam into a full-scale war, never happened. When one is using the pretense of an imagined attack, in an alleged attempt to practice valor, then one is engaging in civic vice. Throughout my work with teen programs, I would have to face the use of this tactic (creating false targets as sources of blame) which was used in defining teens as a problem to themselves and others. The alternative version came to light only when dissident narratives were discovered, and the voices of those who had been recipients of gross violence and injustice in Southeast Asia became entitled to have their stories heard.

B. *Scenario #2: Death at my door. A trauma-inducing incident at home opens a portal for helping others to heal from severe and disorienting shock.*

My learning experiences described in the prior scenario outline my progress in developing a new outlook towards official sources of authority. I developed a body of autonomously derived and dissident viewpoints after my classroom confrontation. I then expanded my sources of information as I gradually became introduced to bodies of opinion in the arenas of local politics and community action through my early adult years. When I first considered becoming involved in youth services at the neighborhood level, and subsequently opened a new after school program, I had already developed the beginnings of a dissident's approach, which I applied to my understanding of educational neglect and denigration of today's youth. [45]

Before describing this second scenario, detailing a shocking incident in which my personal space was threatened, and my will to keep active in community work challenged, I first relate a story from the 1960s, when I was in my early twenties. This experience, in which I found myself shocked and saddened by the loss of a lifelong friend due to violence, would in a sense prepare me, through an acquisition of emotional resilience, for similar types of challenges during my later adult life, including the one to be told in this second scenario.

I start this section with an early episode in my life.

A young person close to me and my family was taken from us by a violent life-ending intrusion. It, too, resulted in a deep wound, affecting my emotional well-being, and violated my sense of connection to gentle souls who mean a lot to me. It is only through the wisdom of the heart, grasping deep grief, and then coming to terms with loss through reconciliation that I have learned to deal with such violent intrusions today.

John Tomlinson was the son of Tommy Tomlinson and his wife Flora. He had one sister slightly younger than himself. His father had served in the armed forces during World War II; in fact, he served in the same unit as my father. Their unit traveled from the South Pacific and Australia, and then went on to Japan after the war had officially ended. After their time of service concluded, the two men maintained a close friendship even while living in different cities.

When my siblings and I were growing up, we heard the telephone ring from time to time, and if one of us answered, we might hear what would become a familiar voice—that of Tommy Tomlinson. After he asked for and conversed with my father or mother, we might learn that Tommy and his family were on a visit to New York, and that they would all be staying with us during their visit to the city. These calls would come with no advance notice, and they were often made from a telephone booth just minutes away from our home, but that did not matter. Tommy and his family were our family, too, and they were welcome.

We remember these visits fondly—they involved excited and friendly chatter, reminiscing about the war, talking about the joy of raising children, and what each family was doing. At the time, my father worked as a brew master at Rheingold Breweries in Brooklyn, and Tommy had become an Episcopalian minister. John and his sister would hang out with us kids, playing games outside, or enjoying board games like checkers and Monopoly in the house. We got on nicely, as close-knit cousins do.

By the year 1968, I was off to college. At the time of the phone call, I wish I had never received, I was visiting home on a break from Whittier College. "It's Tommy," the voice said, but this time it was stern and heavy, nothing like the usual friendly, joyful voice I had been used to hearing. "Please, let me speak to your father," he said.

As my father listened, he quickly responded with, "Oh my God, no, no, no!" He had just received the tragic news that John had been murdered. My childhood friend had enrolled at Trenton State College in New Jersey, where he had been majoring in counseling services. On a night a few days before this call, he had responded to a request from a fellow student, whom he had been trying to help, to have another sit-down. John was loyal to his friends, and was never inclined to say no. The sit-down took place in a car parked in a local lot. I am not sure how this happened, but somehow the young man John was mentoring managed to tie John up; then he repeatedly stabbed John, resulting in his death. As John cried out for help, he turned on a portable tape recorder to make his murder "part of the record." Somehow, John's parents listened to that recording, which shockingly amplified their already unfathomable grief.

As a young man in my twenties, I was dumbfounded. I remained pained and numbed as I struggled to deal with the tragedy. John was so gentle, so giving.… His generosity and inclination to serve had no boundaries. It would take me years to process what had happened to John and the devastation afforded to his family. In some ways, I was able to make cognitive sense of the event, but in my emotional body, a dull ache remained for what seemed to be forever.

I now return to the scene of scenario two, which occurred at the dawn of my kicking off the Southern Heights Program in 1984. My personal encounter with violence involved the loss of a roommate who was murdered. This murder reignited the deep confusion and grief burning inside me. Edith was my temporary roommate before she eventually found a place of her own; I had only cursory knowledge of her, as she, an émigré from Colombia, spoke only a few words of broken English, and I spoke perhaps two words of Spanish. Our relationship as short-term roomies was a product of happenstance; her death, however, and its effects upon me became a life lesson in dealing with sudden and tragic loss, and in instilling in me a determination to move on.

A few years prior to Edith's short stay with me at West 161 Street, I took a break from teaching, and was driving a yellow taxi to make ends meet. On some evenings, I took a dinner break at a Twin Donuts store just south of Columbus Circle. Over the course of a few weeks, I befriended Yvonne, a waitress there, and we would converse about family life, among other topics. She learned that during holidays, I used to travel out of town to visit my family, but otherwise I lived alone. After a bit, she invited me (she had nicknamed me "Teach" by then) to come to her parents' house for a Sunday dinner. The Sunday meal became a weekly ritual. I would get to meet her parents, sisters, and brother, and would bring gifts for the family. The family always fed me generously—I must have gained 20 pounds! Among those with whom I shared the dinner table was Tia, the sister of Yvonne's mother.

In the early 1980s, while I was still living as a single tenant in the Heights, I received a request from Yvonne, asking if I could temporarily assist Tia and her family by putting them up for what they thought would be a few weeks, or perhaps a month. They had been living in a multiple-family house in Queens, but the owner had sold the house, so the family had to move. They were in the process of finding a new home in Elmhurst, Queens.

Yvonne's request seemed to be one I could handle rather easily, especially given the fact that between my work at the school in the mornings and afternoons, and my long hours with the youth program, I basically came home to shower and hang my hat. Besides, the family had been so open and welcoming to me. I told them that, of course, having them stay with me would be no problem.

A few days before getting ready to move, Tia took her son, Ralph, to his new school to enroll. They were accompanied by Tia's niece and her niece's infant daughter. As they walked down the street after leaving the school, they approached a grate in the sidewalk that suddenly exploded in flames. The infant daughter was killed, and Ralph suffered extensive burns over his body; he needed almost a year's stay in a comprehensive treatment burn unit.

As their stay at my apartment continued over the next several months, another son, Tito, also stayed with us. He had a short-term marriage, supporting himself and family with odd jobs in the community. After the rest of his family moved, this time down to Florida, Tito remained with me, along with his new girlfriend, Edith. We had agreed they would find a place of their own in a short while. What I did not know was that his so-called "odd job" consisted of being a "steerer" in the drug trade. After learning of this, I confronted Tito, letting him know that the situation was untenable: he had to leave right away. While he did leave very quickly, he left his girlfriend Edith behind.

I eventually learned she had come to the United States from Colombia to escape her life there, but she had left two children behind. She had taken a job, cleaning offices in downtown Manhattan, in shifts starting in the evening and ending in the early hours of the morning. She told me she understood her stay with me was temporary, and that as soon as she saved up enough money, she would move. She maintained her schedule like clockwork. I had not been home when she left for her job in the early evening, but I would always hear her key turn in the lock just a few hours before I departed for work in Queens every morning. Other than that, we spent little time together, except for our brief conversations, during which she held an English/Spanish dictionary in her hands, on the weekends.

Then, one morning, I heard no key turn in the lock. This continued the second morning, and then the third. On that third day, late in the evening, I heard a loud knock on the door. "It's the police," said the voice. After showing their badges, I invited the detectives in. Brief introductions followed, and they asked me if Edith was my roommate. Then they broke the shocking news to me. They had found a woman's body floating in New York Harbor, and after retrieving it and the handbag she was still clutching, they had determined the body was likely to be Edith. Family members traveled down to the morgue the next day, and the tragic and untimely death was confirmed. The family arranged for Edith's body to be returned to Colombia for services and burial.

After a couple of weeks, I heard another loud knock on the door. This time it was a man who identified himself as a parole officer for one of Edith's sisters. After entering the apartment and inquiring how I was doing, he told me he had doubly devastating news to share. He first confirmed that, yes, Edith had been married to an agent in the drug trade, but that she had broken off with him and come to New York seeking a new life. She had planned to work hard and legitimately save up her money, making it possible for her two children to be brought to New York City. She had already made that turn towards a good life, and had nothing to do with her husband, except for his having fathered her children.

While the memorial service was being held in a chapel, her ex-husband showed up. He was murdered just a few feet from her casket. The parole officer could not be sure, but it seemed to him that the plan had been to somehow get Edith back to Colombia so that her husband's former adversaries could catch up and deal with him. The officer assured me that these people had no business with me; I should go on leading the life I was living even though the course of events the officer had just described was deeply troubling. After he walked out the door, I never heard from him, or anyone associated with this incident again. I saw Tito's cousins, Yvonne's family, on rare occasions, for a while; after a few years, I lost contact with them. But…the incident would come back to me in flashes, in dreams and during my waking hours, again and again.

I continued with my work in school, and for my neighborhood programs, but in my private life, I felt as if I had to isolate myself from others. I would feel hypervigilant and wary during the many moments of anxious reflection that arose at any time. At the same time, I suffered a dilemma common to those in human services offering unlimited help—always taking care of others as much as they can, even as they neglect themselves. In the spiritual practice of studying what is called the Enneagram, this would make me, according to this spiritual paradigm, a 9-Type personality [46]: The service giver and mediator, who stays present for others in times of their need, but who keeps his own needs invisible to others, and who, indeed, keeps these needs invisible to himself as well.

In the late 1980s, I began to investigate what was for me only an occasionally explored and then abandoned territory—that of the heart and its intelligence. As Gandhi is attributed to have held in his belief system - to change the world, you have to be the change you seek. In the outer world, I had long sought peace and justice, fairness, and greater accountability for honoring the complex sets of relationships within that world, but I had spent little time addressing the same types of relationships that exist within. Fighting with a spirit of generosity and reciprocity in relations toward the other is of great value, but what about one's relationship toward oneself? If you seek to be a healer in the world, but fall short of taking care to heal yourself, can you be the change that you seek? Each of us has internal gifts which are claimed and self-validated in healthy practices toward ourselves. As we struggle to bring justice to our neighbors, it is important we observe our assumptions and our methods, rather than simply standing just inside the doorway of denial; otherwise, we will remain isolated on an island of ignorance. Ralph Waldo Emerson touched on this principle when he proclaimed, "Believe in your own thought. Believe in what is true in your own heart, and then that is true for all. That is generous."[47]

In the chapter that follows, which I title Forward/Backward and Inside/Out, I take you on a tour of portions of the new vision and territories I came to explore. While working on an increasingly complex set of issues confronting young people, I learned to strengthen the whole mind—including the heart as well as the brain. The brain, viewed through prior Western models, had been viewed as the sole source of intelligence, and equated as the incubator of one's mind. During the period of my youth service, a new paradigm was emerging. Based on studies promoted by new scientific viewpoints, such as quantum physics and analysis of social/emotional intelligence, the understanding of the mind became gradually expanded to include the input and intelligence of the brain and the heart. When relying on our brain, we hone our abilities for analysis. With the guidance of the heart, we build upon our capacity for empathy, our trust for reconciliation and synthesis of our own viewpoints with those of others. Each source of intelligence, operating in tandem, enhances a more holistic approach to life.[48]

As I explored the systems of social emotional learning, the counsel of the Heart Math Institute[49] and the development of intuitively guided learning, I learned to embrace my inner adversaries, such as self-doubt and negative projections upon others, and moved closer to becoming the change-maker I wished to be. I also had to be sensitive to the reality that "diagnosis" is a process, and not a recipe—and demonstrate the same patience towards myself as I did with others.

I have also gradually come to apply the same lesson for myself as I have been doing in my work with teen empowerment and the recognition that adolescents must be encouraged not to follow remote authority but the inner voice within them. Carl Jung, a depth psychologist who had been a disciple of Sigmund Freud, later broke with his colleague and developed a new approach for developing awareness by making connections among previously undiscovered influences over our lives. Jung claimed that in addition to becoming conscious about personal issues buried beneath our easily accessible awareness, it also helped to establish our connection to universal forms of consciousness shared by individual members of the tribe we call humanity. For Freud, a process of guided talk therapy, in which individuals sought emotional understanding and rational clarity, was undertaken to develop a healthy ego and to uncover the hidden tensions in our early childhood upbringing.[50] For Jung, awareness developed as we discovered our relationship to universal energies present in what he called a collective consciousness. Jung claimed that there were specialized bundles of purposeful energies which he called archetypes. He postulated that there were hundreds of these. Amongst these are the orphan, the rebel, and the lover, which are of particular significance for teens. I describe these archetypes in greater detail in the pages that follow. For now, I simply allude to one's connection to, or communication with, these energies; this connection is manifested when we search inside ourselves. Jung and his disciples held that as we make metaphoric connections to these energies, we discover and become closer to exercising our life purpose. Jung described this process as one requiring deep and interactive refection. Jung provides one example with the following quote from his work titled Memories and Dreams: "The meaning of my existence is that life has addressed a question to me, OR, conversely, I, myself, am a question, which is addressed to the world—and—I must communicate my answer. For otherwise, I am dependent upon the world's answer."[51] As I sit at home, in a position of mandated self-isolation because of the pandemic crisis, I am still scrutinizing the question for myself, and the keyboard of my soul is responding to that inner guidance.

As I came to better understand and navigate the challenges and opportunities raised in the two foregoing scenarios, it was the deeply reflective periods of time—the times during which I became connected to my relationship with the orphan, the rebel, and the lover—that provided me both with motivation and resilience for finding personal meaning in my vocation and the commitment to stay the course over time.

C. *Scenario #3: Streets on Fire. Take back our power to change the community—take back the Pit.*

Beginning in the summer of 1985, our after-school program activities (which had operated during the school year at PS 128M) was shifted to a local park on the corner of West 164th Street and Edgecombe Avenue. This arrangement was as it would be for subsequent summers. Despite its state of disrepair and sanitary neglect, the park was the only outdoor communal space the neighborhood had for family gatherings and young peoples' recreation. The city of New York had named this park the Edgecombe Playground, but the people who used it gave it their own nickname—the Pit.

As mentioned earlier, the area where people played sports was recessed below street level; it had a basketball court and a handball court with uneven surfaces, dirt and grime, and cracks in the cement through which weeds and wild grasses grew. Toward the rear of that area was an abandoned wading pool, partially filled with filthy water as the drains were stuffed up. There were also remnants of an old park office building, but a rest station did not exist at all anymore. Broken glass, used car parts, and needles used in the shooting gallery that dominated the park during the overnight hours lay scattered around the area.

The park had a play area for younger children at street level. The equipment was often damaged and left unrepaired, and children playing in the sandbox would often develop rashes from the debris mixed in with the sand. Just over a mile and a half away, in an area now known as Inwood Heights, stood a more well-known park, Fort Tryon Park. It was home to a museum known as the Cloisters and had manicured pathways and beautiful gardens, as well as a panoramic view of the Hudson River and the New Jersey Palisades. This park, a tourist attraction, was the main uptown recipient of municipal government funding. The differences in levels of attention and care given to the two parks represented, in microcosm, the meaning of the Dickensian phrase "a tale of two cities."[52] Ft. Tryon has been maintained with priority funding from the city, as a jewel amongst parks in the city. The Pit, receiving little funding, and many promises for being attended to on some unspecified date in the future, was subject to decades of neglect.

During the subsequent summers, Coach Dave, founder of a grass-roots youth agency called the 280: Dreamers, asked me to assist him with youth training and supervision in the park. During one such session, I was given the task of supervising a track and field practice for some of his young participants, in the recessed portion of the Pit.

After the session had ended, we ascended the staircase and made our way across Edgecombe Avenue, where we were surrounded by overturned parked cars, which had been set on fire. One of the participants asked me, "Why are all these cars on fire?" Being an unreflective critic of Hollywood excess, I assumed the scene was just another day of filmmaking. As we crossed the street to West 164th Street, where I had to drop the runners off at their homes, Helen Johnson who had been leaning out of her window, her arms propped on the windowsill, called out to me: "Mr. Al, don't you see there is a riot going on? Hurry, get the kids home—and get your butt back to your house in a hurry!" Ms. Johnson was a teacher at the Discovery Rooms Day Care Center run by Dave's mother, Gwen Crenshaw; she was also an outspoken gatekeeper for the block. She looked after helpers who at times acted like fools who did not have a clue.

Tommy Harris, who also volunteered on the block, approached me with wide-eyed concern—and three baseball bats on his shoulders. He told me that I was not to worry and that he would escort me towards the "safe side of Broadway," so that I could get home safely. Helping in the Pit even under the best of times was a challenging rite of passage. This alarming incident was my trial by fire.

Fortunately, my teachers came from a partnership between what Helen wanted to be called the "Grandmother's Club" and what Coach

Dave called "Coaches Who Care." Helen was one of a committed corps of grandmothers who looked after the block, and who often had to become primary caretakers of their grandchildren as family structures sometimes cracked under the twin oppressions of poverty and the criminal injustice system. As profiled in a Native American work called *Grandmother Wisdom* (compiled by Mä Creative),[53] grandmothers serve in subtle ways as counsel to both male leaders in a community and aspiring young people. These grandmothers (elders as leaders) in the southern section of Washington Heights functioned in ways similar to the governance put in place by native nations in the northeast. In their culture, grandmothers were asked to help pick tribal leaders, and to educate the young about their culture and communally supportive tasks. Grandmothers on the block that served as my proving ground during the summer months—those living on West 164th Street and adjacent blocks—were the leaders who worked hard despite little public recognition. Grandmothers kept block associations growing, they kept families that had been fractured by the loss of mothers and fathers more intact, and they served as ambassadors to city agencies and elected leaders from whom desired support was solicited.

As a newbie on the block that I had come to serve, I had to pass muster with the grandmother council of West 164th Street: three leaders, each of whom insisted it was they who were the president of the block, but all of whom looked after the block; they also looked out for the good fortune of people like me who came not to talk at them, but to walk with them.

With the advent of a youth program, The Dreamers' Coaches Who Care, grandmothers on the block eventually adopted eager and hard-working partners. The Dreamers, a grassroots program led by one adult volunteer, Coach Dave Crenshaw, inspired many teens and young children to invest in community improvement. Teens and younger peers came to understand that the price of getting playing time on the courts and being invited to trips such as to the Great Adventure amusement park was their readiness to become reliable contributors to neighborhood improvement, and their willingness to be supportive teammates. As they looked up to and appreciated the guidance of grandmothers on the block, the relationship that eventually developed was an intergenerational partnership between those having fierce idealism and elder teammates with years of developed wisdom.

Years later, in 2010, I met a grassroots community leader from the Bronx who became a fellow in the Petra Foundation, which honors unsung heroes who contribute to the cause of social justice and community improvement. The attractiveness of the Petra story resonates with the appeal of the Dreamers story. From a different background, and living in another neighborhood, in a spiritual sense, the leader I met could have been Coach Dave's twin. Chhaya Chhoum, a South Asian émigré, came to live in the South Bronx. The Petra Foundation produced a directory profiling all its fellows for their 2015 25th anniversary, in which profiles of each fellow included quotes after being interviewed for the directory. As quoted on her page, Chhaya said: "We were dumped in the Bronx when the Bronx was burning."[54] Her response was to lead, to counsel, and to organize, with skillful detail and compassionately based attention. With her work at the Youth Leadership Project, as Chhaya's profile states in the Petra Foundation's *Twenty-Fifth Anniversary Journal*, she helped at "health clinics, built a food and crafts cooperative, and negotiated for translators at after-school centers."[55] She also capitalized on the energies of young people, and as also profiled on her journal page, "Chhaya organized annual intensive programs which trained young people to become organizers."[56]

Dave and his young crew, together with the Grandmothers Club, never gave up on the Pit. In 1986, after an extensive clean-up campaign, and after organizing and running programs for both youths and their parents—the programs included showing films at night against the handball court wall—our coalition was rewarded a first-place prize for Manhattan in the Greater New York Council's Top Job Contest. The

Dreamers' theme for improving the park borrowed a tag line from the Citizens Committee Youth Force program, which was called Take Back the Park.[57] The Youth Force program, under the leadership of former director Kim Mcgillicuddy, instituted workshops for our teens, training them in advocacy and outreach skills. We not only took back the Pit for that year, but our local coalition also took over a commitment to that neighborhood recreational space for years to come. Since that time, organized celebrations honoring local heroes and those who had passed too soon have become part of the tradition for our space. In recent years, as I share later in this book, the persistence of Dave with his youthful allies contributed to a substantial increase in city funding, resulting in remarkable improvements for the Pit. Today, a full-service comfort station is in the works.

D. *Three intuitively instructive scenarios - reflections*

Sarah K. Anderson, who is the Field Work and Place-based Educator Coordinator for the Cottonwood School of Civics and Science in Portland, Oregon has written about her 10 years of involving youth in local and school-based improvements. In a book she wrote, called *Bringing School to Life*, Ms. Anderson describes her efforts as "place-based education projects, which serve as an antidote against distraction in a disconnected world."[58] Her students have worked with hands-on projects, in local parks and in nature-based environments which are valued by the local community. Her pupils learn tender care and the science of promoting plant life. Students today are in large part turned off by traditional school curricula, especially that of social studies. Many are diagnosed with attention deficit disorder conditions. What I will share about my experience with the youth participants I have come to witness and receive testimony about is that it shows deficits of attention start with not paying attention to young people; in fact, as young people become fully engaged with projects that interest them, and which are of their choosing, they embrace commitment because their souls have been set on fire.

A second lesson about motivation is discussed by Paul Hawken, an environmentally inclined businessman who promotes economic and political practices that align with the principles of nature. These practices, which correspond with modern-day biological principles, include working from the roots up, establishing a place for your business that aligns with the best interests of all members of a community, and demonstrating respect for the diverse sources of sustenance and mutual support. Hawken believes in spontaneously derived and continuously sustained local change making campaigns. As Mr. Hawken writes in his book, *Blessed Unrest*," Inspiration is not garnered through recitation of what is flawed, but rather in humanity's willingness to redress, restore, recover and re-imagine." [59]These reassuring imaginings are developed on the ground, and through the travails and triumphs of working side by side with neighbors.

Studies documented in books such as *The Spirit Level*, by Richard Wilkinson and Kate Pickett, advocate for creating systems promoting equality and respect for the value of diversity. They caution against producing social conditions that provide excess benefit to the few and denial of benefit to the many. Wilkinson and Picket provided tons of data showing the deleterious effects of inequality as it contributes to loss of focus, motivation, and a sense of making a difference among those who suffer the unintended consequences of inequality.[60]

The magic of the young is defined by their innate, passionately driven optimism, and their readiness to follow in the footsteps of adults who have trust in them. When this occurs, we have recovered a meaningful rite of passage and restored intergenerational partnerships. This is how revered and equal opportunities for teens, in responding to community need, have become a keystone to the Uptown Dreamer program.[61] The Dreamers were the first community-based youth program to partner with the Southern Heights youth program which I had founded. Over the years, as I have maintained my relationship with the Dreamers, I have learned to implement its primary program approach of including youth-led teams in the planning process. Neighboring agencies from the Heights, after partnering with the Dreamers on special projects, have also chosen to implement this inclusive approach in decision-making.

Finally, these teaching moments, learned in the furnaces of confrontation described in the three scenarios discussed earlier, address the values inherent in authentically experienced and locally based constructions of knowledge. Bob Hopkins is a British author and a founder of the Transition Network, which promotes the inclusion of creative projects in the design of social change. Mr. Hopkins laments the overuse, in educational settings, of tasks requiring simple memorization and completion of fill-in-the-blank answers on exams. One of the roadblocks experienced by teens who I met for the first time was their inability to imagine alternative conditions in their lives. As attested to by innovative program designers profiled in Mr. Hopkins book, *From What Is to What If*, once a person cannot imagine possibilities, they begin to accept life as being impossible to change. As described by futurist Bob Hopkins in his appeal for keeping creativity alive,[62] "Constructing knowledge comes about when we develop a sense of self through relationship and connection to a world around us, with place becoming the 3rd teacher embedded in our companionship of teachers and learners."[63] As Mr. Hopkins further states in his book, teachers, coaches, and mentors for the young need to explain that when we believe in the possibility of making fruitful change, we "have a powerful nostalgia for the future."[64]

As I continued to move forward in my youth work, the classroom confrontation faded for me as a source of troubled memory; instead, it became a fire in my imagination. As I confronted damaging adult dialogue, such as referring to teens as "wilding packs"[65] or institutional actions such as the censure of teen opinion in student newspapers, I came to think of these incidents as a personal affront to my own dignity. As a result of my conversations and meetings with parents and youths who had become traumatized in response to unanticipated violence intruding into their lives, our shared experience and our reaching for recovery merged into a common understanding. My encounter with the riot in Washington Heights, followed by receiving unconditional support by friends and neighbors, later became infused into my body of work and my intervention strategy, as I became one with a team of credible messengers. For each of the three scenarios which I highlighted in this chapter, which I call Induction, (the classroom confrontation, the murder of my roommate, and my experience with a neighborhood riot), I have used reflection upon these incidents to assist me in making sense out of them. As is the case with my civic teammates, who must also process personal diminishment and trauma in positive ways, I have learned to transform vulnerability into valor. The intelligence of our generous hearts would eventually contribute to the infrastructure of communal integration.

We—and by we, I mean the members of the boomer generation—have constructed a world of financial destabilization, while at the same time leaving a burden of overwhelming responsibility on the emergent generation. Innovative and inspired teen leadership is learning how to manage, and to lead, to avoid rapidly descending financial fortunes and planetary demise.[66] [67]

As written about by the eco/spiritual writer Bill Plotkin, in the blink of an eye (compared to planetary time), we have disabled the natural cycles of nature, sabotaged the master plan of ecological balance, and left sustainable futures for our young deeply underwater.[68] We have created a civic and environmental crisis so damaging that we should call it by its true name— betrayal of the young, and crimes against the future.[69]

The next chapter, "Forward/Backward and Inside/Out," provides a chronicle of my personal journey with teen empowerment and teen enfranchisement over the course of 28 years. This path is entangled with the work of many others, all of them working with issue-specific yet interdependent causes in a universe asking for balance, justice, equality of opportunity, and the right to participate in civic affairs for all people, all adults, and every young person. Together, we stand up against the marginalization of person-hood, the minimizing of neighborhoods, and the massacre of democratic integrity and planethood. My path became entwined with many partners seeking to show patriotic duty as love of our highest ideals, to practice unconditional neighborliness and love for strangers. Each of us eventually established place as our grounding point, commitment through our unwavering presence, and guidance through our life purpose. Each new program opportunity with which I became engaged served me as steppingstone of experimental experience along the path. Three of the programs that I write about include the Southern Heights program, where I learned to implement teen co-leadership; the Ivy League programs, which was focused on providing equal opportunities for girls in education and sports; and the Future Voters of America Program, in which high school students were trained to prioritize issues of importance to them. These student leaders would also implement advocacy skills when making appeals to elected officials. Each program was a unique marker for me in learning about new neighborhood initiatives which incorporated differing types of perspectives related to class, gender, and race. Working with teen leaders from diverse backgrounds and identities introduced me to new dimensions of teen leadership training that considered the viewpoints of those with differing but legitimate credible stories. We strove for direct concrete results, but also lived with the challenges met along a meandering course. As partners, those who were teen social change activists, and the adult mentors who guided them, found that the development of mastery and the appreciation of mystery were necessary to help us seek the truth and reaffirm our souls. As stated by the eco-spiritualist and psychologist Bill Plotkin, in his book *Nature and the Human Soul*, by adopting the methodology of the wanderer, we create "a visionary set of experiences necessary to discover the truth and to affirm one's soul."[70] The portal to the teen soul includes the energies of the orphan, once entranced by the illusion of separation from life purpose, and now recovering what had been lost. It is powered by the storytelling projects of the rebel who lights the way on the insightful journey home, protects the power of unique perspective, and demands a place at the decision-making table in the world of adults. The civic lover engineers a passage from old, stifling ideas and institutions to the world of new definitions regarding what is essential in our lives. It is about making connections between people's dreams for the future, and the sharing of possibilities developed through communal organizing which gives shape to optimistically focused change. To paraphrase a saying used frequently by members of the Clinton administration in the 1990s, about the prime importance of economic factors in our lives (Their tag line was, "It's the economy, stupid"), I would argue that it is about our social, political, and cultural relationships, stupid, and not the economy. What counts in becoming a creative person is self-evident in the unique nature of adolescence. Using curiosity to help generate questions, possessing a passionately felt commitment to change, and maintaining an oppositional resistance toward institutional practices which have outlived their usefulness all come with the territory of teen social justice activism. I offer two thoughts next, one concerning the preciousness of the teen mind, and the other a passionately held commitment essential to adult support for adolescent enfranchisement.

One quality of mind inherent to, or self-evident for teen nature, is aptly proposed by educational psychologist Howard Gardner, who has counseled school leaders and policy makers about the value of emotional intelligence: it is the value of immaturity. As Mr. Gardner states in his work about multiple intelligences: "A certain immaturity, both mental and emotional, which goes hand in hand with deepest insight, is not a teen deficit, but an asset"[71] He holds that by being allowed space for experimentation, with non-obtrusive support by adults, teens find an inner source of guidance and develop a sense of personal responsibility.

When I describe teen empowerment as embedded in the process of communal enhancement, I propose that the role of the civic lover is to align the higher talents of teens with the higher angels of democracy. Education and communal improvement necessitate training for those I call prophets under development. By learning to develop insightful inquiry, and to construct alternative approaches for neighborhood improvement, adolescents who are learning the gifts of prophecy and an idealist response to problems do so by maximizing their powers of discovery. To paraphrase a slogan used throughout the Occupy Wall Street movement, real eyes overcome real lies.

Rabbi Abraham Heschel, was, as described by one of his biographers, Edward K. Kaplan, a conservative Jewish theologian and a progressive socially engaged activist. Rabbi Heschel, during a period spanning from 1940 to 1972, was an esteemed religious leader in the Jewish community who was recognized by civil rights leaders such as the Rev. Martin Luther King, Jr. after he joined them on many marches. Using his experiences of having escaped from the Nazis, and his empathetic awareness with those unjustly subject to discrimination in America, he had developed a definitive description capturing the spiritual nature and the on-the-ground- work inherent to the mission of social change-makers. To summarize Rabbi Heschel's thoughts, he held that activists work outside their box of comfort, and are prophets, or iconoclasts who challenge the apparently holy.[72] The elements of the holy include the revered and awesome beliefs that are cherished as certainties, endowed with supreme sanctity, which are to be explored as scandalous pretensions. Change-makers who see the future before it has arrived are people who lead movements for change. In an interview with a reporter who had asked Heschel why he chose to march with Dr. Martin Luther King, Jr., despite the risk, the rabbi stated that if he had refused the invitation, he could not look at himself as a practicing Jew. What has inspired me so much about teen leaders and the co-mentors who guide them is their refusal to shy away from the invitation of making the world a better place for all. Rabbi Heschel is attributed to have quipped that if he did not engage in the civil rights movement, he would not be able to self-identify as a practicing Jew. I feel that if I had stopped short of challenging the demeaning, diminishing, and dismissive beliefs and practices of adults who disable otherwise potent teens, I could not call myself a civic mentor for teens. I gradually learned by walking step by step and side by side, with capable and committed teen activists.

The story of my evolution as a civic mentor for teens follows in the Forward/Backward section of this book. Dr. Mindy Thompson-Fullilove is a professor of clinical sociomedical sciences and a professor of psychiatry at Columbia University. She has also spearheaded community partnership programs such as Hike the Heights, where graduate students invite neighborhood youth to festivities where they discover our neighborhoods' rich parks and historical sites. She has worked side by side with my youth services partner, Coach Dave Crenshaw, for decades. Dr. Thompson-Fullilove speaks to the value of entanglement between people recognized for their assets, and communities which choose to construct invitational opportunities for those willing to commit to change.

Dr. Thompson-Fullilove has also written extensively on how to regenerate healthy and whole communities. She has an understanding about corrosive systems in which the issues faced by local people are defined as problems caused by their deficient habits and their responses to issues. Dr. Thompson-Fullilove sees what some describe as problems caused by human deficiency as symptoms of the system. In her book, *Urban Alchemy*, Dr. Thompson-Fullilove calls these "symptoms of disorder inherent to the mechanisms of dysfunctional governance."[73]

In the section of the narrative that follows, I infuse Dr. Thompson-Fullilove's insight into my book's overarching theme. I also apply some of her additional insights shared in *Urban Alchemy*, not only to my communal perspective but also to my changed perspective on holistic intervention with the teen psyche. In *Urban Alchemy*, Dr. Thompson-Fullilove lays out basic principles of holistically informed intervention. She advises that when addressing local issues, we keep the workings of the entire city in mind. I advise that when intervening with the teen mind, we keep in perspective the role of intuition and the intelligence of the heart as central to the mind. Dr. Thompson-Fullilove's next principle is to find out what you, as a change agent, are for (and not just against). I advise that as mentors, we focus on positive teen assets, rather than the learned problem behaviors of teens. Her third principle addresses the crucial need of creating meaningful places. I propose that we give teens a platform to introduce themselves as meaningfully led participants in their own communities. An additional principle proposed by Dr. Thompson-Fullilove is to show solidarity with all life, and to be creative and joyful in expression of that solidarity.

In the next chapter, which I call Forward/Backward and Inside/Out, I start this section of the book by describing what I call essential assets possessed by teens, with which they learn to challenge themselves to connect to their authentically derived goals, as well as to form partnerships with allies who support them for their positive identities and civic contributions. I will then provide anecdotal experiences during my 28-year course of establishing and leading teen empowerment programs. I separate these into distinct periods, initiated in what I call starting lines, in which I operated teen civic engagement programs. As I previously stated, during my years in teen empowerment work, as I progressed from one time- period to the next time-period, I gradually increased my understanding of teen empowerment work within the contexts of larger and more diverse areas and neighborhoods. In the chapter to follow, the reader will learn about the unique perspectives and talents one comes to appreciate when working in a local arena with activists from multi-cultural and diverse national backgrounds. I had started my teen civic work in one community, Washington Heights, and finished my journey with a teen empowerment project in tandem with allies from across the five boroughs of New York City. Over time, teens, and my civic allies, would help me to develop and incorporate deeper understandings about working with teens related to issues of sex and gender, race, and national origin. I would also learn strategies and tactics for working with governmental authority, starting with local municipal agencies in the early years, and finishing with advocacy to the NYC Council and the New York State Legislature.

I soon moved forward with teen leaders and civic allies, who provided so much essential guidance to me. I reached out by arranging direct meetings with teen leaders and with civic reform advocates from other organizations. I also maintained a discipline of exploratory readings and research about the initiatives of adult and youth leaders from other agencies. I have found that many of these leaders remain dissatisfied with the status quo, and practice thinking outside of the box. I refer to these civic allies as public prophets. Through their teachings, I gained greater perspective from those whose minds considered present needs, such as gender equity and criminal justice reform, as related to the callings of the future. I also increased my knowledge about social justice work through the words and wisdom of those whom I call ancestral allies. These are the change-making leaders, such as suffragists and racial justice advocates, who laid the groundwork for the path I have traveled.

While I focused on changing what lay outside myself with my teen civic empowerment work, such as on institutional change and influencing public opinion, what happened in tandem with this work represented an evolution in my thought processes. What I strove to change on the outside also changed me on the inside. As time moved on, I became less of a forthright director and opinion maker, and more of a team player feeling connected to friends and allies who were my co-leaders and mentors. In this book, I will develop a term to describe these civic change counselors which I call co-mentors. We worked together not as leader and follower, but as searchers and groundbreakers working shoulder to shoulder.

II.

FORWARD/BACKWARD
AND INSIDE/OUT

In this chapter of the book, I will be constructing a chronicle of my experiences as a youth service program leader, and my progressively deeper understanding about how teen services programming should better serve the true nature of adolescence. I will show how my relationships with teen leaders, as well as with the civic mentors guiding them, gradually changed by allowing for more age-inclusive equal participation in the civic change process.

In my previous incarnation as a community leader and organizer, I had worked in a neighborhood arena where community enhancement and political change was organized and led by adults, even when there were youth concerns involved. Although my inclination was to always look forward toward positive possibilities for obtaining community stabilization and political change, I appreciated the insights and social justice achievements of those who had built the road towards a better society in the United States, such as abolitionists, suffragists, and labor reformers. However, as I moved forward in my youth services work, I adopted a new perspective about reformers with whom I agreed with, looking at them as people with strengths and flaws, who were learning to adjust according to what they understood at the time of their contributions, but who had not developed insights which we appreciate today. Twenty-twenty hindsight should not be used to negatively condemn the shortcomings, or as-yet-unrealized goals of those still struggling in those prior time periods. In sum, as expressed by a history teacher I had at Whittier College in 1969 (Dr. Harry Nerhood, chairman of the history department), the fish shall be the last to discover the sea, or it isn't what is that counts, but what man thinks is. When I speak in this narrative about looking backward to move forward, I offer this counsel in the spirit of remaining humble, and respecting the complex realities always faced by people looking to understand the world through a conditioned lens of experience.

In a parallel way, I learned lessons about accessing multiple intelligences during my three-decade long journey. By accessing additional types of intelligences, I increased my perspective and adopted insights which complemented my prior predisposition, in which I had relied solely on my rational intelligence. Rather than focusing only on achieving outer goals, I incorporated intuitive reasoning and emotional intelligence in the context of relationship building. These include obtaining understanding for and learning to apply concepts such as multiple intelligences (physical, social, and emotional) which I will describe throughout the unfolding of this book. What I also came to adopt was appreciation and reliance on my intuition and heartfelt guidance, rather than just following what my rational mind told me was the direction to take. Being exposed to the evolving fields of environmental justice and spiritually diverse worldviews would be added to my civic toolkit previously dominated by the logic of science and the rational lessons of history. As human beings, we build society and dream about the future by using logic, and by feeling the power of myth. I learned these tools by utilizing interior interrogation and search, becoming open to the field of experience, and thought outside of my comfort zone adopted through my childhood upbringing and smaller circles traveled. I traveled deeper inside, and to terrains further outside.

Joseph Campbell (1904–1987) was a renowned philosopher exploring the relationship between mythology and human agency. For human beings staking out a place in life, he saw this interchange of metaphorical guidance and human agency as essential to fulfillment along one's life path. In Mr.

Campbell's reflections concerning the quest of the adolescent, he has written: "The adolescent rite of passage is a hero's journey."[74]

During my decades of work with teen social justice-makers, I have been blessed to be invited to their dance with divinity, the discovery and implementation of their souls' purposes. As a student learning from emergent participants in our common life course, I have been blessed through embracing their insights and wisdom. I have tried not to fail setting their souls on fire, and I have adored their tenacity in creating sustainable communities and a better world. I have interacted with teens who have overcome the obstacles they faced in under-resourced classrooms and overly restrictive policies.[75] I have deeply appreciated and learned from their commitment for the common good. Teen social justice activists are, for me, heroes who have aided me with my program projects as well as along my own life course.

In this section of the book, I outline the stages and steps along my journey, addressing these within the context of moving forwards and backwards. In my work with teen enfranchisement and community renewal, I gradually came to realize the importance of checking in with my past, to assess the influences upon me experienced in my own upbringing. I was born in 1949, in Jewish Memorial Hospital located in upper Manhattan, in a community inhabited chiefly by working class families of Irish, Italian, and Jewish ancestry. In elementary school, I did not see a single Black or Latino in my school. In middle school, I saw a handful. In high school, I encountered people from these different backgrounds a bit more frequently, but mostly within my high school building, and not in most of my classes. Having gone through the experiences I have described in the Induction chapter led me to become aided in developing expanded awareness about my personal integrity, a sense of safety, and the need for neighborhood solidarity. The dissimilarities and multiformity of the people with whom I partnered provided for me a source of cultural and civic education. My working model used in teen empowerment became enriched by the dividends obtained through cooperative efforts with those of difference.

In my childhood and teen years, there were major events in our country and the world that, as I look back, I would say became markers of a changing world for which political engagement would mean broadening of previous boundaries. In the year of my birth, Russia exploded its first nuclear bomb, NATO was established, and the Geneva Convention passed a mandate prohibiting the mistreatment of prisoners. These three initiatives ushered in movements for nuclear safeguards, the need for organized protection against authoritarian threats, and the moral calling for human rights for all. During my teen years, involvement with these movements provided a context for my civic engagement with youth. What I felt, as an adolescent, I also identified as central to the lives of all teens I came to meet, beginning in the mid-1980s. Gary Lachman, who is a writer on spiritual traditions and the evolution of consciousness, uses his words well in his book, *Beyond the Robot*. In his work, he describes an underlying sense of alienation for teens, as "a despair for settling, for being seen as insignificant."[76] In Mr. Lachman's book, he also uses a quote by Colin Wilson, who had written extensively in the 1950s about the need for teens to overcome a culture seeming indifferent to the young, in the eyes of the young. The quote is taken from Colin Wilson's book called *The Outsider*, which describes the motivation for teen resistance: "My life task is to light a fire with damp sticks. The drizzle falls incessantly. Yet I feel that if I could get the blaze started, if would become fierce and large, and nobody could stop it."[77] The language of discouragement directed at teens during my teen civic work fell incessantly out of the mouths of major media pundits and insensitive elected officials. Amongst adults who felt as outsiders to such disabling environments, it was the ability to see past the horizon of limitations which guided them toward what Sarah Van Gelder, who had been an editor for *In Context* magazine, called an ecology of justice. Ms. Van Gelder described this ecology as one of community, where "those who make mistakes are still afforded opportunity and given a chance to be re-accepted so that they can bounce back and make themselves and their communities whole."[78]

My early leadership with community service projects involving teens started in neglected public spaces. These spaces which had deteriorated were transformed by people on the ground. Places that had been barren were turned into fertile areas, into stages of communal gathering and celebration.

My initial inspiration for committing so deeply to my neighborhood lit on fire by one of my first teen leaders named Miriam Payne. I provide an anecdote about Miriam and her contributions in a section of this book I title the Orphan. She was shy and retiring in demeanor, but when called into service for reviving our park, she found her voice and energized a coordinated neighborhood rally for the public good. What was to develop for me as relentlessly driven aspiration for ensuring teen voice to be respected by adult decision-makers was set on fire by her passionately expressed determination. Twenty-eight years later, I had come to partner with adults, some of whom were advocates for teens and others civic decision-making positions, who practiced giving an open ear and respectful attention to hundreds of teen social justice advocates. As teens were increasingly invited to sit at the municipal tables of governance, one benefit attained was that an amendment to Public Officer Law was signed into law in New York State, which now allowed 16- and 17-year-old teens a seat on New York City Community Boards (The previous minimum age was 18).[79] Teens were significant agents for making this happen. Adult co-mentors were essential partners in creating space, allowing teens to flourish in their roles of providing public duty. I will introduce co-mentors further on in this story. I point out here that when adults choose to co-mentor teens in the arena of public service, they access and develop their inner teen as a tool in their civic work. Rather than leaving their teen nature buried deep within, or putting its needs aside, they readily access their inner teen tools such as inquisitiveness, curiosity and idealism. It resembles in some ways those who keep their inner child alive, those who display characteristics of playfulness, creativity, and joy just for the sake of what they are performing. Here I will focus on teen attributes essential to holistic development of the mind, which is alive and well in healthy teen minds as well as evidenced by the spirit of adults who honor teens.

Teens feel empowered and learn to make a difference when encouraged to develop the strengths of their inherent teen disposition; I call these strengths the five essential assets that construct adolescent character. These five are: a distrust of authority, idealism, insistence on inquiry (the questioning of the status quo), hammering the hypocrisy between stated principles and governing practices, and their possession of intersected intelligences aligning with the demands of a new oncoming age of ecological sensitivity and spiritually guided action.

Bill Plotkin has developed a spiritually and ecologically oriented paradigm for understanding the human mind and the dynamics of an ecologically balanced world. Mr. Plotkin calls this mindset one of cultivating individual wholeness and integral community in what is now a fractured world. In what he has called the promise and hope of adolescence, Mr. Plotkin also offers insight about one reason adults feel so uncomfortable about teens: "The adolescent must undergo an initiation process that requires letting go of the familiar and comfortable. She must submit to a journey of descent into the mysteries of nature and the human soul. The descent that the adolescent must undergo is what scares people about teens."[80] In my time serving families, teens as well as their parents, I was told countless times by parents about their envy for their children being allowed to go through a rite of passage which honors their desires and self-expression. When parents decided to join their teens on projects, or just to cheer them on, they would talk about feeling less at unease with themselves, and more joyful about their child's prospects. In a time, beginning in the 1980s and extending through the 1990s, the old paradigm about teens continued to hold sway over public opinion, and was responded to by elected officials with new rules of law, and the creating of funded programs, which focused on the problems teens faced, but not on their inherent assets. I give an overview of their assets in the pages that follow.

The five adolescent assets

Asset One: Idealism:

The first asset guiding teens' dispositions and viewpoints is idealism.81 This golden touch of goodwill is driven by a passionate optimism that one can make a difference, and that the wrongs in the world can be addressed and fixed because one believes they can.82 This energy is poetically expressed in the imagery of Dr. Seuss' Lorax, who came upon a devastated environment yet still believed in creating a greener world. The Lorax is a protagonist who is motivated by a fierce optimism for obtaining positive outcomes (This propensity is what candidate Barack Obama tuned into as he proclaimed, "Yes, we can!"). In a world dominated by collapsing ecosystems and broken financial systems, it has become incumbent for the young to become visionary practitioners. Indeed, during the founding moments of our nation this fierce sense of idealism was articulated by George Washington in his words expressing concern for immigrants being welcomed into our nation's larger tribe. In his parting remarks to policy makers in the early days of our republic, President Washington said: "The bosom of American is not only open to the opulent and respectable stranger, but also to the oppressed and persecuted of all nations and religions."83 Today, the youth-led Dreamers, who were young immigrants who spent most of their lives in America, demonstrate the value of idealist resistance toward nativist prejudice, to being castigated as unworthy outsiders. For community members who value their friendship and community contributions, our Dreamers are accepted as valued neighbors. This practice of American neighborliness was embodied in the spirit of Washington's vision.

In the bodies of our political opportunism and cultural prejudice, adolescents are viewed as strangers and subject to the same mistreatment as immigrants when they are "cast out of the garden of childhood, and against the barrier of an unforgiving adulthood."[84] I am quoting here from a poem I wrote in 2010 that I called *The Arrested Development of Adolescence*. My point here is that in a parallel way to the experiences of unwanted immigrants, teens are disposed of and punished as a category of being the undesirable.[85] As discussed later in this narrative, and as embodied in legal changes such as the 1994 revisions to the criminal code, teens began to be held accountable, and punished according to adult norms. Teens were arrested, tried, and incarcerated as adults, even as they were not allowed to participate in the civic process of analyzing and addressing criminal justice issues. Teens were adults only when *breaking* the law; they were denied access to helping to *write* the law. In a later section of this book, I will introduce you to adults who had been tried and incarcerated, and then after years of appeals, had their original convictions overturned. What has struck me so powerfully is that these folks were originally arrested as teens. Long years of their lives had been stolen. However, once released, they reacted not with thoughts of revenge or with broken spirits. They moved on, determined to turn their lives around in meaningful ways by creating personal stories of redemption. Now assured of their value to others, they chose to become servants for fighting for the prevention of having tragic injustices being visited upon innocent others. What came across to me, as I listened to their new stories, and the determination evident in their actions, that an unreserved energy of idealism kept them resilient.

Asset Two: Inquiry

The second asset guiding teens' disposition is their predisposition for using inquiry—particularly when they are utilizing deeply probing and incessantly revealing questions used by them in their search for truth.86 The backdrop of experience informing this asset is aptly touched upon by Paul Goodman in his classic tome Growing Up Absurd.87 *"Balked, not taken seriously, deprived of great objects and available opportunities, and in an atmosphere that does not require service, it is hard to have faith, or to feel justified in having a calling, or win honors. But what then fits the place of these?" As proclaimed by Mr. Goodman: "For every experience that a human being has—a whole way of being in the world."88*

Teen leaders profiled in my narrative—and, in a broader sense, teen leaders today, such as those in the March for Our Lives, Dreamers, and Black Live Matters movements—are driving deep questioning of institutions and practices by adults. Teen leaders are looking for a justified, recognized way of being in the world of decision-making bodies that impact their lives. Young social justice change-makers determine the parameters of possibility for tomorrow. Teens strive to be respected for their incisive questioning about misguided social policy approach. One example with worldwide repercussions is the manically off-course trajectories for addressing climate concerns. Adult leaders have kept alive yet unwell what cultural critic and American historian Jeremiah Abrams describes as the shadow of America. In a process that runs parallel to that described by depth psychologists such as Carl Jung and James Hillman but that is exercised on a social and political level, the American shadow is a process in which we project what we fail to take responsibility for (thought and feelings we feel shame for, or don't acknowledge as owned by us) onto the unwanted others, that is, people we need to justify as dishonorable or less deserving than we are.[89] In response to our unresolved pain and self-perceived shortcomings and the injustice we received, we misdirect our anger and create stereotypes in which we perceive other people as a danger to ourselves or our community. In justification for our invented identity projected on other people, we scapegoat those we perceive as not welcome or entitled. Our shadow problems sabotage the promise of America and diminish the power of our national soul. Historically, our ultimately destructive practices dismiss and demonize peoples of color, casting out and ostracizing those deemed to be positioned outside of the right to be considered an American. These markers of marginalization are intersected by the negative experiences of being a teen. The use of language expressing negative expectations about teen efficacy was broadly in use, even by professionals in the field of education and counseling. These practices of negative expectations and definitions persisted during my 30-year journey, and continue today, although not as substantially as was true up until the last few years. By those who held or continue to hold on to this reductive profiling, teens are castigated as irresponsible, unnecessarily risk-prone, and held responsible for community problems.

Changing laws with the intention of correcting injustices or creating better living conditions for those who have been denied fair distribution of goods and services is noteworthy and a sign of progress with social justice. However, changing deeply held assumptions and attitudes regarding those who deem teens as primarily responsible for our social problems—namely, adults—is a challenge of greater magnitude. The subtle psychological and social layers of this confraternal daring is aptly described by Dr. Scilla Elworthy. Dr. Elworthy is an international peace-keeping negotiator who has successfully led efforts in defusing local conflicts and slowing down nuclear proliferation. Dr. Elworthy counsels that those who seek to bring constructive change to those inhabiting societies different (and perceived as deficient when compared to our culture) from our own need to account for the appropriateness of our own social and cultural assumptions. As Dr. Elworthy notes in her book, *Pioneering the Possible*, it is important for policy makers to check in on their own assumptions before recommending changes to those from different cultures and backgrounds. As Dr. Elworthy states in her book: "Norms and values are important precisely because they are invisible. What are essentially historical constructs have come to be enshrined as perennial truths. From this arises a sort of mission creep. They become the unquestioned bedrock on which large institutions, corporations and governments make the kind of decisions that are destroying the planet."[90] In short, we assume that our ways of constructing economic and political institutions are the norm, and appropriate for other societies, without considering their unique historical development, customs and socio-political forms of governance. In some international transactions, we impose our way of life to obtain political or economic advantage. However, even when we, with good will, force or impose our way of life on societies with different needs, what some policy people who have grown more aware have come to know is that we wind up causing more harm than good for the intended recipients of our aid.

What even well-intentioned adults fail to understand is that teens today are not navigating their path towards adulthood under the same conditions, or with the same opportunities that existed when they were young. Teens listen to the words describing an ideal path for success, or observe the contradictions between adults-stated ideals, and what exists in one's everyday life. They don't buy into the illusions habitually constructed by political mythology. Adults lose credibility, and teens lose faith in the elders as credible messengers and leaders. Adolescents face a doubly disastrous entendre. In addition to the hypocrites, they identify in their individual relations with adults, as an emergent generation they face a dire threat to the planet they are to inherit. The myths promoted by adults about our society's superior methods, and the inevitability of progress and upward mobility are seen by teens for what they are—wishful thinking and delusional expectations. The indisputable accuracy of science and faith in unending economic opportunity are paradigms promoted by adults, while what remains unaccounted for is the denial and destruction of their true nature. Adults also need to work on their awareness about what teens today, maturing in times different from those that they experienced, and who are from varied cultural and national backgrounds, experience for themselves.

When challenging these inconsistencies, teens are habitually rebuked. A perspective of how women have for too long been judged by false standards was addressed at the very dawn of our nation's quest for independence and self-determination, in the 1700s, by Mary Wollstonecraft. Ms. Wollstonecraft was an American feminist writing in the early days of the American republic. Her classic tome, *A Vindication for the Rights of Woman*, challenged men's ideas and practices, which assumed that women did not possess the capabilities of judgment and reason required for full citizenship. Ms. Wollstonecraft provided a social justice critique of those who advocated for the primacy of reason and personal liberty, but for men only. As part of her critique, she challenged hypocritical men to stop treating women as "toys and slaves."[91] Today, female candidates are still judged in a negative way. Attributes that are celebrated in men while they exercise assertiveness are looked upon as aggressive in women. As stated in Ms. Wollstonecraft's case two centuries ago, women's rights activists today still face the same types of double standards. For social justice advocates today, their imperative is to ask questions beginning with *why*, followed by *how*, *when*, *where* do women still struggle for recognition and equity in the face of sexist-driven hypocrisy. Women leaders today not only populate the streets from which movements are born, but they also organize as leaders in movements against violence. In community-based organizations throughout New York City, women are leaders fighting against the perpetuation of poverty, and against a lack of opportunity.[92] Even today, they need to continually raise the question of why they are not recognized and respected as leaders, not only by those who perpetuate injustice but also by men who struggle to overcome unfair conditions. These specious standards are applied from the streets, and are reinforced in our chambers of governance, corporate boardrooms, and in major media productions. In a parallel fashion, teens are raising questions about the exclusionary practices exercised against teens. Teen-led movements are now being increasingly directed by young women, side by side with young men who embrace them as equal partners.

Young men of color, despite the image of New York City being free of discriminatory practices, face bias administration of law enforced at much higher rates than young men who are White. Youth-led agencies such as the Urban Youth Collaborative challenged the routine placement of weapon detectors in schools located in communities of color. In these schools, the entrances are set up to reflect assumptions by adults that all teens are potentially a source of danger to each other, as well as to adult staff. In lieu of having evidence-supported practices such as conflict resolution, mediation, and peer court practice, schools use X-ray and security guards. Most schools serving students of color have more security guards than guidance counselors. All students of color, male and female, attend schools with fewer teachers practicing their trade in license, and far fewer options to be offered high quality coursework. The Urban Youth Collaborative sheds light on the paucity of Advanced Placement coursework in the "inner cities" neighborhoods; these college readiness courses are routine in schools serving the privileged. The collaborative has created a student bill of rights demanding these benefits for all students.[93] They have recently been invited to locally based civic bodies such as community boards and city council advisory boards to push for these changes. Their advice is often noted, but only slowly and unevenly promoted, as changes in policies and practices are very slow to evolve.

The YA-YA Network questioned the values driving huge budgets for the U.S. military and advanced weaponry for urban law enforcement. Their worked is derived from the source of Dr. Martin Luther King's identification of militarism as one of the four catastrophic pillars of our "modern" version of America.[94] In the community where my youth service started, the Washington Heights and Inwood Teen Council raised questions about our adult-led culture of substance usage and abuse, and our ill-advised policies designed to address these issues. Why, given the fact that tobacco, alcohol, and illegal drug production, distribution, and marketing are led by adults in major industries, had teens been identified as hapless dupes who assume primary responsibility for the associated problems of substance abuse? The Washington Heights Teen Council leadership engaged in research about the methodologies of these industries in New York City. The council exposed the public face of ideologies turning teen victims into perpetrators. It followed up its revelations with research showing evidence that the false approach of blaming teens was used for the enforcement of local laws resulting in punishment of teens, while merchants continued virtually unabated by selling tobacco products to teens. Store owners would post signs declaring their practice of not selling to teens but monitoring for infractions did little to deter access to tobacco products in stores throughout the uptown community. I call this the WHIP approach, the witch-hunt identification project, where victims are judged to be villains.

In response to this inconsistent enforcement, The WHTC council also produced a community map detailing the prevalence of sales in local markets. Shopkeepers who peddled tobacco products to youth and who ran nicotine pipelines in fronts were finally busted for a class of crimes resulting in life-long health injuries for youths. What had previously lain hidden became visible, thanks to what teen whistle-blowers exposed. Prior justifications for primarily blaming irresponsible teen behavior which had been promoted by what I call Tobacco Marketing Anonymous would begin to be challenged by local lawmakers.[95] A similar sequence of first blame teens and then enlist their youth leadership to solve the smoking problem has cropped up across the United States, such as with the Rage Against the Haze project in Florida. In the Rage project, after adult efforts to reduce smoking amongst teens had gone nowhere, teens were put in charge of devising campaign strategy, managing the efforts, and creating the messaging, resulting in consistent decline in teen smoking in only a few years.[96] The invisibly enabled threat to teen health became challenged through teen monitoring and oversight of adult responsibility.

During the advocacy period for the Teens on Community Boards initiative (2007-2014), proponents for teen municipal enfranchisement encountered curious forms of hypocrisy coming out of the mouths of edu-cated and professed progressive leaders. These leaders, who had articulated support for equal justice, supported government mandates that were overly punitive toward teens, especially against young people of color. Liberals, who had spoken for the value of giving people who had made mistakes a second chance, voted for and promoted policies denying educational, housing and job support to those who had been convicted of a crime. Often heard were comments such as "My son/daughter is not interested or capable of serving on Community Boards, so I can't support this change." Or "Why should teens who wear their pants around their ankles be allowed critical responsibilities?" In government chambers at both the city and state levels, we continue to see a steady stream of righteous announcements targeting marginalized popu-lations. The propagation of negative labels, often coded in terms like *single mothers, the inner city, wolf-packs,* and *unprepared teens,* embed egregiously negative generalizations within our public dialogue.[97] If we are to stay true to the scientific method, then when valid questions are raised by youthful dissenting critique, it is essential that pettifogging premises are rebuked, and potential avenues to institute changes in how we frame targeted peoples be fully explored and tested. In the upcoming sections of this book, I will profile youth-led campaigns that engaged in these story-changers. These campaigns include, among others, the work of Students Working Against Tobacco, in Florida in the 1990s, where teens were charged with designing, leading, and assessing an anti-smoking campaign against culpable marketeers who had exploited teen vulnerabilities.

What I was most unimpressed with was the continuing prevalence of prejudice even when countervailing evidence was so self-evident. Adult leaders in youth agencies had already seen and acknowledged teen efficacy in practice. For decades, teens in New York City have been serving as aides in afterschool programs and day camps and have been recognized as invaluable resources to the essential functioning of these programs. Findings by the National Parole Association have documented that youth courts, where teens serve as judges under a model of reconciliation as opposed to punitive sentencing, have a far better track record regarding recidivism (that is, youth courts experience far fewer repeat offenses).[98]

For decades, youths from ages 14 to 24 were included as advisors to local government—from Hampton, Virginia, to the San Francisco Youth Commission. Yet here, in ahead-of-the-curve New York City, opponents to our proposed amendment still insisted that teens, by their nature, were incapable of practicing the skills and responsibilities needed simply for being advisors for municipal governance.[99]

Today, truth be told, except for the blind and those unwilling to acknowledge the changes that have been accomplished, things have vastly improved when it comes to allowing teens participation and advisory roles for city governance. This can readily be seen in at least some community board appointments, the creation of advisory boards to borough presidents and city council elected officials, as well as the creation of advisory boards to the New York City Department of Education and the mayor. Youth advisory models, initially developed in Latin America, constructed under the name of participatory budgeting councils, have now been adopted by most City Council members in New York City. Each participating Council member assigns a portion of his or her capital budget allocation, where residents vote on the distribution of capital budgets for each council district. This spending is restricted to properties that are owned by the city, such as public schools, city parks, and New York City Housing Developments. The adoption of this program, which invites teens as young as 14 to vote on budget allocations, was initially proposed for the Council by then City Council President Melissa Mark-Viverito.[100]

This work, however, addresses the period 1984–2014, and both my experience and the words of allies speak to its relevance—including the relevance they hold even today—later in this narrative. Today, the chief concern is the invisible grasp these older assumptions and attitudes hold on many, but not all, adults with whom I engage and from whom I hear curious commentary. In the recent past, and up until today, the words *raging hormones* and *underdeveloped brains* still dominate much of the analysis of researchers and program practitioners.[101]

Of equal concern, apropos of what we have seen in other justice movements such as the embrace of our immigrants and the guarantees of voting rights, is a sliding backwards to yesterday's worst practices. An additional question is whether teen representation on advisory boards is structured to allow for their full input based upon self-derived suggestions about options for change. There are some advisory boards on which teens sit where they are only tokens, at the table in body, but discouraged or misdirected so that offered changes are watered down. One example includes youth advisory boards for agencies with investments in fossil fuels, industries for which adult members have investments. Suggestions to disinvest are put off to a later date, with the rationale that an agency's best interest is to maximize profits now, rather than conceding that future generations' loss of a sustainable environment outweighs the monetary gains of today. These types of latter-day concerns are discussed in the next two chapters of this book, the "Introduction" and in "Anecdotes Arising." The insights offered in the past about the damages resulting from toxic self-interest still bear relevance today. One example is a point raised by the nineteenth-century French historian Alexis de Tocqueville. He raised a valid point when he expressed his concern that the practice of democracy, when restricted to only certain groups (such as White males) was an entitlement enjoyed by privileged citizens only. He warned about the creation of "self-protective enclaves."[102] The present-day development of gated communities and insular belief systems is driven by practices of prejudice and in-group self-interest that have become a barrier to a fully participatory franchise. The practice of adultism, that is, that of enforcing control in lieu of conversation and containment in place of inclusion reinforces the privileged and protected enclaves of adult-led institutions. Young adult leaders in New York City today represent peers suffering bias against their race and national background, as well as their immigration status. When it comes to adults changing their minds about teens, what little hope remains once the true nature of their minds is discovered was articulated by Thomas Paine, one of our nation's founders. In one of his revolutionary war pamphlets written to support our cause—namely, that of becoming independent—he wrote that "the mind, once enlightened, cannot for long remain mired in its previously questionable ways." (The Age of Reason).[103] It is through the practice of idealistically inspired and insightful questioning that the light of reason and justice can be found.

Asset Three: Distrust for Authority

Norman Douglas, a nineteenth-century social and political reformer, has been quoted as having quipped, "Distrust for authority is your first civic duty." Although these words were said about maintaining a healthy dissent from prevailing political authority, here I stake a claim that in a similar way, teen exhibitions of skepticism for outdated adult assumptions concerning teens contributes to wholesome adolescent development. I had first come to develop this skeptical skill set while a high school student in Jamaica, Queens, in 1965. The advent of this advantageous asset became a signature for the 1960s generation.

The tenor of those times, the roaring and turbulent 1960s, describes escalating tensions between the young generation and the older one; it is artfully described in a piece written by the editors of *Time* magazine in the spring of 1989.[104] This issue was a special edition written to commemorate the twentieth anniversary of the 1960s. In this issue, the editors wrote: "Nineteen sixty-eight had the vibration of an earthquake about it. America shuddered. History cracked open. The air of public life seemed to be on fire. Nineteen sixty-eight was more than a series of compacted events, and more than an accidental alignment of planets. It was a tragedy of change, a struggle between generations, a war between past and future, and even for an entire society, a struggle to grow up."[105] For many of us still working as activists today, the energetic footprints of this time still resonate within us; they contribute to our passionately driven intent to right the imbalances between those with privileged authority, on the one hand, and those with hyper-privileged political and economic standing, on the other.

The pushback, or really push*down*, exercised by adult censorship remains today in full effect. As reported in the *San Francisco Chronicle* in 2019: "In Orange County, California, a high school principal condemned [a] student special publication that focused on teenaged relationships; in a town about 20 miles southwest of Salt Lake City, the school administration deactivated a student website examining the mysterious dismissal of a history teacher, and in a suburb of Dallas, the principal forbade a piece in which students were critical of the administration having scheduled school events during a national school walkout in protest over gun violence."[106] I suppose none of these authorities ever read Benjamin Franklin's concern for democracy when those in power exercise actions that suppress patriotic dissent. Thankfully, there are cracks in the armory of absolute adult authority. Students in another California high school had the courts rule in favor of their right to publish, and the school withdrew its suppression of student voice and allowed the students to publish their article. Black Lives Matter is a youth-led movement that confronts the censorship of young black leaders' viewpoints that racial progress is far from adequately realized. The stark reality about actions and decisions made by single White males is that they have the ability and the authority to exercise privileged power. This has been seconded by New York City Comptroller Scott Stringer, in his occasional quips about preferential decisions by those who are "male, pale, and stale." [107]

The Black Lives Matter leadership has developed policy alternatives that advocate for the inclusion of marginalized peoples in decision-making positions, that promote discussions aimed at addressing not only legal actions but also the mindsets that lie deeply beneath the implementation of discriminatory policies, and that organize face-to-face hearings in hot spots around the country. Yet the philosophy that guides them in addressing everything from racial profiling to inequitable distribution of social and economic resources does not simply ask for power, but for a consciousness shift from "the love of power, to the power of love." As poetically expressed by Alicia Garza, the leader of the Bay Area chapter of the Black Lives Matter movement: "Love is what sustains us through all the hardships that come with this work. Even love for people who disagree…love is what ultimately will get us to a place where we can change the world, we live in."[108]

Ms. Garza's sentiments reflect those of being a citizen-advocate for all peoples, and echo Thomas Paine's sentiments regarding the larger dimension of patriotic presence when he was attributed to have claimed at public gatherings that, "Yes, I am a proud citizen of America, but also a citizen of the world." Ms. Garza's work is an affirmation of Thomas Paine's vision, expressed in a much more connected yet conflicted world than Paine knew—a world where it is more crucial than ever to pledge to be a healer of pain for "the other" and to embrace the wounded by governmental wrongdoing and negligence as you would have empathetic others embrace your if you had been an innocent victim in need of sheltering arms. While the practicing of these values remains antithetical in too many quarters of our older citizens, it is a foundational work in progress defining the intentions of youth-led movements today.

Asset Four: Hammering Hypocrisy

In the 1960s, I would frequently hear the slogan "don't believe the hype" uttered from the lips of fellow youth organizers who had opposed the war in Vietnam. This reminder motivated young leaders in ways that aided teens to be instinctively engaged in actions opposing the war. Given the wide disparities in narrative about the war between major media accounts and out of the mouth of officials with the accounts provided by peace activists, including many soldiers returning from the field, these words about hype often prefaced our critique about the war. In the 1960s, this was our initiation in which we learned to hammer at hypocrisy. In more recent days, the Occupy Wall Street movement had posted the slogan: "Real eyes expose real lies."

The youth movements organizing about racial injustice at home and investments in the fossil fuel industry, to name just two issues, have wide access to independent sources of data and information. These sources include credible messengers on the ground who experience the effects of unjust criminal justice actions continuously, and spokespeople from scientific backgrounds sounding the alarm about our environmental negligence. Adolescents are instinctively disturbed, and reliably informed, about the pretenses of pseudo-facts. I use the term pseudo-fact as derived from a term coined by the American historian Daniel J. Boorstin in 1961. In his book, *The Image: A Guide to Pseudo Events in America*, Boorstin defines a pseudo-event as one that is "not spontaneous but comes about because it was planned or planted (by special interests), [and] its occurrence is arranged for the benefit of the media.[109] In the 1980s, the major media ran continual stories about the irresponsible practices of teens resulting in unusually high rates of pregnancy. Later research showed that these teen trends mirrored the behavior of older adults. During my time organizing in Washington Heights, I would hear countless times from testimony provided by health care workers at local clinics that middle-school girls were most often enticed into sexual activity by men who were in their twenties and thirties.

Even when crime rates were falling in the early 1990s, editors creating daily headlines promoted the increasing dangers of rising crime. The steady drumbeat of this news (or fake news, given that crime rates by the early 1990s were falling) provided justification for overbearing legislation such President Clinton's Omnibus Crime Bill of 1994. Margaret Meade, an early twentieth-century anthropologist who specialized in the study of tribal cultures made an address concerning culture and commitment which is still apropos today. In pursuit of more dollars for law enforcement, public officials created an image about crime that, although existing in the past, was no longer an accurate portrayal of actual crime rates. Mike Males, whom I previously referenced in his work profiling the false narratives created about young people, called this tactic storm and stress campaigning. Ms. Meade spoke to the need of studying past practice as a guide—though not as a means of conscription for enforced authority: "We need a past that is instrumental, but not coercive, which locates our future in the now, ready to be nourished, secure, and protected."[110] We state this in another way when we demand that youth are to be recognized not just as assets under the directed control of adults, but as agents of change whose input and contributions benefit themselves and the communities they serve.

My goal was to work in realization of fully inclusive practices of democracy. This goal assumed the need to recognize the value of leadership representing all peoples of color and nationalities, as well as all people living on the younger side of the generational divide. To remain effective and appropriately practiced, my engagement definitively framed the identity of movements generated during the 30-year course of my youth work. Teen-led types of advocacy, of, by, and for youth have included rights for age-sensitive health interventions promoted at school-based clinics, the call for an end to policies such as "stop and frisk," which discriminated against and punished young people of color, and the rights of all students for equity in regard to the availability of courses such as Advanced Placement courses which prepare high school students to be academically prepared for college. Essential to these asks is to have school governance transformed by recognizing elected student representatives as part of decision-making teams alongside school administrators. The re-organization of school governance, inclusive of students at the table of institutional decision-making, would transform our educational institutions from those of producing passive stakeholders adhering to policies and rules to civic learning laboratories where the young had the right to construct the rules.[111] Teachers, school administrators, and students would construct communities of democratic participation. Just as tribal cultures had prepared the young for initiation into adulthood and leadership roles, democratic schools would serve us as a rite of passage, an age-appropriate opportunity for exercising the rights of citizenship in our communities, states, and nation. Changes put in place resulting in direct leadership experience by students-as-citizens[112] would transform the cultures of school sites. Coursework, historical study, and analysis would include recognition of student status as young people navigating the trying conditions of their neighborhood, and the oral histories of their families and neighbors from their own community. The issues being faced by young people and their families remain more crucial than ever today. Timely and inclusive response to these issues needs to include the input of community stakeholders who are addressing these issues on the ground. Governmental responses to a deadly virus (COVID-19) tragically reveal the stark inequities inherent in healthcare interventions that are determined by race and class. People of color have been far more likely to suffer the effects of the virus, and far less likely to possess the tools to manage themselves in the crisis. Health officials are reporting rises in the record-setting rates of anxiety, depression, and ideations of suicide in the young. While it is true that the impact of being hit by this virus has so far appeared to be less dangerous, physically, for the young, the virus still robs the young in "minority" communities disproportionately from maintaining a sense of connection and emotional security. Their parents and grandparents are suffering with more severe conditions because of COVID infection (for example, intensification of pre-existing chronic conditions such as diabetes and heart disease), resulting in their dying at greater rates than those of White students.[113]

Their classrooms and places to play are being taken away in inordinate numbers. Blacks and Latinos are losing connection to their legacies, gatherings, and ceremonies with their extended families. Their isolation compromises an inherent right to be immersed in close relationships with each other, as well as with mentoring adults. This negatively influences people who historically have been ostracized and traumatized through criminal justice practices and the effects of poverty of families. People who have been perpetually kept apart from the fruit of collaborative enterprise grow up feeling that they alone are to blame for problems because they have personal deficits or inherently developed bad habits. The effects of the Covid-19 epidemic did not initiate adverse psychological and social damage to young people of color. Rather it has intensified and multiplied these conditions of social isolation and despair.

Dr. Bessel Van Der Volk is the founder and director of the Trauma Center in Brookline, Massachusetts. He is also a professor of psychiatry at Boston University. After leading research initiatives and healthcare interventions with patients suffering from trauma, he has developed a comprehensive set of approaches to help patients heal from the damage not just to their minds and conscious memories but also from the hidden emotional impact buried deep in the unconscious and their very bodies, which impede optimal responses in their everyday functioning. He shares a comprehensive history about trauma, and several approaches for healing in his book, *The Body Keeps the Score*.[114] Included in his methodologies is an understanding of trauma on the parts of the brain governing our emotions and sense of social connection, as well as on people's neurological infrastructure and genetic makeup. I will visit his contributions, and a more detailed look at trauma, in the section I title "The Orphan." What I bring up here is a point raised by Edward Tick, Ph.D. who has spent years counseling veterans. He shares his insights in his book, *War and the Soul*.[115] His paradigm about the effects of violence upon the soul holds that when a person is traumatized, his soul feels like it flees the body, and forces people to vacate connection to the mind and soul. In place of a mindful and soulful connection is what he calls "an archetype of war," which induces recurrent responses triggered in situations which remind a person of their initial trauma-induced reaction to extreme threats.[116] During the course of providing services to youth, I have seen young people exhibit explosive reactions in situations which are out of proportion to any real existing threat. Some teens I have conversed with just shut down, exhibiting silence in place of dialogue, and passivity rather than taking proactive measures. Entire sectors of communities had been taken over by drug dealers, who all too often included young people as random targets in their line of fire. In Washington Heights, where homicide rates had exceeded 100 per year in the 1980s, 90 per cent of fatalities included young people who had been shot, either as participants in the drug trade or as innocently mistaken targets. Elected officials and the NY Police Department responded to this crisis with a militarized campaign, which include stop and frisk, and banging down of apartment doors, even of those not involved in the trade. Fathers, sons, and brothers, guilty even of the most minor non-violent infractions, were issued long prison sentences. When released, they returned not as rehabilitated, but rather as those abused within their time of confinement, who learned to adopt violent coping behaviors just to survive. Recent studies done under the rubric of trauma-informed intervention have documented that large majorities of young Blacks and Latinos have suffered the effects of trauma either through direct experience or because their family members and close friends have been affected. The newly found practices of trauma-informed intervention will be shared by me in a section of this book I title "The Rebel."[117] People suffering from trauma have not learned to move on from the original incident and, therefore, maintain its story in present time. The healing process begins when a person takes ownership for changing the story.

When they are cohesive and bonded, healthy communities promote a sense of neighborliness in which residents, even at a distance, still care for each other through their contact and presence in spaces where, as often spoken to by the spiritual educator Parker Palmer, it is safe for "each soul to enter the room."[118] Rather than maintaining entrances to schools with metal detectors and the police patrol of streets as if policing hostile territories, we need to include discipline and justice programs in schools based upon the practices of reconciliation, and neighborhood community policing programs where constituents and officers are partners for community stabilization. These practices of renewal and peace-making would call teachers, police officers and the young into a "calling in accountability and mutuality" and into a "reunion of separated beings whose primary bond is (civic) love."[119]

School sites have always been thought of as safe havens, but the escalation of gun violence has altered that reality. In my youth, schools would hold "shelter drills": students would hide under a desk or crouch in a hallway as preparation in case a nuclear attack was imminent. Teachers would oversee these practices in solemn ways; students would snicker among themselves, wondering who would be foolish enough to believe anyone would survive. To paraphrase a cultural critic active in the sixties, we were practicing survival in a haven of the mindless world. I use a play on words here on the theme of a book called *Haven in a Heartless World* by Christopher Lasch. In his book, he laments the overreach of "social science 'experts' (who) intrude more and more into our lives. The families' vital role as the moral and social cornerstone of society disintegrates—and, if left unchecked, so does our political and personal freedom."[120]

Today, all schools and youth-based agencies are required to hold "shelter-in-place drills" twice a year,[121] as preparation for the potential, dreadful arrival of armed intruders. In these drills, students and teachers practice giving and responding to commands that would be given in a high threat situation, as well as retreating to safe spaces within a building, away from windows and behind locked doors. Unlike the nuclear attack drills engaged in by students of my generation, which in a real nuclear bombing would have been useless, shelter- in- drills are essential, as in a real intrusion this practice can save lives. The point here is that although only a small minority of students will thankfully never experience this type of threat, nobody knows where and when. Preparation for all has become the normal. However, what has adult leadership done to prevent the possibility of this threat?

The hypocrisy lies in the hands of our legislative leaders, who fail to act to prevent such terrifying scenarios from ever occurring. Sensible controls that would mitigate excessive gun violence have been habitually opposed by the National Rifle Association (NRA). The NRA exercises extraordinary influence over federally elected legislators. Even in New York State, a measure to put the tracing of bullets into effect was defeated when a single legislator defected and voted against the bill. According to sources in the legislature, even though the legislator felt the measure made perfect sense, his district constituency strongly believed in pro-gun owner rules. He voted against public interest to prevent a threat to his holding on to his seat. As put forth by March for Our Lives leader Emma Gonzalez, a student at Parkland High School. politicians sit in their safe House and Senate seats funded by the NRA." They survive term to term on the game of pay for play, while their youngest constituents wait every day for the armed madman whose only intent is to slay. This daunting reality remains an example of habitually exercised hypocrisy. To paraphrase a quotation posted in an ad in the socially conscious *Ad Busters* magazine - The dreams of our adult leaders have become the nightmares suffered by our youth.

Asset Five: Interconnected Intelligences

This asset is last on the list but first in importance because it connects the previous four assets to form a comprehensive strategy for dealing with and adjusting to a changing world.

Researching and applying teaching methods that incorporate multiple intelligences has changed our approach to measuring intelligence. Multiple intelligences include measures of logical thinking, creative thinking, emotional awareness, and body sensitivity. Each type of intelligence is a critical element for understanding a wide range of mental capacities. These topics covering diverse types of intelligence have been researched by education specialists such as Howard Gardner.[122] New types of tests which consider the diversity in types of intelligence are now increasingly being applied in classroom practices and in teacher preparation programs across our country.[123]

I especially distance myself from considering popular aptitude or achievement tests and traditionally applied tests assessing cognitive capacity (even though my generation collectively scored higher on IQ tests than my parents' generation, as has each generation arriving after mine). Sander Gilman, a professor of psychiatry at Emory University, and James Thomas, an assistant professor of sociology at the University of Mississippi, collaborated on a research study examining previously constructed measures of intelligence. The authors spoke as well to our nation's political responses to these studies. What they found is that most of these research projects, beginning in the early 1900s, were poorly constructed and resulted in ill-founded conclusions. The mismeasured findings had been used to justify practices of discrimination against Jewish people and Blacks. Poor testing results misdirected policies based upon them; those policies continued for decades. The tests were not thoroughly discredited until after World War II. The extensive use of the tests led these two authors to construct a book title asking, *Are Racists Crazy?*[124]

IQ tests such as those alluded to above were initiated by Henry Goddard. Goddard was a recognized leader in the intelligence testing world. The motivation for this type of intelligence testing was not Goddard's alone. The early 1900s saw a steep rise in testing based upon since-discredited theories based on eugenics—that is, the biological, physiological, and cognitive deficit rationales for assuming inferiority in targeted people. In the early 1900s, tests were constructed to prove that racial superiority and inferiority were genetically preordained. As detailed in the book, *Are Racists Crazy?* Goddard's test results, identifying "backward peoples," found that 80 per cent of Hungarians, 79 per cent of Italians, 87 per cent of Russians, and 83 per cent of Jews were morons.[125] The belief that some religious doctrines hold that God had picked Jewish folks as "his chosen people" should be cause enough to create consternation regarding these tests. In fact, decades after these tests were employed, their methodologies were questioned—and they were found to be seriously defective.[126] But in the intervening years, schools used these results to categorize and rank students, elected officials cited statistics to justify imbalanced and prejudicial policies, and the media used them to stoke irrational fears about the "others" in times of high crime levels and social unrest.

Tests used by institutions of higher education are used to determine an applicant's aptitude for becoming a successful college student. The goal of predicting the success of a future college student based upon a one-day test has serious flaws. As found by education writer Alfie Kohn, tests such as the SAT have failed to predict long-term college success beyond the first year of college.[127] As indicators, they are moderately reliable for the freshman year, and even these results fade substantially after the sophomore year. What these tests do align with is the student's household income: the lower the income, the lower the SAT score. The higher the income, the higher the score. What *is* the score on this?

One important factor is the level of early education support that a current student had been given by the parents during their time as toddlers and young children prior to starting kindergarten. The added preparatory value for becoming a successful student had been attained through richer exposure to story and vocabulary at an early age, and then the availability of higher quality course content in the early years of schooling.[128], [129]

Albert Einstein raised an alarm for the entire education system, when he wrote in his 1949 autobiography: " It is a miracle, given the modern methods of instruction, that a child's imagination is not entirely strangled". This he held to be true even if one considers children of privilege. [130] Mr. Einstein was responding to techniques used in classroom instruction relying on pure recitation from teachers, and rote memorization by students, rather than the use of exploration by using research or experimentation . Psychologist and education historian Mihaly Csikszentmihalyi adds grist to the mill, and seconds Mr. Einstein's concerns in modern schools. His research, shared in his book, *Creativity*, shows that "only 50% of gifted children go on to careers compatible with their heightened abilities," and that for all students "learning to like and experience challenge is crucial to their developing motivation for study."[131] The latter category contrasts sharply with the adjective most students I have come to know use in describing school- it is boring.

So, where do we begin the process of educating teens? First, I suggest that teachers change their focus on obtaining just the "facts," through rational processing, memorization of detail, and similar constructs. We need not jettison these crucial elements, but rather should add to the educational equation the importance of heart intelligence and socioeconomic influences on the process. As counseled in the book, *Your Body and the Stars*, by spiritual and health advisors Stephanie Marango, a spiritually oriented medical doctor, and Rebecca Gordon, a nationally acclaimed astrologer, we need to recognize the heart as our "source for radiating our truths, as well as connecting to the source of the universe for its spiritual knowledge."[132] Carolyn Myss, a writer seeking to reaffirm the heart as a center of learning, emphasizes Marango's and Gordon's observation. In her book, *The Sacred Contract*, Ms. Myss states: "The heart chakra is a poetic chakra, which leads us in our search for beauty and truth, and which helps us to utilize lyricism in our quest for developing sharp insight."[133]

For decades, the Heart Math Institute has created measures that link heart health and heart intelligence (social-emotional intelligence) to outcomes supporting personal efficacy and connections to classrooms, community, and the world.[134] Intuition is one type of skill developed using heart intelligence. Dr. Raymond Bradley, a researcher at the Heart Math Institute, conducted a study examining the differences in heart rhythm amongst entrepreneurs when compared to control groups in the general population. Dr. Bradley found differences in heart rhythm among groups of entrepreneurs when each group was compared to the heart rhythms of a control group. Dr. Bradley's study was designed to test such variations when participants in each group were asked to make decisions regarding hunches concerning the future success of theoretical choices they were asked to make.

J.P. Guilford was an educational theorist and psychologist whose body of work I was introduced to in the 1970s. I studied his theory and paradigm while a graduate student at New York University in 1974. Although I did not hold on to his textbook, his thoughts and methods influenced my educational intervention when began teaching cognitively delayed and emotionally disabled students in the mid-1970s at the Life Skills School Ltd. He proposed a "structure of intellect" model, which included one hundred and forty-four intelligence factors, as opposed to IQ tests, which typically tested only twelve factors. One type of intelligence missed by standard tests is that of interpersonal intelligence, defined as the capacity to understand the intentions, motivations, and desires of other people. These types of intelligence are based upon feelings and emotions rather than cognitive or rational factors. [135]

In 1993, I was introduced to the work of educator Shelley Kessler and her colleagues at the Crossroads School in southern California while attending a workshop at Goddard College in Vermont. Ms. Kessler taught a workshop I attended at a retreat for educators and youth service workers. At the retreat, Ms. Kessler shared this spiritually based perspective: "Our Mysteries Curriculum did not emerge in reaction to adolescent fear, isolation and despair. The Mysteries Curriculum arose and thrived out of a bold re-visioning of the meaning of education.[136] and a sharing of this search for meaning with students, through their questions— "Why do people want to destroy each other, and how can we get to trust each other? I wonder what lies beyond the solar system, a white light, a healing power? When will I stop badgering myself when I make mistakes? Why do we continue to ruin the earth that none of us can do without?"[137] The learning cycle starts with the student's questions about life, rather than with a predetermined culture of answers. Both the educator and the educated thrive when the empires of reason are explored as interconnected with the depths of mystery and heart intelligence.

Verifying the value of the five adolescent assets within the context of teen civic involvement at the municipal level of governance.

A final reference point for multiple intelligence is this—any applied method and philosophy practiced is enhanced when started at the earliest stages of educational encounter. Young activists utilize their assets in responsive school-based governance, as well as through actively enhanced opportunities at the community-based level.[138] Additionally, teens must be allowed to creatively express these assets and put them to communal use, and this opportunity must be shared across the generational divide.

Kathleen Cushman, an educator who, with support from the MetLife Foundation launched a project called "What Kids Can Do," describes learning gains attained when we set fires to the mind: Guided practice results in learning gains that are more reliable than just assuming a particular student has talent[139] The attainment of personal efficacy and social engagement are better enhanced through the models of project-based learning and what Generation Citizen calls "Action Civics."[140] The guiding philosophy behind the "What Kids Can Do" program is that active, constructive engagement by youth, under the guidance of attentive and affirming teachers, increases knowledge and encourages application of learned skills.[141] When students engage in dialogue and debate with each other, and learn to generate questions and create consensus, even during elementary school—when they get to construct approaches and create interventions in their schools and communities, their social/emotional IQs are raised, and their sense of concern for others and capacity for making a difference are enhanced. Their primary grade exposure to social engagement such as community service-learning projects also is a building block for their "action civic" work in middle school and high school when the increasing demands for a life of independence take hold. These projects include making improvements in people's lives such as making sleeping bags for the homeless and beautification projects such as working in community gardens. Many studies have documented the finding that when the responsibilities involved in becoming engaged in the civic realm, including those responsibilities associated with voting rights, begin in high school, then the likelihood of voting as one gets older increases. As a bonus, the likelihood of one's parents voting, even if they have previously been reticent to do so, also increases.[142]

When the world of civic participation is offered to high school students who have practiced civic skills such as brainstorming, guided research, debate, and consensus making while at the same time being engaged with older adults with decision-making experience, the number of quality personal and communal outcomes typically multiplies. This approach, which is known as project-based learning, was implemented by me when I became a director of the Police Athletic League's (PAL) teen services program in 2004.[143] It is also a staple of practice in other teen civic training programs such as the Action Civics approach used by Generation Citizen. This will be more thoroughly described in a section of this book I title "The Civic Lover." In each of these approaches, what is notable is that students would become invested in projects they felt held value and meaning for them. Working together as a team, students were more likely to remain persistent and engage in deliberative practice. The older stereotypes about teens, such as their being chronically disinterested and bored when asked to reach beyond their comfort zones, or that their short attention spans prohibit long-term commitment to a project, were found by adults and teens in these projects to be mythologies whose time had come and passed, no longer relevant to describing the nature of adolescence. The wisdom of elders, combined with the elders' seasoned applications, grew deeper as youth introduced new perspectives based on currently lived experience. As I alluded to earlier in this narrative, the project-based learning approach has also taken place in a world that is now vastly different from the one lived by adults who were teens in the 1960s. When working in civic partnership, a marriage of wisdom and passionately held optimism, idealism and an urge for immediate action arises. Co-leadership and shared advisory, in project-based learning exercises, as well as in places such as community boards, where teens interact with adults on a level playing field, allows for creation of intergenerational partnerships serving the common good for community and beyond.[144]

Adolescent assets are related to social and emotional styles of intelligence. When rewarded, opportunities are created for multiple intelligences to be applied in the arena of community problem solving.

As 16- and 17-year-old teens started getting appointed to community boards in the spring of 2015, their introduction to existing board members was met with cautious optimism and silently expressed skepticism on the part of many older board members. New appointees came in with hopeful expectations accompanied by shades of self-doubt and nervousness. However, once serving, even if for only a few months, the chemistry between the board members would shift. Older adults became impressed with the insights and dedication to serving shown by the younger members. Younger adults became appreciative of the eager willingness of older board members to coach them through the process of learning about complex details and the board's processes. As they increasingly embraced each other, the culture of the board became enriched. Adults had the opportunity to observe the skills and talents of teens in action and listened to the life stories of the young. Community board meetings became a space for equitable participation by teens. Teens learned about the board process, and adults learned how the process in the past failed to account for the feelings and experiences of teens living in the community. This new partnership between adults and teens allowed for the co-evolution of community stakeholders.

I saw this type of shift in expectations in action when I attended one of the many community board orientations led by Manhattan Borough President (BP) Gale Brewer, assistant BP Aldrin Bonilla, and their junior colleague.[145] These sessions were designed to include information about board applications and processes involved in serving as a community advocate. Included were participatory scenarios in which high school students, split into groups representing community board committees, were presented with virtual problems. Teen participants were then asked to come up with insights about the problems, as well as suggestions and possible solutions. There was one problem that was given to two separate groups deliberating independently from each other. In this scenario, each group was asked to rank community need, including the needs for housing and green spaces. After approximately 15 minutes, each group was asked to report back to the larger body as a whole. The assumption was that each group's decision would be based on the recognition that the group had been presented with a forced choice between two options, either prioritizing the need for more housing or for the development of green gardens.[146]

We older folks have been well-conditioned to rank, prioritize, and think in terms of either/or when addressing problems. What happened here, however, was that each group used an "and/also" approach. In their reports, they stated that it was possible to simultaneously address both problems, by building housing—but with added green space, either between the housing units or in the form of rooftop gardens. Gale, of course, summarized the results in her excited and appreciative manner, calling out their genius for looking through the lens of "the third way" and promising to share their insightful input with the currently existing board.

Two observations are in order here. The first observation has been shared with youth providers and educators by the Search Institute, whose staff has studied and dialogued with adults and teens participating in youth agency programs and attending schools across the United States. Beginning in the 1980s, and continuing over a period of decades, the Search Institute has developed a rubric for personally and socially nourishing practices and attributes that maximize holistic teen development and fully inclusive communities.[147] The rubric is designed using categories they define as External Assets. These include analyzing support systems in place for teens, such as family support and caring school climates, as well as practices promoting the constructive use of time by teens. The second major category in the Search Institute rubric measures what they label as Internal Assets, such as a young person caring about his or her school or students learning how to plan. The institute has developed its rubric using measured observations of teen and adult interactions as well as institutions led by adult leaders that have a significant impact on teen lives. In their research into the world experienced by teens, The Search Institutes' researchers found that with adults' reactions to teen behavior, negative commentary or remarks that question the motives and/or abilities of teens had been evident in eight of ten adult responses. When people of differing origins and perspectives are provided the opportunity to work on tasks of mutual benefit, perspectives come to be valued by adults. More affirming attitudes adopted by both adults and young people build neighborhood consensus. Dismissive attitudes which had led to adults questioning the efficacy of the young begin to disappear. Rigid assumptions leading the young to automatically distrust their elders start to melt away. The Search Institute found that when teens are given opportunities for guided experimentation and are supported by adults with positive expectations, the self-image and performance of teens improves, and the nature of the adult-teen relationships becomes more positive. These changed expectations regarding adult and teen relationships introduce a potential sea change in conversations between adults and teens.

The second point is one previously raised by Dr. Scilla Elworthy, whom I referenced earlier as an international negotiator and facilitator. As she has said about her experience and revelations obtained through her work, it is through face-to-face dialogue between differing categories of people that an education process about "the other" begins, and the territories and agreements for common ground are forged.

Most of us are familiar with the inspiring story of Malala Yousafzai, a teen from Pakistan who was working to promote the rights of girls in her country. In an act of revenge by a member of the Taliban, she was shot in the head; thankfully, she was afforded expert medical intervention in England, enabling her to return home and continue her work. Ms. Elworthy has studied the work of the Youth Peace Network (YPN) that Malala became engaged with once she returned home to Pakistan.[148] The Youth Peace Network is a teen agency started in Pakistan in 2010 that incorporates teens into its leadership structure. Assisted by a team of teens, this YPN group has created a grassroots challenge targeting extremist intolerance and deeply rooted gender inequality. The group has trained over 75 activists, who in turn have helped to turn around more than 600 youth at risk of falling prey to the Taliban's radicalization program. Inspired by challenge and a deeply held desire for peace and understanding, and supported by adults who believe in them, they have successfully helped those who are confused and lost to reimagine the world. Young leaders, dialoging face to face with youth of diverse backgrounds in Pakistan, have helped to build bridges of understanding where walls of intolerance existed before.

When I first started with youth organizing, I had to experiment with ways in which young folks from different blocks and diversified back-grounds could be trained to cooperate in helping to solve common problems. Addressing these issues started with organizing basketball tournaments where young men who barely spoke to each other learned to be teammates. As teens began to buy into community service projects, teen leadership teams would be trained to work together on fixing their local park or con-vincing peers to utilize health clinics that most had considered in the past to be intimidating to go to on their own. After a few years of block by block organizing in Washington Heights and as we focused on issues effecting youth across multiple neighborhoods, we also organized training sessions for our teen leaders at sessions with teens from other communities. Our teens would attend retreats, such as one organized by then Commissioner Richard Murphy from the Department of Youth Services. Young leaders would strategize with each other about a range of issues common to each neighborhood, such as how to safely navigate streets under often challeng-ing conditions of random violence. After putting together teen cooperative efforts in neighborhoods in the city of New York, we expanded our scope of cooperative outreach by attending national conferences sponsored by the Law Enforcement Division of the Greater NY Boy Scout Council's Explorer Program. This was a co-ed program for teens. Out teen leaders attended conferences in Colorado, Indiana, and New Mexico, where they would attend workshops, engage in sports, and chow down with teen leaders from across the United States. The workshop training topics included becoming First Aid- and CPR-certified and preparing teens for appropriate intervention in emergencies. Teens also learned the basics of laws enforced on the streets of their communities, and how to de-escalate tensions when things became heated after misunderstandings between people arose. We came to recognize the variations in perspective held by various groups of differing national origins and races. Young leaders taught me how direct engagement between members of diverse groups seeking to solve common problems of public safety, education, and community development could become a source for a commonality of understanding among all involved.

In the following section within this backward/forward chapter, I focus on how the skills of adult co-mentors and teen activists became proactively and fortuitously developed through periods of trial and error. We used mistakes as lessons about what we could avoid in the future. We also carried methods adopted in the early period of our programs as building blocks for establishing a foundation for programs with differing population targets, and/or for application to issues covering a broader area. We started block by block, and as our work continued, we had to apply our approach neighborhood by neighborhood across the five boroughs of New York. In my early years, the focus was on fostering cooperation amongst teens who lived in the same uptown neighborhood and who had diverse racial and national backgrounds. In their lives, just living on a different block from another teen could be seen by them as living in a different universe.

In 1994, we helped launch a program focusing on establishing a girl's right to play sports, and to afford herself of higher education opportunities. Many parents came from backgrounds that made them apprehensive about girls playing in what they saw as boys' games. Once they began to see changes in their daughters, such as exhibiting more confidence and becoming disinterested in temptations leading to adverse outcomes, the parents' views became supportive. Once the girl's boyfriends would come to see them in a different light, capable of playing sports and pursing dreams, the boys would do more to support the girls in their newfound efforts.

After I assumed the directorship of the teen program for the Police Athletic League in 2004, I helped teens to organize citywide conferences. Programs from 16 youth centers, across the five boroughs of New York City, would choose delegates to what we called the Youth Council.[149] The council would decide on issues of interest each year, and hundreds of teens would attend workshops led by teen workshop facilitators.[150] I use this series of period pieces to chronicle the journey in which I developed and refined my skills as a mentor to teens practicing civic empowerment. I title this section of the book "Forward/Backward" because the 30-year journey I reference might, on the face of it, appear to be a steady progression or a series of simple learning stages, leading only to better and better personal developmental outcomes. However, at each stage we had to learn to deal with new obstacles, but with the same fundamental approach. These included letting teens decide on the issues, dialoguing and debating with each other, and then coming to a consensus about how to present the issues and proposed solutions.

Before discussing this 28-year period of my teen enfranchisement work, I offer a few thoughts on my civic work in Washington Heights between 1979 and 1984. Although developed with work in adult-led programs exercised from the perspective of adults only, I did develop community-building and inter-group relationship practices which would also be relevant to leading youth programs. I do this to look backward, in a period just before the initiation of my youth programs. During this pre-youth services time, I had developed organizing skills and enhanced perspective about the nuances of Washington Heights that I would look back upon as applicable and valuable for my work with youth programming. During this period, I was involved in neighborhood volunteer work in which organizations were run by adults, addressing local issues about crime, lack of housing, and overcrowded schools. Although these movements addressed issues of concerns to teens and youth, the membership and leadership were devoid of adolescent representation. However, the Heights and Inwood were well organized at the grassroots level, and I learned lessons that were applicable to my involvement with teen enfranchisement efforts. Some of these included working with folks from diverse backgrounds as people had to come to understand cultural differences. Activists had varied levels of work experience, some had professional administration skills, and others were skilled community organizers. Upper Manhattan stretched from West 155th Street to the northern tip of Manhattan at West 223rd Street, and from the Hudson River Park to the edges of the Harlem River. We have many sections of our community in which individual members of one section, such as the southern part of Washington Heights, would barely know what was going on in a section in the northern edge of Manhattan, such as Inwood or Marble Hill.

In 1979, while living in an apartment complex on Riverside Drive, I was introduced to a local democratic club by one of my neighbors, W. Dwight Murph. Mr. Murph was interested in politics and had also been a college student who had taken courses given by a philosophy professor named Dr. Albert E. Blumberg. In his earlier years, Mr. Blumberg had been active in left-progressive political movements. Nearing retirement as a professor, and active in neighborhood improvement efforts, he was seeking volunteer opportunities in which he could make a progressively oriented yet practical difference. At the time I joined the Audubon Reform Democratic Club in 1979, he had been elected as a Democratic District Leader; he was also the leader of the club.

The executive leadership of the club, comprising three co-chairs and an executive committee, was served by active people who had taken on leadership roles in issue-involved causes. The first lesson I would learn would be about leading strongly opinionated members to come to consensus through continuous exploratory conversations and a commitment to compromise. The causes included reform of institutional healthcare delivery systems. Neighborhood leaders, such as Pricilla Basset from the Uptown Health Council, and David Dubnau from the Riverside-Edgecombe Neighborhood Association, fought to make medical intervention more accessible and more sensitive to people's cultural orientations by creating satellite locations for hospital-related services. Affordable housing and assuring tenants' rights in housing court were also major focuses of the club. In an era that was eventually marked by the election of Ronald Reagan and the rise of the political right, the club focused not only on getting democrats elected at the city, state, and national levels but also worked to get progressive-leaning candidates elected to these positions.

The philosophy of club members was that to ensure fair representation of the community, the club had to have people from diverse backgrounds in lead positions. The club worked to expand its membership from its liberal but Caucasian base to include Blacks and Latinos, especially those with a Dominican-American background. With the population explosion uptown in the 1980s, Dominicans were now a majority constituency. The Audubon Club also pushed to have equal representation by men and women, whether by drafting candidates for office or by appointment to Democratic Party and municipal governance positions.

These values would influence my decisions as I assisted teen leadership within my youth agencies. My organizations served sectors of the community composed chiefly of Dominican-Americans, but also contained a large percentage of Blacks that had both American and immigrant origins. Programs designed to serve girls in sports were very few in number in the Heights. Girls were not provided equal opportunities as were boys to participate in sports, nor to learn leadership skills by serving as captains on a team. Girls remained frozen out of activities which incorporated exercise. Having sufficient exercise promotes positive health indicators, confidence, leadership skills and an appreciation for teamwork. If equal opportunity is not watered at the roots, the flowering of leadership at the top by girls remains sparse.

A second lesson I learned, after the first one teaching me about the value of consensus-building amongst opinionated leaders, was the importance of having as many members as possible who had a variety of interests and issue focus involved in promoting the goals of the organization. The Audubon Reform Democratic Club, for which I was an Executive Board member in the early 1980s, had a comprehensive approach: it organized committees addressing specific issue interests such as public safety, access to health services, education reform, and equitable Democratic Party representation in leadership ranks. When the Audubon Club organized outreach teams for collecting nominating petitions, necessary to get candidates for public office on the ballot in New York State, club members went door to door and engaged neighbors in discussions about these issues. The goal of a progressive political club is to have its leadership focus on policy reform and more equitable delivery of municipal agency services. Challenges coming up in specific situations such as a spike in robberies or low scores on tests given to students would be addressed in conversations. However, the goal of the club was to develop comprehensive policy suggestions for providing remedies to problems. Types of the Club's recommendations would include improving cooperation between the public and the local police precinct and improving the richness of educational resources in local schools. The Audubon Club's intervention advocated for a progression from identifying a problem, to a proposal in action, to adoption of municipal policy.

In our local youth programs such as Southern Heights and the Uptown Dreamers, we scheduled frequent leadership trainings into our calendar. Agency staff listened to and honored the uniqueness of members' individual experiences and stories. At the same time, we encouraged them to see how their own perspective fits into a larger frame of the community in which they lived. This involved helping them to organize in ways that allowed them to be responsive to the interests and needs of their peers, and those of their adult neighbors. Everybody wanted to feel safer when walking down a street after dark. Parents wanted to feel that their concerns had been responded to by teachers and principals.

A third lesson I learned was the importance of brainstorming, getting out of zones of familiarity, and becoming willing to experiment with novel approaches in addressing problems. In 1981, I met Maria Luna who was organizing tenant associations with a housing rights group called the Riverside-Edgecombe Neighborhood Association. With rising crime rates and fear of being on the streets for simple errands becoming the new norm, Maria and I decided to cofound a grassroots neighborhood improvement organization called the Riverside Neighborhood Security Association (RNSA). A couple of years after I had first started community work with Maria, I also introduced her to Albert Blumberg, the President of the Audubon Democrats. With a vacancy in a Democratic Party position for female District Leader opened after joining the club, she agreed to fill that position. A district leader, amongst other duties, places people to serve as election inspectors at polling places and meets with other district leaders to draft local Democratic Party platforms related to crime, education, and housing needs.

Our security association held monthly meetings that served as a forum about community concerns such as crime. The meetings also served as a link via which residents could establish connections with community affairs officers at their local police precinct. While advocating for increased law enforcement presence during difficult times, we also attempted to persuade concerned membership to utilize and build on other community resources that contributed to a better quality of life. Creating active tenant associations and community watch programs helped sustain a communal culture in which people who might otherwise feel isolated established connections and a sense of neighborliness. People learned the value of not just passively waiting on help from professionals but also about becoming active in supporting the goals and programs operated by both professionals as well as by grassroots programs. In my youth organizations, we built this culture of caring, building on the guidance of our brother/sister program, the Dreamers, which promoted the practice of encouraging teens not only to be friends with themselves, but also to be best friends with their peers.

After several gatherings of the RNSA, I increasingly grew weary of repetitive conversations in which the focus on youth involved talk amongst adults who often complained that young people were irresponsible and a problem to others. Perhaps my experiences in my profession at the time, first as a special education teacher and then as supervisor at the Life Skills School, allowed me to see young people who had been labeled as deficient and emotionally challenged in a different light. I had started at Life Skills in 1972 and continued to work there until my voluntary retirement in 1994. The school, which had been housed in a Hebrew school building in Rego Park, accepted, as per contract with the NYC Board of Education, placements of special needs students who resided in all five boroughs of the city. Most students had been given multiple (and sometimes conflicting) diagnosis about how to label their condition, and/or lived in school districts lacking the availability of programs adequate to meet their needs. At Life Skills, founded and led by former Board of Education teachers Howard Greenwald and Robert Singer, staff took heed of each diagnosis and the Board of Education recommended educational programs. However, the school functioned as a deeply caring community, focused on each student's social and emotional needs. Many students had case histories suggesting that their behaviors were extremely resistant to improvement. Often, in a matter of a few months, or a couple of years for those who had been more severely challenged, students abandoned their dysfunctional communication styles and oppositional behaviors and learned to trust in a supportive atmosphere. I had learned that even those labeled as irredeemable could develop lifestyles conducive to their learning to redeem themselves.

The RNSA executive board agreed that I would write a youth proposal in which the association would sponsor a new youth program. In drafting the proposal, I took the lessons learned at Life Skills to mind. These included creating supportive environments, especially for those who had been mislabeled and ostracized. Also important was creating programs where young people, once taking some responsibility for their own lives, and learning to get along with others, could find a place they could call a second home and become recognized for their assets rather than for their problems. The proposed program would draw from diverse communities within our neighborhood, offer sports and recreation, homework assistance and cultural activities, and put together a teen civic team to assist with running program activities.

During the early 1980s, I had also been appointed to the local community board by then Manhattan Borough President Andrew Stein. I would be reappointed by David Dinkins after he was elected to be borough president following the conclusion of Mr. Stein's tenure. During my time at Community Board #12M, I learned about and practiced the measured participation necessary for boards to function; such participation included delegated committee work. I also met members who linked their responsibilities of being sensitive listeners who attended to community members' concerns with offering advice and assistance in getting problems addressed or helping promising programs to get assisted.

One of the committees for Community Boards is called the Youth Education and Youth Services Committee. Members of this committee stressed that given the magnitude and scope of the problems faced by our entire community it was important that individual agencies network to address common issues. Charles DeFino, a liaison to the New York City Department of Youth Services who worked for the Board, advised me during my maiden voyage as a youth service director for what we named Southern Heights: Communities Organized for Public Service. He not only advised, but also arranged for Southern Heights to create partnerships with other agencies. His delivery style was highly animated, accompanied by fast-moving hand-waving—and at times equally fast-moving sarcastic commentary. At the end of the day, after all was said (by Charlie), practical things got done. One example was the supportive programming offered by Project Basement, which operated out of St. Catherine's Church. Project Basement staff delivered workshops to our youth on sex education and developing healthy co-ed relationships. A second example was the Washington Heights Development Corporation, which filmed mock job interviews for our teens, offering tips about their presentation and guidance for preparing resumes. Each of these agencies had their own neighborhood territories and agendas to cover, but also found a way to collaborate to provide extra levels of support for youth.

There are two sets of overarching civic engagement principles that my experiences in local democratic politics and on the ground community improvement efforts provided me. The first set is discussed in detail by authors James G. Gimpel, J. Celeste Lay, and Jason E. Schuknecht in a book they co-wrote called *Cultivating Democracy*.[151] In their survey of successful and challenged attempts for "promoting political socialization" in diverse communities across the United States, they emphasize that the nature of the civic environment in place matters. As the authors, put it in their book: "[H]igher rates of knowledge can lead to higher rates of participation, provided that local environments also provide sources of information, and those actors are engaged in critical social engagement. It is the role of the provider of services to stimulate interest, and once people become motivated, to mobilize people to act." The authors also found that "the greater the rates of conversation, and the less people from differing backgrounds remain segregated from each other, the more people develop a sense of efficacy, and the ability to deal with highly contested differences of opinion." [152]

In the youth programs that I either directed or partnered with, introducing information and strategies involving teen voice were essential. As teen leaders became used to listening to opinions from those of different cultures or distant locales, their heartfelt embrace of others developed as part of their social justice portfolios. Teens were also rewarded with out-of-town trips to college campuses and to specialized recreation facilities in upstate New York such as rock-climbing or outdoor challenge courses. Our programs also scheduled special events that profiled the accomplishments of teen leaders in audiences, including their parents and community partners. Our teen advocates were also included as part of our agency advocacy team when we made presentations to elected officials and municipal agency representatives. When supported by validating adults, and building confidence through experience, teen leaders volunteered to serve as coaches to peers who were newer to our civic participation process. Over time, our teen leaders became recognized as credible advocates for policy change. Documentation about their service also helped in their application portfolios for entry-level jobs and for college. Two brief descriptions of teen leadership programs are offered next, with deeper elaboration to come in the later sections of this chapter.

Having teens offer positive peer influence was a program component developed in our early days with the Southern Heights and Uptown Dreamer programs. Our two programs shared sponsorship for Explorer Post #280, a teen co-ed program that had been developed by the Greater NYC Boy Scout Council. The Boy Scout Council assigned each post an identification number. As the years progressed, the number 280 would be identified as a source of pride associated with the post's many accomplishments. These will be addressed in more detail in the later sections of this chapter.[153] Each post elected officers, a president and vice-president, a secretary and treasurer, and an executive council. These officers served in an advisory capacity to each of the two programs, Southern Heights, and the Dreamers. This was my first program leadership engagement for working along with a teen advisory body. Two of our teen officers, Calvin Thomas, and Dwayne Piper, became instrumental peer facilitators for encouraging increased numbers of teen visits to the Columbia Presbyterian-sponsored Young Men's Clinic. Columbia had set up what was called a Young Adult Clinic, but it was almost only women aged 14 to 21 who took advantage of their services. Dr. Bruce Armstrong, the director for these services, wrote a new grant and obtained funding to start a standalone Young Men's Clinic. After meeting one of the clinics health care workers, big Jim Griffin, who had volunteered to referee basketball games for our boys, Calvin and Dwayne were talked into giving the clinic a try. After they reported back to the peers about how cool the social workers, doctors, and nurses were, they convinced friends to go to the clinic, often accompanying them on initial visits. From that point on, the word spread in the community.[154] The Young Men's Clinic, which, before our Explorer's first visit, had scant attendance, became so busy that they had to open its doors for an additional evening each week. Dr. Armstrong would be invited to conferences when asked to speak to the value of community-based teen clinics. He always brought stories and a slideshow to the conferences when pitching his case.

In 1994, after setting up the all-girls education and sports program called the Ivy League/Uptown WINs (Women in Neighborhood Sports).

This league was co-founded by Ivy Fairchild, who worked as the public affairs director for Columbia University, and me. The teen advisory body for the Ivy League was called Female Finesse. They helped the Ivy League staff to develop education workshops for parents, young people, and folks from other youth programs in the community. These workshops, developed in collaboration with the Women's Sports Foundation and the NYC Girl Scout Council, offered workshops on the benefits of sports participation for girls, as well as legislative mandates such as Title IX which demanded equal funding and opportunities for girls and women in programs paid for by the federal government. The Dreamers, who served as a supportive partner for the Ivy League, also had a teen advisory group called Coaches Who Care. These girls would serve as peer coaches during basketball and softball tournaments, and helped to organize special events, such as the Women's Sports Foundation-sponsored National Girls and Women In Sports (NGWS) Day. At one school in Washington Heights, PS 128M, the NGWS Day would be held on a specified day each year in February. Every girl would get to participate in one school period long clinic for girls only. The boys in their class were cheerleaders, who created posters and banners in support of themes about opportunities for girls. They would also create chants to encourage girls during their time on the clinic floor in the gym. Each session had several skill stations set up (for example, one for shooting baskets, another for passing the ball) which were led by female students. Some were high school students and others were from middle school and the fifth graders attending PS 128M. I will elaborate in more detail about the two stories I just shared, as well as the benefits to teens and community, in the latter portions of this Backward/Forward section.

The second set of overarching factors is aptly described by Jeffrey Stout in his work *Blessed Are the Organized*. This factor has to do with the essential place of programs being embedded in community relationships, and the value of having these relationships being recognized by elected officials. It is important for organizers to articulate and promote their organization's identity and purpose, and to advocate for its benefit to the city at large. In this work, Mr. Stout incorporates the voices of grassroots leaders and makes the case that the character of democracy is enhanced at the community-organizing level. Mr. Stout emphasizes that training programs for local leaders need to instill a "conscious understanding about the social forces acting upon members of a community, and the skills and understandings necessary to be developed in order to become capable of transforming the world."[155] Mr. Stout further elaborates: "[It] is essential to establish meeting spaces with government officials where ordinary people exercise control, are in possession of research, and lead 1 on 1 conversations which overcome the dynamic of their bowing and scraping in the presence of alleged superiors."[156] These attributes need to be developed within a context where "advocates build bridges, i.e., productive and cooperative relationships and form alliances between those who are mutually respectful, flexible, and which increase self-understanding and appreciation for the viewpoints of others."[157] In the latter stages of my journey, when the Teens on Community Board coalition was first being formed, and then when it was being expanded, our fervent belief in our cause needed to be tempered by respect for wholesome criticism or skepticism and by the cultural backgrounds of some that lent them to being less comfortable with generating too much independence for teens.

What I have found, however, is that social justice engagement is a challenging journey, with steps taking us forward and newly arising obstacles that sometimes take us backwards. At points when we think a new social consensus has arrived, such as the amelioration of racist attitudes and policies, hidden motivations and discriminative practices haunt us again. Just when we think society has become more enlightened about the place women hold in society, the hidden horrors of humiliation and abuse are uncovered, and leaders who advocate for a woman's return to the kitchen enter the political scene. In sum, the quest for social justice and equality does not move forward on a one-lane highway of inevitability; rather, it progresses in fits and starts as unacknowledged fears and temptations. Retribution rises to the surface. In writing this chapter, I found that just as I arrived at the point when I seemed to suggest we had obtained positive gains, I fell back into the territories of doubt and the need to look again before approaching the procurement of our aims anew. One truth I came to discover: those we assumed to be naturally or logically our closest allies were our fierce obstructionists, and those who initially objected to our goals became, after constructive and open dialogue, our most passionate and persistent supporters.

I would experience this curious scenario during my outreach and advocacy efforts for teen enfranchisement. Many of those who were veterans of the civil rights movement were sympathetic to our cause, even as some raised the strongest objections, as if teens had no right to enjoy similar gains in civic opportunity. Many educators immediately identified with our goals, while some remained intractable even in the face of overwhelming evidence against their proposed claims that we needed to conduct our approach to teens with the same old "business as usual" attitude. I cannot provide reasons for these dueling dynamics, except to say that people are complex, and our histories reflect our complexities.

Carl Rogers, a psychologist in the humanistic camp of practice, might have responded to this dilemma by saying that in permitting ourselves to understand another person we make a risky decision. Attempting to understand another person is part of the challenge in coming to terms with unconscious and denied influences which operate within our own psyches.[158] Depth psychologists such as Carl Jung called this task learning to take responsibility for what is not readily seen within. Our blind spots are invisibly sabotaging, a process he called shadow work. In doing so, one challenges oneself—a task that is not always taken readily. The decisions not to challenge ourselves are sometimes made consciously, but more often are driven by unconscious forces that, without counseling and/or interior focused understanding, develop within both our personal shadow worlds and the American shadow. I focus next on what I understand to mean by the concept of the shadow and the consequences of failing to address its powerful impact on our actions.

Anodea Judith is a counselor and spiritual practitioner who has a master's degree in clinical psychology and a PhD. in Health and Human Services. In her book, *Eastern Body, Western Mind*, Ms. Judith describes the shadow as "repressed instinctual energies locked away in the realm of the unconscious… (even when we are not consciously aware of the shadow forces below) they do not die or cease to function, but are enacted unconsciously, sometimes with great force."[159] I cite this source to make a connection to analysis that will be offered in later sections of this book, where psychologists will speak to the prejudices held by adults toward teens as driven by unconsciously unresolved issues from the adolescent years of adults as the driving motivation for enacting punishment, and control over teens. Depth psychologists refer to this dynamic as "projection", that is, where, as cited by Ms. Judith, "the shadow chases us, and is projected onto others."[160] As I will point to later in this book, my generation, the Boomer Generation, has constructed and maintained institutional practices leading to the continuous of perpetual wars, the building of historic levels of debt, and the deconstruction of natural processes so severe that the sustainability of life itself may be radically altered within the next 100 years. It is the leadership of the Boomer Generation, which, beginning with the Criminal Reform laws of 1994, put in place punishment and constriction of teens to a degree never put in place against the young before. It is the leadership within our financial industries, with supportive policies put in place by government, which have resulted in record levels of debt that threaten the continued functioning of budgetary allocations ensuring the health and education of future generations. Teens are labeled as irresponsibly out of control, while adults fall back on public images of being prudent and wisely in control. In a book edited by the religiously oriented philosopher Thomas Moore titled *Blue Fire*, he refers to an essay by the late Jungian psychologist James Hillman called 'Notes on White Supremacy.' In his essay, Mr. Hillman refers to the shadow of racism as "a shadow forcefully present in white consciousness itself, as a self-contained psychic reservoir."[161] When the force of this reservoir had been explosively released is when we saw a dramatic rise in the incidences of lynching and riots organized by White people which resulted in death and destruction of Black communities. For adults, it was during periods of fear about ambiguous change, of frustration with crime, loss of jobs, and moral crisis that adults put in place laws and regulations that accused teens of being sources of these problems. Example of these reactions will be described in the section of this book titled "Rebel."

Jeremiah Abrams, a writer, and a depth psychologist edited a book called *The Shadow of America: Reclaiming the Soul of a Nation*. This book includes essays from psychologists examining the shadow present in each of us as individuals, as well as the collective shadow of America resulting in practices of collective irresponsibility. In one of these essays, Sylvia Brinton Perera, who, at the time of the book's publication (1994), was a Jungian psychologist practicing in New York City and a teacher at the C.G. Jung Institute. In Ms. Perera's essay, she addresses the relationship between scapegoating, and the resultant irresponsible social and political consequences that follow. I use the term scapegoating as defined by Ms. Perera: "Scapegoating serves to relieve scapegoaters of their own responsibilities and to strengthen their sense of power and righteousness."[162] The dramatic and seemingly unresolvable tension in this process was aptly described by the Russian dissident and writer Alexander Solzhenitsyn, when he posits: "The dividing line between good and evil cuts through the heart of every human being. And who is willing to destroy a piece of his own heart?"

For now, I refer to a historical reference made by Dr. Bessel Van Der Kolk, M.D. in his book, *The Body Keeps the Score*. Dr. Van Der Kolk examines how World War I veterans, who had been wounded and traumatized in war, and who had been initially promised pensions but never received them were further traumatized by leaders in 1932. Those who enacted violent action against these veterans traditionally have been acclaimed as heroes in our nation's historical lore.

I summarize here the words of Dr. Kolk from his book about the history, causes and promising treatments for trauma. As shared by Dr. Kolk: "In

1932, the nation was in the middle of the Great Depression. In May of that year, 15,000 unemployed and penniless World War I veterans camped in the Washington D.C. Mall to petition for payments of their still unpaid World War I bonuses. A month later, President Hoover gave orders to clear out the veteran' encampment. Army Chief of Staff General Douglas MacArthur commanded the troops. Major Dwight D. Eisenhower was the liaison with the Washington D.C. police. Major George Patton was put in charge of the cavalry. Soldiers with fixed bayonets, hurling cannisters of tear gas, charged into the crowd. The next morning the encampment was deserted and in flames. The veterans never received their pensions."[163]

I share this recounting of extreme injustice to make a point. For the most part, the veterans who fought in World War I did so while still being teens themselves. They offered selfless service and sacrifice, but when demanding what was promised and due to them, they were not only denied but also treated as criminals. Teens in our times who were innocent of crimes, such as the young people of the Central Park Five, had been accused of predatory wilding, imprisoned, and then released. After decades, they have received some financial consideration, but what about the hundreds of innocent young men who have served time and never received any compensation. Many teens provided volunteer community service at their school-based and community-based programs. In adulthood, those who had not been officially cleared even after serving undeserved time in penal institutions remained ineligible for college loans and other government assistance programs. This lifetime of double jeopardy for those who had served their sentences and were now looking for a second chance in life was codified in criminal reform laws passed by national and state legislators. If anyone is guilty of predatory wilding actions, it is the legislators who passed and condoned these immoral acts.

Jane Addams, who was an early twentieth-century organizer in Chicago's settlement house movement, might attribute adults' reticence as a natural foible of human nature shared even by professionals. As Ms. Addams explains in her writings about settlement houses in early twentieth-century

Chicago: "Scholars are not immune from contributing to or initiating a bunch of terrible words from a stance of moral condescension or a historical present mindedness. These add to an already existing mountain of terrible words that bear down on our civic culture. It is important to distinguish between respectable criticism and gravitationally terrible words."[164]

Thomas Paine, an idealistic founding father at the dawn of our nation's birth, describes the chaotic reality perceived by decision-makers who hold on to the fading known to resist the feared unknown future: "In their situation of confusion and despair, the present councils have no fixed character. It is now the hurricane months of British politics. Every day seems to have a storm of its own, and they are scudding under the bare poles of hope. Beaten, but not humble, condemned but not penitent, they act like men trembling at facts and catching a straw."[165] If 2020 has taught us anything, it is that we too are operating in uncertain and turbulent times, caught between the reach for yesterday's remedies, which no longer work, and an aversion towards tomorrow's clouds of unknowing. What follows is a description of my meandering path.

My path starts with my initial days at modestly funded volunteer programs. Southern Heights: Communities Organized for Public Service established an extended day recreation program at PS 128M in the Heights. Sports and camping experiences were the hook. We incorporated campaigns for community improvement, and we invited teens to become advisors through their membership in the Boy Scouts of America Explorer Post #280 Program (membership was co-ed).[166] The Boy Scout Council assigned an identification number to each unit chartered within its New York City organization. That was true for its Cub Scout Packs, its Boy Scout Troops, as well as for its Explorer Posts. The Posts comprised young men and women, ages 14 to 20, and each unit adopted a specific theme. Over time, Explorer Post #280 became known for requiring community service as a prerequisite for remaining in good standing, as well as for earning extra playing time in sport competitions. One of the first initiatives undertaken by Post #280's teen officers was obtaining improved services for Edgecombe Park. Post

#280 partnered with the Youth Force-sponsored "Take Back The Park" program. (Youth Force was a teen leadership training program operated by the Citizens Committee of New York City, a not-for-profit civic improvement organization.) Teen officers made appeals for support at public meetings; they also coached younger peers in sports programs at the park.

As I have stated previously in this narrative, in 1994, my community colleague who was a director of Community Affairs for Columbia University, Ivy Fairchild, and I founded an all-girls education and sports program.[167] In order to lead this program serving girls in Uptown Manhattan, I voluntarily retired from the Life Skills School, after a term of 22 years. Ivy would spend every spare moment at her office helping to organize the administrative tasks required to operate a not-for-profit agency. These tasks made it possible for the girl's empowerment group to organize itself as a not-for-profit to be called the Ivy League: Uptown WINs (Women in Neighborhood Sports). Ivy also utilized her connections throughout the uptown community with schools and other youth programs to help us foster recruiting drives to create teams within our Community School District. Our efforts were supported by another program incorporating sports and community service named the 280: Dreamers, which was founded by Coach Dave Crenshaw. Our girl's program, the Ivy League: Uptown WINS, sponsored softball teams, which enabled girls to level the playing field, thereby gaining the admiration of parents and boyfriends for their new skills and sportsmanship. What was instrumental in procuring our funding was a visit by the New York Women's Foundation to an Ivy League special event (co-managed by Coaches Who Care) called Girls Sports Day. After observing the devotion and sportsmanship displayed by the girls at this event, the foundation made a substantial contribution. Our second advisory group, Female Finesse, worked in collaboration with the Women's Sports Foundation and the New York City Girl Scout Council to organize educational events promoting Title IX rights. Some of these girls starred in a promotional video put together by the WSF and shown on TNT; they also served as panelists at their national conferences.

In the third period of my three-decade adventure, I served as a director of the Police Athletic League's teen service program called IN STEP (In
School Training and Education Program). Cohorts of teen participants,
organized at 16 program sites in the five boroughs of New York City, put
together presentations about issues of great concern in their lives and for
their communities. Topics ranged from teen-on-teen violence, to gentrification, to the prevalence of young people in the homeless population, which
was surging. Each group had to research their topic, develop strategies for
intervention, and make PowerPoint presentations on their issues. We also
partnered with the Future Voters of America (FVA), a volunteer-run civic
advocacy group founded by Fran Baras and Diane Grazick.[168] Classrooms in
high schools hosted FVA curricular presenters; during these presentations,
students discussed issues and learned research, advocacy, and consensual
decision-making skills. Each year, FVA clubs, representing individual high
schools, gathered at a citywide high school congress. The student congress
body, which typically numbered 300 youth participants, would be broken
up into smaller discussion groups, which would address specific issues such
as the quality of high school courses and the relationship of teens with law
enforcement. In the afternoon, the issue groups would gather into a general
assembly. A student would serve as a reporter for each group, summarizing the issue their committee discussed. As each presentation came near a
conclusion, the reporter would introduce a resolution. After resolutions had
been introduced to the general body, all participants would participate in a
voting process in which they prioritized their issues. After taking opinions
and thoughts from student representatives, the resolutions were ranked in
numerical order, beginning with the resolution that the general body recommended was the most important to them as young citizens. The top three
resolutions were labeled as mandates. Adult leaders in the Future Voters
of America, primarily the director, Fran Baras, and the assistant director,
Diane Grazick, would work with high school representatives to formulate
advocacy sessions with municipal agency staff and elected officials. Fran
and Diane would also organize coalitions, which would generate a broader

base of support for mandates. Future Voters of America assisted students in developing advocacy efforts addressed to city agencies and elected officials. In 2007, the Future Voters of America High School Congress (comprising delegates recruited by Future Voters and members of the Police Athletic League's IN STEP program) passed a mandate asking New York State to lower the age of eligibility for full membership on New York City Community Boards from age 18 to age 16.

Between the years 2007 and 2010, the Future Voters Leadership, Police Athletic League leadership, and other civic allies who supported this initiative. lobbied the New York State Legislature to get an amendment of the NY State Public Officer law passed, which was required for allowing a change to age of eligibility for Community Boards. Under NY State law, Community Members were understood to be in a category called Public Officers and, therefore, only the state, though the legislature and sign-off by the Governor, could make this change possible. The Public Officer Law amendment's lead sponsor in the NY State Assembly was Brian Kavanaugh, and in the State Senate it was State Senator Lanza. Despite their best efforts, the bill remained mired in committee assignments between 2007 and 2010.

At the city level, Gale Brewer, who at the time was a NY City Councilperson, was the chief operating advocate on the government side. She introduced resolutions at the City Council calling for a Resolution of Support for the state legislation, as this would be considered by NY State legislators to be evidence of local approval.[169] At the NYC Council, this resolution also remained mired in committees, and during that period between 2007 and 2010, the resolution never reached the full floor for a vote. One of the objections I would frequently hear is that this bill is the brainchild of Manhattan's West Side liberals, which did not resonate with leaders from the outer boroughs of the Bronx, Brooklyn, Queens, and Staten Island. In the summer of 2010, changes in federal regulations resulting in funding reductions for teen programs, and the heavy burden of the financial load for running a not-for-profit resulted in organizational change for the Future Voters of America and for the Police Athletic League's teen program.

In 2010, Future Voters of America folded, when limitations of funding options, which had chiefly been made up for out of Fran and Diane's pockets, made it financially impossible to operate the program. This outcome signified a great loss, as the Future Voters training programs in high school classrooms were one of the few quality options for learning civics in New York City Schools. During the mayoral administration under Rudy Giuliani, the position of citywide director for social studies courses had been eliminated. Fortunately for our campaign, Fran Baras and Diane Grazick remained engaged with the ongoing campaign as public citizens, even though the organization's program operations had ceased. Their engagement was invaluable. Additionally, due to budget cuts at the federal level, put in place by a Republican Party-dominated Congress, the Police Athletic League's IN STEP program was reduced from a citywide program to a smaller one, serving only parts of Queens and Staten Island. Most of the funding for IN STEP was provided through the federal Workforce Investment Act. Under contracts with provider agencies, the subsidies to programs, which had been allocated at a rate of $2,700 per participant, was reduced to the level of $1,250 per participants. In addition to the cost per participant becoming lowered from previous levels of support, the designated catchment area for service (which is determined by the NYC Department of Youth Services and Community Development – DYCD) had included the entire city of New York. Under new provisions for awarding these contracts by the DYCD, the previous catchment area of five boroughs awarded to Police Athletic League was changed to cover only two of the five boroughs in New York City. The Police Athletic League received grant awards for Queens and Staten Island only. Teen programs in the remaining three boroughs would continue to operate on a more limited funding basis (meaning fewer participants, and more restricted program options). However, Police Athletic League site leadership, and teens active in all their centers, remained devoted to the Community Board initiative. The Police Athletic League, as well as the two former directors for the Future Voters of America, stayed true to the cause.

Moving forward, post 2010, and continuing until the successful outcome of our campaign in 2014, teens continued to advocate to officials across the city, writing letters, submitting petitions, and testifying at public hearings. Adult leadership who believed in the teen initiative and who trusted young citizens organized advocacy efforts at their own program sites and provided powerful testimonies of support at public hearings. Adult leaders of other agencies, as well as teen leadership in their programs, became essential partners in our advocacy campaign for getting passage of the amendment to NY State Public Officer Law making 16- and 17-year- old teens eligible for Community Board membership. As our coalition's date for success approached in June 2014, we counted on the work of members from 35 agencies to sustain our momentum and efficacy.

One ally and public servant who exemplified tireless devotion to seeing our bill passed is the Chairperson of the Education and Youth Services Committee for Community Board #12 in Manhattan, Fe Florimon. After our Teens On Board representatives made an advocacy pitch to her committee in 2010, she stewarded our request for a renewed full Board resolution of support, which was passed by the Board membership. Fe's support moved far beyond words to tireless advocacy. She would devote time at each Youth Education committee meeting to pitch support for our cause.[170] When our coalition attended meetings at other Community Boards and civic agencies, including those held in Brooklyn, Staten Island and Queens County, she made it her business to be there as part of the team. Civic devotion by Fe and dozens of additional allies more than made up for loss of dollars.

In the fourth and final period of my 28-year path, we struggled with the Teens on Board initiative at times, yet gradually expanded our advocacy base. Students and adult leaders from numerous civic-oriented groups included partners such as the NYC Girl Scout Council, Global Citizen, and the student arm of the NAACP, containing a total of 10 collaborating agencies. In our annual appeals for the passage of the Public Officer bill, our coalition expanded to a more diverse membership across the five boroughs. Our coalition included 35 youth service and civic partners. Amongst the additions were the Boy Scout Council of New York, The Children's Aid Society, the Asian Student Advocacy Program (sponsored by the Coalition of Asian Children and Families), United Neighborhood Houses, Queens Community House, Staten Island Voice, and an NYC Beacon program in Sunset Park.[171] In the fall of 2013, we began working with a new partner, Generation Citizen, founded by Scott Warren. The partnership proved to be an enormous benefit.

Generation Citizen's programming approach mirrored that of Future Voters of America regarding organizing civic education in New York City classrooms. Generation Citizen also organized innovative additions in its approach. The group partnered college students studying in the field of political science, and/or having a keen interest in seeing students involved in civic education. These college students had a deep interest in community change as did the social studies teachers in the classroom with whom they were paired. The college students, who were called Democracy Coaches, effectively became co-teachers. Democracy Coaches were not much older than the high-school students with whom they worked, and they were looked upon by high-school students as peer mentors. Specific skills in research, debate, and dialoguing, as well as outreach and advocacy, were coached and validated by adults. Generation Citizen called their training package the Hourglass method, which I will address in more detail in the "Civic Lover" section of this book. Students brought their final social studies class presentations to a citywide end-of-semester event called Civics Day. Generation Citizen recruited volunteers from the education community, civic-minded and youth service agencies, and interested public citizens at large to serve as judges at each Civics Day event. Each Generation Citizen classroom would have two or three student reps at a display profiling their issue. The student reps would speak to the process of choosing and researching their project, developing an advocacy approach, and reaching out for support from potential allies and elected officials. These elements were organized into grading rubric, moving from a score of one for those least effectively organized to a grade of four for those more impressively completed. The rubrics were reviewed and ranked by Generation Citizen staff, with the top achievers presented special awards at the event day final assembly. All classes attending were also noted for their efforts and essential contributions to the civic realm in New York City.

Scott Warren was the founder and Executive Director of Generation Citizen.[172] Scott agreed to assign Sarah Andes (who had set up a lunch meeting amongst herself, Scott, and me), the New York City Gen Zen director, with the task of focusing on the Teen on Board campaign. At the lunch meeting, Scott had thoroughly quizzed me about the history, process, and structure of our Teens on Board campaign. Although he paid for my lunch, I never got to finish it, as I was too busy responding to his continuous and focused train of inquiry. The value of Scott's broad perspective concerning the vital importance of having teens involved in civics he addressed comprehensively in his book, *Generation Citizen*. Scott's book is his organization's biography as well as an insightfully constructed roadmap for training and involving young students in politics. In one passage in his book, Scott points out: "Young people learn politics through doing politics, acting on local issues they care about: police brutality, homelessness, the lack of teen jobs, and the dearth of affordable housing options. Collectively, their efforts have impacted policy in a real way."[173] Having Scott and his assigned leaders join our campaign as partners gave us the gift of having campaign associates who possessed a progressive vision about the skills and talents displayed by youth activists, and a comprehensively constructed plan informing our advocacy approach as we moved forward.

In her description of what the author Carolyn Myss uses to describe the archetype of an engineer or builder, her words fit closely to what could be included in a job description for Sarah Andes. Ms. Myss has developed a spiritual schematic that includes archetypes, which she considers to be energetic guides of significance to folks for developing what she calls a Sacred Contract, and I call the soul design of our life purpose. In profiling the archetype of engineer, Ms. Myss states, in her book, *Sacred Contracts*: "The engineer is eminently practical and devoted to making things work.

The characteristics of the engineer reflect the grounded, orderly, strategic qualities of mind that convert creative energy into practical expression."[174]

Through her guidance as a civic engineer, Sarah implemented practical steps in support of visionary goals. These included identifying issues focused upon, platforms, and the legislative record of individual elected officials we were attempting to bring on board as endorsers for the Teens On Board campaign. This would help immensely in identifying the level of support we might expect from each elected official. In cases where an official might be sympathetic, but not sure of committing, our strategy was to ask for increased advocacy support from agencies and constituents within that elected official's district. Sarah developed detailed action plans for suggested use by our campaign allies, including advocacy scripts and templates for requesting letters of support or using social media texts directed at office holders. As a trained leader in advocacy and coalition-building (which she had been implementing with Generation Citizen's Hourglass model), Sarah also developed a strategic advocacy plan for our Teens on Board youth council members to use to recruit new supporters. For example, our spokespeople learned to better define and refine our "ask," by learning to listen carefully to the target audience's statements of agreement and/or reservations. Adult and teen advocates learned to use a pitch emphasizing the fierce urgency of *now*. After the New York City Council received testimonies of support from over 35 community and issue advocacy groups, the council, with near unanimity, passed a resolution of support. From the standpoint of the State Assembly and State Senate, this resolution was a statement of home rule—that is, those representing the area in which the change in age would take effect approved of the change. In June of 2014, the New York State Legislature passed the Public Officer Law amendment.[175] Public Officer Law in New York State governs the rules of membership and organizational procedures for advisory bodies to municipal government such as Community Boards.

As civic partners and allied advocates, our coalition members worked to transform locally based expertise into shared wisdom distributed among those we sought to influence. We benefitted from using the strength of network-based negotiation. We also succeeded, to a significant extent, in having initially skeptical adults dismiss their negative stereotypes about teens; this change in attitude occurred after the adults listened to teens with compassion, allowing them to develop appreciation and respect for the civic work undertaken by adolescents. In the final year of our efforts, we saw a sea change in support among public officials and municipal agency staff, which led to positive changes in public opinion regarding adolescents.

We also succeeded in helping to facilitate changes in the process of adult and teen relationships within the realm of public affairs, in ways aptly described by C. Otto Scharmer, a senior lecturer at the Massachusetts Institute of Technology. One of his major premises, in what he calls his Theory U, states that in effecting change in the arena of social relationships, people need to be present for each other. That is, people need to use active listening, and to develop a willingness to adjust their beliefs when confronted by clear evidence, whether that evidence is presented as newly learned facts or deemed to be present in the testimony of people judged to be credible. Mr. Scharmer describes this process as "that of presencing the future, which is necessary to enable the emergence of an alternative future—with presence, awareness, and resonance."[176] The term *presencing* was invented by Mr. Scharmer to describe the process of being focused on present time while simultaneously using what we know about the past, and what we anticipate for the future, to serve the needs of those in present time. For example, current studies disprove earlier findings that stated negative teen behaviors are attributable to teens' innate nature. Thus, when we implement policies and practices affecting youth, we should link them to what we have, in the present day, come to know about adolescents' assets and challenges, and not act on yesterday's falsely obtained conclusions. In addition, we have traditionally held that teens are our future leaders, but we have assumed that teens will obtain the skills and understandings to lead only after they mature into adulthood. Those of us who have partnered with teen leaders in community improvement efforts serve as credible witnesses to teen leaders who are *already* demonstrating leadership skills. Many highly educated adults (human services professionals, educators) with whom I had conversed at advocacy presentations and at Community Boards from across New York City articulated to me their reservations about teens having the mental capacity or maturity to serve. The typical line these people would give me is that until teen brains are fully developed, or teens' impulsive behavior has been resolved, they would be unqualified to be appointed to Community Boards.[177] (If I had heard that line today, the silent voice in my head would be that the standard these skeptics suggested must not apply to certain members of Congress.) Advocates from our campaign testified about their own productive civic partnerships with teens who contributed valuable help and ideas to their programs. Directors from Police Athletic League centers often spoke to me about how suggestions for program improvement forwarded to them by teen council members were adopted as best practices. I will present examples of these types of teen contributions in the "Civic Lover" section of this book. Adults who had uncompromised belief in teens' civic efficacy impact on communities presented evidence from other cities in the United States where teens had been serving as advisors to government for decades. Some suggestions from teens already serving as advisors to city governments were transformed into policies by elected officials. For example, teens aged 14 to 19 years served on the San Francisco Youth Commission.84 Teens who were called "youth commissioners" were paired one on one with adult members of the city's board of supervisors. Youth commissioners engaged in research on important issues, such as the displacement of LBGTQ teens from their families and came up with practical proposals for funding sanctuaries for teens in danger on the streets. As a result, attitudes of adult policy makers shifted, and supportive policies were put in place. As adults and teens became better at seeing each other, each became more receptive to the other's suggestions, and common ground was established to enable positive and protective change. The hope for a better future unfolded in the *now*.[178] Given the evidence presented by teen council performance in other cities, how irrational was it for adult leaders in New York to hold the belief that teens could *not* be ready?

How resonance between generations becomes amplified and enhanced was observed by me, when I was directing the PAL IN STEP program. In 2006, I was observing a community project being developed by teens (and guided by mentors) to help the homeless in the South Bronx community. The adult and teen civic enhancement team was located at the PAL Webster Center in the Bronx. The experience I had while observing this project is nicely described by Dr. Sven Hansen, who has a background in the special forces, sports medicine, and professional staff development. In his theory about resilience—that is, the ability to persist, to bounce back, and get through obstacles—Dr. Hansen speaks to certain crucial aspects about how lived performance, and not just adherence to abstract theories, informs us about a person developing their potential. One aspect that Dr. Hansen writes about is in lieu of just following advice about what has worked for people in the past. With adult and teen civic partnerships, there is a need for adults to share the challenges of their own workloads with teens, while simultaneously being certain to try to understand the burdens of the teens' own workloads. Through the facilitation of mutual understanding and acceptance of dually offered undertakings between adults and teens, a civic project obtains credibility and becomes effective in the eyes of the whole team. It is through the mutual apportionment of matters at hand that sensitively shared understanding is fostered and becomes adopted as part of the culture of an organization. Adults have learned to share the challenges of workloads while simultaneously being certain to try to understand the burdens of teens' own workloads. In his book about the work involved for keeping partners who are sharing tasks resilient called *Inside-Out: the Practice of Resilience*, Dr. Hansen suggests, that mutually supportive adults and teens practice the art of resiliency through "respectful engagement." Each partner, by "encouraging optimism rather than blame,"[179] contributes to an effort where teens get to work shoulder to shoulder with adults, learning to love their agreements and disagreements, developing discipline through focused and sustained effort. Their advancement, filled with "rejuvenation and novelty" contributes to resiliency for all actors involved."[180] Stated another way, as it becomes okay to share our vulnerabilities, the need to withdraw lessens. When it becomes safe to recognize a different viewpoint, there is less worry, and people can connect more readily.

When testifying at a public hearing at their local Community Board, some of our teen advocates from the PAL Webster program in the Bronx brought this process into sharp focus when they described how their own biased viewpoints were changed in the face of credible evidence. The teen council had been approached, a couple years earlier, about assisting homeless people in the South Bronx. At first, teens were very resistant: they stereotyped homeless people as older, smelly people who nobody wanted to help. However, their teen council was approached by a street outreach program (a local chapter of the Coalition for the Homeless) whose members taught the teens that more than one-third of homeless people in their community were also teens—teens who were on the street after suffering parental rejection or family stress. Once the teens' scope of vision regarding who the homeless were had changed, the previously egregious task transformed into one of necessity. In addition to stepping up with food and clothing drives for homeless victims, the teen group produced a documentary to educate others who were misinformed about homelessness. One of the teen leaders in that Webster Center project was Ramon Spence, who went on to earn a B.A. and an M.A. in business administration. He is currently a center director for the Washington Heights PAL Armory program. Teens in the Armory program are receiving educational support and training for community service from partners to the Armory, the Manhattan District Attorney's Office, and New York Hospitals community outreach program at the Columbia-Presbyterian campus.[181]

Over the course of these 30 years, I also participated in and witnessed change that corresponds to the development of the best teen-enfranchisement efforts, as alluded to by S.R. Arnstein's ladder of citizen participation. Mr. Arnstein, who was an institutional planner, developed his metric in 1969 as a means to evaluate civic experience, which progresses from stakeholder participation (where recipients of information are manipulated to serve the goals of others) to that of being considered a full partner of those who exercise civic control and power.[182] When I first started working with teens as civic contributors, most of them who were invited to join our advocacy groups were asked to do so on the passive end of the participation ladder, that is, participating in projects chosen and designed by well-intentioned leaders seeking to expose teens to intervening in community affairs. After being exposed to and trained by teens and their mentors from Future Voters of America and Generation Citizen, my focus changed to that of having teens identify issues from their own perspective and observing them develop youth-centered approaches for civic change.

In the remainder of this chapter, I revisit the time periods, which I call starting lines, and which I just summarized, both with anecdotes involving civic allies and partnerships with more detail. I will also weave in related research implications and insights gained through my exposure to a wider variety of civic-minded organizations. I introduce important youth leaders, supportive adults, and the civic vision of agencies. Some of these agencies were ones that I led. I also had the privilege of partnering with leadership from other agencies, and their counsel led me toward more increased understanding of the teen enfranchisement agenda. The organization which exerted a major influence over me, beginning in 1994, is the Petra Foundation. It was organized as a family foundation by John Shattuck, his family, and friends to honor the social justice and community work of Petra Shattuck (who died suddenly from a brain aneurism). The Foundation would honor 100 people involved with civil rights, human rights, and community rehabilitation organizing—under-the-radar people the Foundation considered unsung heroes who remained committed despite lack of institutional support and significant financial resources. I will infuse some of the Petra Foundation fellows' stories as this book unfolds.[183] Before getting to these time periods, which I introduce in a format where I use calendar years as stating points, which I call starting lines, I offer two caveats which involve factors that weave their way through each of these four program periods.

My first consideration is that although I initially held and then amended strongly held viewpoints about programming and adult/teen civic relationships, my 28-year journey was shaped just as much by experimentation, unanswered questions, and wandering.

An artist named Joey Allgood, who produces prints and amusing connected narratives, created a work of art which I purchased at an outdoor market in Union Square. The print shows a cat with a ball of yarn. The expression on the cat's face suggests an odd combination of self-satisfaction and inquisitive wonder. The accompanying text reads: "A feline fumbling with its significance in the universe finds relief after observing how the fuzzy sphere it's holding was formed through a series of seemingly-random winds. (The cat) deduces that order and meaning can only be derived from chaos in the presence of intelligent design."[184] I formerly parented a household of cats over roughly the same period as I operated youth programs. This period lasted for 22 years, beginning with a cat I named George III in 1999 and ending with the passing of my youngest cat, Sasha, who had reached the age of 19 years old in 2019. During this time of observation with their frolicking and play, their focused attention on problem-solving (how to reach that food on top of a counter) and their persistence in the face of obstacles, I lived in an experiential world representative both of cats as agents of intelligence, and teens as centered intelligent agents of change. I often had to refigure on how to relate, how to be goal-oriented, and being open to change and the unexpected.

My second consideration is the importance of affirming, again, the primacy of the intelligence of the heart when involved with teen civic empowerment. Especially when serving teens in communities where they are physically and emotionally challenged, a leader learns to recognize that he or she shares in the impacts resulting at times in despair and resignation. As suggested by the psychologist and spiritual pioneer Greg Braden, our work involves building a "resiliency of the heart in order to maintain a sustained recovery of optimism." Mr. Braden cites four tasks identified as factors in fostering resilience: "Seeking knowledge about oneself (and others); sustaining a personal sense of hope; developing an ability to cope in healthy ways; and framing one's work in ways encouraging finding personal meaning in life."[185] The work performed in helping teens to find their selves and sense of purpose is continually on the agenda when engaged in teen empowerment service.

What helps to strengthen the hearts of both teens and their co-mentors involves connecting with a special type of love, as aptly described by the writer James Baldwin about this type of love: "Love takes off the masks that we fear we cannot live without, and we know we cannot live with. I use the word 'love' here not merely in a personal sense, but as a state of being, a state of grace, not in the infantile American sense of being happy, but in the tough and universal sense of quest, daring, and growth."[186] In the communities I served, which had for decades been denied the fundamental elements of governing compassion and access to life-enhancing resources, it is not just personal responsibility and the seeking of individual satisfaction that makes a difference in the lives of our young people. What gives our young a sense of personal meaning and communal connection involves what spiritual philosopher Thomas Moore describes as the qualities of observation and care for one another. This includes paying attention and caring for the heart and the soul, in addition to managing with offerings of healing and devotion. Our tasks include watching out for and honoring others and persisting in the retrieval of lost hope and opportunity. We succeed when we all take back our birthright for these gifts, which all too often have been disowned.

Starting Line #1: Conceiving and launching a new youth program in the Heights

In 1984, after having served for two consecutive two-year terms on Community Board #12 Manhattan, I was asked to write and submit a proposal for an afterschool program that would be called Southern Heights: Communities Organized for Public Service.[187] The program concept involved having community volunteers offering a program providing academic assistance, cultural activities, and recreation to an elementary and middle school-aged population. In addition to providing these basic programs, we proposed adding service requirements to "hooks" (a hook is the offering of a desirable and/or basic program which is linked to other lesser -known types of programs that an agency would like to see young people participate in). Attached to components of our program, which had been traditionally offered to youth, would be short-term projects (some for a day, others for a few weeks) for learning and participating in community service projects.

This proposal was initially met with skepticism. It proposed working on blocks in the neighborhood comprising significantly different types of populations; the blocks were largely segregated by race and/or national background. What was assumed in our modest request for dollars was that our neighborhood's residents would come out in significant numbers to volunteer. The reticence about funding was partially derived from the fact that in the 1980s, it was a very dangerous time to be on the streets. The so-called wise elders told me, "Nice idea, but you really must be a dreamer." However, after some urgently delivered words to her Board colleagues at Community Board #12, Youth Committee member Maria Luna was able to sway enough votes to get our newly proposed program on a list for new funding[188]. After consideration by the Mayor's office, the proposal was funded, albeit for a modest amount. We were granted $9,000 each school year for a period of three years. This level of funding meant that for the program to be launched and managed over time, I would have to be a part-time volunteer director. Despite our high expectations for adult volunteer assistance at the program site, once it opened in December of 1984, I would have an adult staff of— none, for direct staffing needed to guide students in program activities.[189] (We would have one adult volunteer, but only for the first year of our program, whom I will introduce in the narrative below.)[190]

As fortune would have it, Richard Crenshaw, a colleague of mine at the Audubon Reform Democratic Club, offered the prospect of some adult assistance from his son. Richard worked closely with me on tasks typical for a local democratic club—recruiting members, gathering signatures of petitions in support of the candidacies of people we supported for public office, and in organizing public forums about issues of concern to the neighborhood. Although also biased as a proud father to his son, David, Richard's assessment of his son's already impressive leadership with youth was confirmed by established neighborhood leaders for youth services. Looking to connect two people he cared about and respected, Richard proposed a meeting between David and me. The Audubon Reform Democratic Club, representing Washington Heights, was founded in the early 1970s by anti-Vietnam War activists. By the time I joined the club in 1979, the club's leadership positions were held by activists advocating for peace, housing rights for tenants, improved health services, and more multiracial and diverse cultural opportunities for leadership within the Democratic Party. Although David was not a member of the Audubon Club, he would volunteer when called upon to help circulate nominating petitions and literature for candidates endorsed by the club. Richard knew his son well. Richard had witness and heard testimony from credible messengers about how hard a worker Dave was for the causes and programs he believed in. Dave demonstrated an uncanny ability to recruit and motivate volunteers. David had volunteered with sports programs under the guidance of the gym teacher at PS 128M, Michael Kane, while still a high school student. David also knew the streets of Washington Heights, and although now barely out of high school, had wisdom beyond his years about how to navigate the territories of street-corner territorial disputes. David organized youth participation opportunities beyond the school day, such as invites to tournaments outside of the neighborhood.[191] He also encouraged his young members to lend a hand in the community as a way of giving back. David's youth group was organized under the flag of the Dreamers.[192] The one dependable adult volunteer in the early years of our program would be Coach Dave.

The Crenshaws, father and son, and I met in a parlor at Paradise Baptist Church, located on Ft. Washington Avenue just west of Broadway. The pastor, the Reverend Lee Arrington, had offered the space for our meeting, as he always looked for ways for his church to help the community. David let me know he would agree to be an advisor and a trainer but that he could not stay on site as he had his own youth program to run, which was called The Dreamers. At the time, neither of us suspected we would become decades-long partners in the provision of youth services.

A second gatekeeper for my youth program was Steve Simon, a chief staff for then Councilperson Stan Michels. I define gatekeeper as a public servant or agency official with access to resources and potential partnerships for people who are either new to a particular field (such as youth service), and/or who do not have enough money or resources to accomplish what they seek without the aid of outside help. Mr. Simon demonstrated his care and commitment through two types of practices viewed at the time as sorely lacking from public officials—that of showing up and following through. Steve demonstrated an uncanny ability to master intricate details of public law and policies. He was also an articulate bridge-builder between the office of the councilperson and leaders of grassroots agencies in the community. Additionally, he was a colleague of mine from the Audubon Club; he had worked closely in our efforts to fight for neighborhood safety and stability during a time of escalating street violence and an out-of-control drug trade.

Mr. Simon convinced Kevin Garvey, the head custodian, as well as the principal at PS 128M, Mr. Kevin Miller, to give Southern Heights a chance at PS 128M during afterschool hours. In addition to the off-site guidance and tutoring of Coach Dave, we benefitted, during our first year of program, from the experience of the school's head gym teacher, Michael Kane. Volunteering for us at Coach Dave's behest, he agreed to stay on-site after regular school hours to help with sports programming and to guide our volunteer staff of teenagers, none of whom were older than 16 years. Trained by Mr. Kane and Coach Dave, they would undoubtedly become among the ranks of the most committed and knowledgeable staff I had supervised. (My previous eight years of supervisory experience were at the Life Skills School, a school for special needs children. Given the commitment and high standards of the Life Skills Staff, including the teen volunteers, for performing at such high levels of commitment speaks to the high standards met by our volunteer teens). If judged by the current standards of staffing for childcare programs, (two of which include that only people 18 years of age and older can supervise after-school participants, and that they should be high school graduates), this made us the most illegally led program in the Heights—and probably in the entire City of New York.

We were also blessed to have head custodian Kevin Garvey back us up, no matter what the circumstances were: he seemed enchanted by the idea of a program led by teens. (Two of these challenging circumstances included keep the site safe and clean in extended school hours, and Mr. Garvey having to field periodic complaints about our program.) In our second year, a new principal was assigned, Ms. Blanca Battino. She would come to be called the people's principal. She was an absolute godsend—a gatekeeper, an advisor, a creator of a safe space for all who used her site. Indeed, her operating principle was that the building and its resources belonged to the people, and not to her. Even on our limited budget, we functioned with tireless volunteers offered by other neighborhood agencies. These partners would provide us specialized program activities, such as health education and job preparation, which would be provided for an hour, typically one or two days a week. The health education component was donated by Project Basement from St. Catherine's Church, and job readiness component by the Washington Heights Development Corporation. Our menu of services became much more comprehensive than a more limited set of options we would have delivered if operating strictly on our own. Being privy to the benefits of collaboration is a source of agency wealth. Even given our trial by fire in our first year, we would subsequently be ranked tied for first place in recommendations for continued funding by the Community Board each year.

> This period was one of great awakening for me. I came to my new post as a director for a youth program providing services at the community-based level as a well-intentioned professional with no direct experience with working in an afterschool program setting My previous experience working with children had been in a school serving special needs children called the Life

Skills School. Although I had taught and then later supervised a teaching staff and young folks with special needs, the youth at Life Skills had much more serious conditions such as substantial cognitive delays and severe emotional disorders. The Life Skills staff was deeply committed and loved the kids, but the environment was one that was much more self-contained than that of a service program working with a general youth population in a community district.

I have found that at times the art one is drawn to reflects a challenge in life that one has faced or is about to face. I have an art print produced by a street artist named Nolita Graffiti hanging on a wall in my apartment. It shows a young girl, rather distant and disconcerted in her demeanor but nonetheless self-assured. The title of the work is *Grown-ups Are Obsolete.*

For young people growing up in communities besieged by violence, and which are in receipt of inadequate services, the adults insisting on making decisions for them can appear to be obsolete. Parents who have been subject to the trauma of street wars try hard to convince their children to stay calm, attentive, and consistent in their life endeavors. In an atmosphere where chaotic conditions remain unaddressed, where unconscious pain subtly directs a person to make poor decisions, words appear to the young as devoid of significance. Principals and teachers in schools serving under-resourced neighborhoods struggle mightily to provide quality education to their students. Given the typical conditions of classroom overcrowding, turnover amongst quickly demoralized staff, and lack of up-to-date quality educational materials, educational staff and students enter school with one hand tied behind their backs. It is the disconnect between high ideals and the best of intentions with existing classroom conditions which create a necessity for students to develop alternative choices. Some become misdirected under the illusions developed on the street, and others find adult mentors who, in tandem with their students, can rise above the challenges they face. With few adults at all available in the Southern Heights afterschool program, it was the effort extended by teens which served as an anchor to the younger peers during the 1980's and 1990's.

The teens who volunteered daily for the afterschool program demonstrated a commitment and maturity beyond their years. They often pulled me aside to offer me guidance and perspective on how to communicate with our programs' youth participants. Consulting with their adult mentor, Coach Dave, they would also offer program adjustments to make activities more welcoming and exciting for young students. No, grown-ups are not to be discounted or discarded for their significance in the lives of the young participants in our after- school site. However, for the Southern Heights after-school program, adults had to put aside certain attitudes which I shared with other adults (such as sticking rigidly to a clock and adhering to a tight schedule, at the expense of letting an activity unfold according to the developmental needs for different age groups). My expectations about what teens could introduce and manage had to frequently be raised to a higher bar. The more I became exposed and in awe of what teens could do in leadership roles, the less I underestimated the value and contributions of our teen volunteers. I would adjust my supervisory actions and become guided by a new appreciation for their talent. In both my imagination regarding teens, and in my work-a-day relationships with teen leaders, I was making more and more room for them as highly valued co-leaders. I also learned that by my taking time to acknowledge and affirm who they are in their whole personhood (not by the negative stereotype labels so prevalent in the media, but by their tireless care and commitment to our program and community), our mutually supportive relationships became nurtured and sustained over time. The validation of personhood contributes to the nurture of neighborhoods.

In our second program year, beginning in September of 1985, I would confer with the Greater NYC Boy Scout Council, and then decide to organize our teen leadership corps under one of the Boy Scout program options called Explorer Posts. Explorer programs were co-ed. The city-wide Explorer Program council provided invitations to play in sports tournaments and opportunities for overnight camping. Each post was organized around a theme, such as career exploration or law enforcement. Our post theme was community service. The Explorer Program also emphasized incorporating youth leadership into our program. The Southern Heights program was structured to have teens elected to leadership posts such as president, secretary, and treasurer for the post.

I was introduced to this new model of teen leadership, and once our young people served admirably, I began to appreciate our teen volunteers as officially recognized leaders. It was in this venue that I would get to see one of our teens, Miriam Payne, in a new light. In the post's first year, she was elected as the Explorer Post president.

She and her family had emigrated to the United States from Liberia, which had been in the throes of a civil war. They settled in an apartment on West 165th Street and Edgecombe Avenue, smack dab in the middle of street wars invoked in the name of the war on drugs. Despite an atmosphere of constant, imminent danger, Miriam presented herself as a healer, making and sustaining safe spaces in a war zone, and bringing a sense of calm amid the swirling waters of fear that might otherwise have overwhelmed us. While some exploited the differences among peoples of various backgrounds, she helped to make a place at the table for people from diverse ancestry—from the Dominicans living on West 170th Street to the African Americans living on West 164th Street. Breaking bread, and feasting at holiday celebrations, children—and the adults who guided them—became one team in the classrooms at the after-school center, and on the ball fields of life.

I would continue to learn life lessons I had during this early period guiding the Southern Heights program. One of these lessons was recognizing the difference between using numbers to measure us and bringing forth self-discovered values. Our lesson was to learn to treasure oneself and others. My program mentoring was assisted by teens, as well as by my decades-long mentor, Coach Dave Crenshaw. Participants in his program gradually came to identify the fact that the metrics shown on a scoreboard were of secondary value to the game because the game of life is eternally present for each of us, and the numerical outcome of a particular basketball game is transitory. His players would be recognized not by the number of points they produced, but by the grace and dignity they brought to the playing floor, which the players understood was shared among one's teammates, one's adversaries, as well as by all present, even the audience. Dave would counsel the adult leaders he met at tournaments. Dave taught that it is not just adults who lead us by rank and position. It is youth themselves who are *our* boss. Teens who take charge of their personal agendas and our communal tasks set the tone and lead by example. Teens show us all what it means to give and take, shoulder to shoulder, helping to set an agreed-upon organizational agenda. Adults would come to see ethics in action from the ground up. Once our teen leaders understood the value of this lesson, they got it, and practiced it. Adult staff would implement the model of joint decision-making and mutually determined goals. We all learned that cooperation and generosity were sources of wealth.

Young Dreamers played ball, whether it was basketball or softball, with a higher purpose in mind than worrying whether they won or lost a specific contest. The players on each Dreamer team would gather for debriefings after each game and learn to reframe the meaning of what a game presents to them – they began learning the ethical parables of life. Their primary challenge was: how can you succeed with grace no matter the trying circumstances? One's team might have lost a game after being subject to some questionable officiating. The lessons Dreamer players came to understand is that making mistakes in calling a game is not intentional. On the basketball court, as in life, a person may face bad breaks, but what is important is to overcome feelings of anger and resentment. Can one be ambitious and sensitive to the needs of teammates? The young players on our teams might be competing against a team whose members had more advanced skills sets than your team. However, if you saw opponents from a competing team as friends who could model new skills, a young player also had a peer teacher. As young Dreamer participants became engaged with learning and practicing Dreamer sportsmanship, our players would not lose self-determination nor respect for the presence of everyone on the court. Dreamers would maintain gratitude just for the blessings of good health obtained through exercise as well as developing friendships and a culture where fun came first, and winning games came second. Dreamers would come to perceive referees not as perfect game officials, but rather as adults who cared about the flow and quality of the game, who, despite missed calls, had not missed their calling for being there for the kids. This would especially be the case even when referees made mistakes that cost your team the game—albeit sometimes with extra encouragement and counseling from adults sitting on the same team bench. What mattered were the intrinsic values of relationship, by which you developed the inner allies of confidence and trust. You could find yourself with best friends even among your opponents. As expressed in the 280: Dreamer motto: "Be a best friend to yourself, and also to others." Young Dreamers, despite the fact, that like all young people their age, had developing hormones and yet not fully developed frontal lobes, learned in an environment led by adults with high expectations for their capabilities to resist the temptations of instant gratification, to discard exhibition of the behaviors of blame and judgement, and to accept the valued guidance of adults with whom they had developed great respect and trust.

Starting Line #2: 1994–2002—Leveling playing fields and honoring unsung heroes

In the spring of 1993, I took on a project that would become more than running a softball season, for girls, which are typically limited to just one season. With the co-leadership of a community colleague, Ivy Fairchild, who had served as Director of Community Affairs for Columbia University, this pilot program would become a year-round league of its own. Ivy and I had coordinated a girls' program, a series of softball games amongst four teams for girls as an extension of the Michael J. Buczek Little League, which had been serving boys. At the conclusion of the pilot season for girls, the players, coaches, and parents told Ivy and me that they were thrilled with the opportunity for girls to play. They let us know that they would like to see the girls league continue. As one of her many civic tasks with helping the uptown community, Ivy had previously been involved in supporting the Buczek League, as well as many other community programs. (The Buczek League was named in honor of a fallen police officer who had been killed while serving in some of the areas of Washington Heights that had the highest levels of drug violence.) There is an old saying that if you want to see something get done, ask a busy person to do it. Ivy, one of the most involved people in the Heights with community programming, was the perfect person to ask.[193]

Ivy was familiar with the fact that I started up and led the Southern Heights program for a few years, and that I was still assisting the Dreamers.[194] She admired The Dreamers' mission of ensuring that girls got their chance to be included on the court. We had a few girls' sport teams up in the Heights, but for the most part these were restricted to programs that enlisted more elite players. The total number of girls programs in sports was limited when compared to the plethora of sports programs for boys. Ivy appreciated the value of exercise and sports participation for young people for its effects on promoting better health indicators (lower blood pressure, less likely to develop diabetes) and wanted to see young girls experience the joy of participating on a level playfield.

After the 1993 season, Ivy and I talked about what we could do next to ensure equal playing time for girls in our community. What had begun as a 15-minute conversation on the Buczek Field after the final game of the season transmuted into a series of planning sessions. We jointly decided to launch an initiative to expand the short season into a year-round sports and education program for girls. The following spring, a new program was launched: The Ivy League: Women In Neighborhood Sports (Uptown WINS became its acronym). I left my secure job as a special education supervisor for the Life Skills School, which had been in Queens, New York. I agreed to accept the position of director for the league's operations on the field. Ivy took on the responsibilities of not only being a board member for the new league but also, for all intents and purposes, completing tasks normally handled by an entire board. Ivy had strong intention and fierce focus for getting things done. She negotiated with the Department of Parks and Recreation for securing ball fields. She helped the league find an administrative home by assisting in our procuring office space in the Columbia Presbyterian Hospital complex at 60 Haven Avenue. She negotiated a rent-free deal with Lorraine Tiezzi, who was the director for Columbia's Center for Population and Family Health. Ivy, using her powers of persuasion, initiated setting up partnerships with the six Community School District Six schools. Ivy also appealed to the President of the District Six School Board, who at the time was Robert Jackson, and obtained a resolution of support for the league, giving us visibility and credibility. Title IX, which is the name of a piece of civil rights legislation, requires that all organizations receiving federal funding ensure equal time for girls in education and in sports. The Ivy League, as part of its educational program, would educate the community by promoting Title IX. Equal opportunity for girls in sports now had uptown advocates, which would be profiled by enlisting girls as advocates and role models.

After choosing to retire from my 22-year special education career at the Life Skills School, I now had a chance to re-direct my life through creating a novel youth program in Washington Heights on a full-time basis. There is a saying that states, do what you love, and the money will follow. In committing to the program, teen leaders served as supervisors and coaches, at the tender age of 16. Gerry Reneau was trained under the watchful ideas of Michael Kane, the school's gym teacher. Johnny Rosario worked closely with and sought advise from school supervisors and teachers. Gus Cruz engaged with me in close conversations about how best to deal with trying behaviors. Jackie Hurt provided no nonsense supervision over our game room. Yaniris Taveras served as a peer coach for girls in sports and community service. I name here just a few leaders, who though quite young, adopted immense responsibility for their age. At the same time, they commanded respect from their peers and younger students, and also had a feel for what motivated their friends and held meaning for them. Their experiences also helped to shape career decisions. Gerry became a corrections officer; Johnny a contractor in construction; Gus started his own outdoor adventure service company for youth; Jackie embarked upon a career in social work, and Yaniris worked at a community child care center. When I agreed to take a new position as director of the Ivy League, the financial risk I had taken was considerable. I would become wealthy beyond my dreams by working on a mission I deeply believed in, and with adults and teens who were not only positive role models but also people who helped me to develop rewarding and long-time friendships. The money never did follow, but the social and emotional rewards were limitless. I accepted a salary that was slightly less than one quarter of what I had earned at Life Skills School. I gave up the security of having health benefits and a retirement plan. I missed the comforts and friendship of the Life Skills family of students and staff. I maintain some of those Life Skills friendships until today and have an extended web of Ivy League friendships developed on ball fields, Ivy League educational forums, and in the American Dreaming Network which upholds a young girl's right to try hard, learn the value of teamwork, and decide to be a leader for herself and a new generation of girls affirming their right to succeed on their own terms.

What I had yearned for, and now earned, was the chance to make a difference for youth in my own neighborhood. The time had come for me to move beyond policy advocacy to community program viability. In collaboration with Ivy, and by establishing mutually supportive relationships with neighborhood institutions as well as with volunteer coaches, the time had met us as we chose the challenge to create a world anew for girls. Ivy and I exercised determined follow-up, including forging agreements with local agency leaders who decided to adopt a girls' team. We succeeded in expanding what had been a four-team, seasonal league in 1993, into a year-round sports and education program serving 300 girls. The Ivy League had 20 teams in all, serving uptown from the lower end of Southern Heights to the northern tip of Inwood.

As part of my job responsibilities, I served as field supervisor for all games played on our softball schedule. As a reward, I had the blessing of two volunteer umpires for all games (even triple headers). One umpire was a seasoned adult named Warren Boyd who had officiated in sports for many years. His assistant umpire was a teen from The Dreamers program, Ralph Paolino, who umpired on the first base line. He was an umpire in training, who never missed a game, and who worked tirelessly to see that our girls got support from a young man who cared about them. For Warren and Ralph, their weekly pay was a cheeseburger deluxe dinner after the final game each Saturday.

Parents, mothers, and teachers—women—coached the teams. Each coach inspired their players to change their expectations for themselves. If they wanted to be a ball player, they needed to put aside their need to maintain an appearance as a girlish teen while on the ball field. Girls, with boyfriends at their side, initially had shown up at the field wearing lipstick and holding makeup kits in their hands. As these girls learned that sweat was an outcome of trying hard to play well, and that dirt on their leggings was a sign of fierce effort, seeing them dive through the mud to make a play became more commonplace. Some of the boyfriends also changed their expectations about the importance of girls being given the opportunity to play ball. Many young men helped to carry the team equipment, cheer for the whole team, and assist with officiating duties. The screams of delight would echo from the fields at the Dyckman Street ball fields and Inwood Hill Parks, raising alarm by the seagulls strolling near the shoreline adjacent to the edge of the ball fields. Parents who in the initial games showed up with a fair degree of apprehension, feeling as if their daughters had become possessed for reasons they could not quite understand, changed into avid supporters. At the end of each season, every girl received a trophy for showing the courage and determination to get onto the field. Every player and each coach came to exemplify the statement that, as per the motto of the Women's Sports Foundation, it was time to break through sports barriers preventing equal opportunity for girls.

In my role as director, I also reached out to the Women's Sports Foundation after reading about their educational programs promoting advocacy of Title IX. After meeting with the Executive Director, Donna Lopiano, and the Foundation president, Wendy Hilliard (a rhythmic gymnastics gold medalist), they offered resources and technical support as part of their agency mission to assist local programs promoting girls in sports. [195] The Foundation would set up planning meetings with us on a regular basis. They offered us open access to their menu of program supports, including sports clinics, Title IX-related workshops, and invitations to their national conferences and annual fundraising event at the Waldorf Astoria hotel. Our girls and coaches would be granted complementary tickets and sit at their own table.

Ivy and I agreed to the creation of an additional coordinating committee to oversee these events, which comprised players who stepped up—the teen girls, of course. After training was put in place, they adopted the name Female Finesse. They helped organize special workshops, whose theme and agenda were put together by the Women's Sports Foundation. One such workshop was the High School Summit, where girls and boys attended sessions designed to increase sensitivity and support from boys for girls' sports opportunities. Sport stars such as track and field all-star Jackie Joyner-Kersee and girls from the block who stepped up as teen leaders put together workshops promoting advocacy and self-reliance among girls. The Women's Sports Foundation also saw to it that our league was represented in the public eye. They would call attention to our league at annual summits where they highlighted the goals and methods used by community programs. Two of our teen officers, Candice Isaac and Yanel Cordero, also represented the

League and Female Finesse as part of a "Women in Sports" 90-minute profile on the TNT network.

The Dreamers, in addition to operating their own direct programs, also took on the added responsibility of being what I call gatekeepers to up-and-coming youth organizations. As a gatekeeper, the Dreamers offered volunteer assistance and the technical support afforded by sharing their experience with youth leadership. Dreamer teen participants became co-leaders for the Ivy League activities. Dreamer boys set up and assisted with the rookie division (girls aged six to nine) under their banner known as Big Buddies. Dreamer girls, under the banner of Coaches Who Care, coached on the fields, as well as on the gym floor at PS 128M.

In 1995, the league submitted a funding application to the New York Women's Foundation. The application was quite ably conceived and written by Andrew Rubinson, the director of another fine youth service program, Fresh Youth Initiatives. We were awarded a two-year limited grant, which provided for a slight salary increase for me, the assistance of part-time female adult staff members, and additional support for procuring supplies. Two staff members, Ruth Mendin and Nancy Blanco-Frazier became role models of leadership for the girls and provided direct training for our teen councils efforts of organizing special events. What had clinched obtaining the grant occurred when two of their officers came for a site visit. They saw dozens of girls playing on the gym floor—being coached and supervised at skill stations by teen girls. They stayed for 10 minutes and then told us, 'Shh, don't tell anybody, but you are in."

Two notes on the challenges and successes of this program.... There is an old saying articulated by an aboriginal leader from Australia regarding the proper relationship between helpers and the people they seek to assist: "If you come to help me, you are wasting your time. But if you have come because your liberation is bound up with mine, then let us walk together..." [196] Our finest moments came as we learned to get out of the way of female leaders being born. Almost every single member of Female Finesse and

Coaches Who Care obtained college educations. Some went on to careers as teachers, and others as directors in youth programs and counseling projects.

The second noteworthy point is that the good the Ivy League program did for girls with their empowerment programming and messaging also led to transformations for themselves in other types of career paths. This dual benefit was shared with me by Myra Linares, the daughter of ex-City Councilman Guillermo Linares. Myra had played the position of catcher for two seasons. She told me she had come to her team as an extremely shy and introverted person. The demands of her position—to be vocal (and loudly so) as well as to direct her teammates in shifting their positions on the field—had changed how she communicated. When she shared this story with me at a community event, years later, she had been assigned to a community affairs position for Governor Andrew Cuomo. She gave credit to the Ivy League, to her coaches and supportive teammates, for helping her utilize the skills needed for that position. It is only when we find our voice that we get to make the choices that have originated within us.

Shortly after the launch of the Ivy League, my life course would become enriched by another family foundation whose mission was to celebrate and support people they called unsung heroes working at the community-based level. I received a phone call on the landline in my apartment. I picked up and heard a voice on the phone, in which the person asked if I was Al Kurland. When I answered in the affirmative, the caller introduced himself as Steve Tullberg.

He said that he was part of an awards committee for the Petra Foundation. The organization is a family foundation that honors community activists and social justice advocates who work diligently despite having little institutional support. The Petra Foundation award committee selects four new Petra Foundation fellows each year through the efforts of their awards committee. Committee members had researched candidates, and used background checks, as well as listened to testimonials given by people who knew the candidates well. As was the case for all nominees, I had undergone a committee's selection process. In 1994, I would be selected as one of four new fellows from among a larger field of nominees. I was honored to be picked as one of the four new members.

The three other awardees that year were Ellen Baxter from New York City, who had set up permanent and affordable housing for homeless families; Ron Chisolm, a founder of the People's Institute, a national organization involved in training community organizers; and Allan Macurdy, from Boston, who founded a mentoring program called Partners for Youth Disabilities. The committee had made their decision about inducting me based upon what they judged to be my selfless work on behalf of young people in uptown Manhattan. Mr. Tullberg informed me that by the rules of the foundation, the nominator of my candidacy had to remain anonymous, and that I would soon receive confirmation in a letter from Wendy Sommer, who at the time was the chair of the foundation.

These were long days of hard work and scarce money, and for a moment my New York skepticism kicked in. There was a pause on the phone. I wasn't sure of the credibility of this announcement, or whether this was like those magazine-clearing house calls promising large monetary awards. Mr. Tullberg thankfully, had experienced this pause during his phone calls to winners in previous years. He understood my hesitation, and said, "This is not a scam. You can look us up online, examine our criteria for making awards, and then contact us after you receive the letter." He sounded assertive but not pushy, and sincere. I thanked him and asked a few questions, then I agreed to get back to the foundation soon.

While I waited for the letter, and even after I showed up at the award ceremony at Georgetown University in June, the same question kept popping up. Why me? I know so many who do the good work; we all do it for the love of the work and the people we serve. We sat down at a pre-ceremony barbeque where 1994 winners, as well as winners from the previous five years, shared stories. Included in each story was the fact that all of them were deeply grateful for the award, and that each of them had asked the same question—why me?

The answer for each of us was entangled with the life and purposeful living of Petra Shattuck, the wife of John Shattuck, the foundation founder. Petra had been taken from her family by a tragically premature death. The foundation was set up by John Shattuck with his family and supportive colleagues to honor Petra, who had exemplified selfless and passionate social justice purpose in her work. In her work at John Jay College, and with criminal justice advocates, she organized to see justice was obtained for targets of criminal injustice. Included were proposals for changes in the paradigm of law enforcement. Some of these reforms included utilizing input from grassroots activists. Changing the methodology of law enforcement involved moving away from punishment and toward the use of restorative justice practices. In restorative approaches, the entire community of affected peoples, from perpetrators and their families to the aggrieved individuals and the surrounding communities, have their input and recommendations considered when working towards resolution of problems. Verdicts are delivered with liberty and justice for the accused by allowing them to take responsibility for their crimes through community give-back and re-ordering the direction of their lives. Those who had been offended would receive financial enumeration, while also engaging in the healing practices of forgiveness and reconciliation.[197]

Petra Shattuck was taken from her family, friends, and colleagues very suddenly by a cerebral hemorrhage in 1988. She had managed to escape the shadow of Nazi occupation and forged a career in which she fought for Indian rights and human rights. Petra worked to undo the effects of law enforcement on vulnerable persons and stereotyped communities. As stated by Petra to her colleagues, and later shared in the Petra Foundation journal, "I see the problems in America as one with the problems of mass democracy, where people have lost hope that the mechanisms of the democratic process can work, and that to make it work, we have to put its practices up against the ideals, and our values...."[198]

In deep grief, and in response to such a staggering and incomprehensible loss, her husband, her family, her friends, and colleagues sat at a kitchen table and dialogued on how best to celebrate her life by rewarding unsung heroes who personified the dedication, commitment, passion, and vision needed, from the ground up, without significant institutional support that mirrored who she was (and, for that matter, who she is, as we walk with her in her energetic footprints. I borrow the term "energetic footprints" to be understood in a sense suggested by Daniel J. Siegel in his book, *Mind*, when he described still feeling the presence of people who recently passed on. He described the felt presence as one in which the intention of their (both the departed persons and his) work seemed to remain alive and connected in some way, and continued to guide him towards goals that the departed person and he still shared.[199] As I intuitively grasped Petra's path, I saw the travails of my mother, an exile from Nazi-occupied France, and of Miriam Payne, one of my first teen leaders, whose family escaped civil war-torn Liberia. During my youth service engagement in Washington Heights, I met mothers in the Heights who lost their husbands, sons, and fathers to violence. As warriors who had to navigate the effects of trauma, they all walked side by side with Petra.

The Petra Foundation not only brought individual awardees to their table of acknowledgment, affirmation, and embrace but they also invited our friends and families to their annual award celebrations. In the words of Dr. Mindy Thompson-Fullilove, professor of psychiatry at Columbia University's Graduate School of Health, awardees and their closely related celebrants could "address the madness of our sorted-out cities. With inspired hearts, social change agents move from destructive illusions to creative solutions. We create meaningful spaces and show solidarity with all life through the celebration of our accomplishments."[200]

The Petra Foundation had to close its doors as an independent family foundation in 2015, after 25 years of service and the induction of 100 Petra Foundation fellows. Thankfully, the Center for Community Change organization, founded in honor of Robert Kennedy, was able to adopt some of the Petra Foundation's generosity. By linking us to their larger network of activists and social change agencies, they helped Petra Fellows[201] to keep connected to each other and to affiliated sources of information and organizing activities. An encyclopedia would be needed to cover the lives of all those fellows, as well as those of the trustees who committed their lives to support us. I introduce a few of these distinguished people in the coming chapters of this book. A few of the Petra Fellows for which this collaborative opportunity was made available include Bob DeSena, founder of the Council of Unity, which organized leadership initiatives at schools comprising honor students as well as gang members; Ellen Baxter, who converted abandoned buildings into multiservice housing centers for homeless men and families; and James Gilmore, a police detective who interrogated youth on the streets not by using the lens of racial profiling, but rather through the lens of poetic profiling, in order to bring out the youths' hidden capabilities and the higher angels of their nature. I also share the legacy left by the extended Petra family and borrow some of its practices—the meetings that take place at kitchen tables, not conference rooms and the stories that move us in our lives and in fruitful association with others. The most vulnerable and formerly powerless become passionately effective agents of change when adored, embraced, and empowered through recognition and support. Bold and constructive strategies and wisdom arise from authentic and indigenous insight. Those of us who felt isolated and marginalized now feel that they emerge safely "in the company of friends."[202] As so eloquently put by Petra Fellow Linda Stout, who has tirelessly worked to build bridges between communities by establishing the Peace Development Fund:[203] "My own struggle to find my voice helped me to realize the importance of new ways of organizing that are empowering to, and inclusive of, everyone."[204]

Starting Line #3: 2003-2010—My recruitment by the Police Athletic League… "Go where others don't." PAL civic partnership with the Future Voters of America.

Go Where Others Don't is the mission-inspired motto of the Police Athletic League. Where resources are scarce, and socioeconomic conditions challenging—this is where the Police Athletic League chooses to establish youth programming.[205]

PAL had elected to set up summer camps at the Washington Heights Armory in 1995, and again in 1997. The PAL senior leadership, led by Dr. John J. Ryan, Executive Director, had decided to use the two years of providing summer day camp service only as a trial balloon for a possible full-time school year program in future years. In early 1998, Dr. Ryan, in consultation with the PAL Chairman of the Board, Robert Morgenthau, was able to negotiate opening a full-time center at the Armory using funds confiscated from the drug trade. The PAL Armory Center opened on March 15, 1998. I return now to the period when the day camp was first proposed in 1995. In early 1995, PAL leaders decided to open a day camp for that summer. The PAL Sports Director, Jim Dolan, was put in charge of the planning. He had worked in collaboration with Coach Dave with short-term programming before (such as sports tournaments) and was happy with their relationship. He reached out to Coach Dave, and Coach Dave and I decided that he would agree to accept the position of camp director. I agreed to be the man behind the scenes to develop the camp application, identify and maintain compliance with regulations, and help with the recruitment of campers and the training of staff. Both Dave and I provided campers with programming to supplement the standard city-wide programming for all PAL day camps. Two of these standardized programs included a PAL Sports Day (an intramural amongst all camps) and a PAL Cultural Day (a celebration held in Central Park with exhibitions of campers' artwork and dance routines associated with diverse cultures from around the world). The Armory Day Camp opened as part of a city-wide portfolio of twenty-one-day camps across the city. We handed out surveys towards the end of our first day camp season to both campers and to their parents. Camper response, as well as parent communication about the camp experience, verified their appreciation and positive outlook regarding the usefulness of the camp for their childcare needs, and the impact the staff and program had upon the children.

On April 6, 1997, a tragic event involving a shooting of a local teen resulted in a ripple effect of communal anger and grief towards the police. On an early Sunday morning, a 16-year-old high school student named Kevin responded to a call for assistance from a friend of his, who had been in an altercation with teens from another block, who felt himself to be in danger of further retaliation.[206] Woken from his sleep, and harboring resentment towards teens from the world of "the other," Kevin took actions that would result in his untimely death. After Kevin had attempted to chase his perceived adversaries down, and failed in his attempt, he retreated up a poorly lit Amsterdam Avenue with a machete in hand (see note 106), he paid the ultimate price. Units from the local precinct responded and one car pulled up behind him, asking him to stop and drop the weapon. My own personal sense is that Kevin either failed to hear them, or that his response was one of fear and panic. Officer Anthony Pellegrini, crouching several yards behind Kevin, took aim. Officer Pellegrini fired from behind Kevin, and bullets entered Kevin's back. Kevin, who was mortally wounded, quickly fell to the ground.

During this difficult time, in the late 1990s, life seemed almost impossible to handle.[207] The number of arrests and shootings that officers had to respond to left little room for emotional and mental processing, or a space to breathe. At the same time, mistakes made by officers and department policies allowing premature use of force had often severely impacted families and the young in the Heights. As anger and despair amongst community members grew, their confidence in any form of government intervention diminished rapidly, and trust was at a low. In the third scenario, which I shared in the chapter titled Induction, I briefly described the Kiko riots and the conditions in our community leading to distrust between neighborhood residents and the police. I will delve into these social and personal tragedies more deeply in "The Rebel" section of this book, where I elaborate on the contributions of Coach Dave Crenshaw. A neglected section of Highbridge Park, towards its southern end, was nicknamed by those residents living in proximity to this park as the Pit.[208] The Pit was emblematic of the dangers and neglect of public spaces in Washington Heights nicknamed the Southern Heights. The Pit was a nickname given to the Edgecombe Playground located at the intersection of West 164th Street in upper Manhattan. Neighbors who had only this park to access for recreational needs experienced deep challenges for using it. These included severe deterioration of its facilities, having no comfort station for small children, and piles of garbage unattended to which included disposed needles. Not having a safe and clean place for children to play contributed to people not finding any sense of normalcy in their every-day lives. What should have been a simple walk to a playground—simply letting a child play—every day produced high anxiety. What was commonly assumed as part of the package in other, safer communities was the expectation of having access, which included a routine stroll across the street and arrival at a safe space for recreation. What was part of the package near the Pit was experiencing crossing the street as sometimes akin to ducking the crossfire of bullets in the hurricanes of retribution between competing drug groups and managing in a space overwhelmed by dangerous debris.

In the days following Kevin's shooting, the response by one of Kevin's aunts was a call to forgive Officer Pellegrini.[209] As quoted in my local newspaper, she saw the problem as residing not with his actions alone, but with the systematic response to crime, which had been organized by the NYPD, that had cost many families so dearly, even as precincts sought to bring back community stability. The suddenness and intensity of violent encounters saw the good intentions of officers compromised; increasing levels of communal distrust was the result. Events were organized at the grassroots level. Fresh Youth Initiatives, under the guidance of co-directors Andrew Rubinson and Rodney Fuller, organized a dialogue and grieving session for family and friends. The Community League of West 159th Street brought together law enforcement and community stakeholders to search for understanding and common ground. Healing and reconciliation start from the ground up, including all community stakeholders.

As I mentioned previously, the response from PAL, organized by Board Chair Robert Morgenthau and Executive Director John J. Ryan, was to expand its seasonal presence at the Armory. After two seasons of sponsoring a day camp only (in 1995 and 1997), the Police Athletic League program was now reconfigured to include a full-time afternoon and evening center for the entire school year. PAL, under the leadership of Board chair Robert Morgenthau and Executive Director John Ryan, was able to work with Chancy Parker from HEIDA, a federal drug intervention unit that generated funds through confiscated illegal income. Establishing a full-year program, including use of more space within the Armory than what was necessary for the day camp, necessitated negotiating with Dr. Norbert Sanders, whose organization, The Armory Track and Field Foundation, was delegated by the city to manage the usage of space at the armory. (Armory space is owned by the City of New York. In this case the city chose the Armory Foundation to represent it, by contract, in the management of the Armory space.) The opening date was a bit unusual, March 15, 1998, and the space limited, but we took advantage of the opportunity afforded us. PAL, under advisory from Councilperson Stan Michels and Democratic District Leader Maria Luna, hired me as center director. Mr. Michels and Ms. Luna had a close community relationship with Robert Morgenthau in his capacity as the Manhattan District Attorney. A Center Director is tasked with managing the program and fiscal obligation at each program site. The Center Director also has his or her center coordinate with city-wide activities sponsored by PAL, such as sport leagues and special events.

Sergio Larios and Lotti Almonte were assigned as liaisons from Community School District 6 of the Department of Education (DOE) to the communities of Washington Heights and Inwood. Mr. Larios and Ms. Almonte had become familiar with the work of Coach Dave (who, of course, continued to be an off-site advisor and my trusted confidant) and myself through the advisement of Gwen Crenshaw and Robert Jackson, each of whom had served with the Community School District #6 School Board. Mr. Larios and Ms. Almonte invited me to their offices at PS 48M (which housed the school district main office) to discuss PAL and District 6 collaboration. What resulted from conversations and negotiations between Mr. Larios, Ms. Almonte, and I was a signed agreement between our parties (signed off upon by senior management from the school district and Dr. Ryan for PAL). Although the contract contained terms and conditions governing the relationship and responsibilities of all parties listed in the contract, in real life we all worked an on-the-ground, learn-as-we-go collaborative learning enterprise. They assigned one of their experienced supervisors, Lorraine Pacheco, as the point person and manager from the DOE side.

What was the result? The demand for additional enrollment pushed proposed numbers beyond the space capacity available at the Armory site. The PAL Armory thus was assigned an additional space in which to run after-school programming. The Armory PAL became a two-site program, increasing the need for well-coordinated programming. Looking back on her past relationship with the Southern Heights youth program, we became adopted by the school principal, Blanca Battino, and staff at PS 128. Ms. Battino agreed to host our afterschool and summer day camp programs.

After a couple of years of operation, the District Six office and Armory PAL leadership (with crucial hands-on support from Coach Dave from the Dreamers) created programming that extended beyond the traditional scope of services offered by a standalone after-school program. We co-organized sports tournaments for middle schoolers called Fit for Life, in collaboration with the district six coordinator, Lotti Almonte. PAL middle schoolers got to participate in the District Six middle-school intramural involving five middle schools. Our condition, given the fierce insistence of Coach Dave, was that for each male team entered, the schools also had to enter a female team.

After the middle school intramural season ended, PAL leadership collaborated with the district to organize a community service-learning initiative, also for middle schoolers from several schools, with the District Six coordinator Lorraine Pacheco. The stewardship by PAL was coordinated with representatives from schools such as IS 164 in the lower Heights and IS 52 in Inwood. Taking charge at the PAL site located at PS 128M was a program specialist named Aida Ramos. Aida had started as a PAL IN STEP participant (a high school intern) in 1998. Aida had also previously served as a Female Finesse leader for the Ivy League, and as a teen program officer for a leadership program operated by ASPIRA. (ASPIRA focused on serving the Latinx communities around the city, and on grooming leaders from amongst high school students.) After graduating from high school, she was appointed as a PAL staff member. The importance of this learning-by-doing youth services tool (when addressing the needs of a community service-learning program) can be grasped when understanding the connection of well-trained teens transitioning into high-performing staff at youth centers. A description of this occupational education comes next. What Aida had to learn to manage in working with teens and staff from multiple school sites is similar in ways in what I had to learn after becoming the Director for the PAL Teen Services program, which we called IN-STEP (In School Training and Education Program). A key contrast between Aida's responsibilities and what would become mine is that I would be working in-house with PAL staff and participants, while Aida would have to network with staff and participants from schools. I next describe the IN-STEP program to profile the complexities shared for managing staff and participants from multiple sites. We strove to serve multiple sites across the neighborhoods of New York City. Each community had its unique mix of diverse peoples. Differences in national origin and customs resulted in variation about expectations on how youth and adults relate to each other. We strove to understand and honor these differences, and at the same time we endeavored to maintain our goal of having adults and youth better understand how to bridge the generation gap.

My fuller understanding of IN-STEP came about in 2003, when PAL had me transition from being a Center Director for a site to a Teen Services director.[210] What I had come to appreciate from one perspective as a Center Director changed substantially, as I now had to collaborate more closely with sixteen PAL sites, including adult staff and organized teen squads from each site.

As a Center Director at the Armory, I was assigned a cohort of teens each year, for whom I was responsible for supervising at my site. As an IN-STEP director, I would now become responsible for managing its support staff, as well as designing and assessing its program approach and its budget. Our teen enrollment portfolio include youth attending twenty-one centers located within the five boroughs of New York City. IN-STEP initially served about 180 high school students. Each was assigned a 10-hour-a-week menu, which included career and education workshops, internships at PAL after-school centers, and participation in college exploratory visits, as well as planning meetings by designated high school reps, who would serve on a city-wide teen advisory council. These leaders would develop and host an annual summit for all high school students in PAL. Topics included the 2004 theme: "Money, Power, and Respect.", which had been originated by teen leaders under the direction of their program manager named Greg Paul.

Within a year of my assuming the director's position at IN-STEP, we were asked to increase enrollment from 180 to 350 participants. We developed varieties of program options such as RSVP (Recreation Specialist Vocational Program), which gave teens specialized training for becoming group leaders in PAL after-school sites after they graduated from high school. Trainings included learning program activity leadership in sports and the arts, CPR training, and workplace safety training. An additional program, operated by Marcel Braithwaite, was the RAMP program (Rising Artist and Media Program). Marcel and his teen cohort helped to plan and design an annual participant yearbook for the program years 2004 and 2005. Marcel's team conversed with teen leadership and supervisors from each site. The second section of the yearbook profiled graduating high school seniors.

The citywide teen leadership was organized into what we named the Youth Advisory Council. Each program site would have their local teen cohorts select a representative and a back-up to the Advisory Council. The teen council was led under the exemplary leadership of Greg Paul who had college training in the field of education and youth development. One of the projects of the city-wide council was to plan, design, and manage annual youth forums.

At individual program sites, twenty-one across the five boroughs of New York City), teen interns organized into teams of IN-STEPPERS would be trained to become members of neighborhood youth advisory councils for each of their own sites. In addition to serving as high school interns assisting at after-school programs, each team would participate in a civic engagement learning component. Using a project-based learning approach, members of each team brainstormed to develop a project of their choice. Teen health concerns such as drug abuse and exposure to AIDS, youth-on-youth violence, being academically shortchanged by schools not having adequate college transition programs, and gentrification are examples of topics picked by teens over the years. Presentations, via PowerPoint and on-stage delivery, were hosted each spring at the Black Building Auditorium on the uptown campus of Columbia University, thanks to a thoughtful and helpful ally, Sandra Harris.

The process high school students went through opened their eyes to the power of their insights and initiative. This was summarized well by President Lakeisha Rock and Vice President Alex Egalite of the Brownsville Beacon IN-STEP team: "We inform the youth of today about the physical, mental, and social problems in their own neighborhood. We train peer advocates about tactics that are detrimental, and which are vital. We work to have participants understand cycles of mistakes, and actions to take to prevent these mistakes. We seek to help develop leaders for tomorrow by having them flourish and learn from their experience."[211]

A summer piece for the IN-STEP department was managing what is called the Summer Youth Employment Program. Individual agencies such as PAL are awarded contracts through New York City's Department of Youth and Community Development. During my years with the IN-STEP program, our enrollment numbers ranged from between 1,400 to 1,600 teens across the city of New York. Most enrolled teens were assigned to PAL sites, which included summer day camps, summer playstreets, and administrative support at PAL headquarters. The balance of enrolled teens was assigned to municipal departments such as the offices of Borough Presidents and local police precincts. We also assigned some teens to smaller youth agencies, which did not have their own contracts with the city.

With IN-STEP, each cohort of teens had an assigned site supervisor. In Aida's community service-learning project, school district personnel would drop into her site for visits, but Aida was the site supervisor who worked with PAL group leaders in monitoring student volunteer performance. Teens assigned to IN-STEP were enrolled for one year, and often for two or three years. These teens had signed on through their own choice, and not because of being mandated to enroll in the program. Middle-school students assigned for community service were obligated to 25 hours for the semester (as a requirement for graduating from middle school). They could opt to stay on if they found the experience valuable. I make provisional note of these differences here and will address them in more depth when I profile the difference between mandated community service assignments and voluntary community service-learning experience later in this book. What I will address are the differences in experience for the young between these two types of community service. One is a result of being mandated to serve, and the other resulting as a function of personal choice, an expression of the willingness of a participant to experiment with life decisions, seeking alignment with experience and personal values.

During my tenure with the IN-STEP program, I had hired Tamara Chalvire as a program monitor for one of the PAL sites located in South Jamaica, Queens, called the Edward Byrne Center. After one of my senior managers for the Summer Youth Employment Program and special projects for IN-STEP transitioned over the Department of Full-Time Operations for PAL, I chose to promote Tamara Chalvire to that position. She had shown superior ability in managing complex tasks, and unwavering initiative in tackling daunting tasks. I had had high expectations for Tamara, who not only met them but far exceeded them as she developed into a mastermind of programming and supervisory management. The complexities of this program are far too numerous to address in this narrative. However, I will provide a small taste here.[212]

For five months (April through June for planning, teen enrollment, and hiring seasonal staff, and then July and August for program operation), some of the tasks involved included training staff and teens, getting placement sites approved as per Department of Youth Services, Department of Transportation, and Department of Health regulatory codes, and managing a complex payroll system. It is super condensed by short-term reporting requirements, and intense as social problems and conflicts inevitably arise. When a summer finally comes to an end, most participants have had a rewarding experience. For those who have excelled, we extend invitations to apply to the school year IN-STEP program. Some who accept the challenge of serving during the school year move up to appointments with PAL after high school graduation. As the years have gone by, a few IN-STEP alumni have progressed up the career ladder within the PAL organization. Two examples are Ramon Pence, who had been an IN-STEPPER from the South Bronx, who went on to become a center director at the Armory, and Shakeia McPherson, who had been an IN-STEPPER from the Garcia Center on Staten Island, and an officer in our city-side Teen Advisory Council, who is currently a manager for the PAL teen College Discovery Program.

In what would turn out to be my final year as Director of IN-STEP, during the fall of 2006, and at the invitation of the Department of Education (DOE), I attended a conference held at Hunter College looking at partnership possibilities between DOE and community-based agencies. During a break in the workshop action, I found myself eating lunch while sitting on a couch next to two women who were codirecting a program called the Future Voters of America (FVA). Fran Baras, the director, and Diane Grazick, the associate director, ran through the agency's mission and the civic contributory work initiated and led by high school students. Their descriptive conversation resonated with me both on a conscious level and on a deeper level. I spontaneously leapt off the couch and almost bounced off the window.

Once I calmed down and explained my excitement, a constructive conversation began—as did a multiyear partnership between FVA and PAL. What I explained to them was that the approach they had developed extended the scope of fostering teen leadership even beyond the one I had been facilitating with IN-STEP. At PAL, we trained our teens to present to adult staff working at PAL. At FVA, teens were being trained to become advocates of teen issues, which were then presented to elected officials and municipal agency representatives. What also became refreshed in my memories was that years before, in 1974, as a senior majoring in political science at CUNY/York College, I had written my final paper on the theme of training high-school students to learn civics by participating in advocacy at home—that is, in their schools and communities. My exposition had now come home—into the house of FVA.

The broader outlines of FVA philosophy align with research work and summary studies, which clearly pinpoint developmental factors associated with optimal adolescent development and progressions of inclusive teen participation as civic decision-makers. The focus insisted upon by Fran Baras and Diane Grazick was not just to have teens incorporated into what benefits the agendas of adults, but to have adults become educated about the capabilities of teen social justice advocates as well as of the needs of an emergent youth generation. Crucial elements of this process are outlined by Elaine Ho for the Futures Page. This study was a comprehensive overview of best practices involved in social change programs that look at teen efficacy in more inclusive ways. As cited in the Future Page synopsis: "Youth should be invited by adults to participate in decision-making. It is fine and good to be surveyed for opinions, and to be asked to advocate for change. But it is not cool to be left out of the part of a process where young people generate change."[213]

Future Voters worked hard to identify not just schools but decision-makers and teachers who were committed to inviting students into a decision-making process for the issue areas they had consensually identified and chosen to act on. The FVA agenda called upon adults to commit to youth-derived agendas, to encourage initiative by the young, and to develop a willingness to challenge themselves when their own unconscious beliefs belied their stated purpose of developing leaders who could operate in a space where it was safe to be themselves.[214]

Additional crucial elements in fostering pro-active decisions and action by teens were identified by Shawn Ginwright and Taj James, who in 2002 wrote an article for a journal called *New Directions for Youth Development*. At that time, Shawn Ginwright was an assistant professor of sociology and ethnic studies at Santa Clara University, and Taj James was a co-founder of the Movement Strategy Center in Oakland, California. In their comprehensive overview of youth programs seeking to involve teens in organizational advocacy and leadership structures, Ginwright and James proposed that teen involvement, guided by supportive adults, resulted in impactful changes for positive youth development and for significant communal changes. Among the factors cited by Ginwright and James was "the importance of the role definitions applied to youth in the process. Many programs identify teen helpers as assets to the larger organizational body, but what is needed is a shift in self-identification by the young, where they believe and strive to be assets of change with issues that are meaningfully addressed by them. Spaces need to be created where adults can hear what youth articulate, and (where adults) are not allowed to act in judgment and interfere; where the space is safe enough for youth to nourish autonomy."[215]

Future Voters of America organized training sessions for both their student participants and adults who supported FVA programs. Local programs were operated in conjunction with social studies teachers at selected schools, and in preparation for an annually sponsored city-wide event called a High School Congress (to which each individual high school delegation is invited). At each of these annual assemblies, high-school delegations meet in the morning for small group or committee work. Members of each group discuss issues, prioritize them, and prepare to make their case to the entire assembly in the afternoon. Small group work was led by students and not adults, who were respectfully asked to remain outside of the classrooms where each committee met. Fran Baras and Diane Grazick, who led the Future Voters on a volunteer basis, told me, in their own way of maintaining accuracy but also in a relaxed atmosphere with good humor, that rule #1 that there were times that I was not to be allowed to be in the same room with teams as they debated, dialogued, and came to consensual decisions. Teens needed time to be open amongst themselves while not under the gaze of adults. During the times when I was allowed in the space, the rule was to keep at least a virtual piece of tape over my mouth.[216]

At the city-wide assemblies, teams of decision-makers, after having developed their issue priority list, appointed a spokesperson to make their case. Time was allotted to allow for give-and-take between each committee and members of the entire body of the assembly. After all presentations were made, a collective session was held wherein members voted on the priorities presented. If multiple groups came up with identical issues (for example, if four groups came up with the same health issues), the issues were converted into one priority to be considered. The issue areas obtaining the highest number of votes became designated by High School Congress consensus as the top three priorities, which were then labeled as mandates requiring swift and focused follow-up. All other issues were then ranked in order of total votes received and were still considered to be important issues. The three mandates, considered to be the most crucial and/or compelling to be addressed, would be taken up after the city-wide congress by student leaders under the guidance of adult staff and supporters. In some instances, advocacy groups formed to meet with city agencies or elected governmental officials. If an issue was determined to have traction for being seriously supported and advanced within the municipal governance structure, then a plan of action was developed to help navigate its status from a good idea to city agency practice or proposed policy change.

The keynote speech at a congress held in 2006 was made by Gale Brewer, who, at the time of this writing, is Manhattan borough president, but who at the time of the 2006 Congress was a city councilperson. Ms. Brewer was one of the most progressive members of city government; she ardently pushed for maximal participation by members of the public. In her view, this meant teens being respected as credible stakeholders in municipal decision-making processes.

Ms. Brewer spoke a Future Voters of America annual events and worked behind the scenes in support of initiatives created by teens at it's High School Congress gatherings. Ms. Brewer was seen by staff and youth members as a civic godmother in support of their cause. She assisted Future Voters in her capacity as a City Councilperson by getting the mandate submitted to and addressed in the City Council. Ms. Brewer served in that capacity that year and every year afterward, including after taking office as Manhattan Borough President in 2013. The mandate called upon the city of New York to lower the eligibility age to vote in municipal elections to age 16. The High School Congress mandate to lower the voting age to sixteen had scant additional support in the City Council. Council person John Liu, and maybe one or two others came on board. Opposition among almost all councilmembers was unalterable, and the push to have a bill get out of the council's Operations Committee went nowhere. In 2014, an amended version of the High School Congress' initial resolution would be introduced to the City Council in an ask to obtain a resolution of support. The process about how the amendment was conceived and approved at the High School Congress is outlined in the paragraphs below. In 2014, the Council's Operations Committee would approve a resolution of support by unanimous vote, and the full Council vote would reflect only one or two dissenters. The story of obtaining success with both the City Council resolution of support, and the amendment of New York State's Public Officer law is essentially defined by the collaborative efforts of teen activists with their civic mentors and sympathetic government officials.

In early 2007, Ms. Brewer met with Future Voters staff and student leaders and presented them with a list of possible compromises to the full voting rights bill to be considered at that year's congress. Suggestions included having the bill considered as a sunset bill. Sunset bills, once passed, expire after a few years; after that they are either dropped or reintroduced. The consensus among FVA members was that they did not want to have to revisit the issue every few years. A second suggestion was to mandate a civics test to become eligible to vote at age 16. This proposal was roundly rejected as a violation of the 1965 voting rights laws, which stipulate that requirement of any test is a barrier to the right to vote.

The third suggestion was to have legislation passed that would still allow for civic participation by teens. The suggested legislation would allow for 16- and 17-year-olds to be appointed to Community Boards by Borough Presidents and city council representatives. Once appointed, each teen would have full voting rights on the Board and serve under the same terms and conditions as adults age 18 and over. These boards are a network of 59 municipal advisory bodies composed of residents who either live or work in each of the 59 districts. Community board members are appointed by either borough presidents or the city council member representing the relevant district; members serve terms of two years. Each community board comprises several committees, such as Land Use, Public Safety, Parks and Recreation, and Youth Services. All members of the board meet once a month at general board meetings held for their district. These meetings leave room for presentations by public officials and members of the public. Each meeting also has a session in which resolutions, passed by individual committees, are brought to the floor, and voted upon by the full board. If passed by the members of the full board, these measures are passed on to appropriate representatives within the structure of city government in an advisory capacity. Board resolutions are carefully worded to ensure being representative of the board's intent. Board members understand that although resolutions are constructed to reflect community input, they are not mandates but rather advisory statements which, board members hope, will be taken into consideration for policy change or adjustments in municipal agency practices.

This third suggestion for reducing the required age for community board membership (to age 16) resonated with the FVA leadership. The leadership decided to bring this suggestion for consideration amongst teen delegates to the 2007 High School summit, for possible inclusion as a mandate. At the 2007 Congress, it passed by a margin of about 2 to 1 amongst high school delegates. The forum members also decided to make the community board amendment a mandate. FVA leadership as well as their civic allies initially thought this to be a slam dunk to be passed into law. Amongst the thoughts expressed as cause for optimism were the following. Community board processes and protocols very closely resembled those practiced by Future Voters and other youth organizations. This seemed to be a natural progression of skills from individual youth agency civic training process to community board operations and procedural methods. When all was said and done, only a total of 118 teens could be appointed city-wide; it was assumed that those selected would be among the most intelligent and committed teens. Put another way, those selected could be a Mensa population in the civic realm. Mensa identified a small fraction of teens, maybe one or two per cent, as the most intelligent people when measured by traditional IQ testing. The number of teens selected for community board appointments would be even a smaller fraction of the total teen population in New York City.

What had been seen by staunch proponents to be a measure of common sense and civic good instead resulted in highly contested opposition by elected representatives as well as by members of the public. The reasons for the opposition were many. Factors included intractable ideas held by adults about teen capabilities and efficacy, and the existence of mitigating factors such as heavy homework loads and the culture of community boards. Board meetings are cumbersome and demanding of one's time. They were considered by some of the more skeptical adults to be a steeply uninviting atmosphere. This type of judgment, held by adults, disregarded the prior histories in other cities, such as San Francisco and Hampton, Virginia, where teens as young as 14 years of age had joined Youth Commissions working closely with adults since 1996.

The remainder of backward/forward section of this book covers the final period of my 28-year journey that I call starting line #4. This section includes narrative anecdotes and profiles of people with whom I had become involved as a lead coordinator with the Teens On Board campaign in 2010, until the time that NY State Public Officer law was amended and signed into law by Governor Cuomo in August of 2014. Although this period is shorter in duration than the previous period, what I highlight are the cumulative lessons learned which allowed us to achieve success with our campaign. In the starting line #4 section, I highlight successful strategies implemented in seeing our goals realized, as well as the pitfalls and delays for getting our legislation passed. These factors, both those resulting in positive impact and those presenting challenges to us, are all intrinsic to the process of civic advocacy. Successful impacts are generated through obtaining agreements for a goal amongst people from diverse areas of responsibilities. Problems arose from biased attitudes about teen civic efficacy, by adults, initially seemed immovable. When all was said and done, social change organizers, as is the case with all people, lived in their civic experience, with acceptance of inevitable delays and frustrating temporary challenges.[217] Sometimes other types of circumstances, such as illness or injury, or loss of loved ones, add extra layers of challenge for reaching civic goals. As the end of this period neared, in the summer of 2014, we saw the passage of our bill come into place. Becoming involved in civic action, and politics, is, as is said about democracy, a challenge that must be experienced through practice, trial and error, and acceptance of roadblocks on the path of trying to achieve a goal. The point about democracy I make here is that it becomes relevant when practiced, and not solely through the study of history or abstract principles.[218]

Starting Line #4: 2010–2014 Teen enfranchisement and civic collaborations: Negotiating personal loss while helping to forge a new architecture for teen enfranchisement

Before getting into the experiences of the challenging and rewarding civic adventure finale, I now discuss other types of experiences, those of just living life as it comes, with its heartaches and rewards. The beginning of this five- year period was incredibly challenging for me. On a personal level, I suffered family losses and adverse health issues. In the space of three years, I lost both of my parents—my father in March of 2010 and my mother in

January of 2013. I then lost my younger brother, Pierre, the father of three young adult children, as a pedestrian victim in an auto accident. He was 56 years old.

On a personal health level, I suffered ongoing dizziness resulting from a vestibular disorder, three attacks of gout, and fatigue, which in later years was linked to a faulty valve in my heart. In the section to follow, I introduce a few of the people who allied with me not only as civic co-mentors, but also on a deeper level as caring friends who assisted me with life enhancing support.

During this five-year period, there were also challenges on an organizational level for the two agencies that had provided grassroots leadership for the teens on board campaign. As I previously mentioned, the two primary agencies leading the teens on the community board campaign suffered financial downsizing. Future Voters of America closed its program operations and PAL's teen civic component saw reductions in the level of funding per participant. The organizational coverage in the city was downsized from serving all five boroughs to only two, Staten Island and Queens. The point I make here is that even when faced with personal health issues and experiences of family loss, as well as losing some of the reliable support previously garnered from closely aligned allies, a civic change actor and social justice organizer faces choices. Does one give in, downsize, leave the scene for lesser terrains of engagement, or does one access the aid of empathetic allies and re-locate inner sources of resilience and strength? In working with the latter, I believe I lived the words expressed by Parker J. Palmer in his book *Healing the Heart of Democracy*. As I chose to work at healing the heart of democracy, my allies in this effort helped me to encourage healing in my own heart. As expressed by Mr. Palmer: "When we learn to 'think with the mind descended into the heart'-integrating cognition and emotion with other faculties like sensation, intuition, and bodily knowledge – the result can be insight, wisdom, and the courage to act on what we know." [219]

It would take a village, starting with my family and extending out to devoted friends and civic allies, to help me pull through emotionally. It would also take a tribe, those who were my civic colleagues who cared about my well-being and who shared my passion for teen enfranchisement, to encourage and support me as a civic warrior. On days when I was hesitant to get out of bed, my knowing they were there for me provided assurance for my continuing to serve as a determined civic advocate. On the organizing front, leadership within the inner circle of our alliance, such as from the Uptown Dreamers, the remaining teen program leadership from PAL, the help of Generation Citizen, and the office of Gale Brewer, firmed up their resolve and support. As a team, we remained determined to move forward, to look for ways to restructure the inner circle of leadership, to find a wider base of supportive allies, and to develop a new advocacy methodology to help bring sympathetic but reluctant partners on board.

My personal well-being, the maintenance of fierce, determined optimism, and energy to reach out beyond the universe of my own basic living, met the tests of life. To stay committed, one must have a sense of urgency, a hopeful vision, and the obligation to think of others before addressing issues in one's own world. When experiencing loss and suffering, there are many days when simply getting out the door and going through the motions makes your day. On a personal level, my emotional spark needed to stay alight, despite the dampening impact of endless tears. What I review next are the effects of personal injury, and the resolve required to move forward when temporary disability tempers one's desire to move forward.

On February 4, 2010, after my buddy Coach Dave Crenshaw had dinner at Coogan's Restaurant, our favorite haunt for relaxation and informal program planning, we decided to walk the few blocks home, even though a brief snow flurry had left a coating of black ice on the sidewalk and streets. After stepping into the road at West 164th Street and Broadway, I slipped and did a 180-degree flip, landing forcefully on the top of my head. I sustained injuries that required several stitches and a two-day stay at Harlem Hospital for observation. Although I was released after doctors determined that I did not have a concussion, my experience of well-being changed radically over the next three years. I experienced nearly constant waves of dizziness, both at home and at work; my orientation to life tasks, as well as my energy, seemed thoroughly drained. The way I explain this frequently recurring symptom is related to what a child experiences when playfully lifted in air and then spun around in circles. Once put back on the ground, the dizziness continues. For me, a sudden change in the position of my head, looking up or off to the right, would be followed by dizziness and loss of balance, at times for a few seconds, and sometimes for a few minutes. I would often experience this unsettling and fatigue-inducing phenomenon, intermittently, a few times a day. Thankfully, in the Spring of 2014, after I had pursued the advice of several medical practitioners (a chiropractor and an acupuncturist), my god-daughter Aida Ramos connected me to a physical therapist who specialized in balance disorders. After only a few weeks of visits and exercise, my sense of stability became mostly secure; only minor bouts of disorientation reoccurred.

During this same period, I suffered heavy family loss. In March of 2010, my father, at the ripe, young age of 98, succumbed to cardiovascular disease. John Kurland, in addition to being a father who lived to support the lives of his four children, served as my primary role model, as he spoke on behalf of the dispossessed. My father also used story to encourage us to see the differences among people as sources of learning and ways to grow our appreciation for the unique among neighbors with whom we shared common turf. I introduce you to John Kurland in more detail later in this book.

I briefly mention my father's impact upon my adopting the use of story as an organizing tool here. I elaborate on his contributions further in the section of this book titled "Rebel." In this section of the book, I reference my father as an early role model for how a person can use his or her arousal of empathy to connect with people. He introduced me to stories about the lives of people who turned the adverse conditions of denial and oppression in their lives into tools for developing oppositional and transformative resistance. As I learned to practice these amended skill sets, what I had learned from my father was reinforced by putting it into practice while working alongside social change allies during our advocacy campaigns. Coach Dave, like my father, is a practitioner, sharing anecdotal adventures in which he brings together ways in which those who wander through the thickets of challenge come to recognize internal resources. Even in the contexts of the very different lives they lived, their use of the power of story illuminated counseling objectives. For example, African Americans and Dominican-Americans had arrived in their communities from diverse embarkation points. Members of each group sought to embark upon the path towards success. Each sought the same types of social outcomes but traveled different roads on the way to their desired destinations. When cooking for a barbeque, the chicken for meals might be prepared with the skin intact, or with the chickens skinned (dependent upon their cultural preference). The music played at their gatherings might include salsa or historical civil rights songs. Their fortitude for persistence might be connected to the story of Dominican independence, or to the valor of freedom riders in the American south. After sharing their tales involving bias and facing exclusion, community leaders used the familial supports of great food and heart-affirming music. Each group learned to employ the festivities enjoyed by the other group. All groups developed a common ground for celebration and generating hope by incorporating their varieties of celebration into one event. The commonalities centering upon the right to reclaim a space for participation and recognition became apparent; those commonalties became part of their mutually shared recipes, providing culinary excellence and musical beat in support of generating resistance and resilience. New insights contributed to construction of social and cultural bridges that nurtured understanding among them.

Throughout much of our campaign to get teens on board, proponents incorporated research findings and specific facts in their methods of persuasion. Among those who were practiced in historical narrative and research, our positions often became grounds for continuous, contentious dialogue. As we learned to incorporate the stories of young people who had made major contributions despite having to navigate significant challenges, ears began to open, and hearts become more receptive. Later, as we continued to parry the opinion—*but teens do not possess the capacity...*—we introduced the narratives of teens serving on youth advisory committees and commissions in other cities. These organizations included the San Francisco Youth Commission and the Hampton Youth Commission. We shared the process of their mentored contributions, resulting in significant personal gains for participants, as well as for changes in policy more favorable to the young in the communities they served. In the minds of many of those who had previously opposed our goals, youth history was shown in a new light, teen possibilities were now more readily considered, and adolescent historical narrative bent ever so slightly closer to the arc of justice.

Before moving forward, I turn backwards one more time, looking back to my early childhood mentors whose influences and methods remain alive for me even today. First, I reflect upon my father as an example of a person who used story and listening to others as an essential methodology for effecting change. I enter this here as a kind of prelude to what I will share about his life in the section of this book called "Rebel."

When John Kurland told stories, he used them as portrayals of his personal experiences which revealed principles, or larger truths, about the power of using story to inform and inspire people in their work for social justice. My father's passion for resisting discrimination and injustice against marginalized groups were linked in his mind to what he had to endure as a member of a financially challenged immigrant group that had been oppressed and marginalized in the early decades of the twentieth century. John sought to encourage an empathetic response in his skeptical friends when sharing life stories about himself. His goal was to have his friends consider new positions about their beliefs, to open their hearts and minds. After at first laughing and then learning to his personal tales involving intolerance and discrimination faced by John, because he was a Jew and a white working-class man, his friends would loosen their grip on their unforgiving beliefs regarding people of different races and national origins.

My father, for example, told—and retold—a story about his personal experience during a job interview in the 1930s. He had scored well on a job questionnaire and on a selection test, and he had performed admirably in the interview—until the final question was put to him by his interviewer. The interviewer asked, "Not that it makes a difference, Mr. Kurland, but are you Jewish?" My father answered in the affirmative. He never heard from the company again.

Social justice advocates today use an exploratory methodology in which peoples of diverse racial identity, but comparable skill sets, and experience apply for comparable jobs. My father was an intelligent man who had skills that qualified him for jobs, but who was still rejected based upon prejudice against Jews. When I was introduced to anti-racism activity through my church's organized protests, as well as in my later years in adulthood through my political activities, I was motivated to fight injustice not just on principle, but because discrimination against Black and Latinx people felt personal to me.

My father was especially likely to repeat this story with people from his own religious and social group. He was never afraid to confront bigotry expressed by folks from national backgrounds different from his own. He always felt that by packaging the demand for social justice in the context of story people would be more receptive to listening with an open ear. This would be true, not always, but some of the time, and for him, small steps still helped. The requirements for adhering to civil rights code, created in bodies of law, are morally essential and still, to this day, only partially sufficient. Dr. Martin Luther King, Jr., often said that other channels of communication work beyond the reach of legal remedies. When Dr. King spoke to friends and allies about the need to shift people from their positions of rejecting the rights of others, he emphasized something that was more important than simply changing rules. What inspired people to shift from inflexible stances was making it safe for people to open their hearts. Stories involve not just logical precepts, but heart-to-heart communication. People engaged with my father in this way, as his story helped his friends to understand an issue as personal.

John Kurland's partner—and my other primetime, early-life mentor—was my mother, Jane Claire (Millhauser-Johannet) Kurland. On January 25, 2013, on the eve of what would have been John's 101st birthday, my mother, Jane Claire, passed away. This was three years after my father passed. In her younger days, my mother had not only been a social butterfly, but she was also a woman who created a home environment in which all were welcome, even if someone needed to stay with us for a short time. Some were parents from other families: they needed a safe space and emotional solace to help them recover from emotional breakdowns. Others were young people who felt they were worthless and despised after being tossed out of their homes by insensitive or misunderstanding parents. All were made to feel welcome by Jane Claire, and all were not only invited but also encouraged to feel included in the Kurland household. My mother related to them with endless empathy and reserved judgment. We came to name her the Empress of Embrace.[220]

She had come to America in 1940 as an exile, having been run out of her beloved France after living with, and then escaping from, Nazi occupation. During this time, she lost her early-life fiancé, Francois, who died in a labor camp. After arriving in America and establishing a close and nurturing relationship with a man named Alfie Hano, who was like a brother to her, she lost him. He had signed up with the U.S. Air Force and was shot down and killed on his 23rd flying mission over Germany. All that suffering, separation, and loss remained with her on many levels throughout her life. Despite her personal pain, she found ways to adopt the role of a healer, helping others who were hesitant about their futures to develop hope. The people she embraced included young relatives disposed from their home by a parent, and a neighbor suffering a breakdown after years of emotional abuse from her spouse. Like some of the mothers offering sanctuary to disposed children of others in Washington Heights, Jane Claire would open our apartment to those who had been emotionally injured. It was important that those she considered to be, in a way, extended family, have temporary sanctuary and a safe space from which to redirect their lives. My mother had a way of assisting emotionally wounded friends and relatives to transcend the clouds of dark despair and find the silver linings. She helped folks to rediscover their inner source of optimism inherent to the learning challenges of a young child.[221] Readers of this book will learn about her life and contributions in more detail in the section of the of this book titled "Orphans"

Just as my parents were more early mentors during childhood, Coach Dave was my first mentor after I became involved with teen empowerment work in Washington Heights. His specialty has been serving youth who have been rejected by their own families and ejected from the safety of classrooms. Dave and I consider those who are cast out from the shelter of family and institutions to be orphans, in need of nurturance and support. Those youth who have been psychologically injured and who have become distrustful and skeptical about being offered positive alternatives have accepted invitations after engaging with Dave's power of story. I think we share, at the deepest levels of consciousness, a common understanding about young people as orphans and rebels. I think the connection I share with Coach Dave springs from an emotionally oriented and spiritually connected knowingness that has kept us united. Our deep connection has helped us to maintain a decades-long partnership in working with youth in the Heights and beyond. Even as we have, in recent times, worked for different agencies and been geographically far apart at times, we each still look forward to checking in with each other frequently.

To share one scenario here, I write about how Dave brought the love and support of my civic-minded, extended family home to me when he organized a memorial "thank you" service for my parents at Coogan's Family Restaurant. His organizing of this ceremony gave me a chance to share my family stories and express to the audience how my parents' influence shaped my approach to providing youth services. Many of the youth who attended, who at that point were alumni, gave speeches about the meaningfulness of the programs Dave and I delivered, and gave heartfelt messages of gratitude for my parents. Coach had shared similar sentiments with me in the past, in private discussions on many evenings, as we related our daily triumphs and tribulations to each other. On this evening of reflection and appreciation,

Dreamer youth and alumni got to virtually meet my parents through the storytelling and socially engaged type of Internet, and to understand me in deeper ways.

On this same evening, Coach Dave shared with the crowd his gratitude for my parents. He also revealed what he had learned on a trip to Albuquerque he had taken in 2002, when he had come with me to celebrate my dad's 90th birthday. Although we stayed for only a few days, he said each of my parents, through their presence and sharing of life stories, had changed his life in deep ways. My mother shared with him the agony of being forced to leave a home she deeply loved after escaping the Nazis' occupation of her beloved country, France. Her lifelong response had been neither to retreat into isolation nor to desire retribution and revenge—but rather to learn to extend her compassion to others with open arms. My father, who never pursued an education beyond high school, led a selfless life of parenthood, where through guidance, story, and support, he made sure his four children grew up knowing that our life courses were, in fact, ours to choose. He also shared with Dave that he had endured most of the jobs he held despite the lack of their having any personal meaning for him. No matter what the travail had been, he had always found things that were joyful and meaningful to him, even if only in small ways. In a sense, the deep dialogue on that trip was a ceremony about the importance of being included as family, even by people you had never previously met, but that you have come to know as if you will be with them forever. Since then, Dave has taken the time to remind me that even over the course of those few days, my parents changed his life. I cannot help but feeling that when Dave organized that event about my parents, their souls had also entered the room. I profile Coach Dave more extensively in the "Rebel" section of this book, in which I share in more detail about how he generates soul-to-soul connections.

I now share a story of grief and loss for my younger brother, Pierre, with whom I first learned how to be a big brother and a mentor. How does a civic leader, no matter how motivated and determined, adjust when being hit by overwhelmingly and seemingly insurmountable personal loss? I was fortunate in having incredibly committed family and friends offering me crucial aid in dealing with my pain and loss. They guided me in letting me know that I had the power to move on, and that they would be there for me even if I stumbled. Their compassionate listening and support helped me to heal the chaos and wounding I felt inside, but rarely showed to others. As I received aid in navigating the inner work necessary for me to remain hopeful, I was better able to engage in moving forward on an outside path.

On September 19, 2013, I, along with my siblings, my sister-in-law, and my two nieces and nephew, lost my younger brother, Pierre, who was only 56. He had been driving on a quiet street, on a sunny morning in Van Nuys, on his way to work. He received a cell phone call and, acting dutifully for the safety of others, he pulled over to take the call. From the sidewalk, he spoke for a while to the caller. As he attempted to get back into his car, he somehow did not see or hear a car speeding down the street. For some reason, the car was proceeding on a path too close to Pierre's car. Although airlifted by the sheriff from Van Nuys to UCLA medical trauma center, my brother never had a chance.

"It did not make any sense," were the words expressed in anguish by my niece Rebecca. We all felt her words were true—and we will continue to feel so for the rest of our lives. The intensity of the pain, the unexplainable separation, the disorientation may lessen with time, but it never leaves us. Pierre lived a life unselfishly and relentlessly devoted to his families, his immediate tribe, and his siblings. I profile what this meant to his family and work colleagues in the memorial dedication at the front of this book. He was a constantly available source for counsel, which came from his center of uncompromised love, devotion, and limitless understanding. You will also learn more about my brother Pierre in my section of the book titled "Civic Lover."

Just as I have mentioned in the section above, about how Pierre meant so much even to his work colleague, it was my work colleagues at PAL, close colleagues in my teens on board coalition, that offered me emotional, family-like support in distressing times. Even given the depth and detail required for working at PAL, many colleagues let me know their thoughts for me and my family, and of their eagerness to lend support. Through their encouragement alone, I found the strength to move forward. My circle of family-like colleagues and friends let me know that they were there for me 24/7. They came for me during my higher moments of resurgent energy and optimism and cheered me on, and they took up the slack for me when I stumbled through periods of despair. They were each, in their own way, both familial, providing counsel and comfort, and deeply committed friends, pulling me away from poor decisions and missed opportunities. This was especially supportive for me in my work with PAL, when I worked within the unit where I spent hours a day to keep our program sites in compliance with complex codes governing health, safety, and program quality.

At that time, I was working in the Grants, Research, and Evaluation (GRE) department at PAL. The department was led by Director Karen Trank. She reached out to PAL personnel across the agency and organized the construction of a special fund called the Pierre Kurland fund. Karen and our company of friends within GRE had heard many stories about Pierre and my family. A few had even met Pierre and his daughter Rebecca on one of their trips to New York City only a year prior. Karen and company heard about Pierre's relentless generosity and devotion to his children, and they wanted to somehow honor his supportive and sheltering relationship to them. My PAL colleagues were *so* generous! They gave to the fund named in honor of my brother, and they also shared words of limitless value. Besides being such an impressive professional, one of my GRE colleagues, Stephanie Chen, possesses endless empathy toward others. I consider her to be a PAL daughter. Her verbal reassurances to me helped me loosen the bonds of my grief and to keep my feet moving forward, one after the other. From her presence alone, I got the message: *We are here for you.* On her personal consolation note, she wrote me a heartfelt message:

"It hurts me to even try to imagine what you must be feeling with yet another terrible loss. I am glad I met your brother, even if only for that one

time, his strength of character and love of his family are what stood out most strongly to me. For now, take comfort that he was loved, even by those who barely knew him, he was just that type of person."

Adrienne maree brown (ms. brown prefers the use of lower case letters in her name), a social justice organizer with sharp emotional intelligence, expressed the value of family-like embrace in an interview with Nick Montgomery and Carla Bergman (author of *Joyful Militancy*): "[W]e are always emerging, as insistent changes intersect with our lives, and when we falter, pain teaches us, that we are all in these ways recovering leaders, and that by trusting with our teammates providing support, the universe will come to show us pathways of scaffolding opportunities."[222] To this day, my memories of my younger brother arrive every day; on some days, I reread Stephanie's note, reassured by my teammate.

My personal challenges and resilience occurred within the context of political and financial challenges faced by our teen enfranchisement campaign. As I previously mentioned, our initiative encountered a major setback in the form of decreasing funding and loss of partners as allies. Future Voters of America, which had in every sense been the founding organization for the Teens on Board campaign, was forced to disband due to heavy financial challenges related to the activities the agency remained committed to, and limits on how much of their own time and money volunteer leaders could continue to sacrifice.

The PAL IN-STEP program, which had operated in five boroughs and at 21 sites, had to reduce its presence to two boroughs, each with only one site. What was lost to us left room for gain. We had less money, and we had lost the leadership of agencies who could extend their reach on a city-wide level. But we did not lose the passion and commitment of those who remained. Even with our temporary setbacks, our intention and devotion lead to the creation of new partnerships and greater effort to expand our support within the government. In the early stages of advocacy and organizing for our proposed bill (to allow fully vetted 16- and 17-year-olds to serve on NYC community boards), the Republican Party controlled State Senate had passed our bill. However, in the Democratic Party controlled State Assembly, our bill remained mired in the Operations Committee in the Assembly. Historically, bills sent to committees can often remained mired in that committee for years at a time. Our original allies among youth service providers and civic reform organizations continued to remain steadfast. Community boards, primarily based in Manhattan, continued to remain supportive. Our coalition would have to expand upon previous efforts and strategies to draw attention to our bill, and then later create grassroots momentum for having the bill approved by the full State Legislature.

Those who remained as member in our original coalition buckled up and brought a renewed commitment for the new challenge. What we determined in our new planning meetings was the need for engineering on the ground support in the districts of elected officials from each of the five boroughs in New York City.

The New York State Public Officer Law amendment, allowing for full participation on Community Boards for 16- and 17-year-old teens, was initially sponsored by Assemblyman Brian Kavanagh and State Senator Lanza when the bill was introduced in 2008. To give our proposed initiative some teeth, on-the-ground advocates had also offered letters of support from youth agencies such as Global Kids and the Girl Scouts, as well as from some municipal bodies such as community boards. For example, community board #12, located on the northern tip of Manhattan, had passed a resolution in support of the amendment, by a vote of 22 to 4. In their resolution, the body of the resolution pointed out: "Giving youth an opportunity to serve on Boards[223] would give them an introduction to participatory governance, and Board members an introduction to their world of experience, and that their involvement would allow for the introduction of new ideas; in New York State, many sixteen- and seventeen-year-olds pay taxes, and participate as citizens with their work in community service and youth agency-led issue initiatives, and that this gives them the right, and a say, on how those revenues are spent."

Agency allies who also backed our efforts offered convincing arguments for passing the amendment based upon their organization's previous experience with teens with letters of support. The Girl Scout Council of Greater New York had been on board since the campaign's inception. They offered these words of support in their letter: "On behalf of more than 21,000 Girl Scouts and 7,000 leaders, we enthusiastically support this initiative. This allows girls to find their voices, to take an active role in their community, and to learn that they are powerful members in their community." [224]

Dr. Sarah Zeller-Berkman also lent her support, as she had steadfastly done since the early stages of our efforts. At the time, she worked as an organizer, project developer, and advisor on behalf of the Youth Development Institute. She graciously acknowledged me as the string that kept our effort going, starting from its earliest days, and continuing through to our campaign's success. Humbled, I could offer her only this: that although I may have been the string, it was her amazing support, as part of a cord, that was essential to our effort. We each remained steadfast in our obligations to our own work—*and* to the larger task of obtaining recognition of teens as powerful and productive actors in the world of municipal governance reform. Amongst her essential contributions was assisting in getting letters of support from the directors of youth service agencies. [225]

Dr. Zeller-Berkman garnered support from academia and civic organizational research. She culled what was most relevant to our campaign, disseminating the information to us communally. Dr. Zeller-Berkman was the keeper of academic knowledge applicable to grassroots campaigns, helping us to construct youth enfranchisement wisdom "in the commons." In addition to sharing the findings of her sources, she also offered testimony at another level, that of an organizer and trainer promoting youth empowerment on the ground, through after-school-, extended day-, and community-based agencies. Dr. Zeller-Berkman advised youth agencies such as PAL's Beacon program department. (Beacons are community centers offering a focused program for middle-school students.) Sarah provided program support by connecting us to resources and best practices with middle-school teen councils.[226] Dr. Zeller-Berkman developed a holistic approach, connecting positive teen assets as agents of change with the value of their service work at youth centers and in communities. For those of us in the coalition, Sarah's approach, defined and refined through her time at the Youth Development Institute, clarified how to best address obstacles, such as belief systems about teen deficiencies and how to help teens construct deliverable contributions to their neighborhood (for example, teens becoming trained in conflict resolution). She offered step-by-step curricular support, involving teens in civic learning and providing them opportunities to practice its application at a local level. Dr. Zeller-Berkman assisted adult mentors at program sites, training teens to contribute to their parenting agencies through participation in youth advisory councils. Teen youth advisory boards became a centerpiece for optimally functioning community programs. Beacon Centers, funded by the Department of Youth and Community Development, had been conceived and launched some years before by Richard Murphy, who had been the commissioner of the Department of Youth Services (predecessor of DYCD) under Mayor David Dinkins. Mr. Murphy pioneered youth program development through the lens of viewing the young not merely as clients in a specific program, but as participating observers and advisors. Mr. Murphy promoted a mandate of universal inclusion in public affairs. The essential importance of universal inclusion had been introduced on the international stage in Article 55 of the United Nations' charter. Each autonomous community is a building block within a worldwide network of communities. Mr. Murphy worked incessantly in bringing the U.N. Charter mandate back home to New York City neighborhoods. As stated in the article's section on community development: "Development is conditioned upon its being a process of creating economic and social conditions aiming for the progress of the whole community, with its active participation, and the fullest possible reliance upon the community's initiative."[227] Although our movement temporarily faltered, it would rise again, based upon participation of a much larger representation of the youth community from more diversified neighborhoods across New York City. By including community-based agency leaders, and members of their teen participation programs in our advocacy campaign, we established local neighborhood buy-in for making teen representation conditional upon agreed upon and shared endorsement of our teen empowerment initiative. In the early stages of our campaign, we had been perceived by activists in boroughs outside of Manhattan to be proposing an initiative that was a West Side thing. (an item on a wish list of liberal progressives)

Our renewed resilience and determination continued to be crucially supported by our legislative supporters. In January of 2010, what some would have considered a chance encounter may have been the work of the higher angels guiding our campaign. Those of us who remained with the campaign, since its inception in 2006, had been turning over in our heads the need to retain the partnerships we had established, and trying to come up with strategies for improving the momentum we had gained up to this point in time.

On an early January day, in 2010, I had decided to attend a workshop on reducing gun violence. The workshop was hosted by the Quaker Friends House in the East Village and in partnership with New Yorkers Against Gun Violence. I believed deeply in their approach, which involved enlisting youth in their advocacy, and I thought I might find a new and essential ally.

Toward the end of the meeting, after questions and commentary from the audience, the master of ceremonies decided it was important to introduce an elected official who had sponsored legislation seeking to control the spread of dangerous weapons. After announcing the purpose of the legislation, the MC introduced the sponsor—Brian Kavanagh!

Thoroughly surprised, I rushed up to greet Brian as the meeting began to break up. He was as surprised as I was that we were meeting there, and we both were grateful after we conversed. I let him know that earlier in the day, I had had conversations about our wanting to continue the Teens on Board campaign, despite our organizational challenges, and that, given the work already done and the milestones reached, we were determined to regroup, expand, and move forward. A huge smile spread across Brian's face, and he shared with me that he had just had a parallel conversation about moving forward that very same day. He asked me to call his staff; we set up a meeting within a few days. I remember reading somewhere in a Shakespeare play a line stating, in effect, that our faults lie not within the stars but within ourselves. To that end, I believe that the "coincidence" of meeting Brian at the workshop on reducing gun violence was about manifesting fruitful fortune with good work, and that although the proper intentions lay within each of us, guardians among the stars must have been smiling down upon us. Senator Kavanaugh's staff met with me shortly after our surprise meet at the Quaker House and helped to identify elected officials and agency leaders in neighborhoods outside of Manhattan who might be favorably inclined to lend a hand.

The period between early 2010 until the successful completion of our campaign in 2014 was marked by the growth of a coalition comprising many agencies across New York City. Over time, this development would change the way the campaign was perceived: it went from being viewed as "a West Side thing" to being seen as a call for inclusion from multiple city-wide and community-based sources. Large organizations would eventually represent us from a city-wide perspective: the Boy Scouts and Girl Scouts, Global Kids, the Children's Aid Society, United Neighborhood Houses, the Asian Student Advocacy Project, and PAL. These organizations would be joined by locally based groups—The Uptown Dreamers, the Community League of Heights, Harlem RBI, (RBI is an abbreviation for Runs Batted In.), the Forest Hills Beacon, (Staten) Island Voice, the Forest Hills Beacon Center, and the Far Rockaway Youth Task Force. Incorporating the input and counsel of neighborhood-based youth and civic-change organizations kept the campaign closer to the grassroots of citywide activism. Diversity developed democratic inclusiveness on a municipal level.

Some new partners became best friends of the campaign. In the fall of 2013, Generation Citizen, founded by its then executive director, Scott Warren, came to serve us as an organizing machine. As will be described in later chapters of this book, Generation Citizen had organized civic clubs in high schools across the city. Their program model was centered on training students in the skills of issue identification, advocacy, and networking. In addition to intensifying our focus on the mechanics of advocacy; the organization also helped us reconstruct the role teens and their supportive adults might play in changing the perceptions youth and adults held for each other. Of course, Generation Citizen's approach was all youth centered. As Scott wrote in his biography of Generation Citizen, it was high time that "the guppies teach the older fish."[228] His agency's school based action civic programs were learning laboratories for civic practices designed by and for students in service to schools and communities.

I came to learn about Generation Citizen through an initial encounter at a youth forum with Sarah Andes. Sarah was the organizations' New York City chapter director at the time. Her organization, in partnership with the Resiliency Advocacy Project, had, in the fall of 2013, conducted a youth-organized and -led mayoral debate. RAP was, at the time, led by Elisa Kaplan. Ms. Kaplan deferred authority and welcomed youth to plan the debate night. High school students made up the panel which would pose questions to candidates in the mayoral race.

After conversing briefly with Sarah while she was handling a table distributing information about Generation Citizen, she let me know that she was highly interested in our campaign, and that perhaps Generation Citizen might become a partner. Sarah organized a sit-down lunch for the two of us and Scott Warren. Scott bought lunch, but I never finished my salad. I was too busy responding to his two hours of exploratory questions. Within a couple of days after our lunch meeting, Sarah let me know that Scott had agreed with her assessment and was determined to aid our campaign. Even with the huge responsibilities of guiding dozens of school-based Generation classrooms across the City of New York, Scott supported Sarah, lending to the Teens on Board committee her considerable time and invaluable expertise. Sarah helped us to build an architecture of more effective advocacy. Sarah helped to develop an advocacy guideline rubric, which introduced the nature and importance of having teens sit on community boards, and tips on generating letters of support as well as generating appeals to elected officials.

I flush out a detailed picture of Sarah's involvement in a later section of this book titled "Civic Lovers." For now, I offer a few general attributes of mentors who are civic lovers, and then in the chapter civic lovers reveal how Sarah exemplifies those attributes. A civic lover is a social justice advocate who uses the higher assets of one's soul, the quest for connection, empathetic understanding, and inspired creativity with civic engagement practices that enhance mutual problem-solving methodologies and collaborative civic practices. The spheres in which the work becomes applied is that of communal improvement and the deepening of democracy through greater inclusive opportunities and a focus on universal justice. Civic lovers are facilitative leaders who develop youth programming in which the civic actors who receive aid learn to apply, on their own, the tools of democratic advocacy. Among these tools are the compelling arguments as to why our campaigns' goals benefit teen holistic development and construct opportunities to join city governance as effective stakeholders. Sarah did not just deliver important information. She participated in planning and outreach diligently and consistently, showing us that she and Generation Citizen were fully on board with our Teens on Board agenda and activities. She co-led workshops delivered to youth programs and teen advisory councils. She typically arrived to training sites earlier than I did. The one and only time she was late was when I neglected to give her full and accurate subway directions to a planning meeting site hosted by the Isabella Senior Center. Sarah also designed advocacy agendas for Teens on Board volunteer taking trips to the individual districts of New York City Council members and to Albany to meet members of the New York State Legislature. Scott attended one of the timely missions to the New York State Legislature with Sarah, me, and a teen advocate from PAL named Ramon Spence. We had targeted individual state representatives who seemed to be favorably disposed to passing our bill, and whom we sought to have sign on to the legislation. We also had open discussions with those who might lean towards supporting the bill, but who had some questions or reservations. He thanked me for much that he learned on that trip, but I believe we four advocates were teacher/learners for each other. We did our meetings with individual legislators or their senior staff by pairing ourselves in teams of two for each office meeting and taking cues from each other about how to pose a question or make a response to a comment. We also focused on keeping the discussion open to multiple perspectives, and our keeping our ears sharp with active listening about possible objections or roadblocks that might pop up in our campaign.

Sarah also designed agendas and training tools that she and I, or other advocacy allies, would use as a model of information and follow through training to be used by staff and youth members whom we were soliciting for becoming campaign allies. The tool developed by Sarah was adapted from the training model used in social studies classrooms by Generation Citizen's Action Civics programs. Regardless of the audience we were engaged with, our approach remained the same. I will share Generation Citizen's specific steps later in this narrative; for now, what is important to know are the goals of the process. Youth advocates were trained to communicate the significance of their presence as advocates for an issue. By making sensitive and well-informed presentations, advocates were being trained to teach skeptical adults that all young people are not alike, and that what they have to say has importance. Youth needed to present with clear initiative and listen sensitively to the viewpoints and objections of their audience. Teens needed to learn the value of personal contact, and to strive to make the experience one in which those they addressed felt they had spent valuable time listening to them. The content that was discussed varied, dependent on the students' ages, the neighborhoods in which they lived, and their previous experience with civic and/or community service-learning efforts. We used these sessions in places as diverse as a Queens Community House Beacon program in Forest Hills, an extended teen evening program hosted at the PAL Edward Byrne Center in South Jamaica, Queens (that program was also attended by teen leaders from the Far Rockaway Teen Council), and a teen evening program at the PAL Webster Center in the Bronx.

Let me introduce an anecdote relating to one of our visits, namely the training we provided to middle-school students at Forest Hills Beacon. We introduced the session with a warm-up activity: students viewed a video of Barack Obama, then a presidential candidate, talking about the importance of citizen/stakeholder participation. Obama invited audiences to become participants and live the message of "Yes, we can."

We then invited audience members to profile and discuss actions they had taken to advocate for their issues and compare their actions to talking points in Obama's address. As youth members of their Beacon Program, students had previously been involved in campaigns to save funding for Beacon programs and for the Summer Youth Employment Program. It was after this that we introduced the Teens on Board campaign, connecting their ongoing work to this new campaign, and outlining a process used in the Generation Citizens' "Advocacy Hourglass" approach.[229] Again, I do not dwell in too much detail here (major elements are woven into the section of this book titled "Civic Lover"). I highlight here the purposes of the hourglass learning sequences. Some of these include the need to have a well-defined process for adopting goals, which includes brainstorming, debate, research, discussion, and consensus-building dialogue. Student advocates need to establish target populations to which advocacy will be addressed. While holding on to the zeal of their beliefs, students must also be open and sensitive to their target audience's interests and opinions. Sarah incorporated training techniques in which youth advocates developed tactics that were to be used to gain attention and present their case clearly. Young advocates were counseled not to come on too strongly, yet to have enough of an impact so that the target recognizes the value of what they were proposing. The goals were to have one's intended allies feel—and then commit to— "the fierce urgency of now."[230]

This approach aligned with the conclusion educational writer Parker Palmer made from his experience and research covering how impactful outcomes are attained: "It is not just what you teach, but the nature of your presence, i.e., it is how you teach."[231] To paraphrase Gandhi (although here

I apply his statement to a local level), when applying the principles of democratic participation at the local level, we gave both our advocates and our targets the opportunity to play on the community playing field and to be the mutually affirming partners that help to make democracy work at the municipal level. By becoming agents of social change who participated on an equal level with adults, in civic affairs, teens became the change they wanted to see brought about in their own schools and community. Between the fall of 2013 and the spring of 2014, our campaign's momentum accelerated with the infusion of Generation Citizen expertise and the contributions made by all our partners through letter writing and presentations made to the New York City Council. Finally, in June of 2014, the state legislature passed an amendment to the Public Officer Law, authorizing 16- and 17-year-olds to serve as full voting members on New York City community boards. Additional anecdotes and details regarding the passing of this amendment are shared in the section of this book titled "Civic Lover."

The Public Officer Law amendment was passed by the state legislature and signed into law by Governor Andrew Cuomo on August 12, 2014, we had a new goal, letting teens and their mentors know that this opportunity exists. Now that 16- and 17-year-olds could legally be appointed to community boards, our coalition, seeking to encourage teen engagement with the boards, designed and effected a new civic education workshop for orientation and training about community boards, and how to apply for membership. For the design and delivery of these workshops (which came to be named Community Board Boot Camps), we were fortunate to enlist a new ally, Alan Shulman, a retired social studies teacher, and a New York State representative who was also a member of the National Council for Social Studies.[232]

One of the new forums we had designed was hosted at the borough office of Brooklyn Borough President Eric Adams. Students from Brooklyn's Boys and Girls High Schools, as well as teen leaders from youth not for profit agencies, were invited. Also invited were elected officials and their staff, as well as sitting members from some of Brooklyn's community boards.

Presentations were given about the purposes and practices of community boards, including their structure and deliberative processes. Students were then invited to participate in mock community board committee work, to work on virtual issues presented to their committees. The sessions then continued with commentary and reaction given by participants in breakout groups; a session on how, and why, a teen should apply to become a member of the boards also was held.

We repeated offering this training model in additional locations, including at an office space operated by an arm of the New York State Health office in midtown Manhattan. Teen leaders and some of their mentors attended on behalf of programs from the Bronx, Brooklyn, and Staten Island. Reactions were positive, on the part of both adults and teens. Monifa St. Louis, an adult staff member from Island Voice (a youth advocacy and community-builder on Staten Island) attended one of our boot camps in mid-Manhattan. In response to the training she received, she commented: "I am excited to meet young adults from Brooklyn who are committed to bringing about change." In a similar fashion, Meshach Brown, a student/participant at Island Voice, offered: "Students learn the value and power of working together and being involved in their community." [233]

These experiences and reactions would be repeated by adult staff members observing our trainings. At the same training session hosted in midtown Manhattan, a young adult leader, Morris Odilli, representing the Staten Island Voice program, offered these observations on the session: "The youth advocacy training for Teens on Board was both informative and motivational. It helped me realize ways to go about creating effective change in our communities. The motivational part, for me, was seeing the youth who took the time to be here, time that they could have easily allocated elsewhere. Instead of doing something unproductive, they came out to work on some things affecting them. For me, I had the opportunity to hear youth testimony, which brought about a light for 'being for our future generations.'"

Teens began to apply for and become admitted as full members on New York City Community Boards. Victoria Pannell, a 16-year-old junior from Manhattan's Democracy Prep Charter school, was one of the first teens to be appointed to a board; her appointment was achieved through the advocacy and outreach of Manhattan Borough President Gale Brewer. In an interview with Ginger Adam Otis of the *New York Daily News*, she shared her thoughts for what it means for a teen to have been appointed (Ms. Pannell had been appointed to Community Board #10M): "I saw an interview with Michelle Obama, in which she discussed the importance of talking about her experience. This talk was inspirational to me."[234]

When adult members hear teens talk about their experience, they are inspired too. Ms. Pannell, in relating her experiences, shared the following thoughts: "I have been involved in homeless outreach, helped to arrange food drop-offs to needy families, and advocated tirelessly to end global sex trafficking." Add to this Ms. Pannell's maintenance of perfect school attendance as an honors student and I think the adjective *amazing* to describe Ms. Pannell's accomplishments would be an understatement. As a new board member, she was thrilled to see the passion expressed in differences of opinion, and she plans to reach out to the youth and the older adults on the board to work together on issues of importance to the Harlem community.

As Scott Warren asserts in his book *Generation Citizen*, where he also describes the change-making process effected for both community institutions and the actors who adopt leadership roles in the process: "[T] o make real change, we need to persist…This is a process of changing the narrative of democracy and is our political journey…It is a journey which has no end, but it is one which can, and will, define our lives."[235]

Forward/Backward and Inside/Out: Closing Thoughts

In the next chapter of this book, which I call the "Introduction," I include sections in which I delve in detail into another type of ally for teens, which are called archetypes. What an archetype is, and how they are relevant to both the adolescent mind and soul, as well as the heart of democracy, will be fully developed in the Introduction chapter. For now, I just offer a hint: archetypes are windows to the soul, connecting one's life purpose to spiritually organized energy centers which we connect to both unconsciously, and when we become more aware, consciously. Examples of these archetypes, each of which guides us in the methods we use and our purposes for using this energy, include the advocate, the counselor, the orphan, the rebel, the lover, and the visionary. We personally connect to these archetypal sources internally, experiencing them as intuitive flashes of insight, and externally, enhancing our connectively based attention to people and purposes larger than ourselves. Before addressing the nature of archetypes, which for me at first appeared invisibly (that is, beyond my conscious awareness), I offer a few summary thoughts on the preceding words concerning the relationship between positive teen assets and organizing efforts on behalf of teen empowerment. In part, it is the discrediting of falsely held stereotypes that buttresses this effort.[236] I offer this at this point to emphasize that to construct something new, even evolving forms of consciousness and institutional practice, it is also a simultaneous necessity to take down old forms which have become barriers against a teen's holistic development and fetters slowing down the progressive attainment of constructive civic relationships. Many of these barriers were struggled against by social justice advocates in the past, and even today. Teens experience these obstacles as members of marginalized groups, blacks, Latinos, women, etc. The effects of these negative practices are experienced by teens more intensely, because they are adolescents subjected to bias against them based on negative stereotypes about teens, and by prejudice against their larger communities of diverse cultures and differing national origin.

My first thought concerns the obstruction that is introduced by negative stereotyping, and by people holding on to rigidly held false beliefs about other people targeted for civic exclusion. In the 1800s, business associations developed bodies of beliefs about how the disabilities of working people acted as a barrier against their attaining fruitful outcomes in their lives.

The following words from a business journal encapsulate this dismissive disposition: "Wageworkers remain employees of others, because they have not the initiative enough to be employers themselves. They remain poor because of lack of brains, lack of wit to earn, thrift to save, nor knowledge of how to use savings. The superior few and the inferior many scarcely appear to belong to the same species."[237] This is an example of the power of diminishing narrative, which creates a mental caste system even before systems are put into place.

One hundred years later, this outlandish orientation persisted even among highly educated professionals. In 1979, Annie Stein, a community organizer from New York City, threw a light onto this type of false information when she critiqued a textbook commonly used for training in the early childhood education community. Ms. Stein quoted a passage from the text, used for teacher preparation: "Blacks, Puerto Ricans, Chicanos, and to a certain degree, low-income whites…have the following (inherent) characteristics. These include a low motivation for learning, weak self-concepts, and an inability to defer gratification nor to plan. People with these backgrounds are culturally deprived, without hope, and are passive and dull."[238] President George H.W. Bush once criticized the quiet sabotage of low expectations. What he might not have known is that this toxic disposition was foundational to an early childhood education syllabus less than a year before he assumed the office of the vice president of the United States.

By necessity, I worked alongside many adults, generally of good will, who also harbored these disabling belief systems and attitudes. I share two examples here. The first example highlights explicit prejudice in the absence of compelling evidence. The second reveals subtle attitudinal bias, which was expressed in the disguise of humor. In this case the person's actions were directed towards teens; it would never have been put on public display if the target had been adults.

One of the participants in my Southern Heights program was named Michael B. He had been diagnosed by school professionals with behavioral disorders that at times could result in defiant and aggressive behaviors. He was a student during the day at the same school where we operated our after-school program. Over the course of a few days, I received concerns from teachers about his behavior every day. One day, I decided to invite Michael to be my monitor/helper for the program by having him tag alongside me, organizing materials for activities and taking down graffiti from stairwell walls. During the afternoon, he never left my direct eyesight, and upon dismissal, I walked him, in the company of his group, downstairs and then outside, before locking the door at the end of the session.

When I arrived to open our program the next day, I was asked to report to the principal's office. At my meeting with the principal, I was told she had received a report from a classroom teacher who said that her room had been vandalized; after questioning some people at the school, the perpetrator was determined to undeniably be Michael. Michael was to be suspended from school for three days—and the principal was requesting that I, in turn, suspend him from my program.

When I detailed my engagement with Michael from the previous day and challenged the teacher's account, the principal, Blanca Battino, promised to investigate more thoroughly. The following day, both the principal and the initially accusatory teacher apologized and withdrew their claims about Michael's aberrant actions. What Ms. Battino had done was to hold enough room in her heart to investigate the alleged incident with Michael without predetermined expectations or prejudice. Adhering to a strongly held principle for fairness when judging the accused, the people's principal, Ms. Battino, refused to entertain the type of hearsay testimony that had been used to falsely incriminate Michael, and which never should be used to implicate an adult in court. Had Ms. Battino allowed a false allegation to become a basis for punitive action to be taken, the result would have been an unfair consequence for Michael, beginning with a school suspension, and increasing the probability that at the age of 11, he would start on the path of the school-to-prison pipeline.[239]

I make two points here. The first is that according to studies detailing the excessive prejudicial practices inherent to the criminal justice system, during the 1980s and 1990s, public officials routinely created punishments directed at youths of color—punishments that were excessive and often imposed on those who were innocent. My second here is that the teacher who accused Michael was, in general, dedicated to her professional craft, kindhearted, and, when presented with the errors of her ways, immediately open to correcting herself. It took a village of those with poor and destructive intentions (policy makers constructing poor rationales) and those who would most often never wish ill will upon others, but who make an occasional mistake, to create a culture of misunderstanding and misdirected approaches that prove quite damaging to desirable outcomes for youths.

The second scenario took place at a Community Board meeting in midtown Manhattan just over two decades after the incident with the vandalized classroom. Our Teens on Board campaign representatives were visiting boards to obtain their support for changes in the New York State Public Officer Law to permit the seating of 16- and 17-year-olds on the boards. Borough President Gale Brewer sent a staff member to testify at a public session; I presented additional testimony on behalf of our ask. Our coalition strategy was that, by obtaining letters of support from several boards, we would establish a case of home rule; that is, that adult members of boards welcomed this change.

At the conclusion of our joint testimony, the board chair called for a rollcall vote. The result was a flat-out tie: 23 to 23. By rule, it was up to the board chair to cast the deciding vote. With little commentary, he declined to base his vote on opinion; instead, he said he would flip a coin. He then stated, with a wry grin on his face, that if the coin came up heads, he would vote yes, and if it were tails, he would vote no. The coin came up tails, and we lost by the tie-breaking vote. The chair thanked us for our presentation, and he thanked the board members for their vote. There was not a single comment by board members concerning what had just unfolded. Gale's staff and I left in stunned disbelief.

The chair's action represented the trivialization of legitimate civic concerns regarding teen representation. I cannot imagine the same action taking place if any adult group had been making a request about one of their concerns. During their training, board members receive many directives instructing them to show respect for public stakeholders, and to consider requests with sensitively measured responses. They are also asked to base their decisions on evidence or well-supported opinions. Per the presentations we had made to the board members, dozens of cities across the United States had already effected changes allowing for teen participation in advisory roles to municipal government. All five Manhattan boards that had previously been asked to provide letters of support readily agreed to our request. Our problem, as a coalition, concerned how to overcome the prejudicial actions of those people who held pivotal positions and for whom a desire by teen representatives to improve their civic participation did not matter.

The attributes that I have come to define myself with as a youth services organizer specializing in teen enfranchisement developed during my relationship with a communion of souls. The paradigm that I had about the nature of adolescence gradually evolved as I engaged with teen activists and their mentors. As I continually met teens through my years of engagement, I came to recognize them as responsible citizens who demonstrated care and concern, commitment to change, and productive use of their skepticism and idealism. I had a shift in beliefs and attitudes about teen identity and efficacy. I became directed towards shape-shifting and course-changing energies, setting me off in a particular direction, allowing my inner work to shift my perceptions and applied practices.[240] My collaborators motivated and taught me to change the nature of my outer directed work, that is, my leadership methods, where I learned, and where I taught others, to progress from being an influence peddler selling tactics to teens for their own benefit, to becoming a teacher/learner promoting teen civic efficacy in which teens were equal partners in creating the common good. It is true that my changes in beliefs and practices about teens involved redoing my assumptions and practices in the fields of education, psychology, and political science (specifically, civic activism). In my studies, and with my leadership approach, I also incorporated lessons learned at a dimension of understanding which was new for me. Gradually, my deepening dive into the spiritual world, and my evolving relationship with soul work, became the bedrock of my approach for ensuring that teen enfranchisement was obtained. I got here through many stages of growth and discrete periods of experience. My early exposure to the religiously progressive teachings of Unitarianism and the American Friends Service Committee certainly deeply influenced me.[241] Each of these religious denominations encourage deep reflective practices promoting tolerance, as well as social and political advocacy for universal inclusion and participation in public affairs. I consciously incorporated what I learned from the social justice movements they supported, such as anti-war organizing, and addressing the practices of racism. My participation in these projects informed my later civic practice with teens. At the same time, what I had felt and intuitively sensed for some years about the validity of heart intelligence, and the larger context of soul-based practice in civic affairs, moved up into my conscious awareness[242] I studied works describing social-emotional intelligence, and theories holding that the universe, and life itself, is managed and shaped by spiritual energies which inform our decisions about social engagement and civic change.[243] I also engaged in workshops and conversations with spiritually oriented practitioners who proposed concepts that were new to me about the relationship of the unconscious, and what they referred to as the super-consciousness underlying our perceptions of reality. It is from this perspective about my personal evolution in being a youth empowerment advocate that I use the chapters titled "Induction"; Forward/Backward and Inside/Out; and Introductions to focus on my progressively developing approach in supporting teen civic participation. The progressions I experienced reinforced my existing knowledge base about the importance of wholesome development of the teen mind and the need for cutting-edge change in the world of political affairs. During my 28 years on my teen services path, I would gradually incorporate additional perspectives including the importance of working with social-emotional intelligence, grounding civic practice using the ecological principles of inter-connection and sustainability, and honoring the unique soul-based presence of each person with whom I formed civic relationships. My shorthand explanation is about my coming to understand these new dimensions of understanding in intuitive ways, initially, and then learning to categorize and frame them in a cognitive fashion later. The everyday practical work of social justice, and the underlying influence of the soul in our spiritually energized world became my project-based hands-on and heart informed workbook.

I use the chapter I title Induction to impart to readers the significance of episodes prior to and occurring in the early stages of my teen empowerment work. In each turn of event I highlight how the friction ignited for me was followed by my being driven by inspired determination. Initially understood intuitively, these episodes stayed with me and served as reminders and energizers for my youth work where I applied intuitively felt lessons more consciously. The three episodes – which involved for me learning to manage and get past betrayal, figuring out how to manage and get past random violence which had invaded my personal space, and being recruited by friends and neighbors into the process of organizing from the ground up – served me as a learning opportunity from which I would later teach about teen civic empowerment. The fires set in my mind, and compassion developed in my heart, induced me to us my force of evolving willpower as a leader along my path of destiny.

I have used the Forward/Backward section of this book to set the context (that is, the stage) as one of sequential experimental and experiential steps in which my knowledge expands and my toolbox becomes filled with assets. As I previously stated, I call these periods in which I organized youth programs (and became better organized by them) steppingstones. Another way to describe these steps is having lived in unfolding stories side by side with neighbors, and then social justice advocates across the city of New York. My steps forward had begun when I provided after-school service in Washington Heights, with the assistance of teens as co-leaders through the Southern Heights and Uptown Dreamers programs. It taught me about delivering credible services to youth and community with scant financial resources and the unlimited goodwill and assistance of young volunteers. Then, expanding my field of vision and activities, both in scope and purpose, my civic education evolved. The next step started with an all-girls sports and education program called the Ivy League/Uptown WINS (Women in Neighborhood Sports); it continued with my induction into the Petra Foundation, where I formed learning relationships in storytelling and grassroots empowerment. I learned the lessons apprehended by helping peoples from specific demographic backgrounds and diverse places. My approaches had to be refined, and the commonality of enfranchised purpose also had to defined for the benefit of all. As I came to finish the final phase of my learning leader training, with PAL, the Future Voters of America, Generation Citizen, and our Teens on Board partners, I came to develop organizing skills needed on a city-wide basis—skills that used the talents and commitments of other leaders exercising diverse perspectives and suggestions regarding how to move forward.[244]

During that time, I exercised leadership by gradually learning and applying the skills of community organizing and facilitation of optimal personal development by teens. I took from what ancestral allies, modern-day prophets, fellow co-mentors, and teen leaders shared with me about innovation—that is, the practical reform of what exists now, and the instigation of imagination, where what seemed improbable became negotiable and put into practice.

What comes next in my narrative concerns my lessons learned about the soul of adolescence. I also develop my theme on how the soul of adolescence is aligned with the heart of democracy. Each shares support from the archetypes of the orphan, the rebel, and the civic lover, albeit in differing relationships. For the former, the relationship involves the individual civic reformer, and how the archetypes inform and guide them. With the latter, what is discussed is how social justice change-makers possessing these archetypes contribute to the evolutionary calling of democracy, which is to progressively include those who have been orphaned from civic participation, to incorporate new stories which change the nature of national identity and relationships within governance, and finally to infuse the wisdom of the reformer into the practice of democratic governance. In my earlier days, these teachings came to me through a disquieting presence, a whispering from within. The greater the scope of my engagement became while working with youth across variations in class, ethnic origins, and gender, as well as geographic location, the more the soul's quiet influence impacted me as a mindful discipline that was invaluable in shaping my work. No matter the unique experiences of a young person associated with varied types of origins, the spiritual work facilitating holistic individual development and communally based relationships is shared by all people. We each come alive with a unique sense of purpose, a hunger for being connected to other people, our place in community, and life-sustaining collaboration. With my hands-on work, and my studies about intersectionality[245], I came to understand that people's unique proficiencies related to their backgrounds are experienced on multiple levels of group consciousness. For example, female teens with whom I worked in Washington Heights were affected by discriminatory policies as teens, as women, and either as persons from an African American or a Latina background. These young women had to deal with ageism (or adultism), sexism, as well as racism and national chauvinism. At the same time, a young woman's residency also resulted in differential impacts. Residents of Washington Heights are mostly of Dominican background, while those from East New York are mostly African-Caribbean or Latinas from other countries such as Mexico or in Central America.

Imagination is an invaluable asset for navigating steppingstones, and, at first, I considered this guiding voice to be affected by a type of collision between romantic vision and my rational mind. As I came to value the counsel of my inner allies, called Archetypes (which I address in the section of this book I call the Introduction), I used the counsel of what I call inner allies to furnish a deeper source, a soulful-based cauldron of fiery idealism. Establishing a connection with this cauldron is what John Trundell, an American Indian activist from the 1970s, called inherent to the "power of being a human being." As Mr. Trundell further explains:[246] "As human beings, we have [an] energetic connection to original instructions (encoded in our soul-directed life purpose), and to our ancestry." In my teen empowerment work, my energetic connection to spiritual ancestors such as early suffragists and abolitionists laid a foundation for more conscious civic work. Daniel J. Siegel, a writer who describes the mind, and whom I have previously referenced, touched on this idea when speaking of his sustained connection to a mentor who had passed away. Mr. Siegel wrote that the connection allowed him to continue being guided by conscious discovery about the inner working of our minds. [247]

The wisdom of the soul instructs us in a clear light about life purpose. In my case, the establishment of democratic community, and simultaneously inclusive of teen participation brought about in both conscious and mysterious ways, afforded me the opportunity to connect to the higher teachings of our nation's founders and subsequent reformers. These changes in perspective were for me akin to what our nation's founders called common sense. Soul knowledge outpaces, in deeper and wider ways, the substance and parameters of imagination. A few years ago, I was introduced to a responsive reading called "Shout for Joy" by Sara Moore Campbell. I first heard this work at a Sunday sermon at the Unitarian-Universalist All-Souls Church in New York City. Here, I cite a few lines from her poem: "[I]n the tomb of the soul, we wrap ourselves in the security of darkness, which sometimes brings us comfort, and sometimes brings us preparation for experience…as we seek balance for ourselves, we also invite the light to awaken possibilities within and among us, for new life in ourselves and in the world."[248] What may begin in darkness for us also comes to serve us as turning points in our lives.

The turning points in my life are entwined within the steps of my 28-year civic journey and are confluent with the work of activist teens and their civic co-mentors who drive the changes required for entering a new era. Two literary allies put this era into focus for me. One of the allies is active in the reform of governance, the other in the great awakening necessary to guide us under new terms and conditions for our lives. David Korten is a political and social activist who has written about what he calls "the Great Turning." In his work, *The Great Turning*, he criticizes top-down and remotely imposed authority. Instead, he celebrates "our capacity (as agents of co-equal authority in governance) to anticipate and to choose our future, which is the defining characteristic of the human species."[249] Mr. Korten further suggests that we "need to use this capacity with conscious, collective intent, organizing by partnership, and unleashing our potential for human cooperation."[250] Exercised at the conscious level of expansive participation in governance, this principle forms the superstructure in the work of Black Lives Matter, the Dreamers, and March for Our Lives. As I will share in the final chapter of this book, "Anecdotes Arising," there has been an explosion of youth-led social change initiatives in which the energy of heart intelligence and an understanding about people having connections and belonging as human beings. Collectively, this multitude of initiatives being launched by new generational leaders has adopted perspectives which incorporate the principles of sustainable ecological responsibility, the imperative of universal social justice, and the power of the democratic spirit to create a more equitable society. On the spiritual side, Anodea Judith, who has developed paradigms for understanding subtle energies and higher-order consciousness, cites our work as one of "transformation," where "privately we awaken to our true nature, where we find our forgotten selves, and pursue external accomplishments within the boundaries of nurturance, honoring receptive wisdom and creative expression."[251] Each of these writers, Korten and Judith, from their own perspective, attest to values suggested by the convention of the Unitarian-Universalist Association to "recognize the dignity and worth of every person, to encourage a free and responsible search for truth and meaning, and to construct respect for an interdependent web of existence of which we all are a part."[252]

Throughout the course of my civic adventure, I consciously incorporated the above teachings as I came to deeply appreciate the intersection of the rational mind and soul-informed dimensions of our knowing selves. A reference to the need for this type of intersection is pointed out in a book called *The Karmapa*, by Ogyen Trinley Dorje, a Buddhist teacher, on the "the Paradox of our Age." Mr. Dorje discussed this in a dialogue with students from Redlands University on their visit to India. Mr. Dorje said: "While we are technically more connected than in any point in human history, we are still left with vague feelings of being emotionally disconnected and isolated. Our ways of feeling and living in the world are still catching up to this new understanding of our all being connected on so many levels."[253]

What follows in the Introduction is the unfolding of my understanding of the influence of the soul in my civic education and work. In the upcoming pages, I provide a more thorough discussion about this inner-directed and higher-connected agency, and its essential relevance to bringing about the fruits of my life purpose.[254] My nouvelle contributions for civic cuisine were inseparable from the contributions of my allies, ancestral allies, today's public prophets, civic co-mentors, and my soulfully connected teen allies. Each of those who contributes shares a human capacity building and socially conscious set of habits, as suggested by the Unitarian-Universalist principles—connecting human dignity, the right to express one's conscience, and the democratic process.[255]

III.

INTRODUCTIONS

UNDERSTANDING OF THE SOUL; THE THREE ARCHETYPES REPRESENTING THE SOUL OF ADOLESCENCE; THE ADOLESCENT SOUL'S CORRESPONDENCE WITH THE HEART OF DEMOCRACY; AND A MEET AND GREET WITH THE CIVIC CO-MENTORS WHO GUIDE TEENS)

In this introduction, I offer an additional set of considerations about the nature of the teen mind and the role of adults who guide them in community civic reform. Episodes involving dramas of disruption and trauma, when reflected upon with the guidance of one's soul, and especially when supported by empathetic allies, become reoccurring teachable moments providing resilience along the path of civic empowerment work. In the "Forward/Backward" section, I described the positive assets of the adolescent disposition, and how I came to discover and utilize those assets during the sequentially experienced starting points along my path. In this section, I incorporate my discoveries about augmented and supplementary levels of consciousness. This universe of experience starts with the soul, from which I propose we have a spiritually informed outline of our life purpose. We connect to our soul in all periods of our lives. For the purposes of this book, I speak to the connection between adolescents and the adult co-mentors who guide teens. As outlined below, I describe three spiritual entities which are archetypal energies, called the orphan, the rebel, and the lover.[256] Each archetype assists in a person's psychological development and social awareness by offering specialized metaphoric guidance from the soul. Think of the soul as a spiritual general practitioner, and the archetypes as specialists. For social justice advocates seeking a deepening of democratic practices, archetypes can also be referenced when a person becomes engaged on a social level such as in civic affairs. Societal entities, such as nations, also have souls guiding them on a spiritual level. In the case of the United States, the archetypes of the orphan, the rebel and the civic lover are essential to informing our national identity. We started our war for independence because we saw ourselves as orphans. We modified the way we governed people inspired by rebels rejecting a story of exclusion—for women, Blacks, laborers, and adolescents. In our effort to align ourselves as dignified peoples with high potential, with the higher angelic intent of democracy, organizers served through civic love, seeing the best in ourselves and others. To that end, in this section of the book I begin to develop a distinctive paradigm about the underlying, soul-based cradle within which our conscious civic work evolves.

In developing this perspective, I do not reject outright the value and accomplishments of previous reform efforts. Rather, I see them now as having been worked within what are called nesting boxes. Each social justice reform movement has developed analysis and strategies essential to obtaining universal human dignity and social progress. The contributions of social reform have had many accomplishments, as well as limitations and setbacks. All of them have served humanity in its evolutionary quest for balance, equity, and justice.

As I have incorporated discoveries and understanding about soul-based influence. I have come to appreciate an intra-dimensional correspondence among the differing levels of individual, social, cognitive, and intuitive intelligence. Just as our perspective allows for a more inclusive look linking the many levels inherent to human development and civic work, it is also possible to appreciate the multiplier effect that each level provides for all other levels.

If there have been a thousand philosophers speculating on the nature of the soul, there are probably a thousand and one definitions, with the extra one being a definition lying outside any one person's reach. At this juncture of the Introduction section of this book, I offer a modest take on how I view the soul. As I see it, the soul is a "place" (which does not occupy physical space) in which we establish contact with spiritual knowingness and guidance for our lives. The soul, as an energetic presence, encourages us to develop strong feelings and attachment, but does not, in and of itself, offer disabling signals of judgment. The soul is the fountainhead of all non-judgmental guidance and support. The soul also serves us as a mediator and a bridge between universal sources of consciousness and each of us as an individuated person.[257]

Bernie Glassman is a writer and commentator who incorporates Jewish teachings into his viewpoints about establishing nurturing relationships with others. He advises that by adopting soul-oriented practice into our daily lives, we can embrace lofty ideals while we are also facing hard realities.[258] As articulated by Mr. Glassman, "In order to have a real effect (in society), one needs to engage all spheres of our existence, the mental, emotional, the soulful and the spiritual." Dan Millman, a former gymnastic coach and now a self-help practitioner incorporating spiritual perspective into his life, calls Mr. Glassman's description one of "adopting guidance which reinforces each of us in living true to our life purpose." Mr. Millman suggests that we develop this practice when we "trust our wise and beautiful spirits, use our creative energies to reveal our inner gifts, and then share our gifts to establish more harmony in the world."[259]

Dr. Scilla Elworthy has served as an international mediator of conflicts and a peacemaker in dozens of hot spots around the globe. She is a violence-reduction activist who has successfully applied higher ideals to the bedrock work of resolving heated differences on the ground. In her advice about creating connections and mutual understanding among peoples who have grown accustomed to being distrustful of each other, Ms. Elworthy advises her readers that "real change comes when people are enabled to use their thinking and energy in new ways. It is crucial to use different systems of thought, different languages, and to have faith in fresh visions for the future."[260]

Over the course of my work advocating for teen enfranchisement, I had to battle the proponents of old systems of thought, leaders who were led by stereotypic mindsets rather than forward-thinking ideas. You met a small cross-section of these misinformed leaders in the previous section of this book. In the Introduction I touch upon portraits of youth led movements, such as Teens for Food Justice, the Ya-Ya Network, and Teens Take Charge. These teen enfranchisement movements are being generated in a new era which calls upon sympathetic adults to honor the essence of adolescence and the efficacy of teen civic contributions. I profile these movements and organizations through the lens of my anecdotal experience as well as my investigation of progressive research. You will meet those leaders, teens and adults who adhere to the soft whispering of the soul in guidance in a world full of conflicting interests and clamoring communication.

A Buddhist-oriented social activist, Kurt Spellmeyer, aptly describes this highly evolved process, crucial to balanced and equitable adult and teen relationships, as a critical reference point, where "we manage with stewardship, and use our experimentation and experience with a flashing light which reveals our trusted territory."[261] Stewardship requires intervention that is based on empathy for where people are at (not just where we think they need to be). Developing mutual trust is the common currency for both healthy relationships and wholesome social/civic encounters. Mr. Spellmeyer also suggests that in our application of new modes of thinking and uses of language, we operate in a new period of apocalypse. He defines the apocalypse not as a chaotic ending of time, but rather as a "lifting of the veil"[262], enabling us to "consider new possibilities, open-endedness and connection to complex interactions that can be confronted with courage and faith."[263]

The experience of adolescence is complicated, even before we consider adolescents' relationship to soul. This period of life is a flowing juncture in which each teen faces the forceful crosscurrents between childhood and adulthood. Teens also bear the unintended consequences brought upon them by those who insist on the certainties of the past while at the same time refusing to navigate the unknown of the future. Adolescents navigate in the resultant, turbulent present.

The soul extends to each of us an invitation to practice our unique being-ness with a novel purpose. As we search for the deep and beyond, we facilitate relationships through the co-creation of meaningful lives. Today, as never before, given the immensity of tasks we face and the propensity of the soul to whisper to us, its voice can be drowned out or lost in the cacophony of competing messages coming to us through media blasts and warnings issued to us in a dire voice by the propaganda of political parties. Acting subtly, but with significant influence are special agents, archetypes, which I call inner allies. Depth psychologists such as Carl Jung and James Hillman have spoken of these energetically engaged associates as archetypes.[264] Hundreds of specific types of archetypes, each with an identity and assisting us with life purpose, have been addressed by many proponents of this school of thought. I have called archetypes "special agents" because is a soulfully organized reference point and represent a portion of spiritual and soul-related energy that are attuned with elements of a greater consciousness. This attunement is like an intuitive radar. Archetypic types offer a range of possibilities from the perspective of their specialties, from advocates to teachers, from the wounded child to the medicine person, from the artist/engineer to the scientist depending upon their areas of specialization. Each archetype shares responsibility, as a soul-connected team member, in providing us the keys that allow us to develop our full potential. To use another analogy, think of archetypes as both players and coaches on a baseball team. As players, they are outfielders, who patrol the areas to be covered before an opponent can score more runs and defeat you. As coaches, they are those who assist behind the scenes, such as batting and pitching coaches who have offered hours of advice with great patience. At certain points in a game, their advice clicks in, helping with execution of a skill that might have proved elusive before.

Alan Elenbaas is an astrologer, writer and blogger who studies Jungian psychology. Mr. Elenbaas has and M.A. and a B.F.A. in English and creative writing. He has extensively studied the connections between our conscious decisions and the invisible inner allies called archetypes which guide us. He wrote about the musings of another Jungian psychologist and writer, James Hillman. Mr. Elenbaas quotes Mr. Hillman, who wrote in his book, *Re-Visioning Psychology*: "(When a person accesses archetypes) first there is a psychological moment, a moment of reflection, wonder, puzzlement, initiated by the soul which intervenes and countervails what we are doing, hearing, reading, and watching. With slow suspicion and sudden insight, we move through the apparent to the less apparent…as things become clarified."[265] After 2010, I expanded my library to include readings about depth psychology (which practices getting in touch with the longings of the soul as a conduit for addressing psychological issues and social problems). Although the teens I guided faced issues of separation in ways different from my own, we each experienced the journey of the archetypal orphan. We each found our inner selves, and missions, and reasons to shine out to the world. We shared the need to change the nature of our stories from ones imposed by external authority to becoming authors of our own narratives, making us rebels in our own ways. The adolescents whom I came to guide had an unexpressed drive to make a difference. Once fully vested in the theater of social justice and change, we each felt connected to a larger cause and mission for using our inner derived power to make our communities a better place. I call this the mission of civic lovers, who revel in the role of urban patriots linking inner abilities with the life-enhancing mission of conscious communities. Given my focus on the nature of adolescence, I concentrate on three archetypes—the orphan, the rebel, and the lover. I see each of them as essential to teens holistic development, allowing them full participation in the civic realm. Reaching our full potential includes using our multiple sources of intelligence, learning to identify our inner sources of authority and express their truths, and learning to discriminate between what aids us and what deceives us. As we become comfortable and confident about using our inner sources tools, we bring a fuller portfolio to the plate of participation in the civic realm, showing up as a whole person. I more fully flush out the interaction between these archetypes and social justice advocates in this Introduction, in the part addressing the soul-based inherent nature of adolescence. I will also profile how each of the three archetypes, the orphan, the rebel, and the lover, are not only archetypal references for the adolescent soul, but also archetypal references informing the heart of American democracy.[266]

For now, I offer a brief overview of the contributions offered by each of the teen archetypes. The orphan archetype helps teens to establish a presence in society and to recover authentic, purpose-driven identity. The evolved orphan accomplishes this through the practice of conscious and self-determined distancing from beliefs and practices that limit and diminish the orphan's potential. The goal of individuation is not to become perfect, but rather to work on becoming more whole, and to come into one's full bloom.

Once a life purpose is established, the rebel archetype assists by developing, and sharing, a life story based upon a teen's perspective, and interpretation of experience. Using self-determined story is an act of the rebel, to restore what has been captured by others, or lost by ourselves. As the rebel is fully actualized, their actions pull the curtain promoting socially constructed illusions and enable adolescents to reset their life course.

The archetype of the civic lover enhances the acts of embrace, invitation, and validation. Successful connection to the civic lover archetype facilitates our feeling safe with, and rewarded by, our embrace of the purpose and life-story of others. It aids us in aligning our knowing existence within the context of mutually affirming communal relationships, ranging from family to schools, as well as with governance.

I also share here three examples of testimony regarding how these archetypes are expressed in everyday life. I refer to the orphan work through the influence of my first teen co-mentor, Miriam Payne, whom we met in previous sections of this book. Her presence, which is what an orphan seeks to establish, is akin to the Asian myth of Kwan Yin, otherwise known as the Woman in White.[267] According to this myth, Kwan Yin is the "divine feminine riding a dragon and showing the face of a loving mother. In her left hand she carries a willow branch, a symbol of healing. In her right hand she carries a bottle, from which she pours a stream of compassion into the raging waters."[268] Understandably, there is rage developed by teens facing gross injustice, and the misdirected anger exhibited by some adults who ascribe dire characteristics to teens. When social justice activists offer healing and compassion in the face of heated emotional chaos, the part of each of these people which is experienced as an orphan feels safer, and makes it easier for those they are serving to consider coming home.

Dr. Clarissa Pinkola Estes, a Jungian psychoanalyst and poet, has made an urgent call in her writings for welcoming what she calls the "wild-woman archetype" which she associates as being instrumental in women becoming self-actualized and justly identified. In her book, *Women Who Run With the Wolves*, a spiritual book also filled with psychological insights, she uses the power of myth to look at the female psyche. I look at this calling as an example of the female rebel archetype. Here I summarize part of what Dr. Estes counsels in one of her themes throughout her book: [One of the most calming and powerful actions you can do to intervene in a stormy world is to stand up and show your soul in shadowy times like these. The wild woman shows mercy toward others, but also needs to be fierce. Both are acts of immense bravery and greatest necessity.][269] The alchemy of connective action within the construction of community, taken together with insistence upon being honored and recognized, has been a key focal point to my civic guidance and program management with teens. I have had the pleasure of working with many fine young men who have offered wonderful contributions. However, most of the young leaders who have chosen to work with me have been females. For decades, young female leaders have been fighting in the teeth of both sexist and adult-organized repression.

Anodea Judith, Ph.D., is an advocate of spiritually informed self-help and social harmony. She is a former therapist who now teaches courses on energy work and body-related, intuitively based intelligence to audiences across the world. In the book, *Waking the Global Heart*, she makes a connection between one's heart and the need to awaken the global heart. I look at this congruence as the central work of the civic lover. A major theme (which I briefly summarize here) that she returns to again and again in her book is that: [The heart is the center of love. It is the primeval force that calls things into relationship—the source of organizing principles of how we better live together. Individually, culturally, and politically, this necessitates a transformation from the love of power to the power of love.] [270] This heart-informed energy, connecting the intelligence of each of our hearts to the heartbeat of people's movements seeking recognition, respect, and the recapture of honored places in the world is the essence of balanced relationship. As we take ownership and responsibility for this benevolent type of power, we move forward into a new era of mutual concern, taking us away from practices involving power over others to ones that engender power with others through love. Throughout my relationships in support of teen empowerment, it has been leadership, by both adults and teens, expressed through the wisdom of the heart that has resulted in the type of change congruent with soulfully sensitive and ecologically based progress.

I have been addressing the nature of heart-inspired adolescent leadership during a transitional time between the era of power-over to power-with. Just as I had used this new understanding about the power of love, I had also learned about additional transformational practices being developed by allies, relevant to our task of creating a more beautiful world. Below I discuss some of my new realizations contributing to the definition of adolescence being reborn. My narrative also places this process of re-defining adolescent identity within the context of social/cultural and political change. As we moved from the late 1990s into the early 2000s, we transitioned from a declining era of industrial/material mindsets to those informed by eco-logical and spiritual design. Just below I share a peek about this transition, and then develop these changes later in the Introduction section and in the final chapter of this book I call "Anecdotes Arising."

Juliet Schor and Betsy Taylor are environmental activists and writers who co-edited a book titled *Sustainable Planet: Solutions for the Twenty-first Century*. They include selections from environmental activists such as Herman Daly (who has proposed using systems of ecological sustainability in place of our industrial system emphasis on striving for perpetual economic growth) and Bill McKibben (who has analyzed the effects of our industrial practices which have been negatively altering our planet's natural systems in place for millions of years). Their two selections in this book, along with those of other environmentalists' contributions to this book, agree with a central tenant of societal change that is essential to create a sustainable future for our planet. Each contributor to Sustainable Planet calls upon policy planners to: [cast off the nineteenth-century mentality that structures the current system, and...create innovative models of sustainability that neither overstep the limits of nature nor accept current levels of human suffering].[271] The editors of this book refer to a central theme, which is that as people transition to a new era, we must recognize the necessity of moving on from old illusions about progress. In order to establish the sanctity of place, we cannot introduce excessive levels of carbon which disrupt the functioning of the environment. The authors summarize connections between our strug-gling for the attainment of social justice and the need for construction of ecologically sustainable systems. The authors offer their poignant theme of how marginalized peoples still struggle: "Today, although we have a much more sophisticated understanding of what social justice means, low-income families nevertheless find themselves in the same relative circumstances they were in over a century ago. They are struggling to overcome desperate poverty, living in communities that are tragically unhealthy due to pollutant neglect, and laboring against a culture that considers material possessions the absolute measure of social value." [272] As an example, the authors point to a speech given by Congresswoman Nydia Velasquez, from which they extract quotes in a chapter of their Sustainable Planet book titled *In Search of Justice*. According to Ms. Velasquez' research out of the University of Michigan, "In my Congressional District, childhood asthma rates tripled in the 1990's, and the infant mortality rate, at 13 per 1,000, rivals that of Estonia, Bulgaria, and the Czech Republic."[273]

The 1990s are often cited today as a period of improving fortunes for all and for huge advances in quality-of-life outcomes. That was the decade that proved the unqualified success of our system. The 1990s ended nearly a quarter of a century ago. Yet the legacy created during that decade, in which people's value became largely defined by their position within the economy, continues to be conflated with humanistic and spiritual values. I demonstrate in the latter parts of this section that economic indicators promote a materialist viewpoint. It is how much one owns, and his power over controlling manna, which define enduring success and of achieving a better quality of life for all. Continual economic growth and financial expansion constitutes what it means to be a mature and happy person well positioned in society. The grassroots work of advocacy groups, including those led by teens, challenge these assumptions as deeply biased. Teen leaders are challenging the mythologies created through the lens constructed by hyper-privileged sources. Several of these groups, such as Teens Take Charge, Teens for Food Justice, and the Praxis Project, are profiled in detail in the latter parts of the final chapter of this book titled "Anecdotes Arising." Each group is community-based, led by adolescent activists, and produces results that demonstrate the value of teen efficacy as well as meaningful change to society at large. This is a small sampling of the thousands of group efforts occurring across our globe, throughout our nation, and throughout the City of New York.

Each of these initiatives mentioned just above are models for constructing conscious connection between individual need and communal enhancement. What holds true for these efforts is that they are creative efforts for inspired insurrection using dialogue and the urge for transformative experience. Today's movements are born out of the efforts and because of the passion of yesterday's groundswell addressing the needs for evolved forms of thinking and governance responsive to everyday people. The leaders and members of these groups constructed social justice platforms and a path moving closer to what Dr. King referred to as the arc of justice.

The author Chris Saade was born in Lebanon, and his family moved to the USA after experiencing the violent outcomes of war. He is the co-director of the Olive Branch Center in North Carolina which, as his program's profile states, "offers courses of socially engaged spirituality and the mysticism of personal authenticity and inclusion."[274] In his book, *Second Wave Spirituality*, Mr. Saade pays homage to the movements of yesterday, led by people whom I consider to be ancestral allies for our current-day political and social reform organizations. The new movements of today find some room for improvement from the old tactics of defaming others through confrontation assessments and judging the faults of others through the lens of our ideals but not the consequences of our actions. At the same time, Mr. Saade points out that in our current attempts to seek social justice and communal reorganization we need not outrightly reject our ancestral allies, but rather should incorporate the fruits of prior work into the necessities of our new era. As described by Mr. Saade: "Our collective imagination was conceived in the amazing dreams of many social movements. These include laborers, suffragettes, human rights crusaders, and civic rights reformers, those who improved democratic practices and fought for ecological sustainability, among many others. We cannot deny or expunge ourselves from the historical womb that bore us. We know that any freedoms we enjoy today have been forged by the unbounded efforts and the audacity of those who preceded us."[275] In other words, in our striving for social justice today, we benefit because we stand on the shoulders of those who struggled and created change yesterday. We are soulfully connected with organizers of like mind today, and all of us feel in unity with the passionate intention of our justice seeking ancestral allies.

What the collective imagination of groups today is enhancing is described by educational researchers Randi Engel, Lam, and Nix for the journal *The Educational Psychologist.* In their article, they contrast differing educational styles, called "Bounded Framing" and "Expansive Framing."[276] The goal of the former is to achieve improved opportunity and access into existing systems, but in ways that do not result in negative consequences for the individual. Students engage in research and propose solutions, making us more informed consumers in a system that had been designed to create endless demand. Excessive desire harms individuals by facilitating feelings of endless unsatiated desire and greed.

Criminal justice reform advocates propose the hiring of more police despite the expansion of a prison system which produces a propensity for increased use of violence by prisoners released into communities to ensure survival in a perpetually hostile environment. For expansive framing, the goal is to move beyond established systematic boundaries, that although perpetually funded and glorified by proponents, continue to result in unintentional and unwanted outcomes. Significant numbers of black and Latino young people have been shut out of moving on with their lives when subject to harshly punitive laws. Using our bounded framing perspective, our compulsion-producing consumer society has created exploding debt that neither families nor local governments can afford to pay off. Our justice system enforcing the mandates of capture, punish, and then release of prisoners who have been hardened rather than changed has produced escalating levels of domestic violence, and legions of young people excluded from higher education and career pathways.

Those who have utilized the viewpoints enhanced by expanded framing incorporate the findings of environmentalists who caution us on the limits to growth inherent in our natural environments. Social scientists have discovered that transcending up the ladder of material fortune has not resulted in greater satisfaction or happiness in people's lives. Learning to adjust to the counsel of small is beautiful. Meaningful relationships among people are valued as interpersonal possessions which support all involved. is an outcome of expanded framing. Applying the practices of alternative sentencing, such as mandating community service for non-violent offenders rather than mixing them within the confinement of violence-producing spaces has been found to be a practice resulting in less recidivism, and a higher likelihood of ex-offenders being considered for jobs. These outcomes are also a product of expansive framing, proposed by those with open hearts, and mindsets which see possibilities where only roadblocks existed before.

Rob Hopkins is a British author who has written books such as *The Power of Just Doing Stuff* and *The Transition Handbook*. He was also named by *The Independent* as one of its top 100 environmentalists and has co-founded the Transition Network, which profiles individuals who have exercised skills exhibiting creativity and intuitive intelligence. According to his findings, the exclusive use of rational means of learning and tightly structured methods of education has contributed to a decline in creative thinking. What results is that we tend to produce businesses and social organizations creating more and more of the same types of outcomes.

I will highlight specific examples of the contemporary practices and business models he proposes for what Mr. Hopkins calls a "future-oriented offense" in the chapter I title "Anecdotes Arising." At this point, I highlight a central element common to these initiatives.[277] These include the use of stories by leaders which lie outside the paradigm of traditional narratives which propose the superiority of privileged people. In its place, new leaders create spaces in which people feel, whether workers or customers, are safe spaces. These entrepreneurs create stories that inspire imaginative participation which create mutually rewarding relationships and minimal harm to others. No matter the place of a person in a business or governmental relationship, all people are stakeholders in a mutually beneficial enterprise called conscious and connected community, and not just clients or customers.

Also woven into the web of my narrative are profiles of civic leaders who have chosen to guide teens by adopting a role I call co-mentorship. Among their many sources of orientation about what it means to be a co-leader, as opposed to someone who has assumed a position of age-privileged vertical authority, are two articles in the United Nations constitution.

Ms. Roosevelt contributed to the wording used in each of these two articles in the UN Constitution.[278] A summary, or abstract of the principles outlined in these articles appear in Ms. Roosevelt's "Declaration of Human Rights,"[279] which she shared with audiences at her speaking engagements. The first article (Article I) states that "all human beings are born free and equal in dignity and rights. Each is endowed with reason and conscience."[280] One of the premises I share in this book is that this principle, which is included in Article I, not only applies to adults, but also to adolescents. An additional article (Article XXV), which I refer to here, states, "Everyone has duties to the community in which alone the free and full development of his personality is possible."[281] The montage of anecdotes in this book attest to the fact that the work of teen activists and their civic co-mentors, specifically when involving their contributions to communities, proves that this constitutionally based provision, when honored in practice, can come to life.

Just as I profile a new understanding of the adolescent mind and character (that of the orphan, the rebel, and the civic lover), I illuminate the mind and character of the civic co-mentor. What follows is a combination of a job description and a projection of a co-mentor's life purpose. The civic co-mentor, who can be either a teen or an adult, has a mind frame that encompasses that of the new adolescent, that is, their internal adolescent (that of the orphan, the rebel, and the lover) is still active, vibrant, and resourced in the co-mentor's civic work and co-mentoring relationship. In restating these attributes, I use certain guidelines developed by the cultural anthropologist and visionary Angeles Arrien in her classic book, *The Four-Fold Way*.

Here, I summarize a few key points highlighted by Ms. Arrien. Those still navigating their journeys as orphans, those wandering in search of themselves and their allies, assist in guiding partners "along their lifelong journey towards wholeness."[282] They assist their allies in healing and in trusting life. Orphans take a stance, aligning with the sources of inner wisdom, and attuning to the authentic in their allies, reclaiming internal resources as gifts, which had been forgotten and lost. Rebels, who seek to establish an authentic story, and to honor the stories of others, develop a practice of reciprocity and balance in learning how to give and receive. Both teen social change activists and civic mentors, in serving the world as an enlightened warrior, act knowledgeably, respectfully, and kindly. They make evolved use of rebel energy. I call this enlightened rebel energy. Rebels act with modesty and humility for the unexpected encounter with mistakes, as opposed to relying on stated opinion as fact, putting others down, and addressing those with differing viewpoints using dismissive language. When successfully utilizing this rebel energy, he or she learns "to extend honor and respect to others, to use judicious communication, and to manage the right use of power," according to psychologist and writer Carolyn Myss.[283]

What civic-change advocates put into practice as civic lovers involves becoming a "visionary, where each individual is creative and unique. It is important to use non-judgmental truth telling, and to align one's personal insights and vision with those of others," according to Angeles Arrien.[284] Ms. Arrien adds, as part of the four-fold way, that the co-mentor needs to also be a teacher who "remains open to alternatives, practices trust, develops comfort with uncertainty, and who stays attuned, but not too attached, to proposed goals and outcomes."[285]

When I assess the gifts exhibited by co-mentors, I also add two arche-typal attributes in describing their portfolio of talents. As outlined by Ms. Myss, two additional assets are those of the advocate and the eccentric. As described by Ms. Myss, the advocate is "a counselor, but also a person who feels passion for pleading the case of his or her charge. As a supporter, they help to shoulder responsibilities, and as a friend they are confidant and significant other."[286] The eccentric is one who has no problem "deviating from convention or norms when they cease to serve. Often helping their charges from places "on the margins of conformity, they encourage free thinking, and are not shy about adopting the role of the sacred clown, using humor to shed light on the truth."[287] In confluent ways, the eccentric adopts the energy of what Ms. Myss calls the archetype of the alchemist, who "converts conventional form into altered expressions of itself, and who operates in the complete spirit of transformation."[288] Ms. Myss also describes the related archetype of the pioneer, who "is eager to explore new territories, both internal and external, and also to innovate by actually doing what has not been done before."[289]

In a sense, the essence of a co-mentor can be characterized by that of being an oracle. In a classic Greek or Roman sense, an oracle was a highly respected leader and visionary, believed to have great knowledge and wisdom. Through the words conveyed in their voice, a sense of purpose and direction was conveyed to those looking for reliable and trusted advice.

I am playing with this term, the oracle, because I also see it as being used as an acronym—ORACLE—with the letters representing the orphan, the rebel, the advocate, the civic lover, and the eccentric archetypes. In a traditional sense, the oracle is seen as a person with great knowledge and wisdom, who also exposes the truth about existing limitations and the promise of tomorrow. Oracles, whether they are co-mentors or philosophical leaders in the classical sense, also transform the space from which they preach to and practice with their followers. In this sense, the oracle can also be a place, a safe space where a change-maker feels at home, getting to the heart of the matter, and aligning place with one's presence and life purpose. Many of the youth agencies where I had worked, or had partnered with, attracted teens both because of the presence of attuned leaders, and because their youth centers felt like temples engendering a sense of hope and mission. This trait shared by a leader and the place of practice assists the skeptical in believing that what was considered improbable is now within the grasp of the seeker. Benjamin Franklin is attributed to have associated the oracle as a mistress "who can see furthest into the future and who has the deepest love for mankind."[290]

I discovered the soul of adolescence and its alignment with democracy as my consciousness and my understanding about inward development gradually became more consciously apparent to me during my 30-year journey. As I shared in the Forward/Backward section of this book, I came to get my first glimpse of the mutually reinforcing association between a teen's personal development and a community's enhancement by connecting optimal educational approaches with inclusive neighborhood organizing. I would have my sudden moments of realization about this connection, and start to make this association in intuitive, but not intentional ways. In the passages that follow in this section, I incorporate how the archetypes of the orphan, the rebel, and the civic lover significantly influence both personal and communal optimal development. As the stages of my path progress from one period to the next, I gradually become more conscious of the relationship between the inner archetypes and soul purpose, and its application for making civic engagement and social justice work understood on an additional level of soul awareness and spiritual understanding. The starting lines, as well as the steppingstones in each period of my teen empowerment path re-ignited memories described in the Induction chapter. When organizing teen empowerment programs in the Heights, and then across the neighborhoods of New York City, these charged memories would remind me and then validate my intuitive sense about dealing with marginalization, violence-induced disassociation and facilitating communal webs of support. What follows in the Introduction details how I discovered and then contributed to an evolving paradigm about teen identity, the role of co-mentorship in teen civic training, and the alignment between the soul of adolescence and the heart of democracy.

The archetype of the orphan influences us to a felt sense of connection to our life purpose. By *felt sense*, I allude to our intuitive intelligence being accessed as a guide when we drift from our inherently derived intent. When one drifts from the direction suggested by the soul's guidance, we experience an increasing sense of loss. We feel this disassociation when we attach ourselves to values and work that we do not feel at home with.

The process of undoing ourselves, that is, being an orphan, is foundational to our nation's original intent as expressed in the grievances section of our Declaration of Independence. Our ongoing efforts for narrowing our nation's racial and social divides, to ensure equity within the democratic process, are areas of political participation in which we assist with the healing process. We proclaimed our Declaration of Independence from England after leaders in the 13 colonies finally had had enough with being abandoned as loyal subjects to the throne. King George III was becoming increasingly repressive and arbitrary by militarizing communal spaces and imposing unfair taxes. As Americans, such as abolitionists and suffragists marched forward in their quest for obtaining full electoral enfranchisement, elite leaders, through custom and law, strategized to have people, even those who had been emancipated and had always been central contributors to the greater good, remain exiles in their own land.

What we experience in our social and political relations is assisted at an individual level when we utilize aid from spiritual sources. Paul Levy, a writer who has researched the work of an evolving science called quantum physics, describes this process as "accessing the universe itself as a source of information, which is organized invisibly in creating personal meaning."[291] Our first act in inducing a sense of alienation occurs when we walk away from ourselves as primary authors, artists, and scientists interactively engaged with the universe through our inner knowing tools.

In an anecdote I share about my mother, Jane Claire (in the Orphan section of this book), I explain how her felt sense of being inviting to those who had been dispossessed was enhanced simply through the act of empathetic embrace (which is welcoming everyone she met with a sense of loving and understanding). Simultaneously with those she embraced feeling accepted, my mother felt fulfilled. This disposition is part of my social/emotional education and spiritual inheritance. During my leadership activities with teens, when I encountered their having to face censorship of their views, I immediately connected with them through my orphan sense first experienced when I was shut out of expressing myself in a high school classroom. The task of the orphan is to heal the wounds of malevolence directed at oneself, and to heal the maladies imposed on communities.

Managing orphan energy goes beyond what Dr. Richard Katz calls "maintaining professional distance." Dr. Katz adds to his practice with what he further explains is "therapeutic alliance."[292] The orphan heals and, in complementary ways, is healed herself. Together, therapist and patient acknowledge each of our presence, create an inviting space for relationship, and exercise our voice as a reflection of our life purpose.

In his interpretation of Frank Baum's masterpiece, *The Wizard of Oz*, Salman Rushdie, author of the famous novel *The Satanic Verses,* identifies the work of Dorothy as what I would call the mission of the rebel. By choosing to help friends to change their story, the rebel simultaneously changes their own story. Mr. Rushdie's theme of the story of Oz shows how "the weakness of adults forces children to take control of their own destinies."[293] When Dorothy helps the lion to discover his innate courage, the tin man his innate heart, and the scarecrow his innate intelligence, she rediscovers these assets within herself. As her team exhibits these new-found talents, the dispossessed in Oz become liberated both from oppressive control and the misdirection imposed by supposed wizards. A new Dorothy gets to return home.

Chris Grosso, a recovering addict, a spiritual teacher, and a writer with a Zen-like orientation, recounts the trial he went through during his recovery from substance addiction in his book *The Everything Mind.* The essential to the work of recovery, as he writes, involves not only claiming ownership for one's gifts[294] but "also experiencing ownership for our wounds. When we accept our responsibility, we (consciously and unconsciously) create a new identity for ourselves." During the 1980s and 1990s, escalating demand for material possessions became central in the process of our raising young people. Negative stereotyping of youths of color became habitual as we reinforced a mania for prison construction and destabilized the psyches of profiled young people. Co-mentors such as me closely counseled emotionally and socially wounded teens. We became successful only when those who took responsibility for their wounds learned, as counseled by the poet Audre Lorde, "to stand alone, unpopular and reviled, (when working on establishing common cause), with those standing outside of the social structure. (These young warriors work "to define and seek a world in which we all can flourish."[295] Invent yourself anew; transformed collaborators, together, can create a world anew.

After surviving the trauma of an armed invasion of his school, Alex Wind, a high-school student from Florida, proclaimed that "people believe that youth in this country are insignificant. Acknowledging and supporting the voices of teen leaders, such as those addressing the issue of gun violence, affirms that teens have been the only public sector advocates in recent times to create movement and change with gun laws. Adults can show support by honoring their place in the continuum of American social change, by extending respect and creating safe harbors within every school, and by recognizing that the higher purposes felt by teens is aligned with our nation's soul."[296] After 800,000 young folks organized and marched down Pennsylvania Avenue in Washington, D.C., adult leaders listened to their collective voice more attentively, and the National Rifle Association, after years of turning a blind eye to gun violence victims, blinked for the first time in quite a while.

Thomas Jefferson understood where this demand for passionately expressed action in the pursuit of moral accountability originates. Jefferson believed in a creative tension between one's intuition and conscious reasoning. In describing this interactive process, Jefferson wrote: "Man is destined for society. His morality was, therefore, to be formed for this object. He is endowed with a sense of right and wrong merely relative to this. This sense is part of his nature."[297] This sense makes common sense.

The role of the civic lover is to create and invent, and to entice compassionate connection for the genius inherent to each of us and to mutually beneficial outcomes for us all. Ralph Ellison, a Black novelist famous for his work, *The Invisible Man*, described the journey of the civic lover as "traveling on the rock, a terrain upon which we struggle, which also becomes a terrain of ideas, and a compelling force for the ideal."[298]

During our nation's social and political development, civic lovers had to master the terrain. During our colonial time, just prior to and during our war for independence, secret gatherings called Committees of Correspondence developed both strategies for liberation and manifestos in support of democratic ideals. In the 1860s, leaders of the Reconstruction movement had to suffer extreme suppression and danger just to seek basic rights for democratic participation; this was also true of the freedom riders who headed south in the 1960s. After years of organizing, teen leaders finally made a breakthrough in response to governmental neglect. In 2012, teen activists who were members of the Colorado Youth Advisory Council lobbied for—and then succeeded in reforming—teacher licensing requirements. The state legislature, in response to the student-presented case, mandated teacher training in the prevention of teen suicide and in methods of effective intervention to reduce rates of teens taking their own lives. Adult leaders came to recognize teens as creative change advocates. Teens managed to bring about this success using not just their rational intelligence, but also by knowing their social/emotional IQ. As described by the psychological and motivational writer Mihaly Csikszentmihalyi, "The creative person can manage the complexity of creativity, the tension and intensity of contradictory extremes, without succumbing to inner conflict."[299] Chaos, rather than rigid control, is the mother of invention.

For the personally fulfilled and socially responsible teen, navigating the territory of the adolescent psyche involves inviting the counsel of the orphan, the rebel, and the civic lover archetypes. Teens are thus involved in raising their consciousness. Young leaders develop what democracy's strategist, Jean Bethe Elshtain, calls one of the pillars of strength for democratic practice. As Ms. Elshtain writes, part of being successful in democratic practice involves "developing a sense of purposeful individuality, and a group commitment to the civic good that is not the possession of a single individual only, nor to just a small group."[300] As we, the people, in our work for enhancing democracy rise, we jointly awaken, observe, propose, and then experience and experiment in the grand adventure of creating enlightened minds and a socially evolved society.

As I share biographical sketches and anecdotes, I profile the nature of each archetype, and how significant allies of mine during my civic work personified for me those who manifested their efforts through close association with these archetypes. I present the personal civic work of my allies in the context of communities that are dealing with these same archetypes on a social level.

Teens who are subject to the effects of negative stereotypes and deficiencies of crucial resources work on their orphan energy to find the inner resources to develop a positive relationship with themselves. Communities that have been subject to damaging profiles and disruptive interventions that antagonize and divide their residents come together to affirm their neighborhoods' resources and develop webs of relationships in which alienated folks come to trust each other.[301] Before agreeing to participate as a social justice activist, each person changes the self-diminishing aspects that might have damaged their personal story and reinvents their self-assessed personal profiles. As activists from varied backgrounds learn to come together and work on agreed-upon socially affirming goals, tensions, remedies for decline, and positive outcomes are attained. The profile of the community changes in the minds of those who participate, as well as in the assessments of those who observe a community's proactive and constructive actions. When people coming from diverse backgrounds learn to see each difference as a resource for the common good, civic lovers express the effusive goodwill of their hearts and nourish the heart of community.

Before getting to the substance of this section, I share the significance of the value people from different backgrounds bring, not only to learning, but also to being motivated to work together in the commons we call community. I was raised in neighborhoods almost entirely populated by working-class and middle-class Jewish, Italian, and Irish children, men, and women. Even after moving to Washington Heights, the civic work I engaged in, albeit with African American and Latinx leaders, was all experienced in a world of, by, and for adults. Despite not having experience on the streets or in classrooms with "minority" youth, I carried with me an intuitive understanding of why I felt so compelled to do the work I did. This entire book is my attempt to explain the *why*. For now, I share how my intuitively generated commitment can be explained partially by comparing music genres that speak to the alienation of youth, albeit from different cultural perspectives.

When I was a teen, in the 1960s, my everyday world was accompanied by music. One of the artistes who inspired me to become involved in fixing the world made mad by adults was Bob Dylan. His lyrics were a sharp critique about how the adverse effects of adult beliefs and actions led to deep distrust on the part of youths. In one of his songs, the lyrics say: *"Everybody wants to know why he couldn't adjust…adjust to what…a dream that is a bust. He was a clean-cut kid, but they made a killer out of him."*[302]

A generation of teens during my time of adolescence were turned off and largely turned away from the "sensible assumptions" held by adults. In a world where a "noble" war was exposed as horrific and where pictures of Black people being beaten simply for asserting their right to be an American citizen, young people were instinctively revolted, and they passionately *chose* to revolt as well. The common adage held by teens was: *Don't trust anybody over the age of thirty.*

During my early days of youth organizing, I was invited to listen to an artiste very popular with teens. His name was Tupac Shakur. In his expressions of longing and lost hope, he retold what youth in my community experienced every day as a hurtful absence in their hearts. As the lyrics of one of Tupac's songs play out: *"In my mind lies a great soldier, fearless in motion and restless in stride, in search of the intent to destroy paradise from the inside. In my soul lies a great adventurer, ready to die, quick to explore, hungry for change."*[303]

The youth I worked with faced diminished and dismissive expectations, as did the youth of my generation. During the 1960's, when my generation was emergent, they fought back but with racialized and violent expression that seemed to me to be negative profiling on steroids. Too often our frustrations led to violence, and our perception of the suspected other led us to create our own dismissive stereotypes. The current emergent generation is reaching for inter-racial understanding and insisting on peaceful protest as the appropriate means to obtaining peaceful ends. I learned *so* much, from both generations about identifying forms of repression and denial. Learning from my intuitive sense, reinforced through my memories of resistance and song from each generation, has served as an anchor in my determination to serve the better intentions and higher angels of people and our society. Activists are learning that although territories differ, what we strive for in seeking human dignity and social justice is best obtained by considering our separate struggle to be connected in a community justice commons. Whether expressed in anecdotal evidence, short story, or song, it is the connective power of narrative that contributes to creating a society that is simultaneously differentiated and whole. The means for getting to an inclusive and just society is achieved in ways as suggested by a saying from Australia: "community is based upon the 'shared wisdom' philosophy. That mean all members are listened to and their knowledge and wisdom is valued and welcomed."[304] For my work to have meaning for me and relevance for those I organized with, I had to learn the music of their lives.

Paolo Freire, a South American educator who proposed that community education was linked to one's individual learning, proposed as a postulate in his work, *The Pedagogy of the Oppressed*, that to read a book, first one had to learn how to read the world.[305] As I now transition into the world of the adolescent archetype, I share how I learned to read the world of the soul, which subtly informed my experiences early in life and then enriched my efforts through engagement with my teens and their co-mentoring allies as we all learned to navigate the winding road between our intentions and deeply held convictions, finding a place with supportive friends with which to engage on our terms. I begin with introducing many of these teachers and co-mentoring orphans.

A. Orphans of the world, unite!

To paraphrase the words used in the rite-of-passage classic *Iron John* by Robert Bly, founder of the Expressive Men's Movement: "Each child (and adolescent) resides in their own psychic house, or soul castle, and deserves the right of sovereignty inside. When a parent (or esteemed teacher) ignores that house, that sovereignty, the child (the adolescent) feels anger and shame. Without claiming their sense of sovereignty, the child (or adolescent) feels worthless."[306]

Adults, sometimes through extending of goodwill, sometimes with a measure of contempt, bring about this loss of sovereignty. Misdirected good intentions and looking down on another person are negatively impactful when practiced by adults overseeing young people during the crucial period of adolescence. In the chapter titled Induction, I revisited a negative encounter I had in my high school days with an English teacher that I had highly admired and believed in without reservation. I revisit my recollection here to make another point. The firmer the expectation of trust a student holds for an esteemed authority figure, the greater the impact of betrayal. Even as one processes on a cognitive or conscious level, the ripple effect in the emotional body, and on the soul, remains, until one engages in healing practices at a deeper level. The resultant feelings were initially of great disappointment and anger. Over time I utilized a more assertive emotional response to counter the demeaning effects of imposed adult authority. At the same time, for a while in life, I continued in unconscious ways to carry this wound as a source of self-sabotage. Over time, after engaging with the interior work of the mind, I listened more attentively and assuredly to the inner voices affirming the nature of my talent. I constructed a body of interrogation, critical about the imposition of remote and arbitrary evaluation by adults. By developing confidence in my internal sources of potent competency, I preserved my reserves of confidence and patiently became encouraged by those who assisted my drive for self-determination.

My beliefs and feelings were also affirmed by trusted allies. I had these feelings of increased confidence buttressed once again during another confrontation at the school I mentioned previously; this time, the incident involved one of the school's assistant principals. In the spring semester of my senior year, as we gathered in the school auditorium, I refused to salute the flag during the singing of the national anthem. I did this as protest to the war in Vietnam. I was quickly reproached by an assistant principal, who had the reputation among students for being quite the authoritarian. He brought me to the rear of the room and told me that should I repeat my defiant and disrespectful performance, he would suspend me from school and possibly block my graduation. I returned to my seat. When asked what I had been told, I was told by classmates in my aisle that I should not worry. The next day, during the anthem ceremony, I refused to salute the flag again. This time, I saw the entire row of my classmates join me in my gesture. The assistant principal, who had begun walking towards our row, looked stunned and red-faced. He turned away and said nothing. Many of the students who supported me disagreed with my opinion on the war, but they stood steadfast with my right to demonstrate in a symbolic gesture what I believed in. Without that support, I might have become an orphan—if not allowed to graduate—simply from the questionable authority of censorship. My classmates, my extended family of those who believed in freedom of expression, helped justice to prevail.

The youth-led movements that I admire today, such as the students from Parkland High School and across the United States, demonstrate that when those who are members of an abandoned generation stand firm, in unity, governmental negligence can be challenged. When Greta Thunberg stood before the United Nations Assembly and spoke in outrage against the Boomer generation's abandonment of her generation, millions of young protesters from around the globe joined her.[307] By marching and engaging in advocacy directed at local governmental authorities, representatives of the emerging twenty-first century generation spoke out against the Boomer generation's crimes against the future.[308] Modest young people, who had stood tall, empowered each other in gatherings of mutual embrace. Adolescent advocates spoke words of wisdom and warnings about the dire consequences resulting from environmental neglect.[309] Young people who for years have been treated as though invisible in the eyes of governance gathered their energies of resistance from the collective soul of the adolescent orphan. I have learned, as have thousands of youths today, the relevance of the words of spiritual counselor Ram Dass, the late spiritual teacher and promoter of compassionate aid, who had for years brought assistance to dispossessed and injured people residing in India. In his alliances with others offering help, he found that it was not just those for whom we offer aid who are injured, but that those making offers for the common good have also internalized emotional injuries, yet unresolved, which he calls wounds. Mr. Dass counseled us that it is best not to bury our wounds, but rather "to turn the wound from enemy into friend."[310] Rather than remaining in brooding isolation and just behind the psychic borders of self-denigration, it is crucial for orphans to develop a new orientation toward their authentic aspiration and the affirmation of allies. This process of return is a voyage in which we come home to ourselves. I have also learned some lessons about finding connection to friends and allies. Engaging in this process helps those who have felt abandoned and marginalized to find a way to acknowledge themselves with the support of communal compatriots. When reaching out to and connecting with allies, many of whom might be working on orphan issues within themselves, we are constructing an emergent social narrative and a safety net of mutual recognition for emotional issues we share. We extend validation for the value of others who are wounded, in the process of healing, who are real, but never perfect. [311]

I will next introduce people with whom I have networked, whom I call co-mentoring orphans. I call this sub-section of the Introduction chapter "Orphans of the World Unite!" In this sub-section, I first share an anecdote about a person I consider having been an orphan role model in my life. He was closely related to me by blood, and still is affiliated with me in spirit. My late uncle, Pierre Johannet, was my mother's younger brother. I had had physically distanced but meaningful encounters with him early in life (his family lived in Cambridge, Massachusetts). I call him one of my primary orphans, as he deeply influenced me in my early years when I was trying to figure out interests in life that seemed meaningful to me. Stories in which those who made a difference in the world, and who were not afraid to proudly be who they are, resonated deeply within me. My Uncle Pierre introduced me to literary works that I related to, and which in unconscious ways also helped to shape my disposition towards civic empowerment. Three of these works, which I discuss in further detail in the next few passages describe my uncle Pierre's motivation for wanting me to become a rabble-rouser. Those books he gave me I consider gifts, opening a portal of understanding for me in my future civic work. In youth organizations I worked with, staff and volunteers provided introductions to books and incorporated them into their youth programs; we also instituted a requirement for youth to reflect upon the books they read and then write about them. Three books that my uncle gave me included *The Three Musketeers,* the *Lord of the Rings,* and *Pedagogy of the Oppressed.* The aftereffects I experienced after reading these books remain powerful for me today.[312]

Following the exposition about Uncle Pierre, my earlier orphan role model, I tell the tale of two other orphan role models. The first of these two is Kamau Marcharia, whom I had met in 1991 when he became inducted into the Petra Foundation.[313] It is a family foundation which brings recognition and offers support to social justice advocates whom they identify as unsung heroes operating with little institutional support. When Kamau was still a teen, he had been falsely accused, tried, and imprisoned for a crime based on fictitious evidence constructed by racist prosecutors. Years later, after being released (his record was not officially expunged), he devoted his life to finding justice in what I call our criminal injustice system.

The second of the two orphan role models I profile is E'niyah Pazmino, whom I met during my youth service work at PAL in 2016. She had joined a program at PAL called Youth Link, which provided educational support, counseling, and career guidance to young adults who had been disconnected from school and work and were thus subject to injurious consequences from family stressors and institutional bias.[314] At the time, I was a member of the

Robert McGuire Scholarship Committee, which awarded modest college scholarships to graduating high-school seniors.

After profiling the three orphan role models, I conclude the Orphans Unite section by comparing two of the role models who bracket my life journey. The first is my mother, Jane Claire Kurland, one of my childhood exemplars. The second person who served me as a standout for brave and compassionate presence is a teen named Miriam Payne, whom I managed in my first uptown youth service program, in Washington Heights, in the early 1980s.[315] Each of them, as young adults, was a member of families in exile from their native land. My mother came to the U.S. in exile from France, and Miriam arrived here with her family from civil war-torn Liberia. In their own ways, each of them transformed their experiences of loss into life journeys in which they established supportive relationships with distressed others who had been painfully wandering and lost.

A model for the new orphan: My late uncle, Dr. Pierre Johannet

My late uncle, Dr. Pierre Johannet, was one of my primary orphan/teachers. During my early years, as I mentioned earlier, he provided me with books that later provided valuable lessons for me as I entered the path of working with teens. For instance, in the book *Pedagogy of the Oppressed*, I was introduced to Freire's concept of banking education. His theory posits that under the model of banking education, the minds of the youth are empty vessels to deposit beliefs and disposition for practices in which only certain approved thoughts are put in. The goal is to train legions of producers with no say in their workplace conditions, and consumers who respond on demand to the suggestions of marketeers.

While he was still 16 years old and living in Nazi-occupied France, he had to choose between being forced to leave as an exile, or almost assuredly be detained in a labor camp and die. On a tip from a family friend, Pierre's father, Henri-Jacques Johannet, a finance officer with the French Shipping Line, provided his son a plan for escaping from Paris. Although Pierre Johannet had been raised as a Catholic, the religious affiliation of his father, the lineage of his mother, Ida, passed through the German-Jewish family of Millhauser. Under Nazi German rule, my grandmother's lineage resulted in her children to be considered as Jewish. Pierre could not use public transportation, as any male teen was at risk of being shipped to a labor camp. Instead, over a period of four days and a hundred miles, my uncle navigated his escape by walking, crawling, and, frequently, hiding behind trees or in railway beds. He was also assigned the daunting task of hiding and guiding a 14-year-old friend with him. Years later, when he was residing safely in New York City, it took my uncle decades of counseling and reflection to help heal the trauma he had suffered during his escape. After World War II had ended, and he had established citizenship in the United States, he went on to obtain his medical degree from Columbia University. Pierre embarked upon a career as a psychotherapist specializing in helping patients with severe distress as they dealt with their own trauma. My uncle's successes in helping patients in emotional turmoil remain with me as testimony to his awesome accomplishments. Pierre had transformed his inner adversaries into a friend; at the same time, he served as a best friend to others suffering mental anguish and pain. At his memorial service, former patients recounted Pierre's presence and compassionate understanding for who they are and what they had to overcome; their words brought me to tears. Some of my uncle's patients have pursued a profession in the healing arts themselves.

During my early childhood years, at Christmas time, my Uncle Pierre, along with his wife at the time, Judy, sent presents to the children in the Kurland family. In addition to holiday jam prepared by Judy, I received books, sent on Pierre's initiative, that he thought would be interesting to me. When I was in elementary school, one of these books was *The Three Musketeers* by Alexandre Dumas. This story, set in medieval France, profiled three musketeers, who came from financially privileged backgrounds and who served the royalty and country with armed support. This trio had a fourth companion in their duties—his name was D'Artagnan. The commitment shared by the four men was captured in the phrase, "All for one, and one for all!" The type of thinking promoted by the musketeers' phrase informed my youth programming. The heroes in this tale served valiantly for those to whom they had pledged support. After I had established my first teen leadership program in 1984, a major lesson that I sought to have teens learn is that of reciprocity, that is, the receiving and in return giving aid. While it was critical for teens in Washington Heights to receive aid through our program supports, it was also necessary for them to provide beneficial service to their program. D'Artagnan was much younger than his three compatriots, and he did not share their rank or status. In my youth programs, being of younger age did not exclude a teen from leadership opportunities, nor staff gratitude for their service. Teen leaders in our program offered volunteer assistance, making them feel accomplished, proud, and part of a united team. Providing tutoring and coaching assistance to younger peers, our teen interns came to be seen as role models for leadership and support.

While I was in junior high school, Uncle Pierre sent me *The Lord of the Rings* by J.R.R. Tolkien. This story took place in an imaginary land called Middle Earth. Communities of diverse peoples were subject to impending prospect of colonization by dark force masters of imperial power. One of these communities in danger of this fate was populated by a race of people called hobbits, who, it turned out, were short in stature and modest in disposition, but who would exhibit extraordinary courage in resisting occupation and repression. In the end, courage and maintaining hospitality towards allies in the fight would help to subdue the forces threatening them. At the same time, these warriors would also learn to resist a certain temptation known as an addiction to power. This addiction was symbolized by the possession of a magical ring that afforded the bearer invisibility and strategic advantage—but also, although the bearer remained unaware of it, a taste for power, which, once one had experienced it, might lend one to become dependent on using and abusing that power.

Young adult staff and teen volunteers in our youth program were, for the most part, residents of the Washington Heights neighborhood. They came from families with modest financial means. In the 1980s, our community was inundated with street violence, but short on resources such as books, due to underfunding from the City of New York. Younger students in our after-school program attended PS 128. Having limited opportunities to visit local libraries, and few books at home, they looked to our staff and our teen volunteers to be ably prepared to help with school assignments, and to introduce them to new experiences far away from the streets in which they lived. In this sense, teens who faced the same challenges as did their younger peers had to look for ways to be allies to younger students in helping them to overcome the social and political forces creating challenges for opportunity in their lives. Just by showing up to help invested teens with significant responsibility, and power. Adult staff decided to provide training to teens about taking ownership for this empowered responsibility. The training involved having teens become comfortable with reading books, and them sharing books with younger participants in the program. Our staff supported teens with this task by having them also read and share other sources of literature (usually newspaper articles). Some of these articles covered the civic work of teens and young adults contributing to programs throughout New York City. In this way teens not only became big-buddy readers with young children, but they also shared in developing a library of sources profiling the young as role models for civic contribution. After being introduced to written sources about the value of young people to themselves and community, by being conscientious and trustworthy, teens got to see themselves as stakeholders within a larger citywide community. Through their own personal reflections, and conversations with friends, they began to see themselves as actors in a larger story about creating a common good. Most youth members came from households with scarce access to great literature. As school time became dominated by practice worksheets and a focus on testing, the time devoted to reading, and discussing what was read, diminished. Discussions with youth about making ethical decisions in the context of locally situated adventure stories were a fundamental practice in our youth program.

While I was in high school, my uncle sent me a copy of *Pedagogy of the Oppressed* by Paolo Freire. As I mentioned in the Induction chapter, I had already been involved in resisting force of militarism in our country. I personally faced fierce verbal attacks about my opinions, in attempts to de-legitimize my viewpoints. Based upon ill-founded fears based upon negative racial stereotyping, young Blacks face not only verbal assault, but also physical assault when street confrontations with law enforcement unjustifiably spiral out of control. The testimonies of those subject to such harm also are habitually dismissed by authorities in law enforcement and the major media. However, I was not aware of the extent to which the process of schooling was guided by the paradigm that Freire labeled the banking model of education. In this model, once students are programmed to become diligent producers and consumers, they are also sorted into categories which track them toward stratified career opportunities. In addition to information being pre-formed and selected by professional staff, and then fed into the "blank" minds of students, schools were also designed to sort students by race, national background, and class. Using drill-and-test methodology, students advanced on tracks designed to reinforce existing social strata, separating people into those who were business owners, professionals, and other working-class categories.[316]

Freire proposed what he called a "dialogic model," where students are trained to think critically, engage inquisitively, and develop independently derived perspectives on schools, community, and society. The goal was to transform the educational experience into one that was no longer based on a factory model, but rather on a community model, where engaged activism transformed the classroom and neighborhoods. During the time in which I led youth programs, media outlets and elected officials were actively promoting demeaning types of profiling that led to students identifying themselves as potential sources of danger to others; it also led them to inadequately thinking about—and solving—their own challenges. In our programs, our focus was to have young people recover their lost humanity.

It was during the period between 2008 and 2015 that I, as well as my siblings, became much closer to my Uncle Pierre, and his second wife, Meg Turner. We visited each other more often, sharing from our life experiences, as well as from the lessons we learned from our professional experience. Both Pierre and Meg were practicing psychoanalysts who devoted their services independently to communities and people in dire emotional straights. Pierre had consulted with the James Jackson Putnam Center, serving troubled children during the1960s. In the 1970s, he helped to establish the Samaritans, a suicide prevention program. He also provided advice to early learning programs such as Head Start, and to law enforcement drug abuse prevention programs such as Drug Abuse Resistance Education, also known as DARE.[317] Eventually, I came to discover that my work with teens paralleled what Pierre and Meg were working on in Cambridge.[318],[319] Later in their professional careers, they became proponents of an approach articulated by Jacques Laquan, a French psychoanalyst who came out of the Freudian tradition but who later moved on to develop his own ideas (which are far too complex to fully discuss here). What I will mention here is that central to Laquan's work is a belief that what we call the unconscious is "structured like a language."[320] Pierre and Meg held conversations with me at a time when I was developing a sensitivity to, and theories about, the unconscious structure represented by archetypes. After being introduced to this level of consciousness and source of intelligence, this additional layer of perspective serves as a psycho-spiritual foundation for my book.

Pierre and Meg were also committed followers of a spiritual leader named Amma. Among the many premises of her counsel was that of the essential need to see life "from a broader perspective, where people need to not see the forces of nature as inferior (to the inventions of man), and to make protecting nature a part of one's daily routine." The wider field of view envisioned by Amma was one in which the principles of spiritual connections became expressed in the practice of environmental responsibility. I have tried to entwine this interactive relationship around the anecdotes detailed in this book.[321]

In addition to my retaining spiritual principles learned early in life from the Unitarian-Universalist faith and interactions with the Quaker-informed American Friends Service Committee, I have expanded my circle of spiritual advisement. [322] I studied these new sources of spiritual world-views beginning in the 1990s. Significant to me among these readings were those of the psycho/social and spiritual advisor Ken Wilbur. Wilbur developed a matrix of evolutionary learning stages I discuss in more detail in the "Anecdotes Rising" section of this book. [323]At this point in my narrative, I simply reference Wilbur's rubric, where he cites the necessity of willpower exercised by the ego. Wilbur understands the ego as developing within a continuum of evolutionary consciousness. He proposes that the social progress enhanced by ethnocentric belief systems promotes bonding and group-based sources of referenced identity rather than being limited by the individualism of ego identity only. Even as this new source of beliefs, which Wilbur labels as tribal consciousness, becomes dominant and transcends ego consciousness, the ego is not discarded. Rather, it functions within the context of the wider spectrum experienced in tribal relationships and identity. What evolves after the stage of tribal consciousness is that of "world-centric" identity, in which we all share rights and responsibilities as humans.[324] What evolves after that state is what Wilbur calls "cosmo-centric" identity, where we develop mutually enhancing forms of relationships with all forms of life, and with past and future generations. I have borrowed from this essential conceptual rubric of evolving stages of consciousness in my narrative when I describe the evolution of understanding about adolescent nature and teen identity. My aim is not to discard prior concepts, but to incorporate the value produced by ancestral allies, while at the same time offering critique after analyzing old concepts in new contexts. As I will share in the unfolding of this Introduction chapter, the new context is compromised by a fusion of environmental awareness and spiritual considerations in which a new look at teen nature is embedded, and a deepening of democratic practice is understood. Concepts infused in this chapter and in the next chapter titled "Anecdotes Arising" are informed by new wave forms of spiritual practice and the deep ecology movement.

David and Jack Cahn, in their jointly authored book, *When Millennials Rule*, identify two areas of experience describing the evolved perspective of millennials. One is the essential need to address the environmental crisis; the other is the fragmentation of communal relationships.[325] Uncle Pierre understood this connection intuitively and pursued connection with Amma and other civic-minded people with similar philosophy. By "this connection," I mean the connection between ecological sustainability and soul-based integrity. Within each of these realms of life, we encounter naturally occurring processes and energy, which are inter-connected and mutually beneficial to each other. As human beings, we exist as a partner in these larger universes, which are also connected. His contributions toward this understanding enriched my life and expanded my practice immeasurably.

An orphan as civic brother: Kamau Marcharia

Kamau Marcharia, whom I met when I was inducted as a Petra Foundation fellow in 1994, exemplifies civic heroism. As cited in the Foundation's commemorative issue of *Soaring Spirits*: "(Kamau Marcharia) is a compassionate warrior, undeterred by threats and scare tactics by those who oppose their work."[326] In fact, the trauma unjustly imposed on his life occurred at the age of 16: a false arrest and conviction, for which he served an 11-year prison term that gashed his body, mind, and soul. Despite such injustice and pain, Kamau turned his life around. With fierce and compelling advocacy and organizing, he fought to ensure that others subjected to the violence and displacement of our criminal injustice system would free themselves from facing the immorally and socially maladjusted adversity forced into his life. According to his biographic profile in the Petra Foundation's *Twenty-Fifth Anniversary Handbook*, his warrior presence bolstered a fierce resiliency within him, cementing his commitments to "bring justice to the forsaken, and social justice to the most isolated."[327]

After his initial arrest as a teen, Kamau had been accused of serious acts of criminal violence. These charges were put forward despite the fact, as his Petra biographical statement says, that he was "not at the scene," and the "prosecutor's remarks seemed to exculpate rather than to implicate him."[328] In September 1973, after successful appeals, Kamau was physically released from prison. A survivor of the twentieth-century version of a plantation, Kamau learned to adjust after having been abused through the misapplication of the justice system process. A heroic human being, Kamau, released from the bondage of a criminal injustice system, transformed unbelievable pain into a commitment for hope, reconciliation, and reform.[329] He became an impassioned advocate and fighter for unlocking the shackles that keep the innocent and brave locked behind bars. He broke free of the psychological chains of fear, a tool used by oppressors in their vain attempt to keep justice-seekers immobilized and disconnected from allies. He moved forward by challenging the barriers put in place by policy makers and citizens as they remain caught up in the illusions of racist colluders who destroy lives. (Barriers such as being denied social benefits like support for college, ability to work despite prior records, and access to health benefits and public housing.) The "black warrior" (as the Petra biographer describes him) has continued to organize and has held a seat on the city council in Fairfield County, South Carolina. Despite the selfless work he continues to deliver, coalitions of racist forces continue to falsely accuse him. Rather than fostering reconciliation, they seek to bring ruin to his career and to his life. Kamau will prevail, but he still needs those of us with a humane conscience to support him.

Kimberly Crenshaw is a social justice speaker and writer who has brought to the attention of sympathetic anti-racist organizers specific practices that have gone unnoticed when it comes to addressing justice system malpractices towards women of color. Ms. Crenshaw is an anti-institutional violence advocate who had also brought to light the disproportionate lack of attention to female inmates and survivors of the prison system while addressing criminal justice reform audiences.[330] In her writing and speeches where the audience comprised advocates for penal system reform, Ms. Crenshaw convincingly speaks about what we can do. Her eloquent speeches and writing address issues affecting women, yet the points she raises are still apropos to the obtaining of justice for Kamau: "I think there should be a massive response to the incompetence of leaders in the past that allowed this to happen."[331]

In the communities that I came to serve, the types of traumas I have mentioned here arrived in the daily lives of people unannounced and uninvited. Their impacts are overwhelming—from the disconnecting of men who had served prison time from viable routes of re-entry into society, to the emotional trauma of wives and children who had lost primary partners in their lives. Through adverse policy and malpractice, these social and emotional aftershocks remain in their memories, in their bones, and in their very DNA. Recent studies in the field of epigenetics have shown trauma may effect changes in DNA for succeeding generations.[332] Traumatic influences can trigger a predisposition for generating unknown and even unfounded fear-based responses to real life situations. These life-changing predispositions can be engendered by a mother during pregnancy and then passed on to the unborn child. An unconsciously triggered fight-or-flight response arises for even seemingly minor sources of stress. These unintended psychological predispositions and behaviors had become tragically activated during the periods of the intensely implemented wars on crime and drugs. Beginning with President Nixon's launch of the war on drugs, initiated in the 1970s, street harassment of innocent citizens, of those with minority ethnic identities and different national origins intensified exponentially when compared to enforcement practices prior to President Nixon's recommendations being adopted. Arrests and imprisonment also expanded at many times the rate of any other modern democracy. These invasive practices continued to grow exponentially through the 1980s. Families routinely had the doors of their apartments knocked down. In some cases, their places of residence were mistakenly identified as the source of drug activity. Pro-forma apologies regarding mistaken identities (sometimes, but not always) came later. This transgenerational trauma syndrome serves as the psychological background and national tragedy of destructive experience that was common to the everyday lives of families living in communities of color.

An orphan as mentee and civic sister:
PAL Youth Link member E'niyah Pazmino

During my tenure at PAL, I experienced joy and a sense of amazement after being chosen as an awards committee member for the Robert McGuire Scholarship Program.[333] This initiative was managed by esteemed PAL colleague Elinor King. Funded by New York Mets owner Fred Wilpon in honor of one of our PAL board members, the former New York City Police Commissioner Robert McGuire, this initiative interviewed high-school seniors who had been active as a volunteer for PAL. The recipients were all high-school seniors making plans for entering college. Those who were chosen after a rigorous selection process (which included a review of high-school transcripts and reference letters and an interview with the awards committee) were awarded modest motivational grants as a "thank you" for service, and in acknowledgment of the challenging road they were traveling to lead a successful life. To receive an award, each designee had to present proof of acceptance to college.

E'niyah Pazmino was introduced to our committee as a participant of the PAL Youth Link Program, which was conceived and directed by Bobby Ferazi. This program served teens who were "disconnected youth"—that is, those who faced roadblocks on their way to completing school, and those who had been in trouble with the law.

According to PAL staff members and teachers who had written letters of support for E'niyah's McGuire Scholarship application, she had started the program "as a very shy and uncomfortable girl, who was recommended to Youth Link after her arrest for a crime. She was emotionally abandoned by her mother, and in her early program days, found ways to sabotage relationships with peers and adults, lacking trust in the possibility of connection."[334]

After sticking with the program, through periods of personal ups and downs, things began to click for E'niyah. Frequent talks and counseling with mentors, such as Ian Houk, assisted her in drawing a new map about relationships. In her scholarship essay (also required as part of the application),

E'niyah revealed the following insight about her early days in the program: "I wasn't allowing my friends and helpers to get to know me… I was creating my own isolation."[335]

Her counseling, development of positive peer relationships, and engagement with tasks that helped her to redefine her life allowed her to redraw that map. She loved to help paint murals, one of which contained figures and scenes showing happy people and bright backgrounds, and a figurative path with a starting and finishing line. She said in an interview: "[T]he mural symbolized how everyone can have a bright future."[336]

According to letters written by PAL staff and schoolteachers in support of E'niyah's McGuire Scholarship application, she matured into "a young lady who is very reliable, interested in new challenges, and one who is very interested in truth and justice."[337] According to E'niyah's application cover letter, she had applied to and was accepted to Witten College in Ohio. E'niyah also stated that she plans to pursue a course of study fusing law and psychology, so that she "can help other youth caught in the trappings of injustice, so that they do not become excluded from the right of opportunity."[338]

The lesson that each of these people has contributed to my understanding of the orphan archetype is that any wound, traumatic as it can be, will only continue to be a source of resentment, self-sabotage, and unfulfilling wandering if one chooses to stay in the hurtful experience as if frozen in time. When you choose, with the supportive guidance of true friends, to change the wound "from enemy to a friend," the wound, though it may never be fully resolved, can continue to heal, and be managed. What remains is an energetic presence in which one comes to terms, a layer at a time, with the experiences of anger, shame, abandonment, and hurt feelings. The wounded healer becomes a healer of the wound in self and in others.

As opposed to engaging in the practices of control and domination, those who have learned to heal their wounds revel in the nurturance of reconciliation.[339] The practice of reconciliation involves creating emotional separation from the pain of an incident, moving toward extending forgiveness toward those who have caused you harm, and re-framing memories as learning lessons so that one can move on with their lives. Those who move on release their fears about challenging aspects of oneself and disparaging perceptions of the other. The practice of reconciliation involves a willingness to face discomfort and to look at the possibility of change. A person brings seemingly irreconcilable feelings and thoughts into a balanced new perspective. If a mentor or a person attempting to help suggests a new approach, this is helpful. However, the person who is affected must display buy-in, that is, choose to face a problem and be willing to make changes. The experience of reconciliation is nurtured in the sanctuary of un-coerced places and intentionally developed safe spaces of conversation. It involves reaching for our goals while simultaneously being willing to surrender that which does not serve us anymore. Reconciliation is practiced in the spirit of pleasing grace and gratitude, with thoughtfulness about benefits received and given. Managing the experience of reconciliation is one place from which each of us embarks on a path that ensures the pursuit of happiness and the establishment of a beloved community.[340]

Jane Claire Kurland: Maternal model for the orphan archetype

I now come to my interactions with two people with orphan profiles whose impact upon me was significant. Jane Kurland, my mother, had been exiled from France. Miriam Payne's family emigrated to Washington Heights during a time when her home country, Liberia, was in the throes of a civil war. Each of these two role models transformed their experiences of dislocation and disorientation into practices of life-enhancing relationships with members of families other than their own; those family members, in turn, found reassurance and safe havens in my mother's and Miriam's welcoming presence and embrace.

My mother was the older sibling of my uncle, Pierre Johannet, whom I profiled previously. At the time of their forced exile from France in 1940, she was 19 years old and engaged to a man named Francois. After the Nazi occupation of France, Francois joined the French underground, which conducted the hit-and-run resistance to the German army. Jane Claire prepared fruit jams that were put up for sale to support the efforts of France's freedom fighters.

After getting a tip (a veiled threat from a newspaper reporter rumored to be sympathetic to the Germans), my mother and grandmother were, on a day's notice, transported out of France and put on a ship scheduled to journey to America out of a port in North Africa. However, my mother was not initially told that her fiancé had been captured by enemy forces; he was now in a labor camp. My grandfather, Henri-Jacques Johannet, made up a story asserting that Francois had been killed in a bombing. He feared that if my mother knew the truth, she would attempt to return to France in an ill-fated attempt to vie for Francois' release.

Thankfully, my mother and grandmother had family in America, which gave them a safety net once they had relocated. On my mother's maternal side was the Millhauser family (aunts and uncles), including Bertram Millhauser, who was Jane Claire's uncle. In later years, he went on to become a screenwriter, penning a few of the scripts for the *Lone Ranger* television series. He also wrote a screenplay for a movie called *The Black Hand*, which portrayed the terrorizing conditions suffered by law-abiding Italian citizens blackmailed by the Black Hand gangsters. The hero of those exploits was detective Joseph Petrosino, who, despite being assigned few fellow officers (as well as being under great danger of retaliation himself), valiantly fought the mob, until he was executed by agents of the Black Hand in Italy.

My mother and grandmother also turned to the Hano family as a source of extended support. Clara Hano was my grandmother's sister; she had married Alfred Hano, who for a time was a labor lawyer. They had two sons, who were my mother's first cousins: Alfie Hano and his younger brother Arnold. Arnold, over the years, became a prolific writer, finishing 26 books, including *A Day in the Bleachers,* which received substantial recognition. It was an account of Arnold's visit to the Polo Grounds for the first game of the World Series between the New York Giants and the highly favored

Cleveland Indians. The Giants swept the Indians in four games. Arnold's account captured the too-good-to-be-true belief held by Giants fans that their team would prevail, as well as the spirited and clutch plays made by members of the Giants team.

Arnold served for the United States armed forces in the South Pacific. His older brother, Alfie, signed up as a bomber pilot who flew missions over Germany toward the end of World War II. By rule, pilots flew no more than 25 missions; tragically, Alfie's plane was brought down by enemy fire on his 23rd mission. He was listed as missing in action until a couple of years after the war. Alfie's parents then received a visit from one of the surviving pilots, a junior officer on the plane. The junior officer gave the following oral account to my uncle, Alfred, which has been passed down as family lore. He let Alfie's father know that as the senior pilot on the plane, Alfie stayed in the cockpit and made sure his mates parachuted to safety. Alfie went down with the plane. His remains were later recovered. A couple of possessions, including his name tag and his watch, were identified, and given to the junior officer. The junior officer, in turn, searched for Alfie's family. He made his way to Alfie's family home (that of Alfie's father, Alfred Hano) and recounted what happened to the plane. The junior pilot also gave my uncle Alfie's watch and his dog tag. Although Alfie was a first cousin to my mother, they related to each other as brother and sister; the news of his death left her devastated.

In 1947, my mother was introduced to John Kurland. After a four-month romance, they tied the knot on February 14, 1948. They remained in love with each other (and married to each other) until my father's passing in March 2010. My grandparents had been very disapproving of the marriage, as it was between a man of a modest working-class background and their daughter, who came from a family of notable social status and financial privilege. They remained in communication with my mother, but distant, until my arrival on April 19, 1949. With my birth, my grandparents' position began to shift. However, shortly after my birth, Henri-Jacques Johannet died after suffering a massive stroke. My mother had worshipped her father throughout her younger years: he was a completely loving and attentive father who adored his vibrant and headstrong daughter.

In less than a decade, my mother had suffered the devasting loss of three of her beloveds – a fiancé, a close first cousin, and her father. I consider these experiences to be that of becoming an orphan three times over. An orphan is traditionally defined as one who has lost both parents. The trauma of separation, disbelief, and disorientation results in powerful psychological injury after one loses parental figures. The specter of becoming an orphan loomed large in the lives of many of the children and teens with whom I worked. Those who have been separated through traumatic events lose their ability to navigate even small problems and fail to reorient themselves with a new sense of who they are, and where they belong. They break new ground, and break through intense subconsciously owned fears. When the war on crime and drugs escalated in communities such as Washington Heights, the loss of fathers to the prison system and the loss of some mothers with alcohol and drug abuse problems became more common.[341] In our community, young people often had become attached to surrogate parent figures such as grandmothers or extended family members who took a child from a sibling's or cousin's family into their house. The nature of the relationship between the orphan and their loss of a parent, or a surrogate parent figure was traumatic, so long as a sense of devotion and deep love had existed between them. In some cases, young people adopted staff members at youth centers and community leaders who were role models for them, seeing these folks as a mother or father figure in their lives. Having felt my mother's sense of loss, often after having conversations with her about her memories of long-lost loved ones, helped me to become sensitive to the significance of this problem in the lives of young ones in my youth programs. Scores of young people, over the years of my work (I will introduce a few of them in sections of this chapter) referred to me as dad, or father, or godfather, and continue to reference me in this way even today.

Shortly after the conclusion of World War II, Jane Claire attended the University of Michigan for a brief stint. During her college stay she became involved in a short-lived and rocky relationship. After obtaining a divorce, she returned to New York City in 1947 and worked at the Lord and Taylor department store while she contemplated the next steps in her life course. As fate would have it, she would be introduced to John Kurland on a blind date. Her life course would then take a surprise course.

The blind date was set up after a conversation between her aunt and a co-founder of an art school. My mother's aunt and uncle, Alfred and Clara Hano (Clara was her mother's sister) had become benefactors to a newly opened school called the Cartoonists and Illustrators School. (It was later re-named the School for Visual Arts, which remains open for business today). A founder of the school, Silas H. Rhodes, one day in the latter part of 1947, had been approached by Clara, who had sought his advice about getting her niece, Jane Claire, to get out and meet marriage-eligible men. During this period, a man named John Kurland was working part-time at the school in the administrative office. One of his tasks was to keep the office's paperwork organized. Mr. Rhodes was fond of John, and when Clara approached him, he offered to set up John on a blind date with Jane Claire.

Given the different backgrounds John and Jane possessed—for one thing, they came from widely divergent socioeconomic classes—their introduction to each other seemed to be a creative gamble that was unlikely to produce positive results. On their first date, John managed to spill an entire bottle of red wine, splashing much of its contents onto Jane's dress. However, their conversation, in addition to a magnetic attraction, led them to become enticed with each other. After a few more dates, their attraction to each other grew stronger; four months later, they were married. What had initially been viewed skeptically on both sides of the family—this marriage between visitors from differing worlds—turned into a six-decades-plus marriage between two dreamers and idealists who led their lives from the influences of their hearts.

My mother had to adjust to staying with a man from the working class—a man who was still trying to improve his modest financial means. He told his family and friends that he never held a job from which he did not learn, even though he had held jobs that he thought were only temporarily viable and not fulfilling. Any occupational experience he had, no matter how limiting, served as a possible steppingstone towards a future of better fortune. My mother became inspired by—and wedded to—his unending hope for a better future for themselves and the world. John also had to be there for Jane, for the burden she carried from the past, which resulted in a life-long struggle in which she worked with issues of grief and loss. My father's response was to remain steadfast, despite Jane's emotional ups and downs, and to offer his unconditional love to her. Her commitment to her husband, family, and close friends was to be there for them, no matter their world of troubles. She would be a best friend to the people she valued in her life, and in turn would become a best friend to herself.

Jane Claire was anything but a quitter. She and her husband had four children—me, Nicole, Jacqueline, and Pierre. One of the major life lessons she offered us, in partnership with John who adhered to a similar philosophy, was to remain true to who you are, and steadfast in staying on your chosen path no matter the obstacles and the setbacks. Her gift to those she loved was to offer a determined and fierce supportive optimism, which, for those caught in periods of doubt and despair, would be their lifeline.

As we four siblings grew up in the Kurland household, we witnessed episodes in which Jane Claire embraced people in distress—some of whom were relatives or family friends—with reassurance during dark times. When our mother thought it helpful, even our crowded apartment was offered as a temporary sanctuary for those in need when they had become dispirited and displaced. The Kurland children became brothers and sisters to cousins who had been thrown out of their own homes by their parents, as well as to some of our friends whose relationships with their parents had stretched to breaking points. I remember one episode vividly. One of my mother's close friends, whom my mother had gotten to know well while we lived in a Mitchell Lama co-op apartment called Rochdale Village, was in an emotionally challenging and sometimes abusive relationship with her husband. She had a nervous breakdown, and then fled to the safety of our family abode. I still can picture her sitting on the couch in our living room, speaking incoherently while drawing undecipherable images in a sketchbook. She was admitted to a psychiatric facility, and allowed occasional home visits, which often were to our place. Her two daughters virtually lived with us, having meals at our dining room table, and obtaining safety from the uncertain and chaotic atmosphere of their own apartment. Their father seemed to be overwhelmed and, for his daughters, emotionally unavailable. My mother let them know that for as long as they needed, Jane Claire was their mother too. It was after experiencing numerous responses of this type to others in need that we Kurland kids came to know our mother as the Empress of Embrace.

There is a familiar expression: to know another person, one must walk in their shoes. My mother had a knack for fitting into the shoes of others, no matter the size of the shoe. Jane Claire was also a guardian ensuring hope, one who lived in the hearts of those who had had nerve-shattering experiences, their expectations trapped in stressful suspense. Before a person in deep distress is willing to listen, there is a need to engage in conversation within a safe space. This imperative for creating safe spaces reminds me of a saying by Parker J. Palmer, an educator who promotes spiritually based practices in school classrooms. What comes to mind for a person facilitating acceptance by a skeptical or troubled person is the need for the person who is doing the inviting to create a sense of acceptance and calm. The invitee needs to feel welcome to co-occupy the space. Those who invite such a person to enter this space, when helping them, need to help him or her to feel secure. When one reaches out to support those at risk, as a result of being in damaging and fragile relationships, we need to create a sheltering space where it is "safe for all souls to enter the room."[342] Coach Dave, with whom I partnered for youth services beginning in 1984, would often remind me, even recently, about one of the reasons young people, some of whom had an instinctual distrust of adults, would come to talk with me and rely upon my counsel. This would be the case even for youth who had only known me for a short period of time. He often reminds me it was not about my authoritative position, nor my expertise, but rather that when entering a room, people seeking guidance feel safe just by my being there.

As part of my spiritual inheritance, I adopted my mother's disposition for unconditional generosity towards others in trying times. During the years of my work with teens, I helped many who were on the run from dysfunctional households, frightened by the presence of abuse and the ever-present lingering potential for violence. I encouraged staff and volunteers to look past the outward expressions of anger and inward temptations for withdrawal practiced by young folks trying to deal with the emotional chaos in their lives. The facilities in which we housed our programs became identified by youth and their parents as safe sanctuaries and places where they could find supportive counsel. Although the material resources available were not plentiful, the commitment by adults to share what little we had was extended to our youth. We wanted them to feel okay with what we had to offer, to feel safe in the act of asking for what they need.

Our primary means of recruitment was not only word of mouth passing among teens and their families, but also the spread of an empathetic contagion. Making sure that young people felt appreciated and welcome became our trademark. After having been under emotional siege, escaping from the toxic invasion of their personal space, or trapped in agitated addiction to anxiety, young people embraced by our empathetic staff and volunteers developed the courage to take one step forward in changing the course of their lives. Those who had been tested after facing dangerous conditions or unjust action became transformed into feeling like an orphan with no place to go. Once engaging with our staff, they soon thrived in our atmosphere. New arrivals to our program, who were understandably skeptical about reaching out for a new relationship with adults whom they were unfamiliar with, took tentative steps toward developing trust. After a short time, now listened to by attentive adults, having been extended opportunities for sensitive two-way conversations with staff, young people who had arrived with uncertainty realized they had a place to go, and people they wanted to get to know. As suggested by John P. Miller, a holistic educator, we were "breaking new ground, navigating the challenges of belonging nowhere, and learning to make trusted connections in order to heal pain."[343] It takes a village of mutually embracing friends to light the way for a joyful life journey.

Miriam Payne: A model teen leader
representing the orphan archetype

Miriam Payne, like my mother, was a member of a family that immigrated to the United States from a country embroiled in violence. In the early 1980s, after immigrating from war-torn Liberia, and deciding to stay in America, the Payne family settled in an apartment in Washington Heights. They lived on the fifth floor of a building at the corner of West 165th Street and Edgecombe Avenue. On any given night, one could hear the crackle of gunfire. When peering out the window to the park across the street, the Payne family members had a birds-eye view of daily illicit drug transactions. When I met Miriam and her family in the mid-1980s, Washington Heights was recording escalating levels of violence resulting from the drug trade battles that were taking place on the streets. That section of Washington Heights, bordered on the south by West 155th Street and the north by West 165th Street, which was called Southern Heights, was an epicenter of extreme street violence; the violence was beyond the scope of many parts of northern Manhattan. According to the reports released by the 34th Police Precinct, (oral reports given to members attending the 34th Precinct Community Council), those few blocks accounted for "30% of all homicides in the entire precinct, a precinct which stretched from West 155th Street to the top of Manhattan Island at West 225th Street."[344]

Miriam's parents were both health professionals. Her father was a doctor, her mother a nurse. Miriam was one of five sisters; there was also one brother. As is often the case for families whose parents are professionals, the atmosphere was one promoting commitment to educational pursuit, alongside a no-nonsense commitment to religious values. Relative to many of the families in the surrounding area, the Payne family was financially secure and socially stable. This increased the likelihood of success for the children, but it also increased parental caution about allowing the Payne children to become too involved with the surrounding neighborhood. However, at the urging of the gym teacher, Michael Kane, at PS 128M where both girls went to school, as well as from Coach Dave Crenshaw, who assisted Mr. Kane, the Payne parents were persuaded to allow their daughters to enroll in the Southern Heights after-school youth program. The school was three blocks from where the family lived, and the rationale for allowing the two Payne daughters to participate in the youth program was that it would provide a safe outlet for their recreational needs (both girls loved track and field activities); it also provided a safe place to socialize among friends who were doing the right thing. Even after they graduated from PS 128M, in the sixth grade, they continued to attend the program, as their social bonds were tight, and the after-school activities were appealing and satisfying to them.

For the middle- and high-school students who came to the program and volunteered to help elementary school-aged children with homework, and who coached them in sports activities, we organized teens into a New York City Boy Scout Council unit called Explorer Post #280. Participation as an after-school volunteer and membership in the (co-ed) post afforded these teens opportunities to compete in sports intramurals, to go on overnight camping trips at Camp Alpine in New Jersey, and to be invited to special events such as National Explorer Conferences held in cities across the United States, such as Boulder, Colorado, and Tucson, Arizona. Career and self-help workshops were offered at these conferences, as well as recreational activities and, of course, a venue where the teens could meet lots of other teens and chow down on good food.

Explorer Posts would also be encouraged to develop teen leadership, where youth served as Post officers. Explorer Post #280's teen leadership loved sports and recreation, but also recognized that unless they traveled outside of their own neighborhood, no clean and safe outdoor recreation venues were available. The city park just across the street from the building in which the Payne family lived was the southernmost portion of Highbridge Park. Residents affectionately called this place the Pit. This is the same park

I describe in Scenario # 3 in the Interlude chapter. As previously described, the park had no restroom station or attendant building, and its facilities, such as the swings and the basketball courts, were in various states of disrepair. The teen post leadership bought into a local initiative by The Dreamers, the local block association, and others, to do something about making the park safer and cleaner. This effort was supported by the Post, and it led to a presentation by Miriam Payne, who had become the Explorer Post president, to our local community board in an appeal for assistance.

It was a dark and stormy evening on May 28, 1991, when Miriam showed up to what is known as the public session at Community Board #12 in Manhattan. Each board reserves this portion of its agenda to allow individual residents and community-based agencies or other neighborhood spokespersons to state their case for three minutes. These oral testimonies might cover topics such as complaints about existing problems, recommendations for improvement in governmental practices, or an invitation to an agency's upcoming event. In cases where people were asking for a response from the city, board members could ask clarifying questions after the presentation or offer recommendations for a spokesperson's next course of action. Miriam spoke to an audience of 50 board members, as well as government aides who were in attendance, and members of the public. Miriam, by nature a quiet and reserved young person, made her first try at addressing a public assembly. Although presenting to others through a measured tone, she had no reservations about stating her case. Although the city had invested hundreds of thousands of dollars to public parks in affluent neighborhoods, including Inwood Hill Park, which was located less than a couple of miles away from the Pit, the space she and her neighbors counted on remained deteriorating, dirty, and unsafe for years.

Miriam's quietly compelling presence was conveyed to the audience throughout her delivery. For a couple of years, she had been a committed teen volunteer who tutored younger students at our after-school program. She never raised her voice, or made her younger peers feel intimidated. Her intent was recognized by students in need who trusted her intentions. On any given day at the program, I would receive a polite "good afternoon" from Miriam; then a short conversation would ensue in which we discussed her duties for the day. Other than that, she simply got down to business, being focused and engaged with those she helped with school homework assignments. They responded by following her advice. Although Miriam's small cohort of supporters from the program wondered how she would do that night and how board members would respond, and although she probably harbored similar concerns, her presentation was clear, firm, and compelling.

In her short three minutes, she introduced herself and her Explorer Post program, then she described the challenges with using the Pit, as well as the fervent need to have a park space that was accessible to the surrounding neighbors. She also detailed the frequent volunteer clean-ups at the park, and the Post's plans for continuing to help at the park and to run a recreation program there during the summer months. She let the board know that the initiative already had a few partners, such as the West 164th Street Block Association. A second resource she named was a training and technical assistance program called Take Back the Park, operated by the Youth Force component of the Citizens Committee of New York City. Her ask was to have local city departments such as the 34th Precinct and the neighborhood offices of Parks and Recreation step up and pay more consistent attention to the Pit. She also asked that the community board do all it could to facilitate the necessary actions she had enumerated.

As she concluded her remarks, the audience spontaneously arose in a standing ovation. A couple of questions followed, such as an inquiry asking what an Explorer Post was, and how many resources Take Back the Park had to offer. For the most part, the statements of board members were statements pledging support. Chairs of committees, such as the Public Safety Committee and the Parks and Recreation Committee, said they would assist with letters to local city agency managers and to the offices of appropriate commissioners. The chairperson of Community Board #12, Marvin Higgins, was quoted in the "Community Board Report", a page for a local newspaper, *The Washington Heights Citizen and Inwood News*: "Whenever you have young people come to a Community Board meeting, and get involved, it deserves attention, because you hear so many negative things about kids. What Miriam did tonight is so laudable."[345] The district manager for the board, Maria Rivera, concurred with Mr. Higgins.

District managers for community boards supervise administrative follow-through regarding board actions; they also lead special meetings at the board called district cabinet meetings. These meetings are attended by board leadership as well as by representatives of city agencies. Ms. Rivera, also expressing her opinion in the same article, raved about Miriam's presentation. She was ecstatic about the teen's demonstration of adult-like initiative. In her comments quoted in the "Community Board Report," Ms. Rivera remarked: "I have worked with Explorers in the past and they do clean up our parks. These kids are great. They work for hours and hours cleaning the community, and don't ask for anything in return. This is the first time that they have come before us and asked for help. We hear only about bad teens, and not the good ones who work so hard. There was no generation gap when Miriam came before us tonight."[346]

Miriam accomplished so much from the potency of her presentation. Board members had drawn to their immediate attention the discrepancies in the amount of municipal agency care to public spaces located within economically challenged areas. Annual levels of funding were much lower when contrasted to levels of financial support given to parks used by affluent constituencies. For those who had referenced at table of data, they got to know, on an abstract level, the financial discrepancies amongst parks, including the lower expenditures for the Pit. Miriam delivered a story and helped to create a mental picture amongst those in the audience. By bringing the saga of the Pit to Board members in vivid ways, Miriam invoked gut reactions in Board members about the need for due attention and fairness. These feelings were stoked by a credible messenger who not only lived next to the Pit, but who was struggling to remedy ongoing neglect for a public recreation space. The plight of the lower section of Highbridge Park became an urgent concern for action in the minds and the hearts of community board members. Miriam also contributed to the historic record, which now included board communiques to city agencies and local elected officials, and interviews with the press. She also fired up her co-members of Explorer Post #280 as well as other teens and adults living in the nearby area who supported the program.

Anodea Judith, author of *Waking the Global Heart*, is a former therapist who shifted her professional work to a writing career in which she advocates for using energy work to promote physical, mental, and emotional health. She sees that people who come to the civic stage with optimal health on all levels also offer visionary hope for a better world. I believe that invigorated hearts promote a healthy heart of the world. Group consciousness is awakened one community at a time. In her speech, Miriam used what Ms. Judith calls the power of sound through effective communication. Miriam's inspired delivery is a living example which shows that clearly expressed and compassionately driven communication delivers knowledge and inspires the will to act. As articulated by Ms. Judith in her book: "[C]communication is an act of connection, where minds that were divergent develop common subsets after communication has occurred. Communication is a way of extending ourselves beyond our ordinary limitations, and communication creates the future. It creates the world at each moment!"[347]

As a teen leader who stepped up to the stage of neighborhood participation, Miriam started by moving beyond whatever self-limiting expectations she might have held, even if secretly harbored. She served as a community steward, extending the windows of perception for those who did not know her park's dilemma well. Miriam lived by a principle expounded by Christina Fong, who as a teen cofounded a local chapter of the League of Conservation Voters at her school in San Francisco: "If everyone helped with one movement they believed in, whether the environment, health care or civic rights, the world would be in much better shape."[348] Miriam leveraged a few moments of passionate and credible testimony by facilitating a charge for action.[349] In his work *Crossing Open Ground*, naturalist philosopher Barry Lopez stated that "truth requires passion and discipline. Patience is the road to eternal conversation."[350] Miriam's devotion has been uncompromised, and her commitment uncontested. Her testimony remains among my joyful memories, serving as a reminder about what it means for the orphan to return home. The community board pulpit came to be for Miriam a catapult for innate talents now unflaggingly expressed, while at the same time inspiring action for the Pit. Years later (2018) the Pit would be comfortably used as the neighborhood's recreational home, complete with resurfaced and safe playing areas, sturdy recreational devices, and, for the first time in memory, a comfort station, including a changing station for infants. Miriam helped to get the ball rolling when she engaged in what the liberation/poet Audre Lorde called the literacy of survival: "…and when we are afraid to speak, we are afraid our words will not be heard…not welcomed. But when we are silent, we are still afraid. So it is better to speak. Remember, we are not meant to just survive."[351]

Three practices (3 Ps) for embracing orphans:
Acknowledge presence, establish a welcoming place,
and affirm the value of life purpose

An issue which I raised in the Induction chapter concern the importance of tens being acknowledged by adults, thereby allowing them the right off "being there" while expressing their innate ownership of knowledge. When my right to hold a point of view was dismissed so abruptly and contemptuously, I felt disrespected, and my presence was devalued. Jeffrey Mishlow, in his book *Thinking Allowed* (published shortly after our country's national emergency on 9/11), cited Virginia Satir, a marriage counselor, on pitfalls concerning communication. Ms. Satir warned us about a type of trap encountered when husband and wife cannot see each other: "First you make me up, and then based upon your fabrication of who I am, you reject me."[352] In a parallel fashion, based upon misleading stereotypes about teens, adults can similarly fall into a trap of falsely identifying who a teen is or what their intention suggests. When in touch with thoughts, patterns, and messaging from within, teens access information that is already within their psyche.

Spiritually oriented psychologist Chris Saade labels living from inner guidance as a process "opening doors to innate wisdom instead of blindly following rules. Rather, one follows the traces of an inner path."[353] Scientifically oriented psychologist Daniel Siegel looks at this approach as participation in the development of a holistic mind, where inward energies and outward influences become integrated by the mind's owner. Siegel postulates: "[T]he mind emerges as a self-organizing process which is located between an interior mind-sphere and an outer mindscape."[354]

I consider this process of inner-directed referencing of meaning as a natural quality in which the adolescent constructs and creates common sense. Teens learn to transcend both their falsely assumed limitations, as well as the barriers imposed by low expectations for them held by others." The early twentieth-century progressive educator, John Dewey, saw this as a teaching and learning challenge, where, "the needs to harmonize one's inner traits is an ever renewing problem, one in which each generation has to solve it again for itself."[355] The underlying pattern from which adults, whether well intentioned or fearful of teens falsely perceived to being by their nature a danger to themselves and others, is what psychologist Dr. Mike Males refers to as "kourophobia—the fear of false stereotypes about teens."[356] This malpractice is a marginalization of personhood, which is taught to the young as a means of repairing their "deficits." These falsely constructed beliefs and practices are transmitted to adult professions across psychological, sociological, and educational disciplines. As is the case for racism, sexism, and similar issues, the perpetuation of adultism is a transgenerational disease. This passing of torched identity is handed down not just from adults but also among teens who have learned the lessons of diminishment too well.

A 2019 *New York Daily News* guest editorial written by two high-school students at Stuyvesant High School profiled the toxic effects of derogatory statements of biased opinions on student relationships. According to Gordon Banks, then a high-school senior, and Maria Sarci-Pudgen, then a high-school junior, the use of racially dismissive language at their school was routine. Mr. Gordon writes: "[W]hile in a freshman biology class, another student blamed him (because he is Black) for the AIDS virus, and then told him to go back to Africa."[357] Pudgen wrote that she often heard the "N word used against her, and her Black friends and that Blacks don't really care about education. In one heated confrontation, a student threatened a Black student with lynching."[358] As the article continues, it states that to navigate the atmosphere at school, Black students had to deal with "being left out of meaningful conversations about them and being reduced to figments of "hater's imaginations."[359] All this at a "specialized" New York City high school populated by student scholars! The issue the writers of this article advocated for was having bias training instituted as an implicit component of the school curricula, complete with dialogical methods for breaking down stereotypes and building real person-to-real person connections. A bias-reduction practice, they argued, should be extended to provide healing across the relational domains of race, gender, immigrant status, and LBGTQ identities.[360] These rights should be infused and extended to staff as well as students, and be entwined with busting stereotypes that falsely identify the nature of adolescence. The grist of relationship-building concerns mastering the rules of engagement, recognizing oneself and others through the intelligence of the open and accepting heart. As written by the writer Terry Tempest Williams: "[T]he human heart is the first home of democracy. It is where we embrace our questions. Can we be equitable? Can we be generous? Can we listen with our whole beings, and not just with our minds? Can we offer our attention, and not just our opinions? Do we have this resolve in our hearts to use these questions to guide our actions?"[361]

Once we begin to establish open relationships originated and received through authentic presence, we can apply our understanding to establish safe places. Dr. Marvin Hoffman is a clinical psychologist from Harvard University who feels that a teen finds desired place by using their natural talents of doubt and skepticism to first scope out a proposed place of participation: "In the best tradition of Holden Caulfield (the sarcastic protagonist in the book, *Catcher in the Rye*), students…[h]ave a finely calibrated 'shit-detector' whose alarm bells are easily activated by any hint of phoniness or insincerity. It is with our loss of this sense, as we age, that our sensitivity to genuineness atrophies for many of us."[362] Adult educators who value this asset of authenticity in teens operate from what the Latin American educator Paolo Freire called a place of "respect for what students know. This capacity to be critical and curious lends the young to restless questioning, and a search for revelation about something(s) hidden. Their fiercely focused attention, and need for eternal vigilance, in an integral part of their being alive."[363]

When adults hold tightly to appreciating teens for the psychic skills I mention above and construct learning spaces that encourage application of these skills, the typical false narratives used to describe teens' "inevitable deficits," such as boredom, disinterest, and short attention spans, fail to materialize. Sarah K. Anderson, an educator with 10 years of experience with very young students at the Cottonwood School in Oregon, has taught students lessons in "place-based learning environment."[364] Students provided learning experience and community service in gardens and forests develop into people who are avid questioners and focused interventionists. Ms. Anderson states that when students "feel that their guided experiences are authentic, and involve hands-on opportunities closely tied to places holding meaning for them, then [I] inevitably [see] improvement in student achievement and the growth of appreciation for the natural world."[365] Ms. Anderson continues: "[O]ver time, the participatory culture cultivates a desire to serve, and over the longer-run, dispositions towards becoming engaged, life-long citizens."[366] Critical to this process is that students are encouraged "to choose, to implement, and to evaluate their project. These experiences help students to find their voice, and to recognize that they have the power, and the right to participate. Including youth voice in public decision-making is a priority in place-based education."[367]

Once a teen has an established and recognized presence—and a relationship with a trusted ally or mentor in a safe place—his or her focus on living a life of purpose becomes affirmed through embrace and validated through mutual accord. These efficacy-validating practices have been corroborated for years through stories shared on a site called Spark Action.

Teens who had organized a leadership council in Nebraska helped to raise awareness among foster-care youth about their legal rights and the municipal policies that affected them. These young social activists also developed a Foster Youth Bill of Rights, which the government in turn developed into a handbook and resource guide to be distributed among foster care agencies and group homes.[368] In 2012, the Colorado Youth Advisory Council drafted legislation (House Joint Resolution 1004) to reform teacher licensing laws to include "suicide prevention and awareness training"; the resolution was adopted by a unanimous vote.[369] In the Bay Area in California, the San Francisco Youth Commission, whose ages range from 14 to 24, modeled changes in policies, resulting in more safe havens for homeless LBGTQ youth.[370] What these initiatives and dozens like them across the United States shared was the development of youth into emerging citizens. As expressed by Morrison Odelli, an adult co-mentor from the Staten Island Voice Youth Program, "[Y]outh develop civic competence, and confidence, through the attainment of relevant information and participatory motivation. They meet and greet others with common interests, learn how to implement constructive change, and become proud for being a light for future generations."[371]

Becoming guided by being the light for future generations is another way of maintaining the course of one's life purpose. Harriet Beinfield and Efram Korngold are writers who constructed a manual of the use of Chinese medicine. I think their words are also medicine for soul-based searches for finding one's course. Beinfield and Korngold describe each of us as "life-forms who are stations for the reception and transmission of energies, through which we, and others we influence, are nourished. Each person exists to nourish all others, and in return to become nourished. These forces (energies) are not material but include subtle energies of a spiritual nature. In our inner world, we have a central sun which is also the source of life. This inner sun is our true self."[372]

The challenged path begins with obstacles that have been planted internally though our habitual exposure to negative profiling. The combination of feeling blocked by obstacles and at the same time ill-equipped to meet challenges is introduced to teens in subtle and overt ways. Learning to lower one's expectations for self-efficacy is transmitted through the teaching of racial profiling, sexual profiling, and adult's profiling of teens.

The behavioral outcomes have become all too familiar for teens who get trapped by their own responses, which leads to, what leaders of the Icarus Project call, "shadow healing—self-hate, suicidal thoughts, compulsive behaviors, depression and manic episodes."[373] The Icarus Project leads trainings for teens and staff of youth services and human service organizations. Their workshops focus on having folks identify internal obstacles and learn "to cease learning what is internally sabotaging." Icarus has created interactive constructs linking institutions of oppression with the unconscious internal maps, inducing marginalized people to buy into their status as being less than fully human. These negative habits are also promoted and reinforced by modern societies in which there are levels of extreme inequality, such as in the United States. Today we see more and more reviews of numerous studies documenting that varying levels of inequality correspond to decreased or increased evidence of social/emotional problems and disease.

One summation of studies supporting this premise contains numerous citations in a book titled *The Spirit Level* by Richard Wilkinson and Kate Pickett, Growing Up in Societies with High Levels of Inequality. As stated by Wilkinson and Pickett: "(Inequality does not) cause psychological distress, but are socio/economic conditions which multiply the ill effects."[374] Since 1970, when levels of inequalities rose substantially in the United States, these two authors have cited studies showing that the level of anxiety among youth has increased five times over; that teens with limited resources increasingly resort to impulsive and risky strategies in response to stressful circumstances; and that although life expectancies for youth have declined, homicide rates in cities like Chicago have "risen steadily."[375] Wilkinson and Pickett also cite studies that show the effects of stress (both chronic and acute) on the functioning of the mind and body. The influence of acute stress results in changes in the brain, leading to hyper-vigilance and adjustment in the immune system (thus keeping a young person continually primed for defense); it also leads to problematic changes in the circulatory system, "including constricted blood vessels and increased heart rates."[376] When maintained over time, this leads to what the authors cite as chronic stress "with the brain showing impaired memory function, the adrenal glands showing slowed rates of recovery from acute stress, and the development of heart disease and high blood pressure at very high rates when compared to youth from affluent communities."[377]

Education leaders such as James Popham use assessments of students that, rather than focusing only on cognitive development and academic skills, incorporate devices they label "transformative assessments." These devices identify the status of each student's well-being and challenges, "fostering ownership for talents and hope, as well as for liabilities and fears."[378] By using ritual and ceremony, and by identifying parents and on-site staff as supportive and understanding partners, a safety net of compassion and encouragement is constructed as protection in the face of deep challenge.

In their innovative ways, each of the approaches outlined above encourages warm invitations for students to be present—and assertively so. I have previously referenced Parker Palmer who has postulated when conditions are made safe for "souls to enter the room." Each of the above practices has helped to construct spaces/places that are in alignment with soulful needs and natural learning rhythms. Youthful intention and awareness became guided by the natural order—that is, the order in which everything is connected and starts from the authentic center of being. These promote an alluring beckoning for the orphan to feel safe coming home to himself or herself and enthused about extending this same invitation to others. Once feeling at home with one's true self and attested purpose happens—and the person is enthused about accepting the need for this soulful nourishment in others—the heart becomes resilient and strong. A student's first significant encounter with community is in the classroom. Whether or not the space feels safe and invites initiative, taking chances and finding supportive teammates with their peers and teachers makes a huge difference to a child's healthful development, educational advancement, and sense of becoming a future citizen.

The soul-enhancing and character-building education of students is what educational leader Peter Grey talks about in his storytelling sessions concerning the Sudbury School in Framingham, Massachusetts. This school operates on what its founders call a "democracy model." The school's founders have instituted governance structures—which they call "school meeting"—in which administrators, staff, and students of all ages, all of whom are members, have one vote per person. These meetings break out into governance committees; the Judicial Committee, in which school rules are interpreted and enforced, is one example. The committee comprises one staff member, two student clerks, and five student representatives.[379]

According to Peter Grey's account, since its inception in the 1990s the Sudbury School has documented many positive outcomes, both for students (75 per cent of whom go on to college) and for school climate. Additional examples describing benefits include "students who become more self-directed and who take on personal responsibility for their lives; young people who develop high motivational levels for further learning; graduates who have adopted the strategies of using play and exploration in the learning process, and emerging young adults who lack fear of authority figures as a result of having had respectful relationships with staff from the school."[380]

Mr. Grey's accounting of the Sudbury model tells a story about how freedom, responsibility, and creative opportunity contribute to the optimally holistic development of people as well as school governance models aligned with the higher angels of American democracy. Nikhil Goyal is another education proponent from the same school of thought as Mr. Grey. Mr. Goyal gives a promising accounting of what he calls "free school practice"[381] with his description of the Brooklyn Free School in Clinton Hill, Brooklyn. This school was founded in 2004 by a former public school assistant principal. It was dubbed in a 2006 article in the *New York Times* as "arguably New York's most radical learning center."[382] The school "has no metal detectors, security guards, or bells (sounding off for changing classes during the day). Fifty-five per cent of the students are white, and forty-five per cent are students of color (a mini-miracle of integration in New York City, which is one of the most segregated school systems in the whole country)." As described by one student, when she first arrived at the school and then adjusted to the school's routine and atmosphere, it was like "going through a de-tox."[383] "She became more interested in reading books across many topic areas and learned to love books. She dropped her habit of watching television all the time. At the time of her admission, she was a shy student immersed in self-doubt and disinterested in the larger world. Over time, she became a member of several committees on the school, and active in her community."[384]

Each of the previously mentioned anecdotes speaks to rebellious efforts targeting traditional types of educational pedagogies. An older paradigm of teaching and learning organizes the educational experience around method-ologies of abstract learning, supervised and presented as official knowledge under adult control. The rebel schools tell a new story, relevant to the emer-gence of stories honoring individual dignity and communal governance. In the section that follows, in which I focus on the adolescent archetype of the rebel, I share anecdotes about those who have influenced me, beginning early in my life, and extending throughout my youth service career, to tell a story about myself. Mentors exhibiting rebel energy contributed to a shift in my beliefs. My compassionate concern and my irrationally optimistic drive to facilitate youth empowerment was felt with more passion. Each of my rebel role models connected consciously to their inner rebel wisdom and aspired to set their protégé's souls on fire while in search of meaningful connections. My co-mentors, in exercising their rebel muscle through interactive sto-rytelling promoted active dialogue that supports the mutual expression of ideas. The co-mentoring rebels who individually had significant influence with me in their own ways also seemed to become a village which helped to raise me as a rebellious participant in civic affairs. Their teaching prompted and supported my continual search for creating paths of participation for youth. Some of these paths were initiated in park improvement projects that were based upon natural learning rhythms taught to us by nature. My journey became extended to other realms, such as collaborating with teen advisory councils, who taught me about their central place in community and the need for operating as self-governing systems. I came to recognize the central importance of respecting declarations of interdependence. Through the encouragement and construction of civic improvement and community enhancement institutions, our collaborative enterprise would offer teens what I would later call a New Deal for prime-time citizenship. The old story told about the essence of adolescence faded as teen social activists and their co-mentors constructed and shared new stories.

Rebels of the world: Shine a light on your deep story, then give glory to the stories of others

Bill Pfeiffer, a deep ecologist who has shared his vision for a sustainable earthly habitat in his book *Wild Earth, Wild Soul*, draws a distinction between stories put forth to create older ways of thinking and those that visualize new possibilities. According to Mr. Pfeiffer, the old tales hold that the entire world revolves around humans. In our society's construction of rank, status, and social hierarchy, people with high socio-economic status and groups constructed to maintain that status for members of their group are deemed by the media to be significant centers of attention. Others who lie close to the periphery of power and significance get occasional attention with one-shot human-interest stories but are omitted from history as reconstructed for school textbooks. According to the ecological worldview, as held by Mr. Pfieffer, humans, no matter their socially constructed status, are no more and no less significant than any other creature.[385]

Amherst University Professor Penny Gil would say this means that each of us has our own internal organizational systems, each of which is unique and essential to the structure of the whole person. Our task is to realize that each of us has an important spiritual light to offer, which some-times exists in tension with others, and sometimes exists in a creatively supportive relationship.[386]

Mr. Pfeiffer also holds that the universe is constructed "not of atoms, but of stories." What we tell ourselves, how we define our essence and purposes, are the stories. When we take ownership of them, we also resonate with others as authentic.[387] My rebel-archetype teachers taught me the importance of honoring and supporting each story; I in turn learned to use stories in guiding teens. As Mr. Pfeiffer states in his work when describing the emergent story, there are many different stories and ways to live, which reflect the way each of us truly is.[388] What is constructive and mutually beneficial is keeping and honoring personal integrity for all. Each of us has a right to hold our ground, to self-affirm."[389] Our best practices include using discrimination positively in recognition of our being co-habitants of spaces which are our consensual commons. We build community as a confederacy of mutually beneficial souls.

In our current world of incited ideology and instigative attacks on the viewpoints of those we disagree with, we have succeeded in creating a social and political atmosphere of massive, mutual distrust—expressed in loud voices that in the end violate the volition of all. These behaviors are rewarded and punished according to ones rank in society.[390] These tit for tat exclusionary practices remind me of the pessimistic parable in which those who insist on "an eye for an eye" create a world where everybody is blind. When we fail to listen to the inner-based inspiration for our stories, and when we remain deaf to the life narratives of neighbors, we are, in a parallel way, creating a world where everybody is hard of hearing.

A new rebel is stepping onto the stage, one who thrives, who changes the world in positive ways, in part because, as stated by eco-psychologist Bill Plotkin, rebels are wanderers, in a spiritual sense, who, as Mr. Plotkin postulates, have " an understanding, that as a wanderer, we become visionaries, who by necessity explore and experiment with possibility."[391] One of the premises of my book is that although the classroom and school are the first place a young person experiences a complex socially interactive environment, it is the immediate community in which she or he experiences the first socially constructed environment partially embedded in an environmental matrix, and partially divorced from ecologically sound obligations. As our society becomes modernized and more dependent upon manmade elements, a young person loses touch with their innate connection to nature, including its natural rhythms and co-dependent inter-relationships. As the environmental truism states, everything is connected to everything else. For millions of years, humans had a psychological understanding about themselves, and socially constructed relationships, which were perceived to be connected to the laws and mechanisms of nature. The first peoples of North America managed these relationships respectfully for at least 10,000 years. With the invasion of the Americas by Europeans, guided by their mindset which includes obtaining mastery over others, including nature, we have mismanaged, in our materialistically driven solutions, and after only 500 years, to see the beginning of the end of a sustainable planet. Bruce Rich, a critic of the World Bank's financial practices, provides an extensive expose of the rift between the world we think we have created, and the natural world as it is. In his book, *Mortgaging the Earth*, he quotes the late anthropologist Claude Levi-Strauss: "A well- ordered humanism does not begin with itself, but puts things back in its place. It puts the world before life, life before man, and the respect for others before love of self. This is the lesson that people we call 'savages' teach us: a lesson of modesty, decency and discretion in the face of a world that preceded our species and will survive it." [392]

When teens exercise inquiry and hammer hypocrisy, this is their natural way of using discretion. As I will explore in teen program profiles of youth-led environmental and social justice projects, adolescents are less likely than adults from the Boomer generation to put themselves before others, or to dishonor the Earth. In reference to his numerous comments about honoring individual autonomy and respect for voice, Nelson Mandela is often attributed to have said: "What we fear is not our inadequacy, but our inner light. Once we affirm this in ourselves, then seeing the light in others will naturally evolve." [393] As teen change-makers begin to create new stories, about each of themselves and the fate of our society and Earth, they are motivated by and instructed from what they discover by using their inner light. Once teens get who they really are, what follows is that they understand others as different from them but connected to them at a spiritual level. Rebels are creating new stories, and in turn, new stories are guiding them.

To help in their search for meaningful storyboards framing their purposes of civic change work, social activists use stimulating imagination and the attraction of alternative futures.[394] As we jettison those old stories which no longer serve our purposes in the twenty-first-century world, we do so after we come to understand the limitations of narratives constructed solely for self-interest only. We also learn to deconstruct the false assumptions and damaging effects of viewpoints which falsely create negative stereotypes. Teens, when sharing stories about their individual civic contributions and the social capital created by collective teen social change efforts, construct an emergent story about who they are and why they seek change. Young people are offering to share with others the benefits of their good deeds.

I would like to bring to light the words 'painting connection to our souls'. I share here an analogy based within the story of evolution, and how seemingly simple life forms contribute to the evolution of life by connecting to a higher purpose. I take a step back to another "starting line"—a point in time only a few billion years ago. I first encountered this insight in a work by biologist E.O. Wilson; I encountered it again on a website I viewed recently called Understanding Evolution. As shared in Wilson's biography of bacteria: "Until about 4 billion years ago, when life first arose, there was no free oxygen in the atmosphere at all, for life was anaerobic, meaning that it did not need oxygen to live and grow. With the evolution of a bacteria, the Cyanobacteria, Earth's atmosphere became changed into one that could support oxygen-loving (and carbon dioxide producing) organisms like us."[395] Another modern biologist, Mahon Hoagland, expands upon this idea: "Before a single plant or animal appeared on the planet, bacteria invented all of life's essential chemical systems. They transformed the earth's atmosphere, developed a way to get energy from the sun, devised the first bioelectrical systems, invented sex and locomotion, worked out the genetic machinery, and learned how to merge and organize into new and higher collectives. These are ancestors to be proud of!" [396]

The point I am making here, as I bring this discussion back home to adolescent empowerment, is that the drive for self-assertion, improvement, and adaptive relationship in the natural world of relationship building was affected by seemingly simple, under-developed organisms which were central to our species being able to come to life at all. Although they did not possess neurons, nor a brain, the evolution of the species was driven by quest, and an evolutionary imperative to adapt to support new needs in a changing environment. Under our industrial era, thought leaders such as scientists and policy makers created paradigms about the nature of adolescence. Under the influence of these experts, teens came to be seen as under-developed by their primitive cerebral cortexes. What was overlooked was that teens were primarily driven to act by basic characteristics that are central to evolution in life and to healthy human development, and not by hormones or other chemical or physical structures in the body. What scientific writers such as Daniel J. Siegel have pointed out is that connecting bodily structures with observable behavior conflates correlation with cause. As asserted by the biologist Mr. Hoagland in his book, *The Way Life Works*, these life-enhancing attributes are "inherent to the process of life itself."[397] I share here two examples espoused by Mr. Hoagland. The first one is that "life creates itself through accidents, and that accidents ensure novelty, which is essential to adaptation."[398] The second one is that "life competes within a cooperative framework where individual organisms develop a strategy for fitting in. Each creature acts in its own self-interests even as the living world works through cooperation." [399] In our old-school paradigm of intervention with teens, we obsess on having them eliminate mistakes and segregate teens, thus marginalizing them from contributing to society. During the adolescent stage of development, in which teens are vulnerable yet self-assured, it is natural for them to be searching and to start stumbling. Teens do so with their spiritually based propensity and felt sense of connection to nature, to be navigators, which includes postulating, estimating, and adjusting concerning one's direction in life. Yes, teens are often prone to making serious mistakes. In the practice of scientific experimentation, errors contribute to the learning process, and do not signal an end to the search. Despite facing high levels of questioning about them without due cause, and negative commentary on their actions and intentions, teens remain resilient to getting back on the life course for which they were born. The Search Institute, which has been conducting studies for decades on what constitutes positive and negative adult commentary with teens, find that 80 per cent of these conversations fall in the negative range. Teens are role models for self-directed, learning beings.[400] The life process demands of all of us, across tribes, villages, continents and species, that we organize and evolve in ways that, if captured by an artist, would result in beautifully painted pictures reflecting our souls.

An adolescent's mission at this stage of their lives mirrors that of what futurist Marilyn Ferguson describes as that of the outsider: "[T]he outsider wants to be integrated as a human being, to achieve a fusion of heart and mind, to understand the soul and its workings, to move beyond the trivial. The outsider wants to better express himself, to better understand himself (as well as others, I might add). The outsider seeks a way out with intensity and extremes of expression."[401]

What follows in this section are anecdotes about my allies who have facilitated my understanding and strategies for building the traits of the outsider as especially relevant for the rebel as storyteller. Before getting to these vignettes, I take one step back into the nineteenth-century world in which fading paradigms about adolescence were first constructed. I then move forward in appreciation of my twenty-first century-leaning allies contributing to a model of teen nature and prosperous development more in line with both the assumptions of new-wave spiritual philosophy and the deep ecology movement.

Let's step backwards, to the 1800s, when scientists and policy makers at the top of society's decision- making pyramid, driven by the principles of mechanics and industrial organization, created the very concept of adolescence we know today. Our new way of knowing the adolescent resulted in a torrent of social imperatives for controlling them. Amongst their underlying assumptions were those that held that all life could be understood through mastering the management of the rational mind, which is superior to any other form of intelligence. What was assumed, by psychologists and proponents of the most desirable types of thinking, was to utilize rational thought and the conscious mind only. All other modes and origins of thought were deemed to be obstacles to clear thinking, and barriers to achieving social progress. Over-reliance on feelings and emotions were deemed to impede optimal outcome for society, or to lead to outgrowths of superstition. In addition, the findings of scientists were transformed into masterfully produced technologies. Scientists who conducted studies based on evidence determined by the rational mind alone saw their work enthusiastically marketed to serve profitable and material ends. Some of these marketed studies supported the continual oppression of racial minorities and women. Technologies were created as tools that separated humans from the laws of nature, which were indeed designed to transcend and subdue nature. Emotionally derived qualities of thought are serving the new generation of teen activists in driving their energetic response and felt sense for the fierce urgency of now. Most scientists are warning us that as a species we are running short on time for fixing our environmental dilemma, and that if these issues are not faced, the consequences will be dire. For the emergent generation faced with the prospect of losing it all, being passionately fired up is a most relevant and timely response.[402]

In the present day, we now have energy-related technologies that sap the Earth's infrastructure and poisons our air and water. Industries such as factory farms that produce our food and nourishment also contribute to more excessive levels of carbon dioxide than all other forms of energy use combined. The scientific community, whose research led to the development of technologies creating these conditions now have come to a consensus of 90 per cent or so that within 70 years, the damage to our planet's ecology, and all the natural systems supporting it, will be beyond repair. We will then descend into a cycle that might result in the termination of our own species. We created a mythology about the imperative of progress being dependent upon perpetual growth of technologies and economies, and now will live or die depending upon whether we adhere to sober scientific warnings and perennial spiritual wisdom or succumb to the superstitions of mechanical/industrial design. You just cannot stop progress, as my father would tell his children, partially in jest…but mostly in alarm. In just over 200 years, those of us who are "most evolved" have begun undoing four billion years of life and Earth's sustainable history, creating the ultimate counter-story to life itself.

Why do I make a connection between bacteria (and viral agents) and the archetype of the new rebel? In our culture, bacterial and viral agents are most often focused upon as agents of aggression that pose threats to our bodies; in many instances those threats have been borne out. However, new findings in biological research and the field of health have determined that in most cases, microscopic organisms work in tandem with us, helping us to fulfill the requirements necessary for achieving optimal health, and for surviving under challenging conditions. As shared by the science writer and researcher Ed Young in his book, *I Contain Multitudes,* he writes about a variety of organisms within us, that technically are not us. In his book, Mr. Yong reveals how vital microbes "sculpt our organs, defend us from disease, break down our food, educate our immune systems, guide our behavior, bombard our genomes with their genes, and grant us incredible abilities."[403] Those adults still adhering to the old paradigm defining teens tend to see adolescents as foreign, strange, and look at teens as dangerous to themselves and others. Teens, as we do with microbes, are habitually be kept under control by adults, and if seen as necessary, are dealt with to ensure that they do not threaten the established order of our lives. Teens are reframing the established order in hopes of better aligning everybody's lives with the natural order. As we are introduced to social justice movements and teen contributions to those movements, we are learning how these grassroots efforts are reshaping our decaying civic and community institutions, protecting us from the social toxins of racism, sexism, homophobia, and adultism, and guiding us in behaviors with which we honor our unique potentials and dignity as well as the life-enhancing value of conscious and embracing communities.

The new rebels of America are dissenters and critics of the political/economic system of our recent past. They critique exclusionary policies and belief systems for not addressing the bodies of evidence inherent to grassroots and multicultural civic contributions. They are defense agents standing against the attack on their communities. Social change-makers speaking from their positions on the ground shine a light on their true nature as fully capable actors in the fields of constructive social change, and are invaluable in making our programs, our community, and our city a better place for all. Teens are equal partners in the myth-busting team.

Just as those earlier bacteria changed the narrative of life on Earth, teen change-makers and their co-mentors are key change agents in our transitional times. As the wheel of progress is turning, and we are navigating from the industrial/mechanical era to the spiritual/ecological paradigm, civic enhancing teammates are conceiving and producing a new story about the efficacy of adolescence and the expansive evolution of democracy. The Greatest Generation led us, first at the peak and then during the beginning of the unwinding of the old story. The Boomers planted seeds for the new story, but also at times have sabotaged its unfolding.

Put another way, as a slogan in an *Adbusters* magazine had proposed: "The utopia of our parents has become a nightmare for the younger generation."[404] The upcoming generation is the first one in modern history to have seen life expectancies decline, financial opportunities decrease, and the prospects of living on a safe and sustainable planet become subject to cancellation. What has become problematic for teens, and those living with them, is not the nature of adolescence, but the unnatural systems adults have created which diminish our positive outcomes and threaten us all.

As I mention in other places in this book, studies about the effects of economic and political equalities, as detailed in a book called the *Spirit Level* show that researchers have documented that increasing, large inequalities, constructed by manmade and adult-created systems, are also associated with negative risk-taking behavior, impulsive episodes, and attitudes of negativity that inhibit people from buying into the American dream.[405] As I will detail in the section of this chapter called "The Rebel," psychological, social and education research had in large part conflated social construction of dysfunctional behavior by teens with what was falsely assumed to be inherent to their nature.[406] Teens and their co-mentors, when flexing their rebel muscle, incorporate new stories holding adult-led institutions as accountable, and social change-makers as civic accountants, bringing society's ledgers, and our nation, into more responsible balance.

I have also pointed out in other sections of this book the creation of a falsely constructed narrative called "patho-adolescence" by a generation of grown-ups stuck in a dysfunctional arrested adulthood. Patho-adolescence is a concept I have borrowed from spiritual social critic Bill Plotkin.[407] Arrested adulthood is a concept I learned about from the Canadian societal critic named James Cote.[408] The economic, cultural, and social institutions initiated in the late nineteenth century and still active today are ways of life that have become constructs enabling and celebrating the very outcomes that Dr. Martin Luther King, Jr. has decried as toxic to our society. Dr. King summarized these threats to the stability and viability of society as America's "four catastrophes—materialism, militarism, poverty, and racism," which I refer to throughout this book. There are a relatively few (when compared to the population of the United States) whom critics call the 1 per cent today. Through financial opportunism, they benefit with seemingly limitless gain, while the rest of us suffer from the dissolution and denial of our psyche, social glue, our soul, and our spirit. If generations of adults, who have had to power of the vote, find themselves at such a strategic disadvantage, socially, economically, and politically, then the prospects for teens, who have been ill-prepared for voting, or as with 16- and 17-year-olds who cannot vote, the mountain of reform left to climb is immense. For teens seeking social justice, as well as for the civic co-mentors who believe in and guide them, the task begins with constructing evolved stories, honoring the adolescent genius within and the angels of our democracy showing us the way to equanimity in our social and political affairs. Adults suffering from anxieties and fears used to negatively focus on teens need to learn to heal themselves, rather than to attempt fixing those whom they identify as problem teens.[409] Teens need to desist in maintaining complacency and passivity in the face of unjust action directed toward them by exercising, as taught by Dr. Martin Luther King, Jr., "restless determination" in forging civic friendships with adults.[410]

As previously indicated, the Icarus Project is a program with a syllabus empowering marginalized and oppressed peoples. Its leadership provides critique and corrective strategies for all victims of degrading *isms*, including racism, sexism, ageism, and nativism. Icarus Project leaders speak about these negative outcomes as "micro-aggressions." These mini-sized attacks with huge consequences wound our psychic well-being invisibly and in subtle ways. Once a person has experienced and adapted to these destabilizing influences on an individual level, a person creates what they call negative mind maps.[411] These internalized maps sabotage positive self-concepts and become obstacles for generating the will to recover from injuries and attacks. These "mind maps" come to constitute our hidden assumptions of low self-worth. For example, if a black female teen raises the temperature of a conversation at school by complaining about discriminatory practices leveled towards her, she might be labeled by those seeking to maintain the status quo as being *rowdy*, *uppity*, or *disruptive*. Others in control of the educational system, although having some sympathy for her as a target, typically counsel those unjustly discriminated against to adjust their attitudes and behavior. The counsel to speak in more moderate tones is suggested as the primary means of remediation. Failure to adjust to biased relationships with accommodating responses is seen as the fundamental cause of the problem. In this dynamic, the aggrieved individual is tasked with making personal adjustments instead of challenging the functioning of a culture of white privilege sustained by the school system.

The task of the new rebel is to identify these processes of substituting personal responsibility (as the sole answer for change) in lieu of the need for societal change. The rebel's task is then to develop strategies and resilience, allowing injured peoples a new frame, or story, by which to relate oneself and the world. The framers of the Icarus Project identified a challenge that is central "to avoid shadow healing and stop learning what is invisibly sabotaging to ourselves."[412] The act of self-sabotage contributes to our distrust of life-enhancing assets and disconnection from allies who are here to support us. By gaining ownership over fixing the process of one's self-undoing, we also learn to appreciate the goodwill extended to us by others." The new rebel must develop a disciplined practice of personal and social responsibility, which in turn diminishes the likelihood of the dismissive practices of a culture reinforcing business as usual. This involves an internal reconstructive process in which compassionately assertive young people build a proactive identity and perspective, which in the end brings us closer to our true selves and the good of others.[413]

As understood from a spiritual level, this idea of taking on one's personal demons and societal negative stereotypes has been aptly put forward by Rabbi Abraham Heschel when he praises those who take on the role of active outsiders and iconoclasts. In his writings, including his book, *The Prophets*, he calls upon those of us who look for a more beneficial world to learn how to become prophets: "[T]he iconoclasts, challenge the holy revered belief systems in which we adhere to outworn truths without reflection, and contest cherished beliefs supported in the scaffold of certainties. Iconoclasts take on institutions with their supreme sanctity. The prophet exposes all of these as scandalous pretensions."[414] When co-mentors guide their young social change mentees to optimize potential and challenge limiting social beliefs at the same time, I believe they follow in Heschel's footsteps by training prophets under construction.

Our younger sister and advocate, Greta Thunberg, who spoke so eloquently at the United Nations last year regarding her generation's grievances and her generation's concerns about our dying planet, was labeled in many palaces of privilege as a "girl who just has an attitude." They need to check their dictionaries for usage. The correct word is *aptitude*.[415] She has a natural skill set inspired by the full bloom of her imagination. With her hypocrisy-exposing vision, Greta sees through the adult-constructed veils hiding misdirected good intentions and egregiously directed bad policies that threaten the viability of our planetary sustainability.

On my path of delivering civic instruction and motivation to adolescents, I was taught well by many new rebels, some of whom I introduce in this section. To kick off my rebel/mentor profiles, I introduce one rebel/mentor guiding me in my teen years, and one inspiring me after meeting him in my adulthood. The first is Richard D. Leonard, whom I met during childhood and who counseled me for social action during my teen years. The second profile I share is of Kurt Tofteland, an activist for prison reform whom I met in the early 2000s after his induction into the Petra Foundation. Each of them engaged with me at different stages of my life. Richard Leonard and Kurt Tofteland exhibit mentoring characteristics needed for changing false stories.

I refer to the rebel archetype by borrowing from the archetypal profile developed by the spiritually oriented writer Carolyn Myss, which she calls the Storyteller. Her biography of the storytelling archetype also sheds light on the personality characteristics of civic rebels. As outlined by Ms. Myss, the storyteller utilizes a "[r]elay of wisdom and foolishness, mistakes and successes, facts and fiction, and tales of love and the impossible. With our storytelling, we often exaggerate beyond ordinary life. Stories bring us into contact with our inner being and communicate metaphoric learning or experience."[416] The rebel/mentors whom I have learned from had different stories to tell. What they shared was their skills in exposing old narratives, which were disabling or unjust, and enticing those who listened into considering new ways of looking at life, and then changing their assumptions and actions.

After sharing my experiences with Richard Leonard and Kurt Tofteland, I will then use an approach as I employed in the "Orphan" section. I will profile two of my primary rebel/mentors, the first of whom guided me early in life (and remained an influence throughout most of my life)—my father John Kurland. I met the second person early in my youth services career (in 1984). He was (and still is) my closest and most steadfast rebel/mentor ally. His name is Coach Dave Crenshaw.

The first rebel/mentor, John Kurland, was the storyteller-in-chief for my immediate and extended families. He involved me in the practice of using words and language as expressive energies possessing multiple levels of meaning and identity. This facilitated my ability to see variable senses of meaning dependent upon context. In the 1950s, when unexamined and unchallenged authority was in ascendency, he exhorted friends and foes alike to see the point of view of those who had been dismissed as not credible, or who had been excluded from sharing power in the political process. The second rebel mentor is Coach David Crenshaw, co-founder of the Uptown Dreamers in Washington Heights, as mentioned earlier. He trained young people to reconstruct internal narratives about themselves. His storytelling facilitated youths' ability to make connections between their active service for community and realizing their life purposes. As young people learned to construct their authentic story, their commitment to service became more meaningful to them and became acts of love. For now, before introducing these two, I start with a man deeply influential over my civic decisions, who was the Minister of Education at the Unitarian Community Church of New York in my youth.

Richard D. Leonard: A reverend preaching civil rights who walked the walk

After protesting to my parents, when I was about nine years old, that I had no religious training in my life, my mother reached out to a cousin, Randy Rothman. (She is now known as Randy Diner.) Randy suggested we try the Community Church of New York, a member-church of the Unitarian denomination. It was during my Sunday school years, beginning in the fourth grade and concluding with my graduation from high school, that I came to meet—and be deeply influenced by—the church's minister of education, the

Reverend Richard D. Leonard. By introducing me to compassionate social action, and peaceable practice in protest, he helped me to set the table upon which one brings the flavor of non-violent protest to the menu of activism.

Rev. Leonard is a man of many talents and a wide range of interests. For 64 years, he served five churches, including nine years at the Community Church of New York. I was most influenced by him during the mid-1960s, when I participated in anti-war and pro-integration movements. In addition to his religious and social justice teachings, he rounded out his life with creative activity. A long time had passed, after I had been in my early 20s, when I lost contact with Reverend Leonard. It was not until about 2010 that, after visiting the Unitarian All-Souls Church on Manhattan's east side that I connected with him again. After a long and distinguished term of service with All Souls, he retired, but was still a faithful congregant for Sunday services and the church's special events. Rev. Leonard, amongst his many commitments to fighting for civil rights, had joined the first march in Selma organized by Dr. Martin Luther King, Jr. in 1965. Now, 50 years later, the All Souls Church proudly decided to honor his service to the church and the Unitarian movement, as well as his contributions in ensuring human dignity and social justice. According to an anniversary journal that was put together in 2015 by fellow congregants of the All-Souls Church, "Dick Leonard played chess at a grand master level, and competed in an exhibition with the world chess champion Anotoly Karpov. He taught chess to seven hundred young people. For seventeen years, he also played in the Riverside orchestra."[417] The journal also mentions that he had presided over 4,377 weddings. I can attest to one of them, as he presided over mine in 1970 when I married Harriet Kaplan, a close friend of my sister Nicole. As was his personal signature of affirming memories of important occasions, we received an anniversary card each year, on or about February 14.

The social activist as storyteller nourishes aspiring change agents. Through oral and literary means, civic mentors learn the optimal ingredients of social justice activism.

The following is a brief abstract about the reverend's body of work as presented for the 1965 march in Selma. It a biographical piece that appears in a 2015 commemorative journal provided by the All-Souls Church (where Rev. Leonard had served for 34 years, up until his retirement. He remains an active congregant to this day.) As stated in the journal: "Leonard, devoted to the cause of civil rights, decided to join, together with 200 Unitarian and Universalist Ministers, a march in Selma, Alabama, in protest of overwhelming violations of civic and voting rights for African Americans."[418]

"As they gathered during the morning for breakfast, before joining the march, and after then exiting a local diner, one of the ministers, James Reeb, from a Washington, D.C. church, was accosted, physically beaten by a mob, and subsequently died of his wounds. The Unitarian coalition chose Dick Leonard to take his place, marching to honor James Reeb, and his own dedication for the cause. In the words of Rev. Leonard, as written in the All-Souls Program given out at its celebration of his life, "This whole episode involving such tragedy and hope for change radically changed his life."[419]

Rev. Leonard published his own thoughts, in journal form, in a book he called *Wet Cement*. After Martin Luther King, Jr. issued an appeal to ministry across the United States to join him in Selma, Rev. Leonard decided to respond to the call. He shared a thought about changes in life-course in *Wet Cement*: "What I thought would only be a show of support for a few days, turned into a life-changing event for both the country and for the author."[420]

In his telegram of appeal to all forms of ministry, Martin Luther King, Jr., included a reference to a moral imperative for social responsibility: "We have witnessed an eruption of the disease of racism which seeks to destroy America. No American is without responsibility." (This quote is reproduced in the All-Souls Church Program tribute).[421] Dick Leonard responded by not only going to Selma for what he expected to be just a few days, but, as stated in the All -Souls Journal, "was one of the two Unitarian ministers (the other being the Unitarian-Universalist Association president Dana McLeen Greeley) and three hundred other people to finish the entire five-day march.[422] The territory between Selma and Montgomery, Alabama, was dangerous and intimidating. Marchers were under constant harassment and surveillance. As recounted in the All-Souls Journal: "The bloody attack that had included the use of tear gas by state and local law enforcement agents and that had occurred just a few days earlier was still fresh in the marchers' memory…indeed, it was seemingly seared into each marcher's flesh."[423] The march was conducted over a course of 50 miles, but not for one inch of it were these determined champions of justice deterred from or hesitant in achieving their aims.

Then United States Senator Robert F. Kennedy had apt words describing the integrity and grit of the marchers: "Moral courage is a rarer commodity than bravery in battle or great intelligence. Few of us have the greatness to bend history itself but each of us can work to change a small portion of events."[424] Serving as a role model, even with his softly expressed urgent counsel, Rev. Leonard conveyed this sense of responsibility for social justice. As I listened to and ingested his stories, the hunger for justice intensified for me, and the search for an active means of expression for seeking remedy became part of my social/emotional DNA.

In the heated atmosphere of the 1980s and the 1990s, I remained firm in my commitment to stick to my mission, even in the face of annoying and physical confrontation. None of the incidents even remotely approached the danger and violence encountered by civil rights organizers, not only in Selma, but also in segregated cities across America. Marching and organizing despite taking extreme risk were the freedom riders in the 1960s, and Black Lives Matter activists marching today. Transforming socially conscious dreams into reality implies taking considerable risk. It is the young who see the conditions of the status quo as untenable, for themselves or for the quality of the planet, who decide that taking risk is a necessity for heading off potential social and environmental catastrophe.

Although I was never physically assaulted by members of law enforcement during my teen service provider years, I did on occasion confront challenges to my physical space and emotional safety. Except for the incidences I describe in the Induction chapter, describing the murder of my roommate and my escape from and unfolding street riot, most of the threats I encountered during my youth services journey were from law enforcement officers.

In one of these incidents involving being confronted by law enforcement officers, I was stopped on the corner of West 165th Street and Fort Washington Avenue while I was carrying a tall stack of file folders. I did not do a good job of anticipating the loosy-goosy way I was carrying multiple folders stacked one upon another and had quite the time just squeezing them together, keeping a keen eye on them, and walking gingerly toward my office destination. On a sunny morning in the spring of 1995, I had been on my way to the Ivy League office. It was located in the NY Presbyterian complex at 60 Haven Avenue.

An unmarked van zoomed onto the sidewalk in front of me and screeched to a halt. An undercover officer leapt out and identified himself as a police officer. Officers at the time who were assigned to drug busts worked undercover, and in plain clothes. One of the two officers who had alighted from the van had an intimidating posture and an antagonistic tone. He accused me of purchasing drugs in a nearby apartment building located across Ft. Washington Avenue and about a block south of my location. It took some verbal jousting and 15 minutes of conversation before they finally believed my story: I was simply a youth services worker carrying documents to an office I was heading to just a few blocks away. I, at this point in the spring of 1995, was a white, middle-aged man being stopped in broad daylight in front of a hospital building. I was subjected to verbally accusatory and threatening comments (initially, during this encounter, the junior officer threatened to arrest me and take me downtown if I did not admit my guilt). What would have happened, I thought to myself, if I had been a young Black man? Once the second officer (who I believe was the supervising officer) decided to take my account at face value, each offered a cursory apology, jumped back into the van, and went roaring away. A few of my colleagues and friends were a bit critical of me for not asking for police identification and then lodging a complaint. I believe at the time I was just too surprised to react, and also did not want to begrudge the difficulty of enforcement on those trying times. What I could not get out of my head, and still hold on to today, is the privilege extended to me by my white skin.

In a much earlier incident (this one in the late 1980s), I was in a livery car with three of my teen volunteers, whom I was bringing home after an early evening event. During those trying days, it was our practice to deliver door-to-door service to ensure their safety. Once the livery car stopped for a red light on Amsterdam Avenue near West 164th Street, we heard a blaring loudspeaker from a police vehicle: an officer demanded that we pull over. Initially he insisted we were there for illicit purposes. Again, after yelling at me with a suspicious tone, the officer, after 10 minutes of conversation with us, became convinced of the true purpose of our presence. Yet, what I reflected upon after the incident was over is what might have happened if I had been a young Black man in the taxi with those volunteers. Each of my volunteers was a young Black person, and I believe that my being a person of Caucasian persuasion prevented this encounter from resulting in a much worse outcome for them. What had been especially disturbing to me was that my three volunteer, after we had departed from the scene, reacted by just laughing about this incident. Each of the three volunteers told me that what had happened was no big deal. They had made psychological adjustments and considered these types of encounters to be just living life. Abrupt and intimidating encounters with law enforcement officials were just business as usual.

A third example involves an encounter in East Harlem, this one in 1994. I was walking eastward across East 116th Street (near Third Avenue) at a brisk pace one morning. I was on the way to a meeting with the East Harlem Community Council for Improvement (EHCCI) whose leadership had expressed a desire to help sponsor T-shirts for a special event the Ivy League/Uptown WINS agency was planning in promoting the right of equal access to sports by girls. The event was to be a girls' sports clinic organized for us by the Women's Sports Foundation at Riverbank Park (a park operated by the State of New York, between the Hudson River and Riverside Drive at West 145th Street). In the middle of the block, an officer sprung out from a doorway and pushed me forcefully enough that I bounced against a parked car. In response to my verbal complaints about such treatment, the officer responded: "We were looking for a White boy, and you are it." Thankfully, after a few minutes, a supervisor intervened, sized up the error of the officer's actions—and I was off, on my way, only 15 minutes late for the meeting. Had I been a young Black man, running, and then arguing, what might the outcome have been?

As I wrote a bit earlier, some people questioned me about not lodging complaints for this third incident. My response included expressing my sense of the futility of seeking remedy given the climate of the times. As evidenced by contemporary media accounts, crime had been diminishing in the early 1990s, but news stories continued to fan the xenophobic flames of discriminatory notions about Black youth. I rationalized that as a middle-aged White man, even though I too encountered confrontational situations with law enforcement, they were of little consequence when compared to what young people of color had to face every day. I chose to focus on my community allies, and the efforts the young were making to instill change.

My point is, in sharing these three confrontation experiences with law enforcement, and my responses to them, that what protected me first and foremost was my status, that of being sheltered by White privilege. Had I been young and Black in any one of these encounters, I would at a minimum been kept on the hot seat of unauthorized suspicion, arrest, and worse. Given my status, the raised temperatures at first induced by misunderstandings were mediated by cooled-off heads who in the end took the stance that being White made me alright. Teen leaders, both young, White activists and many more young, Black, and Latino activists, had already been organizing during the times when my confrontations occurred. The social justice and civic change efforts by these leaders is documented in a study called "From Assets to Agents of Change." As noted in this study: "[S]tudents organizing in communities to defeat curfews, writing policies, and helping to get them passed (which protected young people), and assuming leadership positions at schools guiding changings in curriculum made those proposing changes in policy and practice more reflective of diverse communities."[425]

Today, years later, my frustration has only gotten worse. I have not personally encountered confrontations with law enforcement in recent years but have heard too many accounts from close friends and in the media which have only heightened my apprehension and concern. In the last few years, the City of New York and the New York City Police brass have decided to reintroduce a program called "neighborhood policing," that had been introduced by Police Commissioner Bill Bratton, under Mayor David Dinkins in the early 1990s. Between the end of the Dinkins' tenure, and changes in approach under Mayor DeBlasio, successive administrations had the approach of community policing withdrawn. This tactic was replaced by escalating invasive tactics, biased records of arrest and imprisonments, fanned by media hysteria and politicians seeing that getting tough was their ticket to being elected.

When community policing was reenacted, I saw an opportunity to work with law enforcement leadership and officers on the ground to propose a method of law enforcement in which the creation of enhanced communication and joint problem-solving would replace the chase-and-arrest approaches that had been predominantly put in place to ensure neighborhood safety. Given the levels of distrust that have endured, we have a way to go. As the old organizer's saying goes, "Organize, don't agonize." Part of the process involves crossing experiential divides and building bridges amongst people who hold different perspectives. My exposure to practices building understanding and in which I gained appreciation for difference began under the tutelage of Rev. Leonard.

Even when Dick Leonard did not teach me directly in Sunday school classes, his guidance and wisdom deeply colored the offerings each Sunday. As the education director for the Community Church of New York at that time, the history, teaching, and practices of non-violent resistance and for promoting socially just changes in society were offered to us in study and through participation. It was at Sunday school class that I was also introduced to multidenominational teachings and practices. People in New York City celebrate both Easter and Passover each year, learning the lessons of sacrifice for the common good and the importance of persistence and solidarity for a good cause. Although the principles and practices for each of these traditions, Christian and Jewish, are taught in public schools, practicing these traditions varies according to a person's religious denomination. At the Community Church of New York, Sunday school students and adult congregants practiced both traditions. We congregants celebrated all traditions through sermon and song. We also had sit-down dinners where we broke bread, and share food and festivities, for both Easter and Passover holidays. As I became introduced to and made friends with residents, young and old, in Washington Heights, not only learning about their traditions, but also sitting down at the table and breaking bread (or matzah) became central to living, learning, and loving in our multi-lingual, ethnically diverse, and religiously tolerant community. Police officers and civilians living in communities of color engage with each other from different perspectives. As an officer, a person has been trained to seek neighborhood safety through the practices of enforcement. For those navigating the social fractures and problems experienced on the street, safety is ensured by building webs of communication and trust with people with whom you differ. As I will share in the section called "Anecdote Arising," the road to reconciliation has begun between these two sectors of community experience. It has involved honest, face-to-face conversations, and ceremonies in which we sit down at the table and break bread, rather than suffering as spirits gone fragile through trauma, miscommunication, and breakdown of trust.

In the early 1960s, Rev. Leonard introduced me and my classmates to Michael Harrington's works about poverty and the invisibility of the poor. He opened the doors of the church, hosting a freedom school, where public school students and teachers came to protest the ongoing practice of school segregation. White and Black students attended a virtual school, one that was integrated, for a day of living proof about the value of shared educational lessons amongst peoples of differing origins and racial background.

When I reached my senior year in high school and was on a learning curve regarding the Vietnam War protest movement, Rev. Leonard guided me through the philosophy of conscientious objection, as well assisting me in completing the application to officially obtain that status with the government. The anti-war protest songs of artistes such as Phil Ochs, Pete Seeger and Judy Collins permeated the halls of worship. These experiences, induced through participation at rallies and exposure to the literature and song of peace activists, informed a functional foundation for my anti-war activities, my search for social justice, and ultimately my seeking voice for young people. Martin Luther King, Jr.'s *Stride Toward Freedom* and Malcolm X's biography were typical of our readings and discussions. It was during these times of civil rights and anti-war education that I was trained to adopt the value and practices of conflict resolution and violence reduction. It was this intense training which would be needed for my work on the streets, in today's times of escalating tensions and divide. The skills I developed remain as essential options for rebuilding community bonds.

Action, practiced with sincerity and conducted with deeply serious intention, are essential to the work of social justice. Yet, if not tempered by doses of humor, one's life work becomes unbalanced, less rewarding, and often results in burnout. For all the serious work that Rev. Leonard prepared me for, he occasionally displayed the value of being light-hearted, of inducing laughter, which was just as important to me

Of course, throughout the church period where I received attentive training in becoming more socially conscious, there were also moments of lightheartedness and humor that let me meet Dick Leonard in a different light. One example stands out to me. One day during an early winter excursion (at some point in the mid-1960s; the exact date escapes me), a group of Sunday school students from the Community Church Sunday school, chaperoned by Rev. Leonard, went on an outing to a church retreat in upstate New York. There were plenty of trees and fresh air, and a frozen lake on which to romp. In hindsight, I think this excursion implanted in me a love for taking teens on retreats to campsites in Alpine, New Jersey, and the Ten-Mile River scout camp as a staple for my youth program approach in later years.

At that age, a teen caught up, to a certain degree, in bravado, I was thrilled to show off my strong throwing arm and being a typical show-off. I ran after my mates with glee, hurling snow bombs, often with great accuracy, as they hid behind trees on the edge of the lake. At one point, during my showmanship, as I turned slightly, seeking my next target, I noticed out of the corner of my eye a long and gangly arm whipping an object towards me from behind a tree. (Mr. Leonard, the thrower, was long and slim; the tree was my assailant's perfect cover!) Before I could react, a snowball crashed into my cheek and jaw; only then did I turn in amazement: Rev. Leonard was all smiles. I was in awe of his arm's strength and accuracy, and at the same time in disbelief that such an unassuming and gentle man was the author of such impressive athletic mischief. At that moment, to me, he seemed to be like Bob Gibson, a professional league pitcher for the St. Louis Cardinals, who was famous for giving many a batter a close shave with his blazing fastball. Both the Rev. Leonard and I had a good chuckle, as did my fellow Sunday school peers who no longer had to run from my random pot shots with ice balls.

Parker Palmer, a prolific writer and spiritually practicing educator ,who I have referenced earlier in this book, often talked about the process of educational encounter as being informed not just by method, but by the atmosphere or social climate of the classroom. The process is not just about what is taught, but *how* it is taught. Dick Leonard was always there—a welcoming and reassuring presence. And never afraid to share his humorous takes on life, either through story…or the accuracy of his now storied arm. From the time I started my first youth program in the Heights—and continuing through my many program progressions—I never forgot the importance of these qualities. If we were on a camping trip, I would join the young in our search for firewood, and not just tell them to go get it. I would join them in gathering wood, tell jokes, and invoke laughter. When we scheduled basketball games at the Pit, a ball court in the Heights, and heavy rain had left puddles on the courts, I would get there early, and, as the kids arrived, invite them to help, joining in as a team effort. As we brushed water off the court together, with the youngest ones also joining us, I would turn it into a game in and of itself and share smiles after we congratulated each other for a job well done. If I saw a young staff person struggling with a lesson, the result would not be a write-up, but a walk into the room to offer modeling and encouragement—and I would be welcomed because I was right there. After I shared stories about my foibles as a young student, the children with whom I shared these tales would giggle. Young people in my program occasionally complained about the curious habits of their teachers or having to complete homework lessons after the teacher had failed to adequately teach the lesson. When children would hear me recount stories, such as my having a teacher who would not dismiss the class at the end of the day until he counted all the windows in the room, they would laugh because they understood that even though a student faces times when classroom situations are strange, or unfair, they could still make it through the trying times and succeed. The young in my program might have started a lesson with frowns, but it was the inducement of smiles that got them through their trials of learning by error and correction. My memory is undoubtedly blurred, but I can't recall seeing Rev. Leonard with any frowns, just smiles.

Rev. Leonard is a gentle soul, but never shied away from "exposing scandalous pretensions" (just as Rabbi Heschel had counseled). Dick Leonard's teaching ranged from the traps of gambling cultures to the veil of hidden poverty. The ethical challenge which became increasingly evident to me was his central teaching. His shared wisdom informs us about the obligation of applied citizenship, constructed through our heartstrings. Empathy leads each one of us to discover the core of our identity. Adoption of mindful neighborliness disposes us to open the door of generosity to others in need. Rev. Leonard's counseling provided me an ethical platform on which I could claim my inner gifts and become healthy and wise among people of diverse cultures in neighborhoods across New York City. Richard Leonard motivated me through his powerful personal narrative so insistent on justice. He encouraged and invited me to develop my path through anti-war and civil rights activism, two channels of social justice activism carried on in resistance to the imposing presence of the four catastrophes.

Kurt Tofteland: Escape from the prisons of the mind

The second co-mentor offering lessons to me on the power of storytelling was Curt F. Tofteland. He founded a program in the prisons of Kentucky called Shakespeare Behind Bars. Curt told prisoners and prison observers of the effects of the prison system, saying that despite being seemingly stuck with the conditions of incarceration, even after being released from behind physical bars and unforgiving walls, finding your true voice is the key to finding your freedom. As stated in the Petra Foundation's *Twenty-Fifth Anniversary Handbook*, Curt, who joined the Petra Foundation as a fellow in 2007, would, in prisons throughout the state, enroll "abusers, armed robbers, and murderers as his actors."[426] He focused on prisoners who had little or no hope of release—and even more diminished odds of escaping the recidivism cycle. Curt would counsel his newly found actors that "the past is gone, and all that remains is the present."[427] He would use, in his theatric backdrop, plays written by William Shakespeare, including *The Tempest,* whose central theme was forgiveness. Those who had helped themselves to their own fate would discover the power of forgiveness toward themselves. Their mistakes and transgressions, which had been hidden behind the veils of rage and grief, would yield to gradually understanding one's personal responsibility for having made self-sabotaging choices. By agreeing to transform themselves with acts of courage and engagement with reconciliation and healing, those who had been wedded to the identities of criminal and prisoner would learn to find their inner guidance, latent talent, and supportive allies. They would come to agree to be there for others as good friends.

In 2015, Shakespeare Behind Bars was in its twentieth year. It has since been expanded to multiple prison sites in Kentucky, as well as to two Michigan prisons. As outlined in the Petra Foundation's Twenty-Fifth Anniversary biographical profile of Kurt, the Shakespeare Behind Bars project at Luckett prison in Kentucky comprised "of 34 actors who had received parole, or who served out their sentences, not one returned to prison.... Each had become apprentice magic users, like Prospero in *The Tempest*, who found enough magic in Curt and Shakespeare, to guide themselves toward a different future."[428]

People in Kurt's program transitioned from being identified as prisoners to becoming spokespeople who had become parishioners. Graduates from the Shakespeare program, as is the case of those in Fuller's *March of the Invisibles*, had learned the lessons of the freedom walk by listening to and expressing their voice.

What free people had now come to learn, as had former slaves and suffragists before their time, is that by incorporating the tool of metaphor in finding one's voice, one learns to become visible. Ancestral allies establishing their voice used the tools of Biblical references and song, and analogous comparisons to what privileged founders had identified as the basic cause of democracy. Participants in the Shakespeare Behind Bars program studied their lines and learned to adapt Shakespeare's words and themes. They felt connected to the play and learned to express Shakespeare's ideas in their own words. Some of the ideas included one's need to establish self-respect, to been seen by others for one's authentic self, and developing a method for convincing others, who had been continuously rejecting you, to find the common humanity you shared with them.

Rollo May, a developmental psychologist, and who was a regents professor at UC Santa Cruz in the late 1960's, described one's condition of psychic imprisonment as a schooling process in negative emotions that results in what he called enforced confinement. A theme of his book, called Love and Will, is that enforced confinement, as well as trauma, results in a reduction/

loss of autonomy, and the will/capacity to organize oneself. There results a false movement away from one's original goal, driven by impulse without strategy, and whim without will.[429] I would add that when we commit to constructing and maintaining institutions called prisons, we simultaneously develop invisible trappings of prison consciousness internally.[430]

Michael Schacker, in his book, *Global Awakening*, contrasts differing types of consciousness and institutional practice dependent upon the era. He sees the era, loosely bracketed by the years in the late 1800s until the beginnings of the 21st century as an era he calls the mechanical/industrial era. Mr. Schacker holds that cultural practices, social understanding, and societal institutions underwent radical changes from the previous era, which he calls the medieval era, through interactive relationship with this new form of mechanical/industrial consciousness. With the rise and constructive design of societal institutions, largely guided by the use (and misuse) of scientifically influenced practices, institutions and practices were developed that relied upon the use of assessment, measurement, tracking and control with the desired outcome of achieving a better ordered and productive society. New values were inculcated into individuals, and these same values were used to assess the success of society. The practices put into place to support attainment of these values included IQ testing, measures of each person's productivity on a job, and developing loyalty to a nation-state. A person's rank and status became shaped by their gender, race, and class status.

In this book, I look at the development of the criminal justice system, including jails, prisons, court rooms and the work of public safety agents as a subset of this larger mechanical/industrial paradigm, albeit tragically skewed with bias against peoples of color, and laden with practices and technologies promoting and sustaining extreme levels of violence. In addition to maintaining sinful assaults on the dignity of marginalized and ostracized people, generations of citizens saw their access to opportunity and rights to just practices erased from their lives. Policy-makers who supported these unjust procedures and institutions also set back our progress for reaching the ideals put forth by our nations founders and subsequent social justice advocates.

I define prison consciousness as the socially constructed awareness where oppressors contain and control those seen by them to be inadequate or dangerous. Detainees, prisoners, and others tragically intercepted by the criminal system's unjust practices, through trauma, internally replicate a consciousness where those victimized by these constructs self-identify as impotent, self-sabotaging, and aggressive.[431] When social justice organizers learn to identify and move beyond the limitations of prison consciousness, they more readily join in Dr. King's march toward freedom. At the same time, these social prophets and learning leaders dance with the higher angels of America's nature. Each empowered and empathetic person revels in the dignities of all people and the wealth produced by the beloved community.

In 2006, during my tenure as teen services director for PAL with its IN-STEP program, I was invited to partner with Jeremy Weller, the artistic director of the Grass Market Project from Edinburgh in Scotland. He founded this program and continued to direct it using tools in ways like those developed by the Shakespeare Behind Bars program. He had worked with people in prison, patients in mental hospitals, and teens on the street. What they all had in common was that they had been self-limiting in some way, and had a story to tell, for which they were only partially aware. Even after beginning to identify their inner story, participants needed encouragement and guidance in learning how to express their story. The leadership at the Armory Center and Harlem Center PAL sites, together with Jeremy and his staff from the Grass Market Program, agreed to put together a collaborative theater project. The project was given the title: "This Is the Real." The project goals included training teens in the use of narrative theater, where they would get to share a memory. What teens became moved to tell revealed inner conflict and damaging choices in their lives. In exercising their imagination and newly found storytelling talents, they sought to have audience members know them in more complete ways. Collaboratively, with peer support and the guidance of the Grass Market staff, young people learned the art of improvisational presentation, stage presence, communication, and developing one's inner voice. Each actor kept a journal of their experiences, and the troupe went to theaters to observe other actors exercising their craft.[432]

The process was at times raw, and at times became a stage for spontaneous and tumultuous upsets. The young actors and their drama-production guides persisted, learning to harness the power of their fiercely released emotions together with a disciplined methodology of on-stage delivery. The troupes in the This is the Real program successfully performed in front of neighborhood audiences. Members of the viewing public were often taken aback by the youths' honesty and powerful messaging. One member of the cast, Geronimo Ruiz, told me that after he had developed new communication skills and with the growing confidence in using artistic expression, he was able to reconnect with an estranged family member. Other actors expressed their feelings that stage training and experience helped them become more focused and mature. Some dreamed of pursuing other opportunities in acting, but all adopted a new attitude that it was their right to have their voice heard and to step on to the stage of life. John Zeiler, a PAL board member who was the project's advocate when meeting with city-wide leadership for PAL, and who was generously invested in this program, contributed this message after closely observing the program's progress for seven weeks: "Many of the stories presented on the stage were ones owned by the actors, and they learned to feel comfortable presenting them on a stage. We have seen firsthand the power of narrative storytelling to transform the lives of young people, and to bring people together in a community where its members transcend social barriers."[433]

Anodea Judith is a counselor and a writer who has developed an approach utilizing methods of tapping into what she called spiritually based but bodily connected energetically constructed centers called chakras. There are several types of chakras, representing seven levels of universal human experience, from the balance and grounding near the feet and the compassionate outreach of the heart, to the connections to the spirit world putting a person in contact with the intelligence of the greater universe. In mastering a connection to and understanding of each chakra, a person learns to transform themselves beyond previously perceived limitations. In my work with teen empowerment, and their essential need to develop a voice and become heard, I have found myself drawn to Ms. Judith's words, describing the fifth chakra, associated with the throat and our innate drive to be seen for our presence and to master the power of communication. Ms. Judith in her book, *The Wheels of Life*, describes the role of the fifth chakra: "Communication is how consciousness extends itself from one place to another. Communication is an essential key to accessing inner planes and for using our multi-dimensional mental levels. Sound, rhythm, vibration, words. Powerful rulers of our lives. Using them, responding to them, creating them anew each day, we are the subjects to rhythm upon rhythm, endlessly interweaving to create a fabric we can all experience."[434]

Kurt Tofteland and Jeremy Weller effected these triumphant gains with creative theater projects. I have also seen teens obtain joy by obtaining meaningful change in the civic realm. As shared in "The Orphan" chapter, Miriam managed desired changes by finding her confident, expressive voice. I experienced this again while helping in pushing the Teens on Board campaign forward. Pablo Vasquez, who had started at the Armory PAL as an IN-STEP intern, was then, upon graduation, appointed as an adult group leader in the after-school program. He was admired by his younger peers and staff members alike. He proactively assisted teens and adults learning new skills and having lots of fun. Shy by nature, and hesitant with his public speaking, he volunteered to work as a youth coordinator for the teens on the community boards campaign. He met with groups of teens from PAL and neighboring programs such as the Washington Heights and Inwood Teen Council. The more he spoke, the greater his confidence became, and the more the desired outcome of our campaign gained traction. As a result of his efforts and influence, we saw lots more of signed petitions and many more volunteer organizers. In the world of civic change, the advocacy stump is the stage.

I now introduce an organizer from the Asian-American community, Mitch Wu, who was a leader in getting teens from diverse backgrounds within the Asian and South Pacific communities feel confident in becoming civic advocates. Under the guidance of Mitch Wu, teen leadership teams became effective in changing deficient policies practiced by the New York City Department of Education. The advocacy campaign, led by Asian high-school students, would bring the fallacies of what is called the Asian Model Myth into greater public awareness.[435] Under Mitch Wu's guidance, teen leaders in the Asian Student Advocacy Program (ASAP) successfully advocate when meeting with members of the NYC City Council. The Council created advisories and regulations calling upon the Department of Education (DOE) to hire more Asian-American guidance counselors. These directives also called upon the DOE to implement trainings so that teachers and their supervisors would understand the diverse cultures and nuances of habits within the Asian diaspora.

Mitch Wu: Leader of The Asian Student Advocacy Project

ASAP is a high-school student leadership program that has been established by the Coalition of Asian American Children and Families (CACF). Although the term Asian-American has, in the American imagination, created a monolithic conception of these peoples, CACF represents people of Asian and Pan Pacific origins from more than 67 backgrounds. These include those who live in places as diverse as the islands of Micronesia, the Philippines, Japan, Korea, and India. China has dozens of categories within its borders alone. Getting Americans and policy makers to move beyond the colonially derived, one-ethnic-type-size-fits-all viewpoint is one part of the myth-busting inherent to CACF's task. In addition to this takedown of stereotype, CACF has also had to address the myth of the universally supersmart, affluent Asian who has little need for societal help because he (or she) can adequately take care of himself (or herself). Adherence to this misconception is called the "Asian model myth." Creating stories convenient for exploiting the marginalized and the vulnerable is as old as colonialism and imperial practice itself. In the 1980s, when the old story claiming that success was dependent solely on individual initiative again formed in the public imagination, the picture of the Asian being better off on their own also took off.

If we look at a slice of demographics for Chinese immigrants to the United States during the 1980s— there are multitudes of ethnic subgroups from this nation. Our preconceived notion and limiting stereotypic suggestion about the nature of a Chinese person as being monolithic in origin or cultural character is not real. More than half of all Chinese working women (ages 16 to 64) in New York City were garment workers. In 1983, over 70 per cent of garments sewn in New York City were my immigrant women. In sum, they averaged 6.5 years of schooling; only 22 per cent finished high school. Although immigrants from Taiwan had a high proportion of college graduates (four times the national average), the reality for immigrants arriving from the poorest of areas in China was significantly different.[436] Yet the availability of assistance to Chinese families, beginning with their schooling, was scant when compared to other ethnic groups. Even when the U.S. Department of Education provided some assistance, it did not have an adequate number of personnel who were trained in Chinese languages, nor were there sufficient staff trained in understanding with sensitivity the nuances of the culture. In 2013, I was introduced to the civic work of CACF's high school program (ASAP). I was also introduced to its inspirational leader, Mitch Wu.

Mitch Wu developed an interactive workshop training program in which high-school students, using PowerPoint presentations, oral testimony, and theater games such as role reversal would lead presentations and trainings. At the time I was introduced to ASAP, Asians and Pacific Asians represented 15 per cent of New York City's population, with one in every two families living in poverty and one in five not graduating high school at all. Twenty-seven per cent of Asian households were led by parents who spoke no English.

After learning about and presenting the real stories of Asian and Pacific Asian peoples, challenges and obstacles worked on several fronts. In addition to providing educational and social assistance to its participants—as well as psychological and school-to-career counseling—ASAP developed a set of strategies they labeled the Campaign Bridge. Its elements, embedded in strategies of advocacy and municipal institutional education, included asking the city to develop standards to improve the ethno-sensitive capabilities of school counselors, increase the numbers of Asian counselors on boards, and increase the total numbers of guidance counselors working in schools. At the time, the typical school had more corrections officers in the building than guidance counselors. ASAP leaders also asked that a more comprehensive and nuanced reference guide be developed, taking into consideration true demographics and the multitudinous variety of needs. (One example demonstrating the variety of needs among Asian and Pacific Asian peoples is that there are more than 300 languages spoken amongst the many nationalities of these peoples.)

During 2017–2018, students extended their ask, advocating before the New York City Council, requesting their intervention to bring about the ask. Using effective presentations, students were able to get the city council to act with the New York City Department of Education. In addition to the goals, ASAP leaders joined with a broader Asian civic advocacy effort to honor Fred Korematsu, who along with thousands of Japanese Americans had been unjustly and tragically interned in labor camps during World War II. Mr. Korematsu, his family, and followers advocated for this honor for years, and on January 30, 2018, the New York City Council officially proclaimed a day of honor for Fred. Twenty-three students who were enrolled in the ASAP program that school year made a difference.

The need to develop civic skills and a commitment to the larger good was eloquently spoken to by one of ASAP's high-school spokespeople, Dennis Yu: "Changes begin with me, and if I want to be an advocate, I need to start making changes happen in my own school, community, and home."[437] Mr. Korematsu taught, by example, that taking responsibility for healing part of America's shadow,[438] the falsely imposed imprisonment of innocent and loyal citizens, was his for the taking. His extended family and community supporters persisted by taking personal responsibility through social action, and the promise of democracy became one step closer to being fully realized.

I first met Mitch Wu after he joined the coalition fighting to ensure teens a seat on community boards. He participated in the fight and brought his troops into the cause, readily stepping up as one of the inner members on the steering committee. What became readily apparent to me as we collaborated was how articulate he was, able to grasp and summarize the immediate actions that were necessary, and to keep sight of the endgame. He remained readily available to us and easily accessible. Mitch was there for us when we presented to the city council's Operations Committee, seeking to move our request for a council resolution of support along to the full council—and he was at the full council meeting to testify in person. I also viewed the end-of-the-school-year presentations made by his ASAP leadership, at which they shared the vision, goals, and accomplishments they had seen come to fruition.

As a Teens on Board committee member, I shared a civic relationship with Mitch in a way that paralleled what was expressed by one of the ASAP leaders, Nada Almagar, who had served with ASAP from 2017 to 2020. Ms. Almagar spoke to the value of being acknowledged and affirmed in civic dialogue: "ASAP exposed me to environments of powerful people who are still willing to listen to our experiences and ideas."[439] Her comment reminds me of what cultural commentators and political analysts referred to as the parade of invisibles, for example, abolitionists and suffragists, among others, becoming "visible" once they found their voice and had experienced it being heard. Each year, the ASAP closing ceremonies incorporated testimony and presentations by teen leaders and showed me that the transformation from invisibility to visibility takes a lot of focused and persistent work. In closing out this peek at ASAP, I next share three lessons learned.

The first concerns the value of using a peer group learning approach when learning about civic and political processes, and how to create a team of advocates in pursuit of social justice. Ina Claire Gabler and Michael Schroeder implement a curricular approach described in their book, *Seven Constructive Methods for the Secondary Classroom*. Ms. Gabler and Mr. Schroeder refer to the seemingly magical approach of co-teaching and learning as "invisible teaching."[440] The authors cite studies showing that the peer approach, when contrasted with the traditional teacher-centered approach, enhances learning for higher-order thinking and understanding, as opposed to the memorization of details, dates, and deliriously intoxicating "facts." Additional studies also show the process results in the encouragement of individuals believing that what he or she has to offer is meaningful to the group. Rather than simply raising one's hand and being complimented for providing a correct, "official" answer, a participant's contributions are carefully listened to, reflected upon, and incorporated into the authority of a peer-centered decision-making body. As Mitch has prioritized to his students and in conversations with me, what is paramount for designing and implementing school curricula and guidance counselor services is taking the issue of linguistic isolation into account. Amongst the sixty-seven nationalities within the Asian and South Pacific diaspora, each has its individual cultures, languages, and social mores. To have educational and guidance intervention become more sensitive and appropriate to student and parental need, Department of Education staff need thorough training in cultural diversity. The Asian American Advocacy Project students and staff were able to successfully lobby the City of New York in addressing this crucial issue.

In orchestrating this type of process on a day-to-day classroom basis, Mitch's articulate guidance—and the fact that he established himself as an accessible presence—has been testified to during ASAP's annual gatherings by high-school students from dozens of campuses. Mitch also demonstrates that his leadership is, in a word, amazing; in some ways it is comparable to being a conductor at a concert. In addition to coming from a variety of school campuses, the personnel of ASAP are as diverse as the population of the Asian and pan-Pacific diaspora. The ASAP environment is a wonderful microcosm of the multi-tiered fabric of constituency making up the heart of the city of New York.

The second learned lesson is alluded to in the sourcebook *Open Minds to Equality,* which was written by Nancy Schniedewind and Ellen Davidson and published by Rethinking Schools. In facilitating the opening of minds to the subtle forces entrapping us in institutions which enforce inequalities and roadblocks for opportunity, we open ourselves to a horizontally based sharing of power and authority in governance. One of these deceitfully discriminatory elements is the perpetuation of a false sense of superiority among favored subgroups in a vertically privileged society. In their book, the authors of *Open Minds to Equality* cite multiple examples of these discriminatory elements, one of which is that boys and girls share the socially constructed belief that boys' ideas about science are better than girls' ideas.[441] As referenced previously in my book, Dr. Elworthy refers to this process as barely under-the-surface embedded false beliefs being mistaken for perennial truths. Political and economic decisions made in the United States of America institutionalize privileged male access to scientific education and careers. The prevalence and persistence of these practices reinforce the belief that the existing stratified value of opinion, organized through gender bias, is based on the nature of whether one is in a superior position of authority as a male or an inferior one as a female. The Asian model myth is implanted within a body of falsely constructed perception, which represents all Asian people as universally highly intelligent and financially well off.

A second, closely related element reinforced in anecdotal form in *Open Minds To Equality* is that when a person is habitually exposed to such misleading stereotypes, that person develops a feeling, commonly disguised in cultural bias, that the false belief is naturally credible.

Mitch guided his ASAP cohort members at leadership trainings in becoming credible messengers who are well-informed and confident in their stated positions on an issue. His lessons were instructive and delivered to his students both with mental clarity and intensely felt purpose. He would continuously reinforce the need for his students to cite reasoned evidence and carefully structured inquiry used to bust unfounded stereotypes. At the same time, Mitch is a labor-intensive listener. His young trainees, even with all the diversity of their backgrounds, practice his persuasive lessons of giving strongly constructed argument balanced with open listening. The narrative construction of a monolithic Asian is an obstacle each of his pupils must face, deconstruct, and expose. At the same time, Mitch welcomes being instructed by the authors of this type of experience, each according to their unique encounter, all in pursuit of demanding full respect for the integrity of who they really are.

I address the third element used by Mitch by referring to *Bulletin 111* put out by the National Council for the Social Studies. In this journal, a task force chaired by Susan A. Adler proposes "a framework for teaching, learning and assessing a national curriculum for standards to be established for Social Studies."[442] Here, I reference a section of this information and training guide in which they outline "knowledges, practices, and products" to be used in support of "narrowing the gap between civic ideals and practices, so that they become more congruent." The authors propose that "learning how to apply civic ideals to inform civic action is essential to participation in democracy and support for the common good."[443]

Mitch guided his civic-minded students, as they, in reciprocal ways, guided him. He introduced processes critical to reforming political malpractice. These included developing a strategy of structured inquiry. What was instrumental in his methodology involved his guidance, not to just recite what they thought to be correct answers, but to develop thought-provoking questions and secondary questions to further clarify points of agreement and disagreement. Mitch's students learned to investigate sources, verify bodies of evidence, and work with those in power so that they jointly agreed to bring the democratically civic ideals of fairness and respect into the reformed practices of New York City municipal institutions of education and governance. Mitch, the mindfully mannered muse, inspired his agents for social justice to temper their passions with reasoned practice. As a result, students were able to see their personal experiences reflected in successfully obtained common goals. As stated by Annu Lu, another ASAP participant, "Initially I saw the conversation I had with ASAP on issues as being relevant for me. By becoming aware of other people's experiences, this became a conversation about everyone."[444] All for one, and one for all.

John Kurland: My father, my primary role model for the rebel, and storyteller.

I was raised by a father, John Kurland, who loved to describe the unusual foibles of families, friends, and workers he had come to know by taking center-stage at our household dining room table. In support of political viewpoints, he read copiously and conducted a great deal of research. In addition to what he learned from the written word, he possessed a natural sense for the predicaments and pride shared by those of the blue-collar working class. He saw himself, and those among his socioeconomic class, as being outsiders in relation to gaining access to the benefits promised by the American dream. Obtaining and maintaining strategic advantage for gaining access to financial opportunity (and then maintaining it) was contingent upon being involved in protecting the place of unions. He worked extra hours to earn enough to keep pace with family expenses.

Just as the stories offered by my father influenced my view of the world, so did the stories given to him shape his expectations about who he is, and what he had to face in society. Tyler Anbinder, an American historian, wrote a historical overview covering the origins and lives of immigrants in New York City called *City of Dreams*, which I previously referenced for demographics and the history of immigration by Asians. I now reference his description of the passage of Russian Jews from their homeland to America at the beginning of the 1900s. In his narrative, he paints a picture of pain and sacrifice endured by these pioneers arriving on American soil. Mr. Anbinder cites poverty, the relentless pressure of anti-Semitism, and the need for organizational resistance as central themes that initiated the passage from Russia to America.

As cited by Mr. Anbinder: "In 1903, a pogrom near Odessa left tens of thousands of Jews homeless and resulted in the murder of fifty people. In the official accounts put forward by Russian authority, it was stated that Jews themselves were responsible for what happened."[445] My paternal grandparents lived near Odessa and told these stories to my father and his six siblings. As Mr. Anbinder continues, he describes the psyche and social orientation of Russians toward Jews, relating Russia's official story after a pogrom in Balta in 1882. Mr. Anbinder shares an account of the aftermath of the pogrom: "[E]verything that had belonged to the Jews had been demolished, destroyed or sacked. No buildings remained standing other than a few walls. The entire Jewish population lacked clothing, furniture, and beds."[446] The author then continues, giving the Russian account regarding why Jews were the ones responsible: "[W]ho takes the land, the woods, the taverns out of your hand, The Jews, wrote one socialist broadside, wherever you look, wherever you go, the Jews are everywhere. The Jew curses you, cheats you, and drinks you blind."[447] So, in other words, both Russian authority and organized socialist resistors shared the same narrative about the place and responsibility of Jews.

In the false narratives about resistance, such as acts of counter actions exercised by Jewish people during the Holocaust and Blacks during slavery, the unsubstantiated and stereotyped storyline was that there was a lack of resistance by these oppressed peoples. Thanks to the sharing of personal narrative and updated historical accounts, these insidious storylines have been revised and updated to show the magnitude for standing up, and the heroism exhibited by the oppressed. This was also true for Jews who organized populist uprisings in reaction to the pogroms. As cited by Mr. Anbinder: "[A]s a result of public opinion pressure, the Tsar signed an October 1905 after granting civil rights to all Russians, including Jews."[448]

By 1905, my grandparents decided to immigrate to the United States; the family arrived in various boats over the course of a few years. They initially settled in Bristol, Rhode Island, where my grandfather, Isaac Kurland, worked in a shoe factory seven days a week, twelve hours each day. He was told by his supervisors that if he did not show up on any given Sunday, he should not bother returning to work the next Monday. After a few years, the family relocated to the Lower East Side of New York City. My father had been born in Bristol on January 26, 1912, the sixth child among his siblings. Shortly after his birth, the Kurland family moved from Bristol to New York City.

By 1929, the year of the great financial crash, my father was 17 years old. His family, poor, and on the margins of being able to establish a stable economic livelihood, became dependent upon his also working. The jobs he procured were obtained through arduous and long periods of effort and did not last but for short periods of time. Jobs during the Depression paid poorly, but this lot was to define his life through the 1930s and into the early 1940s.[449] He was drafted into the U.S. army during World War II. He dutifully sent most of what he earned as an enlisted soldier home to support his family. He was not engaged in active combat during his tour of duty in the South Pacific and Japan, after the Japanese had surrendered. He did, however, see the aftermath of war: the devastated towns...the dispirited people, trying to pull themselves together. These included those whose homelands had been invaded—places like New Guinea and Australia—as well as those residing in Japan. In my father's accounts of this period of his life, he included the Japanese as producing engaging art and aesthetically pleasing environments. He never failed to let us know what good people these folks were and how he had connected to their pain as well as his own. I have no doubt that my repeatedly being exposed to his oral history and viewpoints directly influenced my choice of the narrative edit I put together in my high-school presentation.

During my childhood, and into my teen years, my parents continued to live the life common to those of the blue-collar working class. My father procured a union job with Rheingold Breweries in Brooklyn; he worked in a secure and relatively decently paying job until his retirement in the late 1970s. My mother also worked, beginning in the 1960s, initially as a substitute childcare aide. After a few years she obtained a permanent position at the North Queens Childcare Center in a housing project in Flushing, New York.

Even with two incomes, life in my family was lived pretty much paycheck to paycheck. The family lived comfortably, but always had to budget carefully to meet monthly expenses. However, as my siblings and I have bemusedly looked back, we remember certain days when our lunchboxes contained two slices of bread spread with oleomargarine, and our refrigerator had little more than a quart of milk and a half-used jar of Grey Poupon mustard. My parents lived purposefully, dedicated to providing the basics, and supporting and validating their children's path in following whatever felt true to our hearts.

Under my father's morally measured guidance, and in his telling of story to me, he instilled certain basic themes that became central to my youth services perspective. He shared pictures and books that pointed to the amazing place natural life held on planet Earth and beyond, from the organization of the planets in the solar system to the significant place of microbes.

I recall vividly an incident taking place during my early teens: I was getting ready to chase a cockroach with a can of Raid. Upon spotting my attempt, my father grabbed the can out of my hands, then went to get a dustbin. He carefully swept the insect into the bin, carrying it to a rock garden just outside the door of our garden apartment in Parkway Village, Queens. He came back in, speaking to me in a soft and serious tone, and let me know that the cockroach has as much right to be here on Earth or in our apartment, as I had as a human being. Initially, I found my father's perspective to be somewhat amusing and confusing, but I respectfully adhered to his counsel. Over the years, this instructional episode helped to inform my environmentally oriented political outlook and my infusing a naturalist philosophy into my socio/political approaches to providing service. Participants in my youth programs engaged in numerous weekend visits to enjoy and experience natural environments, complete with forests, foliage, dirt trails, bubbling streams, and the background sounds of chirping birds and croaking frogs. Our most frequent and requested excursions were to Camp Alpine, New Jersey, and to Ten-Mile River in upstate New York. During the early evenings, when the light of the moon and the stars reflected upon the leaves, while I was sitting alongside my fellow volunteers and young people, there were many moments in which the sense of silent awe in the eyes of my fellow observers connected me to my father's counsel, and my young people to the comfort and wisdom of the forest.

My father posited his dissenting viewpoints in the face of ferocious verbal critique by his friends. After World War II, anti-communism's narrative displaced the primacy of the moral imperative supporting the outcomes of the New Deal. During the early 1950s, a senator named Joe McCarthy, with his unjustified attacks on citizens with differing political beliefs seemed to stand democratic principles on its head. Those with whom he debated had forgotten the early struggles of unions. During this decade, and into the 1960s, many people shifted their concern for union rights to a focus on the dangers of communist aggression. In a climate of fear and distrust, in addition to the questioning of the validity of union organizing, what arose was a revival of racial intolerance and antipathy toward immigrants. People who questioned the tactics of union leaders, and those who feared people of different origins, conflated the intentions of those seeking social justice with their supposedly being secret agents sworn to turn America into a communist slave-state. Friends, who had organized with my father on behalf of unions, now ceased to question the unquestionable prerogative of those in privileged positions and power. Those who questioned the fights for economic equity and racial justice put social justice organizers in a box in which they were labeled as dupes to communist manipulation or who were overly sympathetic to un-American causes.[450]

When John had taken my mother to visit the monuments in Washington, D.C, during their honeymoon in the spring of 1948, he also took her to the neglected neighborhoods suffering in the shadows of architectural beauty and subject to denial of the benefits inscribed in their marble. He counseled that this contradiction, if not reconciled, would be a national scar of perpetual shame.

In my youth, my father would take me to the library to study not only the majesty and mystery of microbes, volcanoes, and the nature of the planets in our solar system but he also introduced me to the works of Thomas Paine, including *Common Sense* and the *Rights of Man*. In these works, a nation's co-founder inspired perseverance for staying the course of independence by inducing those who had been outsiders to change the narrative about those who owned an inherent right to life, liberty, and the pursuit of happiness. Paine questioned the validity of unquestioned assumptions about the unchanging nature of social order. Mr. Paine's insightfully sarcastic critique was especially pointed in proposing the need to revolt against the imposition of remotely imposed authority. Paine would not only challenge and insult the arbiters of British royal authority, but also American loyalists whose political dispositions lent them to be more favorable towards limited democracy. My father, no doubt inspired by the writings of Paine, was uncomfortable with and disparaged a partial democracy in which elites denied rights to fellow patriots based on gender, race, and class. These early-onset impressions have become foundations for my later political development.

Through guided study and storytelling, my father inspired me and each of my siblings. He encouraged us to construct our life path based on our developing interests and talent. John would not shy away from offering his sage advice regarding what he saw as career paths for his children. However, he would not insist that his opinions were the final word, nor discount our choices. He had an intuitive sense when it came to allowing his children to define and choose their path. He guided us, but he would never misdirect us based on his personal viewpoints nor his pursuit of his own truth. Thomas Paine wrote scathing critique about the inherent wisdom of monarchs. My father would share his wisdom, but not impose it as absolute or as conditional to our determining our life course.

My dad would take me on visits to the library, where we pored through books on volcanoes and microbes. One day, without announcement, he took me to Cooper Union College and suggested I inquire about studying to be an engineer. Although I was not interested in pursuing earth science nor becoming a biologist or engineer, some of the principles we read about together remained with me. The contours of place would become important to me as a critical factor for respecting the importance of attachment to the spaces people inhabited. Respecting the ground walked on became honored by me as representing a source of identity. When people with whom I collaborated sought improvements to communal space, they did so to help future generations, and in honor of generations before them who had celebrated on these same grounds. My father pointed out to me the importance of basic biological principals, such as the interactions between small entities—for example, the way cells and organs use two-way communication to enhance survival.

One pillar in my approach with managing teen empowerment programs was to have young people learn to honor everyday people as unsung heroes. contributing to the successful practice of democracy at the community level. Local activists were modest people, working under the radar of wider forums of public attention, such as newspaper stories and television profiles. However, by offering their small gifts of public service, their acts became central to improving the lives of their friends and neighborhood families. Humble and unselfish acts, such as coaching a younger peer having difficulties with managing emotions learn to identify sources of stress, and then take personal responsibility for adjusting, were huge in the lives of emotionally conflicted children. His friends lived by modest means yet held on to big dreams and large ideas. Two of his friends who changed my course life included Bob Lynch, a very tall man who was married to a dwarf. He would, on his visits to our home, give me bundles of old issues of the *Nation* magazine, introducing me to progressive political critique not available in school textbooks or in popular films. The second set of friends were Miriam and Karl Klapper, who introduced me to the anti-war movement in the beginning stages of the conflict with Vietnam. They also coaxed me to join a local chapter of the American Friends Service Committee, set up in East Harlem. It was here that I had my first experience as a peer mentor to younger children. As I further studied universal consciousness through the lens of seeing all people as part of one human tribe, I connected to the role of using energy when addressing issues of the world. While those living in fear and practicing the art of separation might choose division and building barriers of misunderstanding as one way to use of energy, I was guided on a different path that honored inclusion of all. I was influenced to look for connections across difference as a source of appreciation for life.

As I recall again that day with my roach encounter and surrendering the can of Raid, I also make a connection between the sanctity of respecting life for all, and the central application of this precept to social relationships. As is counseled in the basic precepts of Buddhism, whether you are engaging with nature or peoples from backgrounds differing from your own, first do no harm to others, honor all life, and take action that is beneficial to others. John Kurland, in his life, walked the talk. As my youth services career progressed over the years, I had tried my best to do the same.

This is what rebels do. They change stories that are destructive for oneself and others. Rebels transmit new stories that promote healing instead of hatred, and informed interrelationships rather than isolation. In a rebel's urgent work for changes, a place for you and me at the table of empowering dialogue is essential.

Coach Dave Crenshaw: My rebel-partner through 28 years of teen empowerment service.

I now get you to meet my primary co-mentor, with whom I still consult today, Coach David Crenshaw. I was introduced to Coach Dave during my early days of youth organizing in the Heights. What I now realize is that in meeting Coach Dave, and beginning to do youth agency work with him, I would be starting a long-term partnership with a point man who understood a young person's message derived from their own point of view. Coach Dave, himself a compelling storyteller and compassionate companion, has an endless appetite for listening to stories expressed by young people, using their authentically derived vision about themselves as a guide for assisting them with decisions. He also engages in attentive conversation with his close friends and allies. He has become not just my civic ally, but a best friend during the decades we spent providing youth services. As I eventually came to learn, Coach Dave's philosophy about the inherent goodness of people and their right to life were remarkably aligned to what my father had taught me. My father and Coach Dave were born in different eras, and they were from different backgrounds. However, what they share is a common philosophy about every individual's right to live by their own story. Dave's practices and perspective have helped to cement a brotherly bond between us—a bond that endures, no matter the distant stages upon which we have worked, to this day.

Dave had his own journeys and course of civic development, part of which I share here. Dave's parents instilled in him the habits of being open and honest with others, and for keeping commitments to communal engagement that are practiced with virtue. By *virtue,* I mean that when intervening in the life of another person, it is essential to recognize their integrity even as they make mistakes, and not to introduce an opportunistic agenda in lieu of acting in the next person's best interests.

Coach Dave's father, Richard, introduced me to Dave in 1984, just prior to my launching my first uptown youth program. I had come to meet Richard in the early 1980s while serving as a co-chair with him at the Audubon Reform Democrats. He served the club by expanding its circle from beyond a core of anti-war Democrats to one that addressed the needs of multicultural residents. He helped to expand the club's leadership corps to include those who were in the trenches of social justice, which included the right to safe and affordable housing, access to quality health care, and ensuring enough seats for senior citizens in need of support services. He had an open ear with which he carefully considered people's opinions, responding with a soft yet persuasive voice, which he used to create reconciliation amongst activists with strongly worded and opposing viewpoints. He was welcome into the conference rooms of Democratic Party leaders and afforded a space in community decision-making for credible messengers from grassroots organizations. He strongly supported progressive ideas underlying social and political policies, while tempering his expression of these thoughts with respectful tolerance for difference.

When I shared with Richard my concerns about having little experience with community-based youth services, he let me know that he had a reliable person with direct knowledge of both our community and the needs of young people, who might be willing to help. Richard proposed that I meet with his son, David. In a parlor at the Paradise Baptist church, which had often offered its space for community meetings, Dave and I introduced ourselves and dialogued about each of our own experiences. I believe David recognized me as green—but authentically wanting to do the right thing. He agreed to advise me, and to provide the support of teen volunteers. I refer to this meeting as one in which a hero of the Heights met Mr. Rogers.

Dave's mother, Gwen Crenshaw, was a co-founder of the Discovery Rooms for Children childcare agency. Its principles were guided by those that had been developed at Goddard College, which emphasized both the need for social reform and the need to provide child-centered approaches sensitive to each child's social, emotional, and cognitive needs. Gwen led from a spiritual center and was sensitive to each child's and parents' spiritual space. A civic partner of mine, Alan Shulman, who became involved in later years with our Teens on Board campaign, relayed to me, in the form of a historical remembrance, how Gwen practiced principles of child-care, which included maintaining respect for children no matter where they were at mentally and socially. In her dealings with adults, she still utilized these same principles, even for folks she did not know personally.[451]

In the early 1980s, Mr. Shulman had been a social studies teacher at George Washington High School, located on the northeastern fringes of Washington Heights. He was also attuned to—and involved with—the work of our local school board for Community District #6. At the time, Gwen Crenshaw was president of the board. A president of a school board presided over meetings. If a board had to conduct a vote, such as hiring and firing school principals, and it resulted in a tie, the president would cast the tie-breaking vote. At one of these meetings, she presided over a contentious meeting that posed ethical challenges regarding the board's actions. A teacher in one of the district schools had come to the attention of the board as being gay. A resolution was on the table to have the teacher fired because of his sexual preference, which at the time had come to be falsely associated with representing a threat to children's well-being. The resolution was supported by some board members, even by those who had been radical in their approach to educational processes and the pursuit of social justice. Ms. Crenshaw, who was also a devout member of a Baptist Church (which was not exactly a leading voice for protecting gay men at that time), stoutly refused to have the board pass the resolution. Gwen Crenshaw proudly proclaimed, and stuck to her opinion, that a person's chosen identity, which is a personal choice and a free expression of who that person is, should never be the basis by which others devalue that person. The only thing that counts is a teacher's performance. The resolution was introduced in the throes of intolerance—which became stillborn by Ms. Crenshaw's persistence in upholding the rights of human dignity.[452] Now, after I have shared these brief profiles of Dave's parents, I begin with a short introduction about Dave's life.

Coach Dave had been accepted to Hunter College High School as a member of its first co-ed class. When he learned that, he was accepted for admission to Hunter, Dave initially resisted attending the school. He had agreed to take the admissions test, under the guidance of his parents, and with prodding by his teacher, Mr. Robinson. As is the case with so many people, both old and young, he had felt comfortable socially with his circle of friends. He was hesitant about making a change. Dave's parents and Mr. Robinson listened to his concerns and gently nodded. They then prodded persuasively, and Dave agreed to make the move to, what for him would be, a brand-new world. Dave was, and is gregarious and curious, and it did not take long for him to adjust and to foster a set of new friends. As he engaged with classmates at Hunter High School, he learned to turn those who originally had been unknown to him, and different from him (the student body was almost universally White) into friends. By stepping across what could have been imposing boundaries, Dave became motivated to modify the story he had known about educational settings and who he would welcome into his social circle. He came to see himself as being a person comfortable with making friends even with those who initially had been strangers. Dave was not only a member of the first matriculating Hunter College High School class to include males, but he also was the only new student from uptown Manhattan. Dave entered the Hunter College High School campus holding tightly to his identity as a proud Black man, while becoming buddies with proud young men and women from backgrounds different from his own. He began developing relationships with diverse students, not in spite of racial and national background differences but with curiosity and acceptance for them because of their differences.

One of Dave's close classmates was Cynthia Nixon, who as a high-school student was leading a campaign to allow a high-school club for gays and lesbians. (Ms. Nixon later achieved fame as an actress on the television series *Sex and the City*. According to a local story, Dave, being a close colleague of hers, taught Ms. Nixon to dance). Dave, sensitive to the importance of pride in one's African American hetero identity, leapt into the cause of establishing a gay and lesbian high-school club. He felt that if Blacks, Latinos, and women could have their clubs, then it was correct for gays and lesbians to have the same. As was the case with his mother at that contentious school board meeting, for Dave this was a moral imperative. After a campaign of fierce student advocacy, the adult leadership at Hunter College High School agreed to adopt, and later embraced, the right for gay and lesbian students to have a club of their own.[453]

Shortly after graduating from Hunter High School, Dave established himself as a director of his own youth program he named the Dreamers. After I established the Southern Heights youth program in 1984, Dave quickly became my trusted colleague. He became not only a professional associate, but also a friend whom I identified as having a devotion to youth service, and a management style with a distinctive flavor that was all his own. I share here three elements of his management style.

The first element is that as I worked more closely with Dave, he reminded me of my dad's ability to establish his presence in a room. With Dave, as had been true for my father, his voice filled all the available space in the room, including the nooks and crannies. At the same time, he engaged his audience with sensitive understanding about who they are. As a speaker, he made his voice readily apparent while connecting to his audience. Appreciation for his message became indicated by thralls of laughter. These reverberations of joy were a sign of mutual understanding. Coach Dave's voice is like my father's, but with even stronger amplification. Dave's voice dominated not just a room, but all the buildings three-quarters of the way down the block. His projection was closer to that of Stentor, the mythological figure whose voice filled entire atmospheres but whose message was clear and welcomed. Even as members of Dave's audience processed his volume, he led them through a series of "aha" moments, when ideas that had befuddled them earlier suddenly achieved clarity. When all is said and done, joyfulness is the quality that defines the relationship between Coach Dave and his young participants.

About five years ago, I reconnected with an Uptown Dreamer alumnus named Jackie Hurt. She had been a teen in the 1980s, and in addition to being a Dreamer member, she also attended the Southern Heights program almost every day. When I ran into Jackie at a special event sponsored by Manhattan Borough President Gale Brewer in 2010 or so, she shared her memories of being led by Coach Dave and me. Jackie told me: "You and Dave showed me that you always loved us, and we loved you too."[454] Today Jackie practices in the social work field. Dave's messaging to the young taught them that it is important to be compassionate with oneself, and at the same time equally essential to be compassionate with others.[455]

The second element of Dave's style is that although he is, when reflecting upon his mission and operating his programs, serious about his work, he uses playtime and celebration promoting joy as a method for getting his message across.

When Dave shared an anecdote about his life, or when a young Dreamer participant listened to one of his Dreamer program stories, you could always hear the accompaniment of laughter as the story progressed. Even when he was expressing a story with an important lesson, the channels of communication were opened through his use of amusing anecdotes. Dave would also lighten up the serious atmosphere of instructive workshops, infusing chants and songs to ensure that programming designed with merit would also include its fair share of merriment. While walking a trail on a camping trip, under the heat of summer, Dave would have his troops pause under the shelter of a tree, break out water and fruit, and tell a story taking his audience's minds far away from the blazing of the sun. The walk to a destination would always seem more tolerable.[456]

Dave's style as a narrator is aptly portrayed by Carolyn Myss' archetypal description of the Storyteller, as "one who relies on foolishness but with wisdom, who accepts mistakes as pathways to success, and inspires one to retell the tale of life with acceptance and love, so that what comes to pass is what one once thought to be impossible."[457] As is the case with so many in our underserved communities, the youths that Dave works with, after being subjected to negative stereotyping and, too often, dark expectations, learn to internalize these voices and to harshly criticize themselves. Dave named his program the Uptown Dreamers because, while guiding his participants along practical pathways, he also had them focus on working the dream rather than jerking themselves with diminishing expectations. Whenever one of his young people did something in error while attempting a task and started to come down hard on themselves, Coach Dave reminded them that one of his nicknames was "the master of mistakes"—meaning one who uses whatever has gone wrong to get back on the horse and move on.

A third element inherent to Coach Dave's mentoring approach is the practice of guiding his student athletes to look at sports, not through the lens of scores and statistics, but rather as a metaphor for life. In his talks, he asks his players to consider themselves valuable teammates not in association with the points scored in a specific game, but rather in relation to whether they had developed a new skill, such as dribbling the basketball with their non-dominant hand or learning to look to pass the ball instead of dribbling in circles or into defensive traps. He also asks that each player be a coach and an enthusiast for all players on their team. Learning to help build confidence in them when they make a mistake, like turning over the ball, is Dave's approach.

Coach Dave also counsels that opponents—that is, members of each of the opposing team—are not enemies, but friends. The harder they play, the more adjustments you make in your own game; therefore, your adversary is helping you to develop as a player. Even more importantly, Dave lets his players reflect on the fact that most of the teams they play face social and financial challenges at the same levels as their own. The lesson Dave provided to his young players was to honor each other on and off the court. The game of life contains lessons about the treasures of friendship, which count far beyond the measures of a scoreboard.

Writing essays and contributing community service are the two most important things Coach Dave looks for in his players. He reads each essay diligently. The essay might summarize the flow of a game and its highlights. It might also be about a friend a player made from a team in a neighborhood far from home. Maybe from Brooklyn, or maybe from Berkeley. In addition, many opportunities are provided to players to provide service to others. This might be done as acting as a peer coach to younger players or helping a student struggling with math. Players are also invited to provide service at special events, such as an interagency sporting event, where volunteers assist in managing the event or showing up at a food pantry to help distribute goods to families in need.

One story that sticks in my mind is about the cherished value of being a friend to others. An example of one of Dave's players learning this lesson was shared with me by a Dreamer alumni named Carmen Guzman. Carmen would share about her learning this lesson after she had become an alumnus after playing on Dave's basketball team in the 1990s. While still in high school, Carmen was discovered by Elvin "Lefty" Torres, one of Coach Dave's volunteer assistant coaches. He spotted her behind an apartment building, shooting a basketball at a hoisted milk crate hanging on a fire escape. Lefty invited Carmen to Dave's gym. Carmen initially had a hard time keeping up with the rigorous demands of the program, which included keeping to a busy and challenging schedule. Most of the time made available for Carmen on the court was for developing a focus for mastering basic basketball skills, and not just playing for the sake of playing. Carmen would have her playing time reduced if she did not take her development as a player seriously, or if she put her ego ahead of being an attentive and supportive teammate. Most important to Dave, and an understanding gradually adopted by Carmen, was the importance of exercise to increase stamina and flexibility, as opposed to looking flashy on the floor. At the same time, Dave was focused on Carmen's desire to play, and on her inherent abilities. By the time Carmen reached her sophomore year, she had made her high-school basketball team. In Carmen's junior and senior years, her school, Murray Bergtraum High School, won the NYC Public School Athletic League citywide championship. In her senior year, her high school bested a Catholic school in a New York State championship game, a victory that had been held by the Catholic school for years. Carmen was named Most Valuable Player for the statewide tournament.

In an interview with a reporter from the *Washington Heights* and *Inwood Monitor*,[458] for which I was present, but no longer have a copy of the newspaper issue (it also stopped publishing years ago), Carmen was questioned about her championship experiences. The initial part of the interview was then followed by an inquiry about her time developing as a player with the Dreamers. In response to the question, "What is the most important memory you have about being on a team?" Carmen paused for a few moments then answered: "What I liked most was Christmas Day mornings, when the Dreamer teammates would go door to door, and deliver gifts to families that had few toys or possession. It made me happy to see the smiles on their faces, and proud to be a person who made a difference in their lives."[459] Coach Dave would remind his players about the value of using Dreamer math: one plus one equals eleven. When one person on a team helps a neighborhood, the community also has a teammate contributing to its well-being. Coach Dave was a prime leader in promoting Title IX practices, which guaranteed equal access and program quality for girls as those for programs running services for boys. This civil rights requirement not only addressed the law and ethical recognition, but also set a bar for girls to realize optimal development of their skills and talents.

Coach Dave understood his role in partnering with other youth programs. His was an effort exercised not as a commander but as a gatekeeper. Gatekeepers facilitate the adoption of practices which may be challenging to what one is accustomed to. In being a role model and a sharer of methods and resources, outcomes for which a leader may have been hesitant or skeptical, were reached in surprisingly quick time. When Coach Dave shared his Dreamer program model which kept girls in the forefront of receiving quality services, and having teen girls serve as co-leaders, the emerging Ivy League was able to adopt tried and true practices. When the all-girls Ivy League/Uptown WINS program was launched, Coach Dave encouraged girls to become peer coaches and boys to support the maintenance of fields and supplies.

In the second operating year of the Uptown WINS program, I submitted a funding application to the New York Women's Foundation with major help from Andrew Rubinson, the Executive Director of a neighboring youth community service program called Fresh Youth Initiatives. The mission of Andrew's agency was to organize community service opportunities such as food drives, community gardens, and neighborhood beautification murals. His agency involved youth not only in delivering assistance to those in need but also in continuous personal and group reflections about one's role as a community citizen. When Fresh Youth Initiatives started in Washington

Heights in 1994, Coach Dave served as a gatekeeper to them, offering the volunteer assistance of himself and his youth members.

After the application was submitted to the NY Women's Foundation[460] on behalf of Uptown WINS, the foundation sent its officers to observe an activity at our school-based site. When two of the foundation's program officers entered the gym at PS 128M, they saw a tightly organized sports clinic for girls that was supervised by older female peers. One hundred elementary school girls were leaping and screaming with joy as they learned and practice basketball shooting, dribble and passing skills. Ruth Mendin, a young adult volunteer with the Dreamers who had been in that program for a decade, was supervising the gym. She and Coach Dave trained event captains, female high-school students who would assist on the floor that day. The gym had six individual basketball backboard areas, each of which was set up as a training and practice skill drill area. Leading the drills at each basket were trained middle-school students. The event was thus led by a team of young female coaches.

The interview conducted by the program officers with me at the end of their visit was brief. Their excitement about what they had seen going on was readily evident by their smiles and animated response. As they got ready to leave for the day, the program officers turned to me and winked, telling me that although not yet an official decision, we got the grant. Consequently, the Ivy League was funded by the foundation for two years, which was its maximum funding period. The NY Women's Foundation grant provided for the creation of a female teen advisory group, which we called Female Finesse. Working closely with the Women's Sports Foundation[461] led by Donna Lopiano and Olympic rhythmic gymnast gold medalist Wendy Hilliard, the program's neighborhood was provided workshops promoting the value and practice of Title IX. Coach Dave's assistance as a program friend and gatekeeper allowed Uptown WINS to step up in its program options, and young girls to step into new opportunities for leadership.

In the early 2000s, Lottie Almonte, a Community School District #6 sports program director, was tasked with organizing a middle-school sports intramural program. She asked for Coach Dave's assistance in training coaches and observing the games played. Once again, he embraced the opportunity to be a gatekeeper. He readily accepted, with one proviso: for every boys' team entered by each school, a girls' team must also be organized for the tournament. Six middle schools took on the Title IX challenge, and the school district launched a middle school version of the city's high school Public School Athletic League program. Just as the clinic at PS 128M became an annual tradition (it is still being held), organizations in the Heights such as the Inwood Little League, which traditionally had sponsored all male teams only, re-organized and set up teams for girls.

The energy of Coach Dave inspired and often instigated activism and connection by his mentees and program colleagues in ways suggested by Camille de Toledo, an author from Europe who writes extensively on generational change and moving on from outdated practices. In her book, *Coming of Age at the End of History*, Ms. Toledo focuses on crucial habits needed by youth to overcome old-school obstacles blocking their paths. These habits included being open to constructing new perspectives and developing trust for their choices and for each other. As Ms. Toledo writes: "Doubt more than you believe, explore before you jump to conclusions, embrace more than you exclude."[462] Our youth were subject to almost constant messages of diminishment, from the media as well as from the inner critics besieging them. Coach would actively listen to the stories related by young people, and he would counsel them and introduce them to people who would change their underlying assumptions. Girls, in making what was once unbelievable to that which is possible and then done, became co-participants in changing their lives.

Coach Dave also counseled the young to become resistant to seeing themselves as victims. He offered his counsel in the spirit of Chicago organizer Jane Addams, who in an interview shared her advice to the most discouraged of her clientele: "Self-pity keeps us circling relentlessly in our own narrow orbit."[463] Dave distanced himself from organizations whose leadership offered help largely because they had pity for the people they sought to serve, and he zeroed in on the habit practiced by his youth of habitually pitying themselves. Dave had little room for victim consciousness; he helped those he loved to push such thoughts out of the inner rooms of their minds. Like Jane Addams, Coach Dave understood the futility of "merely turning the tables of those using authoritarian control." He also maximized enthusiasm on the part of his young leaders by nurturing a resource that Adams called "youth ebullience…which needs to be sustained over time."[464]

Coach Dave was a committed team member and co-leader of our steering committee for the Teens on Board campaign. Serving as an organizer and spokesperson in our seven-year effort, Coach Dave motivated youth and adults alike in getting petitions completed and spreading the word within their own circles of influence. He was also a best friend to our cause, helping to convince leaders, who had seen helpful initiatives blocked without due cause previously, to put aside their reservations. Coach Dave, at public meetings such as community boards and open sessions at the NY City Council, spoke with clarity and vision, helping to get public officials and elected representatives to see the value of having teen representation at the community-based level. Those serving in these government capacities, after receiving Coach Dave's words, would respond with renewed resolve to support our initiative. Those who had been hesitant or unsure would switch their positions to ones of more reflective consideration for our cause. One example is the testimony offered by Coach Dave to the NY City Council Operations Committee, which had to approve a resolution of support for our legislation before it would be considered by the full council membership. Coach Dave brought to life the relevance of our cause by relating it to what he found to be true for his Dreamer youth, even in the tough days of the 1980s and 1990s. As Coach Dave offered in his testimony to the committee on the opportunities to be granted if offered the right to apply to community boards: "…although we offered a lot of games, tee shirts and trips, what they (the young) appreciated the most were the workshop, the mentors, and the projects which helped them to grow. Projects that helped them with the storms of life, remembering the community service projects where adults did not show up, but they did… (these experiences) provide the motivation to stay in school, to strive for a scholarship, (and to make a difference)…. If I want to be a ball player, I am gonna (sic) try to be on my high school basketball team…but what happens if I want to improve my community… there is no real mechanism for me to stay in and get with it."[465] City Council members paid close attention to Coach Dave's words, expressed in a tone reflecting his own ebullience. The Council members responded affirmatively with the nodding of their heads and loud applause. The Operations Committee, with a unanimous vote of support, passed the Resolution on to the full Council, which in turn passed the Resolution with only two abstentions.

What Coach Dave spoke to here is the importance of invitation, affirmation, and validation in public venues in which teens are involved. To wrap up this brief biographical statement about Coach Dave, I refer to a commemorative statement I wrote for one of Coach's best friends and program allies, Ray Pagan, who in his professional life with the New York City Parks and Recreation site in the West Village, lived the values of making his house a home for others. Ray was the floor leader at a Parks Department recreation facility that at the time was named the Carmine Recreation Center, which was located at the intersection of Carmine Street and Seventh Avenue in the southwest section of the Village. After many years battling health challenges, Ray passed away, leaving a big hole in Dave's life. Coach Dave continues to celebrate Ray's life as he fills that hole in his heart by practicing what Ray preached. I share here some of my commemorative words, in praise of Ray, which in part explain why Dave felt he had to work side by side with him: "For Ray Pagan, the gracious gatekeeper and humble host. For every team invited to the Carmine Center, no matter its point of origin, when one played hard, maintained respect, and competed in recognition of the dignity of your playful adversaries—all are welcome. At Carmine, there was no downtown or uptown, only our town. In Ray's house, the Dreamers had a chance to exercise their bodies, their minds, and their dreams. Scrubs developed into stars, and troubled characters became coaches. Ray, you are missed. But what is not missed is your eternal presence kept in the memories of our hearts."[466] It is with this energy of empathy and civic embrace that we who struggle valiantly for teen enfranchisement maintain our dreams and realize our goals.

Civic lovers: Build an internal architecture of compassion and share your vision with the world—facilitate hope by training teens and their mentors to become helping hands.

Drawing from his teachings about his spiritual tradition, Rabbi Michael Lerner shares the practice of "chesed." Rabbi Lerner sees this practice as an enabler of resiliency and compassionately centered action. In his book, *Jewish Renewal*, and also offered in a magazine he co-founded called *Tikkun*, Rabbi Lerner elaborates on the significance of compassionately offered mutual recognition: "Chesed is where we practice with and embrace each other with loving kindness, affirm one another's complexities, recognize each other in our inner and outer obstacles, and face the issues that we all face by giving and receiving recognition."[467] This practice integrates the best practices of a healthy heart on personal levels, in political practice, and on spiritual levels.

To be a civic lover, one uses a second practice which is to become infused with what spiritual leaders from the Christian community define as agape.[468] Agape is exercised as the spontaneous and altruistic love for community and humanity. Creating humanistic community starts with getting in touch with our self compassionately, and then seeing compassionately expressive people build a community. It is akin to poet Sam Keen's treatise on love. In his poem, *Hymns to an Unknown God*, he eloquently states: "Soul grows in communion. Word by word, story by story, for better or worse, we build our world. From true conversation—our communication deepens into compassion and creates community."[469] To understand teens as natural allies for the social good, we strive to get to know their intentions, and capabilities. We, as concerned adults in the lives of adolescents, investigate them for their positive qualities, and remain open enough to have them to investigate adults for their life-enhancing offerings also. We learn that our yearnings can be mutually felt, and our stories overlapping in productive encounter.

In pursuit of deep knowledge, which affirms the resources available from within and the valuable assets of trusted allies in our outer world, the civic lover displays understanding and the use of skills sets in three significant ways. The first resource for a civic lover is to develop and listen to a story from both your own deep places and those of others. This is done with the courage to act in the spirit of an amateur, one who acts just for the sake of the love of it, rather than out of the certainties of being an expert. To look at the second set, we can consider the use of integral leadership exercised in our colonial days by revolutionary ancestral allies.

Gordon Wood, an American historian exploring the motives and character of our early civic pioneers, describes a second skill set, a resource crucial for civic lovers seeking a new paradigm of governance. What is assumed for leadership exercised on behalf of constituents includes adopting the practice of what they called "disinterest."[470] Wood explains in his book, *Revolutionary Characters*: "Doctor Johnson (one of the early revolutionary characters) describes directive disinterest as assuming leadership positions with virtue and self-sacrifice, where a leader remains superior to the privileges of private advantage and private profit."[471] The political and economic leadership developed under the stewardship of the Boomer generation has become so invested and dependent upon technologies which are corrosive to our environment, and anti-democratic practices of extremism in service to positional advantage that we hardly know the practice of disinterest in governance today. In the perception of the younger generation, this dissolution of disinterest appears to them as uninterest in their futures on the part of their elders.

A third resource can be defined as a form of patriotism, which, by utilizing a love of civic imaginative exercise, seeks to align the best of democratic practices with our nation's higher ideals. Civic lovers accomplish the merging of practice with principle by effecting a congruency of mutual interests between those who govern with those who are governed. As shared in her book, *The Power of Their Ideas*, by New York City's education reformer Deborah Meier: "By investigating an appreciation and ownership for shared, multiply derived stories."[472] , Ms. Meier breaks down student experience and story as becoming better understood through what she calls five intellectual habits in need of development: "concern for evidence (how do we know that?); viewpoint (who said it and why?); cause and effect (what led to it, and why); and hypothesizing (what if, and supposing that)…but most of all is the fifth habit—who cares? Becoming convinced that it matters, and if it makes a difference."[473] As I will share in the anecdotes to follow, under the old practices of condescension by adults toward the young, they have been too prone to ignore evidence presented and viewpoints of the young, attributing cause and effects for problems to teen deficits, and not even looking at alternative ways of seeing teens. As for making a difference, it has been the politics of indifference that has weighed so heavily in perpetuating chronic misfortune for our emergent generation.

Ancestral allies to our movement for adolescent enfranchisement and holistic recognition offer some additional thoughts about the practice of civic love. Frederick Douglas, an eighteenth-century abolitionist, described a prescription for curing the disease of indifference as practice by "one who does not excuse, but rebukes, the sins of our country."[474] Given the magnitude of the planetary crisis, for the young the Age of Reason has become defined through a culture of rebuke.

The outcomes derived through civic lovers' contributions are sustained through commitment, as described by a physician's assistant who had participated in Socratic dialogue sessions with the educator and writer Christopher Phillips. (Phillips describes these sessions in his book, *Socrates in Love.*) As put forth by one of Mr. Phillip's students named Rachel (her last name is not mentioned in the book), "All commitments are a type of marriage. They entail responsibility and devotion. But the best ones have a romance to them. They are creative and loving."[475] The failure to substantially address the challenge of generational transition today could be more aptly described as reactive and ducking the issues. The practice of civic lovers can also be viewed as poetic politics, as referenced by the mystic and poet Rabindranath Tagore. In Tagore's poem (quoted from Goodreads, with the poem reference unidentified), he pens the words: "I slept and dreamt that life is joy. I awoke and saw that life is service. I acted, and behold, service is joy."[476] In our world today where the good life is defined through the parameters of self-interest, it is the young, in record numbers far exceeding that given by prior generations, who see service as the joy of seeing the benefits of alternative futures.

Some of our ancestral allies built communally embedded institutions in creation of a culture and cooperative system based on these beatific practices. The atmosphere of place created in organized and protective environments contribute to the benefits of individual mental health as well as facilitating safe spaces for the disposed. One example is the work and legacy left by Jane Addams, the founder of Hull House in Chicago whom I profiled in the past few pages of this book. In the 1900s, she created a multi-service agency that served the needs of individuals, family, and community holistically. Her extended home addressed the mental and emotional needs of her "residents", as well as helping people to build relationships through workplace education, housing support, and united advocacy campaigns. The social/emotional culture of Hull House drew people to it and kept them supportive of new arrivals, as articulated by two Hull House alumni, Ruby and Maria (last names are not used in the book): "They paid attention to us as individuals. Everything was personalized. You weren't just some kid. They wanted you to be the best you could be. And, a lot of the time, you didn't even know you were learning—it was done in such a loving and a caring way."[477]

Rose Chea and Catherine Payne, alumni from my early days working with the Dreamers and Southern Heights, expressed the same types of sentiments. They came here with their families from Liberia. During the time of their youth participation, they told me, "We had two fathers, you, and Dave, one White father, and one Black father, but... [W]hite and Black did not matter, as you both helped us as a father."[478] As I previously mentioned,

Jackie Hurt had affirmed this at a dinner we attended in honor of Muslim Americans when she told me that the program was quite special to her: she loved us just as she was certain that we loved her. Steve Ramos, a neighbor of the family of Johnny Rosario, who was one of our teen group leaders at the program, visited us and lead young students in chanting and song. Steve reminded me that the reason he volunteered with so much enthusiasm was that he was doing so not as much for an agency, but rather as part of a family.[479] (I recall this in comments he made directly to me at the time.) I have come to love these communities for being there for me and offering me their compassion and enduring embrace. Two sisters, Yaniris and Eli Taveras contributed hours upon hours to service projects. Their mother would often wryly complain to me that they spent more time cleaning up parks than tidying their own room.

New York City and America are flush with programs that motivate youth to affirm their true selves and their life missions while encouraging them to embrace the "other" as sister/brother. I propose that civic change work done from this perspective—the congruence of the empowered self and the assurance of fully enfranchised community—is soulfully guided by those in touch with the archetype of the civic lover. In the following pages, I share anecdotes about three civic lovers who co-mentored me as role models for exercising the energies and power of the civic lover archetype. The energy works by making others feel close to one's heart and at home in the same space. The power is exhibited through statements of affirmed recognition and embrace for another person's presence. I learned about their teen enfranchisement work either through personal witnessing of a civic lover's work or the trustworthy testimonies of those whose lives felt enriched through a civic lover's intervention and influence. After sharing these three profiles, I will then develop a deeper profile of Sarah Andes, formerly the New York City Director for Generation Citizen. In her capacity as citywide Program Director, Sarah helped to design and have Generation Citizen sponsor hundreds of middle- and high school Action Civic programs in social studies classrooms in the five boroughs of New York City, and for advocacy campaigns championing teen enfranchisement. Sarah, although decades my junior in age, was my principal co-mentor during the final two years of my 28 years of work with teen enfranchisement. I call her a civic-minded soul-sister. I met Sarah at a youth-sponsored Mayoral forum in 2013.

Each project in which she sought civic improvements and/or educational reform was perceived by me to involve the civic lover within Sarah, who worked with a cognitively derived understanding of history and social structures, and who related to those she served from her heart. These levels included fostering cognitive and emotional levels of intelligence and working on present-day issues with the future in mind.[480] All of them had a special appreciation for the need to foster creativity within a framework of diverse populations. Their programs, and the communities effected by those programs, became motivated and energized because of the input of young people who molded new possibilities with their helping hands.[481] Before delving further into Sarah's profile, I share the work of other co-mentors close to me who share characteristics of the civic lover that I also observed in Sarah.

Ellen Baxter: Finding homes for the homeless.

Ellen Baxter is a Petra Foundation fellow who was inducted into the Foundation in 1994.482 I had met Ellen a few years earlier, while she was serving her community by advocating for and creating attractive and sustainable housing options for those most in need. In uptown Manhattan, we had a very quickly expanding population, and shrinking housing options within our physical infrastructure of abandoned, neglected, and increasingly expensive apartment options. On the day of her induction, I sat in the living room of a Petra Foundation trustee named Scott Armstrong, from Washington, D.C. Petra Foundation trustees, amongst their many types of support for new and existing fellows, opened their homes for foundation receptions. A mainstay gathering was always a barbeque in

which we feasted on delicious food and had the joy of hearing stories. Petra Foundation fellow, trustees, and financial contributors to the Foundation broke bread and conversed at these barbeques annually on the night before the Saturday evening Petra Award dinners. Not known to either of us until we sat down next to one another is that each of us had become a Petra Fellow. I was proudly surprised when I discovered who was sitting on the floor right next to me, but Ellen! After expressing happy hellos, we asked each other, "What are you doing here?" We at that point learned that each of us had been invited to be fellows. With the foundation's recognition of Ellen, whom I had long admired for her tireless work on behalf of challenged community members, the raison d'être for the foundation became crystal clear to me in just those few moments.

The following profile of Ellen's work is drawn here from the pages of the *Twenty-Fifth Anniversary Petra Fellow Journal*. Ellen fought for and designed "alternative housing options to those that were living in overcrowded and often dangerous shelters or single room occupancy flop-houses."[483] Her first accomplishment was to convert what had been a long-abandoned hot sheet motel at 10 Fort Washington Avenue into a complex of modest apartments for single, homeless men. The building common areas (such as the lobby and hallways on each floor) and each apartment provided a warm and attractive atmosphere and comfortable space. Ellen added additional buildings soon after, the first on West 135th Street and Riverside Drive, providing housing to homeless families; the most recent being that has been added is located on West 155th Street and Edgecombe Avenue.

Ellen had said that her mindset for putting together these projects was based on the insight she had while living in Geel, Belgium, that "the mentally ill and the destitute can co-exist in a community with others."[484] Her modus operandi was to set up a recruitment process for individuals and families in need, but also to engage in conversations with them "about the responsibilities of community."[485] Folks living there were encouraged to exercise choice, such as choosing their rooms and encouraging their voice through their creative work. The entrances and the hallways of each building are lined with the residents' works of poetry, drawings, and paintings. Residents were encouraged to be trusted neighbors to each other. This sense of neighborliness was experienced in an environment of beautiful surroundings that reinforced each person's motivation for being there as a participating member of a larger community. Amongst the many qualities promoted by Ellen's housing managers is that of having a welcoming and beautiful space. Artistic pieces, paintings, and drawings done by each housing developments residents created a beautiful allure for the space. Creative contribution is a key element for maintaining purposeful community. Prized spaces matter. In the 21st Century, space has become expanded and shared as a common space by stakeholders from around the world.

Yanel Cordero, teenage global explorer.

I first learned about the youth program called Global Kids after being introduced to it by Yanel Cordero in 1995. Yanel had been one of my mentees in the Ivy League in the early 1990s when she served as a teen leader in Female Finesse.486 Yanel's vision of community expanded beyond her home neighborhood of Washington Heights. Yanel eagerly joined youth programs which appeared enticing to her, with her inquisitive and curious nature. Yanel engaged very quickly in youth-led service projects, each comprising a leadership population with diverse cultures and national backgrounds. I do not think my resume listings, at age 36, came close to the length of hers, even when she was just 16. Amongst her invitations to explore distant places was a chance to take trips to places like Venice, Italy, to meet youth leaders abroad, which was offered by the Global Kids program. Yanel, whom I considered to be my spontaneity-loving and wonder-induced wanderer, was a natural. Her vivid imagination, eternal

questioning, and enthusiastic participation lit up any room and brought joy to her co-leaders.487 Yanel also attended a special event sponsored by the Black Women's Sports Foundation in Atlanta, Georgia. This event was organized under the auspices of the U.S. Olympic Committee, which in turn invited the Black Women's Sports Foundation as an organizational participant. This initiative was called the F.L.A.M.E. program (Finding Leaders Among Minorities Everywhere). Under auspices of this program, aspiring student athletes were connected to female Olympic sport stars.488

As per mission statement objectives developed by the Global Kids leadership, led by the Executive Director at the time, Evie Hantzopoulos, (I source the quote here from their mission statement), Global Kids "taps into young people's interests and leadership potential" by fostering an inquiry-based environment, which promotes critical thinking, academic achievement, and global competencies. Each youth leader is inspired and trained to take direct action "based upon their intrinsic desire to make a difference." (quote from the Global Kids website)[489] This approach is based on what I call aspirational agitation for the common good, expressed in the spirit of agape, which I understand as the love of community simply for the sake of owning and experiencing this love. In helpful cohabitation, all give generously without expectations of personal return.

Global Kids alumni have spoken eloquently about the personal achievements they attained while embedded in an activist culture of doing the right thing for others. Testimonials from their website speak to their insights and discoveries. Alejandra Ruiz spoke of this experience as "changing the course of her life through her direct activist work on changing the laws on immigration." Anisah Miley's testimonial stated that "at the age of 16, working with their Global Action Project, she traveled to Northern Ireland to work with youth, from both Catholic and Protestant backgrounds. She learned she had to exercise empathy in herself and among others who came from traditionally conflicting tribes. The Global Kids program taught young people to extend the practice of being a good neighbor across cultures from around the globe. Despite having grown up in neighborhoods that were chiefly segregated by ethnicity, national origin and class, these twenty-first-century explorers had learned to be planetary citizens. The culture of an organization is driven by the character of its leadership. With Evie, she always made decisions by keeping in mind that some of the founding board members for Global Kids had been Global Kids themselves, and that all subsequent boards were to include membership drawn from the agency's pool of youth participants.

Adam Bukko: occupying space with soul.

I learned about the homeless youth advocate Adam Bukko's innovative work in helping homeless teens via his testimony included in his jointly authored book *Occupy Spirituality*. The genesis of Adam's career and impact of his agency's work is profiled throughout this book, from which I provide the following descriptors.490 In partnership with Taz Tagore, Mr. Bukko cofounded the Reciprocity Foundation in lower Manhattan. The foundation serves homeless, formerly incarcerated, and trauma-damaged teens. Some of the teens have been rejected by parents and negatively impacted by family collapse under the weight of poverty; many had aged out of the foster care system. As articulated by several practitioners of trauma-informed intervention, many types of adverse experiences involve some degree of trauma. In addition to the wounds inflicted upon the body and mind, what results is a soul that is induced to vacate the body. The soul becomes encouraged to return by holistic programs designed to welcome it back into the room of one's heart and the spaces of one's relational living. The Reciprocity House interventions include alternative and healing modalities such as acupuncture, meditation, massage,

trauma-informed therapy, and communal gatherings. The culture of the program encourages the serving of home-cooked meals, the engendering of friendships, and the reassurances built through communal bonding. Adam Bukko sums up the totality of his strategy with the following words: "I begin my work with considering the streets as an extension of my living room."491 Once he and his staff connect, the wanderer gets welcomed in the Reciprocity home. In effective youth intervention practices, safe space matters, beginning with a healthy body and soul, as does the rewards of mutuality between you and me.

What these three approaches I just profiled share is a vision of what Krishna Das describes as "seeing with the unique intelligence of the heart."492 Krishna Das is a spiritual practitioner who teaches through the artform of singing and chanting with group participation. The more one uses this type of intelligence, the more one sees the scope of the "heart expand to be as large as the living world."493 This is both personal medicine and mutually based empowerment.

Heart intelligence is also addressed by Catholic Worker founder Dorothy Day, who also taught about the value of heartfelt giving. As Ms. Day says, this is "what we have known as the long loneliness after which we have learned that the solution is love, and that love comes best with community."494 On my path traveled from Southern Heights to the Dreamers, from the Ivy League to the Police Athletic League and Future Voters, I have come to love these communities for being there for seekers, with compassion and enduring embrace. I have come to love them, as the participants whom I have engaged with have always loved me.

The orphan, the rebel, and the lover became for me the primary constructs, spiritual and metaphorical in nature, through which I came to view and work with teens. I consider these three archetypes to compromise the Soul of Adolescence. In working with these archetypal energetic allies, I do not look at spreadsheets or solely at the results of research studies. I intuitively sense their presence, which, while invisible to the eye, is felt at a spiritual level. I peer through a lens of intuitive channels, using poetic profiling. Identifying issues through the piecemeal perspective of a specific type of discipline, such as psychology, sociology, or political science is essential, but not enough.[495] One must look between the notes and at teen qualities derived from previously invisible and mysterious aspects of their true nature, which, when explored and brought to conscious understanding, inform us about life purpose from an additional perspective. For instance, when working with the archetype of the orphan, the origins of one's experience are unique for every individual. As I wrote in the Induction chapter, my sense of alienation which was developed after suffering through adverse encounters with overly judgmental teachers is fundamentally different than those of what a 14-year-old Black or Latino student has to process today. In addition to being bombarded with dismissive language by teachers, which is psychologically damaging, minority students are continuously under the threat to their physical safety in their confrontations with school and law enforcement authorities. They are also far more likely than white students to be forcibly relocated to juvenile correction facilities where they are abused. However, the common denominators between the two experiences involves learning how to demand that one's presence is respected, whether in a classroom (as in my experience) or on one's block (as in the Latino's experience). In addition, just as my disenchanting encounter led me to develop empathy for others who had similar classroom experiences during my time as a youth service director, many directors of youth programs who grew up on the streets and had to face youth-law enforcement confrontations also respond from an experientially based point of view. For me, working with and developing common understanding for teens coming from across a variety of backgrounds helped guide my resistance and rejection of generalized assumptions constructed out of abstract and laboratory-based findings. Working from a soulfully based spiritual perspective has also deepened my understanding about the sources of abandonment faced by the orphan, and the rewards garnered when we stand true to our life purpose. The orphan gathers resilient power when connected to others navigating the same terrain of abandonment and wandering. I let go of paradigms viewing the fundamental nature of teens as primarily defined by the structure and processes of their brains and hormones. Our mistaken adoption of these paradigms had been derived from scientific research, and policy makers' interpretations of this research. So much of science has advanced the health and well- being of humanity. However, within the fields of youth study and recommended practices for governance, the dominant bodies of research from the late nineteenth century until well into the twenty-first century have been used by the media and policy makers to put forth socially constructed interpretations that have been misleading when used to define the nature of teen characteristics and abilities. I profiled some of this research and resultant policies in the orphan section of this book, and re-visit those as contrasted to more modern research in the "Civic Lover" and "Anecdotes Arising" sections of this book. For now, I simply point out that the agreed upon point of view, based on old paradigms of adolescence, was what I, my co-mentors, and teen civic-change agents had to challenge in our arguments for effecting changes in the balance of authority between adults and teens. Advocates for teen representation on community boards were often rebutted, despite our submission of new scientific evidence and stories about successful teen participation in other cities, because, even though highly educated, and disposed to liberal social policies, these people could not let go of the old paradigm of adolescence. To provide one example here, I speak to the so-called expert opinions of civic leaders based upon unfounded assumptions and denial of evidence. One type of objection which I would frequently hear (including from educators and civic volunteers) is that teens could not participate in the type of civic governance required for community board members because science has shown that they are developmentally inadequate for the task. When I would present examples of this specific type of teen civic efficacy, such as the San Francisco Youth Commission, where youth aged 14 through 24 had served officially as youth advisors to that city's Board of Supervisors since 1996, I would get a slight nod or shrug of the shoulders, but not a modified opinion. Today, we see this same practice of attachment to non-substantiated beliefs in the popularly expressed rejections of reality (exercised by adults with mature cerebral cortex) in the dramas of climate change denial and dismissal of the existence of structural racism sabotaging democracy. As conceptual changes, essential to constructing a new paradigm of adolescence, became more widely adopted, agreement with corresponding policy changes for teen civic engagement were more readily put in place as well. It is with this understanding—namely, changing the definition of the inner teen to correspond to changes in public opinion about, and policies over, teens—that is a major theme of this section of my narrative.

Shortly, I will discuss the soulfully based construction of society, which I view as transitioning from the mechanical/industrial to the ecological and spiritually embedded. I believe the emergence of a new paradigm for adolescence is crucially embedded within the latter paradigm, and crucial for obtaining social justice and progress.

A historical and cultural interpretation addressing the need for our psychological and political evolution is explained in a comprehensive way by placing human evolution and social progress in the context of the "Great Turning," a term David Korten, who is a member of the Club of Rome and president of the Positive Futures Network, develops in his book, *The Great Turning*, when referring to this transition.[496] Mr. Korten had for years served as director of U.S. foreign aid to developing countries. He changed the policy approach he used when deciding whether conditions were sufficient to approve the provision of aid to a given country.[497] He came to realize that it was the very conditions imposed on recipients that weakened already vulnerable economies. These adverse conditions had been fostered by austerity measures that limited government support for their citizens and international loan agreements, keeping poor nations under perpetual debt obligation. It is not until approaches are changed and local advice and leadership is incorporated that investments are made to support locally driven development. In a parallel fashion, when teens who have been stuck in cycles of poor decision-making and risky friendships are counseled in ways that maintain their dependencies on adult-led suggestions and conditions, they remain dependent on these adults. When teens function as decision-making stakeholders analyzing conditions and facilitating changes, they guide their peers and adults in charge of policy making. In developing new approaches for teacher-student relationships, and after assessing the deficits of old-school practices and benefits of new supervisory styles, a great turning of school culture and governance becomes unleashed. Encouragement of teen power supersedes outdated guidelines and plans keeping the young dependent and acting as perpetual followers. Students are encouraged to adopt graduated levels of independence in thought and action, and to enter teacher-learner partnerships by practicing equal levels of interdependence.

Sarah Andes, architect for new generational leadership.

I discuss, in the final part of this section, a civic lover profile of Sarah Andes and her teen enfranchisement contributions. In this section of the book, I speak to the influence of Sarah Andes (whom I met in 2013) on my co-mentoring skills and perspective. Her contribution to campaign strategies was deeply instrumental in seeing our desired amendment to Public Officer Law being passed. The guidance and re-assurance of her presence also helped to improve my focus and increase my confidence in seeing our campaign achieve its goal.

As a curtain-raiser for my profiling of Sarah and her civic work, I offer a few thoughts on what I mean by the term "civic lover." With these thoughts, I utilize a perspective on consciousness that was inherent to the philosophy of ancestral peoples, and increasingly being speculated upon as possible by scientists from the new physics disciplines. I use analysis and insights from both schools of thought to develop a biographic and archetypal short take on the civic lover.

Mario Kamenetzky is a philosopher, and a former science and technology expert for the World Bank. He wrote a book on consciousness, where he referred to the energy of consciousness as an invisible presence with which we interact. Mr. Kamenetzky has tracked socioeconomic development issues for almost 50 years. In writing his book, *The Invisible Player: Consciousness as the Soul of Economic, Social and Political Life*, he added consideration of his spiritual orientation and poetic reflection to his looking back on his career. He considers this orientation and reflection as crucial to evolving beyond a consciousness aligned with just mechanical and technical metaphor. He writes about the character of consciousness as "ever-present, although often our unacknowledged companion. It fires our vision of human nature… flashes intuitions…and strives to keep satisfied our instinctual drives and our social needs…(and) transmits messages from and to the spiritual universe."[498] In other words, consciousness plays a role in our life in subtle ways, yet substantially influences how we come to define ourselves (our identity) and decide on approaches to life. As we progress toward a new era, in which ecological interdependence and political changes mandating greater empowered representation are now arising, we need to develop an evolved consciousness. It is one of the assumptions held by me in this book that in our materialist society, where people cede personal authority and decisions to outside sources, we overlook the influence of consciousness on our personal development and chosen course in life. We need to learn the lessons taught by nature and the environment about learning to live within the context of nature's rhythm and let go of the dictates of machine consciousness which led us to believe we can function outside of the natural environment. This holds true for my perspective and understanding about teens, who have a unique niche in the evolution of humans. When we overlook the role of the archetypal civic lover in the lives of adolescents, we miss out on the insights and contributions available from compassionately interconnected activists. The new cohort of teen activists has already moved beyond the limitations of the Boomer Generation's more limited consciousness. They are our teachers now.

Carolyn Myss in her book, *The Sacred Contract*, does not include an archetype called civic lover, but does describe an archetype called the Advocate (attorney, legislator, lobbyist), which aligns closely to why civic lovers do what they do, and where they choose to give expression to this energy in their lives. Civic lovers engage with great empathy and passion for managing and reforming the civic and political institutions which govern our lives. In the bio-statement Ms. Myss gives to the advocate, she writes: "Ram Dass would describe the work of the advocate as that of compassion in action. Compassion in Action is a life-long devotion to championing the rights of others in the public arena, a passion to transform social concerns, specifically on behalf of others."[499] This description aptly describes the work of Sarah, who practiced with strong commitment, extraordinary persistence, and an attitude of making the injustices toward teens a matter of her personal concern.

Matthew Fox, a spiritual activist and writer, quotes a founder of the Catholic Worker movement, Dorothy Day, which I use here as an example of a civic lover taking personal ownership for the harm done to vulnerable people: "Dorothy Day was arrested for picketing with militant suffragists in 1918, and was thrown in jail for the first time. She writes about what she learned from this pain: 'The blackness of hell was all about me. The sorrow of the world encompassed me. I was like the one who had gone down into the pit.'"[500] As I will soon share in my stories about Sarah, I observed in her conversations with teens that she displayed an instinctive sensitivity to the pain suffered by teens, and then put together carefully constructed strategies, to be adopted by teens, for navigating around the imposed pitfalls of dependency.

Sarah Andes, like all deeply empathetic civic lovers, is driven by a passionate drive to act. As shared by Susannah Heschel, who wrote a book of compilations written by her father, Abraham Joshua Heschel, staying stuck in a condition of insensitivity and indifference toward those subject to injustice is an issue of moral concern. Susannah Heschel shares an essay describing the ethical stance and passionate drive for Rabbi Heschel's opposition to the war in Vietnam: "I concluded in 1965 that waging a war in Vietnam was an evil act…(this involved) the discovery that indifference to evil is worse than evil itself…I learned the niggardliness of our moral comprehension, the incapacity to sense the depth of misery caused by our own failures."[501]

Sarah combined a careful construction of methodologies for teens designed to reinforce a belief in their own efficacy, with teens in developing arguments persuading adult leaders to escape the trap of maintaining the disabling traps of business as usual. As part of her program design, she included exercises for teens assisting them in overcoming their internalized misconceptions of inadequacy. In turn, teens learned to make presentations to adults which turned their hearts and minds closer toward perceiving adolescents as credible and valuable civic actors.

In summing up this transition to Sarah's story, I suggest that Sarah also combined the mission of stimulating imagination with then using a construction of step-by-step practical approaches. Everyday tasks were enacted within an anticipatory context of what is possible. The naturalist writer, Barry Lopez, in his book, *Of Wolves and Men*, proclaims that "it is imagination that gives shape to the universe."[502] Sarah inspired the young, and adult mentors working with the young, to dream about the possibility of alternative futures. At the same time, she considered herself not only to be a conscious advocate, but also a conduit in which the young participated in the process of both borrowing the best of approaches used by those in other movements and reinventing them to serve the arena of adolescent lives.

Before continuing with Sarah's profile, I discuss another important issue: granting legal permanent residents the right to vote in New York City. The issues concerning civic enfranchisement contain some parallels between teen civic participation and that of electoral participation by immigrants. In New York City, a large number of young people are either immigrants themselves or born to parents who are newly arrived at our country.

In our historic struggles to expand the franchise, the history of struggle for women and blacks has gained more visibility in modern times. What is not known to many people is that legal residents had had the right to vote at the dawning of our democracy, and then had that right removed. This disenfranchisement began in the late 1800's and came into full effect in the first two decades of the twentieth century. Young people and their families, recent immigrants to the United States, constitute a majority population in neighborhoods in New York City. I raise this aside here, because one of Sarah's primary concerns was the denial of the natural right of a person to feel grounded in their communities by participating in the process of advocacy and decision-making in governance. To feel safe in their bodies, recognized for their minds, and secure in family and communal/civic relationship, community stakeholders need to participate in the operation of our city's agencies and the formulation of responsive policies. I consider the organizers of granting voting rights to legal residents to be conducting a campaign for civic patriotism. Using traditional means of dissent and locally based organizing, advocates are fighting for the right to democratic participation for those who sustain the very society that refuses them the right to enfranchisement. The causes of advocacy in this campaign contain ethical parallels to those in the campaign to allow teens the right to vote.

I was introduced to the initiative for the right to vote for legal permanent residents during the early 2000s, during the same period I was spearheading the teen enfranchisement campaign. At the time, the campaign was led by David Andersson, an organizer for Queens Community House, Ron Hayduk, a professor at City University, and additional faculty from CUNY.

In an online journal hosted by the Migration Policy Institute and written by Ron Hayduk and Michelle Wucker, the authors lay out central points of support for allowing residents with Green Cards to vote. They pointed out that those who are now current residents but born abroad "now constitute 11.8 per cent of the total U.S. population, the greatest absolute total since the great wave of immigration between 1880 and 1920. Their presence is significant in numbers alone."[503] However, as the authors continue, "Most of the 12 million residents living in the United States cannot vote, although they may work, pay taxes, send their children to school, and serve in the military. (40,000 now serve)."[504] Teens pay taxes also, attend schools which often are providing deficient levels of service in their underfunded districts. Active adolescents serve their communities in community service projects, peer courts, and as advisory board members to community-based agencies. Unlike

New York City, other cities such as San Francisco and Hampton, Virginia allow teens as young as fourteen to serve on advisory boards to municipal government. The present generation of teens contributes community service at higher levels than any of the comparable generations preceding it. Until recent reforms in criminal justice codes, minors could be arrested, tried, and incarcerated as adults. They were held accountable for breaking the law but had no participatory avenue for making the laws affecting them.

In an article in another online journal called *Student Union*, posted by Voice of America on March 9, 2020, Nico Zviovich paints a portrait of one immigrant who personifies the great struggles immigrants have in getting to the United States, and their ethic of hard work once they settle here. Mr. Zviovich wrote: "Garang Majouk left the Sudan during that country's civil war, forded the Nile River during his escape, washed dishes in Lebanon, and came to Iowa at 19 years of age as a refugee."[505] Nico has been involved in the fight for the right of legal residents to vote. As related in earlier sections of this work, my Uncle Pierre Johannet escaped from Nazi occupation at the tender of age of 16. Miriam Payne's family escaped a civil war in Liberia. Many of the teens who were the backbone of leadership in my youth program were teenage, first-generation immigrants. Sixteen-year-old teens, such as Gerry Reneau, Gustavo Cruz and Johnny Rosario were at the afterschool program when it opened its doors each day. After I would arrive, they would assist me as floor captains over the gymnasium, the game room, and the homework assistance classroom for the balance of each program day. The program had a youth enrollment of 140 and averaged about 100 children in daily attendance. At the time, I was still working at the Life Skills School in Rego Park, Queens, from the hours of 8 a.m. until 2 p.m. I traveled by subway and could not guarantee my arrival to the program by 3 p.m. each day. They were also my captains, whom the team of teens volunteering to help followed and respected. Selfless teens helped this program to thrive and served as role models for younger peers.

Immigrant voting rights movements are beginning to find success today. In an article for *Newsweek* written in September 2017, John

Haltiwanger covered a success story in College Park, Maryland. College Park lies just outside of Washington, D.C. It has a diverse population that in total numbers 32,000 people, 21 per cent of whom are foreign-born. College Park is also home to the University of Maryland. The vote to approve voting rights for legal residents was passed by College Park's City Council; its mayor cast the tie-breaking vote. A few other cities in Maryland have already passed right-to-vote laws. In response to this victory, Ron Hayduk, who is presently a professor at San Francisco State University, commented: "For most of U.S. history, and in the vast majority of the USA, voting by noncitizens was the norm, and not the exception."[506] Perhaps we are rising back to the norm. Immigrants are increasingly becoming a substantial part of our nation's total population as we move on through the 21st Century.

In Tacoma Park, Maryland, 16-year-olds have been granted the right to vote. The same has been true for years in municipalities located in New Zealand, Israel, and member-states of the European Union. The questions for these countries have not been regarding whether 16-year-olds may vote, but rather about encouraging teens to come out in satisfying numbers. Once a person votes early, they tend to vote often later in their lives.

The right to vote for legal residents was introduced again in January 2020 by Councilmember Ydanis Rodriquez. Ydanis' family roots began in the agricultural fields of the Dominican Republican; he currently serves as a public official in New York City. Years ago, Comptroller Scott Stringer was appointed to a community board at the age of 16 (how I am not sure, as it wasn't legal yet), and now he is running in 2021 as a candidate for Mayor of New York City. As cited in a story by Kelly Maura for CNN Politics on January 23, 2021: "[T]here are currently 1,000,000 legal residents in New York City who cannot vote. If Mayor DeBlasio signs this bill, they would become eligible to vote in 2021."[507] This is a year when 27 council seats are being turned over due to term limits. Also, up for election are positions for mayor, the comptroller, and borough presidents.

Two closing points regarding immigrant voting rights are worth noting. The first is summarized by Ron Hayduk in his classic book, *Democracy for All*: "The overwhelming number of immigrants in the USA pay more in taxes than they receive in benefits. In total, immigrants (in 1997) paid $133 billion in taxes. There is one city council district in Queens, New York, where legal residents, compromising 45% of that district's population, cannot vote."[508] Teens who are not in school, but who work diligently in support of their families, pay taxes. The items they purchase are also subject to sales taxes which are a large component of income for municipalities. Teens, who are excluded from the right to vote, are therefore civic stakeholders subject to taxation without representation.

The second point has been addressed by Robert Snyder in his book *Crossing Broadway*, a definitive biography of Washington Heights. Mr. Snyder discusses how generations of everyday people, including immigrants, have kept uptown Manhattan viable and thriving. He also refers to aspects of immigration that reflect the items I iterated above. As Mr. Snyder writes: "All of these contradictions and challenges are abundantly in display in New York City…where immigrants have played a role in the rising population and vitality of New York City since the bleak years of the 1970s."[509] Here in the Big Apple, what Nelson Mandela would have called the "multiplication of hope" has risen to the power of our seeing greater fortune for all. Permanent legal residents and teens have shown civic responsibilities inherent to good citizenship and contribute to the public treasury, yet neither has obtained the right to vote. In neighborhoods across the city, teens exemplify the qualities of citizenship. The current youth generation offers thousands of hours per month of civic contribution through community service, peer mentoring, and youth council projects.

The leaders in the immigrant-centered movement called Democracy for All share the need for urgency and justice that are the commitments of leaders partnering with me for the Teens On Board movement. The leaders from both movements also share tactics and a world view, as aptly summarized by Ann Tacket and Beth Crisp in their book *Practicing Social Inclusion*, about incorporating participation by the ostracized into policy making. In one section of the book, the authors list critical elements of fostering social inclusion that have been observed and documented through their surveying of social justice movements in Australia; these elements include "authentic trusting and relationships; subjecting the status quo to critical scrutiny; being willing to work for change; being flexible and adaptive in your methods: and using language that is sensitive and inclusive."[510]

When I refer to Sarah Andes as an architect, I do so in a specific sense: she is a civic architect. I weave in some of her engineering traits in this archetypal portrait of the Engineer, which I associate with Sarah. For this I borrow from the archetypal description developed by the psychologist and writer Carolyn Myss. Ms. Myss describes traits of the engineer archetype in her book, *Sacred Contracts*: "[T]archetype of the engineer/architect is that of being eminently practical, hands-on, and devoted to making things work. It is grounded, orderly, and has a strategic quality of mind which turns creative energy into practical expression. It designs solutions to common dilemmas."[511] The civic architect or engineer has to design learning environments, which are in line with teen assets and not based upon false assumptions about their learning characteristics, such as the misguided belief that teens by nature have short attention spans.[512] As I attest to later in this section, Sarah possesses an uncanny ability to quickly organize civic engagement training processes, such as planning a workshop or an advocacy trip. Advocates in training need to learn to expect that when reaching out to people, whether they are potential allies for their cause or elected officials, they cannot automatically assume the position a person holds on an issue. Advocates deal with civic actors with unknown or varied agendas, as well as articulated positions on an issue. Students learning the trade of lobbying must adjust their expectations, and not expect simple yes or no answers. Student advocates need to adjust to the reactions of others who state that they are not sure and will get back to you. Inherent to advocacy campaigns is developing a thought-out strategic plan and outlining steps a, b, and c to be ready for multiple possibilities. As civic program students experience ambiguity and uncertainty common to the political realm, they develop a muscle of patience, which is so crucial for navigating life's ups and downs.

Sarah facilitates the acquisition of new habits and strategies for teens, which are crucial to developing not only approaches in civic advocacy but also social-emotional maturity in life. As I work through this section on Sarah, I will weave in some of these lessons learned by young change-makers. For now, I describe one practice she uses, and encourages in young people, as well as with adults, which is to first listen, then listen, and then listen again. Sarah practices with patient and open ears and is a role model for her students. She also has students learn to become active listeners, both in what is called scenario-practice (for example, mock sessions for outreaching to officials) and by having classmates engage in mutual reflection in which students' critique and support each other.

Matthew Fox is a theologian and religious reformer who has written critiques of religious doctrine and practice. In his arguments, Mr. Fox reinterprets religious text to demonstrate how people can become validated and empowered through allowing for multiple interpretations of words and phrases, and not assuming any oral or written expression of ideas has to be set in stone. In one of Mr. Fox's books, *A Spirituality Named Compassion*, he has a section in that book called "Politics and Education: Educating for Compassion." As Mr. Fox states in this section of his book: "We have reduced education to job preparation and diploma getting, making it one more commodity that a consumer consumes."[513] Mr. Fox quotes educator Mary Richard as offering an alternative purpose for education: "a process of waking up to life."[514] He elaborates on this perspective: "Education is about the way to solve problems and celebrate it mysteries...to the obstacles entrenched in economic and political shibboleths that prevent our waking up."[515] Experiencing the back and forth of civic engagement, and reflecting upon the shifting of tactics or viewpoints held by an advocate help the young to wake up to life. Nobody is the action hero model used to describe leaders in traditional history textbooks, nor rigid stereotypic people stuck with low intelligence or inherent habits. People who are being served are complex, being receptive to some ideas and programs and resistant to others that are new, unfamiliar, and uncomfortable for them. In a compassionately designed template for delivering human services, staff and volunteers are trained to represent themselves as models for managing change.

Sarah also addresses another point in her civic trainings, which is the power of using questioning as a roadmap for discovering information, and not just relying on prefabricated answers offered by outside authority. The value of adopting a healthy practice of guided questioning is well summarized in a book by the writer and policy analyst Andrea Batista Schlesinger, *The Death of Why*. In addressing the need for youth for having unedited venues for participation, I summarize the words of Ms. Schlesinger: Authentic participation by youth depends upon) not having the imposition by adult leaders of preemptive, prescriptive 'solutions' for youth problems. Youth do not need to routinely be given answers built upon inert knowledge which addresses neither the call for community nor participation in a democratic community. As Ms. Schlesinger has stated, "In working with youth, their answers need to be constructed (by them), and not retrieved. Inquiry is risky. Resiliency is the reward."[516] Sarah designs a youth-engagement experience where they exercise reflection and are heard, design their own projects and strategies, and produce results that are an affirmation of their abilities and rewarding to the community at large.

After meeting Sarah, I learned that she has a twin sister who was raised with her in their early years in Chicago. Her family migrated to Texas, where she grew up and completed her college degree, which included much course-work in French and geography. After graduation, she served for a year in the Mississippi Delta through AmeriCorps; then, after applying for a position as New York City Director for Generation Citizen, she began her tenure in New York City. I believe that her experience and exposure to such a variety of cultural and social contexts helped to shape Sarah's appreciation for the richness of possibilities offered when engaged in diverse environments. When a person is dealing with changes in location and environments, differences in the menu of life at any time can facilitate the habit of questioning to help make sense out of difference. Clients in youth service programs have to adjust to change and establish new reference points for participation when specific activity menus are new and challenging for them. A youth program's responsiveness and effectiveness are invariably enhanced when staff and volunteers ask questions of those they serve, which creates a barometer for how those served are dealing with changed expectations and activity goals. Staff, volunteers and youth participants derive an appreciation for the value of differences in climate and program delivery in a format of participatory experiential education. What Sarah had shared with me on occasion is her need to work on being grounded. With the influence of place being so critical in people's lives, the experience of feeling grounded, even in new, strange, and fast-changing environments is part of the experience of feeling connected to others in your immediate surroundings. Many young people face issues with this sense of stability. Their families may have been forced to move because of rising and unaffordable rent, or evictions, or family crisis resulting in their being forced to live from shelter to shelter. In their own search for feeling grounded, I think they found a soulmate in Sarah.

Sarah has an innate sense, and an ethos, for the primary task of encouraging young people to develop their full potential. Sarah approaches this task as a construction project. During the initial periods of deciding on an issue, students also engage in self-reflection to assist them in identifying skills and talents that can be applied to the task of civic improvement work. One student in a group might have a talent for drawing, which can be utilized in the construction of outreach materials such as fliers. Another student might have an insatiable desire for detail, and this person can be invaluable for sticking to the patient search necessary for thorough research. Students have varieties of highly developed internal assets, which are turned into strategic tools of action.

Classroom civic environments are engineered in ways to support student discovery. Students with similar learning styles and talents work together in sub-groups amongst the classroom population. In addition, dedicated time is built into the schedule, so that small groups can report out to the larger body of the classroom, with allowance for questions and then adjustments in response to other student's observations. Multiple studies on classroom approaches have shown that cooperative learning leads to improved recall for detail, and the ability to take specialized content and apply its relevance in a larger context.

Ms. Andes sharpened and expanded her portfolio, along with those of her colleagues at Generation Citizen. Their organization's syllabi and lesson plans were diligently organized after studying research by organizations such as the Center for Information and Research on Civic Learning and Engagement (CIRCLE).[517] The staff of CIRCLE completed hundreds of studies in the fields of politics, education, and youth development. They also advise youth empowerment and leadership practices. They have found that when youth are given meaningful roles within an organization, they develop a sense of efficacy, which contributes to their holistic development and empowerment. The results obtained though their release of newsletters has helped to dispel urban myths diminishing the capability of teens, such as the myth that they are inclined to apathy or, when they are engaged, that they do not have a measurable impact on community improvement.

Sarah's responsibilities for training staff and students located in diverse communities and in schools with differing cultures of learning were tempered by an appreciation for learning about each school and adjusting the application of a syllabus devised centrally to the needs of each place. By matching local experience with best practices derived from national research and history, she strove to maximize opportunities for fully engaged learning by students.[518] Sarah has been a proponent for the efficacy of place-based education.

Generation Citizen has also constructed specific training tools that have proved to be highly effective in creating motivated teen advocates and policy change-makers. Generation Citizen, in its classrooms, uses what they call an hour-glass model. It promotes intensive exploration, discussion, and planning at sequential stages of participation. These activities start with looking at community issues, choosing a focus issue, and then researching and beginning to formulate an approach to the chosen issue, starting with identifying its root cause. From that point, a group collaboratively adopts targets and tactics for pursuing its goal.[519] Schools from all over the city of New York participate, including the Staten Island School for Leadership, which in the past addressed the issue of drug abuse among the homeless, and the Mott Academy in Manhattan, which examined the issue of police accountability.

In the autumn of 2013, I began traveling with Sarah to youth service programs, soliciting their support for our Teens on Board initiative. One such program operated out of a middle-school program at Beacon Center in Forest Hills. It was sponsored by the Queens Community House, which ran scores of youth and adult service programs throughout the borough.

When a civic co-mentor walks into a classroom proposing engagement with a specific cause, she or he engages with students who presently are engaged with standardized classroom work; adult civic trainers also dance with emerging engineers of social change, and step together with them as co-equal partners.[520] Each teen member co-constructs according to their varieties of mental agility.[521] Teens also teach adults according to the parameters of their own learning styles.[522] They open one's heart to new possibilities; together we reassure unsettled souls.[523]

The Beacon program youth participants (in this workshop, except for one high-school student, were all middle-school students) had been active in campaigns organized by the Campaign for Children.[524] Each year, budgets for middle-school after-school programs are typically threatened with budget cuts, and sometimes with elimination. Youth helped to organize petitions and letters to city government officials and elected representatives. Students also traveled, participating at rallies in front of City Hall. They already had some familiarity with planning advocacy approaches. Almost none of the youth Sarah and I met with during our visit to the Forest Hills Beacon knew what a community board was.[525]

After we had finished introducing ourselves to one another, and learning about their experience, Sarah had the group watch a video showing part of a speech given by then U.S. Senator Barack Obama at the Democratic Party Convention in 2004. The video highlights included a call to civic action, in which he proposed a frame of reference for the importance of "we" in garnering benefits for "me."[526] Sarah then introduced a written outline speaking about the frame, constructed by her specifically for the Teens on Board campaign. The students identified their interests and talents, and role played in directed conversations about learning about the part they might play in the campaign on behalf of their Beacon site. I followed Sarah's presentation with an introduction to the group about the structure, functions, and purpose of community boards. This included informing them about how boards work at full monthly meetings, and the place of individual committees, such as public safety or youth services and education in prepping the full board body for specific issues. The students then participated in a short mock session about how they might present an issue to a committee, appeal for the urgency of now, and enlist the attention and support of committee members.

Patrick Pinchinat who was the Queens Community House Forest Hills Beacon director, and Marlena Starace, who was the lead supervisor for the program, stepped out of the room during the process to allow their students independent space to come up with their own viewpoints and suggestions. After the students were dismissed (after first chowing on pizza), Sarah and I asked if the students had provided them any commentary about the workshop, we just gave them. Patrick and Marlena each let us know, with broad smiles and an enthused voice, how, even after such a long day for their youth members, they loved the session and were excited about helping. In the weeks following this workshop, their student members collected hundreds of signatures on petitions. The leadership at the Forest Hills Beacon also communicated its institutional support to the Department of Youth and Community Development, which provides funding for and monitors Beacon programs, as well as to city elected officials representing their neighborhood area.

Sarah and I, along with the Beacon youth participants, had started in conversation and learned from each other in revelation. In our outreach, we succeeded through thorough preparation, but ensuring that folks who initially were strangers felt safe in the same room also helped. It would take another year for our Teens on Board bill to be approved. However, after just a few short years, those, who as middle-school students had helped to make the public officer law amendment come into being, would then be eligible to apply for community board membership. They made the road while walking.

Sarah has counseled her staff, and kept true for herself, that whether one is assessing oneself, or allies and adversaries for one's cause, if an action civics practitioner is to operate with integrity, then condemning judgments are off the table.[527] Her mission is one of promoting "urban patriotism," in which students proposing civic reform source their inner authority, listen to and form alliances with allies, and adhere to the highest principles of inclusive democracy. To be a patriot for the democratic process, it is necessary to exercise decency, respect, and tolerance for differences of opinion. Jean Bethke Elshtain, in her book, *Democracy on Trial*, offers a lament and a critique about the absence of practices enhancing democracy. She calls the practices of respectful disagreement amongst people with differing political mindsets "democratic dispositions." Ms. Elshtain identifies these three dispositions, and reinforces her precepts throughout her book, as follows: (The practice of democracy requires) a propensity to work with others different from oneself toward shared ends; having a combination of strong convictions and a willingness to compromise; and having a sense of empowered individuality and at the same time a commitment to the common good (no one person's or small group's agenda takes precedence over the value of coming to consensus).[528] Students under Sarah's leadership in New York City, counseled by their social studies teachers in partnership with college students whom Generation Citizen called Democracy Coaches, were not just learning about these dispositions, they were experiencing becoming predisposed to those best practices of democracy by performing them. My point here is that, if you were to teach students to play the piano, you would not just have them study previous musicians or the theory of musical form. Piano students need guided practice in playing the piano. By utilizing the theory and practice of what Generation Citizen calls Action Civics, young proponents of social change get to hit the right keys and induce harmony in the world.

With the consent of her boss, Executive Director Scott Warren, Sarah had agreed to serve as an additional primary co-coordinator for the Teens on Board campaign in the fall of 2013. Through her example as a role model, and her teaching me new approaches for civic advocacy, Sarah helped me to develop the twin capacities of adhering to a vision and building infrastructure, which became pathways for getting to our goals in practical ways. What she brought to our decision-making and strategies was fueled by a psychic resonance she shared with potential allies, and at the same time a tool-building kit for getting to goals that were mutually agreed upon by partners. Before sharing the details about Sarah's suggested strategies, I share two thoughts about Sarah's presence.

The first is Sarah's confluent approach as practiced by the American-based Quaker founder George Fox, who began his leadership at the age of 16. These small but inner-oriented congregations shared in the practice of developing what they called clearness community. Each of their parish members work on being guided by their own inner teacher and at the same time supported by a community of fellowship. When people such as I visited the semi-annual presentations of student Generation Citizen clubs, the room allowed for emerging civic reform proponents, who participated in both internal interrogation and the questioning of external structures that governed their lives; this was universally shared among the students and became self-evident through the students' oral presentations and visual displays. In student presentations I witnessed, they shared about their own characteristics and practices, such as harboring homophobia or being too controlling. They described how they had to self-reflect, reexamine, and then assess ways of becoming accountable to themselves before they could feel good about advocating for change in others.

When training the staff of Generation Citizen, Sarah practiced with an approach integrating her intuitive sense of understanding the teen mind. Matthew Stewart is an American historian who examines our nation's early frames of mind as establishing precedents for today's political practices. In Mr. Stewart's book, *Natures God*, he makes reference to many samples of written correspondence between elected officials, and also amongst political activists, in the early eighteenth century. Although life in each of the states resulted in many differences in culture and political priorities, these letters of correspondence stuck to a central them. The wording in the letters always linked the concept that the laws of governance are ideal when they are aligned with respect for the autonomous mind. I make this point here to emphasize that when we rely too heavily on narrow ideology and viewpoints, or subject citizens to marketing techniques (whether in commerce or in pursuit of political advantage), we aim at shaping minds and controlling choice rather than honoring autonomously derived personal perspective. In a letter written by James Madison, in which he refers to the work of Thomas Jefferson as validation, he states: "The opinions of men, depending only on the evidence presented in their own minds cannot follow the dictates of other men." Mr. Stewart elaborates on the thought: "To demand a certain kind of belief, or to impose any faith, to 'pass laws for the human mind,' is not to direct understanding but to attempt to destroy it." correspondences to best practices for the Age of Reason and the laws of nature. In this work, Mr. Stewart writes about the naturalist essence of the teen mind: "The teen mind is a laboratory, just as nature is a laboratory, and is by its nature guided by experience and experiment, one of not knowing and of wandering." Sarah encouraged a sense of safety as well as wonder in wandering as part of a learning process. This allowed students to engage in a process shared by policy makers as they reformed our experiment with democracy, overtaken by doubt as much as by knowing, and of wandering/ stumbling towards desired ends.

At Generation Citizen's semiannual gatherings, which they called Civics Day, leadership clubs from middle schools and high schools from around the city shared their discoveries and obstacles in developing their issue-based strategies. When people such as me visited the semi-annual presentations of student Generation Citizen Clubs, the room allowed for emerging civic reform proponents, who participated both in internal interrogation and the questioning of external structures that governed their lives; this was universally shared among the students and became self-evident through the students' oral presentations and visual displays. This model for internal interrogation and seeking consensus reminds me of a methodology used just before and during the times when colonies fought to become independent. These were called Committees of Correspondence. These committees were scattered among the 13 colonies. They were forerunners to individual state delegations to the Congress. Each body informed a larger decision-making body of their positions, and then sought to shape a consensus supporting their position. In the students' case, the process was one of peer politics. When student groups, originating from differing schools, adopted similar stances on a particular issue, it could create a momentum for a larger decision-making body adopting the position initiated by a smaller body. Just as the entire Congress could eventually adopt a position initially proposed by a state delegation, a larger body within Generation Citizen, which leadership put together as a teen advisory board to the city-wide agency, could address an issue from a wider perch of influence. At the individual school level, Generation Citizen was supporting the young for having their viewpoints and suggestions not only respected, but also as expressions of voice that could change school policies. Generation Citizen has, in the last few years, initiated and organized a nation-wide campaign to have states and/ or cities reduce the voting age to age sixteen. Legislators at both the federal Congressional level, and in the New York State legislature, have introduced bills which lower the voting age to age sixteen. The wording in this legislation includes acknowledgement that teens already demonstrate a type of citizenship as reflected in the new generation's record levels of volunteering and community service. This verbiage also mentions that teens contribute to government treasuries by paying income and sales taxes. A last point that is frequently included is that teens master academic and cognitive skills which are often at an equal level or surpass the tested performance of older adults. (I will discuss these initiatives in the section of this book called Anecdotes Arising.) Thomas Paine has been attributed to having said, when referring to the right of governance being retained by those who are being governed, that with the success of the American Revolution, the time for its implementation had met us. This has been said, in another way, in recent times, as noted by Scilla Elworthy, an international observer of mediation and conflict resolution strategies around the world: "The future belongs to those who can see it."[529]

This approach, advocating for inclusion of the young in decision-making, also adheres to sage advice given by Andrea Bautista Schlesinger, a policy analyst who worked for a brief time in Mayor DeBlasio's administration in New York City. In addition to writing books, she has done extensive training with New York City Youth Councils and is a fierce proponent for allowing space for youth opinion and teen leadership. She points to a central tool, suggested by the title of her book, *The Question Of Why*: "We cannot know everything, as knowledge changes. Absorbing and acting on today's answers is simply not enough. The future is a moving target, and the ground beneath us is never still."[530] Assumptions about what works in the world, or is best for most people, have always been implemented as policy and an institutional practice by adults, who often miss the shifting grounds of reality. It is time to stop living the present as a wannabe construction of the past.

Mary Parker Follett, in her book, *The Creative Experience*, written in 1918, was an advocate for more participatory practice at both the corporate management level, and for democracy. I see Ms. Follett's words as still appropriate today and lining up with Sarah's work. "Democracy is an infinitely inclusive spirit. We have an instinct for democracy because we have an instinct for wholeness…[D]emocracy is a self-creating process for life…projecting itself into the visible world…so that its essential oneness will declare itself." [531]

Co-mentors: Gatekeepers for personal potential
and conscious community

What follows next are additional attributes I observed in co-mentors with whom I have had civic empowerment relationships, as well as for those serving as co-mentors in social change venues across the United States. Why, is might be reasonably asked, do I coin the term co-mentor instead of using the traditional term of mentor ? Historically, mentors are those with a trusted relationship with a mentee, who offer guidance, support, and the wisdom gained through experience to assist a person in learning about and adjusting to customs, culture, and rules of governance. The responsibilities for guiding mentees toward successful assimilation into society remain as a responsibility for co-mentors as well. However, what is different about learning to navigate and master social responsibilities in the 21st Century is different from what was required by mentees for thousands of years.

In prior times, mentors had a relatively stable society, and rules that were passed on from generation to generation with relatively no change, or gradual change. Except in the case when there was a major change in socio/economic structures, and in the consciousness and adaptive behaviors necessary to thrive under significantly changed conditions. For example, when our nations co-founders gave counsel to emerging leaders, the medieval structures governed by elite and remote authority were giving way to a new set of relationships where authority was vested in the consent of the governed. This was a radical change in conditions of rule, as well as for the responsibilities of everyday people who now had to exercise choice in lieu of either faith or adherence to externally imposed rules.

In the 21st Century, we are experiencing another set of radical changes. I speak here to some of these changes, specific to civics, governance, and socio/economic relationships. Our era is defined by continuous cycles of change and instability. No one person, or group of persons now has legitimate claim to represent all of society. For hundreds of years, in European nations, societies had been relatively homogeneous. Those who were granted ultimate ruling authority were always white males with considerable financial advantage and high social status. Political authority resided in the heads of elite leaders, and not in the sovereignty of each and every person. The idea of individual sovereignty for all was introduced in evolving democracies as a unique and radical concept. Politically and socially constructed rules of law, and for living, were adopted and assumed to be either congruent with human nature, or in the enlightened best interests of all.

Today we live in a world, a nation, and a city, that is comprised of stakeholders from multi-cultural backgrounds and diverse national origins. People who had been excluded from equal opportunity and civic enfranchisement, women, blacks, Latinos, native Americans, peoples of Asian and Pacific Island descent and GLBTQ peoples now have an inherent right to participation and for obtaining positions in governance. These new mandates are considered to be self-evident. What is being proposed in this book, and which has been demanded by teen-led empowerment and enfranchise programs, is that teens also have the rights for autonomous decision-making and collaborative civic responsibilities as do adults.

What separates co-mentors from traditional mentors is that these trusted relationships are no longer based on top-down relationship, with the adult being assumed to have exclusively valued sources of wisdom and preferable practices for governance. Co-mentors are in a side-by-side, or shoulder-to-shoulder relationship with teens, where adults respect and respond to the perspectives, knowledge and offerings given by teens. This new basis for adult-teen relationship, in addition to involving new cultural understanding and political agreements, is embedded in the soul nature of adolescence. Adult co-mentors retain an active, accessible and relatable presence of the adolescent archetype, the orphan, the rebel and the civic lover. A former civil rights activist and presidential candidate named Jesse Jackson promoted a slogan to live by for responsible and compassionately-based citizenship – keep hope alive. Co-mentors, those who are adults and those who are teens, continue to live by this principle of active hope.

What each also keeps alive are the adolescent soul attributes which assist in helping individual people, and our society, to thrive.

Civic mentors guide teens in recognition of all the dimensions of their identity and character. Co-mentors honor and attempt best practices aligned with the principles of our ancestral allies, such as the first peoples of the Americas. They also study and integrate the emerging understandings of science revealed in disciplines such as quantum physics, which have brought into question the validity of basic operating principles of the universe assumed under older scientific models. Co-mentors use a blend of ancient wisdom and opened ended experimentation as we move into the future. Co-mentors, rather than leaving their adolescent archetypes (the orphan, the rebel, and the civic lover) neglected or dormant, consciously work on nourishing them even into their elder years.

They also choose to involve teens in self-discovery in tandem with learning how to be pro-active contributors for the betterment of their schools and communities. Civic co-mentors can be either an adult or a teen. For each person, grown up or still developing, the inner adolescent is alive, who finds a path for expression and remains committed to making a difference in the world. Miriam Payne, Coach Dave Crenshaw, and Sarah Andes have been, for me, in my evolution as a teen empowerment advocate, role models for co-mentorship. Each of these three has been significant to me at critical periods of time and helping me to move forward with major transitions for my thinking and practices. However, as profiled in this book, I have been blessed with help from co-mentors young and old who are facilitators for bring forth the improbable as medicine for a wounded world.

Co-mentors begin with these ends in mind: Be eccentric, go forth as a navigator, and adhere to a dedication for enhancing holistic development of self and society.

What are the natural instincts of eccentrics—uneasy with and defiant in the face of the thoughts and practices that diminish creative and inventive ways of being in the world. Teens, when they challenge the problems brought about by stubborn adherence to business as usual, also allude to voting habits that bring about a diminished democracy. What is perceived as normalcy to adults resistant to change is an attachment to habit which is so powerful that change, even in the face of necessity, is rejected through insistence upon conformity. This inner sense of being a refusenik, when it comes to not conforming just for the sake of conforming, was poetically put forth by E.E. Cummings in his letter to a high-school editor in 1955: "To be nobody-but-myself in a world, which is doing its best, night and day, to make you like everybody else—means to fight the hardest battle which any human being can fight, and never stop fighting."[532]

Teen social justice fighters and their civic co-mentors persistently resist in a world whose financial security is embedded in branding, and whose political actors succeed by diminishing and dismissing others in the fight for equitable representation. This instinct for having the right to be seen and heard, and to make a difference, is felt as a survival of self and allies, and is dependent upon deviation from the norm. Insistently inquisitive inform-ers promote new sources of knowledge and action derived from emergent information arising from the changed conditions and tensions of a changing world. Change-makers of all ages wear their eccentricity as a badge of honor, insisting upon remaining included in the circle of decision-making even as they remain off-center.

Co-mentors are navigators: they encourage their partners to seek guidance in the practices of ancestral allies who had been involved in social justice; collaboration with present-day prophets who are civic cousins, such as those who fight for electoral inclusions for legal residents; and restitution for peoples robbed of their heritage and blocked from participation in the American Dream. Co-mentors mingle with the promises of the past, the potential of today, and the vision of tomorrow. They cross inter-disciplinary boundaries in the academic areas of study, and they move back and forth between the parameters of consciousness-informing science and spirit. They encourage a "marriage of sense and soul," as the postulator Ken Wilbur calls it in his book with the same title. In *The Marriage of Sense and Soul*, he brings cohesion and agreement amongst the theories of practitioners which seem, when looked at from a limited perspective, to appear to conflict with each other. He suggests that these theories, and the practices they help to produce, about the physical world and the spiritual dimension, are in a complementary partnership when seen through the lens of holistic relationships and the evolving consciousness of mankind.[533] One example of this type of partnership is between the rational and the intuitive minds. The rational mind is validated with scientific measurement. What is true for co-mentors, who have aligned their suggested practice with their lived experiences of being credible messengers, is the value of experimentation and willingness to move forward with the unknown, and mystical search felt through the heart. This process of congruent enterprise is learned through our invisibly sourced energies connected to nature, the higher order of the universe, and by using proven techniques and the scientific method.

Dr. Richard Katz, who has taught at Harvard for 20 years, has studied the indigenous scientific practices of interpersonal relations and community-building. Mr. Katz speaks to the difference between seeking control over patients or establishing equitable ways to share power with each other: "This navigation involves learning to discriminate between the drive for power, in which we seek domination and control over others, and wisdom, where we acquire the right way to live."[534] Dr. Katz respects boundaries and honors the wisdom on both sides of the line.

Co-mentors practice keeping personal and social holistic development in mind. David Korten, the former U.S. AID worker turned international economic justice advocate, speaks to the personal when he speaks to the essence of what it means to be human: "Humans innately have the capacity to anticipate and to choose our future. This is the defining characteristic of the human species. We add to this our capacity for conscious and collective intent. We organize by partnership, and unleash potential for human cooperation, using our expressions of higher order capacity and responsive service."[535] Mr. Korten does not respond from remote places of power, but respects the wisdom derived from grounded sources and local imagination.

The scenarios I have encountered and co-led, from the advocacy in the Pit, to IN STEP Project-Based Learning, to Generation Citizen's Action Civics classrooms, provide witness and testimony to David Korten's insights.

The drives for individually mindful integrity and for contributing to beneficial communal adhesion to common goals are basic to supporting the practices of co-mentors. It is with this focus from the mind, the heart, and the spirit that co-mentors find success with the institutional forms they help to create. As articulated by Buddhist-oriented observer Dale S. Wright and paraphrased by me: Critical thinking must be engendered within the spirit of open engagement, and engagement which must be cultivated, so that we can capitalize both on our rational power, but also by reaffirming and reformulating our spiritual sensibilities.[536] Co-mentors have been guides in aligning the organizational genius of the brain with the wisdom of the heart. Co-mentors teach how to untangle the knots of the mind, and re-weave the fractures of community. Co-mentors teach the wounded on how to read dysfunctional mind maps and transform them into fruitful currents and fortuitous blueprints for supportive changes in the world. In the contours and energies inherent to the teen psyche and the workings of democracy, they help to build bridges that enable authentically directed intervention with democracy by the young. As thousands of emergent young activists learned algebra and navigated the mysteries of this creative confluence, they too became navigators, even if eccentrically disposed, as we crossed the bridge to a new age. In the closing chapter of this book, titled Afterwards: Anecdotes Arising, I will cover a few social justice leaders and organizations, each of which has its own founding stories. Each civic mentor and teen activist (whom I consider to be participatory patriots for expanded democracy) contributes to an emerging body of nascent narrative.

Part of the joy in collaborating with co-mentors is that our relationship partially reminds me of creative fiction, that is, believing in the impossible about others whom I hold in high esteem, yet which still contains an intuitively perceived ring of truth. As I continued to work with Sarah in a series of youth program site presentations, I also joked with her about her secret identity as Wonder Woman. Sarah's superhero weapons taught me to formulate cohesive ideas and approaches which account for a co-mentor's abilities which originate from sources that extend beyond the five senses. Use of one's intuitive sense helps to facilitate manageable outcomes by youth. She encourages youth, and adults, with the heart of a teen, to feel the power of their civic agency. Her determined belief in adolescent agency is shaped through adolescent heart to adolescent heart communication. She communicates her strategies and suggestions with a soft yet determined voice. I believe that she also possesses and uses her secret weapon to snare young people into believing in themselves. For Wonder Woman, this weapon was known as a Lasso of Truth.[537] The lasso is wielded invisibly—yet is felt and affects deeply those who work closely with her. The more I experienced her in action, the greater my confidence in my own sense of purpose and effectiveness became. Through this purposefully focused technique of capturing me by having me capture my own power, an innate sense of optimism grew within me. In the past, a measure of self-doubt and uncertainty would at times creep up for me and be expressed as self-sabotage. Encircled by the lasso, I dropped the lies, and told the truth about my talents to myself. Sarah also values and utilizes the innate intelligence of the teen, assisting them in adopting their approach to situations and problems by using a novel orientation—that is, the unique perspective that is present in the eyes and minds of the teen beholder.[538]

Coach Dave often told me that on a team that is successful in winning championships, it is not just the level and talent of a superstar that counts, but the effect that person has on raising confidence and performance among each of his or her teammates. One of Sarah's colleagues, Yuen, speaking in confidence with me, told me then when in doubt, she just reflects and then follows a lead by doing what Sarah would do.

Our campaign had been going on, becoming gradually more successful over the course of six years. After Sarah's participation and teamwork with our Teens on Board campaign, we reached our objective of getting the Public

Law Amendment providing for teen membership on the board approved in just the subsequent six months.

Ms. Andes also utilizes her lasso by getting teen leaders to embrace their own innate intelligence and power of efficacy by encouraging teens' natural skepticism. She guides teens away from automatically and unreflectively embracing unquestioned assumptions and the bias of truths derived from the past.[539]

A Buddhist-oriented learning specialist named Ellen J. Langer refers to this utilization of one's inner-based resourcefulness as "mindfulness learning, which is developing the ability to observe without grasping too eagerly or becoming unduly attached. Langer also calls this the "maintenance of an intelligent ignorance."[540] Practitioners of empirical practice such as rational or cognitive therapies and those advocating for integral spiritual pathways embrace this practice. Young people today are far less likely than previous generations to become biased by the diseased truths of the *isms*, from racism, to sexism, or to homophobia. When confronted with those proposing these false beliefs, teens I have worked with simply say they are ridiculous, and that it is time for us to move on. In Anecdotes Arising, I will profile movements launched in opposition to previously held limiting beliefs and practices, which have become co-facilitators in helping us to navigate toward more promising future.

In closing out this profile of the civic co-mentor, I now share one more anecdote about Sarah Andes. In March 2014, working closely with the office of Assemblywoman Nily Roszik (who was representing a district in Queens, and who was lead sponsor for our bill on the Assembly side), Sarah organized a lobbying schedule with state legislators in Albany. Sarah, Scott Warren, and I were the designated lobbyists. The three of us split up for some meetings, but we all attended a meeting with Assemblywoman Vivian Cook from southeast Queens. She was amenable to the idea of helping young people but deeply skeptical about community boards, even joking at one point that if we cared about teens so much, it would not be fruitful if we would we send them to that type of forum. I remained an observant listener, for the most part, and let Scott and Sarah take the lead. Both Scott and Sarah were thorough in their discussion of teens' ability to navigate challenging environments, and the benefits boards can derive when presented with evidence from a young person's perspective. Ms. Cook began to nod her head with increased affirmation. Suddenly, Ms. Cook stood up quickly, and pointed at Sarah while simultaneously looking over to her aide, who was sitting at a nearby desk. In an excited tone, she called out to her aide, "Sign me on to this bill!" She then pointed at Sarah and said, "I'm signing on because you told me to do it!" We all laughed together, then stood up and warmly shook hands. Then the three advocates moved on to the next case. I think that Assemblywoman Cook realized, in a flash, that Sarah's belief in and practice for the efficacy of teens, trumped any reservations about the challenging environments of Boards. Ms. Cook closed out our meeting by stating that if Sarah followed the lead of her high expectations and strong beliefs, both teens and community boards would be better for the new relationship. In that room, I believe, the Lasso of Truth had worked its magic.

In my relationships with the co-mentors, whom I profiled previously in this section, beginning with orphans then rebels, and finally civic lovers, there was a sense I held about the bonding power of our relationships. Our bonds had their source, on some levels, in the world of narrative construction. At times, it seemed that what we sought to achieve began in desired creative fiction, which through our focused action became real. Each co-mentor was able to transform constructs of personal diminishment and isolation into vision and practice for empowered selves and mutually enhancing relationships.

In the Orphan section, I described how my Uncle Pierre transformed the fixated attachment of trauma into designs of templates to develop tactics for personal self-realization and healing engagement. Kamau Marchuria transformed his life from one of being a disabled target of bias and discrimination to civil rights warrior where he defined himself as a public defender and a visionary helping the wounded become self-assured leaders. E'niyah

Pazmino had to jettison her internalization of self-sabotaging stereotypes and move on from the terror of public rejection. She came to live the joys of personal and communal reconciliation. My mother, Jane Claire, moved on from being a victim in exile into a helper known to the outcast as an empress of embrace. People in turmoil were invited by her to leave behind the storms of inner and outer life and to welcome the sanctuary of safe space.

The rebels whom I profiled were all change-makers using the power of story to develop self-confidence and a welcoming place in meaningful relationships. Rev. Richard Leonard, who walked the walk at the first march in Selma, and again 50 years later, has used talk, his power of speech and story to teach his students that the need for the walk goes on. The road to social justice is still broken, from the downtown district of Brighton on Staten Island, where so many still cannot breathe, to the isolation chambers on Rikers Island. Kurt Tofteland helped the incarcerated to transform the theater of personal degradation and the sanction of terrifying imprisonment into stages of personal discovery and communal redemption. Mitch Wu enabled policy makers to progress from the language and misinformed practices turning Asian people with needs into imagined ineligibles into dialogically informed democratic practices where elected officials and affected stake-holders joined hands in the process of participatory pluralism. My father, John Kurland, used the power of heuristic humor and illuminated cause for indignation to aid those who were privileged by immunity to the practices of bias and discrimination learn to feel the pain and need for justice by the marginalized in our city and nation. Coach Dave would recognize, and induce the young to locate within themselves, the indigenous and ingenious sources of their identity. Once empowered with their newly fostered talents, the young would build bridges with supportive allies to make the road in achieving mutually beneficial civic outcomes.

In reference to my relationship with Coach Dave, I recall our initial meeting at the Paradise Church and call it "The Hero of the Heights Meets Mr. Rogers." Although I had zero previous experience working the streets with youth, Dave would come to believe in my still unpracticed methods and innate idealism. At the same time, I would be repeatedly reassured, that despite his being so young, he practiced with the wisdom of social justice elders. In his unreserved drive to see justice for the young, he would learn to overcome pitfalls induced by his mistakes. To be willing to try again, and get up from the fall, to march forward on a path resulting in better outcomes for those you serve defines what it means to be a hero.

In my admiration and appreciation for my co-mentors, I also value the sense in which we all started from a place that seemingly seemed a fiction, and often a nightmare. Through the ripened exercise of self-determination and public partnership we saw what was only imagined, fruitful outcomes, begin to bloom. In describing this phenomenon, I borrow a concept I learned from Jeffrey J. Karpel, which he calls "indeterminate potentiality." Mr. Karpel is a professor of philosophy and religion at Rice University. In his book, *Mutants and Mystics*, he profiles the works of science fiction writers, the imagined heroes in superhero comics, and the escapades of those practicing in the realms of the paranormal. Mr. Karpel describes "indeterminate potential" as a kind of field of potential ideas which take form through our determined intervention. Some of the ideas introduced in science fiction, for example, the submarine, and experimentation with changing the make-up of humans, are practiced in science today.[541]

In examining the realm of political and cultural norms, this transition from what is seemingly unattainable becoming quickly accepted as real can also be increasingly seen in our times. Many voters who had believed, in early 2008, that a Black person might be a president at some time in the future, believed it to be unrealistic to support the notion that Barack Obama could become president of the United States. After his victory in the Iowa caucuses, the belief system held by the skeptical quickly shifted into a shared hope for social just change. For as long as I can remember, the belief in marriage equality seemed to be a goal not to be obtained in my lifetime. However, after the under-the-radar organizing and advocacy of LLGBTQ activists, and a surprise Supreme Court decision, within a few months what had seemed untenable as per public opinion polls shifted when new polls showed super-majority support.

In the spirit of recognizing the invisible and fictional-based support of imaginative narrative, I mention here a few key elements which operate as tools for the critical work achieved through social justice action by our ancestral allies, present-day public prophets, and civic co-mentors. Each of these civic change types of difference-makers have these abilities in seed, or potential, but don't necessarily find it on their own without first committing to inner search and establishing public partnerships.

The first element is the unshakable belief, in the face of obstacles that seem so daunting, in one's efficacy as a social justice change-maker. In her book, *No Citizen Left Behind*, Maira Levinson included a chapter called "A Living Narrative." Ms. Levinson includes a quote from a Lebanese-American activist named Abed Hammoud: "...what drives me is to pave a way for a new generation of Arab-Americans. I think I am the transitional generation, and I believe that if everybody (just) waits, then the transition will never happen."[542] In other words, Abed believes that through his intervention, the process of change is happening now, and that his participation matters. As further elaborated upon by the book's author, "...narrative is not just a construct of educators spinning out radical and counter-cultural narratives that have no traction in the real world, but that narrative is (a living history, constructing) an empowering American History and identity from the building blocks of struggle..."[543] What seems improbable to attain needs the support of strong belief and determined action.

A second element refers to the actors effecting change. Are they individual heroes or social change actors aware of their relationships with supportive civic partners? Do they act to bring future benefits home to the present or remain stuck in the matrix of perpetually waiting until tomorrow? As suggested by Krista Tippitt, in her work *Becoming Wise*, she suggests that those who act on behalf of future possibilities being brought to life in the now, position themselves not in the safe system of established belief, but at the edges of possibility. As stated by Ms. Tippitt, who has interviewed and worked with change-makers around the world: "I have learned that people in the center are not going to be big change-makers. You have to put yourself at the margins and be willing to risk making change."[544] Teen social justice activists, working on behalf of their peers, who as a generation have been pushed to the margins of progress, and who have been criticized for exercising too much risk, know better. It is not about business as usual, but rather transitioning to the future with new consciousness. As stated on the back cover of Ms. Tippett's book: "The enduring question of what it means to be human has become inextricable from the challenge of who we are to one another...the possibility of personal depth and common life for this century, nurtured by science and 'spiritual technologies' with civility and love as muscular public practice."[545]

David S. Reynolds, in his book *Beneath the American Renaissance*, describes the influence of subversive literature in the 1800s, which, as described by Sean Wilentz in his foreword to Reynold's book "used demotic dialogue, encouraging a good ear, and using the voice of democracy's champions: (those writers) were so ardently devoted to the American ideals of American democracy."[546] Problems we face are real. They are not a tomb, but rather a womb, from which we foster the birth of life-promoting practice.

Charles Eisenstein, writing in modern times, has, in his book, *The More Beautiful World our Hearts Know is Possible*, aptly described the position and narratives expressed by social change activists sitting on the edge of two worlds: "Even as the old world collapses around us, or even as we leave it in disgust, still we carry its conditioning...we have become colonized through and through, born into its logic, acculturated to its world view...we take for granted the very things that are which actually are the roots of our crisis."[547] Our new era change-makers provide medicine for the disillusioned and entranced, so that what can be seen today unfolding are manifold variations of Dr. Martin Luther King, Jr.'s beloved community. As pointed out by Dr. King: "Learning and practicing the virtues of citizenship and the democratic process must happen from childhood occur when we speak truth to power and we keep faith that change is possible."[548] As we identify, observe, and practice with the heart of democracy, our more beneficial futures show their face to us today.

How the soul of adolescence aligns with the heart of democracy.

I now introduce the section describing how the heart of democracy, engaged with by local civic activists, teen social justice advocates, and the civic co-mentors guiding them, aligns with the three archetypes which are supportive of the Soul of Adolescence. With the soul of adolescence, the orphan, rebel, and civic lover become accessible to social justice actors within their personal psyche, and then they use these new orientations to guide them in achieving communal and civic reform. The heart of democracy is a social and political construct, using the reference points of the orphan, rebel, and civic lover from the larger perspective of creating and sustaining inclusive and just communities and society. When institutions and political practices are created and sustained under the guidance of the wisdom of each archetype, the formerly excluded and ostracized feel welcomed and embraced. The stories of diminishment and enforced dislocation are replaced by those of communal validation and inclusive participation. Communal and political partnerships are engineered amongst mutually appreciative partners who construct public options of benefit to one and all. In each case, they share the energies of the orphan, the rebel, and the civic lover, although outcomes are manifested on different levels, the psyche and the socio-political.

For Miriam, Coach Dave, and Sarah, as well as for other civic co-mentors, the dialogue that counts occurs when teen social change activists, who are working on their personal and social awareness, engage with the wounds perpetuated when society ostracizes perceived outsiders, constructs deaf ears to alternative stories, and builds walls prohibiting us from seeing and getting to the future. Varshini Prakash, a young person writing an article titled "Teach Your Elders Well," stated the case succinctly in the January/February 2021, issue of *Sierra Magazine*: "We are young people who have witnessed the world in chaos careening toward climate catastrophe. We have watched and waited our entire lives for people much older and more powerful than us to take care of the crises that were emerging. Yet little has happened. Now, the new kids on the globe are bursting forth with engrossing energy and novel ideas. Teen leaders in the emergent generation are standing up to say: "We are ready to be adults in the room. We are ready to take the future in our own hands. We are ready to envision reality in a different way."[549] M. Scott Peck, a religiously oriented visionary speaks to the relevance of a teen's soul-based guidance and the place of today's teens on the evolutionary path of human beings.[550] Co-mentors such as Miriam, Coach Dave, and Sarah have flourished by being taught by the young. They each understand, that to a certain extent, because the young are more attuned to the future, they are leading us, those who are members of the Boomer generation. Mr. Peck holds that both modern biologists and theologians appreciate the place of establishing individual identity and purpose as central to the ongoing progress of evolution. Teens, as individuals, and as an emergent generation, feel that call, in these urgently disruptive times, and are rising to the challenge.

For those of you in the Boomer generation (which includes me), to whom Ms. Parashar's article is chiefly addressed, if we are to be guided toward adopting co-leadership relations with teen activists, we need to listen to an old saying. The young need you not only to be joined at the hip with their life-affirming agenda. Cooperatively enhanced work for progress is facilitated through the sensitive correspondence of adolescent souls. When advocates for change adopt healthy civic practices, members of the emergent generation and the Boomer generation all flourish. The Uptown Dreamers thrive on pro-active partnerships between adults and teens. Applications for co-mentorship as Democracy Coaches at Generation Citizen are open. As I will discuss moving forward, similar invitations offer co-mentoring opportunities across multitudes of youth-led and civic changing making organizations, but each is crucially relevant in helping to obtain social justice and environmental balance in the United States. Take the challenge.

We are not drowning at the end of the world, but re-awakening in oceans of possibility as we imagine and construct viable futures.[551]

What I had shared in the preceding section is a biographical sketch of the soul of adolescence. One major message from that section is that our adolescent hearts are empowered through the guidance of the soul. Now, in the next few pages I discuss the intersection of two powerhouses related to spiritually based insights and understandings about civic life, the personal soul of adolescence, and the political heart of American democracy. I do this to help clarify why I believe that the personal soul of adolescence and the collective soul of democracy, though operating on different levels, are closely aligned. These next few pages will also serve as a transition to the final chapter in this book, called Anecdotes Arising.

As I have alluded to at the beginning of this section of the book, I will now further elaborate on my interpretation of a teen's relationship to the personal archetypes of the orphan, the rebel, and the civic lover, and propose a correspondence or synchronicity with how American democracy has evolved. I will be drawing comparisons to those three archetypal influences on our methodology of governance today which have origins throughout our history.

I use the concept of correspondence or synchronicity by borrowing from a Jungian concept—that what happens inside an individual's consciousness has a corresponding presence in social/political identity. For instance, I perceive teens as being influenced in part by the archetype of the orphan, cast out of childhood's innocence but blocked from adulthood recognition and power. I see the United States as having been an orphan in the last stages of its colonial dependence on Great Britain, not allowed the full rights of British citizenship while also being defined as not prepared for independent governance. I see the history of our nation's dissidents, the suffragists, abolitionists and so on, as being a progressively unfolding chronicle about civic rebels, undoing the contradiction of allowing only those who are privileged by class and race to enjoy the fruits of democracy. I see the work of simultaneously working on obtaining the highest mindful potential of oneself and one's friends and neighbors with the mission of aligning our democratic practices and ideals as the crux of a civic lovers' work.

During the 1960s, when I was beginning, as an adolescent, my work in social justice and civic reform, I was experiencing the tensions in societal transitions that teens face even today. As described in *Time* magazine's special issue on the significance of volatile times in the 1960's -we sat at the epicenter of an earthquake occurring along two intersecting fault lines. We are at that place again, and together, we can navigate safe passage for all.

The first fault line represents a transition away from the old archetypical portrait of adolescence that was generated during the age of industry and machine consciousness, which defined teens through brain capacity and level of hormones. The eruptive energies evident in teen enfranchisement efforts have activated the first sets of differences in belief about teen nature, shaking the edifice of falsely derived scientific findings and misdirected policies adversely affecting teens. Evolved understandings used to define teen nature have emerged as the ecological and spirit-based constructs of adolescent nature based on current scientific research and sociological studies, for instance, those I previously covered, such as the work done by Epstein, Males, and Seale.

The second fault line shaking up the precepts of our older belief systems, represents a period defined by David Korten, the former U.S. AID worker mentioned earlier, as a call for changes in practice which diminish and attempt to control people with different cultures and political systems. Mr. Korten holds that we are transitioning from our prior mechanical/industrial paradigm shaping our social and economic institutions. Under the old paradigm, privileged groups (who consider themselves to be superior simply because of being a member of a certain race, or socioeconomic status, who institutionalize their privilege with exclusionary policies and practices) create and maintain superior levels of wealth and status. Those who benefit from widening class divides and the instigation of racial division also manufacture ideologies and belief systems to justify the continuance of the status quo. For instance, these systems reinforce the belief in the power of any person to rise in status predominantly through personal effort. According to this belief, those who fail to succeed suffer because of personal deficits in character and ability. This belief system also celebrates personal benefit as foundational to the greater social good, even if a relative few benefits disproportionately at the expense of most of us.[552]

An additional set of beliefs adding disruptive fuel to the declining efficacy of old beliefs includes the unfettered faith in the value and practice of efficiency, without taking into consideration the hidden costs and unintended consequences of an invention, such as the automobile, television, and extraction of natural resources. While a small number of adults benefit financially from these practices, it is the general population, and the newest generation, which will pay the price of environmental neglect through having to face increases in taxes to pay the costs of remediation. The youngest members of our nation are facing decreasing levels of positive health indicators and indicators of a good quality of life.

In exercising the consciousness and practices of the emerging ecological/spiritual mindset, we account for small actions implemented in local places having a ripple effect on everything else. Even given the diversity of our ethnic and national identities, which defines our splendor as a multi-variant species, our prime connection is that of being human. We, the majority, are stewards with responsibility for each other, and for the planet coming first. Mr. Korten describes a need to transform our mental concepts and social institutions as "a Great Turning" in which we adopt practices of ecological responsibility in place of acting like automatons in service to the invisible hands of the great machine.[553]

It is a time for those of us with a mature orphan archetype to heal the incorrectly defined identity of what eco-psychology-oriented Bill Plotkin calls "patho-adolescence."[554] I mention this concept here, as in addition to the damages caused to the teen psyche, a continuous cycle of instability and dysfunction results in parallel ways for our societal institutions. Under the constant barrage of adult-led invalidation practiced by our political leaders and media sources, teens look for alternate sources of participation, cooperative enterprise and communion. Adolescents, rather than being looked at as drop-outs, should be considered as those who are pushed out. Marginalized and displaced, struggle to optimally function in settings put in place by adults. When suffering the effects of trauma, the pain they suffer from sources not identified by either themselves or their health providers contributes to subpar institutional performance, or just leaving the field of participation. One of his examples cited is that of confusing the goals of marketers and advertisers for maximizing consumption with the nature of being a teen.

The teen who has adopted a patho-adolescent identity has adopted the demeaned and dismissive characterizations as inherent to himself or herself. He or she has also bought into the toxic practices promoted by the industries still dominant today promoted in marketing and sustained through tax benefits. Today, a teen's identity is conflated with a pathological identity—which, in turn, conflates the excesses and social toxins generated by adult-manufactured institutions. Compulsive consumption and the reinforcement of impulsive responses for retaliatory action through our "war on for morons" policies, are mistaken for the true nature of the adolescent soul. Out-of-control desire for material things has been created and sustained by advertising and marketing, reinforced by parents as a tool of conditioning and control, infused into what Paolo Freire describes as our "banking system"-constructed schools, and then promoted and funded by our elected officials.

As explored by Bill Plotkin, the very term and concept of "adolescence" was not even used until the ascent of the industrial age, between the late 1800s and early 1900s. This concept of adolescence, which society until recently understood to be universally applicable, conceptually keeps teens in a place considered to be frozen, inadequate, and stuck in delayed development until a mature state of adulthood is reached. This concept about adolescence was created to hold human beings, who do evolve and progress in consciousness and habit during the time zone (or fulcrum) between childhood and adulthood, in a place where underdevelopment is considered unalterable until mature adulthood is reached. According to Mr. Plotkin's analysis, the symptoms of the "problematic adolescent" are rooted in the arrested development of supposedly mature adults (whose behaviors serve as models for teens) and the exploitative and toxic practices of our society, For example, out-of-control spending, explosive levels of debt, and unprecedented levels of pollution in our environment. In contrast to these interpretations, Mr. Plotkin holds that the period of adolescence is a time for people to develop evolutionary advantage through the unfolding adolescent advantage, which includes the urge to inquire deeply, to be part of community, and to share the gifts of creative imagination. Mr. Plotkin quotes the author and wilderness explorer Geneen Marie Haugen: "[W]e cannot intentionally create unless we can first imagine."[555] Teens have been at the forefront of converting barren plots of land into community gardens and challenging the destructive effects of racism, sexism, nativism, American exceptionalism, and impulsively managed addiction to using violence as a solution for social problems. The term "wilding," which was invented in the 1990s and then applied in policy initiatives punishing teens, arose through social paranoia exercised toward teens, especially those who are people of color. The term wilding was popularly used, in the 1990's and beyond, by elected leaders and news stories which contributed to creating an image of adolescents as being out of control, dangerous to themselves, and a threat to society. When adults had participated in episodes of wilding, such as the draft riots in the early stages of the civic war, or attacks on members of minority groups, these were justified at those times as necessary to challenge injustice, and to protect the sanctity of civilization. When colonials rebels dressed up disguised as Native Americans and engaged in the criminal act of dumping tea in Boston Harbor, these scenes were later glorified as being acts of patriotism preceding our war for independence.

I am not proposing that violent acts of wilding are justified, either by our ancestral actors nor teens. What I do hold is that the energy of wilding, when expressed in creative and peaceful ways, is essential to building a healthy sense of autonomy, and sets precedence for establishing new cultural norms which protect positive forms of identity and group solidarity. Many of the writings in the Romantic period of literature promoted ideas about developing alternative lifestyles and practicing civil disobedience. The periods of the Harlem Renaissance and the Beats created spaces for freedom of expression, and protection from the invalidation of imposed will. The positive forms of Hip Hop and Rap function in similar fashion. They provide its performers and audiences with a language and a stage for resisting intolerance towards its members, and medicine for healing the effects of weaponized discourse attempting to define them, as well as from institutional violence. My larger point here is that counterculture supports the development of cognitive and social/emotional growth. Growing into their enlarged capacities for positive self-identification and group pride, their hearts and minds are set on fire, contributing to hopeful and enthused vision, healthful communion, and a shared language which becomes a facilitating influence for defining what is meant by the common good, the authentic, and portraits of beloved community. Participation in countercultural experience comes to both precede and complement later participation in the civic and political realm.

It is the premise of my book, which intersects the work of Mr. Plotkin and Haugen, that the archetype of the orphan centers us in our evolutionary task of discarding the nonfunctional and in imagining change. The rebel guides us in developing its emerging story. It is the archetype of the civic lover that allows us to align our higher potentials of realization with the higher angels of democracy. As Haugen continues: "Imagination might be the most essential, uniquely human capacity—creating both the dead-end crises of our time and the doorway though them."[556] Mr. Plotkin alludes to this when he explains "the distinctiveness of adolescence" as "a radical time which can be expressed in archetypes, developmental tasks, centers of psychospiritual gravity, inherent contributions to community, and circles of identity."[557] In this book, I refer to these elements as the confluence of mindful change performed as an extension of the works of ancestral social reformer allies and public prophets today guiding us in our journey aligned with the Great Turning. Civic co-mentors for teen activists facilitate the vision and action of social justice-producing change agents. To quote Mr. Plotkin one more time: "Puberty is a rite of incorporation into a larger social community, where teenagers learn to create an authentic social presence. Confirmation is a rite of separation OUT of that community and into a time of mostly solitary wandering, there to prepare for true adulthood.... Teens become adults who (as Plotkin quotes the poet David White) '[become] visible/ while carrying/what is hidden/as a gift to others.'"[558] Coach Dave's constant theme in his practice of assisting teens is that the task for mentors is to dig for the gold that inherently shines in each teen. The time has come today for the rebel to generate a new story about self and community in which our centers of individual purpose and communities of social conscience thrive, and in which autonomously affirmed teens and adults share their energetic motivations as they develop new paradigms of partnership.

An additional balancing act, as we move out from the old paradigm and in the beginning stages of the eco/spiritual age, is described further as an education about the nature of social ethics and responsibility. Taking larger responsibilities for the social good and for planetary sustainability involves a deepening of participatory practices in governance. When fully in effect, previously marginalized people take a place at the table in the chambers of decision-making. Seeking just and ethical improvements for our experiment in democratic governance is a quest.[559]

Those who had at one time been excluded from participation in our democratic practice—women, laborers, and people of color—in seeking to foster change in what our nation's founders held would always be an imperfect democracy, aided all Americans in aligning our governance practices with the higher angels of our nature. When America adheres to its ideal as expressed in its motto: government of, by, and for the people, we do so by ensuring universally inclusive participation and representation at all levels of government. There is no longer any bias, discrimination, or exclusionary practice based upon one's racial background, national identity, gender or sexual orientation, or age. Individual stakeholders (that is, those who establish residence, pay taxes, and contribute to the communal good) facilitate great leaps forward for our society. We, as a nation, after being counseled and pushed by the leadership of marginalized peoples, generated, and then experienced great leaps forward during our post-Civil War Reconstruction, the women's suffrage movement, and the civil rights and peace activities of the 1960s. Today, teen-led movements such as Teens Take Charge, Generation Citizens Vote 16 project, and others (which I will profile in the Anecdotes Arising section of this book) are inventing and managing assurance for civil rights and inclusive rules of official authority. People are developing administrative, legislative, and judicial outcomes which bind us all together as one nation. Though our multicultural influences and social/political maturity, our nation is beginning to ensure personal space for individual dignity. It is a time to shed the addictive habits as I previously outlined, by Dr. Martin Luther King, Jr., as the "4 catastrophes, materialism, militarism, racism, and the continuing cycles of poverty."[560] How have our ancestral allies and current social justice leaders had their footsteps followed by a new generation of youth leadership in addressing Dr. King's concerns?

An environmental movement, which became resurgent in the 1970s, led to a flowering of eco-responsibility in which we take accountability, in part, by addressing the intersection of responsible consumerism, honor for the Earth, and personal obligation engendered at the local level. By developing an environmentally sensitive and spiritual connection to things, and the process by which we obtain things, we bring remedy to the excesses of the obsessive-materialist syndrome of hyper-consumption, over-production, and the destabilizing of natural life process. One example of this is the creation, by the Earth Island Institute in San Francisco, of the Brower Youth Awards, in honor of David Brower, a founder of Friends of the Earth, the Earth Island Institute, and the first Executive Director of the Sierra Club. Young people, from ages 15 to 25, are selected for their hands-on difference in making their immediate school and community an example of environmental responsibility and social justice. In 2020, Chander Payne, from Bethesda, Maryland, was an honoree. Among the projects he devised and led were "connecting his school pantry with a local roof top farm, bringing twenty pounds of produce to his school menu each week." Mr. Payne also helped to establish an "Urban Boot Farm in his high-school courtyard, which enlisted the volunteerism of marginalized youth such as those from Washington D.C.'s Homeless Children Project." Through Mr. Payne's initiative, those marginalized from access to wholesome foods came to know about healthy diets and taking local responsibility for the local production of food.[561]

Opposition to militarized strategies conducted through larger and more destructive war took off with the growth of the Conscientious Objector movement during World War I. Objectors developed their pacifist belief system from the doctrines practiced in the faith, such as those of the Mennonites, Quakers, Amish, and Jehovah Witnesses, as well as those practiced by humanists and other secular-based movements like the International Workers of the World. Objectors faced beatings, imprisonment, solitary confinement, and social ostracizing, but maintained their practiced integrity for living through the philosophy of non-violent resistance. Today, the intrusion and violence of structural racism and extreme economic inequalities have resulted in marginalized people living under conditions of colonization that we know today as segregation, community disinvestment, and economic policies which favor the privileged. A youth organization called the Ya-Ya Network has been providing leadership training, and opportunities to lead, to youth activists aged 15 to 25 in New York City. Promoting a new wave of "youth activists and youth allies," they help budding leaders to "unpack their identities, deconstruct implicit bias, and to lead in safe operating spaces both inside and outside of their own communities."[562]

Resistance and the re-visioning of strategies to fight structural racism has been, in the last decade, experiencing a strong resurgence from coast to coast. In 2014, Fania Davis founded the Restorative Justice for Youth Project in Oakland, California. Ms. Davis had been a civil rights lawyer for 27 years, and earned a Ph.D. in Indigenous Studies, making her a prime candidate for training youth in the law, and the necessity of operating from boots on the ground in their classrooms and community. The Youth Project has been instrumental in changing the practices of seeking school safety from one of retribution or punishment, to one of restitution or one of "counseling, conferencing, and making amends." They utilize the tools not of retaliation against falsely constructed youth demons, but of negotiation where the offender and the victim dialogue, forgive, and re-construct a web of community.[563]

In New York City, the Urban Youth Collaborative (UYC) facilitates the "transformative power of youth organizing" for establishing grassroots social change coalitions and recognizes youth contributions toward constructive change. UYC partners with grassroots social justice organizations such as Make the Road New York, Sistas and Brothas United, and the Future of Tomorrow. The youth leadership council at UYC has also helped in the "passage of the Safe Student Act of 2015, which ensures accurate reporting of arrests and suspensions in schools," and had procured "$2.4 million in funding from the NYC Council for the Restorative Justice Initiative."[564]

While continuing to partake in the lessons of various forms of counter-cultural experiences, teens are now increasingly joining adult-led social justice movements, as well as staring up and steering movements led by young people. Young adults are learning to address the root causes and consequences of militarism, materialism, poverty and racism. One example here is the work of Maya Salcedo, who was a Brower Youth Award recipient in 2012. Three years later, she attended a youth summit sponsored by an organization called Youth Rooted in Community (RIC). The RIC Summit brought together "a national grassroots network of activists, adults and youth, working to facilitate community resilience through rural and urban agriculture, community gardening, food security…and environmental justice work." This story about inspired idealism put into the construction of social policy is laid out in a piece written for *A People's Curriculum for the Earth*, edited by Bill Bigelow and Tim Swinehart from Rethinking Schools.

A maker policy statement and statement of principles constructed by the summit were 17 basic principles, including "the right to have healthy food at school, the right to use locally sourced food, and the right to empower more youth with the knowledge of food justice."[565] Historic movements such as the Women's Rights Convention in Seneca, New York, Dr. Martin Luther King's March of Washington, the Stonewall rebellion demanding rights for LBGTQ people, and Native American initiative at Standing Rock. Each of these movements for inclusion and social justice have become milestones contributing toward the development of forward- looking consciousness and institutional reform. These movements are celebrated and studied by youth leaders today, who still struggle to maintain the civic and political gains obtained yesterday. In addition, they are organizing, as marginalize peoples, who are also ostracized because they are teens, and developing new strategies for gaining social and political equity.

Teen leaders are exercising their muscles of multiple intelligences and informed supportive coalition-making infused with authentic sources of sight, passionate optimism, and love for the common good. They are developing the ability to see, and to lead, through their own volition, and not as dependent upon disguised conditioned obedience, in which they fake being to be able to see (to please adults). Youth leaders are acting from spaces of autonomy and respect for horizontal power-relationships rather than spewing of yesterday's disproved truisms and today's questionable conclusions.

Students learn the benefits of participation beginning with the transformation of school culture and practices. The young, not by choice, had always participated in the process of socialization in the classroom. For 12 years, they have encounters with adult authority other than that of their parents. This authority has, until now, been absolute and resolute. In our changing times, youth voice is changing the nature of educational institutions, as well as those of teen and adult learning/teaching relationships. Classrooms are now developing curricular approaches, which teach the intersection of classroom and community. Classrooms and school environments are still their primary places of interaction, but new stories have been created, and they have created chances for tomorrow's vision to be realized today.

The structure and processes of school governance vary, from highly authoritarian to gradients of participatory opportunities. Whether a student's dominant mode of experience lies closer to that of becoming a programmed first responder to remote authority (akin to what is known in some circles of advertising as creating conditioned consumers) or a reasoned stakeholder within whom participatory authority resides, determines their status as either conditioned and a controlled civic consumer or a creative subscriber for the social good.

The confluence between empowered teen citizenship and deeply participatory democracy is aptly described by Neil Postman when he asks a question: What is the end of education? "Does the creating of the right kind of public schools contribute toward strengthening the spiritual basis of the American Creed. This is how Thomas Jefferson understood it, how Horace Mann understood it, how John Dewey understood it. The question is NOT whether public schooling creates a public. The question is: What kind of public does it create? A conglomerate of self-indulgent consumers? Angry, soulless, directionless masses? Indifferent, confused citizens? Or a public infused with confidence, a sense of purpose, a respect for learning, and a tolerance for difference and diversified outcomes?"[566] Each of these types of elements, those of the lingering fetters that hold us back and the emergent possibilities that shape us as enlightened change agents on a promising bridge between now and the future is flushed out in the sections that follow.

In the preface to this book, I recounted three periods in my life that set the table for the civic work that would be a path I traveled in my 30-year journey. Each challenge presented me with opportunities to retreat from engagement or build resiliency for compassionately supported participation. In the Forward/Backward section of this book, I presented a picture of my 30 years of youth empowerment experiences as a series of periods in which I refined my approaches under the influence and guidance of allies from backgrounds and geographic areas of diverse and varied compositions. Through my interactions, I developed more nuanced understandings of multicultural variation and the needs of community based upon the perspectives of class, race, gender, and identity. I developed skills and understandings for communal organizing and teen empowerment based upon intersectional needs and capacities.

This chapter is a psychological/social/civic progression into how we took a comprehensive look at civic work accomplished by teen change agents and their co-mentors by examining their deeper connection to and support from archetypal inner allies. This chapter develops a concept of the congruity between the potential of a holistically developed self, embedded in the body and mind, to the heart and one's soul in attaining the achievement of deep democracy. What I have developed in the anecdotal piecework for the orphan, the rebel, and the civic lover applies both to the adolescent soul and the heart of democracy. Throughout the course of our history, and during today's chaotic transitory period, reformers—those who contest the inequities of the status quo—have been America's orphans, seeking to bring us back home to exercise our ideals. New stories have been created, not just by elites, but by those living and contributing close to the ground. Harmony and balance are gradually coming into place between the dreams of idealist minds, and the mission of living our lives uncontested for participating in the experiment we call democracy.

As I progressed through this chapter, I shared my recent reflections and moments of realization based on the reconsideration of episodes in my early life and applying new thoughts about those early lessons throughout the later stages of my journey in which I helped to develop conscientious community practice guided by soulful principles. I describe, through sharing of insights and inspiring anecdotes experienced on my journey, how my soul-based and spiritually based learning contributed towards an evolution in my consciousness. I eventually came to see my civic empowerment practices in terms of a multidimensional perspective. These practices include historical contributions from change-makers and dissenters from the traditional practices of indigenous peoples, and an appreciation for the importance of social/emotional information in my decision-making. I further improved my organizing practices when taught by present-day advocates and co-mentors who come from differing racial and national backgrounds than mine. These allies, past and present, teens and adults, helped me to infuse my civic reform portfolio by helping me to see the underlying foundation of our souls. Our souls are, by their very nature, accepting of difference and multitudes of variety, instructive and forgiving, and expressive of a prime function of having love for life. Our real self is an extension of our soul.

As stated by mystics, and as I learned by myself and my allied co-mentors, if you are an orphan, your challenge is that when you abandon your life purpose and your dreams, you continue to remain lost in diversions and on false pathways away from personal and social fulfillment. Nelson Mandela has given us hope and courage through advising us on staying true to our inner instigated message. A central theme of his work is not to fear the darkness, but to embrace your inner light. As one puts aside fear, you engender love for yourself, and inspire others. The "beloved community" thus becomes ours to co-create and receive mutual benefit.[567]

If you are a rebel, the task is to transform story, and to have your authentic rendition seen by others. The messaging of our soul's purpose might initially be experienced as a discomforting whisper, or a flash of insight lost in the business of ceding authority to others. With practice and patience, adherence to the stories imposed upon us fall away. The personal patterns and habits ingrained in us through social fiat give way to the quiet yet persistent messaging that has been available to us all along. As we stay aligned with our internally sourced messaging, we are empowered to use authentic voice. Once balanced and centered, we develop a habit of loving to hear the voice of others. The Buddha brought this mandate of enlightened presence and relationship into one of his teachings called the Ambathta Sutre: "Whoever is in bondage to the notions of birth and lineage, or to the pride of social position, or connection by marriage, they are far from the best wisdom of righteousness."[568] Two shamanic counselors, Linda Star Wolf and Nita

Gage, propose breaking the chains of this bondage when they write: "Break from attachments to the broken treaties of separation inherent to our social institutions, and listen deeply to the entreaties from the soul, provided to us through connection to our bodily signals, our heartfelt guidance, and our minds broadened beyond the illusion of separated and isolated individual consciousness."[569] For teens today, those who break the bonds of "perpetual preparation, and the resultant continuous dependencies" speak this truth to both personal and generational power.

Thomas Paine articulated the Buddha's insight using a clause advocating for the right of an emergent generation to govern: "Every age and generation must be free to act for itself, in all cases, and from the ages and generations which preceded it. The vanity and presumption of governing from beyond the grave is the most ridiculous and insolent of all tyrannies. Man has no property in man, neither has any generation a property in the generation to follow. It is the living, and not the dead, that are to be accommodated."[570]

Paine, celebrated for his inspirational writings during times of our dark soul, challenged his fellow rebels for their contradictions exercised in chasing the rights of life, liberty, and the pursuit of happiness. For him, if these were not available for all, then they were to be scorned as the privileges of the few. He would later be buried in an unmarked grave, scorned by President Roosevelt as a "filthy little atheist," and have his contributions unaccounted for in our historical narratives until brought to light by dissident historians in the middle of the twentieth century. Stories addressed by the ostracized and presented by those who are diminished by those in power introduce a fierce contesting force against the status of the privileged. The dreams and the social reform actions initiated by the young never disappear but are reborn in the narratives of idealistic change agents who walk in the energetic paths of Mr. Paine.[571] Modern-day public allies for teen enfranchisement march in the energetic footprints of ancestral allies such as those of abolitionists, suffragists, labor organizers freedom riders, and farm worker advocates like Cesar Sanchez. Modern-day public prophets like Black Lives Matters activists, Dreamers, and Call the BS organizers are co-creating today's ener-getic hubs. Today's social change proponents are constructing inspirational milestones, suggested by Thomas Paine, which guided the wounded heroes against the unchallenged orders of complacency and tyranny. As they have "detailed the design for justice," they have presented to me as not only large in my life, but larger than life itself."[572] Both the designs of deep environ-mentalism and spiritual activism correspond with the reconstructive and restorative intentions of social justice organizing.

The civic lover constructively creates pathways that connect our inner purpose and the validating practices of a deep and inclusively participatory democracy into the very habits of our everyday lives. As I have previously mentioned, in his observations about democracy in America the nine-teenth-century social commentator Alexis de Tocqueville insightfully stated that "it is the inward habits of the heart which informs the infrastructure of democracy."[573]

In the following chapter of this book, which I call Anecdotes Arising, I introduce additional co-mentors whom I met and greatly admire post the period of my 28-year journey. Here, I briefly acknowledge the significance for me of one co-mentor, whom I collaborated with and who continues to exhibit the propensity for being an artistically oriented citizen. She excites the imagination of her teens and civic allies and builds creative pathways for inducing social change. In my heart of hearts, there is no me without us. This co-mentor is Yvonne Stennett, who is now the Executive Director of the Community League of the Heights, whom I met in the early stages of my youth services career in Washington Heights. Among the many tools for which she has encouraged the young to express their community connection is that of historically referenced street art.[574] Her teen activists have presented their voice in the form of community murals in which each community stakeholder concerned with social justice and communal improvement is artistically depicted as walking shoulder to shoulder with the grand marchers, our neighborhood's early movement pioneers for social reform. These murals, conceived of and constructed by teens, are designed after conducting surveys with neighbors and having conversations with those versed in local history. The images move us, and the walls speak to our shared historical significance.

I elaborate on these projects here to emphasize the importance of art, and creativity, in promoting social change. The aha! moments induced by artists as citizens encourage the eye to see in novel ways, the ear to receive voice with expanded sensitivity, and the enhanced wisdom and guidance of the heart. Whether expressed in paint or orchestrated voice, each of these methods is a creative work of art.[575] As proposed by Rob Hopkins, an environmentalist and proponent for a resurgence of imagination, these teen-led creative initiatives represent a "weaving, through experiential testimony, of the lessons of history combined with the imagined possibilities for the future."[576]

Social climates involved in creating new cultures and practices are embedded in the evolution of our democracy. Creating expansive and welcoming space facilitates social change that promotes, as written by Anodea Judith, the "power of love over the love of power."[577] The design of love enhances mutual appreciation and support. At the dawn of the twentieth century, labor organizers, those who fought the resurgence of a Jim Crow culture, those who worked to get voting rights for women, pacifists guided by the philosophy of the Quakers and their philosophy of nonviolent resistance, all contributed to the foundations of our current path for recognizing human dignity and socially embedded rights. As pointed to by Sean Wilentz, an American historian who has profiled our nation's labor movement history and the progressive evolution of our democracy, these movements were "a set of living, breathing relations that involved real people in often challenging and bewildering circumstances, trying to make sense of the huge forces which were beyond their control."[578]

Today, civic efforts, led by passion, reinvent themselves. Movements today are led by those who have moved away from revolutionary confrontation by seeing an evolutionary congruence of divergent and conflicted lives. This new type of social justice vision and action is written about by adrienne maree brown, a writer and social activist. A part of the orientation for becoming evolutionary-oriented change-makers involves a methodology driven by the "urgency of making kin: I have a circle of friends and family, with whom I am radically vulnerable, and trust deeply, we call it co-evolution through friendship."[579] When we develop friendships on a personal level with those from our neighborhood, we embrace those who understand us, and accept their foibles and missteps as part of the package when being a friend. Within our tightly interconnected world, the planet is now our neighborhood, and those whom we may have feared or distanced ourselves from in prior times are now becoming our best friends in ensuring the safety and sustainability of our common shared home called Earth. During the period of the Teens on Board campaign, leaders from organizations with varied missions understood the fierce urgency behind the push to get teens included in municipal advisory roundtables. We were brought together seeking the passage of principled policy, and we came together in a spirit of friendship. We felt a common affinity for the cause, and after getting to know each other better, enjoyed each other's common experiences of struggles and triumph. We also saw our civic tasks as being worked upon within the company of friends.

How do two soul-driven strategies, those of ensuring the holistic development of adolescents and fighting for universally inclusive practices of deep democracy (each of which emanates from the engines of the heart) become mutually reinforcing scaffolding experienced in the intersections of synchronistic understanding?

One lens that I use to frame this question is to examine the dynamics common to each realm—those in the personal realm which help us toward fulfillment, and those in the social/political realm which contribute to commonly shared benefits. I propose here four dynamics, each of which, on the negative side, can either stifle us or, on the positive side, lead us toward exercising constructive and creative change. Here I refer to choices, those commonly attributed to teen nature under the old paradigm, as contrasted to those practiced by teens working on developing the new paradigm. These choices involve four dynamics which can either be self-deflating or life enhancing. The first choice is whether to remain invisible or choosing to establish one's visibility. The second choice is between agreeing to remain silent in the face of misrepresentation, or insisting, using strong voice, to present your true self to the world. The third choice involves whether to decide to shrink into a world of inaction and passivity, or to choose to shine a light on your inner assets as well as the benefits of your social contributions. The fourth dynamic involves choice in both the personal and civic realms of experience. Do you surrender into a state of perpetual paralysis or insist upon breaking the bonds of psychological and civic imprisonment through the practice of passionately driven participation.

Dynamic choice—down with the old and up with the new.

The first dynamic choice concerns whether we remain invisible or become visible. In the personal domain, do we surrender to and adapt self-destructive concepts that sabotage us and hurt others? If we do, the positive potential within us remains untapped, perhaps momentarily felt, but blocked from being developed. We live with the undisclosed story that will forever haunt us. Yet, if we develop the trust and courage to look within, and if we have the compassionate support of others, we can change what has not worked for us into a mandate for discovery and validation. The gold within us comes forth, and our true light shines.

On a social level, do we relate to teens as perpetrators causing harm to others because of their undeveloped brains, and/or, do we relate to them as predators populating wilding crews running amok among us due to their supercharged hormones? Alternatively, if we consider induced behavior using the perspective of social and institutional impacts, do we understand these choices of self-sabotage and aggressive actions as motivated by unconsciously driven choices developed in the throes of personal and household trauma? At a conference cohosted by the NYU School of Health and the New York City Department of Youth and Community Development in 2018, health care and youth services presenters shared the statistic that 90 per cent of youth living in underserved and besieged communities either directly experience traumatic incidents or are closely affiliated with those who do. The unexamined prevalence of trauma becomes the unaddressed factors contributing to social dysfunction. As noted by a director in the NYU health program, the misconnection between underlying causes of behavior and displayed behaviors highlights the need for medical and psychological clinicians to identify the root causes of self-destructive and aggressive behaviors, and to reassess for proper intervention. Recent research which reveals the impact of unaddressed traumatic events has led us to understanding that the underlying emotional condition leading to destructive and anti-social behaviors is that of experiencing chronic depression rather than that of being disposed towards using aggression. The continuing work on the causative effects of trauma, being brought to light by DYCD and NYU, have allowed the invisible sources of pain and disassociation to become brought to the surface and become visible.[580]

This new research will undoubtedly confirm the findings of Scilla Elworthy, the international peacemaker who effects change through the arts of mediation and conflict resolution, and who has done pioneering work. This will re-affirm the benefits of using an approach of reconciliation rather than punishment. As suggested in new guidelines developed by the Centers for Disease Control and researchers from the New York University Medical School, professional practitioners, joined by others in the social service and youth agencies, need to develop "trauma-informed" interventions in which people are healed. Those suffering from the effects of trauma need to identify the root causes of their behavior and to learn to manage their feelings and behavior, rather than being given inappropriate medications, punished, and eventually being incarcerated.

By adopting a trauma-informed approach, policy makers and human service professionals will avoid the reactive chain of personal crisis and social tragedy as cited by Dr. Bessel Van Der Kolk in his book, *The Body Keeps the Score*: "If you have no internal sense of security, it is difficult to distinguish between safety and danger. If you feel chronically numbed out, potentially dangerous situations may make you feel alive. If you conclude that you must be a terrible person…you start to expect other people to treat you horribly. When disorganized people carry self-perceptions like these, they are set up to be traumatized by subsequent experiences."[581] People who are stuck in the condition of being traumatized remain on the unconsciously motivated wheel of victimizing others.

As a society, do we discard those damaged by trauma, or do we invite wounded healers to become active agents who also reform the tragic policies in which we diminish, demean, and dismiss unwanted others? In our quest to pursue a "more perfect union," do we enact policy that confirms that none of us is perfect, but each of us is real? Those of us who have become falsely stereotyped and marginalized suffer from constant wounding implicit to institutional practices of structural racism, sexism, and adultism.

A youth program with which I became familiar with in the late 1990s, called the Council of Unity, was founded by Petra Foundation Fellow Robert DeSena. As profiled in the Petra Foundation journal called *Soaring Spirits*, Mr. DeSena "grew up in Brooklyn street gangs where he experienced the 'darker side of life'. (And) after the suicide of his mentor, who had always tried to convince him not to waste his potential in the streets, (Mr. DeSena) turned away from violence and became determined to make something of his life."[582] As the journal profile continues, (Mr. DeSena) went on to earn a B.A. from St. Johns College and an M.A. in English from New York University. He then became a teacher at John Dewey High School and decided to bring groups of disaffiliated students and student leaders together to mediate their differences and to reduce violence." Mr. DeSena, working in tandem with his teen leaders at the Council of Unity, put together an approach at the school site level in which student leadership teams comprising teens who are doing very well in school, and who are on trajectories for college entrance and well-paying careers, serve together with teens who have been in trouble with the law, and/or undergoing counseling to put their lives back together. By working as a team in which individual leaders have different life experiences and perspectives, teen councils manage to figure out how to make their school climate and culture work for everyone. Students who are identified as 'in trouble' and peers who identify with the school goals of maintaining high grades and assuming positions as student role models get to communicate with students with different lifestyles and life trajectories, making young people on all sides of pre-established equations of difference more visible to each other.

Within our shaming and blaming institutions constructed by and inhabited by adults, both in our political halls of power, and in our media's decision-making apparatus, policy makers need to include teens in the game of governance and change. Adults need to decide whether they are managers informed by their open-minded maturity—that is, their ability to be fair-minded and considerate of new possibilities—or grown-ups with "arrested development" and infused with the demons of our insecurity-industrial complex. Assumptions and behaviors which are included in this syndrome of developmental delay are perpetual cravings for material abundance which far exceed personal need, the worship of celebrity and status, and the allegiance to militaristic mindsets, whether aligned against falsely perceived foreign enemies or the feared projections in our subconscious. These socially constructed and personally adopted attributes of diminishing people seen as different and dismissing folks who without warrant are seen as dangerous, have also become the modern-day markers of maturity in grown-ups. When these same markers are displayed by teens, they become denoted as signs of immaturity and character deficits for teens. As I previously discussed in this book, this type of reinforcement and training provided by adult-led institutions produce what the eco/spiritual teacher named Bill Plotkin describes as "patho-adolescence."[583]

The second gear, or dynamic, involves asking: Are teens to remain silent, induced to cover their voices through the adult commandments of "just listen" and "wait your turn," or are they to choose to be heard and have their viewpoints and wisdom validated by adults? I suggest that us adults of the Boomer generation—we who have constructed institutions and fast-approaching dire destinies—should look closely at our reflexive, institutionally reinforced practices of silencing. We who have constructed collapsing economic and political infrastructures, leaving all of us, but especially the young, with diminished economic outcomes and underwater futures, those of us who have undone millions of years of functional ecosystems and poisoned air and water, really need to look at ourselves, rather than at our Wall Street indicators. We need to listen to the young leaders, from Black Lives Matters, the Dreamers, and those looking for ecologically based natural solutions, to youth councils at the local level, people involved with Make the Road While Walking, Teens Take Charge, and a myriad of other organizations across our city and our nation. They have already introduced interventions with promise, and solutions that work. I am saving profiles on the work of these youth groups and leaders for when I will highlight them in the passages of the Anecdotes Arising chapter. For now, I point out that in listening to and responding to the voices and guidance of teens during each youth program I had led across the starting line periods described in the Backwards/Forward chapter, each program felt more owned by its teens. My decisions became informed by young people themselves, who were credible messengers concerning how they thought, why they acted out or withdrew, and how adults could make programming more responsive to and guided by teens. In the Southern Heights program, teen leaders such as Jerry Reneau, Johnny Rosario and Gus Cruz identified with their peers, and commanded respect when, as leaders, they counseled their colleagues at times to practice patience in trying situations and to try out new programs that at first appeared out of the comfort zones of their friends. Young women such as Candace Isaac and Monalisa Fermin participated in programs such as Female Finesse, which help to construct education workshops for girls, and as leaders in Coaches Who Care. In both educational and sports experiences for younger girls, leaders such as Candace and Monalisa became opinion leaders amongst the young. During the Teens on Board campaign, teen leaders such as Ramon Spence and Shakia McPherson from the Police Athletic League and Pablo Vasquez from the Washington Heights and Inwood Youth Council not only circulated petitions by themselves. They spoke to their peers, who in turn helped to organize petition drives. They spoke up at public forums led by adults and became seen by teen peers as impressive voices on behalf of teens.

The third dynamic is about seeking to exercise social change, abandon passivity, and adopt passion. The promotion of constructively proactive engagement shows promise as we have realized positive changes manifested through the third dynamic—that of rejecting passivity and adopting the habits of socially engaged agency. Greta Thunberg has been criticized for having an attitude problem because of her outcries about severe injustices imposed upon the new generation. These misguided critics have conflated attitude with aptitude. Ms. Thunberg, in dialogue with youth leaders from around the globe, has successfully analyzed the deficits of our declining and flailing social and political institutions. The emergent generation, rather than gaining and progressing with the assistance of the Boomer generation, has seen their health indicators decline, the prospects for prosperous career possibilities larger disappear, and the fortuitous functioning of our ecosystems begin to disappear. Adults from the Boomer generation, who had been introduced to unprecedented good fortune by the Great Generation which preceded them, need to get a grip on reality. Rather than becoming judgmental and insulted by the presentation of urgently felt grievance on the part of the young, adults need to focus on the gifts offered by aspirational agents of change such as Greta. As stated by Greta in her speech to the United Nations, "You have a right to dream, and so do we."[584]

Young leaders have, in the spirit and practice of unconditional love for the other, exercised socially empathetic practices, as identified by medical professional and social activist Mindy Thompson-Fullilove, to "upgrade the fractured space, create meaningful relations with place, and to show solidarity with life."[585] Dr. Thompson-Fullilove is a professor of Sociomedical Science and of Clinical Psychiatry at Columbia University who has extensively researched the "mental health effects of violence, segregation, urban renewal and toxins in inner-city communities."[586] As I spoke to in the chapter describing the uncertainty of tomorrow experienced by youth and families in the Heights in the 1980's, the specter of unexpected and sudden violence upended faith in the security of one's own apartment or the probability of seeing your father in the near future. Family and community relationships became frail and eternally transient. Dr. Thompson-Fullilove is also a leader in promoting social conscience and engagement amongst her colleagues and students. Dr. Thompson-Fullilove accomplishes this by having those in the professional community become engaged with those who live in the neighborhood, with campaigns such as Hike the Heights in Washington Heights. Participants march and recreate an expanded historical account together, as they walk from local historical markers to our local parks, while conversing and being co-taught by each other.

In considering the options of the third dynamic, the choice between remaining passive or proceeding with passion, overcoming a sense of perpetual loss experienced in the throes of isolation and passivity can be managed through the practice of self-aware reflection and rewarding engagement with neighbors. The mood that is prevalent before one finds oneself though finding supportive others is expressed as a dilemma by Palestinian student activist, Lema Khalilia: "(Being Palestinian) means that you are kind of, that you are, that you know you are, but nobody else does…trying to find an identity and having a place in the world."[587] Lema describes the struggle encountered here of finding balance between oneself and one's new home despite feelings of having "unsettled belongings." To be trapped in cycles of ambiguity about who you are, and where you belong, is a surrender to despair. Its companion is indifference. Lema neither surrendered nor remained in despair but embraced the value of her place and consciously organized relationship as a practice of inclusion and embrace.[588]

Activists like Lema Khalilia, as shared throughout this narrative, are organizing in many places and spaces. They are also connected either through the study of youth activist history or by practicing an intuitive understanding for it. As suggested by the words of ancestral ally and 1966 activist Mario Savio on the campuses of San Francisco: "There is a time when the operation of the machine becomes so odious, makes you sick at heart, that you cannot take part. And you must put your body upon the gears, upon the wheels, upon the levers, upon the apparatus, and you've got to make it stop. And you've got to take a stand with the people who run it, and value that unless you are free, the machine will not be prevented from working at all."[589]

As I write these words, thousands of young activists are protesting in the streets, decrying, and putting their bodies against the gears of an unforgiving set of institutions that promote the execution of young Black men and women, with neither moral authority nor legal standing. These non-trustworthy practices, put in place by remote and irresponsible authority, desecrate our sense of what it means to be human and commit fratricide against the higher angels of democracy.

The fourth gear or dynamic is the question of whether we choose to operate under the crushing weight of paralysis, or through the energies of participation. Paralysis is not a choice made by people acting under the guidance of free will nor is it soul-inspired guidance. It is an artifact that seeps into our hands, our bones, our minds, and our hearts, induced by social constructs and institutions to which we have become addicted. One type of paralysis is that of conspicuously practiced consumption, in which we conflate being consumers with being citizens. Impulse purchases do not define free choice. There are driving forces behind the "successful" indicators of our economy, which lie behind our illusion of free choice, compelling us to procure seemingly endless piles of possession. I refer here to market research and advertising designed to have customers learn to become "prisoners of envy." Our institutions, which promote market research and marketing devices to ensure the continuance of this practice, are designed, sustained, and profited from by adults...as is the mythology invented by adults, about teens, that they are by nature creatures of impulse and unregulated desire.

Passion in and of itself is not the problem; it depends upon why it arises, and the type of issue and method we choose to pursue. If we choose the type of body of thought that is divisively dismissive of others, as are typical of racialized and ultra-nationalist narratives, our passion will only lead to stronger social silos and separation from our human family relations. If loving passion accompanies our awe for peoples of difference and embrace of qualities which brighten our multi-cultural world, we will delight in nourishing possibility. Our hearts grow, and our minds become enriched. The nature of passion linked to honoring difference and embrace of the other is poetically profiled by Rumi, a Persian poet from centuries ago whose works are shared by spiritual activist Andrew Harvey in his book, *Radical Passion*: "Passion burns down every branch of exhaustion; passion is the supreme elixir, and renews all things; run my friends, run far away from false solutions; Let divine passion triumph, and re-birth you in yourself."[590] Today, youth activists connect with this message, as shown on a poster at an Occupy Wall Street rally: "Real eyes expose real lies." When activists in teen led groups such as Teens Take Charge and adult led groups such as Make the Road begin to network in common cause, they discover friendships across the boundaries of generations, because members of each group learn to admire and count on each other. Kinship in place of alienated relationship induces a sense of familial passion and support.

Passion provokes that "emotional spark" that powers us past the obstacles and problems encountered when activists are involved in contesting limiting walls of misunderstanding. We all gain by appreciating the beauty of acting in a world of wide acceptance for the unknown and the new. This problem-solving technique was put forth by Teilhard de Chardin in his *Phenomenon of Man*, written in 1955: "This is the problem of action, which is for our mind to adjust itself to lines and horizons beyond measure, and it must renounce the comforts of familiar narrowness, the sickness of the dead end, the anguish of feeling shut in, and the modern disquiet of uncertain outcomes."[591] When teen led initiatives such as improved school policies advocated for by the Urban Youth Collaborative, and when more sensitive guidance policies fought for by the Asian Student Advocacy Project become enacted, teens learn to believe in the efficacy of action.

In this book, I have referred to the research conducted by, and a landmark book, titled the Mismeasure of Man, written by Stephen Jay Gould. In this work he carefully dissected and dismantled the false proposition that Blacks, according to the analysis of IQ tests, naturally tend toward lower intelligence that white people. New research shows the mismeasure of teens based upon false interpretations of brain scans and hormonal presence.[592] Poorly constructed and inaccurate interpretations of research, when popularized and promoted by the media and politicians, sap the belief in possibilities, the vigor and willpower that are key indicators of encouraging participation.

The new research will undoubtedly confirm the findings of Scilla Elworthy, the international peacemaker who effects change through the arts of mediation and conflict resolution, and who has done pioneering work in helping to reduce the use of violence for resolving problems. As Dr. Elworthy has led negotiation teams across the globe, she has found one obstacle to resolving heated differences. This obstacle is defined by the belief that what is has been an eternal truth and cannot be changed. For participants on both sides of the argument who believe that direct action and building mutual understanding can result in positive change, what *is* does not matter as a final determinant of the future. Rather, what creative people in oppositional positions think can be *is* what matters. Ms. Elsworthy has come up with a universal principle, or starting point of understanding, necessary to move negotiations forward, and that is the idea that "unfounded assumptions are social constructs, and not perennial truths."[593] In the past, people have been conditioned to distrust others, to see them as different, and therefore deficient and possibly dangerous to ourselves. As we instill new beliefs and incorporate new attitudes of inclusiveness, tolerance, and equanimity, the desire for peace and prosperity is being increasingly seen as common to one and all.

This principle should also be applied in the field of teen studies. Recent research by social science investigators and teen empowerment activists such as Dr. Mike Males have challenged the validity of social constructs based on ill-founded research findings. International research aligned with findings recently proposed agree with those of Dr. Males, who has detailed the findings of his studies over decades in the state of California. Dr. Males' summary of findings shows that many undesirable behaviors such as criminal violence and substance abuse are more prevalent in older adults than in teens.[594] Additional studies by Robert Epstein, who was formerly a consultant to the magazine *The Scientific Mind*, show that many of the negative behaviors prevalent in American teens are either absent or occur at very negligible rates in about 140 nations around the globe.[595]

Additional research and the arrival of more logical assessments about adolescent nature and behavior are crucial. In addition to brain-centered research, other types of scientific studies of heart intelligence complement these. What must complement this is—in fact, I say it must lead this change— is allowing the wisdom of the heart to freely enter our lives first.[596] We have a heart-felt sense that inspires us toward achieving reconciliation and drives our passionate response to solving problems of discomfort and pain inflicted upon our friends and neighbors. Heart-focused research is beginning to help us understand how the heart does this. Because we feel the need to end suffering and bring about joy, the emotion of intelligence complements the cognitive problem-solving of the brain. The heart is our entry way to the wisdom of the soul, and as put by Ralph Waldo Emerson, it is the soul which guides us to be a unique star amongst a universe of stars and renders us to be true to ourselves.[597]

We must find this initiation for change by allowing for participation by youth. In the challenging days of our fights for rights in the early 1900s, this concept was put forth in a poem called *Chants Democratic*, which reads, in part, "where outside authority enters always after the precedence of inner authority, where the citizen is always the head of the ideal, and where children are taught from the jumpstart that they are to be laws unto themselves, there the greatest City stands."[598]

Alfred H. Kurland

The United States founder's declaration of grievances and the public-school shadow: Colonized students or student/citizens?

As our 13 colonies prepared to launch a war to achieve independence, the document that served as their mission statement contained a list of grievances in which our founding fathers itemized their issues by experiential category. Our public school system, founded with the intent of providing preparation for citizenship, has been an institution that has guided millions of citizens over the course of decades to lives of greater fortune. Syllabi used in social studies classrooms have contained civics content about the nature and process of democratic governance. The practices of how democracy operates are not incorporated into classroom practices—educational institutions have delivered this knowledge in ways that are non-democratic. The "how" of democracy, the way it ideally functions, fails to align with school governance. Decisions about the 'what' of school syllabi, and the 'how' of teaching methods, are now being openly questioned, and their hidden agendas being revealed. What has been coming to light is that the content of courses has been established by remote authorities – textbook publishers and administrators who neither live or understand the world of teachers and students. What is being demanded now is input about course content and teaching methods, by students, teachers, and credible messengers living in their communities.

The implementation of school rules put in place to define good and unacceptable behaviors is being drawn up without the consent of the governed. Without input from students, this undermines a sense of appropriateness and legitimacy in students, and is an example of imposing rules without the consent of the governed. Disciplinary measures and procedures, which are not conceived or agreed to by students, are punitive and discriminate in a negative fashion against students of color, who are recipients of overly severe sanctions. The young are allowed to make decisions about the trivial, such as the color of school uniforms and the theme song for a prom but have little or no input into the design of school rules nor the content and focus of coursework. The nature of rules and school experience train students to be compliant rather than exercise dissent, thereby preparing the young to follow the arbitrary dictates of remotely imposed authority. It is not just students, but teachers who are adversely uncut by this educational system.[599]

Policies and practices guiding teens for participation (or lack thereof) more nearly align with those of the British crown regarding their colonial subjects. In the grievance section of our Declaration of Independence, the founding fathers itemized offenses justifying our need to separate from, or become independent from, Great Britain. In a parallel fashion, the civil rights activist Fanny Lou Hamer gave sage advice to youth when it came to urging young people to establish autonomy and throw off the constraining shackles of old systems.[600]

British soldiers, without due cause, were routinely stationed in the homes of colonists and were sanctioned to harass them on the streets. Today, school authorities, without due cause, routinely station excessive numbers of security agents in our schools. Throughout the New York City school system, teachers, deans, and principals practice racialized discrimination, with overly punitive measures against Black and Latino youth. The Crown created laws subjecting colonists to unfair sanctions and taxes. Colonists engaged in peaceful protest, but the unfair taxation practices remained unaddressed. Today, civil rights advocates such as the New York Civil Liberties Union have teamed with teen leadership groups like the Urban Youth Collaborative to peacefully call for changes to unfair policies directed at youth, such as the overuse of school suspensions and expulsions. This collaborative effort has resulted in teen led education programs about understanding their rights under school discipline policies, and resisting unfair censorship imposed by school leadership. The policies that have wounded citizens and civic stakeholders, whether those which had been imposed by eighteenth-century British royal authority or which are those routinely put in place by school administrators today, share a common quality of ignoring justified grievances.[601] Criminal injustice policies, felt by the young in schools and on the streets, have contributed to a trauma-inducing syndrome which leads people astray from the underlying causes of dysfunctional behaviors, and increases the probability of continual tension and conflict with society.[602]

In each era, starting with the American revolutionary movement, in which we transitioned from colonial to independent rule, and continuing with the oncoming Aquarian age epoch being born today, prophetic leaders take the lead in adopting new mindsets about the needs of individuals and political relationships. In the early 21st Century, as we move on from the mechanical/industrial era to the ecological/spiritual one, it is the change-makers and reformers who shape the culture and practices of our newly emerging institutions. Organized stakeholders seek to forge their own destiny through active and inclusive participation of all stakeholders. Activists, whom I also call participatory patriots, imagine a natural right for autonomy in civic affairs within the context of inter-dependent social and political relationships. When governance is based upon the consent of all the governed, citizens are being prepared for what the American historian Bernard Bailyn calls our perpetual American drama, working towards "beginning a world anew", where authority resides in the consent of the governed, and not the arbitrary decisions of monarchs or elected officials enforcing racial codes. He describes the way our early patriots were viewed by the British: "Again and again they (colonists) were warned of defying the received traditions, the sheer unlikelihood that they, obscure people on the outer borders of European civilization, knew better than the established authorities who ruled them."[603] Teen leadership today faces the same type of obstructive counsel. Teens are defined as undeveloped in the skills for governance and are urged to remain in a state of perpetual preparedness. Teens are continually instructed to just listen, do as you are told, and to wait your turn, until such time, as fully vested adults, they are qualified to make autonomously derived and collective obtained wise decisions. What I propose throughout the course of this book, and highlight in the next chapter, are the similar characteristics shared by America's early revolutionaries and teen social justice change makers today. The shared traits are for being cunningly self-serving, yet idealistic and crucially foundational to the need for change; doubted for the probability of their desired outcomes, which defies the existence of generational change effected by new leadership. Each group, our founders and teen leaders today, were and are delegated to the margins of receiving rights and constructing representative governance, yet it is from outside the margins of official authority that a more democratic form of governance is being created by ostracized stakeholders.

What those who manage our existing system of teen "occupation" and the former rulers of colonized subjects missed was the character of the dissidents who saw through their rationalized agendas. Our founders, though dismissed and disparaged, were cunningly self-serving, yet idealistic. Doubted for the probabilities of their proposed enterprise, our freedom-fighting warriors were guided by powerful messages expressed in Thomas Paine's tome called *Common Sense*. For Paine, common sense meant that the rights to life, liberty, and the pursuit of happiness were not just abstract ideals but inherent human rights. The right to life meant the ability to define and construct conditions which informed a desired quality of life. Liberty meant the inherent right to express opinions and to negotiate solutions with mutual respect. The pursuit of happiness meant the right to pursue one's dreams with dignity and the active support of fellow citizens. The creative constructionists putting together our nation's Constitution started a process of ensuring our human rights. Movements such as those led by abolitionists and suffragists decried unjust exceptions to our national ideals and governance and forced change which made the rule of just law universally applied. Today, we still reside in an imperfect union, and new movements such as Black Lives Matter and the Dreamers are devising amended systems to ensure the autonomy of their citizenry and effective institutions of government which ensure and protect the inherent rights of all.[604]

What those who conceive and develop modes of school governance miss is the true spirit of the adolescent soul, as well as the heart of American democracy. As previously described in the sections discussing the adolescent archetype, the work for realizing our full capacities, whether in the realm of holistic personal development or fully inclusive democracy include the precept of self-governance. When fighting for this right, adolescents are nonconformist, boundary-breaking, and unconventional spirits.

When school leaders hold on to outdated and misinformed caricatures of adolescence, they are missing the mark on the essential nature of what it means to be a teen. They conflate disobedience with an adolescent's natural inclination to be somewhat eccentric, and in search of meaningful connection.

School leaders and teachers have also failed to take into consideration an additional inherent need for teens. Besides having teens pursuing sets of skills resulting in mastery, they should also be encouraged to be engaged in exploring the mysteries of life. Bill Plotkin is a developmental and spirit-oriented writer who has developed a model of evolutionary progress for the soul, include teen souls. In his book, *Nature and the Human Soul*, Mr. Plotkin proposes a process that is essential for adolescents. This process of exploration and navigation motivates teens to "undergo an initiation process that requires letting go of the familiar and the comfortable. She must submit to a journey of descent into the mysteries of nature and the human soul. It is this descent that the adolescent must undergo that scares people about teens."

Adult leaders were denied this right of self-exploration, no matter what period they lived in; today, the teenager who was buried in adults' subconscious, if given the right to emerge, angry and demanding, is what scares them. It is not the responsibility of a teen to retrieve what an adult either fears or has lost, and then substitute that set of thoughts in place of their own autonomously derived guidance. Teens in recent times have been involved, in record-setting numbers, with community service learning, reconciliation models of justice, and efforts to reform our worn-out methods of governance. What had been suggested by visionary leaders, from Thomas Paine to W.E.B. DuBois, and being proposed again today by the under-the-radar youth leaders in local movements, is allowing for the space and integral practice of self-defined presence. What this means at the cultural/social/political level is building societal structures that encourage generational adaptation and the adventure of experimentation with how governance works.[605] Democracy has been described in many ways; the point, however, is always to be invited in as a stakeholder, and to participate in advisory and decision-making processes. Schools need to establish processes in which, as articulated by Jean Houston, "each of us (including students) has a natural right to their autonomous presence and uniquely expressed voice. We need vision, and community ritual in support of ensuring inclusive space, where students occupy what had been their disowned places. By empowering themselves, students also empower their peers.[606]

I now transition in this book to its final chapter, which I call Anecdotes Arising. This part of the book is my contribution in offering an answer to one raised by Anodea Judith in her book, *Waking the Global Heart*. Ms. Judith asks, "How do we come of age in the new age?" In a chapter of her book, she titles "The Drama of Our Time," she introduces challenges and opportunities teens now grapple with in changing their minds about who they are, as well as the type of world they seek to co-create. As Ms. Judith points out: "…transformation begins with a shift in the archetypal framework that tells the story of who we are and why we are here. Our current age of power has delivered vast knowledge, (including)…sophisticated technology and personal freedom, (and at the same time)…our shadow side has created pollution and tyranny."[607] Ms. Judith provides a glimpse of the next steps into the doorway of the future in a chapter of her book titled "Don't Agonize, Self-Organize: Better Living Through Living Systems": " If there is one continuous theme throughout creation, it is that everything comes into being through relationships…when we see relationships as a self-organizing web, we move from a linear chain of command to a multi-dimensional field of possibilities…relationships are participatory…Your power does not come from your role, but from the quality of your relationships."[608] It is people, who act, one individual at a time, who possess unique and creative consciousness. Emergent teen leaders are acting with non-judgmental form, within the context of a worldwide web, who are creating essential steppingstones toward communal and planetary stewardship. The stories that follow in the next chapter - Afterwards: Anecdotes Arising, are written to paint a picture of environmentally adaptive and soulfully sensitive possibilities and practices.

IV.

AFTERWARDS

ANECDOTES ARISING: Emergent narratives and interjoined civic relationships are being born and nurtured in the transition to a new era of social justice, ecological balance, and spiritual guidance. The wisdom of ancestral allies and the public prophets of today become woven into a fabric of the future —put in place by civic co-mentors and adolescent activists living the realities of stewardship and change.

In the period following the signing of the Public Officer Law amendment, and our coalition efforts to have teens sign up for community boards, I began to search for means by which I could remain involved in promoting teen enfranchisement. Beginning in those post-2015 years and up to the present, my journey has connected me to teen-led projects via research, online exploring, and networking. I continue to support allies from the past and, at the same time, looked at initiatives beyond my immediate sphere of influence and direct experience. One of the consequences of my post-2015 search has been paying more attention to finishing this book, which in prior years had been squeezed by my agenda. This chapter, Anecdotes Arising, presents some of the findings of my search, and suggests that while I stay on my journey, I also remain open to new vistas, surprise, and participation in places that I had not imagined before.

It is in the pursuit of this vision, of turning dreams into operational reality, that youth-led groups such as Future Voters, PAL IN STEP, Generation Citizen, the Asian Student Advocacy Project, and others described in my previous anecdotes have transformed students from passive consumers of knowledge into active critics of well-intentioned but unfounded counsel. Unfounded and misapplied sources of knowledge have led us to construct unsupportable institutions that have taught in ways that "homogenize history" and "colonize student life."[609] Free to wander and to ponder, teen activists have turned toward a bend in the arc of justice, replacing remotely derived and arbitrarily created narratives into indigenous local stories. Authentically derived narrative and grassroots communal agreements populate a "people's history," Adolescent activists are being trained to " make the world anew".[610]

Key to the social justice and personally transformative work of teens is aptly described by the psychologist Otto Rank in his book, *Beyond Psychology*. Mr. Rank had a book published, his first written in English, in 1941, during a critical historical juncture where personal dignity and democracy were being defended with the launch of a world war. Mr. Rank makes a connection between the authentic authority of a human, and the discovery that values are as much uncovered as discovered for the first time: "The new values that have to be discovered and re-discovered every so often are old values, the natural human values which over the course of time are lost in rationalizations of one kind or another. For such a re-discovery of the natural self of man…it is necessary to live it."[611] Suffragists had to become self-assertive and overcome the rationalizations of sexism, abolitionists saw the world through their own lens, and rejected the rationalizations of racism. Teen-led movements today are taking down the out of date and dismissive rationalizations of adultism.

At this point I share what our nation's founders proclaimed with the Declaration of Independence as corresponding with what student civic activists bring forth in their declarations of interdependence. In the Declaration of Independence, and specifically in the fourth paragraph which lists the grievances of the colonists against the British Crown and its appointees, the colonists complained of remote and uncomfortable laws, and compliance by force.[612] Today, the laws of governance over the lives of youth are enforced in schools under a rubric that education critic Peter Grey, in his book *Free to Learn*, calls the Seven Sins of Forced Education.[613] When hyper-enforcement and control is imposed on teens in the theater of life beyond schools, such as on the streets with law enforcement, it is conceived and promoted though in media narratives, which have been referenced by Mike Males, whom I have covered earlier in this book, as "storm and stress". Bodies of law and rules imposed by municipal agencies are based on negative stereotypes that are created through excessive enforcement of rules, and perpetual attempts to control every detail in teen lives. To use the NYC Department of Education as one example, there are more law enforcement agents patrolling schools than there are guidance counselors. Paragraph nine of the declaration criticizes "remote judicial decisions and arbitrary enforcement." In 1994, President Bill Clinton and Congress reformed the criminal code, thereby reinforcing a system that for decades had allowed judges to become bound to rules such as "three strikes and you are out"—regulations that radically deconstructed positive life course options for the young, who were prohibited from receiving student loans, housing assistance, or quality career opportunities.[614] Students who are pushed out of school are far more likely to become ensnared in the downward spiral of life they encounter after going to prison, and are far more likely to work in perpetually low-paying job sectors. In New York City, policies such as stop-and-frisk were arbitrarily enforced on young Blacks and Latinos—a discriminatory practice on steroids. Paragraph 13 in the Declaration of Independence points out the hypocrisy of allowing "taxation without representation."[615] Today, teens who are out of school pay a full share of taxes, and all teens shop and pay sales taxes. These points do not even account for the social capital teens create through volunteering and community service, which aid communities, not-for-profit youth agencies, the poor, the hungry, and public spaces that benefit all residents collectively. The National Parole Association has documented that peer courts, in which teens serve as judges and jurors, are far more effective than the traditional court system in preventing the reoccurrence of violations and recidivism.[616] The chapters describing civic rebels and civic lovers are populated with anecdotes bringing forth their work in creating alternative futures.

As previously discussed, John Dewey counseled that we need to organize classrooms as "cooperative societies."[617] Paulo Freire's approach trained students to read the world, to give the reading of books meaning and relevance.[618] The programs highlighted in this chapter exemplify practical application of Dewey's and Freire's teachings. Agency by agency, and project by project, the initiatives covered in this chapter are parts of a larger national and worldwide movement redefining the deepening of democratic practice. Just as folks working to elevate themselves by showcasing the higher angels of their nature, new era social justice and teen empowerment undertakings take us closer to reaching the higher angels of democratic practice. Practitioners in this pursuit may make mistakes, take a few steps backward, and even cause harm while pursing the common good, but these seeming contradictions are grist for the mill as we tread in the challenging work of governance.

Jon Meacham is an American historian who interprets former actions of our nation's leaders as somewhat contradictory to our perceived ideals, but which, with the aid of hindsight, can be seen as supportive of pursuing a path more aligned with the higher angels of democracy. Meacham has written a master work, *The Soul of America* (which I believe should be required reading by every American History student), in which he offers insights into the character and contributions of historical actors. His book shows how these actors "battle for living by the standards of America's higher angels."[619] Americans have instituted terrible programs to obtain justice, but at the same time, out of our shared wounds, new shoots of alternative approach in the justice system have also bloomed. By maintaining our basic American instinct for procuring justice for all, and resilience for the struggle, we should not lose our way by wandering from practices promoting the common good. Toward the end of the book, Mr. Meacham recommends several orientations that would help us to navigate this path. I discuss three of those orientations here. To move forward towards a more perfect union, it is also useful to move backward, to contemplate upon wisdom shared by our political ancestors, as sources of wealth we might best hold on to.

Meacham's first insight is the mandate he calls "entering the arena." To participate, one needs to be there. He offers an insight by President Theodore Roosevelt: "The first duty of an American citizen is to enter the arena of politics, his second duty is to do this in a practical manner, and the third is that it shall be done in accordance with the highest principles of honor and justice."[620] There are ample anecdotes to illustrate what the ancient Greeks described as " a person who refuses to engage in public affairs", which they used to define " an idiot". In schools across the five boroughs of New York City, action-oriented civic programs are training students in ways that improve school menus, reduce school violence, and advocate for improved coursework aligned with the demands of college success. The previously mentioned Future Voters of America and Generation Citizen, as well as public purpose-minded affiliated programs have their core concept of training public citizens woven into the fabric of this book. Constructing classrooms according to the principles of democratic community and utilizing the community as a classroom for civic responsibility are essential arenas for teaching enlightened citizenship.[621]

Meacham's second insight describes the social practice to "resist tribalism." Here, Mr. Meacham quotes the insight offered by Chicago's settlement house organizer, Jane Addams: "We know instinctively, that if we grow contemptuous of our fellows, and consciously limit our intercourse in order to contain other kinds of peoples, we not only tremendously circumscribe our range of life, but limit the scope of our efforts."[622]

Today, youth, trained by professionals, volunteer in scores of schools and community-based agencies involved in conflict resolution and mediation programs, intergenerational programs, and celebrations of multicultural communities and history. Notable among these types of programs are those that have been operated by the Mailman School of Public Health. One example is a program initiated by Professor Robert Fullilove in his classrooms at the Columbia University Graduate School of Public Health in Washington Heights. Dr. Fullilove, a five-decade veteran of the civil rights movement, involves his students in experiencing the community as a classroom.[623] His graduate students volunteer to serve in grassroots programs such as the Uptown Dreamers, whose participants give back to the neighborhood and who also study the history of civil rights. The Dreamers co-sponsor an annual celebration called Hike the Heights, in which neighborhood residents, including youth, learn the lessons of local history and the contributions of locally grown urban patriots. Students celebrate the value of this history within the venues of cherished green public spaces.

A third insight of Mr. Meacham is suggestive of a best practice for education. Cited by Jon Meacham is the need to "find a critical balance." Here, he turns to Thomas Jefferson: "Whenever the people are well-informed, they can be trusted with their own government, and whenever things go so far wrong, as to attract their notice, they may be relied upon to set them to rights."[624] Training in using these practices is essential for cultivating positive attitudes in the facing of enduring obstacles.

In New York City, our public universities and health providers work closely with students to provide personal health and neighborhood-based best practices for environmental sustainability. Programs at organizations and institutions such as the New York Civil Liberties Union, the Society of Friends, and New York University promote violence reduction, civic rights education, and youth empowerment training programs. These programs, amongst others, will be profiled in this chapter as it progresses. What they each share are adopting habits as suggested by the Chicago public housing organizer, Jane Addams, in the early 1900s—to connect a person's habitat with the larger community, and to incorporate the enthusiastic participation of youth.

Before delving into the anecdotes arising profiles, I mention a few things. The first point I cover is by offering a couple of observations on the nature of curiosity and surprise as being part and parcel of the process of discovery by those engaged in civic change work. The second point I make is offering some additional commentary on the assets and character of civic co-mentors. As I will be covering youth-led movements in Anecdotes Arising, I will be sharing some general observations about what youth leaders from differing agencies share as part of their character profile. With my third preliminary point, I share further observations offered by organizational theorists which suggest that the character of co-mentors becomes infused with the identity and nature of the agencies which they lead. I will then lean into the profiles of social reform agencies.

Over much of the course of my three-decade journey, I, together with my god-daughter Aida Ramos, raised a total of 12 cats, many of whom were born in my household, and all of whom were adored. As I recall once again the print I purchased from Joey Allgood, and its companion testimony, I am provided with a reinforcement for observation about cat nature and behavior that I have come to adopt for myself, in acknowledging my "inner cat."[625] As I reflect on my journey of twenty-eight years, there were many moments when doubt, uncertainty and chaos seemed to be the order of the day. However, with sustained effort, faith, and my delving for the deeper meaning and sense of purpose in my work, an intelligent design slowly revealed itself.

In looking back at my three-decade-long adventure, and in sharing the next anecdotes, I now see that what I had seen as random flashes of insights in my earlier years of teen program practice, in fact have order, meaning, and significance for informing and improving the methodology of my practice. One understanding about civic life and civic service that I have come to be sensitive to is that in the soul's world, its intelligent design has informed my serving of higher purpose. As I will share in anecdotes to follow, in many ways these have become more crystalized for me, understood as tools which can be applied to practice. What I need to continue to be open to is remaining sensitive, and ready for new perspectives, surprises, and opportunities. Enriching my body of understanding is necessarily dependent upon continuous experiential teaching and experimental search. As is the case with scientific practice, informed conclusions dance eternally with inevitable error. In soul work, social activists call upon an integrated set of intelligences, and start from the local environment of community and then work their way up. The relationship between acting out of feelings in the bones, and sensing the wisdom of the ground, is aptly described by David Abram in his book, *The Spell of the Sensuous*. Mr. Abram, Ph.D. was a professor and ecologist working at SUNY Stonybrook. As he states in his book: "Communicative meaning is always, in its depths, affective. It remains rooted in the sensual with the landscape as a whole…meaning sprouts in the very depths of the sensory world, in the heat of meeting, encounter and participation."[626]

For teens who have been engaged in service, partnership with a specialized species of public prophets whom I call "co-mentors" has been essential to their development. Eccentric and empathetic navigators for challenging territories and the pathways leading to inner knowledge, they remain a teen's best friend in their search to achieve their highest potential and the creation of a more beautiful world. I offer their job description next.

A few additional thoughts on the valuable contributions of co-mentors in rapidly changing times: Co-mentors are prophets bringing the promise of the future into present-time practice.

Co-mentors, in addition to being oracles, are also public prophets. Prophets are those who can deconstruct the present day and intervene with its fading efficacies. In addition, prophets reconstruct in ways that facilitate the marriage between transformative practice and embarking on the first footsteps of our dreams. Co-mentors stride alongside energetically enthused and focused teen agents of change. By managing open-ended optimism, we come to the realization of conscious, inclusive, and sustainable community. Adult co-mentors march shoulder to shoulder and hand in hand with teens, not seeing them just as mentees, but rather those who are also co-mentors offering novel guidance, unique perspective, and boundless energy. What they graciously offer keeps each of us on the road we make while walking.[627]

As adult co-mentors assist teens in finding their life purpose, constructing their authentic stories, and helping them realize the alignment of self-actualized activists and embracing communities, they can be seen in some sense as public prophets who are developing prophets-in-progress. As profiled by Rabbi Heschel, a prophet is one who "suffers from severe maladjustments to the spirit of society with its conventional lies and its concessions to man's weak needs. Compromise is an attitude which a prophet abhors."[628]

Greta Thunberg is a prophet. Organizers in social justice movements and environmental stewards are her co-mentors. Greta sees the future through a promising lens and calls upon all of us to bring back that optimal future to present time, to ensure that our destination to that place becomes more probable. She made her way to delivering an address to the 2019 United Nations environmental summit, traveling from Sweden to Madrid on a sailboat named *La Vagabond*. The label *vagabond* had been brought about in the 1800s as a term used to distinguish between people who were from the local town and in need while living in the street, and others, outsiders, who were considered disreputable. Vagabonds had traveled aimlessly, carrying a story that people in control did not want to hear. Greta's voyage was in part a representation for a generation wandering in a sea of indifference toward crucially needed environmental action. Greta, like ancient prophets who had wandered in the desert, arrived at halls of power with an ethically vital message about society changing its practices to save themselves from themselves. Before taking her trip to Madrid, Greta had called out world leaders at the World Economic Forum and their empty messages of hope: "I want you to panic. I want you to feel the fear I feel every day. And then I want you to act."[629] Greta's generation of new environmental actors have been in on the act. Dozens of ecology advocates, including those of "the leaders of Fridays for the Future in Labor, Pakistan, to the protesters with Extinction Rebellion in Europe, to the middle and high school students in New York City walking out of school and participating in a die-in," all are exemplars of co-mentoring prophets, mentoring their parents and adult policy makers on what needs to be done to exercise personal and planetary responsibility.

Seen from the viewpoint of spiritual healers, transformative leaders such as co-mentors can be understood as "soul whisperers." As introduced to us by Linda Star Wolf and Nita Gage: "Becoming a soul whisperer is far more complex than training to be a psychotherapist or counselor. Becoming a soul whisperer is first and foremost, a calling. The path chooses you. If you respond, it means embodying spirit and developing a deep connection to your soul purpose. Second, it is a path of training that is spiral, as you dive into your own discoveries, you will learn from masterful people if you learn to remain humble and teachable.[630]

I knew my calling from an early age, and at that time manifested its progress in simple and humble ways. In fifth grade, I took over an abandoned garage behind a complex of garden apartments in Kew Garden Hills. I set up tables and chairs, helping younger peers in first and second grade with their homework—a warm-up for my time spent supervising after-school centers during my career. In junior high school, while at summer camp with the Boy Scouts at the Ten-Mile River reservation, I had been voted in by my patrol to be the patrol leader. I was a first-year scout, called a tenderfoot; out of respect I deferred to an older scout with a couple of years in. On our very first hike up a hill, he slipped on wet grass, tumbled down, and had to return home with a sprained back. At my patrol members' request, I stepped up as patrol leader and successfully guided older scouts to earn merit badges in cooking, first aid, and Morse code. After my episode in high school described in the preface of this book, I accelerated my anti-Vietnam War activities, not only in high school, but also at Whittier College in California. In each of these cases I persisted with a passionate determination and a feel for taking responsible action. During my course of youth organizing uptown, my co-mentors wore these qualities on their faces, in their bodies, and through their uncompromised and relentless actions. At the St. Rose of Lima School, Nancy Davis worked all day at the school and then volunteered to supervise the afterschool and evening youth programs until nine o'clock every night. Eddie Silverio at Alianza Dominicana shepherded multiple programs—from after-school centers to those serving disconnected youth, to parent support programs at La Plaza, Alianza's Beacon program. His schedule was basically to take 30 minutes a day for meals and four hours a night for sleep. The rest of his time belonged to the community. On one of my excursions to the Boy Scouts Ten Mile River campsite, Eddie and I chaperoned teens who enjoyed nature and the company of friends in a natural setting. After that time, as we shared our memories about this, Eddie would affectionately refer to our teen's experience at Ten Mile River as the adventures of hoods in the woods.

As a Police Athletic League director, I watched countless directors from other youth centers—from the Rockaways to Staten Island, to Brooklyn—show up at 10 in the morning, supervise afternoon and evening programs, often on weekends, and then stay late to help clean up. Nobody had to ask any of these people why they were there. Being there for the community, for youth and the parents, was their calling card, and their life mission.[631] Having co-mentors like these people meant that I could never give up or give in.

I collaborated with many other co-mentors who kept their resilience and focus strong by keeping in touch with their calling. Yvonne Stennett, the leader of Community League of the Heights, feels in her heart and her bones the deep intersections between cultural heritage and communal wealth, as well as the essential connective support provided by participatory education practices, safe housing brought about through tenant organizing, and the need for accessible and affordable health centers. On the other side of our city, on Staten Island, a borough on the bay, Bobby Gigi, leader of Island Voice, understands that to help Blacks overcome the obstacles put in place by unresponsive and insensitive governments, stakeholders organize and—as former members in the parade of invisibles—find and offer their voice. It is a collective effort, exercised with persistence and pride, in which a disenfranchised people expand their lung capacities so that, free at last, they can breathe. Both assume, and insist upon, youth forums and youth councils as vitally integrated into the process of their advocacy.

What both Ms. Stennett and Mr. Digi understand is the critical importance of studying existing social conditions from the perspective of those who live its consequences and incorporating their viewpoints into policy practices. W.E.B. DuBois, who is recognized today as a father of sociology, was initially disparaged by authorities in universities and governance. Years later, his insights into racial dynamics have become standard to the practice of sociology. Naomi Schneider, in her historical biography of DuBois, *The Scholar Denied*, describes the insights of DuBois: "DuBois and his largely volunteer labor force did more through his Atlanta school to produce Black scholars who offered an alternative scientific analysis of race, than did rich white universities and their famous professors. They constructed a sociology that conceptualized a set of social arrangements where racial equality could dethrone racism."[632] Today, co-mentors such as Ms. Stennett, Mr. Digi, Mitch Wu, and those leading from the ground-up youth -ed efforts, are conceptualizing a new set of social arrangements where equitable youth participation dethrones adultism. Between the two of them, Mitch, and Yvonne, they have assisted scores of black and Asian students to graduate college and become scholars.

In my development as a co-mentor, I also came to understand what had been provided to me by other co-mentors - masterful skill development and unconditionally rewarding opportunities to serve. By accepting these gifts, and partaking in their practices, I simultaneously expanded my civic consciousness. Where previously I had referred to myself as a capital I, now considered myself as working modestly and harmoniously from the self-identified vantage point as one with a lower case i. I became grateful for the grace of the mysterious yet real presence of civic allies, whether experienced by coincidence or synchronicity, or through their determined intention to assist me. Over time, I made connections between lessons offered by early life and those provided by change-makers I met on my three-decade path. In the previous sections of this book, I described the convergent pathways between my early experiences, my 30-year journey with teen empowerment, the energetic footprints of ancestral allies, and the collaborative civic contributions of a diverse field of social justice workers today. What follows next is a deeper look into a few of the movements led by adolescent leaders and their civic-oriented organizations that are building bridges between what has worked for us today and what is necessary for us to thrive tomorrow. The civic leaders and social enhancing programs I describe foster need-to-learn attitudes and about environments where it is okay to learn from and then master the consequences of mistakes. In a sense, they are civic change-makers who are alchemists, transforming what no longer serves us into new institutional forms and cultural narratives. Simply arriving at what tomorrow offers us, as passive recipients, is no longer tenable in our fast-changing world. We co-invent tomorrow by envisioning and beginning to construct infrastructures and habits that already begin to align with evolving forms of relationships.

Michael Schacker, in his book *Global Awakening,* his thoughtful work about visionaries implementing "new science in search of twenty-first enlightenment," had this to say about old thought patterns: "They are the dogma of absolutism that also supports the various chauvinist dreams that each culture creates for itself, leading to history's endless series of war."[633]

In this section of the Anecdotes Arising chapter, I intertwine positive outcomes of work accomplished with co-mentors and other allies with whom I had direct partnerships, with the social change work introduced and managed by teen-led programs with which I did not directly engage. The latter leaders and their organizations worked independently, operating on their own self-determined, specific issue campaigns, but are also interdependently connected on the larger stage of consciousness and policy change. When teens are invited, trained, and then accepted as equal social change partners, leaders expand upon their perspective to include the realities experienced by the young, and share their wisdom learned in their own lives. Interdependently yet collectively, we all have contributed to what Thomas Paine had called creating the world anew.

Dr. Sven Hansen is a medical practitioner with a background in special forces and sports medicine who has constructed a paradigm he calls "inside/out." Since his founding of what he calls the Resilience Institute, he has taught thousands of those in leadership positions around the world about four elements of resiliency that he views as crucial for participating in and managing change work. His interventionist strategies include learning how to adjust to adversity, staying in a calm center while also being courageous, cultivating body, mind, one's emotions and the spirit, and learning how to connect to others. Dr. Hansen believes that each of these elements exists within a spectrum between best practices, warning signs for decline, and dysfunction.[634] By implementing strategies aligned with the stage a person is at with each element, a person can move up to beneficial conditions and away from the trap of decline. The first element involves the development of courage, which he does not see as attained on battlefields, be they military conflicts or differences in cultural perception; rather, he defines courage as the capacity to embrace an open-ended future with a curious mind, an open heart, and a commitment to action with meaningfully shared goals.[635] The second element is to work on the creative abilities possessed by oneself and the larger group with which one is involved. He suggests that those working on creativity should know "that experiments will fail, but to fear failure is to settle for mediocrity." Our goals must align and stretch our talents and capabilities. We need to accept the need to compromise in ways that help us to see that all involved should be afforded the opportunity to reach their full capacity. This involves inner and outer work on self-awareness, skill-mastery, and perseverance.[636] This leads to the third element of resilience, that of attaining the ability to bounce back after hitting a wall. Working with allies and critics alike, we need to focus on what we can achieve rather than on blaming each other. We need to take responsibility for our bias as we act and to develop supportive networks integrating the needs and viewpoints of all.[637] The fourth element requires us to acknowledge that the need for connection is inherent to humanity's quest. As stated by Mr. Hansen, "Broken connections cause pain."[638] I add that the continuous and habitual infliction of pain contributes to the illusion of false separations. What we need to do is to be mature, and to take responsibility for the greatest possible good for ourselves and for the common good. Doing so shows responsibility through the exercise of respectful engagement on the inside, as Mr. Hansen states, "with our bodies, our thoughts, and emotions, and our life purpose. We need to extend this exercise to our family, our friends, our workplaces, school places and community. We then can then build up nature's habitat and our planetary connections amongst thousands of tribes."[639] As we connect with and learn from purposeful tribes seeking to create common good, we also work on the outside, and thus also enhance our development on the inside.

In my teen empowerment efforts over three decades, the absolutist dogma proposing the necessity of continual war at home hung over our communities in New York City and across the United States. A teen-led organization called March for our Lives questions the dominion of authority in the National Rifle Association (NRA), where an organization's governing elite override the will of its members. March For Our Lives also challenges the decisions of elected officials who buckle to the NRA lobbyists (who advocate against restrictions in gun ownership) and ignore the will of constituents who want to see common sense gun safety measures put in place.[640] The remediation of reckless gun policies has been accomplished in a few states, but NRA obstruction continues to rule our lives at a national level.

Black Lives Matter has challenged the sheriffdom of police departments across our country. They have also brought to light the overbearing burden placed on Black people and their families, who are routinely subject to random law enforcement violence, shattering their lives. Black Lives Matter has succeeded in getting an increasing number of White people to challenge unquestioned assumptions behind unconscious sources of racism that has fueled the specter of violence against Black people for hundreds of years.[641]

Here, I mention the right to vote for legal residents once again. I do this to make its connection to the work of Black Lives Matters for enhancing equal opportunity in civic participation and recognizing this voting rights campaign as a precursor to the work being done now on behalf of young immigrants by the Dreamers. Until 1918, immigrants could legally vote in municipal elections and national elections in the United States. The principle underlying this right to vote, which was in place since the late 1700s, was that if one had established residency, and paid taxes, one could vote. The right to vote was not solely determined by the status of one's citizenship. In the 1920s, in parallel fashion to the rise of lynching and terrorism against Blacks, nativist sentiments and laws against immigrants were passed. One's legitimacy in being allowed participation in the electoral process was (and still is) becoming increasingly determined by having White privilege. Today, the privilege is being increasingly reserved for older Whites, as new anti-enfranchisement legislation in many states is taking the right to vote away for youth under the age of 25. Just as the right to vote was taken away from immigrants in the early 1900s because they were not White enough—and because they leant too far left in the political spectrum—today even White youth are being removed from the voting rolls because of their allegiance to social justice and environmentally sane policies.[642]

Today, the Dreamers, a student-led coalition of young activists, came to the US as young children. They were then raised here, with many having graduated in college or having served in the armed forces. Dreamers have been part of the labor force, while dutifully paying taxes. Many have also labored in volunteer organizations, creating improvements in communities. While their initial rite of passage was involuntary because they had been so young, as new Americans they have faithfully and earnestly committed to the traditional rite of passage described as the American dream—work hard, help yourself and others, and then become a valuable stakeholder to communities and to our nation. The Dreamers have rallied allies, including many from majority populations, to fight against the false practices of ejecting immigrants. These allies support their friends, neighbors and fellow Americans who have lived honorably, befriending others in need, and the American creed.[643] Falsely generated beliefs about immigrants have traditionally been part of what I have previously described as the American shadow. In prior historical periods, as is the case today, upheavals in the workforce and fear of decline in status have led people to erroneously attack targeted peoples.[644]

Clearly, as we all move forward, what also accompanies us are feelings of uncertainty.[645] In her counsel to young activists, the late Detroit-based activist Grace Lee Boggs, who at the time was 100 years young, had this to offer: "The world is always being made, and never finished, activism is a journey, and not a destination. Struggle not in confrontation, but in search for the common good. Value small, incremental action within our exquisitely interconnected world."[646] Many of the activists of old, such as those who had the law changed to end segregation or policies changed to mitigate against unilateral decisions by presidents to start a war—all of whom built bridges toward justice, equality, and peace for us—lived with a fixed dream in their sights. Once protective and progressive laws were passed, it was felt that our job as advocates and protesters was finished. I count myself as subject to this illusion. Yes, true believers and sympathetic supporters affirmed an inner vision, a commitment to the common good. But the certainties of yesterday fade in the face of our changeable and ambiguous world. Organized reactionary forces and the rising presence of fear and resentment challenge the progress in making our democracy, economic outcomes, and social relations more equitable and neighborly.

Given our reality, that of interconnection and the intersectional puzzles of our lives, even the pursuit of happiness has taken on a new dimension. Susan Wilcox, who was a rights activist for Sister Sol, postulated that a new vision for what it means to be happy is an essential component for teaching about freedom: "Happiness is interpersonal, we are aware that all generations of our ancestors, and all future generations are within us, we are aware that the joy, peace, freedom and harmony are those of our ancestors, our children, and their children, we are aware that this understanding is very foundation of love."[647]

Just a decade before my initiation in grassroots youth work in 1984, Hans J. Morgenthau , a sociological and political analyst who wrote policy papers in the 1970s, issued a dire warning about the loss of social glue holding our relationships in a democratic society together: "The governments of the modern state, are not only, in good measure unable to govern, but where they still appear to govern (and appearances can be deceptive) they are perceived as a threat to the welfare and very existence of their citizens. National governments, once hailed as the expression of the common will, and promoters of the common good, are now widely perceived as the enemy of the people, a threat to citizen's freedom, welfare, and his survival, it is the great political paradox of our time."[648]

Sound familiar? In our recent times of financial collapse, the Boomer generation is leaving a whole succeeding generation behind. With their institutionalized ethic of neglect, those who were such idealists in the 1960s are demonstrating irresponsible stewardship regarding our planet's natural systems, which threatens to leave our species permanently behind. The glue that is essential for working together, the glue that is essential for this nation of "divided selves," is trust. A popular slogan held among the young in the 1960s was don't trust anyone over the age of 30. In some ways, we must have been clairvoyants peering through a glass exposing the parenting and governance of the 1980s and beyond. Trust bonds the customer and business owner, which is exhibited in a handshake, and the trust building creates confidence by constituents for their elected officials work. The unspoken assumption behind this trust is that people serve in public office for the benefit of the little person and the invisible. This trust, in these times, calls for a reinvention.

Who is leading the way but young people and their emergent generation, who have created civic reform organizations and social justice movements? Before March for Our Lives, people had given up on the prospect of the NRA so much as blinking. Elected officials are finally inching towards safer and saner gun policies. When the Dreamers were threatened with draconian measures of expulsion, American patriots flocked to the airports to block egregious methods of enforcement against their beloved neighbors. For decades, denial on the part of policy makers and agency heads created the false narrative that the cancerous threads of racism were no longer with us. Black Lives Matter has cut the cords that bind us to the mistaken belief that racism no longer exists. When the curtain is pulled back and people respond to injustice with their hearts, trust begins anew. Today, 57 per cent of the American public sympathize with the protesters even as national leaders rattle their sabers. Building trust begins when we learn to trust in each other. Trust is a currency which sustains democracy, and that means of survival has faded since the 1950s. According to a Pew poll on whether people trust the government, about 75 per cent of people answered in the affirmative in 1958. In the year 2019, that positive figure had fallen dramatically to just 19 per cent."[649] According to one piece of Native American philosophy, if a people's vision vanishes the inevitable result is that the people perish. Today there are movements arising, in locales around our nation that are releasing our transformational energies, at the grassroots level, block by block. This soul-based energy, processed through the linking of our hearts, is a welcome source of alternative energy.

Everyday people acting through modest means but with great compassion and courage are retrieving Dr. King's dream of beloved community and seizing the time to "grow our souls." My journey was sustained by such hope and thrived during activists seeking life-enhancing pathways in which the dignity of individuals and the viability of community remains. Rabbi Michael Lerner, a founder of the spiritually progressive *Tikkun* magazine, attributes our progress to our adopting a "globalization of the spirit," which "requires that we overcome the false dichotomy between changing ourselves and changing societal structures." Rabbi Lerner calls this spirit an "Emancipatory Spirituality encouraging a living synthesis of individual and social transformation."[650] Dr. Charles M. Johnson was a psychiatrist and artist who was also a director of the Institute of Creative Development. In his book, titled Necessary Wisdom: Meeting the Challenge of Cultural Maturity, he has grappled with the ambiguities and paradoxes we face as we create alternatives and tackle hard to grasp problems. We have moved on from an age of one answer fits all, and must face uncertainty not as an obstacle, but a task to be looked upon with open minds and through collective cooperation amongst individuals with multiple viewpoints.[651] My work with teen enfranchisement provided this medicine for myself and for those whom I strived to create civic benefit with. I was also guided by a thousand points of light along the way.

The 30-year string described in this narrative "ends" with the attainment of success in changing the Public Officer Law, which now allows fully vetted 16- and 17-year-olds to serve on New York City community boards. Yet what is felt as an "end" is in fact a beginning, as we now transition into an ambiguously perceived age of promise and problematic obstacles.

During the days of organizing for getting teens approved for community boards, we also generated the possibility of promise in the face of doubt. Getting a vision for teen engagement passed into law is a political good for the teen generation; it resulted in getting adolescents on a path of officially sanctioned municipal engagement. Although we were successful in recruiting teens to serve on boards—teens who have inspired success—if gauged strictly by the number teens placed throughout New York City, we fell short of our anticipated outcomes.

In the fall of 2014, a coalition of advocates that we initially called the Teens on Board Group and then called Project 118 sprang into action, providing orientations and information sessions concerning the board application process. Calling this effort Project 118 was the brainchild of Alan Shulman, a retired social studies teacher and active member of the New York City chapter of the National Council for the Social Studies (NCSS).[652] Based on his experience as a tireless and well-informed advisor to student governments such as that at Boys and Girls High School in Brooklyn, he succeeded in extending their school-based focus by fostering partnerships with community-based allies. Once learning about and joining our Teens on Board campaign in mid-2014, Mr. Shulman eagerly looked forward to extending the model and its working principles, which currently aligned with the principles of school-based student governance, to a larger collaborative model involving community boards. He envisioned having student councils as well as individual students with a high interest in community improvement become actively engaged with the boards.

The amended Public Office law allowed for no more than two 16- or 17-year-olds to serve on any one of the 59 community boards in New York City. The total number of teens who could find community board placement was 118. Alan Shulman, Sarah Andes, and I served as coordinators for the introductory sessions about board applications and membership.

Working with the office of Brooklyn Borough President Eric Adams, we scheduled a session at Brooklyn Borough Hall, which we called a Community Board Boot Camp.[653] Participants included teens involved in their schools and neighborhood groups in Brooklyn, members of community boards in Brooklyn, and residents interested in learning about the initiative.

We organized the day so that it included an overview of the purposes and functioning structure of boards, the duties of board members, and the nature of board committees, which worked on issues aligned with the concerns of neighborhood stakeholders—schools, sanitation, public safety, and land use. We separated the audience into breakout groups comprising youth and adults, who worked on mock problems representing the types of problems typically seen at board meetings. We concluded the day with a walkthrough about the board application process. Participants were pleased with the opportunity to meet each other and optimistic about the prospect of our outreach efforts.

Manhattan Borough President Gale Brewer, whom we had previously nicknamed the Godmother of our movement, held an initial orientation, using the same model, that was attended by over 70 teens. The buzz was one of optimistic anticipation. Gale, a devoted guide for this effort, has held orientation sessions at the Centre Street office every year since, and had also helped us to organize additional sessions, such as those at the PAL Washington Heights Armory and the downtown Manhattan Beacon School.

Ben Kallos served as chair of the New York City Council Operations Committee and had, at the strong urging of Washington Heights Councilperson Mark Levine, engineered a Council resolution of support, which was after a few days approved by the full City Council. Under the leadership of Manhattan Borough President Gale Brewer, four borough presidents also signed on with a letter of support. As a result of the hard work of these City Council members and Borough Presidents, along with the tireless advocacy of allies from 35 community and civic reform agencies, we developed a network of vocal supporters for having teens apply for board membership.

In our first year of outreach and enrollment, we successfully placed 19 teens on community boards. Five teens were placed from the Bronx, six from Manhattan, and nine from Brooklyn. None were placed on boards in either Queens or Staten Island. A good start for Year One. In succeeding years, the total number of community board-enrolled teens had hovered at about 19. In more recent years, starting in 2019, interest has declined.[654] From the stark perspective in which success is measured solely by the number of placements, the outcome has been limited. What follows is some reflection on underlying obstacles, as well as more optimistic sharing about initiatives involving the expansion of youth involvement as civic participants and active actors.

In presenting a point of view that is critical of community boards, I look at the broader picture of factors facilitating a disinclination for civic participation occurring in public venues other than that occurring just with community boards. One of these indices of public reluctance to become involved in public affairs is aptly pointed to by the political scientist and democratic theorist Benjamin Barber. In his body of thought about institutional practices that discourage trust in government, he cites the deficits in dialogue between elected officials and constituents. Mr. Barber feels that for a public conversation to be genuinely political, it must contain certain qualities. These include public talk fostering a sense of commonality, eliciting common ground and overlapping interests. The conversation needs to be two- way, fostering deliberation as participants engage in reflective practices and learn to withstand critical cross examination. What needs to be encouraged is a climate of inclusiveness, where multiple voices are welcomed, and dissent valued.[655]

Although the efforts for outreach and recruitment remained strong on the part of advocates such as Manhattan Borough President Gale Brewer, even into the year 2020, the same commitment and attention to detail has not been exercised by other elected officials nor from support movements on the ground. This may partially be due to the socioeconomic graphics of New York City, leading to great decline in electoral participation at the local level.[656] In some districts, we elect State Assemblyman with turnouts as low as 12 per cent in Democratic Party primaries. What has also, thankfully, emerged has been a flowering of grassroots movements, seeking to influence the direction and governance of our city. Outsiders, officially taking to the suites of government the messaging and energy of the streets, have revived the type of movements which historically have been responsible for leading the efforts for social justice and change.

Of course, community boards are not controlled by ruling elites nor managed by spin doctors. Yet the background influences present in the communities and the nation in which we all live, are. In New York City, 108 billionaires take in 40 per cent of all derived income.[657] These financially privileged stakeholders also contribute funds to the electoral process disproportionately. These billionaire contributors construct sophisticated, high pressure lobbying efforts which exercise great influence on political parties in the choosing of candidates and the policy direction of the Democratic Party. The viewpoints of these affluent actors have dominated the government at both the municipal and state levels. Until recently, through their lobbyists and private pressure campaigns, they have also dominated the agenda and policy formulations at the city and state level. Progressive initiatives, such as having a more progressive income tax structure, a fully functioning education and health care system, and an electoral process which invites voters in rather than discouraging participation had remained stalled for years. In the years 2018–20, elected officials with progressive vision and agendas have finally emerged into positions of greater influence and power.

In 1970, the percentage of residents living in poverty was 11.5; by 2018 this rate had increased to 19.6 per cent. Study after study has shown that "living under the aegis of extreme inequality" depresses participation—voter turnout confirms this trend.[658]

On a national level, the voter participation rate has hovered in the upper 50 percentage range, reaching a high of 63 per cent in 2008, supposedly an explosive year when voters were excited to turn out. By 2016, New York State had ranked in the bottom half of voter turnout for the previous two decades, and in the 2016 election, it ranked the eighth worst in turnout among all states in our nation.[659] Additional studies show that when a society is in the throes of anxiety-producing suspicion, people are inclined either to retreat or, as recent history has shown, to follow highly manipulative leaders with a severe distaste for supporting the healthy mechanisms of a functional democracy.

The second factor I bring up here is one first raised by Mary Wollstonecraft, a late eighteenth-century feminist voice who staunchly objected to the exclusion of women in the voting process. In her classic tome, *The Vindication of the Rights of Woman*, she posits: "Perpetual subordination creates eternal dependency."[660] This syndrome was certainly true for women in Ms. Wollstonecraft's day, as they were defined as naturally weak and in need of following male guidance. It was not until 1974 that a legal ruling granted women control of their own financial assets, independently of their husband's control. In 2020, women are now forced into rear-guard organizing to protect their rights for protecting their bodies and exercising their will. What appeared to have been achieved in legislation decades ago has resurfaced as a steep climb just to maintain rights earned in the 1970's.

In differing ways, institutional foundations, called schools, keep students in a state of provisional readiness. The effects of this situation are spoken of by professor of theology Dorothee Soelle: "To be constantly and overindulgently 'prepared for' is to enter into the contest pared of the essential recognition of one's authenticity and the implementation of one's voice."[661] In our public-school curricula, students' experience in social studies classrooms had been dominated by the study of homogenized heroes with no flaws, who had come from origins of being members of the racially privileged class.

Especially for girls in school, not only are their voices overlooked, but their presence and needs as females are often trivialized or treated as non-existent. When girls express emotions, such as anger or frustration, they are looked at as trying to be too much like a boy and disciplined for not being appropriate.[662]

History was rarely portrayed as being driven by a stakeholder membership living close to the ground, and it was always challenged by financial shortages and negative stereotypes about them. In history class, Helen Keller was portrayed as a deaf and blind young woman, prone to unkempt behavior, who overcame great obstacles under the guidance of a sympathetic teacher. This is all good, but what has been traditionally omitted is her later work in serving the blind. What Helen Keller found is that it is primarily poor women driven to prostitution who represented an inordinate number of women going blind. For her this meant that blindness was not only a personal health challenge, but a socially constructed issue. This understanding was what put her on a road for allegiance to socialism and the American Civil Liberties Union (ACLU).[663] The contexts of history defined by class interest also contain and control our knowledge about what is "real" in the world. As youth are increasingly discovering that history taught in schools omits full disclosure, either about the historic intent of heroes or by omitting local heroes from official historical accounts, they also question the relevance of participation in public affairs. In the community of Washington Heights, as well as in other communities suffering from the effects of disinvestment and government policy creation of segregation, health issues such as elevated levels of asthma, diabetes and cardio-vascular disease for Blacks and Latinos (as compared to Whites) are personal-health issues driven by disparities in resources according to race and national background. Even before developing health issues, schools routinely ignore the health needs of girls.[664] It is within this context of discriminatory political decisions and financial red lining that youth activists and their mentors must define their civic reform approaches.

(Redlining is a banking fiscal practice which severely limits funding to areas of the city typically populated by Blacks and other minorities.) The community of the South Bronx is one of the poorest districts in America and suffers some of the most significant health disparities.[665] It also is also true that New York City has amongst the highest levels of economic inequalities between upper tiers of wealth and financially distressed peoples and happens to have the most segregated school system in America.[666]

When it comes down to the ground, we are still talking community boards whose members operate with the mindset that their goal is to provide valuable guidance to city government. Board members (as I have witnessed for years at Community Board 12 in Manhattan) are exceptionally dedicated to board service and to their communities, are highly intelligent and articulate, and exhibit character traits and possess institutional knowledge of potential value to teens as board mentees. Yet, to the public at large, unless they are neighborhood stakeholders who come to meetings with specific complaints, suggestions, or presentations about promising programs, community boards are little understood or invisible to the larger adult public, let alone to teens.

Histories about boards allude to both their deficits and their assets. Deficits have been identified when examining community board member demographics, and profiled in critical news accounts, leading to questions about the effectiveness of boards. A combination of socio/economic factors, and community board practices being brought under scrutiny, contribute to the decline in participation at community boards. As mentioned in a study profiled in the *Gotham Gazette*, "David Rogers found that boards in communities with higher median income tend to do better at getting their proposals implemented by city agencies than Boards in communities with lower median income."[667] Add to this the fact that even within boards representing communities of various income medians, board members tend to trend toward older age medians; for example, in the past members have tended to be in their 40s and 50s, although there has been some movement toward the 30s now. Board members are recruited from among business owners and agency professionals—and, to a much lesser degree, service workers and those marginalized by lack of work or education.

In a recent interview carried in a progressive newspaper called the *Indypendent*, Alicia Boyd of the Brooklyn Anti-gentrification Network revealed that "[b]y March of 2015, 52 out of 59 Boards had voted to reject Mayor DeBlasio's Mandatory Inclusion Housing policy, but nothing happened."[668] Members of community organizing efforts, as well as some of their constituencies, had often expressed their reservations about introducing teens to boards, in which these types of experiences might only reinforce a sense of lack of efficacy already experienced by teens in other venues, starting with their schools.

Yet, there have been successes too. As detailed in the same article in the *Gotham Gazette*, "A 1992 plan by Community Board 3 in the South Bronx provided for amendments to enlarge the urban renewal area, the Melrose Commons, and…a plan for Brooklyn's Red Hook neighborhood triggered the formation of a committee to monitor bank response to the Community Reinvestment Act, which ultimately resulted in the location of a full-service bank in their previously underserved area."[669]

The gains made by teens who did serve on boards, and the benefits derived by boards and communities resulting their input, are also indicators of hopeful change. Mahfuzar Rahman, who was appointed to Community Board 11 in East Harlem, stated in an interview that "prior to his invitation to apply, he did not even know Community Boards existed." Submitting his application after attending a Community Board boot camp was a good starting point. Mulan Burgess, who was appointed to Community Board 3 in Brooklyn, "chose work on the Board addressing the issue of displacement of residents and mom and pop businesses."[670]

I close this very brief look at the pros and cons of community boards with this thought. The electoral process in the newly founded United States started out as voting rights for White men of property ownership only. Over 200 years later, while the electoral franchise has been significantly expanded, we are still witnessing mammoth efforts to suppress and restrict voting which targets minorities and young people for exclusion. The inequities do not mean we withdraw our efforts to ensure voting rights for all; they motivate us to work ever harder to keep justice and hope alive for the fairest voting rights agenda possible. The same logic can be used for promoting involvement on community boards. They have structural problems and deficits in representation, but they also have members, and some boards, which represent valiant efforts for keeping municipal involvement informed, just, and effective. With community board participatory improvements, the seeds of enfranchisement for adults and teens have been part of the total package of fair representation being planted amongst our myriad of social justice movements. Within the garden of democracy, many blooms are taking root.

In New York City and across our nation, many movements, seeds being planted, and flowering of civic possibilities calling for teen empowerment and civic enfranchisement are arising. Some are led by adults who are working hard to incorporate adolescent participation; others are led by teens demanding that adults come on board by infusing teens with indigenously derived recommendations to deepen our democracy.

A specter is haunting the artifice of adultism—of the evolved adolescent mind and the emergent movement of teen enfranchisement. The controlling power of the old adultizing mindset, along with its institutional protocols embedded in outworn beliefs and practices, still manufacture attempts to thwart the progress made toward honoring the integrity of the teen mind and the enhanced benefits in creating a fully inclusive democracy. Fetters holding back the achievement of progressive outcomes, as well as the profusion of silos of reactionary reason, keep springing up. After lying on the dusty shelves in the libraries of reactionaries, they are presented to us as new lies in deceptive packaging. Modern-day marketing has been put into service the mania of keeping America late again, a nation which ranks close to last among modern democracies for constructing equitable financial and socio-political conditions. Movements led by grassroots activists and teen leaders today are generating hope, and provisional results, that we soon will overcome appeals to fear and retribution, which will then be fodder for the idle gnawing of the mice, leaving only meager remnants. What has become dysfunctional is giving way to the symmetry of intergenerational collaboration and embrace.

C. Otto Scharmer is a senior lecturer at the Massachusetts Institute of Technology who received the Jamieson Prize for excellence for his teaching at MIT. In Mr. Scharmer's book, *Theory U*, he connects our capacity to pay attention to our interior world and be fully present with our efficacy in creating organizational change. He proposes an organizing system of connecting the inner and outer worlds of experience, which he calls "presencing."[671] Adolescent change-makers, as they become increasingly self-aware and responsive to the callings of the future, are "presencing the future."[672] I postulate that teens' visionary inputs are visualized prospects under construction, which enable the emergence of what Scharmer calls an "alternative future—with presence, awareness and resonance."[673] With increased levels of presence, from issue-focused advisory boards reforming educational practice and criminal justice practices, to youth advisory councils working hand in hand with municipal government agencies and elected officials, teens are making their contributions felt at the civic table. Working face to face with teen change-makers, adults, and teens themselves, are raising their awareness. Young activists are becoming more attuned to the specific realities of "the other," connected at a soul level where all of us are united. Our efforts now resonate with rising expectations, celebrating power realized from the altitude of high potential and congruent with the higher angels of democracy.

Sven Hansen, in his book, *Inside/Out: The Practice of Resilience,* which I spoke of earlier in this narrative, elaborates on his concept of resilience by describing how reformers stay focused, strong, and persistent: "Courage is developed when we participate in the healing of psychic and public wounds; creativity is manifested through the full spectrum tapping of our guts, our brains, and our hearts. Connections are reinforced as partners develop discipline through focused and sustained efforts. Compassionate collaborators are remaining mindful and in prayer for ourselves and our allies. We bounce back from adversity when our fractured perceptions and civic institutional practices become more coherent. We rebuild, revision and reconstruct in present time."[674]

After I was afforded the opportunity to coordinate the Teens on Board campaign, and co-lead in its advocacy in 2010, I fashioned a commitment to seeing through to its conclusion the passage of the amendment of NY State Public Officer Law allowing for teens to serve on community boards. Coordinating meant persisting with my commitment, building on small victories, overcoming obstacles, and remaining close to supportive allies in this campaign. I not only got to lead the campaign, but my allies in this civic reform movement also enabled me to discover my strength and develop discipline and persistence over a four-year period. While some, in their questionable practices of falsely demeaning teens and their efficacy, came to be viewed by me as joining the ranks of idle gnawing of mice, others joined me in viewing teens as being in storytelling partnership with adolescents on a mission, such as Dorothy, the star of the *Wizard of Oz*. According to the writer Salman Rushdie, the theme of the film was about adults abandoning young people, and their lack of responsibility as elders. In turn, Dorothy must strategize and learn to survive using intuition, her wits, and her developing wisdom. She succeeded in her mission of returning home, although home was a different place from what she had experienced prior to arriving in Oz. Dorothy also encountered and received aid from three curious allies, a Scarecrow looking for a brain, a Tin man looking for a heart, and a Lion looking to find his own courage. Using Mr. Rushdie's take on this film, the Wizard of Oz is prophetic. Adolescents today are affirming their inner derived intelligence, opening their hearts to discovering authentic life pathways, and manifesting courage in the face of historically daunting challenges.[675]

As I spoke to earlier in this book, Ann Taket, et al, (*Practicing Social Inclusion*) is an advocate for putting teen civic engagement programs in place where "youth obtain control over input and outcomes; where they are delegated power to shape policy and agency practices; and where they serve in equal partnership with adults."[676] In the last few years, organizations setting the standards for meeting this objective, professional organizations who provide guidelines and training and grassroots-based initiatives operating on the ground, are redefining what both teen engagement and what mentoring of teen social change agents mean.

The National Council of Social Studies (NCSS) has a membership comprised of seasoned social studies teachers and school department heads from across the United States. The NCSS members have constructed a syllabus for grades one through twelve, which incorporates student reflection upon issues of importance to them and how to respond to need, research initiated by and analyzed by youth, and participation in project-based learning. Youth activists are changing how to understand history by learning to connect their civic action procedures with historical lessons identified in the classroom. NCSS calls the model the "C-3 Framework for Social Studies State Standards, enhancing the pathways toward College, Career, and Civic Life. This guide is a graduated and integrated structure in which students become aware of, and actively engage in, best practices, and become capable of reflecting upon the process of their participation and the products they produce. These begin with learning how to brainstorm and formulate questions, then how to verify accurate information, and then moving towards creating consensus and targeted action. Students also learn how to evaluate the benefits of the outcomes designed, as well as to adjust, as needed, in the future. As stated in the NCSS introduction to civics in the C-3 Guide: "Students demonstrate civic engagement when they address public problems individually and collaboratively and when they maintain, strengthen, and improve communities and societies."[677]

For instance, when we look at one dimension of the C-3 paradigm called "Communicating and Critiquing Conclusions," they establish guidelines about what students will do by the end of Grade 12. These evidenced-based practices include "constructing arguments using precise and knowledgeable claims (the White House, please take note); learning to acknowledge the strengths and weaknesses of the explanations they derive, and present adaptations of arguments and explanations that feature evocative ideas and perspectives on issues and topics which appeal to a wide range of audiences."[678] Under this model, students engage in researching original sources and consider varied perspectives about what they mean and their relevance to today; they then make claims using evidence-based support.[679]

The Southern Poverty Law Center is an organization that was founded to protect black people and other minorities targeted by hate groups and subject to discriminatory policies. They have an educational arm of the organization which has developed a syllabus for school students covering this topic, as well as the history and civic rights methods available today. They highlight techniques already successfully used by civil rights organizations. [680]

When joining the Teens on Board campaign, students and their mentors chose to study the structure and process of community boards and advocated for making these local advisory bodies more responsive to the needs of teens, as articulated by young people themselves. When the Urban Youth Collaborative advocated for safer school climates, they did so after researching information about the impact of over-policing in schools on both school culture and adolescents' sense of control over their immediate environment.

Starting with historical records from the1930's, and based upon her sociological observations conducted today, Dr. Mindy Thompson Fullilove has been helping to lead a social justice initiative in Orange, New Jersey. As part of her project construction, she critiques the impact of racialized inequalities on that city's Black citizens. These government records show that governments promoted red-lining and under-investment in sections of that city where Black people had created a community for decades. Research, reflect, and re-act are all responses which are essential to the practice of democracy and the implementation of socially just policies.

A question that lingers throughout this chapter is why we see uneven application of reform when we contrast civil rights and protective policies between those offered adults as opposed to those offered teens. Why do these discrepancies persist? Are the practices of civics and democratic principles applied consistently and uniformly to real-life issues and concerns in schools? Where governance designed and led by adults has fallen short, teens have taken the helm. Civic reform campaigns organized by teens are applying the principles of democracy, as they address concerns impacting their daily lives. Teens are taking the lead in New York City, and across the country. If a student seeks to learn how to play the violin, s/he practices on the instrument. If a student seeks to apply the principles of algebra, s/he practices the formulas. If a student seeks to understand the principles of democracy, and graduate school prepared as a fully informed and prepared citizen, s/he must also practice the tools necessary to keep democracy alive.[681]

The New York City Mayor's Administration, under a new program developed by NYC Service, has been in the process of providing these opportunities by advising existing youth councils and assisting community-based agencies and elected officials in developing new councils. This expansive network of youth civic participation began with the founding and expansion of New York City Leadership Councils under the administration of Mayor DeBlasio. To date, the focus has been on "policy, practice and advocacy, and issues such as mental health support, preventing gun violence, and environmental sustainability."[682] One of their teen leaders, Ayesha, 15, put it well, when she explained: "I found how to serve my community by joining the NYC Youth Leadership Council, by not only advocating for Mental Health services, but by writing a grant, which became funded, and set up sexual abuse awareness classes at 3 high schools in New York City."[683] Beyond the learned skill of advocacy mentioned by Ayesha, students in this program write grant proposals. For a proposal to be considered for funding, the writer must demonstrate a knowledge of the history around a specific issue, the impact upon people if there are existing social deficits to be addressed, and a convincing plan of action to address the problem. Ayesha also helped to develop classroom experiences teaching students about the causes of sexual abuse, how to identify when this abuse is present, even if very subtly, and how to get support for solving the problem. When young people buy in to naming and addressing a problem, the approach gains credibility in their minds.

Manhattan Borough President Gale Brewer and Brooklyn Borough President Eric Addams have been pioneers in establishing teen advisory boards at their respective borough halls. These teen advisory boards meet monthly at the borough president office, identify issues of concern to them, and give recommendations for remediating the problems. Adult staff at these offices considers teens to be equally valuable partners in the process of civic reform.[684]

Each of these two borough offices has also hosted "boot camps" to which high school students are invited to learn about community boards, and how they can apply to become members. These information sessions incorporate community board scenarios amongst small groups, which include teens and community board members in the dialogue. In these times of rising tensions between youth and the police, the Manhattan and Brooklyn Borough President offices also initiated face-to-face discussions at roundtables addressing the breakdown of communication and trust between young people and members of the law enforcement establishment. Using face-to-face encounters and open-ended and respective dialogue reflective of differing experiences, those who have become distanced can learn to appreciate the perspective of each side. As each of these sessions has end, many participants have testified that they now came to realize their common interest in clear communications and a desire for peaceful outcomes. A former colleague of mine, Bobby Ferazi, who was the director of PAL's Youth Link program has shared with me the experience of building bridges of understanding between teens and police officers during their supported dialogue sessions.[685] In many cases, officers, somewhat hardened by dispiriting confrontational street encounters, and teens who had been subject to arbitrary and intrusive invasion of their bodies and homes, would, after sharing their vulnerabilities and actively listening to their conversational partners, drop their walls of skeptically induced rejection and enter the experiential house of their partner.[686]

Training teens to engage in best civic practices also contributes to a formation of their holistic development (both personally and socially). Similarly, higher educational experiences focused on asset-based teen models and equitable intergenerational partnerships are crucial for adults entering the field of youth services. A civic education and social justice advocate with whom I have collaborated for over a decade is Sarah Zeller-Berkman.[687]

Dr. Zeller-Berkman is a director at the CUNY Graduate Center's Collaborative for Youth Development. I met Sarah Zeller-Berkman around 2007, when she was an organizer for the Youth Development Institute. She worked to assist both the Department of Youth Services and Community Development, and its provider members, in creating teen advisory programs at the local level. Dr. Zeller-Berkman, together with her research and advocacy teams, had developed rubrics outlining the best strategic practices for us in constructing teen councils, which advise governing structures in human service agencies and the offices of governance officials.[688] A rubric is a graduated progression of behaviors outlined on a continuum towards achieving a desired outcome, usually outlined in a sequence of four or five steps. The first step indicates a complete absence of a behavior necessary to move towards a goal. The next step indicates a behavior in which a participant is taking a first step, or some initial steps. The third step describes a set of behaviors which are close being fully adequate, but perhaps missing one crucial element. The rubrics top level includes a set of desired behaviors which interact to ensure achieving a goal. By focusing on any stage in the rubric, those who implement civic participation projects consider each stage to be indicative of a process where leaders can reinforce and strengthen a particular step to make progression to a higher step more feasible. Dr. Zeller-Berkman wrote a white paper titled *Rolling Thunder*, in which she identifies the goals for "enhancing the collective impact of intergenerational youth policy making."[689] In the guide, she identifies several considerations that an agency needs to think about, whether starting a new youth council or enhancing an existing one. As outlined in the Executive Summary for *Rolling Thunder*, these are "including young people not just as beneficiaries, but as co-creators of youth policy; activating networks of youth councils by using media technology; collecting research based and in-practice results of existing youth councils, and then applying a cross city analysis to inform youth-policy making."[690] As we look at behaviors described in each level of the rubric, an initial stage would be including young people as beneficiaries, but not as co-creators of youth policy. A subsequent level would have youth act as co-creators, but not engage in networks of support. The third stage would reflect establishing a set of neighborhood connections, but not having a plan for following up. The highest stage of the rubric would include having students' participation in all the steps just outlined in *Rolling Thunder*. In the final section of the *Rolling Thunder* guide, Zeller-Berkman also includes extensive data bases on "the history and structure of youth-led models, as well as their purpose and duties, and which municipal agencies t are advised by each one of these councils."[691] This rubric includes " youth commission models, from Hampton, Virginia to San Francisco, and youth council models abroad from the Dominican Republic to France."[692] Each model contains a description of issue focus. By sharing and advising with progressive practitioners, Dr. Zeller-Berkman has enhanced their ability to apply informed practices on the ground, and in collaboration with supportive partners.

I take a step back here, to the year 2010, when I attended a gathering of the New York City Department of Youth and Community Development Beacon programs. Also present were all youth agencies hosting Beacon programs. I was invited to make a presentation about the Teens on Board project. My goal was to recruit new participants in our campaign, including Beacon Center Directors, as well as possibly getting teens at these sites to circulate petitions of support for the Teens on Board initiative.

At the time, Dr. Zeller-Berkman was an advisor to the Department of Youth and Community Development Beacon programs, providing trainings on how to initiate and support after-school-based middle-school teen councils.[693] After the meeting, Dr. Zeller let me know that she would be an enthusiastic supporter. Immediately after that meeting, and continuing until the fruitful conclusion of our campaign, Dr. Zeller-Berkman not only supported us, but also volunteered as an essential member of our coordinating committee. Dr. Zeller-Berkman moved forward with us during our Teens on Board advocacy, and she generously shared bodies of research which she had gathered in her studies that supported and validated our cause.

Today, in her role as Director for the Collaborative for Advancing Youth Development at the CUNY Graduate School Center, she has assisted in creating a state Education Department-approved course in youth studies, including both a certificate study program and a master's program. As highlighted by a program description, written in a brochure prepared for the CUNY Graduate Center program, the knowledge and skills students will develop include "examining the intersections of age, gender, gender identity, sexuality, race, class, and immigration status. Students look at the regional impact on youth development. Graduate students are exposed to analysis of current youth policies through managed opportunities and best practices. Educators under development are learning to apply principles and best practices in program management as well as facilitation and evaluation. With hands on participation, they practice engagement with multiple stakeholders to ensure positive youth development of youth, staff, and communities."[694]

In the last few years, Professor Zeller-Berkman has also coordinated annual conferences (hosted at the CUNY Graduate Center) that have facilitated collaborative support for youth empowerment. Attendees have included agencies such as the Citizens Committee for Children, Girls for Gender Equity, Integrate NYC, and the Intergenerational Change Initiative. This collaboration also includes NYC Service and Teens Take Charge, whose programs I elaborate upon next. The work accomplished already, in such a short time, by organizations such as Teens Take Charge, showcases a changing world in which teen leaders and their organization's participants have already led the way in developing teen leadership models for the 21st Century. In this book, for those whom I have only read accounts in news articles and online, and researched, but with whom I have not collaborated with, I offer only a taste of who they are, and contact info. Doing justice to what they have contributed to socially- just civic participation would require a separate book for each of them. The balance of this chapter, after providing brief mention of these pioneers in youth leadership, will follow up on promising teen empowerment initiatives with which I have had direct involvement or close collaboration, as well as some thoughts by writers and researchers supportive of our new era revolution, facilitated by many, and affecting us all.

Teens Take Charge (TCC) is the embodiment of a youth advocacy organization that operates by, for, and with the leaders who are actual members of the young generation it seeks to serve. As stated in its mission statement posted on its web page, TTC seeks, through its "unscreen the schools initiative," to work for "the elimination of decisions made by schools without the voice of youth, and the inclusion of student recommendations by including them in policy-making structures."[695] Social change agents who have worked closely with me in the past and who have witnessed the work of TTC have told me that their on-the-ground projects include organizing against segregation in schools (New York City is at best the second most segregated school district in America) and instituting an agenda fighting for more equitable resource distribution in underserved schools. TCC has already done a great job of bringing students and policy makers to the table to share ideas, and to implement changes in procedures and protocols exercised by institutions, such as the Department of Education. Agency leaders have been actively supporting teen collaborative input which affects the well-being and civil rights of young people.

Another youth-led agency, this one operating in the Bronx, in New York City, is called Teens for Food Justice. The teen leadership has been trained by adult-led agencies addressing issues of healthful food scarcity in economically challenged neighborhoods, and the questionable content of public-school food options high in sugar and fat content. This program has been successful in influencing Bronx school districts to change menu options at four middle schools in the Bronx. [696]

Similar models of advocacy and decision-making, such as those practiced by Teens Take Charge, have already been established in some schools around the country, such as Constitution High School in Philadelphia. According to a school profile included in an NCSS bulletin, the Constitution High School governance model is based on equal participation by students, teachers, and administrators using the separation of powers between executive, legislative, and judicial bodies as mandated in the US Constitution.[697] At Constitution High School, governance of, by, and for the people (in this case students) is described on the school's website as including participation by students on "executive councils which preside over the development of curricula and school discipline; legislative bodies which design and propose school policies; and judicial councils which administer peer judicial decisions based upon reconciliation approaches and not just arbitrarily enforced rule."[698]

These participatory approaches represent an ethical powerhouse capable of effecting forceful change that may help to undo the underlying traps of apathy and indifference in New York City. As I had mentioned earlier in this book, in New York State, voter registration and turnout in national elections had ranked among the lowest in the nation until the most recent elections. (We are now closer to the middle of the pack amongst all states.) In some local races, such as for city council and the state legislature, turnout can be as low as 12 per cent. In a quote included in the NYC Service website, a critique of our present deficient voter participation condition has been aptly expressed by Naia Timmons, a student at Beacon High School, who also participates in NYC Service: "People don't want the system to change because this will stop their benefitting from the status quo."[699]

As quoted in the book titled *The Virgin Vote*, after President Abraham Lincoln started advocating for an end to slavery and extension of the franchise to blacks, he said: "Allow all the governed an equal voice, and that, and only that, is self-government."[700] President Lincoln had been an advocate for getting young people involved in electoral politics. An equal voice for all would become an optimally expressed representation of generational voice. In the late 1800s, long before 18- to 21-year-old people were granted the right to vote, elected officials encouraged youth participation in the electoral party process and in promoting the responsibility of voting for their elders. During those times, voter turnout ranged from 70 per cent to 80 per cent of the voter eligible population.[701] Were we adults to encourage and put in place universal and high-quality civic education in every school, the disposition to become involved in civics and voting would become enhanced. What would be essential is having the civic classes be inclusive of incorporating their interests and active participation.

In 2019, 14 students, led by an activist lawyer named Michael Rebell, initiated a lawsuit against the state of Rhode Island for not guaranteeing, for every student, civic education that is an informative and inspiring platform for the joys and responsibilities of citizenship. (Mr. Rebell had been the legal representative for the NY State Campaign for Fiscal Equity, which sued the state of New York for underfunding schools in New York City.) The plaintiffs center their claim on the belief that unless students are given the right to an enhanced civic classroom experience, they will graduate unprepared for the knowledge and responsibilities necessary for citizenship. Between the years 2012 and 2016, there had been a decline in total voter turnout in New York State. Mr. Rebell hoped that this legal challenge would be part of a larger effort to increase turnout by allowing sixteen- year- old teens to become part of the electoral franchise.[702] Although the presiding judge ruled against the student claim of having their constitutional rights violated, he also praised their initiative for bringing to light the deficiencies both in public school social studies education, and the problems with democracy itself today. The U.N. Treaty on Children's Rights includes the right to civic education among their planks, as do most governments—they include this right in their constitutions.

The lawsuit, if it had been successful, would have helped to create an educational environment where student voice is intrinsic to the process of social studies education and civic participation. In the 1960s, student activists from Columbia University had released a policy declaration proposing this right for inclusive voice as part of its mission statement. The lawsuit filed by Mr. Rebell and his allies has however, opened a door to follow up legal grievances suffered by students today. What was started in the 60's as street protest and campus organizing by members of the Boomer Generation when they were still teens provides perspective on the importance of youth organizing today.

The Port Huron Statement, drafted by the leadership of Students for A Democratic Society (SDS) in the early 1960's, proposed that: "At whatever cost to cause or doctrine, one must care for the uniqueness and dignity of each individual, and yield to what his consciousness demands in the existential moment."[703] Student leaders in SDS, many of them veterans of the anti-war and pro-civil rights movements, after doing extensive research, found that university boards and trustees were not encouraging dissident critique of institutional attachments to corporations profiting from the war economy, but rather complicit in what we called the military-industrial complex. They also exposed the many officers of university campuses who sat on boards of companies producing armaments. The support of university governors for inappropriate and excessive military spending was one example of Dr. Martin Luther King's four catastrophes, that of an escalating militarism at home and abroad. To our shame, Students for a Democratic Society abandoned its roots of democratic ideals, pursuing a course of rigid left-wing ideologies and inflexible movement tactics. It splintered and self-destructed under the weight of its angry diatribe culture and increasingly narrow viewpoints. Out of the ashes of a fading youth movement, and organizing in more special-ized ways, other movements would follow—such as those of environmental movements, welfare rights groups, the women's rights movement, and other reform movements within political parties and our larger society. However the embers of social justice for youth, initially lit decades ago still burn brightly, and when analyzed and given remembrance by today's youth leaders, provide energy and inspiration for picking up the torch.

The youth-led movements such as Black Lives Matter and March for Our Lives have been inspired in part by the idealism and magnanimous efforts of historically affirmed youth movements in in the 1960's, such those led by the Student Non-Violent Coordinating Committee (SNCC) and student followers fighting for voting rights in the American south. I have had conversations with Dr. Robert Fullilove, a professor at Columbia University's Graduate School of Public Health. who also serves as an organizer and director for graduate school student's volunteer contributions in Washington Heights. Dr. Fullilove's legacy includes his deep roots as an organizer for the Student Non-Violent Coordinating Committee (SNCC), which organized for ensuring civil rights and obtaining voting rights in the American south during the 1960's. These civic guarantees, and the practice of civic empowerment, are mandates that Dr. Fullilove, with alliance from his students, continues to fight for today. In these conversations with me, and in his public presentations, he stresses the importance of learning about electoral disenfranchisement and our nation's shadow history of discrimination and harm toward minorities and marginalized people. By learning about these lessons, connecting the past to conditions still in existence today, it becomes an imperative to promote the goals of achieving a more inclusive democracy. Our nation's leaders, and constituents in our communities, must practice using the tools of democracy. These ways and means include insightful, fierce critique, accompanied by on-the-ground assessment and follow-through.

Today's youth leaders are learning how to both oppose the injustice and shortcomings of the system, and how to use the better elements of the system to change for obtaining a more equitable society. While fighting against discriminatory policies and invasive actions, which have remained immune to remediation for decades, youth leaders have been making changes within themselves which facilitate critical examination of falsely held beliefs. By being honest, open, and flexible, teen leaders have increased their determination not to give up on goals for improving community and national outcomes. The moment has come for our teen leaders, and the urgency of our supporting them now calls us. To the Boomer generation I say: keep your inner adolescent alive. The continuance of indifference is unacceptable.

Enlightened activists, with an evolved consciousness about the uniqueness of each of us, and the interconnection amongst all of us, no longer accept the unacceptable given as perpetually a given. Together, activists have expressed their civic reform demands with a civil rights movement sensitivity which insists upon non-violent resistance, inclusion of leadership rising from multi-racial and diverse ethnic backgrounds, and an appreciation for having the benefit of standing upon the shoulders of our ancestral social justice allies who helped pave the road we walk on now. No longer still the teen I was in the 1960s (although I have kept my inner adolescent alive), and having just gotten to my 72nd birthday, I reflect upon the words of an elder political and spiritually progressive activists seeking to provide wise counsel to other adults questioning the efficacy and the actions of teens.

The writer and eco-spiritual counselor, Bill Plotkin, calls for establishing a renewed practice for rites of passage and ritual which connect adolescent nature and assets to the need for having teens transition into participation in society.[704] In the 1960s, Theodore Roszak was a cultural and political critic who wrote prolifically, composing articles of dissent both from an ecological and a spiritual point of view. He received a PhD from Princeton University in 1958. Even having achieved such high status in the world of academia, he did not lose his appreciation for the energy and perspectives of an emergent generation. He was critical of governmental institutions' proposed interventions for the public good. He shed light on the unintentional consequences of subverting on-the-ground personal participation and perspective based upon alternative cultural and spiritually based perspectives. Roszak called the surrender of civic responsibilities by people outside of traditional policy-proposing institutions (that is, citizens) grounds for surrender to "subliminal totalitarianism, elitist managerialism, and the production of frivolous abundance."[705] Dr. Roszak admired the rabble-rousing stance of young activists and saw them as potentially filling a generational role crucial to challenging authority. He described youth action as being derived from "an illuminated commonplace,"[706] in contrast to entrenched experts. Roszak identified two teen traits as being healthy for their development, as well as for democracy. The first was young people's "commitment to a wise silence, in the face of the strong preachiness of Christianity."[707] (To this I would add the strong preachiness of elite policy makers who better know what is good for teens better than teens themselves.) He also saw in teens a "justified discomfort"[708]from which the adolescent needs for freedom to search and freedom of expression were a healthful antidote to rigidly congealed opinion and uncontestably proposed policies.

Grassroots and youth-led movements today are incorporating insights and practices derived both from our ancestral allies and advocates for future-leaning ideas. In an essay written by John Mohawk, he speaks to practices developed by the Iroquois Confederacy. According to his account, change-makers known as peacemakers urged tribal members to stop treating those who had been seen as enemies as "those who cannot think."[709] Rather, as he writes about peace-maker councils, the task was to develop an understanding for difference, and then to develop agreements supporting commonly shared goals.

In a book looking forward in time, the writer Chris Saade in *Second Wave Spirituality*, outlines six concepts essential to what he calls an "evolutionary convergence" crucial in our twenty-first-century world: "The main evolutionary tasks of our generation seem to be seeding the ideas of global inclusion and of social engagement arising from a profound and compassionate spiritual vision."[710] In both the old and new philosophies just mentioned, it is the practice of respect for difference, mutual embrace, and the development of agreement which define our broader needs for our interconnected planet. In our efforts for promoting respect for individual dignity and collective rights, as we look backward and forward, we construct desired outcomes today.

My journey with teens and my affirming allies was a trial run conducted among a myriad of communities across New York City, our nation, and the globe. Each operates with its own integrity, and all are associated within an unspoken agreement to honor autonomy within the context of coterminous means. At the midpoint of my youth agency experience, I also saw Mr. Roszak's perspectives from the 1960s reconfirmed in the work of Alan Seale.

Mr. Seale is a leadership coach who also is a director with the Center for Transformational Presence. Our present-day youth-led movements incorporate principles of ecological awareness, spiritual openness, and thriving celebration of diverse cultural creativity. During my 30-year path of discovery, I followed four principles outlined in Mr. Seales book, *Create A Works*: "…engage your own intuition, claim your power, practice collaboration, choose wisely for the common good."[711] When I began my journey, and continuing throughout it, I led while engaged with what I intuitively felt, that something was missing from youth service practice, and that young people owned wisdom essential to fixing the problem. I claimed my power by creating opportunities for young people to claim their power. Whether getting attention for a neglected park or promoting attention to redefining teens as agents of change, both my professional wisdom and teens' civic power increased. In seeking improvement to a park's condition, I enlisted collaboration from embedded street associations led by elders, and agencies training youth in advocacy. When local conditions changed for the better, we all had chosen wisely to promote the common good. My journey and affiliated movements seek pathways towards what Mr. Seale calls "creating a world that works, by developing tools for personal and planetary transformation.[712] Our goals are to develop awareness at the soul level, live your life in congruence with your essence, and construct your practices with awareness and intention for yourself and the world." Mr. Seale also utilizes in his teachings the spiritual "principle of correspondence."[713] Briefly stated, what this means is "as above, so it is below"; that is, we need to get through barriers of separation, both internally (barriers between cognitive knowledge and emotional knowledge) and externally (barriers between abstractly derived conclusions and indigenously held truths). Finally, Mr. Seale speaks to the need for our relying not only on ego-intelligence, but also on what he calls "eco-intelligence" (everything has its place, and we are all interconnected in life-sustaining enterprise).[714] As I increased my understanding for the relevance of ecological laws within the context of soul awareness, I saw the connections between natural law and spiritual reality as means of incorporating my teen program-organizing approach as advised by universal sources of wisdom. In the anecdotes to follow, I profile the contributions of a few more teen-led initiatives that grow out of the roots of soil and community bedrock, and which succeed through the construction of best practices informed by our vision for the future.

The subsequent history of what our Teens on Board coalition accomplished in 2014 (opening the door for teen participation at the municipal advisory level) intersects with the work of other teen-led initiatives developing across New York City and the world. Although the advocacy work for the Teens on Board campaign was led chiefly by adult co-mentors, and then supported by teens, what kept me motivated to persist was my memory and appreciation for the fact that I was acting in support of a civic empowerment mandate that had been created and launched by teen initiative. Throughout the later stages of my support for what teen decision-makers had initiated, I felt highly motivated and compelled to do whatever I could to support and finish what teen leaders had started. My intention was that if I could see their civic mandate result in their ability to legally serve on Community Boards, then my mission would be accomplished. It was a high-school congress, comprising 300 students in 2007, which conceived of, approved, and launched this campaign, after which I pledged not to give up until their goal (which I adopted as my goal) was achieved. I had heart-felt allegiance to this cause (supported in my bones, and by my sometimes-aching feet as I organized around the five boroughs of New York City), but this issue belonged to them, and would be inherited by 16- and 17-year-old teens after them. The Teens on Board effort was like a stream of consciousness, strong intent, and effort flowing in a river of other powerful teen-led movements, which has resulted in an ocean of greater teen involvement and equal decision-making status for adolescent civic participants.

Training for the responsibilities needed in civics, grooming civic understanding and skills in ways that students can become enlightened and effective participants are the goals of emergent learn-by-doing civics programs. A national campaign, designed to apply these skills and knowledge on a state-by-state basis, proposes that teens be allowed to exercise their civic skills in the broader context of the electoral franchise. Generation Citizen is seeking to obtain the right to vote for 16- and 17-year-olds across each of the 50 states of our nation. Generation Citizen (whose origins and work I have described in the Civic Lover section of this book, has in addition to its supervision of a myriad of action-civics programs in seven states, also conceived and organized a national campaign called Vote 16. A full description of this campaign, and an invitation to join it, can be found at the Generation Citizen website at https://generationcitizen.org. The materials on their website include a detailed history of arguments pro and con concerning the issue of lowering the voting age to age sixteen, a description of cities in the United States and countries across the world that have already lowered the voting age, and supportive tips for creating or joining a campaign in one's specific state. The civic enfranchisement work led by adult and teen leadership at Vote 16 seeks to shift the voting age to sixteen, spur conversations on the importance of youth political participation, and to create changes in policy that can drive the demand for civics education.[715]The Generation Citizen Vote 16 staff has been successful in partnering with allies at the local level, such as with a teen voting rights initiative still active in San Francisco. As noted by the Vote 16 and Berkeley High school student, Melena Fike, four cities in the United States have already passed measures allowing sixteen-year-old teens to vote. Ms. Fike notes: "Lowering the voting age in any election doesn't just promote civic engagement but gives teenagers who clearly are paying attention the right to vote on matters directly affecting them.[716]

A referendum for the goal of lowering the voting age was narrowly defeated in San Francisco in 2016. In 2020 a voting rights alliance, including leaders in the Vote 16 initiative, tried again, working with the local youth leadership of the San Francisco Youth Commission and other local allies. The referendum fell short again though with a narrower margin: losing 51 per cent to 49 per cent in 2020, compared to 48 percent to 52 percent in 2016. In the neighboring city of Oakland, a similar referendum allowing those who had reached the age of 16 to serve on school community boards did pass.

In San Francisco, adult support amongst elected officials has been growing. Unlike in 2016, when the voting rights referendum had the support of some elected officials, the 2020 initiative had the unanimous support of the San Francisco Board of Supervisors. The northern California coalition for teen voting rights will continue to organize, and hopefully be successful in 2024.[717]

In New York State, on January 23, 2019, legislation introduced by State Senator Brad Hoylman proposed lowering the voting age to 16 and mandating action civics classroom experience for every high-school student. At the national level, Congresswoman Grace Meng has introduced parallel legislation in the House of Representatives. The speaker of the House, Nancy Pelosi, has issued a statement of support for lowering the voting age to 16. In New York State, the legislative branch became even more progressive after the 2020 elections were decided. On-the-ground organizing will begin again in earnest in 2021. Changing minds and opinions about who should have the right to vote takes time.[718]

Manhattan Borough President Gale Brewer is on board with this lowering the voting age to age 16. Her advocacy and organizing skills made such a difference in making the dream of getting teens on community boards a reality. The current level of teen advocacy ensures the time for change on a broader electoral front might be today. Ms. Brewer would be, at any levels she chooses to help, an instrumental and influential organizer for our 2021 campaign. Municipal elections will be a tidal change for New York City governance, from city-wide positions and borough-wide positions to dozens of seats on the city council. All present-day serving elected officials are limited to two terms, meaning that all seats in this year's elections must turn over to new representatives. Our campaign for teen voting rights, led by teens and supported by their civic co-mentors, will visit the office of every elected official, and will work on the ground to build and sustain communal consent.

The testimonials of progress and notable accomplishments achieved in the movements I have just described have eloquently defined our agenda and helped in the advancement toward universally inclusive civic participation.

The fight for teen enfranchisement has roots, some of them flowing out from the efforts of ancestral allies, and other connecting us to present-day public allies. These emerging initiatives, which are flourishing in an expansive and more inclusive civic universe, are filled with many rising stars. However, even the nature of leadership has changed, dismissive of focus on solitary heroic efforts, but rather celebrating modest contribution in the context of collective effort. The nature of these movements is aptly noted by ecologically influenced businessman Paul Hawken in his book, *Blessed Unrest*. Among some of the characteristics which Mr. Hawken writes about is an analysis which shows that these began and were sustained in a meta-movement of blessed unrest, thousands of them across our nation and the world. These did not have leaders as much as agreements involving consensually generated decisions and inter-connected webs of change. Mindful reform was embedded in environmental sanity and social justice. As stated by Mr. Hawken, all change is initiated from the bottom up, coming about because we are all linked at the grassroots.[719]

In a parallel fashion, I have experienced a personal evolution, one in which my writing has become associated with the footsteps taken toward pursuing my life purpose. In a sense, my writing has progressed in correspondence with evolving organizing experience. My writing has also been informed by the civic change work of allies within the youth enfranchise movement.

My first draft of the *Soul of Adolescence* was emailed to Future Voters of America founders Diane Grazick and Fran Baras in 2008, shortly after they had invited me to become a board member for the Future Voters of America. After reading my long string of words, they described my draft as written in a style expressed as a "continuum of consciousness. It was written down as one continuous sentence with a thousand commas and a few periods." Since 2013, this draft has been redone about 13 times. Only now, after revisiting the steps on my journey, do I look again with a more seasoned perspective. I am viewing the ways in which work and relationships which I encountered during that period are valuable in and of themselves. I am now also experiencing models of teen empowerment that were initially unknown by me, or later seemed only to be distant goals up until 2014. Now that I have a clearer perspective about the past, and connection to today's teen empowerment initiatives, I am ready to present an account of my civic work in a book. This version has also been approved by my inner allies with the self-aware and expressive support of my inner teen. I am now expressing myself by asserting myself with active awareness. I, have gradually learned and adopted this practice of spiritually guided active awareness, beginning with mentoring I received from Stephanie Marango, who is a medical doctor and a friend who counsels for using spiritual awareness and guidance.[720]

By developing empathetic soul-awareness I learned to adopt a more seasoned organizing approach and express my intentions with a more holistic worldview. I have been writing this book with gratitude for Dr. Marango's input, as well as under the collective influence of teen change agents, civic co-mentors, and public allies who have been rewriting me.

This book is an offering, engineered from the footprints of my 30-year journey, and counseled from my soul, which has had many advisors. Some of these civic comrades-in-arms are those whom I did not cover earlier in this work. Others are those for whom I have now discovered deeper dimensions about why we felt so closely affiliated. As science fiction writer Jeff Krispel points out, the perspective and teachings of the soul "eclipses the reach even of imagination."[721] Krispel, in his book *Mutants and Mystics*, explores the ways that paranormal experiences, dismissed in scientific circles, have shaped the creative works of storytellers in books and visual media. My point here is that I am not advocating for locating aliens just around the corner from our homes. I did have moments, and more extended periods of time, when after encountering threatening situations personally, or becoming shocked by circumstances endured by those whom I worked with and held in high esteem, it would feel as if what had just transpired could not be real. When a person becomes emotionally unsettled, due to high stress and/or deep remorse, becoming balanced and re-oriented is a task in and of itself. When I was more predisposed to proceeding with action based upon only abstract principles or rational thought, preparing myself to explore open-ended engagement with energies or people whom I did not completely understand was more of a challenge. That which I did not rationally diagnose successfully seemed in part as alien to my nature, and hard to navigate. Krispel, using the genre of science fiction and comic books provides counsel about the need to become safely oriented when experiencing troubling encounters. As Krispel states, "The 'Other', however, is not simply alien, foreign and scary, but, by definition, what one is not."[722] I had found, while I was listening to public opinion about teen identity and nature, many expressions about teens which negatively stereotyped them as seemingly foreign and scary. It took years of advocacy to convince adults with false perceptions about teens that these labels did not describe teens at all. However, after developing social-emotional intelligence which was in part inspired by the insights of science fiction writers such as Jeff Krispel, I simultaneously experienced an increase in soul-related guidance. I more readily found pathways for embracing those whom I did not fully understand.

My dabbling in science fiction works encouraged me to explore obscure and mystical energies as another source leading to greater understanding of human interactive dynamics. My exploration and experimentation led be to re-read and consider insights by some astrologers, who base their practice not on fundamental causation between planetary influences and human behavior. They use astrological counsel as a method of reading life and its mysterious properties and processes through the lens of metaphor and soul connection.[723] As I played with these types of interpretations, I gained additional insight about my inner nature and motivation for action.

My insights were constructed both by adherence to secularly informed civic practice, and by observance of spiritual possibilities and mystery. This requires focus and faith. Eric Toshalis has been a high school teacher, a teacher trainer, and a curriculum writer. He is also a recipient of a Certificate of Distinction in Teaching from Harvard College in 2002. Mr. Toshalis has this to say on the appropriate place of faith in the practice of teaching adolescents: "I argue that faith is an important developmental and pedagogical consideration due to the adolescent need for: (1) belonging for community; (2) separation and individuation; (3) self-transcendence of purpose; (4) narrative meaning; and (5) understanding his or her place with the post-modern world."[724]

As noted by William Kenower, in his advisory work for aspiring writers called *Fearless Writing*, FDR's adage that "there is nothing to fear but fear itself" is especially relevant to both the community organizing and the writing experience. People writing at length for the first time encounter a plethora of "internal and external critiques which have us shy away from embracing the inherent value of our work."[725] Mr. Kenower advises adopting an assertive stance, in which even in the shadow of doubt, we "create boldly and write with confidence because writing is intricately connected to what we have lived."[726] Mr. Kenower suggests the following perspective about the connection between living your life and writing—I have come to understand that all learning is connected. My imagination does not care whether I am writing an essay or talking to a friend. When I stop differentiating between writing and the rest of my life, I come to understand that what it takes to write a book is also what it takes to lead a life that I most want to lead. My whole life becomes a writing practice. I read a similar type of observation made by Daniel J. Siegel in his book on the mind, in which he stated that he was not sure if he was writing the book, or if the book was writing him. Reflecting upon my 30-year journey, it seems that at times the journey was directing me towards staying true to my life purpose, even as certain obstacles I had faced could have potentially led to my making decisions taking me off course.

One of the lessons in life that I have learned through the writing process is practicing empathy with myself as much as I seek to empathize with others. My writing initiatives have become a complementary practice to my continued community organizing. In my civic work with teens, I learned about strengths and deficits of character, in myself, as well as those whom I chose to serve. In each case, developing a relationship with myself and others is a source of learning how to adapt and balance seeking change with accepting life as it is. As I have worked through the writing process, I have, through the awakening of memories, and perceiving life using a fresh perspective, learned to establish moderation in how I judge myself, exercising less severe criticism and more tolerance toward the inner Al. In a sense, the people I refer to in my book have become my allies, and I have learned to be my own co-mentor.

As my acknowledgment and embrace of my inner adolescent has developed, my efficacy in aiding teen enfranchisement has been enhanced though the expansion of empathy. As I learned to embrace my inner demons and allies, those in the outer world became less intimidating to me. My work with teen empowerment participation has evolved, in tandem with the effusive expression allowed in the adolescent bias in my writing.

Adolescent development and civic efficacy each evolve successfully when subject to a full measure of attention. Using this focus, one comes to recognize one's own advocacy skillset, and more fully values recognition by other adults who clearly see you for who you are. In both measures of healthful and holistic development, applied to personal awareness and understanding of others, stakeholders need to exercise buy-in, and to adopt a willingness to become part of the solution. When applying these practices of critical evaluation, rather than identifying teen as people to be repaired, community leaders need to heal themselves and fix their relationships with the young.

In promoting these changes in perception and relationship at the civic and political level, local providers have adhered to principles and practices, both in late eighteenth-century and mid-nineteenth-century New York City, as well as in New York City in the late twentieth century. Sean Wilentz, a labor historian, cites words in a poem describing an affirming and validating set of practices with youth called Chants Democratic. What the poem emphasized was seeing inner authority taking precedence over external authority and allowing children to be authors of self-determined destinies.[727]

Benjamin Barber is a political scientist writing about what constitutes quality civic relationship in the late twentieth century. Mr. Barber advocates for creating nurturing practices in democratically informed relationships. He views inclusive participation as being contingent upon creating spaces that are welcoming to ostracized souls. Mr. Barber refers to these spaces as "those of providing a civic architecture that provides spaces which provide a mutuality of you and me."[728] As stated by Michael Waltzer, a "space of uncoerced human association and sets of relational networks."[729]

I also consider myself blessed to have begun my journey in Washington Heights. This community was a learning laboratory for using difference amongst people as an asset and not a liability, and the benefits of reaching across comfortable barriers to experience success in the realm of the previously unknown. Robert Snyder, in his book, *Crossing Broadway*, provides a masterful account of why and how Washington Heights not only survived in turbulent times, but also thrived in the throes of seeming chaos and danger by learning to embrace others who were previously unknown to them. As described by Washington Heights historian Rob Snyder: "Even as each block seemed to be thought about by local residents as its own universe of experience, residents reached out 'across Broadway,' as well as all other boundaries, and appreciated that although their origins and cultures were different from each other, we all faced common problems which were best addressed through extending our scope of vision for each other and sharing the burdens as one community."[730] For me, despite my place of origin being so different than those whom I came to engage with in community improvement, I was embraced by my neighbors, and Washington Heights became my foundation of grassroots expertise and guidance through my decades of community organizing.

What has been gradually becoming a reality for our teens and communities in 2021 is that once a social justice advocate's sphere of experience is nourished, the sphere of community benefits. The flowering of civic accomplishments for teens and the establishment of positive outcomes for a community is a mutually beneficial relationship which has been proposed for much of our history. John Dewey proposed this connection when he spoke about constructing classrooms as democratic communities, and communities as laboratories for education. The United Nations charter, in its Article 55, established this partnership as a basis for worldwide stability. As proposed in the mission statements of youth-led agencies such as the Urban Youth Collaborative and Teens Take Charge, teens today are adopting these principles in practice, and are emerging as equal actors in civic affairs.[731]

Modern methods for ensuring maximum participation by the young are enhanced through the establishment of invitational community practices. One type of this practice encourages a young person to at first wander from the safe harbor of community, and then navigate his or her way back to it through experimentation and wandering. Ritual provides for experiential practice in the affairs of adults. Rather than just memorizing historical facts and societal rules, this experimental experience makes communal membership meaningful and rewarding to both the young family member and the larger clan. One example of this ancient source of wisdom has traditionally been practiced by our planet's first peoples from Africa. Malidoma Patrice Some, a medicine man from West Africa who holds three master's degrees and two doctorates from the Sorbonne and Brandeis University, refers to the essential ingredients of "power, healing and community."[732] In a major theme of Dr. Some's work, he points out that "The community is where we draw the strength needed to effect changes inside of us…What one acknowledges in the formation of community is the possibility of doing together what is impossible to do alone."[733] In our society increasingly dominated by professional specialization, habitual segregation, and retreat into tribal protective enclaves, we need to move on towards working together and believing in the impossible. As Mr. Some states in his describing the value of honoring a twin presence of uncertainty and mindful determination: "What we need is to be able to come together with a constantly increasing mindset of wanting to do the right thing, even though we know very well that we don't know how nor where to start."[734] As the poet Robert Bly might have said, you must walk the limp in order to stay with your purpose.

One of the beautiful truths I have discovered in working with teens is that we all were born, and then will pass on as imperfect. It is not the positing of an answer for everything that counts, but the joy of creating questions and engaging in the search which provides for meaning and a sense of purpose in life. In our modern-day society, we do not have a ritual for democracy established at the high school level, in which teens can use the tools of democracy to discover related inner assets and a develop a desire to participate communally.[735] We need to develop these forms of civic ritual while recognizing the autonomy of teens, and the unsolvable as a basis for valuing the imperfection of life.[736]

In my personal observations, years before my engagement with my first youth service project called Southern Heights, and prior to my recent exposure to well-developed action civics initiatives such as IN-STEP and those constructed by Generation Citizen, were the experiences shared with me by others whose rites of passage were defined by consumerist and militaristic agendas. The young are exposed the thousands of hours of advertisements on television and print media. As the get ready for graduation from high school, students receive invitations to apply for credit cards. The pitch shows an easy path to the nirvana of endless possessions, but not the consequences of failing to exercise discipline in credit card usage. Our society has constructed a billion-dollar empire which provokes endless desire as a pathway to a satisfying life. Ours societal cliches continue to portray adolescents as lacking in self-control, even as financial institutions profit from excessive spending.

Young men, if not exempt from being drafted into military service, had gone through boot camp before entering a division of the armed services. Young people I conversed with did learn the value of teamwork, albeit with learning skills of using weaponry in theaters of violence. As these people told me, what motivated them to join was the belief that all this training was in service of protecting democracy here and abroad. Today, this option to join the military forces is offered and then taken up as a personal choice of individuals, and not mandated by a draft selection, as was the case when

I was a teen. Yet even given changes in how one joins the military, it is the culture of militarism which has divided our world into staging areas of good and evil, guarding against the dangers imposed by others. It is a culture informed by creating a band of brothers (and sisters) protecting us against the dangerous and unknown other which has framed this form of initiation and ritual. I would not for a minute question the valiant aims and bravery of those who choose to join, but I do question the continuing dominance of the militarized approach to world problems by elected leaders and policy makers.

As documented by Scilla Elworthy, the policy analyst who wrote the book *Pioneering the Possible*, "…the volume of international transfers of major conventional weapons grew by 17 percent between 2003 and 2007 and between 2008 and 2012.[737] I find this decidedly odd, because this is happening at precisely the same time that "major wars and episodes of mass violence worldwide have become far less frequent and deadly."[738] As Dr. Elworthy continues, we can see that "the cycle of violence can be turned around—(by adopting conflict resolution and violence diffusion strategies, such as)…peacekeeping by the United Nations Peace Keeping Force; building political security through mediated solutions; building psychological security through cross border initiative such as Doctors Without Borders; and by working at a spiritually transformative level—for example in Truth and Reconciliation Processes."[739]

What has been proposed in the civic education lawsuit that I mentioned earlier in this narrative, led by Mr. Rebell, and by legislation in New York State, is a mandated action civics classroom experience (one semester in length). It is a graduation requirement for all high-school students designed to prepare students for the practice of citizenship. Universal adoption of this civic ritual would constitute a period of transition from being high-school students learning about democracy as practiced by others to one in which students become participants in the process. Democracy has been studied in many ways. The point, however, is that in learning to become a citizen in a democracy, one must first practice the art and science of civic participation. When looking at the congruent benefits of personal development and neighborhood enhancement, as well as the overlap of ancient wisdom and modern-day insight, I see Dr. Barber as a political scientist advocating for a culture of interactive democratic practice and Dr. Some as a medicine man connecting the health of a teen mind with the continued benefit of fully informed community participation. Dr. Elworthy proposes taking valuable ideals into the world of institutional and political practice.

This book has elaborated on the use of traditional civic rituals in our classrooms and communities in pro forma ways (such as commercialized venues for age transitions and graduations from school) or in destructive ways (such as gang initiations and smoking your first cigarette). It has also celebrated the institutional implementation of civic learning ritual in which teens can contribute in ways that utilize their internal resources while promoting social good.

Institutional ritual in which the value of the individual, and connection to communal good, has been a longstanding practice by tribal communities in Africa. This is a traditional and indigenously experienced ritual that was founded and practiced in Namibia, Africa. This spiritual- centered rite of passage is designed to have adults comprehend the oncoming life purpose of the newborn. This ritual is artfully described in the *Naked Voice* by Chloe Goodchild. Ms. Goodchild poetically writes: "Just before child is born, the mother sits, in silence, under a tree. She calms and centers herself and becomes receptive. She listens until she hears the song as sung by the still unborn child and memorizes that song. She then shares this with the father and her community. Together, they sing this song as the child enters the world."[740] It is the receptive welcome of message, representing life purpose, by parents and tribal community that sets the table for understanding why a newly arriving child is here.

Obviously, I am referring to a life transition different in chronological time from that of the transition between childhood and adulthood. However, what I see as having relevance is a sort of correspondence between two unique transitions that serve a symbolic purpose in our evolution as socially conscious human beings. Just as the newborn is transitioning from the spirit world before birth to become a new member of the welcoming tribe, a teen transitions from the protected world of childhood (that is, the womb of adult custody) to the world of adulthood, with its demand for personal efficacy and social awareness. The point, as suggested by Parker Palmer in his works on soulfully practiced education, is not merely that what we teach (or preach) matters; rather, *how* we deliver what we teach (or preach) that has the greatest impact on what a young person comes to know and remember as significant.[741] Do we encourage learning through rewarded memorization of facts and shaping of desired beliefs about the perfection of the past? Do we recognize learning as a process defined as in the original meaning of education, to learn from within? In both the Namibian account I just shared, and in instituting a civics rite of passage for teens, the newly arriving participant is awarded safe and meaningful passage to community, and the community learns through sharing the perspective, and listening to the voice of the emergent participant.

An early influence on my vision for youth-led efficacy and empowerment—one that began when I was only 18 years old—has remained with me to this day. That influence is referenced in the quote I shared earlier in this book, by Robert F. Kennedy, about the crucial need to involve youth as leaders, to create new terms of living, and to move on from words and conditions which are obsolete. I recall his being a role model for me when I was still a teen. As an adult teen service proponent, I have adopted his message and carry it in my heart.

As indicated earlier, Gale Brewer served as a city councilperson on the West Side during the early stages of my youth work, and for the last seven years she has served as Borough President of Manhattan. Gale is a visionary messenger who listens to the experiential messages offered by those she serves. The injuries her constituents suffered and the gifts they have to offer are crucial ingredients informing her decisions about political service. She has been a co-mentor for me, teaching the lesson of combining the grist on the ground with principles of responsive governance. I have been blessed by her counsel. She has been, as she has often told others at community gatherings, virtually joined at the hip with me as we each advocate for teen enfranchisement. She also lives by her ideals. Co-mentors and allies who align pursuit of ideals with authentic democratic practices matter.

An article in *City and State* recounts how Gale defines her priorities as an elected official and describes the essence of her contributions: "As a community organizer, I know the importance of elected officials showing up for their constituencies and agencies...."[742] She has been a mentor to thousands of interns throughout her career, many of whom went on to serve in the public and private sectors—Emma Wolf, who served as Bill DeBlasio's Chief of Staff; Mark Peters, who had served as a Commissioner in the New York City Department of Investigation; and Benjamin Howard Cooper, who served as an assistant principal and manager for Moody's, an investment firm.[743] I also learned more about Gale Brewer after attending her first town hall as borough president in 2002. Mayor DeBlasio, in his opening remarks giving praise to her, revealed an aspect of Gail's life that had not been known by members of the audience. In her private life, during the time of her marriage, she also has served as a guide for several foster children whom she had taken in. Taking in the disposed, helping them to heal wounds suffered from fractured relationships, and guiding them to develop productive pathways in life was central to her being a parent. This disposition also shaped her practice as a trusted public official.

Whether aiding a future office holder or smaller, more modestly driven youth organizations such as the Future Voters of America, she has, and will, always be there. It was through her leadership as an advisor to Future Voters of America that 300 teen leaders launched an initiative to have teen voice and membership formally made official on community boards. She served Future Voters as a public, spirited godmother in support of the teen leaders' efforts. After I chose to become a lead grassroots coordinator of the Teens on Board campaign in 2010, Gale showed up at every meeting; between meetings, she lent her staff to us to serve as mentors and guides for informed advocacy. It did not matter if 300 people showed up at our gatherings—or only three. She simply was there for us.

Gale's sense of public obligation for offering unqualified support flowed from her familial practices. Just as after becoming a foster parent to many young people she did not allow children to become orphans, she did not let the efforts of young leaders in need of additional support to be cast adrift, without guidance or direction. Her style was not to take control but to offer herself as a facilitator, a guide on the side. With her wisdom and limitless giving, with her uncommon commitment to remain "joined at the hip" with me, and with our cause, she never gave up or gave in until the goals we sought had been achieved by her colleagues in city government. She provided unwavering support for the young and for co-mentors such as me who thrive with acknowledgement, affirmation, and the embrace of common goals.

As I have previously cited in this book, Eleanor Roosevelt had posed a question to an assembly at the United Nations, where she asked the question: Where do we all begin? In this book, I propose that we begin by educating teens to obtain holistic development and full potential, as practiced in the forum of action civics. At the same time, we establish co-equal partnerships, as co-mentors, teaching and learning from each other, and striving to form a more perfect democracy beginning at the level of community. As we engage in this type of experiential and experimental practice, we find that it is in the nature of the teen mind, which remains alive in healthy adults also, to nourish the deepest practices of democracy.

We live during a time in which we have abdicated our responsibilities for enthused participation and compassionate relationship in our worldly affairs. My generation, the Boomer generation, has, in passing the torch, fallen far short of the goal of continuing the arc of justice and opportunity for the emergent generation that follows us. It has been a stormy night—a night that to the young appears to be the eve of Armageddon, where the approach of never-never land is drenched in fear and is immersed in the clouds of failed expectations. The danger lying ahead is the possibility of falling fast and hard as we drift into a period that I call the dictatorship of the dire: a dark time where flailing people address society with occluded hearts and obsessive minds. If this dictatorship were to obtain its ends, the false solutions proposed would be driven by fanatics with fundamentalist mindsets. Angry and wounded people would react to the resulting realities with no remorse, impotent in their attempts and vengeful in the failed aftermath. Rather than seeing a future with promise and positive energy, the social/political atmosphere would be entropic, defined by collapsing energy and peoples devoid of hope. Our language would be the language of Apartheid, which demeans, diminishes, and casts out the "other." Our relationships would be constructed according to the parables found in sins of separation. The sins of separation include holding on to the illusion that each of us is a totally autonomous being, disconnected and not responsible for others' fortunes, honoring their pursuit of happiness as if it were our own. An additional sin is in perceiving ourselves as superior beings, who are above respecting the needs of all participants on our small planet, as well as considering ourselves as beyond the repercussions of violating ecological process that governs all of us. We continue to live in societies populated by colonized souls, under the jurisdiction of the syndicate of the American shadow. The shadow is constructed by hidden fears deep within our psyche which induce us to alienated means of survival. The more we remain stuck in denial, the greater our use of the determined methods of distancing from others different from ourselves. We construct internal barriers preventing us from developing empathy, and external walls leaving us in culture and social enclaves of isolation, despair, and resentment. Alienated and suspicious, we consider these terms of living to be an assurance for obtaining an unrestricted share in the fruits of life. Decisions made under the invisible umbrella of the shadow condition us to separate ourselves from the higher angels of our nature, and the promising potential of democracy.[744]

As responsible elders, we need to practice relating to teens with a sense of civic adoration, where we strive to have them light their souls on fire, helping them to provide a beacon for the world. As referred to earlier, we should listen to the sage advice of Thomas Paine, who, in his body of work, suggests that every age and generation must be free to act for itself. In his critique of monarchy, he abhorred the vanity and presumption of governing from beyond the grave as the most ridiculous and insolent of all tyrannies. Thomas Paine firmly believed, "Man has no property in man, neither has any generation property on the generations to follow. It is the living, and not the dead, who are to be accommodated."[745] This vision and call to action was seconded by one of my early life models, whom I mentioned earlier, Senator Robert F. Kennedy, when he called upon adults to cast off the no longer useful slogans and practices of yesterday and allow the younger generation to lead. It is being spearheaded today by teen leaders such as Greta Thunberg, who, as previously mentioned, is demanding the right for her generation to build the roadway toward tomorrow. Her vision has been seconded by hundreds of youth-led groups, such as March for Our Lives, asking that classrooms be shielded from violence, and elected officials be held responsible for ensuring safe spaces for the young. Teen social justice advocates and their co-mentors have re-written the outworn script defining what it means to be an adolescent and have delineated the need for teens to experience horizontal relationships within civic affairs.[746] We need to participate with them, bringing the wisdom of our elder experience and the knowledge inherent to our revitalized inner adolescent.

Celebrating the civic value of teen contribution, and participating with them in municipal affairs of governance, are acts which suggest adults are now validating the adolescent archetype. We are more comfortable with extending the hand of partnership to those who had been orphans. We are ratifying the validity of a new story offered by rebels. Municipal leadership, urged on fervently by civic co-mentors, are opening their hearts to the latent genius and high potential of teens, anticipating changes for which a deepened practice of democracy shall flourish.

Once upon a time, in a land that was lost, we lived in fear, and saw democracy diminished under the shadow of our criminal injustice system. Sadly, the worst of our instincts to punish and deny legal rights are on the rise again today. As suggested by W. Scott Poole, in his book, *Monsters in America*, teens in the later decades of the 20th Century were being redefined as monsters. Today, teens, especially those of color and origins from places other than Western Europe are again being profiled as monsters. In the preface to his book, Mr. Poole places the concept of the monster in historical perspective: "In American history, they have been symbols of deviance, objects of sympathy, and even objects of erotic desire."[747] As shown in the progressions in this book, teens have been subject to excessive rules of law seeking to contain the rule-breaker. During the 80s and 90s, the US medicated its youth in attempts driven by goodwill to tamper down the ill-effects of raging hormones. We medicated teens at five times the rate of other countries. We have seen developing bodies exploited and used to excite the imagination, beginning with the introduction of *Lolita*.

Yet, as also put forth by Mr. Poole, the word "monster" has its origins in the word "monstrum," the literal meaning being "that which appears, or reveals itself… monsters have been living messages to those unlucky souls to whom they appear."[748] What monsters reveal, as what teen activists have been exposing, as followed up by Mr. Poole, "The monster is a metaphor for revealing the deepest fears and truths about ourselves. The defective, the impure, the alien, constructs about what is unwanted about being human."[749]

What has become well known to civic co-mentors for teen activists, and become increasingly understood by elected officials, it that teens, like people, are complex. It does not serve our understanding of one another by using stereotypes, whether positive or negative, to draw conclusions about who we are. As poetically put by Ani DiFranco, a songwriter who self-publishes: "Yes, us people are just poems…we're 90% metaphor, with a leanness of meaning."[750] We enrich our souls and enliven our hearts when we eliminate the impulse to see one another though racial profiling, or mansplaining (the habit of some men of explaining a woman's life through his own lens and language). When perceiving the other, it is best to consider the multiple levels of complexity defining a person, and to accept what perplexes us in understanding another person as part of the mystery of human existence, and potential mastery in constructing beloved relationships. In my construction of the soul-informed perspective for understanding adolescents, I propose what I call poetic profiling as a creative means to cleanse ourselves from misunderstandings.

This is a generational marriage, one in which successful practice is enhanced by civic- and soul-enhancing dreamwork. Together, we rewrite the narrative of civic education and social studies, ensuring inclusion of a teen studies component, documenting the contributions for the common good made by teen activists and their teammates promoting social justice. We have a world to win by incorporating a history of the social capital gained by our alliance with them, just as we have nothing to lose but our shame by discarding the dysfunctional, which is now obsolete.

Co-mentors also get those teens who are hard to reach because they either choose to stand outside the circle of expectations, or we push them there. In either case, they use their assets and their civic allies to help them navigate their way home. It is not through fiat that we get cooperation, but rather through kinship. As we dream about this, and work with them as friends, we engage in a practice of kinship, as described by the writer and gang intervention specialist Gregory Boyle in his book, *Tattoos on the Heart: The Power of Boundless Compassion*. Mr. Boyle describe the practice of kinship as when "we imagine no one standing outside the circle, moving ourselves closer to the margins—so that margins themselves will be erased. We stand there with those whose dignity has been denied…At the edges, we join the easily despised and readily left out."[751] As an organizer who has successfully brought the exiled and the ostracized home, Mr. Boyle understands that it is by choosing " the power of unconditional love"[752] that we show our respect for the sanctity of teen territory, and our willingness to have teens make their way home on their terms as well as on ours.

Isabelle Wallmaw, now aged 20, is a young person who has studied the lives of incarcerated youth, and the value of place in the process of healing. Ms. Wallmaw is a winner of *Earth Island Journal* magazine's New Leadership award for 2020. At the age of 18, while still residing in Warrenville, Illinois, she helped to found a program in which a space became one of healing for incarcerated youth. This was a gardening program incorporating holistic methods of growing plants (for example, no pesticides) and a community-oriented approach. (Recruit local youth as gardeners, under the guidance of neighborhood mentors.) As stated by Ms. Wallmaw, "At the forefront of running the garden are the voices, visions, and dreams of incarcerated youth."753

Rebels, whom I have co-titled the bringers of new story, can also be understood through the present-day expression—become awoke. A Persian poet and mystic from the middle ages, Jamaluddin Rumi, hinted at this concept with his poetic words: "Don't go back to sleep; Don't go back to sleep; where the two worlds touch; don't go back to sleep."754 Today, we live again in a period where two worlds touch—that of the mechanical industrial age and of the oncoming eco/spiritual age. When we fall back on definitions and concepts apropos the former, what was previously appropriate and useful can become out of touch, as we touch the new age. This is part of human habit, not to let go of what worked previously, even when conditions and contexts change. Dr. Gabor Mate, author of the book *Hungry Ghosts: Close Encounters with Addiction*, describes how this compulsive holding on plays out on both the personal and the social level. On a personal level, denial can become a perceived tool for alleviating or avoiding pain. As Dr. Mate point out, on a personal level, "Just about every mental affliction is an adaptive response that becomes a source of a problem later… (for example), to become acceptable to the nurturing environment, the child pushes down their feelings. Thirty years later they are diagnosed with depression."755 The same thoughts and practices which gave rise to the old era in its ascendency, such as endless expansion of spending and settling social problems by locking people away, have become sources of problems in the oncoming age which now threaten our planetary stability and communal sustainability. We have not yet developed either language or societal practices to deal with what is now perceived as chaotic and nonsensical, and as a response, those still stuck in old paradigm types of responses are becoming increasing angry and depressed. On a social level, our political and economic policy responses are intensifying the problems, rather than solving them. As Dr. Mate continues in his book, "A society that erodes communication and isolates people, which this society does in major ways, is itself going to create insanity… That is insanity."[756]

Small doses of active listening, to the counsel of our ancestral spiritual and social justice allies, to our environmental prophets, and to all who see the new world coming, might go a long way in avoiding seemingly unresolvable problems over the next decades. Unfortunately, in times of uncertainty and fear about the future, one of our disingenuous habits is to dismiss the messenger. In the 1930s and early 1940s, when a great depression and an impending world war diminished our hope of seeing a way forward, President Roosevelt chose a forward-leaning thinker, Henry A. Wallace, as his vice-presidential partner. At first, the public and his public office allies were enthralled with him. As profiled in a book called *American Dreamer*, authors John C. Culver and John Hyde wrote: "No word was more commonly attached to Henry Wallace's name than dreamer. The word almost became part of his resume. He was sort of a dreamer archetype. He was the king of all dreamers."[757] After the outbreak of World War II, the world, and the public's perception of it changed. Policy makers and elected officials began to see the need for war against first the Nazis, and then the Communists, and saw danger everywhere. While Henry Wallace proposed, "Self-determination for people living in colonies, including India,"[758] economic interest and political opportunism created a new path, of opposing independence movements, and seeking more subtle ways to keep foreign lands under control. President Roosevelt had initially agreed to this line of reasoning, but when deciding to run for a fourth term, changed his mind. Henry Wallace would be dumped for Roosevelt's fourth term, and Harry Truman, a hardline cold warrior would be the new vice-president. The cult of militarism would become the optimal course for a nation founded on the principle of non-intervention in foreign affairs. The United States, born into independence by opposing colonization and remote military control, became its chief enforcer. Teens living under conditions of undue containment and control live in disguised colonies in lieu of learned classrooms and inclusive communities.

The youth movements of today are part of a larger web of activism seeking to escape from the yolk of enforced intervention, chronic control, and dependencies on allied leadership, whether in foreign lands or on domestic front, which seek self-interest in place of the interests of their own people. Teen-led movements today, from those led by college activists seeking disinvestment from industries profiting from toxic pollution or the suppression of civil rights, to those led by students in local schools seeking restorative justice and syllabi aligned with greater opportunity, were birthed by what Paul H. Ray and Sherry Ruth Anderson call the "waking up of two generations."[759] Ray and Anderson call the first generation (of consciousness-raising) which began in the 1970s as "focused on what might be called personal waking up new psycho-therapies, and the body-work and spiritual approaches."[760] As the authors continue, what followed in the 1980s and 1990s was "growing into what might be called a cultural growing up…broadened the personal into a strong concern for the social and planetary good… Those who became parents wanted communities that included their children and began to feel a longing for elders."[761] In this book, I have described the blossoming of youth-led movements which focus on both levels of experience, on what the two generations had worked on separately. I also highlight the birth of co-mentoring, where a longing for elder guidance is fulfilled by those who support teen initiative in leading us to the future.

Both teen social justice leaders, and their co-mentors, focus on avoiding yesterday's dependence of militaristic style, or the other isms, such as racism, sexism and adultism, and on conducting their reform efforts by not sticking with business as usual. These leaders have learned to practice what the social analyst Krista Tippitt has described as mystery and art of living. One of these elements include, as described by Ms. Tippitt, that "I have learned that people in the middle are not going to be big change-makers. You've got to put yourself at the margins and be willing to risk changing. More importantly, you have got to approach differences with this notion that there is good in the other."[762] Youth leaders have taken these tasks on to their political plate, and surge forward with full realization that it is the responsibility of adults to catch up. In an anthology put together by the NY Times Learning Network, Katherine Schulten quotes the feeling and tactics adopted by leaders from Generation Z: "Today's youth have come of age in an atmosphere where encroaching problems of climate change, global terrorism, economic crisis, and mass shootings, to name a few, have opened our eyes to reality…the weight of fixing it all is on our shoulders…we've got to experience the world from everybody's point of view. We are not limited by the danger of a single story and aren't held back by our own ignorance."[763]

If I were to summarize the perspective taken by Rabbi Michael Lerner on how the social justice activist establishes civic identity, I would use words he has spoken about, what he calls "emancipatory spirituality,"[764] as practiced by change-agents he calls "spiritual progressives."[765] Throughout this book, and the course of Rabbi Lerner's work, he holds that the globalization of spirit requires that we overcome the false dichotomy between changing ourselves and changing societal structures…emancipatory spirituality encourages a living synthesis of individual and social transformation.[766] I use these words to further describe what I call the civic lover, who after becoming fruitfully engaged in the tasks of the orphan and the rebel, now engages in reflective change using poetic inquiry and prophetic discourse. On all three levels, after authentically identifying the orphan, and adoring new story, the civic lover helps us navigate across the great divide between conscious action enabling people and the unconscious sabotaging us.

The poet Steve Earle and the prophet Jean Houston shed light on this rewarding journey. As artfully queried by Mr. Earle: "When will we ever learn; when will we ever see; we stand up and take our turn; and keep telling ourselves we're free."[767] Jean Houston tells us where we need to start in answering Mr. Earle's question: "We each have unlimited access to that (which) is the Great Friend who oversees, guides and loves us. We each can read a mythic map, to find our life's compass, and understand the signs that guide us. We each can celebrate the fact that we already possess everything we need to create a burgeoning new Renaissance—a rebirth of self and society."[768] This is what civic lovers do.

In the realm of social relations and politics, we apply our civic lover's skills to re-tell stories and create social capital, that is, shared wealth distributed equitably to all. Robert D. Putnam and Lewis M. Feldstein have co-authorized a book called *Better Together: Restoring the American Community*, which speaks to the value of communal partnership: In the theme of their book, they stress that organizing is about transforming private pain into a shared vision of collective action…community builders need to start with what participants really care about, not some external agenda. That is why storytelling turned out to be a crucial technique for building social capital.[769] Cornell West, a university professor and political theorist, adds that stories and activism are best when proclaiming fairness and being future-oriented. As Professor West teaches, prophetic witness consists of human deeds of justice and kindness that attend to the unjust sources of human hurt and misery, including the evil of being indifferent to personal and institutional evil. The prophetic goal is to stir up in us the courage to care and empowers us to change lives and our historical circumstances.[770]

Teens Take Charge uses the gift of prophecy, looking into the future for guidance, and weaves it in to building evolved communal events appropriate for living in the 21st Century. The Teens Take Charge activists do this by organizing events in which adults become attuned to issues that matter to the young and become motivated to take action to support the needs of a new generation. In 2018, they sponsored an event called "A Day in Our Shoes" in which race and equity issues were raised. They sought partnership with adults to end the toxic practice of segregation in our schools. The leadership at Teens Take Charge also forged a working relationship with journalists from the Hechinger Report. Students learned multimedia skills and created a microphone calling out the inequities they see in their schools.[771]

I have been blessed to study civic-change methodology, and apply my knowledge, in a wonderful civic theater also known by the name of New York

City. I have benefitted by applying my skills in this place, which itself has been so enriched by its historical legacy of change-makers. Steven H. Jaffee has edited a guide for the Museum of the City Of New York called *Activist New York*. He put together historical sketches of social reformers and justice movements. He starts in our nation's colonial period with coverage of such cases as the Zenger trial where a publisher fights for freedom of the press, and finishes with a profile of the Occupy Wall Street movement, which has changed the conversation about equitable economic distribution, not just on the street, but within the corridors of power in Washington D.C.[772] In the foreword to this book, the progressive historian from Columbia University, Eric Foner, outlines the history of civic rebellion in New York City: " Every generation of New Yorkers has witnessed the emergence of some kind of collective popular activism. Their movements have helped to make New York, and America, a freer and more equal society. The history of activism in New York City reinforces the insight of the sociologist Max Weber about how social change takes place: "What is possible would never have been achieved if, in this world, people had not repeatedly reached for the impossible."[773] Youth-led movements, such as those fighting for responsible policies governing the use of firearms, equitable racial policies to be practiced in our schools and on our streets, and the right of immigrants and LGBTQ stakeholder to be received in our communities as beloved neighbors, are steering us ever closer to the territories of what seemed impossible only a few years ago.

The civic efficacy of youth leaders, indeed of all students exposed to active civic experience, is described in the testimony of one teacher, Robert Kunzman, in the book Stories of *The Courage to Teach*: "I am stick struck by the focus and gravity that students brought to their projects—their stirring wisdom, and the earnest and genuine questions that their peers offered after they finished…I was there to listen and to appreciate, and quite frankly, to be exhilarated by their sharing."[774]

As I celebrate and support the work of teen public prophets, I peer into a window and see the first glimpses of the future. It is in looking through this window that I see three candles still flickering, illuminating the potent promises of yesterday, today, and tomorrow. The flames of each candle are in a dance of co-habituation. The first candle leads the wanderer to safe harbor. The second sheds light on authentic stories inspired by ignited souls. The third brightens the room for possibilities, celebrating the generous-of-heart gatherings that welcome best friends. Together, they weave a fabric of wonder, embracing us in networks of hope.

An additional way to express the significance of anecdotes arising is to call them developing seeds of teen enfranchisement which best thrive in a garden tended by attentive and appreciative civic co-mentors. In the last few years, many initiatives have sprouted, and fill our civic landscape with promise and hearty additions for our civic common good. Stephan Dinan, a Stanford University graduate is a founder and CEO of the Shift Network which deliver summits and trainings to university faculty and thought leaders around the world. In his work, he makes distinctions between old world revolutionaries and new era evolutionaries who ignite civic change. Mr. Dinan states: "An evolutionary is much more of a peaceful pilgrim, leading more patiently to a new terrain. An evolutionary may hold up a strong mirror to the status quo and work to end injustice but does so with more respect and non-violence."[775] (revolutionaries have too often justified violence to obtaining socially just ends) As Mr. Dinan continues: "An evolutionary is a builder, taking the given cultural foundation and growing it into the next form. He or she is invested in training successors, building capacity, and ensuring healthy societal structures to make sure positive changes endure."[776] (Revolutionaries have tended to rely on charismatic leaders and/or self-appointed vanguards) New era, evolutionary movements are being grown across our nation and the city of New York.

Artemesio Romero y Carver, at age eighteen is a 2020 Youth Poet Laureate from Santa Fe, New Mexico. He won a Brower Youth Award for his stewardship of Youth Unite for Climate Crisis Action (YACCA). This agency is a "youth-led non-profit working to hold this country's elected officials accountable for the health of the planet, future generations, and

BIPOC communities... In 2021, Artemesio Romero y Carver, serving as YACCA policy director, helped to lobby for (and saw passage of) three bills seeking climate change remediation.[777]

In San Antonio, Texas, a youth-advisory council organized under the umbrella of Healthy Futures Texas works to "empower teens to become leaders of change in their community...College students mentor teens for outreach, education and advocacy to increase access to evidence-based sexual health education and to teen-friendly preventative health care. They successfully advocated for updated sex education curriculum standards in Texas schools, which had not happened in twenty years."[778]

In the city of New York, an approach for allowing community stake-holders to make decisions on the allocating of capital spending has grown considerably since its introduction to the city council. This approach, called Participatory Budgeting, originated in South America, and then was adopted by the NY City Council. It allows residents from each council district, begin-ning at the age of eleven, to participate in a process called assemblies, where proposed capital programs are presented, vetted, and ranked by assembly members. City Council members adhere to these recommendations. As posted on the NYC Participatory Budgeting website, in the year 2018, "More than 99,250 residents aged 11 and older participated in the largest local civic engagement program in the U.S., deciding how to spend $36,618, 553 across New York City."[779] Councilperson Carlos Menchacca elaborated: " PB isn't just about choosing winning projects, it is also about creating opportunities for civic participation and stronger communities.[780]

In Takoma Park, Maryland, the city granted the right to vote for legal residents in local elections twenty years ago. Takoma Park had been suffering from low turnout in local elections, which is "part of the reason that they also decided recently to allow residents as young as age 16 to vote in local elections."[781] According to some sources, " 16 and- 17- year -old's voted at four times the rate of adults.[782]

Generation Citizen has been an avid supporter of lowering the voting age to sixteen. However, they are also dedicated to doing thorough research, and seek to establish the efficacy of lowering the voting age in U.S. cities which have already implemented this change. As posted on their website, "Generation Citizen and Vote 16 USA helped launch a Vote16 research network to analyze the impact of lowering the voting age in the United States…Generation Citizen CEO Elizabeth Clay Roy said we can think of no better way to advance the conversation then to bring together key leaders from Maryland's pioneering cities- plus scholars and advocates who have shaped the debate."[783]

In the meantime, one key player, the Speaker of the House of Representatives, Nancy Pelosi, has already weighed in on this issue. According to an account on the news outlet called the Hill, Nancy Pelosi has stated, " I myself have always been for lowering the voting age to 16…I think it is really important to capture kids (sic) when they are in high school, when they are interested in all of this, when they are learning about government, to be able to vote."[784]

This book is a testimonial for the right of inclusive and equitable participation by teens in the institutions and governing bodies which define the quality of their lives and futures. The Boomer generation has some leveling to complete, as aptly put forth by Meira Levinson in her book *No Citizen Left Behind*. As Ms. Levinson, an associate professor of education at Harvard University proclaims, "Tackling the civic empowerment gap today expands the ranks of active citizens both now and in the future. This long-term, communal, and equitable arrangement is essential for achieving a 'more perfect union' to which we all aspire."[785] We Boomers, who have left behind the aspirations of our inner adolescents, have the power to re-capture the marriage of our ideals with our practices. We need not leave behind the emergent generation who will govern us in our elder years. We have a world to win, and nothing to lose but our shame.

ENDNOTES

1   Adultism... The Free Child Project provides a comprehensive on-line overview of adultism, defining terms and providing examples of its use in our society. With adultism, teens are conditioned to evaluate and respond according to the validated viewpoints of adults, based upon their bias and experience. The case made is that like other 'isms' such as racism and sexism, adultism is a social construct. Socially derived constructions amongst the various 'isms' contribute to problems with development and identity with individuals, as well as institutions of oppression and damaged social relations. info@ freechild.org "Understanding Adultism," pp 1–9 (2003). https:// freechild.org

2   Abdication of adult responsibility...It is part of the American dream that each adult generation is responsible for creating conditions in which an emergent generation is better off than the previous generation. One of the premises of this book is that the Boomer Generation (those born between the years of 1946 and 1960) is leaving the next generation a world I which indicators of personal well-being and social sustainability are going south. The Free Child Project maintains a website with detailed data on the decline of favorable prospects for the emergent generation. The site has a section named "We Are The Debunkers". The authors of this site provide statistical charts and compelling narrative documenting how the Boomer Generation has irresponsibility blown its obligations to the young.

The site is managed by Dr. Mike Males, Professor of Sociology at UC Santa Cruz. info@freechild.org Personal indicators such as life expectancy and improving economic status are down when compared to the Boomer Generation. https://freechild.org

3   Teens and municipal change… the Boomer Generation has helped to promote viewpoints about teens which masquerade as fact, even when proven my recent scientific studies, as well as the testimony of those working with teens, not to be true. One example of this is the misreading of data from limited studies which lead to a conclusion that teens are developmentally unprepared to participate in responsible social policy making and change. Recent scientific studies have questioned the conclusion of misleading studies, but social prejudice continues to support unfounded findings. In fact, teens have been co-leaders effecting policy change for decades in cities across the United States. A White Paper prepared for the Public Science Project at the CUNY Graduate Center has documented teen advisory board contributions and adult leader's recognition of teen governing councils in cities across the United States and throughout the world. The White Paper is titled Rolling Thunder, and its research and production were coordinated by the project director, Sarah Zeller-Berkman, Ph.D. See Rolling Thunder, pp 2 – 13 at szb@publicscienceproject.org

4   The four catastrophes: militarism, materialism, racism and poverty are adverse socio-economic and political conditions referenced by Dr. Martin Luther King, Jr. in many of his speeches. The particulars describing how institutions and policy makers construct and sustain these negative conditions will be described though out the course of this book. For now, I mention that each of these come about because of specific historical narratives which result in excessive implementation, for example, relying too much on military intervention rather than negotiation, and/or deficient response, for example, not taking responsibility for destructive consequences triggered

by biased policies and practices. A review of Dr. King's concepts is summarized in "Consortium News," Vol. 26, Number 58, dated February 27, 2021. pp 1–2. The article is written by Laura Finley. https://consortiumnews.com

5   Patho-adolescence… is a term coined by Bill Plotkin in his book, Nature and the Human Soul. He defines patho-adolescence as the conflating characteristics attributed to teens by adultists with socio-economic conditions produced by institutions and policies created by adults. For instance, teens are described as naturally impulsive, yet our economy is built in part by the industries of lending and spending which manufacture financial profit by suggesting greater and greater need for material objects. This makes it easier for adults and teens to spend first and live with the consequence later. Mr. Plotkin describes attributes of our patho-adolescent society on pages 8–10 in his book. He also describes how we remain stuck in this dilemma on pp 224–226. Nature and the Human Soul (New World Library Press, 2008).

6   An emotional e-spark… is a term used by Daniel J. Siegel in his book, Mind: A Journey to the Heart of Being Human. Dr. Siegel is a clinical professor of psychiatry of the UCLA School of Medicine. The emotional e-spark is one of the characteristics of what Dr. Siegel holds is evident in the natural and healthy teen mind. He describes these traits as the essence of adolescence, encouraging a teen to explore, engage in creative learning, and seek meaningful connection to others. A description of this reference about teen essence appears on pp 119–120 in his book Mind (WW. Norton & Co., 2017).

7   Containment, but not conversation and consultation… describes one type of practice put in place which delays a young person's practice of having exploratory and problem-solving relationships with adults until a date at some undetermined time in the future. I raise this practice here as a point of contrast to existing education and civic

models which promote civic conversations between adults and teens. I will reference these types of models promoting inter-generational consensus as this book unfolds. For now, I refer you to one reference titled: A Teen Empowerment Model, 2002–2008, produced by The Center for Teen Empowerment. Pp 1 –11. https://teenempowerment.org

8   Contempt as a weapon of the weak is a concept analyzed by the Swiss psychiatrist Dr. Alice Miller in her book, Thou Shalt Not be Aware: Society's Betrayal of the Child. This concept is flushed out by Dr. Miller throughout her book by citing examples of adult and child interchanges based upon what she calls a sometimes conscious and sometimes unconscious contempt held by adults toward children. Dr. Miller postulates that these interactions, common to traditional child-rearing in the West, result in life-long insecurities and a person's disorganized relationship with their true self. Dr. Miller's book was subsequently re-released under the title: Drama of the Gifted Child (Basic Books, 1996).

9   Negative news about teens, prevalent in the 1990s…is raised by me in this book in many places but is referenced here as informed by a book written by Mike Males, The Scapegoat Generation: America's War on Adolescents. In his book, Mr. Males produces quotes made in the speeches made by public officials which reinforce negative stereotypes and result in policies directed at the young which are overly punitive. For example, in one section of his book he calls "Distorting teen pregnancy," he quotes passages from President Bill Clinton's 1994 address in which he demonized unwed teen mothers as practicing personal irresponsibility. The Scapegoat Generation (Common Courage Press, 1996. pg 16).

10   Debunked studies discrediting teen efficacy… Robert Epstein has written a couple of books and contributed articles to journals and magazines in which he develops a theme called the Myth of the Teen

Brain. In brief, he questions the practice of jumping from pictures of sections of the brain to recommended social policies, and also identifies new studies on teen behaviors and capacity which debunk falsely derived findings suggesting teen deficits and dysfunction. A useful source is an online article written by Dr. Epstein for the Scientific Mind, April/May 2007, pp 1–15. www.sciammind.com.

11   Science-based research findings... which are based upon poorly constructed research models leading to disastrously unjust social policies. Many of these policies took decades to reverse, and/or still promote unconscious bias. Understanding about how deficient research models contribute to discriminatory policy making is made clearer when studying the history of these practices. One excellent source is a book called Are Racists Crazy? co-authored by Sander L. Gilman from Emory University and James M Thomas from the University of Mississippi. They provide numerous examples in their book. I reference one anecdote they provide, that of the research, in the early 1900s, led by Henry A. Goddard, in which he used poor samples of Eastern European, Jewish, and Russian populations to draw generalized conclusions about whole groups of those peoples. These studies were used to justify and fuel highly discriminatory immigration and domestic social policies. Are Racists Crazy? (NYU University Press, 2016, pp 90–94).

12   Cultivating the positive attributes of teens... results when institutions provide models of civic participation and teen development which assume the presence of these positive attributes. I will introduce several of these models in this book. For now, I refer to one model titled "Act for Youth," which has been published by the Upstate Center for Excellence. This curriculum identifies positive teen assets, such as creativity, optimism, and looking for rewarding connections. It suggests follow-through activities which reinforce these attributes, and which give teens a chance to apply them for the purposes of institutional enhancement and community renewal.

The curriculum is titled "A Positive Development Resource Manual" and was produced at the Family Life Development Center at Cornell University. Jutta Dotterweich was a coordinator for producing this manual. https://gradschool.cornell.edu

13 To begin the world anew... is a United States founding theme, identified by a national book award winner, Bernard Bailyn, in his book of the same title. This theme, about re-constructing the current world and seeing possibilities in the future, was held by our nation's founders as a motivational force. This visionary stance is one which is, as I hold forth in this book, also constructive motivation for teens seeking inclusion in our attempts to improve upon our communal affairs. In his book titled To Begin the World Anew, (Vintage Press, 2003), Bernard Bailyn writes about the assumptions held and commentary offered by apologists for the continuation of British rule over the colonies. Amongst these assumptions were that those who proposed independence from Great Britain were too inexperienced and unqualified to lead a new nation. I make a reference here to point out the parallels when adults use dismissive arguments to marginalize and exclude civic commentary by teens, who are otherwise capable people from participation in governance.

14 Teens on board success... was made possible, when adults, who are asked to share a civic stage with teens, and who had been initially concerned and skeptical about teen efficacy, change their minds after sharing in the process of advocacy with teens. One example of this transition and process is profiled in a piece in the New York Daily News, which highlights the rewarding experiences of 16-year-old Victoria Parnell at her newfound civic home at Community Board 10 in Manhattan. The piece is called "Harlem Teen Joins Community Board To Tackle Neighborhood Issues," and was written by journalists Kerry Burke and Ginger Adams Otis. In appears in online form at the NY Daily News website and is dated May 7, 2013, pp 1–3. http://www.nydailynews.com

15   The need of the time has met us... is just one inspirational quote attributed to one of our nation's founders, Thomas Paine. Thomas Paine was in some ways marginalized even by allied advocates for independence, based upon his roots differing from others whose origins were embedded on aristocracy, and whose beliefs were less radical than Mr. Paine's. Thomas Paine believed that transitional changes are initiated when people step out of the comfort zone of tradition, and into the challenge of re-visioning and re-making society out of the ashes of an unjust world. After passage of the New York State Public Officer Law amendment in 2014, allowing for fully vetted 16- and 17-year-old teens full membership on community boards, many teens stepped up to the challenge of making modest changes at the neighborhood level by applying to become board members. A survey covering a few of these teens is provided in an online addition of The State, in an article titled "Teens Now Have Their Say In New York City Government." (November 29, 2014. Article is written by Jennifer Peltz of the Associated Press. www.pbs.org/newshour/nation/new-york-teens-will-new-say-citysgovernment

16   Teen's civic rite of passage (or civic rites of passage) suggests that to promote the habits of democracy in teens, they need to experience institutional practices in which they "do democracy or activate civic opportunities." Put in a simple way... if a teacher wants to teach a teen to play the piano, it is not enough to study former music masters nor the sequence of musical notes or position of the keys. They need to practice playing the piano under the informed guidance of one who is skilled. This is just as true for learning the skill sets of practicing democratically. I provide samples of organized opportunities for civic practice and mention one here. Generation Citizen offers an "Action Civics" classroom experience in dozens of schools across the city of New York and in seven other municipal locations in America. The elements of this action civics approach, and opportunities to adopt it in classrooms, is outlined in a piece

from their website called "What Is Action Civics?" www.genera-tioncitizen.org.

17   Research and written testimonies.... also covers providing opportu-nities for willing but untrained teachers to improve upon the social studies model provided in public schools. The National Council of Social Studies (NCSS) has put together a training syllabus called "C-3k Framework: College, Career and Civic Life," which informs Social Studies State Standards. www.nationalcouncilofsocialstudies. org

18   Walking away from myself.... is an observation that has been attributed to a 15th century mystic poet from India named Kabir Das. Briefly this viewpoint holds that when a person becomes dis-tanced from their own intentions and sense of purpose, then relating to the rest of the world becomes problematic. I interpret his counsel to mean that when you ignore the counsel of your inner voice, you step away from work aligning to your true purpose in life. There were moments in life where I made spontaneous or intuitively pro-posed choices that made no practical sense but had steered me in a direction in which I got to provide service to others which brought me riches beyond those of the material ones alone. To see a sam-ple of Kabir's poetic works, see 100 Poems by Kabir, translated by Rabindranath Tagore (Handpress Publishing, 1973)

In 1976, I faced a choice. The first choice was buying a loft in the Soho district for about $16,000. In 1986, its selling price was about $1 million. The second choice, which is the one I followed, was to move to Washington Heights, which would soon be in the throes of street shootings, and at the same time would afford me the gift of befriending neighbors (with very scarce resources) who would guide me in the process of developing and leading teen programs. Years later, when asked, given what I know about what my financial fortune would have been, had I chosen Soho, would I have changed my choice, my answer was a definitive no! The wealth I obtained through the work I had uptown is priceless.

19   Assert yourself with active awareness... are words of guidance extended to me by one of my mentors, Dr. Stephanie Marango. Dr. Marango is a spiritual practice professional who also obtained a medical degree. I had initially visited her while she was offering mentoring services using a therapeutic technique, she called The Doctor is In. Among the many tools she helped me develop was that, in making a rational or conscious decision, it is also important to check in with your body messaging, your intuitive voice, and your heart intelligence. She guided me with mind mapping (the mind being composed of each of the above-mentioned influences), interactive dialoguing assisting me in developing questions to help initiate search into unfamiliar territories, and exercises to open the energies of the heart. Put in other words, the title of Dr. Marango's practice could also mean The Doctor is Within.

Close to the time in which I met Dr. Marango, I also met Rebecca Gordon, who is a nationally acclaimed astrologer. I had decided one day to stop in and get an astrological reading from her, making that decision just on a whim. After taking a quick look at my birth chart, and also at a chart called a progressed chart (assesses your planetary configuration in present time, as compared to what the configuration was at your time of birth), she looked startled and asked me: What exactly are you doing now that is going to affect so many people? I had not said a word to her at that point about my involvement in the Teens on Board campaign. I decided without delay that although I have little expertise or knowledge with Ms. Gordon's specialty, I should engage in dialogue with her using the tool of active listening. With active listening, one takes care to carefully note not just information, but the speaker's intention for transmitting that information. In Ms. Gordon's approach, she was guiding me in developing metaphoric interpretations useful to one's life work, which expands understanding beyond the scope of the rational mind or the use of measuring provable factors. It also means having appreciation for the speaker's integrity in managing the body of knowledge being offered. In actively listening to and learning from Ms. Gordon, I came to understand that there are sources of knowledge which originate from many differing levels of conscious awareness, and that by being open and totally engaged, I also get to enhance understanding for diversely sourced levels of multiple intelligences. For information on Dr. Marango's practice, see https://www.stephaniemarangomd.com For information of Rebecca Gordon's astrological guidance support see https://www.rebeccagordonastrologer.com

20   Malpractice falsely determines needs (such as the need for war) … and a teacher's uncritical acceptance of misguided polices defined a starting point for me in challenging arbitrary and enforced authority. I developed a body of work used to buttress my arguments in opposition to our nation's intervention in Vietnam, under the guidance of a local chapter of the American Friends Service Committee. One example is their setting up discussion groups with high-school students, including my close friend at the time, Karl Klapper. We were introduced to the history of invasions launched against the Vietnamese, and to a close reading of the 1954 Geneva Accords, which explicitly called for the gradual cessation of hostilities and the reunification of North and South Vietnam. For a summary look at arguments critical of our misguided involvement in Vietnam, I offer two sources here. The first is an article "What Went Wrong in Vietnam?" in the New Yorker magazine. It was written by Louis Manand for the February 26, 2018, issue. The second source is an online article, "The Best Intentions: The Legacy of the American Friends Service Committee and the Vietnam War" written for a site called Professor Nev. It was under History 107, Section 7, written by Benjamin Temple on November 12, 2004. The New Yorker

magazine website is https://www.newyorker.com The site, Professor Nev, which I had found while writing this book, does not seem to be posted anymore.

21   "My country, right or wrong"—pro-war commentary... was a majority opinion in the first few years of American involvement in Vietnam. Positions taken on both sides of the argument were intensely felt and heated. "My country, right or wrong", "and if you don't love it, leave it" were slogans frequently tossed at those of us opposing the war. I have included one source here that addresses what the authors call "blind patriotism" by those supporting the war, and "critical loyalty" by those opposing the war. The name of the book is Pledging Allegiance. Joel Westheimer is the editor of this work containing essays on numerous issues related to the question of what defines patriotism (Pledging Allegiance, Teachers College Press, 2007).

22   Censorship of a student article on porn... is one of the more controversial topics students face when insisting upon the right to write about issues which interest them, take positions, and express opinions. The article I reference here concerns the censoring of an article (by a school district) written by a 17-year-old student who was exploring the motivations and financial necessities of young women involved in the porn industry. The name of the article is "Stockton Teacher Battles District Over Article On Student Porn" for the San Francisco Chronicle. (Written by Nanette Asimov, April 26, 2019).

The is also an outgrowth of literature in the educational community concerning the place of the classroom, and the role of teachers, in managing decisions made about introducing controversial topics. I share one excellent source here: McAvoy, P., and Ho, L. (2020). Professional Judgement and Deciding What to Teach as Controversial. Annals of Social Studies Education Research for

Teachers, 1 (1),pp 27–31. I was introduced to this source after taking an online course with the Harvard Graduate School of Education called Civic Education and Youth Participatory Politics. www.gsc. harvard.edu

23   Police Blotter... was a bi-weekly column carried in a Washington Heights and Inwood local paper detailing specifics of crime incidents during the turbulent times of the 1980s. The Uptown Dispatch July 3–18, 1984, Volume 1, No 4, pg 11.

24   Heroes of the Heights... was central to the theme of a book I call a biography of social action in Washington Heights. It contains amazing detail and captivating anecdotes about heroic actions taken in dangerous times by everyday people who were both modest and determined. The name of the book is Crossing Broadway and the Promise of New York City and was written by uptown native and scholar Robert W. Snyder (Cornell University Press, 2015. pg 7).

25   The Kiko Garcia riots. Crossing Broadway by Robert W. Snyder. Ibid, pp 180–183.

26   The culture of the 1950s was a period noted for rising tensions and confrontation between superpowers, escalation of a domestic political civil war between progressives and conservatives, and the rise of newsprint and television media which became instruments of conditioning for people taking opposing positions across the political divide. I use a source here, a book titled Beyond the Robot: The Life and Work of Colin Wilson, written by Gary Lachman (Penguin/ Random House, 2016). The author profiles Colin Wilson's personality and work as that of the consummate outsider, who inspired those with unique and dissident views seeking to have their opinions heard and respected. Mr. Wilson's first book, The Outsider, has been acknowledged as a literary source of cultural and political uprising. Mr. Lachman's introduction to Beyond the Robot is a

fine encapsulation of the 1950s and Colin Wilson's position as an outsider. pp xi–xvi.

27   Credible knowledge by official sources… refers to a concept that much of what passes for accurate news and legitimate sources of information is promoted by spokespeople for elected officials, university think-tanks, and corporate owned press and media companies. Dissenting sources and opinions are carried far less frequently in the mass public universe, and are often discredited by official sources, diminishing their legitimacy within the corridors of public conversations. A source I refer to here is a book, Educating the Right Way: Markets, Standards, God, and Inequality by M.W. Apple. pp 14–27 (Routledge, 2006).

28   The White High School" … is an article written by the journalist Pete Hamill for the NY Post, at that time owed by Dorothy Schiff. I followed him closely with his many columns which were written in fierce opposition to the Vietnam War, but he also wrote eloquently on topics affecting his beloved New York City. In the 1960s, the gross disparities in quality education had been one of the issues focused on by Mr. Hamill. I saved a copy of this article in a scrapbook but have been unable to locate its exact date of publication, which was within a period covering my final two years in high school. (1967–1968).

29   The White High School Ibid.

30   The White High School Ibid.

31   Misdirected classroom practices and community problems… is an area of concern that had been spoken to by progressive educators beginning in the early 1900s and continued during my exposure to controversies about educational practices in the 1970s. John Dewey, an innovator for educational reform practices, believed that "children must be educated for leadership as well as for obedience" (pg 32), and that school "classrooms should be organized as informed communities" (pg 35). The source for these quotes is

a work published called "Dewey's Laboratory School, Lessons for Today" by Laurel N. Tanner (Teacher's College Press, 1997). Paolo Freire was a South American progressive educator who proposed teaching practices where the student learner is trained to develop "critical capacity, curiosity, and an autonomous space in the educational environment" (pg 33). The book cited here is Pedagogy of Freedom (Roman and Littlefield, 2000).

32 The Other America Influencing President John Kennedy… also was a revelation and work of enormous influence for my developing dissident point of view. In this work, which profiles the problems and strengths of economically challenged people, Mr. Harrington profiles diverse populations of hardworking and persevering peoples who had been invisible to the public. Through negligence, prejudice, and design, these people had been left out of safety net coverages such as social security and guarantees of a minimum wage. The Other America (Scribner, 1962 and then 1997).

33 Representation of a fair and equitable society… is another patriotic theme reinforced through selectively presented information in textbooks and literature that is selected by school authorities. In the work I source here, Founding Myths, by Ray Rafael, the author presents juxtapositions between what official sources cite as actual events in history, and alternative historical accounts which are invented. One example discussed in Mr. Rafael's book is the historical account of Paul Revere's ride, in which he is portrayed as a solitary hero warning colonies residents about the impending arrival of British troops. This version of that event was taken from a poem written by William Wordsworth, which romanticized the account of Paul Revere's ride, but did not reflect an accurate historical record. Mr. Revere made it to Lexington, but never made it to Concord as he was intercepted by British troops. The warnings about impending encroachments by British troops had been organized by local committees in towns and villages. This tactic was a collectively conceived

and executed strategy. Much of what passes for American history in schools is not about having students research and debate contested original sources, but rather regurgitated romanticism. See Heroes and Heroines: Paul Revere's Ride (pp 11-27) in Founding Myths by Ray Rafael (The New Press, 2004).

34   An anthology is a book organized with short stories selected by a book company. The anthologies typically available in schools emphasize themes such as patriotism, individual hero worship, and extreme bravery. I consider my book to be an anthology reflecting the vision and contributions of unsung heroes, working communally at the grassroots, who until recently rarely showed up in official accounts of U.S. History. For works offering dissident historical accounts, see Educating the "Right" Way by Michael W. Apple (Routledge, 2006) and The Wages of Whiteness: Race and the Making of the American Working Class by David R. Roediger (Verso Books, 1991).

35   High-school curricula designed by outside sources... speaks to the fact that in the 1950s and 1960s, and even beyond, textbooks were the primary sources of understanding government and history. They were chiefly designed to present "history as a morality play" (pp 220–221), to inspire patriotism (pg 231) and to present social tensions as "optimistically as possible" (pg 242). I source here the dissident education classic, Lies My Teacher Told Me: Everything Your American History Textbook Got Wrong (Chapter 8, Watching Big Brother, pp 219–242) written by James W. Loewen (Simon and Schuster, 1995).

36   Challenging teachers and authoritarian practices... refer to those teachers and school administrators who organize lessons to teach the value of organizing for justice by people on the ground rather than urging obedience to arbitrary authority. In this educator's instruction manual, called The Learning Leader, author Douglas B. Reeves outlines practices in which students are discouraged from

"blaming victims" (page xxiii) and where students and teachers learn the "primacy of interpersonal relationships as key to organizational effectiveness" (page 21). The source I cite here is published by the Association for Supervision and Curriculum Development (ASCD) and is titled The Learning Leader: How to Focus School Improvement for Better Results (ASCD Publications, 2006).

37   Demonstrate heart… is a practice advocated by educational reformers who believe that the best practice for encouraging inspired learning includes understanding that as teachers and students, "we are all in this together, that we need to develop appreciation for the value of the other, and to cultivate the ability to hold tension in creative ways (pg 44). Healing the Heart of Democracy, by Parker J. Palmer (Jossey Bass, 2011).

38   The heart is cited by Dr. Stephanie Marango and astrologer Rebecca Gordon as an organ referenced by ancient Egyptians to be "equated with character" (pg 84) and seen in Chinese medicine as a "house of the spirit which gives meaning to life" (pg 85). For the role of the heart in shaping our consciousness, also see Your Body and the Stars by Stephanie Marango, MD, RYT and Rebecca Gordon (Atria Books, 2016) pp 81 – 85.

39   Opening of the psychic wound—guidance for the soul… is a process agreed to by spiritual activists. The basic premise is that altering our relationship to this wound, from that of being a victim of circumstance, to becoming an initiative-taking healer who manages our wounds, enhances our personal responsibility, and results in our becoming more effective in healing the wounds of those we care for in our communities. I cite two references here. The first is Johanna Macy, a Buddhist-oriented activist. She introduced me to a concept she calls apatheia, one in which a person experiences progressive deadening of the mind and heart. We establish festering wounds with no active and positive interaction. Wounds are, in

part, a signpost or messaging mechanism guided by soul wisdom asking us to tend to our own pain and confusion with compassion. Ms. Macy weaves thoughts and practices addressing tending to the wound throughout her book. The name of the book is Coming Back to Life (New Society Publishers, 2014). See Chapter 2, pp 25 -30. The second reference, a book written by Julie Tallard Johnson, speaks to the positive effects upon those with whom we engage as we heal our wounds and "make meaning with life as life creates meaning through each of us." The Zero Point Agreement, 2013. See the Introduction, pp 1-8.

40   When we stop fearing the light within us (attributed to Nelson Mandela) … is a thought that serves as a touchtone throughout his engagement in South Africa with both social justice campaigns and the empowerment of activists. Although the quote is attributed specifically to Nelson Mandela's Inauguration Speech, it does not appear there. The concept does reflect the spirit of his work and was popularized by motivational spokesperson Mary Ann Williamson. An account of this is covered in Town and Country Magazine in an article written by Caroline Hallerman on June 28, 2019. Find this article in the online archives for Town and Country magazine at https://www.townandcountrymagazine.com

41   Counter-story telling…. is an obligation and a skill set crucial for those engaged in advocating for social justice, and in helping potential allies find a place for themselves in movements. Connections to issues are not always made simply by citing facts and figures, but rather make sense when embedded in the context of a story which resonates with the person listening or reading a story. Construction of a web of counter-stories also helps to build a foundation upon which an emerging consciousness can take root in the ground of experience. One nice accounting of this was covered in a journal called Rethinking Ethnic Studies (2019) by Rethinking Schools Publications. The name of the article I am referencing is

"Counter-Story Telling and Decolonial Pedagogy" and is written by Anita E. Fernandez (pp 33–37). https://rethinkingschools.org

42   See Teaching What Really Happened by James W. Loewen (Teachers College Press, 2010) pp 141 – 145.

43   See Teaching What Really Happened by James W. Loewen (Teachers College Press, 2010) pp 141 – 145.

44   See Teaching What Really Happened by James W. Loewen (Teachers College Press, 2010) pp 141 – 145.

45   Clinton and Obama, comparative speeches denigrating youth. As is the case with many adults, what is conflated are the sources of adult neglect with young folks supposed deficits in teen character. I cite two sources here that reinforce our understanding of the practice of using alarmist speech. These sources challenge suggestions about innate youth traits being the primary cause of social problems. The first source is a speech given by then President Clinton, in which he deplored the existence of "thirteen-year-olds…with customized weapons…for whom we must initiate a crackdown." Youth who fit into this category were exceedingly rare, but by emphasizing the stereotype, he contributed to an exaggerated climate of fear about youth-initiated violence. (Associated Press release covering this speech, September 14, 1993). Mike Males, in a blog called "Not Youth Violence Again," April 4, 2011) lamented the linking of youth as a primary cause of violence by then President Barack Obama. Although the presence of "youth perpetuating unacceptable levels of rising violence" was specifically noted in President Obama's speech, according to the FBI's Uniform Crime Rate Report, the rate of violent crime among youth ages 10 to 17 had declined to its lowest level since 1971. Find Mike Males' commentary on Obama's speech at Youth Facts: We are the Debunkers https://www.youthfacts.org

46   Fighting the good fight while choosing to remain invisible… is a choice made by modest civic activists, including myself, in which

one chooses to minimize one's importance in the role of leadership or in being effective enough when fighting for a cause. I found some insightful commentary on this habit of humble people hiding under the umbrella of humility to avoid attention to oneself. I cite here one type of analysis, which is called an Enneagram, a personality system first proposed by pre-Christian sources and popularized by therapeutic communities in Latin America in recent times. The habit I just described in attributed to those who have an Enneagram (an inner source of energy) called the Peacemaker. The Peacemaker works hard on improving the prospects for others while at the same time diminishing one's own self-importance. Fascinating descriptions of nine types of Enneagrams is found in a book titled The Enneagram: A Christian Perspective, written by Richard Rohr. (Crossroads Publishing, 2002) The specific pages referenced are in the Peacemaker chapter, pp 181–184.

47 Believe in your own thought… is a theme promoted by Ralph Waldo Emerson, a transcendentalist writing in the nineteenth century. He believed in listening to your intuition, and "nourishing yourself through communion with nature." His contributions to the field of higher order thinking are covered well in a book titled Global Awakening: New Science and 21st Century Enlightenment by Michael Schacker (Park Street Press, 2013). I refer specifically here to a section in his book on Emerson, pp 190–192.

48 Our minds include the brain and the heart… with each of them coordinating with the other through neuron networks of communication. An apt description of these enhancements to thinking is aptly covered in a book titled Resilience From The Heart by Greg Braden. He is a New York Times bestselling author and a pioneer for bridging science and indigenous knowledge. The pages I cite here, speaking to the complexity of neuron development within the heart, the harmony between the brain and the heart, and their

relationship contributing to intuitive thought, are referenced by me for pp 11, 13, and pp 22–23.

49   Research by the Heart Math Institute... beginning in the 1980s and continuing until today has shown promising results for validating what the Institute calls "non-local intuition in entrepreneurs and non-entrepreneurs." One type of study is one in which entrepreneurs are shown to have a differential in the rate of heart beats for about 12–4 seconds, making a spontaneous decision to pursue an outcome. Some of the major decisions I made to change the course of my life were inspired by these moments. One example is my decision to leave a financially comfortable position at the Life Skills School (a place that I loved) to gamble, with little planning, for personal fiscal viability. This was my co-launching of the all-girls' education and sports program called the Ivy League (in 1994). See the Institute Of Heart Math (Boulder Creek, Co.) website to review some of their research initiatives. https://www.heartmath.org

50   Freud and the start of "talk therapy" was a breakthrough for doctors and patients developing a methodology for getting in touch with places in our unconscious domain to remediate psychological problems. Freud's work, as well as the progression of therapeutic approaches for dealing with trauma, is extensively covered in a book called The Body Keeps the Score by Bessel Van Der Kolk, M.D. (Penguin Books, 2014). I reference here excerpts for this book, pp 185–186, page 196, and pp 234–236.

51   Carl Jung's descriptions of multiple dimensions of consciousness and their energetic connections to each other were developed by Mr. Jung (initially a student of Sigmund Freud) as he extended his approach to therapeutic treatment. I reference here a book covering the history and work of Jung, called Memories and Dreams, edited by Meredith Sandini (North Atlantic Books, 2002). Some of what is covered here are the connections between humans and nature

on a subconscious level (pg 24) and the existence of archetypes as invisibly organized bundle of purposeful energy (pg 27).

52 A Tale of Two Cities, by Charles Dickens, is a classic fictional book, which came to be known as a "historical fiction," as it also aptly described actual conditions, such as the wide divide of haves and have-nots living in the same city, and the existence of class struggle and fights for social justice. The summary of the book can be seen at www.britbox.com.

53 The value of grandmother wisdom… was adopted by me in my work on the streets of Washington Heights, as it was often grandmothers who took over the responsibilities of becoming heads on house-holds, or crucially supporting young mothers in distress. Amongst their many roles with supporting family members and adopting leadership positions for on-the-ground efforts to keep community alive was their creation of special events and ceremonies celebrating the tradition on a specific block, which helped to give a cultural framework to local identity. The contributions of grandmothers in neighborhoods across NYC closely mirror those I read about in a book I reference here, called Grandmother's Wisdom: Living Portrayals, which was compiled and produced by Ma Creative in 2014. Included in this book are mini stories of grandmothers from tribes across the world and how their use of ceremony, ritual, prayers, and training contributed a sense of identity and resilience for com-munity members. As is the case of stories profiled in this book, grandmothers in neighborhoods which had become demoralized and fractured are provided a socio-psychological glue, helping folks to keep themselves and their neighbors together.

54 An informed immigrant's counsel for indigent power and resolve in challenged community… is a story personified by Petra Foundation member Chhaya Chhoum in the South Bronx. Her philosophy and selfless work for families and community is referenced here

from the Petra Foundation's Twenty-Fifth Anniversary Journal: 100 Heroes, 25 Years (pg 37). This journal can also be found online: http://petrafoundation.org/fellows/index.html .

55   Petra Anniversary Journal Ibid, pg 41

56   Petra Anniversary Journal Ibid, pg 41

57   Taking back parks and creating beauty in the community describe countless initiatives launched by on-the-ground leaders who utilize architectural skills and artist flair in making our communities anew. What I reference here is the groundbreaking work involving the transformation of local space. One example is the project called Take Back the Park, created by the Citizens Committee of New York City in the early 1980s. The Citizen's Committee provided mini-grants, resources, and training for our teen leaders looking to make Edgecombe Park (the Pit) accessible, safe, and a place to be proud of. To find out more, go to citizenscommitteefornyc.org. The spirit and vision for initiatives such as Take Back the Park are a theme addressed in a book called Urban Alchemy: Restoring Joy in America's Sorted Out Cities, by Dr. Mindy Thompson-Fullilove. (New Village Press, 2013). In introducing this theme, Dr. Thompson-Fullilove quotes a French urban planner, Michel Castel Dupart, who inspired her: "The key to city life is making public space more beautiful…pulling people in and using the space together." Pages referenced here from Dr. Thompson-Fullilove's book, pp 24–28.

58   How do we link the classroom and the community, and bring each of them back to life? Stories and strategies are shared by Sarah K. Anderson in her book, Bringing School To Life: Place-Based Education across the Curriculum (Roman & Littlefield, 2017). I cite her specific sections covering the need for developing vision through community mapping (pg 14); the development of community science through collaboration with experts and hands-on learning (pg 41); and facilitating authentic integration of student understanding

with project goals through learning local history and maintaining personal journals (pg 81).

59   Local stories are created in a web of ideas manifested across the planet. Paul Hawken, an entrepreneur, and an environmentalist, covers the scope and depth of this worldwide movement, which he claims includes five million citizen-led projects which form the core of humanities immunity. These projects are designed to heal rather than hurt, and to facilitate hope rather than harm. Project builders facilitate recovery and restoration of wholesome and holistically derived relationships (pg 143). I also highlight here the commentary of Mr. Hawken detailing the need for addressing environmental and social justice issues as a whole package (pg 12). Quotes are from Blessed Unrest by Paul Hawken (Penguin, 2007).

60   On the effects of inequality... which dampens prospects for personal achievement and for psychological health. In a book called The Spirit Level, by Richard Wilkinson and Kate Pickett (Bloomsbury Press, 2009), the authors point out specific negative indicators for personal health and efficacy which are found with more prevalence as cities and nations are assessed with deeper socio-economic levels of inequality. Just three of the many indicators they cite are an erosion of trust in community life and social relations (pp 49–62), declines in physical health and life expectancy (pp 73–87), and lower levels of educational performance (pp 103–117).

61   I briefly reference the Uptown Dreamers Program here, founded and led by the director, Coach Dave Crenshaw. (Coach Dave and his community-building projects will be covered in more detail in sections profiling him in "The Rebel" section of this book). Here I just reference one of the themes of his program, that his community service projects include a build-a-friend component, and his emphasis on exploration and self-expression. You can find his program online at www.uptowndreamers.com .

62 On the negative role of disruptive relationships and the positive role of participation in a positive space. I refer here a book titled From What Is to What If: Unleashing the Power of Imagination, by Bob Hopkins, a British social entrepreneur who founded a training network called Transition Network.(Chelsea Green, 2019) I briefly reference here what Mr. Hopkins calls the "pre-traumatic syndrome," where he documents that even relatively low levels of stress maintained over time leads to shrinkage of parts of the human brain and increases of chronic anxiety (Mark Cocker, Our Place , London: Johnathan Cape, 2018, citation on pg 58). Mr. Hopkins also covers the positive work of youth offender programs, such as Landworks, which has obtained decreased rates of released prisoners being trapped in the return-to-prison process. Participants are allowed to share their vulnerable condition and stay close to nature while tending to vegetable gardens (as one nurtures the ground, one nurtures the self). See pp 60–62.

63 On the negative role of disruptive relationships and the positive role of participation in a positive space. I refer here a book titled From What Is to What If: Unleashing the Power of Imagination, by Bob Hopkins, a British social entrepreneur who founded a training network called Transition Network.(Chelsea Green, 2019) I briefly reference here what Mr. Hopkins calls the "pre-traumatic syndrome," where he documents that even relatively low levels of stress maintained over time leads to shrinkage of parts of the human brain and increases of chronic anxiety (Mark Cocker, Our Place , London: Johnathan Cape, 2018, citation on pg 58). Mr. Hopkins also covers the positive work of youth offender programs, such as Landworks, which has obtained decreased rates of released prisoners being trapped in the return-to-prison process. Participants are allowed to share their vulnerable condition and stay close to nature while tending to vegetable gardens (as one nurtures the ground, one nurtures the self). See pp 60–62.

64   On the negative role of disruptive relationships and the positive role of participation in a positive space. I refer here a book titled From What Is to What If: Unleashing the Power of Imagination, by Bob Hopkins, a British social entrepreneur who founded a training network called Transition Network.(Chelsea Green, 2019) I briefly reference here what Mr. Hopkins calls the "pre-traumatic syndrome," where he documents that even relatively low levels of stress maintained over time leads to shrinkage of parts of the human brain and increases of chronic anxiety (Mark Cocker, Our Place , London: Johnathan Cape, 2018, citation on pg 58). Mr. Hopkins also covers the positive work of youth offender programs, such as Landworks, which has obtained decreased rates of released prisoners being trapped in the return-to-prison process. Participants are allowed to share their vulnerable condition and stay close to nature while tending to vegetable gardens (as one nurtures the ground, one nurtures the self). See pp 60–62.

65   What contributes to planetary demise? The practice of "wildling" by the adult generation. The term "wildling" was common to public statements during the 1990's in reference to teens being out of control and stealing the sense of safety on the streets for adults. Stealing the dreams of the young and committing crimes against the future is another form of wilding. I reference here Greta Thunberg's issues addressed in her speech to the Global Climate Summit. See coverage in the New York Daily News article, "You Have Stolen My Dreams And My Childhood" written by journalists Kayla Epstein and Juliet Eilperin from The Washington Post. (NY Daily News, page 8; September 24, 2019). http://www.nydailynews.com

66   Bill Plotkin's commentary on the disruption of natural learning rhythms in individuals and chaotic consequences of instability on a cultural and social level. These obstacles result from being stuck in what Plotkin calls an Ego-Centric era. He contrasts the deficits of the Ego-Centric era with the evolving benefits derived as we

progress into what he calls and Eco-Centric era throughout his book. For examples of the disabling consequences for individuals see pp 9 and 10. For examples of societal challenges see pages 225 and 226. On the essential experience of wandering that has become crucial to finding to find one's purpose and place in life... Nature and the Human Soul by Bill Plotkin). I address three of his thoughts here: how wandering allows one to dive deep into self (pg 24), why the human soul is pre-cultural and pre-linguistic and is a person's first home (pg 40), and how the mature soul is necessary to allow a person to occupy their own space (pg 41). Nature of the Human Soul by Bill Plotkin (New World Library, 2008).

67   Bill Plotkin's commentary on the disruption of natural learning rhythms in individuals and chaotic consequences of instability on a cultural and social level. These obstacles result from being stuck in what Plotkin calls an Ego-Centric era. He contrasts the deficits of the Ego-Centric era with the evolving benefits derived as we progress into what he calls and Eco-Centric era throughout his book. For examples of the disabling consequences for individuals see pp 9 and 10. For examples of societal challenges see pp 225 and 226. On the essential experience of wandering that has become crucial to finding to find one's purpose and place in life... Nature and the Human Soul by Bill Plotkin). I address three of his thoughts here: how wandering allows one to dive deep into self (pg 24), why the human soul is pre-cultural and pre-linguistic and is a person's first home (pg 40), and how the mature soul is necessary to allow a person to occupy their own space (pg 41). Nature of the Human Soul by Bill Plotkin (New World Library, 2008).

68   Bill Plotkin's commentary on the disruption of natural learning rhythms in individuals and chaotic consequences of instability on a cultural and social level. These obstacles result from being stuck in what Plotkin calls an Ego-Centric era. He contrasts the deficits of the Ego-Centric era with the evolving benefits derived as we

progress into what he calls and Eco-Centric era throughout his book. For examples of the disabling consequences for individuals see pp 9 and 10. For examples of societal challenges see pp 225 and 226. On the essential experience of wandering that has become crucial to finding to find one's purpose and place in life... Nature and the Human Soul by Bill Plotkin). I address three of his thoughts here: how wandering allows one to dive deep into self (pg 24), why the human soul is pre-cultural and pre-linguistic and is a person's first home (pg 40), and how the mature soul is necessary to allow a person to occupy their own space (pg 41). Nature of the Human Soul by Bill Plotkin (New World Library, 2008).

69   Bill Plotkin's commentary on the disruption of natural learning rhythms in individuals and chaotic consequences of instability on a cultural and social level. These obstacles result from being stuck in what Plotkin calls an Ego-Centric era. He contrasts the deficits of the Ego-Centric era with the evolving benefits derived as we progress into what he calls and Eco-Centric era throughout his book. For examples of the disabling consequences for individuals see pp 9 and 10. For examples of societal challenges see pp 225 and 226. On the essential experience of wandering that has become crucial to finding to find one's purpose and place in life... Nature and the Human Soul by Bill Plotkin). I address three of his thoughts here: how wandering allows one to dive deep into self (pg 24), why the human soul is pre-cultural and pre-linguistic and is a person's first home (pg 40), and how the mature soul is necessary to allow a person to occupy their own space (pg 41). Nature of the Human Soul by Bill Plotkin (New World Library, 2008).

70   Bill Plotkin's commentary on the disruption of natural learning rhythms in individuals and chaotic consequences of instability on a cultural and social level. These obstacles result from being stuck in what Plotkin calls an Ego-Centric era. He contrasts the deficits of the Ego-Centric era with the evolving benefits derived as we

progress into what he calls and Eco-Centric era throughout his book. For examples of the disabling consequences for individuals see pp 9 and 10. For examples of societal challenges see pp 225 and 226. On the essential experience of wandering that has become crucial to finding to find one's purpose and place in life… Nature and the Human Soul by Bill Plotkin). I address three of his thoughts here: how wandering allows one to dive deep into self (pg 24), why the human soul is pre-cultural and pre-linguistic and is a person's first home (pg 40), and how the mature soul is necessary to allow a person to occupy their own space (pg 41). Nature of the Human Soul by Bill Plotkin (New World Library, 2008).

71 Immaturity is a positive aspect necessary for the development of healthy adolescents… this position is developed by Howard Gardner, a developmental psychologist, in his book called Intelligence Reframed (Basic Books, 1999). Dr. Gardner speaks to the importance for those aspiring to be creative to be able to "hold the tensions of conflict comfortably…and to work with people who experience discomfort while taking risks in an environment" (pg 121).

72 Revealing and overcoming scandalous pretensions is a theme that Rabbi Abraham Heschel addresses in his reference to the orientation and work of prophets throughout his book. Prophets reject the assumptions and institutions established by those whose privilege undermines the development of new ideas and the life prospects of those who are locked out of pathways leading to privilege. He considers this viewpoint and motivation for social justice work to be essential to the nature of being a prophet. For a look at this perspective on prophets, specifically related to his Jewish ancestral roots, see The Prophets, Volume II by Abraham J. Heschel (Harper Torch books, 1962).

73 Here I reference what I call Dr. Thompson-Fullilove's periodic table of civic reform elements, such as finding out what you are

for, unpuzzling the fractured space, and creating meaningful places. See page 3 for the itemized list of elements, and chapters for each of the above listed three elements: Finding out what… (pp 102–119), Unpuzzling… (pp 142– 163), and Creating… (pp 194 –219). See Dr. Fullilove's book: Urban Alchemy: Restoring Joy in America's Sorted Out Cities (New Village Press, 2013).

74 The adolescent rite of passage is a hero's journey… Experienced on a stage, as noted by Joseph Campbell, on which "aging patriarchs typically have become tyrants, enslaving everyone around them." I am a member of the Boomer generation, and like many others in the1960s, battled against the restrictions imposed by aging patri-archs. Too many of us have "grown up" and become the new class of aging patriarchs whose governance and institutional practices con-tinue to contain and marginalize those dispossessed from the process of making meaningful choices about our lives. In this chapter, I will profile unsung heroes in our communities and nation, teen leaders and their civic mentors who have taken back the definition of ado-lescent mind and heart and are reconstructing webs of community. What is being reclaimed is addressed by Clarissa Pinkola Estes, Ph.D. in her book, Women Who Run with the Wolves: "What had been captured and stolen, our great treasures within, and access to great opportunities in our lives." What had been severed, an alignment with our spiritual wisdom, and the spirit of mutually supportive communities is under acts of reconstruction, being woven into nets of purposeful and empowering movements. See Joseph Campbell, Hero With a Thousand Faces (Princeton University Press, 1968, pp 17–18) and Estes, Women Who Run With the Wolves (Ballentine Books, 1992, pg 283).

75 Policies leading to deficiencies in public schools is but one exam-ple of how the Boomer generation in large part have been fellow travelers for sabotaging a viable future of the emergent generation. George Bernard Shaw, who was a school dropout and won a Nobel

Prize for Literature in 1925 had this to say about professionals in charge of schools: "Schools and school-masters, as we know them today, are not popular places of education and teaching, but rather prisons and turnkeys in which children are kept to keep them from disturbing and chaperoning the parent" (Bing.com images). We are just beginning to get out from under the deficiencies of public education. The problem started with loss of funding for public schools as the middle class fled urban areas. As an example of this problem, I refer here to an article in the Utne Reader Magazine (Issue #41, Sept/Oct 1990). The title of the article is "How The Middle Class Has Helped To Ruin The Public Schools," excerpted from an article in the Washington Monthly. It was written by Joseph Nocera. In New York City, we have finally, after 30 years of advocacy and court battles, spearheaded by Robert Jackson, first as a city councilperson, and now as a NY State Senator, begun to see an opening with the restoration of equitable funding for our public schools. See the Brennan Center for social justice website for the history and accomplishments of the Campaign for Fiscal Equity. https://www.brennancenter.org

76   A despair for settling and not being seen as insignificant are psychological and conditions of spiritual impoverishment which have been constructed in the young generation's webs of resistance for decades. In the 1950s, Colin Wilson, in his classic work called The Outsider spoke to the choice of those feeling so alienated of becoming a rebel: "(The outsider) seemed to be a rebel, and what he was in rebellion against was the lack of spiritual tension in a materially prosperous civilization." (Beyond the Robot: The Life and Work of Colin Wilson, by Gary Lachman (Tarcher Perigree, 2016, pg 24). For a deeper perspective on the corrosive effects of "consumerism as a belief system (which is seen) as a way to self-development, self-realization, and self-fulfillment," see my reference to the book titled Hooked! Buddhist Writings of Greed, Desire, and the Urge

to Consume, which is edited by Stephanie Kaza. (Her introduction to the book is a good overview of what contributors to this book have to say. (Shambala Books, 2005, pp 1–13).

77   Ibid. Beyond the Robot, pg 147.

78   A good community ecology allows for the opportunity to make mistakes. I refer here to an article in a magazine published in the 1990s which was called In Context. Sarah Van Gelder, its editor, stated: "In a community that works, those who make mistakes have an opportunity and an incentive to make amends and be accepted." (In Context, No. 38, Spring 1994, pg 11). In this chapter, and the chapter to follow, which I call Introduction, I will delve into specific practices which discourage the value and importance of making mistakes. Our obsessions for obtaining officially sanctioned "correct answers" and our policy approaches for youth development which define teens as problems to be solved will also be highlighted as socio/cultural examples of how we deter curiosity, creativity, and alternative pathways in education.

79   What are community boards and what is Public Officer Law? In New York City, there are 59 boards, each of which has 50 volunteer members who are appointed by Borough Presidents and City Council members. Members serve for renewable two-year terms, meeting once a month in a general meeting, and twice more each month on committees to which they are assigned (for example, Public Safety, Education/Youth Services, Parks). Board members listen to and advise residents in their communities, offering advice, and sometimes resolutions of support for proposed programs. Boards operate in a purely advisory capacity to NYC agencies and its government representatives. For more information on community boards, see https://www.nyc.gov/cau/community-boards . Although community boards serve in New York City, the process of selecting board members is governed under State Law under a provision called the

NY State Public Officers Law. Up until our amendment to this law was approved in 2014, community board members could be no younger than the age of 18. The Public Officer Law defines a public officer as a person who has been legally elected or appointed who exercises government functions. For a further look at the Public Officer Law, see www.dos.ny.gov/corps .

80 Teens and their need for an initiation process. I refer here to one type of initiation process, that of a soul initiation, as spoken to by Bill Plotkin in his book, Nature and the Human Soul (New World Library, 2008). In Mr. Plotkin's description of this initiation process, he writes: "...a teen must undergo an initiation process, letting go of the comfortable...which transforms your life by virtue of the truth at the center of your soul image or story...your commitment to truth results in a radical simplification of your life..." (pg 307). Until recently, a student's experience with school classes in civics and history was informed by a curriculum which spoke to participation by adults, and then mostly adults privileged through their gender, class, and race. What has been gradually introduced very recently are civic participation opportunities in which the young learn to practice the participatory skills essential to democracy, sometimes failing and sometimes succeeding in the process.

81 The first asset of adolescence is… a characteristic of one of many teen capabilities in which they are recognized for their potential and contributions, and not their deficiencies. One example of this approach is a curricular design introduced by New York City's Department of Youth and Community Development, which they call a Framework for Civic Engagement. Amongst the constructs of this curriculum are tools ensuring that adults create the conditions conducive to promoting teen participation and engagement. A few of these include maintaining spaces that are safe, physically, emotionally, and psychologically (pg 3), encouraging supportive partnerships and relationships (pg 3), and fostering a process of reciprocal

communication and collaboration (pg 3). A few of the positive habits adopted by teens embraced in this atmosphere include "developing positive attitudes about the process; asking and listening to questions; and learning to respectfully disagree" (pg 2). To read to full description, see DYCD Framework for Civic Engagement at www. nyc.gov/assets/dycd .

82   The asset of idealism… is promoted when adhering to practices as suggested by the humanist and spiritually oriented psychologist Bill Plotkin in Nature and the Human Soul. He contrasts practices where "teens are conditioned as per adult's institutionally approved practices and needs, (to ensure) obedience training" with a spiritual practice in which teens are encouraged through a "process of healthful individuation and psychic growth… and finding fulfillment in one's totality." Nature and the Human Soul, pp 99–102 and pp 174 –175.

83   George Washington on the importance of welcoming newcomers. Washington advised that an inviting infrastructure of involvement is inherent to the heart of America, and that we should also be open to the oppressed and persecuted coming here from other nations. Find his quote in the book called Democracy for All: Restoring Immigrant Voting Rights in the United States, by Ron Hayduk (Routledge, 2006, pp 16–17). I find the quote, and Mr. Hayduk's thesis compelling, because so many of our young generation are immigrants. In the neighborhood where I started my youth work, over 70 per cent of the total population are immigrants who are driving our economic engine of success through hard work and small business ownership, who have children attending our schools, and teens contributing thousands of hours of community service to our neighborhood. For a great anecdotal history and overview of Dominican-American contributions in the Heights, see Crossing Broadway by Robert W. Snyder (Cornell University Press, 2013), and specifically pp 144–147 where he details the vital community

work of agencies such as the Community Association of Progressive Dominicans, and the Dominican Women's Development Center. To view civic contributions by teen-led initiatives, see the website for the Washington Heights and Inwood Youth Council, which organized anti-smoking campaigns, and which participated in the Youth on Board campaign (https://www.facebook.com.Washington-Heights-and-Inwood-Youth-Council). Also look up the website for Alianza Dominicana/Catholic charities that set up several youth service and cultural enrichment programs, including La Plaza, a Department of Youth and Community Development Beacon Program and a Dominican-American Cultural Center. (https://cccs.ny.org/alianza).

84   Cast out of the garden of childhood" is one line in a poem I wrote in 2010, in which I lament the downsizing of adolescent capabilities and identity.

85   Punishment of immigrants and youth—legal codes. For our nation's history of drawing up and enacting punishing legal codes against immigrants, see Alexander Kayssar's book, The Right to Vote (Basic Books, 2000) where he document several examples, such as the literacy and education tests put in place after World War I (pp 139–140) and a series of measures outlined in a section of that book called Immigrants Unwelcomed (pp 136–146). For a litany of codes posing restrictions on young people, see Teen 2.0 by Robert Epstein (Fresno Books, 2016) in its Appendix 5 section, pp 388–390. Some of these include a Massachusetts Law put in place in 1641, "Prohibiting people under 16 from 'smiting' their parents, to a 1970's Supreme Court decision restricting a young woman's right to an abortion, and a federal law passed in 19097 making involuntary commitment of teens easier by requiring school systems to pay for their hospitalizations."

86   Citing the teen disposition for using inquiry utilized in a civil rights lawsuit. Students, under the guidance of experienced mentors, are launching lawsuits against the state government whose policies deny

basic rights enjoyed by adults. I reference one lawsuit here that was submitted in Rhode Island, led by high-school students, and advised by legal advisor Michael Rubell, who successfully sued NY State for underfunding schools in New York City. Although in the district court hearing the student case holding that lack of adequate civic education violates their constitutional rights was ruled not unconstitutional by the judge, the judge's commentary was supportive of the student's initiative and concerns, and he strongly stated that the state of civic education in the schools needs a drastic upgrade. In statements made by the U.S. District Judge William Smith, he said that the problems exposed by the student lawsuit "indicates a deep flaw in our national education priorities and policies." (Washington Post, "Federal Judge Rules Students Have No Constitutional Right…" by Valerie Strauss, October 22, 2020). In the book I previously cited, the whole title reads The Right to Vote: The Contested History of Democracy in the United States (Alexander Keyssar, Basic Books, 2000). In this scholarly history documenting the history of success in expanding democracy, he also points out the many obstacles that had to be overcome to finally get a desired result. Mr. Keyssar sites one example with the women's suffrage movement. As he states: "In 1895, Massachusetts even underwent the demoralizing spectacle of a mock (non-binding) referendum on municipal suffrage that was overwhelmingly defeated, as only 23,000 (out of a possible 600,000) women came out to vote (page 200). In our judicial system, it can take years, and even decades of contested cases and organizing on the ground, no matter the righteousness of case when judged now, but still struggling for legitimacy and traction in earlier years.

87 Balked, but not being taken seriously, is part of the commentary about youth alienation offered by Colin Wilson in his classic book called The Outsider. In a book by Gary Lachman (who was a friend of Wilson), Beyond the Robot: The Life and Work of Colin Wilson (Tarcher, 2016), Mr. Lachman, provides a biography and

an examination of Wilson's thoughts conveyed in his writing. Not being taken seriously is a theme that Wilson reinforces throughout his book. Mr. Lachman revisits this theme in his book, Beyond the Robot. For one example, see pp xiv-xv in the Introduction to his book.

88   Beyond the Robot Ibid. A whole way of being in the world... illuminates Colin Wilson's points made throughout his writings about the narrow scope of consciousness experienced in the 1950s, and the yearning for a new way of seeing life. Gary Lachman offers us quotes to point out Wilson's perspective. As Lachman paraphrases Wilson: "Our everyday consciousness is...a liar. It gives us a severely limited picture, then asks us to believe it is the truth" (pg 148). Wilson offers a new perspective in his book, The Black Room: "Meet the challenge...of no challenge...maintain a high level of purposeful consciousness without the aid of an external stimulus" (Beyond the Robot, pg 147).

89   Projection of the shadow onto the unwanted other... is a concept in humanistic psychology developed and applied by Carl Jung in this therapeutic practice. In short, this theory holds that people have unconsciously held beliefs and feelings that they believe are negative and unflattering. Until they become aware of their ownership, they remain unconscious of its presence in our psyches. These thoughts still have energies which we express in a process called projection, where we see these negative characteristics in the actions of other people we disapprove of. Jeremiah Abrams is a Jungian psychologist who applies this concept to societies. People who consider themselves to be the rightful owners of privilege and exclusively held rights use projection to dismiss and diminish unwanted other peoples. Abrams edited a book called The Shadow in America: Reclaiming the Soul of a Nation (Nataraj Publishing, 1994), which includes chapters by two writers providing social-political examples of this process. See the two chapters: The Archetypal Dilemma: The

LA Riots by Jerome Bernstein (pp 239 – 251) and Gender Wars by Aaron Kipnis and Elizabeth Herron (pp 79–113).

Another source identifying an example of our nation's practice of consensual contradiction is profiled in a piece written by David Treuer for the Atlantic Magazine (May 2021). In a piece he titles "Return the National Parks to the Tribes" (pp 30–45), he writes about President Theodore Roosevelt, who conceived a legacy of establishing our national park system to preserve the majesty of our natural areas, while at the same time holding terrible views about Native Americans. He advocated for their expulsion, using extreme violence in massacres. As written by Mr. Treuer, "Contained in the person of Theodore Roosevelt was a wild love for natural vistas and a propensity for violent imperialism; an overwhelming desire for freedom, and a readiness to take it away from other people." https://www.theatlantic.com

90   Historical constructs are presented as perennial truths… is a phrase coined by Scilla Elworthy, Ph.D. in her book Pioneering the Possible (North Atlantic Books, 2014). Dr. Elworthy is a three-time Nobel Peace Prize nominee who has negotiated internationally for peace agreements amongst people who have been in eternal conflict. One of the obstacles to overcome in efforts for conflict resolution is to have people on opposing sides realize that their own culturally embedded beliefs have been developed and held as a social construct, and that those with whom they disagree have different social constructs. For a peek at Dr. Elworthy's comments on overcoming this obstacle, see her chapter in this book called "Changing the Values that underlie our Decisions" (pp 75–105).

91   Men's belittling of women based in their negative stereotypes… is another example of how embedded false beliefs about the other come to shape behaviors toward those whom we consider to be incapable and inferior. Sheila Row Botham in her book called A

Vindication of the Rights of Women: Mary Wollstonecraft (Verso Books, 2010) shares the insights of Ms. Wollstonecraft, who was an eighteenth-century pioneer for the American women's rights movement. In her writings which were critical of men proposing democratic rights for men, but not for women, Ms. Wollstonecraft cited examples of how men unjustly portray the character traits of women as being inherently dependent and childlike (pp 11–13). She also points out how our society ingrains these beliefs into young girls, guiding them to become habituated as "slaves and playthings" (pp 158–159).

92   Women have become the leaders needed for fighting against the imposition of injustice… both in America and in the international area. For profiles of women from across the globe, see Rad Women Worldwide by Kate Schatz (Ten Speed Press, 2010). Some chapters in her book include Venus and Serena Williams (pg 58), Eniac Programmers (pg 64), and Guerilla Girls (pg 68). The point emphasized in this book is that the transition to more equity in social and political relationships is brought forward by heroes in the sports world, artists, and ordinary people who step up to the challenge. In his book, Young Radicals: The War for America's Ideals (Random House, 2017), Jeremy McCarter profiles the contributions of women off the radar of national fame and not necessarily in textbooks, who nonetheless helped to lead in the women's suffrage movement. Two of these leaders include Alice Paul, a leader in the American Peace Party active in the early 1900s (pp 162–163) and Rose Winslow who, like Paul, was force-fed in prison after protesting about the lack of women's enfranchisement (pp 200–203).

93   The 4 Catastrophes, Martin Luther King (Consortium News, February 27,2021 https://consortiumnews.com

94   For Urban Youth Collaborative see https://www.urbanyouthcollaborative.org Washington Heights and Inwood Teen Council…

I have observed these comments and work while attending meetings at the council. For the teen council, see https://www.facebook.com/Washington-Heights-and-Inwood-Youth-Council-613560715337855

95   For Urban Youth Collaborative see https://www.urbanyouthcollaborative.org Washington Heights and Inwood Teen Council... I have observed these comments and work while attending meetings at the council. For the teen council, see https://www.facebook.com/Washington-Heights-and-Inwood-Youth-Council-613560715337855

96   Tobacco marketing anonymous... describes a teen-led campaign in Florida in the 1990s against the tobacco industry. Tina Rosenberg, in her book, Join the Club (Norton and Company, 2011), describes how teen leaders assisted in lowering smoking rates amongst youth. Earlier attempts had been unsuccessful after being conceived and led by adults. See Ms. Rosenberg's notes on the successful teen campaign, which used the exposure of marketing practices and the hidden agenda for tobacco company profits to motivate record levels of teen participation in the campaign and lowering of smoking rates amongst youth. Ms. Rosenberg describes the teen-led anti-smoking campaign called Rage against the Haze, on pp 55, 56, and 81).

97   The propagation of negative labels describing teens... is a theme of a book by Mike A. Males called Framing Youth (Common Courage Press, 1999). The research and advocacy for teens still serves as a model on how diligent research and enthusiastic advocacy, when practiced by teen leaders, can help to move adults away from the delusions of negative stereotypes about teens. Two samples from this book include sections titled "Teens are Violent Thugs" (pp 283–285) and "Teen Moms are Ruining America" (pp 179–182).

98   But teens are not capable... is an example of generalized statements about teen efficacy which are not true, but still held on to by some

adults even when faced with evidence about the inaccuracy of this diminishing type of distortion. The National Association of Youth Courts is one example of an adult civic enterprise which has helped to bust negative stereotypes. This organization has advocated for and helped to organize Youth Courts, which have an established record of providing positive alternatives to punitive sanctions for first-time offenders. Peer courts nurture a respect for law amongst youth, encourage civic engagement by youth, and foster responsibility for their own actions using positive peer pressure. (Pressure created when youth serve as judges and jurors). For information on youth courts: https://youthcourts.net/the-signficance-of-youth-courts .

99   Assumptions held by adults that teens are not aware enough, or suitably well-informed, to serve as advisors to elected officials in municipal government have been reflected in statements I heard frequently by those skeptical about teens serving on community boards. In some cases, when I had conversations with skeptics showing proof that teens had been doing this for decades in other cities, their intransigence on this persisted. One sample of the historical record profiling teen civic capabilities was sharing the annual Policy and Budget Priorities put together by youth serving on the San Francisco Youth Commission. Individual youth members report to the Board of Supervisors, after meeting amongst themselves in committee work. Examples of some youth proposals that were considered and then approved by the Board of Supervisors include Priority # 6: Free Muni for Youth: Priority # 9, calling for improved dialogue between law enforcement authorities and representative of youth-led agencies. The city government also approved the production of a pamphlet for youth called Know Your Rights. See https://sfgov.org/youthcommission .

100   Participatory voting opportunities are listed on the websites of each city council member participating in the program. In November 2021, there are NYC elections which will result in the replacement

of sitting council members with new office holders, as result of NYC code limiting elected officials to two consecutive terms. See https://council.nyc.gov/pb

101   Adults as advocates for teens… research disproving the unsupported "fact" proposing that raging hormones and undeveloped brains are the cause for teen problems. For two samples of this research, see The Myth of the Teen Brain by Thomas Likona (www.mercatornet.com) and Debunking the Myth of Adolescence by Daniel Offer, M.D. et al in the Academy of Child and Adolescent Psychiatry (Volume 31, No. 6). For Thomas Likona article, see https://www.researchgate.net/publication/240227089_The_Myth_of_the_Teen_Brain For Dr. Offer's article, see https://www.jaacap.org

102   Self-protected enclaves are one of the many concerns shared by Alexis De Tocqueville even as he admired our propensity for local self-rule. As pointed out by Isaac Kramnick in his introduction to the book Alexis De Tocqueville: Democracy in America (Penguin Books, 2003), De Tocqueville stated: "(He was concerned about) the subtler despotism of public opinion in America…The individual is irresistibly pressured in America to accept the opinions of the multitude, since public opinion surrounds, directs and oppresses. De Tocqueville knew of no other country where there is generally less independence of thought and real freedom of debate than in America." (pg xxix) This observation struck me, given that the American people congregate in segregated conditions according to class and class, and depend on news sources which keep people attuned in ideological bubbles with extreme and unforgiving viewpoints.

103   The mind once enlightened… was a phrase used by Thomas Paine. It expressed a belief that once a person adopts a position established through the faculty of reason, they will not return to superstition or subscribe to unsubstantiated beliefs. See The Life and Major

Writings of Thomas Paine (Citadel Press, 1974) which is edited with commentary by Philip S. Foner. In the introduction to this book, Mr. Foner summarizes the origins of this type of thought which inspired Paine and other founders such as Benjamin Franklyn: "He was influenced by the intellectual revolution achieved by Newton and Locke in their discovery of a systematic and harmonious universe whose laws can be ascertained by human reason" (pg xxxvii).

104   "Life on fire, and a struggle to grow up" is a line from Time magazine's editorial notes in their twentieth anniversary edition looking back on the 1960s. As they continue in their description of the generation arising in the 60s: "The spasms almost seemed psychologically coordinated, as if a mysterious common impulse had swept through the nervous system of an entire generation: challenge authority, change the world." (Time Magazine, Special Issue, Spring 1989). This line strikes me as apropos in describing the generation arising today, although, as I will describe in the Introduction chapter and Anecdotes Arising, their common impulse seems to be imbued with a lot more common sense than that which we rabble rousers possessed in the 1960s. https://time.com

105   "Life on fire, and a struggle to grow up" is a line from Time magazine's editorial notes in their twentieth anniversary edition looking back on the 1960s. As they continue in their description of the generation arising in the 60s: "The spasms almost seemed psychologically coordinated, as if a mysterious common impulse had swept through the nervous system of an entire generation: challenge authority, change the world." (Time Magazine, Special Issue, Spring 1989). This line strikes me as apropos in describing the generation arising today, although, as I will describe in the Introduction chapter and Anecdotes Arising, their common impulse seems to be imbued with a lot more common sense than that which we rabble rousers possessed in the 1960s. https://time.com

106   Censorship of student voice is still a practice being challenged today. See the article by Nanette Asimov in the April 26, 2019, edition of the San Francisco Chronicle: Stockton Teacher Battles District Over (A Student Produced) Article On Student Porn." Unlike with my high-school experience, in this case a teacher is defending a student's right to express a controversial point of view, and not crushing it. See San Francisco Chronicle site at https://www.sfchronicle.com

107   Male, pale, and stale" is a quip I would hear from Scott Stringer, who is now the Comptroller for New York City. He would visit a local Democratic Club in Uptown Manhattan, named the Obama Democratic Club of Upper Manhattan, and share his frustration with decisions made for all New Yorkers by small groups of elites who were not representative of the diverse peoples in our city.

108   Black Lives Matter organizing face-to-face hearings. One of the strategies organized by BLM, as well as other dissident groups challenging the roots and practices of injustice, is to engage with policy makers with smaller, face-to-face conversations, not in place of but in addition to the large rallies which protesters from my time in the 1960s depended upon. For coverage of one example of this dissent expressed in conversation and not just confrontation, see "Rebellion's Work" by Jamon Jordon in YES! Magazine (Fall 2020, Issue 95) pp 16–25. See Yes! Magazine site at https://yesmagazine.org

109   The Image: A Guide to Pseudo Events in America… is the name of a body of work produced by Daniel J. Boorstin under the same title. (First Vintage Books, 1992). Mr. Boorstin describes how issues come to be defined, and movements launched, based upon ideas which are organized to manipulate people towards pre-defined outcomes determined by self-serving groups of people. The whole book describes episodes in which these strategies have been used. He outlines the elements of a pseudo-event as having four central

features: "1. Something that is not spontaneous, but rather planned, planted or incited; 2. It is planted primarily (but not exclusively) for the immediate purpose of being reported or reproduced; 3. It's relation to the underlying reality of the situation is ambiguous; and 4. Usually it is intended to be a self-fulfilling prophesy" (pp 11–12). These essential qualities could be applied to the attack in the Gulf of Tonkin, (which was misrepresented) justifying our country's expansion of the war in Vietnam, as well as the evidence supposedly presented (the validity of that evidence was later found to be at least highly ambiguous) that Iraq was a clear and present danger to world peace prior to our invasion of that nation.

110   A past that is instrumental and not coercive is a plea made by the anthropologist Margaret Meade in her book, Coming of Age in Samoa (Perennial Classics, 2001). In her study of relationships between an incumbent generation and those in a new generation being trained to govern one day, she compared some practices in the South Pacific Islands with those practiced in "advanced nations." In one line of her book, urging those training the young to be sensitive to their needs in a changing world, she states: "We must turn all of our educational efforts to training our children for the choices which will confront them. Education, instead of being a pleading for one regime, or a desperate attempt to adopt one habit of mind, should train children to be prepared for all outside influences, allowing them to choose wisely and be healthy in mind and body" (pg 169).

111   Teen-citizen identity movements arising today are using cultural resources to help better understand the nuances of organizing. Youthprise, a civic awareness project organized by students at the University of Minnesota, has produced a civic awareness guide under the stewardship of Humphrey Fellow Paul Sheth. A few models they shared include: 1). Defend Black Lives—cultural organizing. org which posts the works of civil rights artists; 2). A distinction between equality and equity. Under models of equality, all schools

would receive equal funding. Under an equity model, some schools would receive additional funding to make up for opportunity gaps. 3). Understanding the discriminatory continuity in history, that is, from slavery to Jim Crow, to redlining. See https://youthprise.org

112   Comments are found in the Police Athletic League IN-STEP Yearbook, 2005–2006 edition. The pages in this yearbook are not numbered, but student experience with peer leadership is commented upon by members of the IN-STEP program throughout the book. See https://www.palnyc.org/

113   Health disparities between Blacks and Whites result from socially constructed discrimination and not from inherent physiological/biological cause. The resultant differentials result in deficits of available opportunities, and even the capacity to take advantage of opportunities. Black people, living in under-served and segregated communities have higher rates of diabetes, hyper-tension, and heart disease. Black children have 500 per cent higher death rates from asthma compared to White children. See the source: Health Disparities Between Blacks and Whites Run Deep, Harvard T.H. Chen School of Public Health. Authors of this study were David Williams, Florence Norman, and Laura Smart. (2010) Website: https://www.hsph.harvard.edu

114   The effects of trauma on body and soul. In The Body Keeps the Score(Penguin Books, 2014) by Bessel Van Der Kolk, M.D., numerous studies are covered showing the disastrous and long-lasting damage caused by trauma. One study covered was covered in the American Journal of Preventative Medicine (Volume 14, No. 4, V Fellitini, et al), which shows how adverse childhood experiences affect adults even much later in life. According to this study, "Women who had an early history of abuse and neglect were seven times more likely to be raped in adulthood… and children who had witnessed their mothers being assaulted by their partners had vastly increased

chance to be victims of domestic violence." The Body Keeps the Score (Penguin Books, 2014, pg 87). Studies produced by the NYU School of Health and by the NYC Department of Youth and Community Development have documented that up to 90 percent of Black and Latino children have either directly experienced trauma or have been subject to influence by close family members and friends who have been victims of trauma. Each of these agencies has advised that no intervention with children should lack thorough consideration and intervention, which is not advised by what they call Trauma Intervention strategies.

Poorly constructed research and testing results in erroneously applied policies. Sander L. Gilman and James M. Thomas have documented the dangerous effects created in the link between poor academic studies and policies based upon those findings. In their book, Are Racists Crazy? (NY University Press, 2016, pg. 73), they tell a story about intelligence testing which became mainstream in the early 1900s. Henry A. Goddard, who was recognized as a leading authority on intelligence testing at the time, claimed that he had tested average immigrants from various subgroups with intelligence testing measures. His sample was chosen from people who had been in prison or had been hospitalized with serious adverse conditions. He evaluated these targets, and then generalized about whole sub-groups of ethnically diverse populations. He concluded that "80% of Hungarians, 79% of Italians, 87% of Russians and 83% of Jews were morons." In 1924, government leaders, influenced by findings such as Goddard's passed restrictive immigration laws to protect the sanctity of American progress (pp 90–91).

115   War and the Soul, by Edward Tick, Ph.D. (Quest Books, 2005), pp 5–7

116   Ibid War and the Soul, by Edward Tick, Ph.D. (Quest Books, 2005), pp 5–7.

117   These comments are from my recollection of a DYCD Conference co-sponsored by the NYU School of Health at the NY Law School in 2008.

118   To Know As We Are Known, by Parker J. Palmer (Harper& Row, 1983) pg 9 ("Calling us in our accountability and mutuality") and pg 32 ("knowing becomes a reunion of separated beings whose primary bond is love").

119   To Know As We Are Known, by Parker J. Palmer (Harper& Row, 1983) pg 9 ("Calling us in our accountability and mutuality") and pg 32 ("knowing becomes a reunion of separated beings whose primary bond is love").

120   Haven in A Heartless World (Basic Books, ISBN 0465038845) by Christopher Lasch is the original source. I found the quote at www.goodreads.com/book/show/724188.Haven-in-a-heartless-world .

121   Shelter in Place Drills are exercises for public safety in buildings where a safe space for keeping out of harm's way are used either in the event of an armed intruder or presence of a person of danger outside of the building. Two shelter-in drills are mandated each calendar year by the New York State Office of Children and Families as per their Part 414 regulations. 414.2(a)(4) and 414.2 (a) 10. Find more at https://www.ocfs.ny.gov/programs/childcare/regulations .

122   Intelligence Reframed (Basic Books, 1999), Howard Gardner. Defining multiple intelligences, pp 27–46.

123   Intelligence Reframed Ibid. Using multiple intelligences in schools, pp 135–155.

124   See Are Racists Crazy? How Prejudice, Racism and Antisemitism Became Markers of Insanity, Sander L. Gilman and James M. Thomas (New York University Press, 2016) pp 2-4 and pp 89-90.

125 See Are Racists Crazy? How Prejudice, Racism and Antisemitism Became Markers of Insanity, Sander L. Gilman and James M. Thomas (New York University Press, 2016) pp 2-4 and pp 89-90.

126 On the overuse and misapplication of testing. See Beyond Measure: Rescuing an overscheduled, over tested, underestimated generation, by Vicki Abeles with Grace Rubenstein (Simon & Schuster, 2015) pp 97 – 111.

127 As socio-economic status goes, so go Scholastic Aptitude Test scores. In his book, The Schools Our Children Deserve (Houghton Mifflin, 1999), educator Alfie Kohn cited a study which showed a correlation between a student's family socio/economic status, and the measure of their SAT score. "For students living in a family with an income of $10,000 or less, the average score was 873; with an income between $10,000 and $ 20,000, the average score was 918; between $20,000 and $ 30,000, the average score was 972; between $ 70,000 and $ 80,000 the average score was 1,062; and for incomes of $ 100,000 plus the average score was 1,130." (pg 262, note 4).

128 Creativity (Harper Perennial, 1996) by Mihaly Csikszentmihalyi. See specifically the section titled "creating creative environments", pp 139 -147.

129 A curriculum called CLASS is used by the Police Athletic League Head Start Program. This guide helps teachers ensure students having an increased probability for early childhood students enjoying school success. The United States Congress created an intensive education and social-emotional learning program called Head Start in 1965. This model has been adopted in selected early childhood programs, but its availability is not made available for all pre-school children. According to long-term studies on the impact of Head Start programs, which uses a CLASS curriculum, application of its suggested lesson plans is having "strong social/emotion support, strong classroom organization, supportive instructional guidance, and

guidance for productive parent-child relationships which supports optimal outcomes for young children. ("Use Of CLASS Assessment In Head Start," June 12, 2019, cited from Police Athletic League Head Start training program). www.palnyc.org

130   Enhanced education opportunities, and support for a new generation, requires thinking with a new level of consciousness... transcending the limitations of our mechanistic/industrial age and moving forward with ecological/spiritual sense. Michael Schacker, in his book, Global Awakening (Park Street Press, 2013), speaks to the need to move from old institutional agendas to evolved ways of thinking. As Mr. Schacker writes in his critique of militarized mindsets, "Endless stories of war and national chauvinism only perpetuate a culture of war. What we need are stories that nurture the healing culture of peace" (p 67). He cites Albert Einstein in support of his assertion: "You can't solve a problem on the same level that it was created. You have to rise above it to the next" (pg 11), In Creativity, Mihaly Csikszentmihalyi concurs: "Creativity generally refers to the act of changing a source or aspect of a domain—to painting a picture that reveals new ways of seeing." (Harper, The Domain of the Future, 1996), pp 291–292.

131   Enhanced education opportunities, and support for a new generation, requires thinking with a new level of consciousness... transcending the limitations of our mechanistic/industrial age and moving forward with ecological/spiritual sense. Michael Schacker, in his book, Global Awakening (Park Street Press, 2013), speaks to the need to move from old institutional agendas to evolved ways of thinking. As Mr. Schacker writes in his critique of militarized mindsets, "Endless stories of war and national chauvinism only perpetuate a culture of war. What we need are stories that nurture the healing culture of peace" (pg 67). He cites Albert Einstein in support of his assertion: "You can't solve a problem on the same level that it was created. You have to rise above it to the next" (pg 11), In

Creativity, Mihaly Csikszentmihalyi concurs: "Creativity generally refers to the act of changing a source or aspect of a domain—to painting a picture that reveals new ways of seeing." (Harper, The Domain of the Future, 1996), pp 291–292.

132   Dr. Stephanie Marango and the astrologer Rebecca Gordon speak about inner energies and stars as role models... or as the ancients say, as inside, so outside. In addition to receiving counsel from Dr. Marango in 2013 with her The Doctor Is In Sessions, I have had sage advice from her in conversations and online course interactions. Dr. Marango is spiritual diagnostician who follows the advice of indigenous healers to use one's inner wisdom to heal oneself. She has emphasized with me that the messages we receive from our unconscious, our bodies, and our hearts are often expressed in very subtle ways, but that this does not make them any less powerful or relevant. She also pointed out that with free will, we get to choose to respond to and use the energetics we receive, and that when we stay passive, sometimes the energy chooses us. In my early days of running youth programs, Enoch Stackhouse, who was an aide to then-Assemblyman Herman 'Denny' Farrell, and a supporter of my program, used to kid me about how people I could use to assist me would just seem to show up. He gave me the nickname, Magic Man. In a similar vein, when I had first met Rebecca Gordon at a random and spontaneous session, I shared with her some solar information on a civic colleague who seemed extremely interested in teen enfranchisement. Rebecca told me that this person had some solar indicators which closely aligned with mine. She said, in jest, that these were so close that she felt jealous. This person so closely aligned to me showed indicators in her reading that corresponded closely to sectors in my reading associated with service and influencing many people on a social issue. This person is Sarah Andes, who became my closest civic associate in our Teens On Board campaign. Dr. Marango has moved on since the days of her the Doctor Is In

mentoring clinics, although many of her techniques and practices are incorporated into her present-day approach. For her current work see https://www.stephaniemarangomd.com Ms. Andes work with Generation Citizen will be covered in the Civic Lover section of this book.

133   "The fourth chakra is the physical center of our spiritual anatomy, and it governs the heart." These are words written by Carolyn Myss in her book, Invisible Acts of Power (Free Press, 2004) pg 26. As Ms. Myss continues, "Our heart's primary task, of course, is to recognize our own spirit in every stranger and to 'love our neighbor as ourselves'" pg 27. When I felt that I was living in the center of this energy, good times just seemed to flow. When obstacles arose, reading and reacting from my heart seemed to give me the energy to persist until problems faded and promise reappeared.

134   See the website for the Heart Math Institute - https://www.heartmath.org/

135   Alternative designs for intelligence testing See the website describing the approach used by the Structure of Intellect https://www.instructionaldesign.org/theories/intellect/

136   The Mysteries Curriculum The Crossroads School Human Development Department by Shelley Kessler (The Mysteries Sourcebook, 1922-1990), Chapter I, pp 1-14. I was introduced to this curricular approach in 1994. For an updated look on how this curriculum has been applied at the Crossroads School in Santa Monica today, see the Crossroads School site and their section on a curriculum overview at https://www.crossroadsacademy.org

137   The Mysteries Sourcebook Ibid pp iii – v. This is cited from the sourcebook I was given in 1994.

138   Fires in the Mind (Jossey-Bass, 2010) by Kathleen Cushman and the What Can Kids Do Club. On out of school commitments, see pg 8.

139   Fires in the Mind Ibid pg 8.

140   Civic discussions between parents and children build civic-minded dispositions... In a journal article titled "The Influence of Family Discussion on Youth Civic Development," authors Hugh McIntosh, Daniel Hart, and James Younis postulate that civic discussions in families contribute to the development of civic competence is the young (Journal of the American Political Science Association, July 2007). In their article they state: "Evidence suggests that the growth of civic roots in adolescence may be crucial to the long-term development of citizenship...and one interesting finding is...the apparent importance of discussion to the development of civic competence" pg 495. In youth service programs where, adult mentors become second parents to the young, and where youth facilities feel like a second home, involvement in civic affairs has helped teens to become more rooted in their communities, as well as feeling confident about their own civic efficacy. See the Wiley online Library at https://www.onlinelibrary.wiley.com

141   Collaboration For Student Success is the title of a 2009 survey administered by Met Life. A sample of this survey is in Appendix A of the book Fires in the Mind). Met Life documented the positive effects of guided practice, which they called the Practice Project (pg 159). Met Life also took care to acknowledge the contributions of students for this project (pp 173–175). See notes 138 and 139 above.

142   Generation Citizen promotes generosity with adult mentor's civic spirit and the through encouraging the capacity to make a difference by youth. Tara Kini, who is a social studies teacher at the Buena Vista Horace Mann School, partnered with Generation Citizen to create an Action Civics program in her classroom. In her observations about the impact of this program, she stated: "By learning about our system of government in a project-based, firsthand way, my students learned the skills they will need to meaningfully participate

in democracy." In surveys administered by Generation Citizen in their programs across the country, the responses showed that "79% of students improved their civic knowledge; 73% improved their civic skills; and 82% now believe in the power of collective change." See Generation Citizen website: Spotlight 2018–2019. https://generationcitizen.org .

143   Police Athletic League's (PAL) Project-Based Learning approach and its impact on obtaining civic skills. PAL adopted a project-based civics curriculum from the Association of Supervision and Curriculum Development during the years 2004–2007. There are four key objectives identified in this curriculum critical to becoming effective civic actors: 1). Demonstrate effective people skills.

2). Identify and assess appropriate alternatives when taking a course of action. 3). Learn to apply academic skills in a variety of contexts. 4). Students learn and apply strong content knowledge outlined in the common core standards for social studies and learn to appreciate them from various perspectives. www.palnyc.org

144   Global Kids programs emphasize the connections between inter-cultural appreciation and the development of twenty-first-century leadership skills. As stated by then Executive Director for Global Kids, Evie Hantzopoulos, "Our youth participants, also known as Global Kids Leaders, are the guiding force behind the organization's mission and management. Two students and one graduate are on our Board of Directors each year. Through these programs, we have observed that youth develop leadership skills that positively impact their community." From everyday activities to board directives, it is the energies of diversity and multi-cultural wisdom which blend into a universally appreciated guiding force. This quote is extracted from a support letter for the Teens on Board initiative by Ms. Hantzopoulos in 2013. https://globalkids.org

145   Manhattan Borough President Gale Brewer attests… the test of effective teen leadership has already been tested in cities across the USA—with productive results. While Ms. Brewer was still a city council person (District 6 in Manhattan–circa 2008), she was still the governmental mentor for our Teens on Board campaign. In her letter of support, and in many speaking engagements to constituents and to her council colleagues, Ms. Brewer pointed out that what already works in other cities can also be successfully applied in New York City: "Many states, including Massachusetts and Maryland, have already involved 16- and 17-year-old students in their governments. Since 1974, Maryland state school boards have an open seat for a senior student each year. In Massachusetts, a student member serves each year, and has the same voting power as all board members." (Gale Brewer support letter for Teens on Board, June 30, 2008. gbrewer@manhattanbp.nyc.gov

146   Manhattan Borough President Gale Brewer attests… the test of effective teen leadership has already been tested in cities across the USA—with productive results. While Ms. Brewer was still a city council person (District 6 in Manhattan–circa 2008), she was still the governmental mentor for our Teens on Board campaign. In her letter of support, and in many speaking engagements to constituents and to her council colleagues, Ms. Brewer pointed out that what already works in other cities can also be successfully applied in New York City: "Many states, including Massachusetts and Maryland, have already involved 16- and 17-year-old students in their governments. Since 1974, Maryland state school boards have an open seat for a senior student each year. In Massachusetts, a student member serves each year, and has the same voting power as all board members." (Gale Brewer support letter for Teens on Board, June 30, 2008. gbrewer@manhattanbp.nyc.gov

147   Data found on the Search Institute website. For an example, find the Search Institute findings concerning what they call internal assets

and external assets needed by teen for holistic development and fruitful relationships with adults. Many of these assets were identified as being lacking in teens and adolescent-adult relationships after the Institute conducted a national survey with 6,000 teens across the United States in 2020. Internal assets included having a feeling of personal power over one's life. External assets included having confidence in interpersonal relationships with adults. To see the full results of this survey, see www.searchinstitute.org

148   See Pioneering the Possible: Awakened Leadership for A World That Works by Scilla Elworthy, Ph.D. (North Atlantic Books, 2014) pp 171 and 172.

149   Credible messengers must be included in the ranks of communal civic participation… In 2016, The National Academy of Sciences, Engineering and Medicine held a workshop on "Community Violence as a Population Health Issue," which was coordinated by Darla Thompson and her colleagues. At the conference, one of the speakers, Howard Pinderglass from the UC San Francisco School of Nursing, testified about proposed change coming from the bottom up: "Change is not about the government stepping in and taking control. Community members need to be actively involved in decision making that informs community change." Constructing spaces and processes where informed youth can participate in community decision-making is a ritual long practiced by traditional cultures. Malidoma Patrice Some is a medicine man in his Dagara tribe in Burkina Faso, Africa, and holds three master's degrees and two doctorates from the Sorbonne and Brandeis University. He had this to say about the crucial place of ritual in the lives of the young as well as for adult community members: 'Where ritual is absent, the young one's are restless or violent, there are no real elders, and the grownups are bewildered. The future is dim.'" (Ritual: Power, Healing and Community by Malidoma Patrice Some. Penguin Press, 1993). See

https://note.nep.edu/2018/03/01/violence-related-research for the Academy of Science notes.

150   Pablo Vasquez, a young adult, and a mentor to fellow teens. This note is based upon my fond memories and appreciation for his selfless contributions to PAL and to the uptown community. Pablo came up through the Police Athletic League site at the Washington Heights Armory. As a teen, he assisted staff with after-school activities, and as a young adult was appointed by supervisors as a Group Leader. While still a teen, he participated in the PAL Project-Based Learning programs, and helped to gather letters and petitions in support of the Teens on Board campaign. He also went on to become an advisor and a mentor to young people involved with the Washington Heights and Inwood Teen Advisory Council.

151   Communication about one's democratic assets must be adjusted for audiences and cultivated as attitudes amongst change-makers. Meira Levinson, Associate Professor of Education at the Harvard Graduate School of Education, in her book, No Citizen Left Behind (Harvard University Press, 2012), presents anecdotes profiling best practices in teaching youth the skills and understandings for becoming participants in community improvement and democratic change. One point that she makes is that for students from "minority" populations, such as Black and Latino students, to be heard in a coherent fashion by audiences composed of "majority populations," they must practice the skill of what is called "code-switching." Language-based nuances are different, depending upon one's racial, ethnic, or national background origin, and words or concepts with seemingly obvious meaning may be interpreted in differing ways. For instance, the words "community service" may mean engaging in a voluntary activity to help one's school and community in some circles, but for those involved in the criminal justice system, it may mean government-mandated alternatives to sentencing. (Code-switching, pp 87- 92). Another point raised in the Cultivating Democracy book is

one by Aaron Watson, who was a lawyer and the former president of Atlanta's Board of Education. As Watson is noted as practicing in this book - it is important to own an aspirational and self-assertive attitude when engaged in the work of social justice. In his relationships to students and their advocacy, Watson lets them know that "You have a right, and an opportunity to struggle, and a right, and an opportunity to succeed." pg 123 In other words, when teachers encourage and facilitate the right of offering self-determined advocacy, this provides young people to opportunity to offer what Levinson calls " a living narrative'. pg 123 This civic opportunity assumes the right to hold positive expectations, and the right to resist when opportunities are blocked or denied are inherent to being a human, seeking to match one's reality at least closer to their dreams.

152   Communication about one's democratic assets must be adjusted for audiences and cultivated as attitudes amongst change-makers. Meira Levinson, in her book, No Citizen Left Behind (Harvard University Press, 2012), presents anecdotes profiling best practices in teaching youth the skills and understandings for becoming participants in community improvement and democratic change. One additional point that she makes in her code- switching observations is that students from "minority" populations, such as Black and Latino students, need to be coherently heard by audiences comprising "majority populations," As Ms. Levinson points out, " …instead of teaching kids that they do things wrong, or that they and their families have nothing to offer the world of school or a wider public, educators should teach codeswitching as a powerful tool that kids can use in addition to their 'home languages' and their cultural forms and knowledge." Pg 88 Language-based nuances are different, depending upon one's racial, ethnic, or national background origin, and words or concepts with seemingly obvious meaning may be interpreted in differing ways. I have observed instances in mixed audiences, where the words "community service" may mean

engaging in a voluntary activity to help one's school and community in some circles, but for those involved in the criminal justice system, it may mean government-mandated alternatives to sentencing.

153   Explorer Post #280 won the Top Job Award. The award ceremony took place at home plate (in Shea Stadium). When the NY Mets and Proctor and Gamble created the Top Job Award, the intent was to reward youth groups engaged in commitment to community that resulted in observable positive change. Teen members in Explorer Post #280 came to believe that each one of them could be effective, even when facing challenging odds, and that teamwork increased the odds of success. When the Post's youth members marched behind the American flag to home plate at Shea Stadium, the eyes of corporate America, established major league stars, and admiring fans cheered them on, providing a public stage for recognizing the dignity of their humble work. (NYC Scout Magazine, Greater NY Council: Boy Scouts # 345.

154   The unmuting of students and their communities is spoken to by social justice education advocate Maxine Greene in her introduction to the book Teaching for Social Justice (New Press, 1990, Ayers et al). She states the case that motivation needs to be expressed in affirmed voice that is heard by authority: "What situations can be created to motivate students to combat the endless process of silencing found in so many schools—what Michelle Fine calls the muting of students and their communities?" In schools, and communities, the key words are "create situations," because both in schools and in under-served communities, voices need to be not only heard, but also provided a strategic means for turning critique into constructive solutions (pg xxxi).

155   Attaining change assumes owning the means of production for change. Jeffrey Stout, in his book titled Blessed Are the Organized: Grassroots Democracy in America (Princeton University Press,

2010) quotes Donna Rodriquez, who was a community organizer in Brownsville, Texas, about the need to own the space to set the pace of change. In her words of advice to other community organizers, she recommends that they "be in charge of the meeting place and be able to set the agenda" (pg 97).

156   Attaining change assumes owning the means of production for change. Jeffrey Stout, in his book titled Blessed Are the Organized: Grassroots Democracy in America (Princeton University Press, 2010) quotes Donna Rodriquez, who was a community organizer in Brownsville, Texas, about the need to own the space to set the pace of change. In her words of advice to other community organizers, she recommends that they "be in charge of the meeting place and be able to set the agenda" (pg 97).

157   Attaining change assumes owning the means of production for change. Jeffrey Stout, in his book titled Blessed Are the Organized: Grassroots Democracy in America (Princeton University Press, 2010) quotes Donna Rodriquez, who was a community organizer in Brownsville, Texas, about the need to own the space to set the pace of change. In her words of advice to other community organizers, she recommends that they "be in charge of the meeting place and be able to set the agenda" (pg 97).

158   Humanistic psychology is guided by a philosophy of counseling (or teaching)—learning to listen and learn from who traditional counselors call patients. Carl Rogers, who was a humanistic psychologist, emphasized the need for a therapist not only to just hear a person describing problems, but also to listen for their perspective and co-counsel. As Dr. Rogers describes many moments in his practice: "Time and time again, I have seen simple people become significant and creative in their own spheres as they have developed more trust in the processes going on within themselves in unique ways. They have become those who live by the values they have discovered

within" (On Becoming A Person by Carl Rogers (Houghton-Mifflin, 1961), pp 108–109. Empathetic civic co-mentors have also learned that youth members with whom they work provide crucial guidance and wisdom for communal problem-solving.

159   On chasing one's inner tail (and hidden tales) … is another take on the process of projection with one's unseen shadow that is discussed by Anodea Judith. Sometime the enemies whom we identify outside of ourselves are not a problem, rather it is the shadow of unresolved issues within. Inner shadow boxing leads us to expend energy chasing down false targets. In her revised edition of Eastern Body, Western Mind (Celestial Arts, 2004), she describes the process of projection as an unconscious casting call for repressed instinctual energies, which results in a lot of drama with others on one's stage of life. As Ms. Judith states: "The shadow represents repressed instinctual energies locked away in the realm of the unconscious. They do not die or cease to function. They are enacted unconsciously, sometimes with great force. The shadow chases us in our dreams… and sabotages our work and relationships…energizing compulsive activities" (pg 116). Put another way, the shadow does not die and causes us to live with the consequences of our lie. They do not cease to function, but they do increase the probability of dysfunctional consequences. They chase us in our dreams and induce us to create living nightmares.

160   On chasing one's inner tail (and hidden tales) … is another take on the process of projection with one's unseen shadow that is discussed by Anodea Judith. In her revised edition of Eastern Body, Western Mind (Celestial Arts, 2004), she describes the process of projection as an unconscious casting call for repressed instinctual energies, which results in a lot of drama with others on one's stage of life. As Ms. Judith states: "The shadow represents repressed instinctual energies locked away in the realm of the unconscious. They do not die or cease to function. They are enacted unconsciously,

sometimes with great force. The shadow chases us in our dreams…
and sabotages our work and relationships…energizing compulsive
activities" (pg 116). Put another way, the shadow does not die and
causes us to live with the consequences of our lie. They do not cease
to function, but they do increase the probability of dysfunctional
consequences. They chase us in our dreams and induce us to create
living nightmares.

161   The Jungian psychologist James Hillman describes White supremacy
as a "self-contained psychic reservoir" where suppressed anxiety
and inner hatred is projected onto Black people. He states that it
is "present in white consciousness itself, even before it is projected
onto others." White supremacy utilizes the unacknowledged angst
to produce undeserved anger toward Black people that "de-con-
structs everything" in fantasized terms. It can yet "allow each thing
to reveal itself in its fullness," but only after taking ownership and
responsibility for the psychic and social construction of White
supremacy. This is a citation from the introduction to the writings
of James Hillman by Thomas Moore, the editor of this book, Blue
Fire: Selected Writings of James Hillman (Harper Perennial, 1991),
pg 8.

162   On the unexamined power of self-righteousness and construction
of the scapegoat. Silvia B. Pereira, in her essay called the Scapegoat
Archetype, describes the misdirected acts of those engaged in projection and the misfortunes of those who are falsely recreated as
scapegoats. As Ms. Pereira explains the scapegoat process: "(When)
individuals and groups (are falsely) accused of creating misfortune,
this serves to relieve others (the scapegoaters) of their own responsibilities. This strengthens the scapegoaters' sense of power and righteousness." Ms. Pereira continues with the resultant consequences
for those who have been scapegoated: "When individuals are identified as scapegoats, they suffer the symptoms of negative inflation,
exile, and splitting." When scapegoating is allowed to endure in the

dysfunctional times in our nation's history, the bootstrap has been rendered as only the whip, and the property of individual responsibility has been surrendering to the destructive tendencies of denial. Perhaps this practice of scapegoating should be subject to a select Congressional committee investigating un-American activity.

163   The unbearable heaviness of not being (remembered). In his book, The Body Keeps the Score (Penguin Books, 2014), Dr. Bessel Van Der Volk addresses many forums of violence that result in life-long episodes of dysfunction and pain unconsciously associated with trauma. Trauma induced stress leads those in severe pain to censor memories in order to survive. Some of these are instigated by childhood abuse, others by domestic violence, some after suffering severe injury or loss, and many because of being a survivor in the theater of war. In one chapter of his book, which he titles "The unbearable heaviness of remembering," he shares a historical anecdote in which World War I veterans, years after the war ended were still seeking deserved benefits but instead were subject to being turned invisible, and as a final act of betrayal, brutalized and attacked despite their valor. As Mr. Van Der Volk recounts, the government had persisted for decades in "refusing to face the damages caused by the war (i.e., debilitating injuries to vets and justified their lack of response as) an intolerance for weakness." The decade of the 1930s "played a key role in the rise of fascism and militarism around the world (by governments, but in the case of the protest to be described, also ascribed to by some elements amongst the protesters). As Mr. Van Der Kolk continues, "A cascade of humiliations of the powerless set the stage for the ultimate debasement of human rights under the Nazi regime." By the time of the 1932 protest by World War I veterans in Washington D.C., we had been in the beginnings of the great Depression, which caused even more significant harm to veterans struggling with disabling disabilities. The response of the military was severe. As described by Van Der Kolk, "President

Hoover ordered troops to clear out the veteran's encampment; Army Chief of Staff Douglas MacArthur commanded the troops; Major Dwight D. Eisenhower was a liaison to the Washington Police; and Major George Patton oversaw the cavalry. The troops surged in with bayonets and tear gas, and the next morning the encampment was deserted and in flames. The veterans never received their pensions" (pg 188).

164   See Jane Addams and the Dream of American Democracy by Jean Bethke Elshtain (Basic Books, 2002). Ms. Adams celebrates the essential work of ordinary people struggling to enhance their communities. Jane Addams, who helped to found and organize the Settlement House movement in Chicago in the early 1900s, never lost sight of the heroes who made these endeavors for safe housing and pro-active communities' work. As Ms. Addams stated: "If the powerful lose their legitimacy that their authority confers, their power may crumble before their eyes" (p 86)/ In its place, Ms. Addams understood that it is "the growing good in the world which is partly dependent upon the unhistoric acts" of the supposedly powerless and humble (pg 31).

165   Outdated ideas and rule by monarchs, which also impairs the development of democratic governance, is a theme repeatedly alluded to in the works of Thomas Paine. Mr. Paine often refers to the monarchal ruler's situation of confusion and the condition of despair by those who suffer from the effects of unresponsive and ineffective rulership. Christopher Hitchens, in his book, Thomas Paine's Rights of Man: A Biography (Grove Press, 2006) offers this quote by Thomas Paine: "It (monarchy) appears under all the characters of childhood, decrepitude, dotage, thing of nurse, in leading strings or on crutches." pg 9. Mr. Hitchens cites this quote from the book Tom Paine, A Political Life (Bloomsbury, 1996) pg 451.

166   Explorer Post #280 is a co-ed teen program organized under a teen program division called Explorers by the Greater NYC Boy Scout Council. Each Explorer Post is assigned an ID number. When a youth agency charters an Explorer Post, they also choose a mission under which the Post will operate. For Explorer Post #280, our mission was to develop teens as community coaches and to contribute to the betterment of our community. We developed a program approach which include sports, camping, and community service. https://nycscouting.org

167   Ivy Fairchild and girls' empowerment. Ivy and I had admired the response of girls who had been invited to participate in a short softball season that we had put together. After we had observed players who had initially been somewhat reluctant but willing to try, we knew that young women, once exposed to a positive experience taking them out of their comfort zone (in those days, it was dance and cheerleading which were the primary theaters of exercise for girls), would quickly adopt new attitudes about their joy of being on a playing field. For Ivy and me, after a few enthused conversations, looking forward to the attitudinal shift and the participatory rite of passage was reason enough for us to provide an opportunity for young girls to break through some barriers of exclusion. At the time Ms. Fairchild was the director for Columbia University's Office of Community Relations. https://www.gca.cuimc.columbia.edu

168   The PAL IN-STEP Program partners with the Future Voters of America. After a year of holding trainings and doing advocacy work for lowering the voting age to 16 in New York City municipal elections, a new resolution would be offered to PAL teen leaders and to participants in the Future Voters of America program. The annual Future Voters High School Congress would be jointly sponsored in the spring of 2007, hosted at the PAL Harlem Center. The new resolution introduced proposed lowering the age of eligibility to be appointed to community boards to age 16. I don't have access

to the written records at this period, but written correspondence between members of our Teens on Board Coalition, Gale Brewer, and the New York City Council is reflected in the minutes of a NY City Council hearing after which the full Council would endorse a resolution supporting our goal. Go to the New York City Council website, Committee on Governmental Operations (Ben Kallos, Chairperson) to find the minutes under Worldwide Dictation (June 11, 2014). https://council.nyc.gov

169   The Teens On Board support letter from Councilperson Gale Brewer… this letter of support also listed the agencies in support of the resolution to lower the age to 16 on community boards. The letter of support was submitted on behalf of four Borough Presidents to the Operations Committee at the New York City Council. https://www.manhattanbp.nyc.gov

170   Community Boards enlist their volunteer appointees to serve on two committees during their tenure as a Board member. Committee topics range from Aging, to Parks, to Public Safety to Education and Youth Services. Fe Florimon was, and still is, the Chairperson of the Education and Youth Services Committee at Community Board #12M. For information on Community Boards, go to the website for the NYC Community Assistance Unit at: https://www1.nyc.gov

171   Youth organizations and civic reform agencies who wanted to document support for the Teens on Board campaign submitted letters to our organizing committee. These letters were also forwarded to committee chairs in the State Legislature and to the New York City Council. My go to City Council representative who initiated the effort to gain a City Council resolution of support for our campaign was Mark Levine of City Council District #7. His contact is: https://council.nyc.gov/district7 The NYS Assembly representative who coordinated our campaign to amend the NY State Public Officer

law was Nily Rozic from Queens. Her contact is: https://www.nyas-sembly.gov/mem/Nily-Rozic

172   Scott Warren's biography of Generation Citizen... Generation Citizen: The Power of Youth in Our Politics by Scott Warren (Counterpoint, 2019).

        Scott Warren is a co-founder of Generation Citizen. He was its chief operating officer from the time he founded it in 2009 until the fall of 2020. In his book, Generation Citizen, he reviews his adventures in life leading him towards teen empowerment work, as well as periods of organizational learning, development, and expansion for this beloved brainchild. There is a lot which I relate to in his book. One thought that really struck me was his difficulty in relating to peers with similar demographic profiles as his own because his embedded experiences growing up in cultural milieus different than his own (his father worked for the State Department, and Scott spent time abroad, including in Africa) had changed his expectations and worldview (pg 11). The second is the idea he expounds upon throughout his book. He states that "protest is not enough," and that we must expand our participatory repertoire by optimizing the tools of participatory democracy in order to effect changes in governance. (pg 16).

173   Sarah Andes and the archetype of the engineer. When I refer to the archetype of the engineer, I refer to the description of the engineer developed by Carolyn Myss. For Sarah, I consider her engineering as being applied as a specialist, that of being an architect, a builder, and a schemer. This archetype represents, as written by Ms. Myss, a "learning experience which is a process that guides us throughout our lives". Sacred Contracts: Awakening Our Divine Potential (Three Rivers Press, 2002). See pg 384.

174   NY State Public Officer Law is amended... 16- and 17-year-olds are now eligible to get on board. In the final days of the NY State

legislative session in June of 2014, the agenda was still packed, and bringing attention to a bill with relatively narrow focus was not easy. After the NY State Assembly passed the Public Officer Law amendment, Assemblywoman Nily Rozic (herself a recently elected representative, and the youngest member of her chamber) "lived on the floor of the State Senate"—according to what Borough President Gale Brewer told me. After the State Senate also passed the amendment, it was then passed on to the office of Governor Andrew Cuomo, who signed the bill into law on August 14, 2014. See Nily Rozic contact at: https://www.nyassembly.gov/mem/Nily-Rozic

175   NY State Public Officer Law is amended… 16- and 17-year-olds are now eligible to get on board. In the final days of the NY State legislative session in June of 2014, the agenda was still packed, and bringing attention to a bill with relatively narrow focus was not easy. After the NY State Assembly passed the Public Officer Law amendment, Assemblywoman Nily Rozic (herself a recently elected representative, and the youngest member of her chamber) "lived on the floor of the State Senate"—according to what Borough President Gale Brewer told me. After the State Senate also passed the amendment, it was then passed on to the office of Governor Andrew Cuomo, who signed the bill into law on August 14, 2014. See Nily Rozic contact at: https://www.nyassembly.gov/mem/Nily-Rozic

176   C. Otto Scharmer and his Theory U concept of "presencing" (This is the correct British spelling.)

In the fall of 2020, I came across Mr. Scharmer's book, The Essentials of Theory U (Barrett-Kohler, 2018) for the first time. In reflecting upon his wisdom and advice, I was amazed about how I as well as many civic mentors I had known were already applying his concepts. Some spiritualists refer to this parallel occurrence of practice synchronicity. Mr. Scharmer's theory and suggestions are presented in a deeply coherent and well-organized body of work.

In this book, he elaborates upon his Theory U, and gives specific applications concerning the need to become aware of the process and stages of internal conscious development. Part of this includes practicing what he calls a "cycle of presencing," which includes nurturing curiosity (through opening one's mind), practicing compassion (by opening one's heart), and developing courage (using curiosity and compassion in developing one's will) (pp 29–32, 105–111, 102–106). As written by Mr. Scharmer: "Our capacity to pay attention co-shapes the world. What prevents us from becoming more effective if that we are not fully aware of that interior condition from which our attention and actions originate" (pg 31).

177   Objectionable objections about teens posed by adults… including repetitive phrases describing teens such as "they are not ready yet; they have bad habits and follow poor influences; and they are just disinterested in public affairs." These are comments I heard ad-nauseum repeatedly during my course of teen program service. This type of commentary has been characterized in the book, Madness and Oppression, by the Icarus Project (A Mutual Aid Publication by the Icarus Project, 2015) in a section in which they describe comments such as those above as types of "micro-aggressions" which are typically used against all marginalized peoples. In summary, the Icarus lists these as commentary which "in casual conversation uses negative labeling; is often delivered with impoliteness or rudeness; or (if not) is given through the imposition of unwanted help" (pg 16). What these adults had not yet seen, and what is profiled in this book, are the myriad examples of civic work by teens who are changing history. To quote Meira Levison, a youth empowerment advocate, who works for teen civic involvement supported by empathetic mentors: "History is seen as a conversation, and not a fixed truth. Learn not about citizenship, but through citizenship." (No Citizen Left Behind by Meira Levinson, Harvard University Press, 2012), pg 135).

178   San Francisco Youth Commission and its impact upon LBGTQ policies. In the Commission's Policy and Budget Priorities for 2014–15 and 2015–16, the Youth Commission's executive committee recommended (In Priority 12 of the Budget) … "100 new slots of intensive care management, subsidized employment, and the expansion of housing funds to prevent evictions of LGBTQ youth." See www. SFGov.org/yc LGBTQ committee, pg 33 of Policy and Budget Policy.

179   Dr. Sven Hansen and his theory of resilience corresponds with the work of C. Otto Scharmer and others in linking internal awareness and practices with obtaining desired social and political goals. Dr. Hansen proposes four elements contributing to the establishment of resilience: "1. Bounce back—focus on achievement and not blame; 2. Courage—manifest optimism and not blame; 3. Advance through rejuvenation and novelty; and 4. Respectful engagement with what is inside and outside." (Inside/Out: The Practice of Resilience, The Resilience Institute, 2015, pg 13, for a summary of the four elements, which are further developed in later chapters in the book).

180   Dr. Sven Hansen and his theory of resilience corresponds with the work of C. Otto Scharmer and others in linking internal awareness and practices with obtaining desired social and political goals. Dr. Hansen proposes four elements contributing to the establishment of resilience: "1. Bounce back—focus on achievement and not blame; 2. Courage—manifest optimism and not blame; 3. Advance through rejuvenation and novelty; and 4. Respectful engagement with what is inside and outside." (Inside/Out: The Practice of Resilience, The Resilience Institute, 2015, p 13, for a summary of the four elements, which are further developed in later chapters in the book).

181   PAL Webster Teen Council presentation on homelessness in the Bronx. This teen council had adopted the issue of homelessness in the Bronx, and prepared a PowerPoint presentation, which included

a short video or a PSA on this topic. (PAL IN-STEP program year, spring of 2006 www.palnyc.org

182 Arnstein's Ladder of Participation: development of autonomy and opportunity to fully engage in civic affairs. Ann Taket, in the book Practicing Social Inclusion, describes what getting to the upper rungs of this ladder means: "…achievement of the upper rungs of the ladder has far reaching consequences for those involved: autonomy, how much control you have over your life, and the opportunity you have for full social engagement and participation. (p 5). Arnstein's ladder is cited in Practicing Social Inclusion from the work of S.R. Arnstein (1969), the Journal of Institute Planners, No. 35, pp 216–234.

Practicing Social Inclusion by Ann Taket, et al (Routledge, 2014).

183 On social justice organizers as unsung heroes. This commentary was contributed by Petra Foundation trustee Scott Armstrong in tribute to Petra Shattuck, who celebrated unsung heroes as "one voice in a chorus of those willing to stand up to injustice." Mr. Armstrong is quoted in John Shattuck's introduction to the Petra Foundation Journal: Twenty-Fifth Anniversary Edition. https://www.petrafoundation.org

184 An existential dilemma, shared by my cats and learned by me. In 2016, I had purchased a print and commentary in Union Square. The artist's name is Joey Allgood.

185 Greg Braden is author of the book Resilience from the Heart: The Power to Survive in Life's Extremes (Hay House, 2014). Mr. Braden was the first operations manager for Cisco systems and has done advisory work with the United Nations and Fortune 500 companies. Mr. Braden, as part of his work, has identified practices which help to reinforce a person's resiliency even in particularly challenging times. When working with others in the community, Mr. Braden's method identifies the needs of the whole community. He addresses

questions about why we get together, using our strengths and skills to do as much as we can for ourselves. As we improve ourselves, we do so in complementary ways to others in the community. Mr. Braden's approach emphasizes remaining open to change and transformation, while at the same time respecting ecological limits. (pp 108, 109, and 120).

186   A quote from The Fire Next Time by James Baldwin ("Love takes the mask off") which I found at https://www.goodreads.com/book/show/464260.The_Fire_Next_Time.

187   Southern Heights: Communities Organized for Public Service was a youth program what was approved and funded by what was then called the Department of Youth Services (DYS). Today it is known as the Department of Youth and Community Development. It stayed in operation from December of 1984 until June of 1990. Official records, kept by DYS, about Southern Heights, are no longer in my possession. The approval for this program might be archived in the records kept by Community Board #12 Manhattan, and/or found with a search at www.nyc.gov/site/dycd/index page if they have maintained historical records going back to that time. My reference to this program is largely drawn from my fond memories, a couple of newspaper articles about the program, and a copy of a program calendar produced by Southern Heights in 1989. Maria Luna, in addition to serving on Community Board #12, and as a female district leader for the Democratic Party in uptown Manhattan, would later volunteer to serve as the chairperson for Southern Heights. The contact for Community Board #12Manhattan is: https://cbmanhattan.cityofnewyork.us/cb12

188   Southern Heights: Communities Organized for Public Service was a youth program what was approved and funded by what was then called the Department of Youth Services (DYS). Today it is known as the Department of Youth and Community Development. It stayed

in operation from December of 1984 until June of 1990. Official records, kept by DYS, about Southern Heights, are no longer in my possession. The approval for this program might be archived in the records kept by Community Board #12 Manhattan, and/or found with a search at www.nyc.gov/site/dycd/index page if they have maintained historical records going back to that time. My reference to this program is largely drawn from my fond memories, a couple of newspaper articles about the program, and a copy of a program calendar produced by Southern Heights in 1989. Maria Luna, in addition to serving on Community Board #12, and as a female district leader for the Democratic Party in uptown Manhattan, would later volunteer to serve as the chairperson for Southern Heights. The contact for Community Board #12Manhattan is: https://cbmanhattan.cityofnewyork.us/cb12

189   The regulations in force today governing the operation of afterschool programs can be found at the Office of Children and Family Services site under OCFS New York State Code Part 414. A few sections of this code include Part 414.8: Supervision of Children (pp 17–20); Part 414.13: Staff Qualifications (pp 41–45), and 414.14 Training Requirements (pp 45–47). https://ocfs.ny.gov/main

190   Community board recommendations for funding of youth programs. In the first few years of Southern Heights operations, community boards were required to make recommendations for funding both new and existing programs in rank order of priority for a district. They would derive these recommendations after visits to program sites and interaction with youth agency leadership at committee meetings. Contact for Community Board #12: Paola Garcia at pgarcia01@cb.nyc.gov. With the tireless volunteer support of Coach Dave, Southern Heights would remain in good standing with the Community Board. The contact for Community Board #12Manhatttan is: https://cbmanhattan.cityofnewyork.us/cb12

191   Invaluable allies come in many forms, and Ray Pagan was one who was a best friend to Southern Heights and to the Uptown Dreamers. What was once named the Carmine Recreation Center (located at Carmine Street and Seventh Avenue South in the West Village) is now named the Tony Dapolito Center. It is operated by the New York City Department of Parks and Recreation. During the 1980's and 1990's, this site had been under the stewardship of the late Ray Pagan. Under his invitational presence, the Carmine Center became a second home for the Uptown Dreamer program. At the time of Ray's passing, I wrote an obituary for his passing in which I included the thoughts and words that Ray had been a "gracious gatekeeper and humble host". He did not divide folks according to the geographic area from which various teams competed, but rather united competitors in an arena of friendly competition and sportsmanship. No matter the level of ability possessed by players and coaches, all felt that Ray's place was a place for us. A major theme of his stewardship was that girls would be provided an equal opportunity as boys for getting on the playing field. https://www1.nyc.gov

192   The Uptown Dreamer program was founded by Coach Dave Crenshaw in the early 1980s. The culture and team-making thread which kept young people motivated and prepared for life's challenges included a full menu supporting the program theme of Education Through Sports and Community Service. This included submission of essays and reflections on a weekly basis, all of which were read by Coach Dave. Contact for the Dreamer program: teamdreamersuptown@gmail.com.

193   I met Ivy Fairchild when she was the Director of Columbia University's Office of Community Affairs. Under her stewardship, she would travel to programs to meet teens on their territory, and keep her door open in providing advice, assistance, and rewards. In recent times, and today, this office and its programs are managed

by Sandra Harris, the Associate VP for an alumnus of the Alianza Dominicana program. Their office, amongst many other support services, coordinates a small grant program for locally based youth service and community service programs. Ivy generously shared her vast networks of resources as well as so much of her time. The current Director for Columbia University's Office of Community Relations is Sandra Harris, Contact: Sandra Harris at sh533@columbia.edu.

194   I met Ivy Fairchild when she was the Director of Columbia University's Office of Community Affairs. Under her stewardship, she would travel to programs to meet teens on their territory, and keep her door open in providing advice, assistance, and rewards. In recent times, and today, this office and its programs are managed by Sandra Harris, the Associate VP for an alumnus of the Alianza Dominicana program. Their office, amongst many other support services, coordinates a small grant program for locally based youth service and community service programs. Ivy generously shared her vast networks of resources as well as so much of her time. The current Director for Columbia University's Office of Community Relations is Sandra Harris, Contact: Sandra Harris at sh533@columbia.edu.

195   See the website for the Women's Sports Foundation on the relationship of sports experience for girls with improved health and social-emotional indicators. www.womenssportsfoundation.org

196   Practicing Social Inclusion (Routledge, 2014), edited by Ann Taket, et al. See specifically the section in this book titled "Inclusion in participatory research", pp 237 – 246. This section includes commentary by Lila Watson, an Australian Aboriginal Woman on pg 245.

197   Restorative justice and reconciliation programs are alternative practices used in place of exercising confinement, punishment, and retribution. Amongst the positive outcomes of these practices are: 1). These programs place both perpetrators and victims at the center of the problem -solving process (pg 185). 2). The offender

is afforded initiative-taking responsibility for addressing the crime committed. The goal is healing, and not punishment (pg 189). 3). The benefits are good for all, and greatly reduce the probability of recidivism (pg 191). Source: Restorative Justice: Healing the Effects of Crime, Jim Considine (Ploughshares Publications, 1995).

198   Petra Shattuck's comments quoted in the Petra Foundation Twenty-Fourth Anniversary Journal. Her quote is in the introductory part of the journal. There are no page numbers in the journal. https://www.petrafoundation.org

199   Engaged walking in energetic footprints (or continue making the road already started). The author of this statement is Daniel J. Siegel, M.D, and was used in his book, The Mind: A Journey to the Heart of Being Human (Norton and Company, 2017). Dr. Siegel used this is reference to a person named John, who was immersed in healing work and deeply influential for Dr. Siegel. After John passed away, Dr. Siegel would still feel his presence, and attribute this, in part, for their both still walking the same pathway. As stated by Dr. Siegel: "Our essence of mind is truly relational…the self-organizing aspect of John's mind may certainly still be alive even though his body is gone. That is the relational aspect of mind" (the eternal footprint) (pg 262).

200   Address the madness of our sorted-out cities. This is a concept developed by Dr. Mindy Thompson-Fullilove in her book, Urban Alchemy (New Village Press, 2013). In the book, she quotes E.B. White's description of life in New York City, where "if a person lives on a block, and then moves two blocks away, then he has gone to a different neighborhood" (pg 147). In New York City, different neighborhoods, and even blocks, are forced to compete for scarce resources, or may not ever receive sufficient resources at all. As I interpret Dr. Thompson-Fullilove's allusion to madness, if an individual were to develop multiple personality disorder, amongst the

consequences would be that each personality would be seeking competitive advantage, and embark on behaviors seemingly of benefit to it, but in detriment to other personalities. This is an individual personality disorder, which makes it difficult, and at times impossible, for the whole person to function in a healthy way. When we set up a system of financial funding and preferential social policies that favor one place to the detriment of others, this is a social personality disorder, of dire consequence to the whole city. Amongst the recommendations that Dr. Thompson-Fullilove makes (which are expanded upon chapter by chapter through social theory and community anecdotes) are: 1). Open our perspective so that we can see our local place in context of the whole city; 2). Establish connections to allies so that we can operate more effectively and freely; 3). Share resources in ways that ensure equity for each unit of the city (pg 145).

201   The Center for Community Change became the new home for the Petra Foundation. The year 2015 became the last independently operating year for the Petra Foundation, which was a small family foundation that had expanded its net of support to include 100 awardees over 25 years. The Center for Community Change agreed that the Petra Foundation archives and reporting of present civic work by Foundation Fellows would be covered in the Center's website. The Center for Community Change had been founded in 1968 in response to civil rights concerns and in honor of the memories of Robert F. Kennedy, who had been assassinated in June 1968. https://communitychange.org

202   Emerging safely in the company of friends is a type of educational environment encouraged by the educational activist and writer Parker Palmer. In his book, To Know As We Are Known: Education as a Spiritual Journey (Harper San Francisco, 1993), Palmer advocates for a teacher-student relationship where the teacher practices empathy by connecting to the authentic being of a student, and

not his or her status as defined by socio/economic factors. As Mr. Palmer states, "To teach is to create a safe space" (pg 65) where a teacher needs to "honor ignorance (not as a deficit) as an invitation to an adventure into the unknown" (pg 72). Mr. Palmer continues, "Precisely because learning spaces can be painful, it must exhibit hospitality" (pg 73), (where a) space (is created) where it is safe for your feelings to emerge" (pg 85).

203   Linda Stout is a Petra Foundation fellow and a 13th generation Quaker, activist and visionary who founded a social activist organization called Spirit in Action. This agency trains participants "to develop tools and resources for creating a visionary and progressive movement." (Source: Petra Foundation Twenty-Fifth Anniversary Journal). https://www.petrafoundation.org

204   Linda Stout is a Petra Foundation fellow and a 13th generation Quaker, activist and visionary who founded a social activist organization called Spirit in Action. This agency trains participants "to develop tools and resources for creating a visionary and progressive movement." (Source: Petra Foundation Twenty-Fifth Anniversary Journal). https://www.petrafoundation.org

205   "Go Where Others Don't" was the Police Athletic League motto at the time I became employed with this agency. It suggested that as part of its work ethic, the agency should locate areas in the city where people are under duress and struggling in challenging circumstances. In the PAL mission statement, it is stated that the PAL program should work closely with New York City's NYPD in developing a community approach for promoting neighborhood safety, and that its youth participants should be trained to become productive citizens. Source: Police Athletic League Mission Statement www.pal.nyc.org

206   Kevin Cedeno: I woke up to a television news blurb in April of 1997 about the shooting in the back of 16-year-old Kevin Cedeno

by a police officer. I heard the words and watched the images, but the reality of it all just would not register for me. Years before the shooting, Kevin and his twin brother Kern had been invited to our afterschool program. He had accompanied us on one occasion to a camping trip at Camp Alpine in New Jersey. After a few months his being with our program, we could not hold on to him, nor his twin brother Kern, or keep them engaged even occasionally. We at Southern Heights had lost track of them, until this tragedy broke. After the community mourned with Kevin's family, we received an account via an official report issued by the Manhattan District Attorney Office, which placed no blame on the police, and which presented an account that did not align with witness statements from people from the area who had been on the scene. They were designated in the official account as unreliable witnesses. Despite the trauma and pain suffered by Kevin's family, and the shock expressed by the local religious community, the response of these actors was a call for understanding, reconciliation, and justice. As spoken to by the Reverend George Barfield from the Church of the Intercession (located on West 155th Street and Broadway, nine blocks from the location of the shooting), "The family offers forgiveness, as difficult and painful as that is… this is not an indictment of the entire police department, but against a police officer who did not protect the life of Kevin Cedeno." Almost a quarter of a century later, the larger society is only beginning to grasp the lesson and insist on justice delivered by the law enforcement community. I received this oral testimony from members of Kevin's family shortly after this tragedy.

207   Life seemed impossible to handle at times… the seeds of chaos planted in the 1980s and 1990s, and the legacy of officially sanctioned violence—fear and disconnection for the young. In an article written by E.R. Shipp called "Tough Love in the Big City," the consequences of fear and mistrust were highlighted. Early in the article, Ms. Shipp asks: "Kids in New York have a lot of fear. So how did we wind up

afraid of them" (pg 9)? It was in reaction to this irrationally and misplaced torrent of expressed fear about the young that I became even more motivated to work on behalf of young people. In a sense, I became, as did the co-mentors I came to network with, defense attorneys, and creators of alternative stories to counter demonization. As Ms. Shipp continues: "According to the Community Service Society, some 220,000 people are disconnected (ages 16–24), neither in school nor in jobs" (pg 10). Although the pages of the calendar have flipped since the printing of that article, the prospects for that disowned population continue to be flipped upside-down. As Ms. Shipp concludes toward the end of her article, "Many of them (young people) don't believe that education holds the key to their success" (pg 13) All too often, I hear this belief expressed by youth today, many of whom have agreed to the educational game, who graduated from college and still struggle with debt and unsatisfying jobs rather than feeling successful. Source for the quotes: E.R. Shipp, Tough Love in the Big City, City Limits, Vol. 34 No. 3.

208 The challenges of the Pit, recreational space as a place to gain footing.

In one of the talks I attended by Dr. Stephanie Marango, she asked the audience the question: "What is a foot anyway?" I made notes in response to her commentary, and recorded the following thoughts, some hers, and some a reaction to hers. The foot provides us an anchor and a pivot in life. The foot, in its capacity as an artist, centers us, and as a scientist provides us with stability and balance. It provides us with a still point, allowing us to focus on the horizon, propels us in a direction toward which we wish to live, and gets us to the finish line and the chorus of celebration. The Pit is a place where children and families get to jump, and run, and twist, guided by the wisdom of feet. (I did not write down the place and time of Dr. Steph's presentation. It still has an inspirational impact for me, so I assign it to the category of timeless wisdom.) An outdoor recreation space is also a school, educating the mind, the body, and the spirit.

The Pit was also a place where people celebrated their relationships and history. In an issue of a magazine called Encounter, they dedicated the issue to providing education for meaning and purpose. In the introduction to the issue, the editor referred to "the pedagogy of place, which integrated schooling with the day-to-day life of a community." (Encounter Magazine, Winter 1998, Vol. 11, No.4).

209   The loss of Kevin and the ongoing need for healing… was addressed by community-based agencies such as the Community League of West 159th Street. They organized conversations, meetings in which the family, friends and neighbors of Kevin could come to terms with the trauma with its sense of loss, pain, and disassociation. As noted by the holistically oriented teacher Gerald Crow, "…when life energy is blocked, it must be freed to bring about healing, i.e., unaddressed acute and chronic anxiety and stress can bring on personality disorders…" (Holistic Education Review, March 1994), p 11.

210   Police Athletic League IN-STEP program—its constructivist civic curriculum. Teen participants organized their local engagement projects using a Project-Based Learning approach. Marcel Braithwaite was a program manager for the PAL IN-STEP program at the time. Marcel designed a Project-Based Learning syllabus in 2005 which assured students experiencing touchpoints, such as having an instructional encounter that was centered upon them as learners allowed for in-depth investigation of an issue, encouraged teens to produce artifacts (poems, documentaries), and guided teens to shape their own projects, and exercise autonomy and responsibility. (Marcel might still have a record of his curriculum in his files.) mbraithwaite@palnyc.org.

211   Commentary of IN-STEP participants at training sessions during the program years from 2004 – 2007. I would hear this commentary while I was the Director of the program attending training sessions.

212   The IN-STEP program after 2007 and until 2018 was stewarded under the Director Tamara Chalvire who not only tirelessly studied the best practices for teen programming, but also felt the imperative of working with teens holistically, as a product of wisdom gained from her own professional journey. Tamara wove the practice of active questioning into her programming. Some examples, as suggested on a website for The Unbounded Spirit.com included having students question the source of their beliefs, the reasoning use for holding on to beliefs, and asking whether a belief or set of beliefs is limiting in ways, or whether they help to elevate the quality of one's life. I did not know about this website during the time I got to meet and later work with Tamara, but I attest to her ceaselessly engaged work ethic being energized by her unbounded spirit. The site for Unbounded Spirit is: https://theunboundedspirit.com

213   The future is constructed in the present… Young people don't just get involved in creating change, they need an environment which encourages and trains them as change-makers. One study on the qualities of youth-led social change was profiled on a website called The Futures Page. Amongst these are ensuring that youth are engaged in "meaningful participation and sustained engagement where they can explore solutions and sometimes influence decision makers" (pg 3). A second program quality is that when seeking to influence decision-makers, there should be a direct connection for teens "in taking action as individually motivated change-makers" (pg 5, Table 1: Relationship Between Strategy and Impact) on the Future Page website. I have an old copy of this study but cannot find it on the web.

214   Future Voters of America Fact Sheet on Teens (May 14, 2009).

        As part of their support efforts for getting Teens on Board, the Future Voter of America circulated a Fact Sheet to buttress our arguments. One point they made is that at the age of 16 or 17, teens can obtain learner's permits, and in some cases are charged as adults in trials, hold jobs, and pay taxes. Against the charge that teens don't have enough experiences, they highlighted teen service on youth councils in community service and conflict resolution programs, and as governmental advisors in other cities such as San Francisco. As a third point they referenced research studies, such as one that showed that a powerful way to build citizenship skills in the youth is to have them participate in citizenship activities during their high school years. As the FVA organization no longer exists, I am not sure where a documented record of this Fact Sheet might still be accessible.

215   New Directions for Youth Studies by Shawn Ginwright and Taj James, "From Assets to Agents of Change" (2012). https://pubmed. ncbi.nlm.nih.gov/12630272

216   A conversation I had with Fran Baras and Diane Graszik at the 2006 Future Voters of America high-school congress. Their lesson: keep open ears and not open mouths. The Future Voters of America program is no longer posted on the web.

217   Media studies… youth under the gun and on the run. Henry A. Giroux is the Waterbury Chair Professor and Director for the Waterbury Forum for Education and Youth Studies at Penn State University. He is also a prolific writer, and has a book titled Fugitive Cultures: Race, Violence and Youth (Routledge, 1996) as part of his bodies of work. Amongst the observations made in this book is that "for many youths, showing up for adulthood means pulling back on hope rather than taking on the modern challenges and trying to shape them" (pg 33). He provides scenarios in which racist and sexist stereotyping in the media discourage and disparage young people rather than showing them as contributors to our society. Professor Giroux also provides numerous critiques of films, in which youth are seen to participate in cultures of nihilism and violence which is emblematic of a whole generation (pg 40). In one chapter,

"Racism and the Aesthetic of Hyper-Real Violence" (pp 55–88), Professor Giroux states: "Cinematic violence, whether it is ritualistic or hyper-real, is not innocent. Such violence offers viewers brutal and grotesque images that articulate with broader public discourse how children and adults relate, care, and respond to others. (pg 83). Distorted representations of reality produce untruth.

218   Democracy and its discontents… undoing democracy for the many.

What I refer to as the shadow of democracy is held together, in large part, by discriminative legislative policies which undermine the right of participation and the ability to pursue the right to life and happiness. In the book, The Right to Vote: A Contested History of Democracy in the United States by Alexander Keyssar (Perseus Books, 2000), an example is given showing a contrast between efforts to expand voting and to restrict it. In reviewing voting rights legislation in the late 1700s, state by state, Mr. Keyssar documents that while some states expanded the right to vote, in "New York State, local elites sought to prevent voting, and to impose restrictions for municipal suffrage. (p 21). A second source I cite is taken from a history of legal restraints formulated by government ordinance. The Color of Law: A Forgotten History of how our Government Segregated America by Richard Rothstein (Liveright Publishing/ WW Norton, 2017) documents our nation's history of legislation promoting segregation. He cites one case where "Frederick Ecker, who was the president of Met Life Insurance Company, issued a report that was adopted and published by the federal government which recommended deed restrictions which would prevent 'incompatible owners' from occupying properties" Read incompatible owners as Black owners. ("Own Your Own Home," p 62).

219   See Healing the Heart of Democracy by Parker J. Palmer (Josey-Bass, 2011). This quote is taken from a section in this book called "The Farmer's Heart", pg 55.

220 The Empress of Embrace is a title I gave to my mother in a eulogy I wrote about her when she passed on in January of 2013. I expand upon her presence as a source of safety and comfort for friends and family suffering the trauma of dispossession in a section of this book called Orphans.

221 Trust in (family members and) teammates... joy is always emerging. When trusted others extend compassion for us and facilitate joy, our social, emotion, and mental capacities expand. In Joyful Militancy, Nick Montgomery and Carla Bergman speak to this when describing "a toddler's increase in capacity...those first steps that mark the emergence of something new—is sufficient of itself. It is a joyful moment, worth celebrating, not because it is some part of a linear process of development, but because it is an emergent power for kids." (, AK Press, 2017), pg 217. Teen years are not toddlerhood but are an age of transition where young adults are practicing civic skills and expressing and giving joy in the process with each of their first successful steps.

222 Trust in (family members and) teammates... joy is always emerging. When trusted others extend compassion for us and facilitate joy, our social, emotion, and mental capacities expand. In Joyful Militancy, Nick Montgomery and Carla Bergman speak to this when describing "a toddler's increase in capacity...those first steps that mark the emergence of something new—is sufficient of itself. It is a joyful moment, worth celebrating, not because it is some part of a linear process of development, but because it is an emergent power for kids." (, AK Press, 2017), pg 217. Teen years are not toddlerhood but are an age of transition where young adults are practicing civic skills and expressing and giving joy in the process with each of their first successful steps.

223   Letters of support…bringing joy to the Teens on Board organizers.
Our Teens on Board leader received 35 letters of support for our
campaign, which also gave us joy, and encouraged us in our steps
toward success. The NYC Girl Scout Council offered words of affirmation with the words: "Our young people offer valuable perspective and bring new ideas and energy to the public policy arena."
(Barbara Murph Washington, CEO, June 19, 2013, letter of support).
In another example from the Children's Aid Society, encouraging
words included that in observing teen civic participation, they see "a
graduated series of experiences that encourage them to take initiative
and make healthy choices." (Each footstep by step with the other!)
(Richard Buery, CEO, September 4, 2013). All letters of support
were submitted to the office of the Manhattan Borough President
in 2014. https://www.manhattanbp.nyc.gov

224   Letters of support…bringing joy to the Teens on Board organizers. Our Teens on Board leader received 35 letters of support for
our campaign, which also gave us joy, and encouraged us in our
steps toward success. The NYC Girl Scout Council offered words
of affirmation with the words: "Our young people offer valuable
perspective and bring new ideas and energy to the public policy
arena." (Barbara Murph Washington, CEO, June 19, 2013, letter
of support). In another example from the Children's Aid Society,
encouraging words included that in observing teen civic participation, they see "a graduated series of experiences that encourage
them to take initiative and make healthy choices." (Each footstep
by step with the other!) (Richard Buery, CEO, September 4, 2013).
All letters of support were submitted to the office of the Manhattan
Borough President in 2014. http://www.manhattanbp.nyc.gov

225   Letters of support…bringing joy to the Teens on Board organizers. Our Teens on Board leader received 35 letters of support for
our campaign, which also gave us joy, and encouraged us in our

steps toward success. The NYC Girl Scout Council offered words of affirmation with the words: "Our young people offer valuable perspective and bring new ideas and energy to the public policy arena." (Barbara Murph Washington, CEO, June 19, 2013, letter of support). In another example from the Children's Aid Society, encouraging words included that in observing teen civic participation, they see "a graduated series of experiences that encourage them to take initiative and make healthy choices." (Each footstep by step with the other!) (Richard Buery, CEO, September 4, 2013). All letters of support were submitted to the office of the Manhattan Borough President in 2014. https://www.manhattanbp.nyc.gov

226   The Department of Youth and Community Development has, as part of their youth services portfolio, the inclusion of youth advisory councils. As per their Beacon Center/Youth Council description, these programs foster "positive youth development, social/emotional learning/, leadership skills, academic enhancement, and civic engagement. Middle-school students attending Beacon programs sponsored by the Center for Family Life (Sunset Park, Brooklyn), the Police Athletic League (Goldie Maple in Rockaway, Queens), the PAL Beacon at IS 218 (East New York, Brooklyn), the PAL Brownsville Beacon (Brooklyn), and the Queens Community House Beacon (Forest Hills, Queens) provided a lot of support for our campaign by circulating petitions to parents, students, and staff. https://www1.nyc.gov/site/dycd/index.page

227   UN Charter, Article 55. (Ibid). www.un.org

228   This allusion comparing newbie teen civic engagement with guppies, suggests a metaphor between learning needs of the young across species. The Hourglass model developed by Generation Citizen is designed to introduce civic learning skills that are in line with a teens curiosity and developmental needs. The philosophical approach inherent in this model is suggested by the National Council of

Social Studies(NCSS) in a section of their civic curricular guide called "Developing Skills for Civic Discourse." In their description of participatory civic engagement, they write: "The next generation of voters need models for constructive discourse, creating a sense of trust, encouraging participants to speak and listen to each other, and making time for silent reflection" (pg 273). See www.generationcitizen.org for the hourglass approach. For a vignette on how a newbie civic action learner makes progress, see Scott Warren's book describing the step-by-step progress made by a fifth-grade student named A'niya pp 4-7. Generation Citizen by Scott Warren (Counterpoint, 2019) In the cases both for guppies and young learners, there is a learning challenge between thinking you know the environment, and then adjusting to its unanticipated nuances. There is also a natural tension between wanting to accomplish goal and learning new skills making achievement more likely. See the full curricular guide developed by NCSS: College, Career and Civic Life: The C3 Framework for Social Studies State Standards (published by the National Council for the Social Studies, Silver Spring Maryland). Also see an additional reference in the guide called Taking Informed Action in Table 30 on pg 62.

229   This allusion comparing newbie teen civic engagement with guppies, suggests a metaphor between learning needs of the young across species. The Hourglass model developed by Generation Citizen is designed to introduce civic learning skills that are in line with a teens curiosity and developmental needs. The philosophical approach inherent in this model is suggested by the National Council of Social Studies(NCSS) in a section of their civic curricular guide called "Developing Skills for Civic Discourse." In their description of participatory civic engagement, they write: "The next generation of voters need models for constructive discourse, creating a sense of trust, encouraging participants to speak and listen to each other, and making time for silent reflection" (pg 273). See www.

generationcitizen.org for the hourglass approach. For a vignette on how a newbie civic action learner makes progress, see Scott Warren's book describing the step-by-step progress made by a fifth-grade student named A'niya pp 4-7. Generation Citizen by Scott Warren (Counterpoint, 2019) In the cases both for guppies and young learners, there is a learning challenge between thinking you know the environment, and then adjusting to its unanticipated nuances. There is also a natural tension between wanting to accomplish goal and learning new skills making achievement more likely. See the full curricular guide developed by NCSS; College, Career and Civic Lie: The C3 Framework for Social Studies Standards (published by the National Council of Social Studies, Silver Spring, Maryland). Also see an additional reference in this guide called Taking Informed Action in Table 30 on pg 62.

230   The fierce urgency of now generated by the enthusiastic determination of communities. Paul Hawken, in Blessed Unrest (Penguin Books, 2007) celebrates the expansive potential of community as emergent movements divorced from fighting too narrow agendas. As Mr. Hawken talks about with this emergent development, he writes about: "movements as communities, instead of 'isms' offering processes, concerns, and compassion. This movement offers a pliable, resonant and generous side of humanity...It is a reimagination of public governance emerging from a place of culture and people" (pg 18).

231   Not just what you teach, but how you teach it... is a concept contributed by Parker Palmer in his book, To Know As We Are Known (Harper SF, 1983). As Mr. Palmer offers: "In a civic community, you learn how to compromise, creating norms within community for tolerance and civility" (pg xiii).

232   Civic participation Boot Camps... was a forum for introducing community board structures and processes to prospective teen

applicants which was given its title by Alan Shulman, a retired social studies teacher who is a member of the National Council of Social Studies. After our community board amendment had passed, he was instrumental in organizing these information sessions, such as one that was hosted by Brooklyn Borough President Eric Adams. Mr. Shulman was quoted in BP Adams press release: "Our young adults are assets and stakeholders for the future. They must be given genuine opportunities to join, with influence, organize, and be prepared for cooperative engagement where the future is being planned" (Brooklyn BP Press release by Eric Adams, November 19, 2014).

233   Training approach validation from Sherese Mullins, Staten Island Voice. One of the boot camps we organized was hosted in midtown Manhattan and was attended by 30 teens and a few of their adult advisors. After the session had been held, Sherese Mullins, who at that time was the PR/Marketing manager for Staten Island Voice, emailed me with commentary from three of her participants. One teen participant, Monifa St. Louis, wrote about "being excited about bringing about change." A second teen participant, Mesach Brown, wrote that he was pleased to learn about "the power of working together, and being involved in community." Morris Odelli, who was a staff member from Staten Island Voice, wrote that he was impressed that so many young people were "taking time to work on something effecting them, and that he saw this as youth testimony for being there for future generations" (Sherese's email to Al Kurland: January 22, 2014).

234   On the value of talking about experience... points made by Victoria Pannell in the Daily News Article "Harlem Teen Joins Community Boards" by Kerry Burke and Ginger Adams Otis (May 7, 2016). Posted on line at: https://www.nydailynews.com/new-york/manhattan/harlem-teen-joins-community-board-tackles-neighborhood-issues-article-1.2628

235   To make real change, we need to persist… is another observation offered by Scott Warren in his book, Generation Citizen (Counterpoint, 2019). As Mr. Warren notes: "To make real change, we need to persist…change takes time…this process is our political journey. It is a journey that has no end, but it is one than can, and will, define our entire lives" (pg 19).

236   Busting stereotypes supporting rigidly held beliefs. I cite a couple of examples from the book Great Myths of Adolescence by Jeremy Jewell et al. (Wiley Blackwell, 2019). One entry rebuts the assertion that teens involve themselves in an inordinate number of risky behaviors (pg 69) and the other refutes the notion that teens engage in more texting than adults (pg 177).

237   Stereotypes defaming wage workers. This quote was originally printed in Poor Richards Legacy in American Business Values and is by James Prothro (NY William Morrow, p 241) and is quoted in The Legalist Reformation by William E. Nelson (University of North Carolina Press, 2001), pg 15.

238   Low economic status students and low motivation for learning… is a line from a teacher training manual commonly used in the 1970s. This line is quoted from a speech given by the social critic and policy reformer Annie Stein at an event sponsored by People Against White Supremacy. I found the quote in a magazine called The Radical Teacher, May 1985, No. 28 from a summary of Ms. Stein's speech (pp 24–29).

239   Michael Banks, former student at PS 128M, and false accusations lodged against him by a classroom teacher. This account is filed in my memories.

240   Shape-shifting and course adjustments… inner work by teens and contributions to community each involve the inherent right to participate. Looking at Arnstein's Ladder of Participation, an expanding opportunity to be involved defines its central thesis, as stated by Ann

Taket et al. in their book Practicing Social Inclusion (Routledge, 2014): "The ladder tracks a continuum of public participation, from the least participatory to the most inclusive" (pg 11). A healthy adolescent mind is nurtured by providing ample chance to be involved during one's life, and the decisions of one's community.

241   Conscious teens and conscientious adult mentors prevent teens from become marginalized, minimalized, and mesmerized by false narratives. We have moved on from the chaotic times when storm and stress drove social policies effecting teens, and now embark on a new era, as defined by teen leadership at the American Friends Service Committee as #WeAreNotAtRisk, https://www.afsc.org/notatrisk.

242   An emotional asset applied by teens is aptly described as radical empathy. An emergent generation is flexing its brain muscle—using mirror neurons to "expand their capacity for relation, empathy, and altruism," as stated by Richard Katz, Ph.D. in his book Indigenous Healing Psychology (Healing Arts Press, 2017), pg 316.

243   I use the term "radical empathy" not as a new addition, but as a classical understanding of traditional ancestral cultures who felt connection with all beings in the world through the bodily awareness and intuition. Our growing awareness about the role of mirror neurons in enhancing our capacity for empathy is driven by new scientific discovery that is catching up the ancestral wisdom. We are getting back to our roots, which is a radical act. For a good source on bodily awareness and intuitive intelligence, see The Spell of the Sensuous by David Abram (Vintage Books, 1996), especially the mindful life of the body, pp 44-49.

244   Intersectionality... a cognitive acknowledgement "of all my relations."

Patricia Hill Collins, in her book, Intersectionality As a Critical Social Theory (Duke University Press, 2019), analyzes the work of a social justice advocate, Crenshaw, as she has been addressing the fragmented ways in which we approach criminal justice reform. Ms. Collins sees the application of intersectionality as a process of "taking a snapshot of complex social relationships (for example. racism, sexism, and other complex systems of power), in the context of solving social problems" (pg 28). As Ms. Collins continues, "We use intersectionality as a metaphor, a cognitive device for thinking about social inequality" (pg 29). I see this as an ecological application of knowledge applied to the field of social justice.

245   Intersectionality... a cognitive acknowledgement "of all my relations."

Patricia Hill Collins, in her book, Intersectionality As a Critical Social Theory (Duke University Press, 2019), analyzes the work of a social justice advocate, Crenshaw, as she has been addressing the fragmented ways in which we approach criminal justice reform. Ms. Collins sees the application of intersectionality as a process of "taking a snapshot of complex social relationships (for example. racism, sexism, and other complex systems of power), in the context of solving social problems" (pg 28). As Ms. Collins continues, "We use intersectionality as a metaphor, a cognitive device for thinking about social inequality" (pg 29). I see this as an ecological application of knowledge applied to the field of social justice.

246   Go back to our roots and maximize the fruits of our future, exercise our gift... the power of being human. An urgent appeal for exercising this awareness of human power is presented in a chapter of a book titled Original Instructions edited by Melissa K. Nelson (Bear and Company, 2008). The chapter "The Power of Being Human" is written John Trundell, who is of mixed tribal heritage, an activist in the American Indian Movement, and a spoken word artist. He states that the power of being human underlies everything about each one of us, occupying the spaces between the hyphens of cultural and national identity. As stated by Mr. Trundell: "As beings, we are energy, we are spirits in the form of humans. In the ancestral genetic

memory, we understood that this is the spiritual reality that we are in. It is not a physical reality, it is a spiritual reality because it is the reality of being, with physical things in it" (pg 320).

247   "Mindsight" is a concept developed by the psychologist and writer Daniel J. Siegel. With this approach Mr. Siegel describes interactive mind maps, which though our reflection upon thinking about how we think, we develop a tool for becoming aware of our awareness. As stated by Mr. Siegel: "Mindsight is a kind of focused attention that allows us to see the inner workings of our own minds…it allows us to get ourselves off the auto pilot of ingrained behaviors and habitual responses." pg ix. Also see the introduction pp ix – xii. The book is: Mindsight: The New Science of Personal Transformation, by Daniel J. Siegel, M.D. (Bantam Books, 2011).

248   These lines are from a poem which I heard recited at a morning service at the All-Souls Unitarian Church in the spring of 2018. I cannot find the specific speaker delivering the sermon; however, one can learn about the All Souls Unitarian-Universalist Church philosophy and principles at https://www.allsouls-nyc.org

249   The mind reflects, and the world turns… emergent modes of consciousness and societal relations. David C. Korten in his book, The Great Turning: From Empire to Earth Community (Barrett-Kohler, 2006) highlights the transitions which have begun from the old era of mechanical/Industrial mindsets and institutions to forms of relationships corresponding to ecological and spiritual principles. For example, he states this case for our financial transactions, which need to be "life-saving economies that satisfy our basic material needs while maintaining a sustainable balance with Earth's natural systems. Our fiscal dealings must keep in mind the need to strengthen bonds of caring communities and to support all persons in the full realization of their humanity" (pg 303). Mr. Korsten's economic/political approach is congruent with a spiritual approach advocating

for transitioning to ecological and spiritual principles written about by Anodea Judith, Ph.D. See her book, Waking the Global Heart: Humanities Rite of Passage from the Love of Power to the Power of Love (Elite Books, 2006) See chapter one, "The Curtain Rises: The Drama of Our Time" pp 17 -37.

250   The mind reflects, and the world turns... emergent modes of consciousness and societal relations. David C. Korten in his book, The Great Turning: From Empire to Earth Community (Barrett-Kohler, 2006) highlights the transitions which have begun from the old era of mechanical/Industrial mindsets and institutions to forms of relationships corresponding to ecological and spiritual principles. For example, he states this case for our financial transactions, which need to be "life-saving economies that satisfy our basic material needs while maintaining a sustainable balance with Earth's natural systems. Our fiscal dealings must keep in mind the need to strengthen bonds of caring communities and to support all persons in the full realization of their humanity" (pg 303). Mr. Korsten's economic/political approach is congruent with a spiritual approach advocating for transitioning to ecological and spiritual principles written about by Anodea Judith, Ph.D. See her book, Waking the Global Heart: Humanities Rite of Passage from the Love of Power to the Power of Love (Elite Books, 2006) See chapter one, "The Curtain Rises: The Drama of Our Time" pp 17 -37.

251   The mind reflects, and the world turns... emergent modes of consciousness and societal relations. David C. Korten in his book, The Great Turning: From Empire to Earth Community (Barrett-Kohler, 2006) highlights the transitions which have begun from the old era of mechanical/Industrial mindsets and institutions to forms of relationships corresponding to ecological and spiritual principles. For example, he states this case for our financial transactions, which need to be "life-saving economies that satisfy our basic material needs while maintaining a sustainable balance with Earth's natural systems.

Our fiscal dealings must keep in mind the need to strengthen bonds of caring communities and to support all persons in the full realization of their humanity" (pg 303). Mr. Korsten's economic/political approach is congruent with a spiritual approach advocating for transitioning to ecological and spiritual principles written about by Anodea Judith, Ph.D. See her book, Waking the Global Heart: Humanities Rite of Passage from the Love of Power to the Power of Love (Elite Books, 2006) See chapter one, "The Curtain Rises: The Drama of Our Time" pp 17 -37.

252   Quote from Unitarian-Universalist statement of principles www. uua.org

253   Quoted from the Buddhist text called the Karmapa. For one source of information about the Karmapa, see the website: https://kagyuof-fice.org

254   The soul is a visionary, the ego is the strategist. This is a concept developed in Alan Seale's eco/spiritual vision for tomorrow, in his book Create A World That Works (Weiser Books, 2011). He states that our soul is connected to the deep insights of universal wisdom, and that if the ego strategizes on behalf of constructing goals considering this wisdom, that the nature of work for people will also become transformed. As Mr. Seale states: "(An) ego and soul partnership where the soul is visionary and the ego a strategist" (pp 50–53). He continues, "We embrace the soul's vision, insight and wisdom and our ego's ability to harness them for creation and accomplishment as transformative workers" (pg 49).

255   The Spiritual Principles of the Unitarian–Universalist Association have helped me develop a bridge between my work on behalf of holistic education and teen empowerment embedded in communal and political relations. Three of these principles are those that "uphold the inherent worth and dignity of each person; the search for justice, equity and compassion in human relations; and ensuring

the right of conscience as we use the democratic process within our congregations and society at large." www.uua.org

256   Using Carolyn Myss model to describe the three archetypes of the teen mind.

The orphan (or wounded child) "holding memories of abuse, neglect and trauma which can awaken a deep sense of connection and a desire to find a path of service" (pg 373). The rebel "anarchist, revolutionary, protester or non-conformist can aid in breaking tribal patterns, see past tired old preconceptions" (pg 409). The civic lover is "anyone who exhibits great passion and devotion" and "needs to play a significant role with the overall design of your life and self-esteem" (pg 396).

These archetypal bios are developed by Carolyn Myss, Sacred Contracts (Three Rivers Press, 2002).

257   In constructing my concept of the soul as a bridge between optimal personal development and connection to the higher angels of our democracy, I relate to constructs used by depth psychologists and a variety of spiritual insights. One way of highlighting my understanding of this bridge is by looking at the spiritual principles of the Unitarian–Universalist Association. I was exposed to these practices beginning in early elementary school and continuing through the time of my high school graduation. I have also used these principles as guidelines during my twenty-eight years engaged with youth services and teen empowerment work. These core principles about human dignity have helped me to develop a bridge of understanding between my work on behalf of holistic education models and teen empowerment models embedded in communal and political relations. Three of these principles are: 1. "Uphold the inherent worth and dignity of each person;" 2. "The search for justice, equity and compassion in human relations;" and 3. "Ensuring the right of conscience as we use the democratic process within our congregations

and society at large," as printed in the All-Souls Unitarian Church Program service brochure on Easter Sunday, March 27, 2016. A theme that I will develop throughout this book is that these principles also reflect one's work done in guidance from the soul. As we tap into this guidance, we in turn develop our religious practices. I believe that these same principles also apply to our communal, social, and political relationships.

258   For a teen to be fully engaged in civic affairs, and for an adult civic mentor to effectively guide them… each must participate from all levels of experience (physical, mental, emotional, and spiritual). While undertaking this process, it is not just what we know that counts, but living with what we don't know that also matters. As brought up in a conversation recorded between spiritual practitioners Bernie Glassman, Jerry Brown, and James Gimian (a chapter in Mindful Politics [Shambala Press, edited by Melvin McCleod]), "Energy is produced by not knowing," as we bear witness to mystery (pg 78).

259   Incorporating spiritual perspective to live in one's life purpose. Social change activists, teen mentors, and teens themselves are increasingly searching for spiritual reference point aligned with their personal development and communally directed action. Carolyn Myss, whom I referenced above, has introduced me to an organized system of archetypes for which I have great affinity. Another practitioner who has influenced me is Dan Millman and his work, The Life You Are Born to Live (HJ Kramer, 1993). He uses a system of numerical arrangement associated with your date of birth which he suggests hold deep influence into one's personalities and life course. I use my formula for an example here. My birthdate is 4–19–1949. Using Millman's method, I combine the numerals and get 37. You then add up the 3 and the 7 to 10. The type is 37/10. The opening for this type is written by Millman: "Those on the 37/10 life path are here to work through issues of creativity while learning to trust the wise and

beautiful spirit in themselves and others, and to apply their inner gifts to create harmony in the world" (pg 123). This corresponds closely to what I have worked on in my progression of youth service programs—relating to teens and their mentors, heart to heart, and in appreciation of their soulful challenges and gifts. This description also constitutes a subscript for this book.

260   The unchallenged assumptions of the receding mechanical/industrial age are sabotaging the path for establishing coherent practices in our emerging eco/spiritual age. Scilla Elworthy, in her book, Pioneering the Possible: Awakening Leadership for a World That Works (North Atlantic Books, 2014) speaks to the need for new-era leaderships to practice as responsible stewards creating harmony in the world. As she points out the trap of perceiving cultural and political truisms for universal truth, Dr. Elworthy states, "What are essentially historical constructs have come to be enshrined as perennial truths. From this crisis we see a kind of mission creep, they become the unquestioned bedrock (for) the types of decisions which are destroying the planet" (pg 75). During the three decades being covered by this book, teens had often demonstrated the skills and understandings necessary to participate in municipal advisory and decision-making capacities, but in New York City outdated beliefs and institutional resistance were on-going obstacles faced by teens who had contributions to make in municipal governance.

261   Using experimentation as a flashlight on trusted territory is an additional practice recommended for those helping to steward us into a new era. Kurt Spellmeyer, in his book, Buddha and the Apocalypse, (Wisdom Publications, 2006), alludes to this as a person projecting their vision for the future in a way making it safe to pilot visionary practices now. People who have been able to grasp a future-oriented practice, join the ranks of change-makers for whom the present-day outcome is contingent upon realizing that "the future belongs to those who can see it" (pg 14). Mr. Spellmeyer defines apocalypse not

in terms of being the end times, but rather an experience in which people are "lifting the veil" (p 4), that is, seeing through practices meant to misdirect or deceive us, and letting go of old attachments to those systems.

262   Ibid Buddha and the Apocalypse The territory known as the commons is not just a place, but a period. Spellmeyer also proposes that "it might be revealing to think of the future as what biologists refer to as the 'commons. Put shared interest ahead of self-interest" (pg 148).

263   Ibid Buddha and the Apocalypse Staying home in a period of multiple tasks and complex decision-making involves dealing with learned attention deficit disorders. Mr. Spellmeyer also addresses the dilemma-prone society we live in, constructed with over-specialized disciplines, and educated ignorance concerning seeing a problem from an unfamiliar perspective. When utilizing a methodology called "emergent systems paradigms," we learn to avoid "involving a single link between one cause and effect and bring together multiple events interacting with each other" (pg 7). Mr. Spellmeyer suggests that we move on from looking only for predictability to considering possibility and that we focus less on predestination and more on open-ended outcomes.

264   What are these archetypes anyway? One way to define an archetype is to look at the patterns of energy they produce and its effects on us. James Hillman provided a reference point using patterns: "(Archetypes) are the deepest patterns of psychic functioning which represent the roots of the soul governing the perspectives we have about ourselves and others." James Hillman, "Revisioning Psychology" (pp xi, xii-xiv), cited in the book Blue Fire: Selected Writings of James Hillman (Harper Perennial, 1989), introduced and edited by Thomas Moore (pp 23–24).

265   Adam Elenbaas, who has an M.F.A. and an M.A. in English and Creative writing, and is a practicing astrologer, has another slant on making meaning of archetypes. In an article he wrote for The Mountain Astrologer (Feb/Mar 2016, Vol. 29, No. 2), he wrote about what the legacy of James Hillman contributed to astrological understanding. In that article, Mr. Elenbaas speaks to the significance of facilitating imagination and re-visioning as central to understanding archetypal purpose. He sees archetypes as mentoring entities which present "cycles of insights through the medium of myth making and poetic interpretation." (Archetypal Phenomenology and the Astrological Imagination: Reflections on the Astrological Legacy of James Hillman, Elenbaas, pp 33–39). One of the themes I speak to in my book is the importance of mythmaking to the lives of everyday people, including teens, for understanding who they are in metaphoric ways. Rather than looking at them through the lens of racial profiling, see who they are through poetic profiling.

266   The influence of archetypes is not identically experienced when looking at the adolescent psyche and our societal institutions. Rather, its effects reflect out in synchronistic fashion. For example, when a teen is made to feel inadequate, and not seen for their worth, they experience being an orphan. When socio/political practices intentionally exclude marginalized people based upon their gender, race, or national origin, etc., then whole groups are turned into those orphaned from our society.

    I agree with the philosopher Ken Wilbur that archetypes have impacts with differing types of consequence on the teen psyche and our social institutions. For the individual, the interaction has an impact on the self, as a person moves on a spectrum of evolving forms of consciousness ("The Self and Fulcrums," pp 130–132). With institutions, the impact is reflected in changes on culture. In both cases, we "see change, and also a return to home" as Wilbur points out. Old consciousness is not totally rejected, nor disposed of, but is incorporated into a new level of consciousness and related to from an evolved perspective.

Ken Wilbur, The Eye of the Spirit: An Integral Vision for A World Gone Slightly Mad (Shambala Press, 2001).

267   In this book I incorporate infusing social and personal change with the perspective of mythological influence. For example, when I write about some of my allies who master navigating the turbulence of our times from a personal space that evokes calm, and which promotes balance and healing, I refer to the mythological presence of Kwan Yin as being apparently existent within that person's psyche. To briefly describe Kwan Yin: "Kwan Yin, or Quan Yin, is the 'divine mother' riding the dragon, who provides a role model for remaining grounded and celebrating one's gifts." (Description is from the Sedona Journal website, posted in 2012).

268   In this book I incorporate infusing social and personal change with the perspective of mythological influence. For example, when I write about some of my allies who master navigating the turbulence of our times from a personal space that evokes calm, and which promotes balance and healing, I refer to the mythological presence of Kwan Yin as being apparently existent within that person's psyche. To briefly describe Kwan Yin: "Kwan Yin, or Quan Yin, is the 'divine mother' riding the dragon, who provides a role model for remaining grounded and celebrating one's gifts." (Description is from the Sedona Journal website, posted in 2012).

269   Most of the teen leaders I worked with were young women, caught within the crossfire of traditional expectations for them held by their parents, and the new-era invitations to fully express themselves and align their talent with society's institutions. Clarissa Pinkola Estes, Ph.D. in her book Women Who Run with The Wolves (Ballentine Books, 1992) refers to the experience of a young woman's self-revelation and affirmed recognition as originating with "the fairy tale

knock at the door of the deep female psyche" (pg 5). Rather than, as Dr. Estes wrote, living "life as a disguised creature" (pg 4), young women have, just by being themselves and demanding to be seen, been using "bravery to obtain the call of necessity." As is reflected in Dr. Este's book, young female leaders are "showing up, and showing their souls."

270   The love of power, or the power of love. This is a theme running throughout the book Waking the Global Heart: Humanities Rite of Passage from the Love of Power to the Power of Love (Elite Books, 2006) by Anodea Judith, Ph.D., who is a former therapist now teaching spiritual classes world-wide. She considers the practice of the power of love instead of the love of power to be part of the emergence of a new social consciousness which is a rite of passage. For Ms. Judith's introductory commentary on her books theme, see pp 17-19.

271   An expression of love in creating our evolving consciousness and emergent institutions is described by Juliet Schor as "casting off 19th Century structures (such as belief in unending expansion and perpetual growth) and creating models of sustainability (maintaining balance and honoring modest means of survival)." See the editor's opening comments in the Preface to their book, Sustainable Planet, Solutions for the 21st Century (Beacon Press, 2003), edited by Juliet Schor and Betsy Taylor. pp ix – xi.

272   Sustainable Planet Ibid. Cited from one of this book's chapters, "In Search of Justice" by Nydia M. Velazquez (pp 33–44). Quotes are referenced from pp 33–34.

273   Sustainable Planet Ibid. Cited from one of this book's chapters, "In Search of Justice" by Nydia M. Velazquez (pp 33–44). Quotes are referenced from pp 33–34.

274   Honor the loom of the future under construction—remember the womb of the past which constructed the foundation and path

of our efforts. An appreciation for this intention-based connection is brought home by Chris Saade in his book, Second Wave Spirituality (North Atlantic Books, 2014). Mr. Saade had been a native of Lebanon, who established the Olive Branch Center in North Carolina after emigrating here. Mr. Saade honors the memories and the continuing relevance of our ancestral social justice allies: "Our collective imagination was conceived in the amazing dreams of many social movements: labor, suffragettes, human right, civic rights, democratic reforms, and ecological sustainability, among others. We cannot deny or expunge ourselves from the historical womb which bore us. We know that any dreams we enjoy today have been forged by the unbounded efforts and the audacity of those who preceded us" (pg 124).

275 Honor the loom of the future under construction—remember the womb of the past which constructed the foundation and path of our efforts. An appreciation for this intention-based connection is brought home by Chris Saade in his book, Second Wave Spirituality (North Atlantic Books, 2014). Mr. Saade had been a native of Lebanon, who established the Olive Branch Center in North Carolina after emigrating here. Mr. Saade honors the memories and the continuing relevance of our ancestral social justice allies: "Our collective imagination was conceived in the amazing dreams of many social movements: labor, suffragettes, human right, civic rights, democratic reforms, and ecological sustainability, among others. We cannot deny or expunge ourselves from the historical womb which bore us. We know that any dreams we enjoy today have been forged by the unbounded efforts and the audacity of those who preceded us" (pg 124).

276 An appreciation for the promise of the past and potential for the future should be infused into history courses and civics training to expand the perspective about human agency as being connected across the bounds of time. In an article titled "How Does Expansive

Framing Promote Transfer" (transfer of skills and applied understanding), this value is highlighted in its abstract: "When contexts are framed expansively, students are positioned as actively contributing to larger conversations that extend across time, places, and people." The article was written by Randi Engle, Diane P. Lam, Xenia S. Meyer, and Sarah E Nix. (Educational Psychologist, July 2012, Vol. 47, No. 3).

277　A "future-oriented offense" is a term coined by Jon May of the University of Pittsburg: "Memories of the future really are what we are talking about. The idea that by briefly or temporarily putting yourself in the future, and thinking about what it is like there, and then coming back to the present, influences the decisions you make" (pg 177). Mr. May is quoted by Rob Hopkins in his book, From What Is To What If (Chelsea Green, 2019).

278　My point here is to acknowledge Eleanor Roosevelt's contribution to drafting the "Declaration of Human Rights." At the time she was chair of the United Nations Human Rights Committee. www.nps. gov/elro/index.htm

279　The international community affirmed its commitment to assuring the right of dignity to each person when it ratified its Constitution on December 10, 1948. As stated in the Constitution's Article I, Chapter I, "Each person needs to be assured of free and equal dignity, each person endowed with reason and conscience." www.un.org/ en/universaldeclarationohumanrights

280　In the first draft to the U.N. Constitution, there was also a clause stating, "Everyone has duties to the community in which alone the free and full development of his personality is possible." Ibid, U.N. www.un.org/en/universaldeclarationohumanrights

281　In the first draft to the U.N. Constitution, there was also a clause stating, "Everyone has duties to the community in which alone the free and full development of his personality is possible." Ibid, U.N. www.un.org/en/universaldeclarationohumanrights

282   Angeles Arrien, in her book, The Four-Fold Way (Harper San Francisco, 1993) introduces us to archetypes and reminds us that their wisdom is embedded in the collective memory of our intention for creating a more beautiful world. Within the chapters in her book, she profiles the "Warrior (show up and choose to be present); The Healer (pay attention to what has heart and meaning); the Visionary (tell the truth without blame or judgement; and the Teacher (be open to outcome, but don't be attached to outcome)." Cited from the book's Table of Contents. For Ms. Arrien's introductory comments in the chapter on The Healer, see pg 49; for the Visionary, pp 79-80; and for the Teacher pg 109.

283   Carolyn Myss, Sacred Contracts. One of the archetypes influencing the actions of civic co-mentors is that of what Ms. Myss calls the Eccentric, or Non-Conformer. Ms. Myss claims that periodically, circumstances produce a breeding ground for eccentrics. Ms. Myss describes two archetypes which are peculiar to the eccentric person. The first is her archetype called the Alchemist (see pp 366-367) and the second archetype is called the Visionary (see pp 421 – 422). Writer W. Puck Brecher calls these breeding grounds places of creating many "moments of strangeness" inspiring the energy to transform mainstream culture. The instability, imbalance, and chaos existing in period of transition between eras lends many a change-maker to feel that we are all living in those moments of strangeness. See The Aesthetics of Strangeness by W Puck Brecher (University of Hawaii Press, 2013).

284   The Four-Fold Way by Angeles Arrien on non-judgmental truth-telling pages (Harper-San Francisco, 1993), pp 120–121.

285   Ibid The Four-Fold Way This is a reference to the author's comments on remaining open and developing trust (pp 109–111).

286   Page 223. The Sacred Contract, by Caroline Myss Ibid The Advocate (pg 366).

287   The Sacred Contract Ibid The Eccentric (or Sacred Clown). pp 377–378.

288   The Sacred Contract Ibid The Alchemist (pg 366).

289   The Sacred Contract Ibid The Pioneer (pg 404).

290   See the book, 100 Key Documents in American History, by Peter B. Levy (Praeger, 2004). Declaration of Independence… "inalienable rights to life, liberty and happiness… just powers of government are derived from the consent of the governed… grievances listing abuses of government (for example, remote and arbitrarily constructed laws, refusal to respond to petitions)"—all of these are basic tenants of our founding principles (pp 461–464).

Benjamin Franklin stated that an oracle is a mistress who can see farthest into the future (pg 4), and it has been the mistresses throughout our nation's history of dissent who have fought to keep our founding principles to be applicable in the future.

Sojourner Truth was a freedom fighter who in 1867 protested the exclusion of women for the right to vote. In her protest she proclaimed: "I have as good rights as anybody. There is a great stir about colored men getting their rights, but not a word about the colored women…if we wait…it will take a long time to get it going again" (pg 174).

In 1962, the authors of the Port Huron Statement (Founding document of the Students for A Democratic Society) included these observations about the state of our society's commitment to democracy: "We began to see that what was perceived as the American Golden Age was actually the decline of an era. The world-wide outbreak against colonialism and imperialism, the entrenchment of totalitarian states (whose leaders are supported with American funds), the menace of war, these trends were testing the tenacity of our commitment to democracy and freedom" (pg 415). All citations are from the book, 100 Key Documents in American History edited by Peter B. Levy (Praeger, 1994).

291   "The universe as a source of information" (pp 96–97) is a concept introduced by Paul Levy in his book, The Quantum Revelation: A Radical Synthesis of Science and Spirituality (Select Books, 2018). He documents theories and findings from the scientific field of quantum physics and finds their speculative findings and some conclusions to be closely aligned with those of indigenous and ancestral wisdom traditions. One question that has been raised by ancestral philosophers and quantum-theory oriented physicists is about the validity of total objectivity being possible. As one scientist Levy covers states: "What we observe is not nature itself, but nature exposed to our method of questioning" (pg 4). One of the concerns brought up with scientific research today is that if the questions and proposed theories of a research study are based upon unconsciously held bias, the findings at the end of a study may be filtered through this bias, and lead to what scientists call "confirmational bias."

292   Establishing a therapeutic alliance. In his book Indigenous Healing Psychology: Honoring the Wisdom of Indigenous Peoples (Healing Arts Press, 2017), Dr. Richard Katz, Ph.D. questions using the practice of doctors and patients (with its professional rules for maintaining objectivity—that is, strict application of a therapeutic theory governing communication). He holds that in indigenous practice, practitioners honor the "wisdom of patients" (pp 24–27). As Dr. Katz continues: "I listen to the painfully earned knowing from those called 'patients,' an establishment label that marginalizes them. The term 'patient'…highlights the power structure that puts doctors and therapists in charge, not only of the patients but also of all the knowledge that might lead to their recovery—in essence of knowledge generation itself" (pg 24). In a parallel fashion, I hold the position in my book that the label "student" marginalizes young people. The

alternative is to adopt the model proposed by the Latin American educator Paolo Freire, which proposes an educational alliance where the teacher is also a student, and the student a teacher.

293   "The futility of looking for solutions outside of ourselves" (pg 51) is a theme developed by the writer Salman Rushdie. In his take about the theme of the book and the movie The Wizard of Oz, he proposes the story speaks to "the weakness of adults, who have abandoned their responsibilities for the new generation" (this quote is on the back cover of Rushdie's book). It is as Dorothy begins to identify assets being sought by her three allies (the scarecrow – brains; the tin man – heart; and the lion – courage) as already present within herself that she grows more self-confident and achieves her aim of returning home. The Wizard of Oz by Salman Rushdie (BMI Film Classics, 2nd edition, 2012).

294   "Obtaining ownership over our wounds" describes a process spoken to by Chris Grasso in his book, Everything Mind: What I Have Learned About Hard Knocks (Sounds True Publications, 2015). Mr. Grasso, in sharing the trials and triumphs along the road of recovery to addiction, details it is in how we gradually take responsibility, that is, taking ownership for our condition, that we develop a new sense of identity. ("For the love of the wounded," pp 39–44).

295   Learning to stand alone, unpopular and reviled, is a popular saying amongst marginalized peoples first written by Audre Lorde. Ms. Lorde originally expressed these words in her speech "The Master's Tools will never dismantle the master's House" delivered at the Second Sex Conference in New York (September 29, 1979). See the website: https://www.bighivemind.com and the post " Audre Lorde Quote from Feminism to Self-Care", posted on March14,2018. The thought of standing strong, on your own, is cited in another way from her book, Sister Outsider (Crossing Press: Crown Publishing, 1984). See pg 113 on " reaching down into that deep place."

296   People believe that youth in this country… is taken from a quote cited from the article "The Disrupters: How the Youth Activists of #NeverAgain are Upending Gun Politics," The Nation Magazine, May 7, 2018, Vol. 306, No. 13.

297   The "sense of right or wrong…is part of his nature" is a quote made about Thomas Jefferson, which is cited by Matthew Stewart in his book, Nature's God (Norton, 2014), pp 353–354. It speaks to Jefferson's belief that civil rights are embedded in every person's natural right for life, liberty, and the pursuit of happiness.

298   "The rock, the terrain, a compelling force for ideas" is a concept expressed by Ralph Ellison in his book, The Invisible Man (1952). With this thought, Ellison expressed that it is as a person struggles on a rocky road that they develop a compelling force for reaching their ideals. The fact that this person may remain invisible to others does not diminish the value of his or her struggle.

299   The complexity of creativity is developed in books I have referenced by two people involved in psychology and human potential. The first person is Howard Gardner who has developed theory of what he calls multiple intelligences—cognitive, physical, emotional, and others. He looks at certain characteristics of emotional intelligence in teens, which are portrayed in a negative fashion by adults, as actually being positive attributes essential to personal development and useful for social progress. One of his thoughts is that adolescents have an ability to "move from one extreme to another" which he sees as useful in learning to adapt (pg 57). Source: Intelligence Reframed: Multiple Intelligences for the 21st Century (Basic Books, 1999). The second person, Mihaly Csikszentmihalyi, in his book Creativity: Flow and the Psychology of Discovery and Invention (Harper Perennial, 1996) notes, "In his study of the major creative geniuses of this century, a certain immaturity, both emotional and mental, can go hand in hand with the deepest insights" (pg 60). He

also attributes the philosopher Goethe as having said that a certain naiveté is the most important attribute of genius (pg 60).

300   Purposeful individuality and commitment to a whole group in search of the common good is an underlying process essential to a healthy democracy. Jean Bethke Elstain, in her book Democracy on Trial (Basic Books, 1995) cites three pillars of a optimally functioning democracy: "A preparedness to work with others different from oneself toward shared ends; a combination of string convictions with a readiness to compromise in the recognition that one can't always get what one wants; and a sense of individuality and a commitment to civic goods that are not the possession of one person or one small group" (pg 2: Democratic Dispositions).

301   One of the positive legacies in Washington Heights is our having benefited from folks with differing points of origin agreeing to pursue common destinations.

Coogan's Bar and Restaurant, located at West 169th Street and Broadway, was a safe haven for people from all walks of life. Coogan's, founded by Dave Hunt and Peter Walsh in 1986, although only a few feet away from a potential shootout on any given evening, provided a sanctuary with great food, a homegrown ale, and, according to one of its most loyal customers, Steve Simon, the best apricot pastry desert in town. The walls of Coogan's were covered in pictures, posters, and banners celebrating the histories of Washington Heights diverse residents, from the Irish, Germans, Italian, and Jews in the early 1900s, to Blacks and Puerto Ricans also finding a home, to Dominicans, Central Americans, and Russians arriving in large numbers beginning in the 1970s. Walls provided a layered history, and the tables and the bar a place for diverse peoples to break bread, drink, and share stories. A memorable legacy for Coogan's was its sponsorship of the Shamrock, Salsa and Blues 5K run, where adults and children of every national stipe ran along Ft. Washington

Avenue, from the Armory Center to Ft. Tryon Park and then back home again. The "most integrated place in NYC" proudly hosted this event for well over a decade. Reference: Crossing Broadway by Robert W. Snyder (Cornell University Press, 2015, pg 177.) For link to Coogan's, which is now permanently closed, but active online, see www.coogans.com

Jeffrey Stout in his book, Blessed Are the Organized (Princeton University Press, 2008), speaks to the ongoing value of institutionalizing integrated practice and celebrations. As Mr. Stout proclaims: "(This) provides a sense of democracy (as) we have seen in grassroots democratic organizations endeavoring to institute distinction and cultivate excellence (pg 139). As Mr. Stout continues, "Ordinary people cooperate in the spirit of mutual recognition and accountability" (pg 14).

302   Bob Dylan's song… Clean Cut Kid on the Empire Burlesque Album, Special Rider Music, 1984.

303   Tupac Shakur's song… The World Ain't Ready To See. I cite from the film Resurrection and the Underground (Lauren Lazin, Preston Holmes and Kenolyn Ali) Paramount Films, November 16, 2003.

304   Practicing Social Inclusion, Edited by Ann Taket, Beth Crispo, et al. (Routledge, 2014) Australian elders commented on the need of peoples from different origins to practice marching shoulder to shoulder. Continuing with the cited quote in the text, the editors go on to say: "Decentralized and inclusive networks are built upon a spirit of collegiality and collaboration. We work on short- and long-term projects with people sharing key responsibilities and collective ownership." pg 103.

305   Pedagogy of the Oppressed (30th Anniversary edition: ISBN 10-082641279), Paolo Freire. One theme that is reinforced throughout this book is that student knowledge is best constructed by their analyzing, studying, and suggesting intervention in their own immediate

environments and community. This helps them to connect knowledge and theory through academic experimentation and direct experience. Mr. Freire reiterates the need to allow student responsibility in reconstructing the world in his book titled Pedagogy of Indignation (Paradigm Publishers, 2004). See his chapter " Second Letter: On the Right and the Duty to Change the World, pp 36-37.

306   The following quote represents the sense of each person having roots and drawing identify from their own inner sanctuary. "Each child lives deep inside his or her own psychic house, or soul castle. The child deserves the right to their own sovereignty inside that house. Whenever a person ignores that sovereignty and invades (that space), the child feels not only anger, but shame. The child concludes that if it has no sovereignty, that he or she must be worthless." Although our nation's founders did not specifically use this language, in essence this is what they referred to with their insistence upon recognizing each person's dignity and rights as "inalienable" in the Declaration of Independence. Source for the quote: Iron John by Robert Bly (De Capo Press, 1990), pg 147.

307   Each teen deserves to realize their dreams, as derived from their "soul castle" and worked on in unison with their peers. When this is sabotaged or denied, Greta Thunberg describes the response of teens: "You have stolen my dreams and my childhood with your empty words. Yet, I am one of the lucky ones. (Still a victim but suffering less severe consequences by those in her generation suffering the effects of poverty and racism.) What our entire generation must now face (without recognized voice and because of the adult generation's neglect) is entire eco-systems in collapse. We are in the beginning stages of mass extinction, and all you talk about is money and fairy tales of eternal economic growth. How Dare You!" Cited from: PBS News Hour website, Gretchen Frazier, September 9, 2019.

308   Environmental neglect and crimes against the future. In a chapter of his book, Neck Deep in Denial, Derrick Jensen provide these powerful words meant to keep resistance alive and to wake up those sleep-walking toward dead futures: "(Those who construct a combine of) an extractive machine economy with infinite demand (ensure) that you've got the death of pretty much everything it touches. Instead of hope being a comfort, it deserves to be in a box with plaques (honoring) sorrow and mischief so that is serves the need of those in power.") Endgame, Volume I: The Problem of Civilization by Derrick Jensen (Seven Stories Press, 2006), pg 329.

309   A famed Russian dissident echoed these words on the international stage (which are quoted by Jensen): "We do not err because the truth is difficult to see. We err because this is more comfortable." (Alexander Solzhenitsyn, cited from his words quoted in the Sun magazine, March 2004, pg 48). When Solzhenitsyn refers to as "this" in his reference to " more comfortable" is conflating habitual responses and allegiance to misinformed and malignant practices with establishing autonomous efforts to see the truth.

310   I have seen these words, "Learn how to turn your wounds from enemies into friends" attributed to Ram Dass at a few meetings I have attended over the years. Ram Dass was a spiritual seeker and activist for human dignity who also cofounded the Seva Foundation. www.seva.org

311   The health rights campaign profiled in this article is one example of an emergent social narrativeprofiling teen empowerment. In an article documenting the training of teens to become grassroots health workers, it is shown how the progressive actions of a medical school results in a generationally collaborative effort for more equitable health outcomes. In the article, "High School Health Workers? It Works!" the story from Atlanta, Georgia, highlights the innovative program launched by Arletha Livingstone, the Director of

the Innovative Learning Laboratory at Morehouse College. (YES! Magazine, Spring 2020.) The staff from the Morehouse Community Health Worker Program became mentors to trained teens who served as credible messengers and gatekeepers for positive health outcomes for their peers. www.yesmagazine.org/issue/world-we-want/2020/02/19/high-school-health-workers February 19, 2020.

312   My Uncle Pierre as a literary guide and an influence upon my future career and civic engagement decisions. Although each of these three books differ (between fiction and policy narrative), they seem to have had (considering the clouds of interference inherent in recalling childhood memories) compelling messages (somewhat conscious but also subliminal). *The Three Musketeers* represented to me the value of loyalty in a team defending dignity and idealistic expectations. *The Lord of the Rings* took this to a new context, where little people accomplished big things. People of modest means succeeded in forming a coalition of diverse allies, including tree-like beings, bringing an eco-justice dimension to this tale where those who valued tradition and the right to autonomous resisted monolithic and sometimes invisible forces seeking to subvert their cause. I read *Pedagogy of the Oppressed* while in high school, and was, especially given my experience of being in educational places managed by remote control, impressed that places existed where teachers and students worked collaboratively and with equal power. I have no idea which editions of these books were in my possession during my youth, so just provide three references of more recent publication here. The *Three Musketeers* by Alexander Dumas (Wordsworth Classics, August 1, 1997); *The Lord of the Rings* by J.R.R. Tolkien (boxed trilogy), Mass Market Paperbacks, September 25, 2012. *Pedagogy of the Oppressed* by Paolo Freire (30th Anniversary Edition) ISBN 10-0826412769.

313   A national network of leaders working to build a more just society" are words included in the introduction to the Petra Foundation's

Guide: Soaring Spirits: Petra Foundation Fellows, 1989–2015. www.petrafoundation.org

314   A profile of the Police Athletic League's Youth Link Program (serving young adults 16–24) can be found at the PAL website: www.palnyc.org .

315   Southern Heights Youth Program description, presented in a book titled Youth Participation Directory, Volume II – Program Models in New York City, was completed in May of 1992 by the New York State Youth Council (pg 71). I am not sure if this edition, put together by Nan Kreger, EdD and Evelyn Rivera, still exists, either in hard copy form or online.

316   The banking model of education" is a concept referenced by Paolo Freire in several of his works and is a central theme in his critique of traditional education. Being reintroduced to this theme was done with my recent reading of Pedagogy of Indignation (Paradigm Publishers, 2004).

317   Testimony was provided about the life and service of Pierre Johannet at his memorial service - A service of remembrance and thanksgiving at the Bigelow Chapel at Mount Auburn Cemetery, Cambridge, Massachusetts on December 13, 2015.

318   Amongst the conversations with Pierre, his wife Meg, and me, was the topic concerning the relationship between narrowly devised measure of intelligence and the practice of sorting and tracking students according to intelligence levels. In her book, Keeping Track: How Schools Structure Inequality (Yale University Press, 1985), Jeannie Oakes references sources of putting sorting and tracking practices in place as standard educational practice. One example I cite here: "We picture the educational system as having an important educational function, as a selecting agency, for providing a means of selecting those men of best intelligence from the deficient and

mediocre." (Scientific Monthly, January 2021, pg 71) and referenced in Oakes' book, note 41 on pg 304.

319   A second topic in our conversations was on the letdown of drug abuse prevention programs... I reference one source here, presented by Kenneth R. Rosen in his book, America Troubled: The Failed Promise of Behavior Treatment Programs (Little A, New York, 2021). Mr. Rosen speaks to his experiences with these programs, when he emphasizes in his book that these types of programs would be the last in a string of camps and schools all striving to 'fix me'. I realize that I have carried this winter with me ever since. I gave myself that scar. The numbers are still etched in my skin today. It is a police code for child delinquent. This quote is one sample of testimony on the damage created to young adults when punishment and adverse programming is justified for use against young victims of trauma-induced experiences.

320   Philosophic influence on the therapeutic approach used by my Uncle Pierre. My uncle, Dr. Pierre Johannet, was influenced by the Freudian French psychoanalyst Jacques Lacan. His approach assumed that "the unconscious is 'structured like a language.'" (JSTOR journal article, Vol. 9, No. 2, Special Issue of Jacques Lacan, Spring/Summer, 1996, pp 77–104). The point made here is that there are thought constructions and types of logic inherent to every level of consciousness, including the hidden sub-conscious levels, which still influence according to its structural suggestions. When unconsciously held fears, such as fears about " the other," or anxiety about economic uncertainty threaten deeply held fear about survival, are responded to using subconscious sources, a person may not be consciously aware or even consider or process responses that lead to "fight or flight" programs lying deep within us. A Lacanian reference to this syndrome can be found in an article, "Trust No One, A Conversation with Michael Burkun," pp 64 – 70 in The Lacanian Review (Issue 01/

Spring, 2016)). This type of unconsciously derived reaction is what I refer to in this book as a kind of shadow-based mythmaking.

321   The forces of nature are not inferior, but rather essential to life. Amma's philosophy was shared with me and my siblings, Jacquie and Nicole, by Pierre Johannet and his wife Meg Turner. This belief is also discussed in a book called

Nature's God (Norton, 2014) by Matthew Stewart, he postulated that "Nature's God was the presiding deity of the American Revolution… when Jefferson inserted it into the Declaration of Independence, (he) assumed that it the powers on earth for which men are entitled derive from the laws of nature" (pp 138–139). For an overview of Amma's teachings, see https://amma.org/teachings

322   Significant to me in extending my scope of understanding about the importance of ecology, soul and our relationship with those realms were readings in environmental connections to social justice, and the practice of spiritual activism. There is an evolving intersection between environmentalism and spiritual responsibility. In his introduction to the book, Eco-psychology: Restoring the Earth/ Healing the Mind (Sierra Club Books, 1995), Theodore Roszak, an editor of this book states: "The ecological unconscious, a greater ecological intelligence, is deeply rooted in the psyche" (pg 14). In other words, ecological structures, processes, and relationships exist not just in natural external environments, but also with the natural environment of the psyche. As inside, so it is outside. The holistic education writer Susan A. Schiller puts this in another way in her chapter called "Contemplating Great Things in Soul and Place." This chapter is a contribution to the book called Holistic Learning (SUNY Press, 2005, edited by Theodore Roszik, et al): "…balance, inclusion and connection (which we perceive) as photos of outdoor scenes invoke (within us) poetic images as the starting point of imagination" (pp 162–163).

323   In my understanding of a concept developed by the spiritually oriented philosopher Ken Wilbur, consciousness evolves not in a linear sequence of totally distinct autonomous structures but as a spiraling series of "nesting cubes," where old paradigms continue to exist and have relevance, but within the context and with new perspectives gained in an evolved level of consciousness. This is a theory developed by Ken Wilbur in his book, A Brief History of Everything (Shambala Press 1996). So, for instance, as Mr. Wilbur has pointed out, we humans had a period in our evolution where a tribal consciousness promoted a functional development of survival against daunting odds, where people with affinities developed habits and institutions of cooperative support. This kind of thinking kept people perceived as possibly a threat to survival at a distance, and when it was thought necessary, tribes went to battle to secure territory. We are now engaged with an evolved level of consciousness, where we realize that we are all part of one extended family called humanity, and that to survive, we need everybody else. The tribal consciousness still exists and is functional on some levels (ease of communication amongst those who are most familiar with each other) but becoming dysfunctional on a planet where joint planning and respect is crucial for solving problems (environmental degradation) that affect everyone no matter their differences.

324   In my understanding of a concept developed by the spiritually oriented philosopher Ken Wilbur, consciousness evolves not in a linear sequence of totally distinct autonomous structures but as a spiraling series of "nesting cubes," where old paradigms continue to exist and have relevance, but within the context and with new perspectives gained in an evolved level of consciousness. This is a theory developed by Ken Wilbur in his book, A Brief History of Everything (Shambala Press 1996). So, for instance, as Mr. Wilbur has pointed out, we humans had a period in our evolution where a tribal consciousness promoted a functional development of survival

against daunting odds, where people with affinities developed habits and institutions of cooperative support. This kind of thinking kept people perceived as possibly a threat to survival at a distance, and when it was thought necessary, tribes went to battle to secure territory. We are now engaged with an evolved level of consciousness, where we realize that we are all part of one extended family called humanity, and that to survive, we need everybody else. The tribal consciousness still exists and is functional on some levels (ease of communication amongst those who are most familiar with each other) but becoming dysfunctional on a planet where joint planning and respect is crucial for solving problems (environmental degradation) that affect everyone no matter their differences.

325   The emerging generation has more evolved viewpoints on the reasons for and responses to critical issues in our transitional era. For example, the millennial generation consensus on the environment. In the book, When Millennials Rule: The Reshaping of America (Post Hill Press, 2016), authors David and Jack Cahn hold that the millennial generation has a more progressed viewpoint on the urgency of fixing damages to our ecological infrastructure than those of the preceding generation. As stated by the Cahn's: "Millennials say climate justice is an issue divided along generational rather than political lines. Three of four of us recognize that global warming is real, as compared to 61% of Americans...Two-thirds of young Americans say they plan to vote for a candidate who supports cutting greenhouse gasses and increasing financial incentives for adopting renewable energy. Just half of seniors agree" (pg 77). As the authors continue, this new generation of voters makes decisions about why to vote based upon what they see as our present-day elected officials' dysfunctional divisive behaviors: "Realism manifests in a tendency to compromise...millennials came of age during one of the most politically polarized times in American history...Party politics has torn Washington apart. Instead of fighting ideological wars,

millennials want to unify around common-sense ideas: we need better jobs, safer streets, and stronger schools" (pg 244).

326   Kamau Marcharia biographical sketch in the Petra Anniversary Journal - Soaring Spirits (pg 75). See www.petrafoundation.org and click on to download the journal. (This sketch can also be found at the Petra Foundation section in the Center For Community Change website).

327   Kamau Marcharia biographical sketch in the Petra Anniversary Journal - Soaring Spirits (pg 75). See www.petrafoundation.org and click on to download the journal. (This sketch can also be found at the Petra Foundation section in the Center For Community Change website).

328   Kamau Marcharia biographical sketch in the Petra Anniversary Journal - Soaring Spirits (pg 75).See www.petrafoundation.org and click on to download the journal. (This sketch can also be found at the Petra Foundation section in the Center For Community Change website).

329   Kimberly Crenshaw, a black woman, and social justice advocate gave an interview in which she discusses young black people's negative hyper-visibility and the invisibility for injustices of our nation's criminal justice system. In the interview, Ms. Crenshaw also states that we need to "rethink (our) reliance on inequality as a product of (individual) deficits and cultures. Rather, it is a problem of damaged institutions that have never really recon-structed themselves after segregation." (the online interview does not have page numbers) See Forbes Magazine interview online. Marianne Schnall is credited in the byline on June 15, 2020. See https://www.forbes.com/sites/marianneschnall/2020/06/12/interview-with-kimberle-crenshaw/?sh=42abf3a1427c

330   Kimberly Crenshaw, a black woman, and social justice advocate gave an interview in which she discusses young black people's

negative hyper-visibility and the invisibility for injustices of our nation's criminal justice system. In the interview, Ms. Crenshaw also states that we need to "rethink (our) reliance on inequality as a product of (individual) deficits and cultures. Rather, it is a problem of damaged institutions that have never really reconstructed themselves after segregation." (the online interview does not have page numbers) See Forbes Magazine interview online. Marianne Schnall is credited in the byline on June 15, 2020. See https://www.forbes.com/sites/marianneschnall/2020/06/12/interview-with-kimberle-crenshaw/?sh=42abf3a1427c

331   Kimberly Crenshaw, a black woman, and social justice advocate gave an interview in which she discusses young black people's negative hyper-visibility and the invisibility for injustices of our nation's criminal justice system. In the interview, Ms. Crenshaw also states that we need to "rethink (our) reliance on inequality as a product of (individual) deficits and cultures. Rather, it is a problem of damaged institutions that have never really reconstructed themselves after segregation." (the online interview does not have page numbers) See Forbes Magazine interview online. Marianne Schnall is credited in the byline on June 15, 2020. See https://www.forbes/com/sites/marianneschnall/2020/06/12/interview-with-kimberle-crenshaw/?sh=42abf3a1427c

332   Our society's leaders have for too long stuck to old scripts attributing a predisposition for violence amongst blacks as innate, rather than the result of the deep wounding suffered because of trauma. Recent studies in a field called epigenetics have shown that "genes are not fixed...life events can trigger biochemical processes...making it sensitive to the messages of the body. Life events can change the behavior of a gene, but do not alter its chemical structure. Patterns, however, can be passed along to offspring, a phenomenon known as epigenetics." See the Body Keeps the Score by Bessel Van Der Kolk, M.D. (Penguin Books, 2014) pg154. Social messages can also

sabotage the use of life supportive responses after a person is subject to a traumatic incident. See the book Mind: A Journey to the Heart of Being Human, by Daniel J. Siegel, MD (Norton and Company, 2017). Dr. Siegel exposes the misuse of cause and effect. He shows how "The brain structure is molded by the messages it receives". pg 320. The stress of trauma, combined with the misdirection and abuse of ill-informed messaging, have created the socially shared illusion about young blacks being a danger to themselves and others, rather than addressing the reality that undiagnosed trauma is a danger to our social cohesion and stability.

333   The Robert McGuire Scholarship program provided for personal testimony from scholarship applicants which were submitted to the McGuire committee. The applications included an applicant summary page of information, the applicant statement, an educational record of coursework from the applicant's school, and two recommendation letters, one from a PAL staff member and one from a schoolteacher. The stories are often awe-inspiring testimonies to the strength of spirit some teens exhibit in overcoming obstacles. In one year alone (2018), the committee I served on awarded a teen who had lost her mother at a critical juncture in her life, teens who had started high school with very low grade- point averages who turned coursework around after finding a mentor, and another teen who had taken a wrong turn on the streets, correcting his course and then becoming a role model for peers. Today, the chair of the McGuire Committee is Dana Wheeler. dwheeler@palnyc.org . For PAL see www.palnyc.org

334   Each of these notes contain excerpts of quotes from the E'niyah's hard copy application package which included her application essay, and letters of support from her PAL counselor and a schoolteacher.

335   Each of these notes contain excerpts of quotes from the E'niyah's hard copy application package which included her application essay, and letters of support from her PAL counselor and a schoolteacher.

336   Each of these notes contain excerpts of quotes from the E'niyah's hard copy application package which included her application essay, and letters of support from her PAL counselor and a schoolteacher.

337   Each of these notes contain excerpts of quotes from the E'niyah's hardcopy application package which included her application essay, and letters of support from her PAL counselor and a schoolteacher.

338   Each of these notes contain excerpts of quotes from the E'niyah's hard copy application package which included her application essay, and letters of support from her PAL counselor and a schoolteacher.

339   The practice of reconciliation is an alternative method of judgment used in the justice system. When used as an alternative to punishment, going through the process of reconciliation can have a deep impact on those for whom the traditional justice system might label incorrigible or lost. For the person aggrieved, there can be a meaningful consequence for the perpetrator in the face of loss by the aggrieved. For the perpetrator, he or she is extended the opportunity to accept responsibility for his or her acts, and to abide by an agreement to compensate both the aggrieved and the larger community. One of the PAL programs, called Youth Link, referred young adults for consideration of awards by the McGuire scholarship committee. All these referrals were made as mandates, that is, a requirement to attend the Youth Link program in lieu of serving time in a correctional setting. Initially, many of these participants were reticent, suspicious, or oppositional. However, after gradually developing a trusting relationship with a Youth Link staff member and participating in a program where other young adults served as peer role models, young people would decide to take a new course, develop resistance skills against relapse to self-sabotaging

and harmful behaviors, and graduate with a ticket of acceptance to a college. See www.palnyc.org

340   Making its safe for all souls to enter the room. In advising on creating classroom space, which is an inviting experience for students, Parker J. Palmer describes this space as "a place where it is safe for your feelings to emerge. Teaching and learning is a human enterprise. We must use human emotions in the learning process rather than letting them use us" pg 85. An example of a classroom lesson which might raise the temperature for students is one in which the topic is controversial. If the topic is one such as immigration, and in teaching the lesson the teacher allows for expression of opposing positions on immigration, between that of being open to all who seek exile and one which calls for imposing harsher restrictions, this can invoke emotional reactions, both overtly and hidden. A teacher in a classroom with a diverse student body, some born here and some either immigrants or the children of immigrants, needs to check in with all students on their cognitive, emotional, and bodily responses to words that are triggers. See the book, To Know As We Are Known by Parker J. Palmer (Harper San Francisco, 1993)

341   In order to ensure safe space, internally and externally, we need to break new ground, navigating the challenge of belonging nowhere. Students who have come to the U.S. to escape danger and harsh conditions, who also encounter dismissive comments or threats because of their identity, often remain in a state of feeling perpetually unsettled and unsure of where they stand with others. In a sense, it is as if they are orphans from the homeland and their new habitat. To read further about Parker Palmers methods for creating a safe space, see a chapter in his book, To Know As We Are Known (Harper San Francisco, 1993) called 'To Teach is to Create Space'. I refer here to his thoughts about approaching relationships with openness, respecting the boundaries of another person, and creating at atmosphere of hospitality in a space. See pp 71 -75. As noted by

an educator named F. Christopher Reynolds, "...the orphan path comes with the challenge of belonging nowhere." pg 207. Quote is from an article by Mr. Reynolds called "A Gathering of Orphans" in the book Holistic Learning and Spirituality in Education (SUNY Press, 2005), edited by John P. Miller et al.

342   In order to ensure safe space, internally and externally, we need to break new ground, navigating the challenge of belonging nowhere. Students who have come to the U.S. to escape danger and harsh conditions, who also encounter dismissive comments or threats because of their identity, often remain in a state of feeling perpetually unsettled and unsure of where they stand with others. In a sense, it is as if they are orphans from the homeland and their new habitat. To read further about Parker Palmers methods for creating a safe space, see a chapter in his book, To Know As We Are Known (Harper San Francisco, 1993) called 'To Teach is to Create Space'. I refer here to his thoughts about approaching relationships with openness, respecting the boundaries of another person, and creating at atmosphere of hospitality in a space. See pp 71 -75. As noted by an educator named F. Christopher Reynolds, "...the orphan path comes with the challenge of belonging nowhere." pg 207. Quote is from an article by Mr. Reynolds called "A Gathering of Orphans" in the book Holistic Learning and Spirituality in Education (SUNY Press, 2005), edited by John P. Miller et al.

343   In order to ensure safe space, internally and externally, we need to break new ground, navigating the challenge of belonging nowhere. Students who have come to the U.S. to escape danger and harsh conditions, who also encounter dismissive comments or threats because of their identity, often remain in a state of feeling perpetually unsettled and unsure of where they stand with others. In a sense, it is as if they are orphans from the homeland and their new habitat. To read further about Parker Palmers methods for creating a safe space, see a chapter in his book, To Know As We Are Known

(Harper San Francisco, 1993) called 'To Teach is to Create Space'. I refer here to his thoughts about approaching relationships with openness, respecting the boundaries of another person, and creating at atmosphere of hospitality in a space. See pp 71 -75. As noted by an educator named F. Christopher Reynolds, "…the orphan path comes with the challenge of belonging nowhere." pg 207. Quote is from an article by Mr. Reynolds called "A Gathering of Orphans" in the book Holistic Learning and Spirituality in Education (SUNY Press, 2005), edited by John P. Miller et al.

344   From the mid-1980s until the early 1990s, there was concentration of crime in pockets of the Washington Heights neighborhood (areas about 5 square blocks, one entered on Amsterdam Avenue in the West 160th Street blocks, and the second on a corridor along St. Nicholas Avenue in the West 170th Street blocks). As part of my civic engagement in the Heights, beginning in the 1980s, I would attend meetings at our local 34th Police Precinct called Precinct Council meetings. These councils were made of civilian volunteers who served as officers. The captain of the precinct would give a crime status report at each meeting. For an overview of the purpose and functioning of NYPD Precinct Councils, see the website at www. ojp.gov/pdffiles1/Digitization/145633NCJRS.pdf

345   Response of Marvin Higgins, the Community Board #12 chairperson, to comments made by Miriam. Community Board Report in The Washington Heights and Inwood Citizen News, June 15–June 29, 1991, pg 13.

346   Ibid. Washington Heights and Citizen News Maria Rivera, District Manager of Community Board #12 response to Miriam's presentation. pg 13.

Both Higgins and Rivera's commentary speaks to the vital need for service equity for city parks. Councilperson Mark Levine has been representing constituents in City Council District # 7, which extends from north Harlem at its southern border to West 165th Street in Washington Heights. As Chair of the Parks Committee for the Council (2014–2017) he has advocated for and seen to the allocation of more equitable funding for parks, which, in the past, had not received a fair share. City Councilman Ydanis Rodriquez represents City Council District #10, which includes the territory of the Pit. Mr. Rodriquez, in the early 2000's made major financial contributions to the city budget resulting in a total rehabilitation of the Pit and the adjacent park area. To contact Councilman Levine, see https://www.marklevine.nyc To contact Councilman Rodriquez, see https://council.nyc.gov/district-10

347   On the relationship between energy work and a person's health. Anodea Judith (Eastern Body/Western Mind, Celestial Arts, 2004) describes energy centers called chakras as "a center of organization that receives, assimilates and expresses life force energy. Chakra patterns are programmed deep in the interface of the core of the mind/body interface and have a strong relationship with our physical functioning" pg 4. We have several chakras in these interfaces, such as the Crown chakra, which governs functioning of the head, and the Heart chakra, governing our heart and our emotional intelligence.

Communication is an act of construction" is a comment written by Ms. Judith in her chapter describing Chakra Five, which governs the throat and interfaces with our healthy or unhealthy forms of communication. When this chakra is operating in "balance, one communicates clearly, using a resonant voice and being a good listener. When a person is subject to abuse or trauma, this person might resort to lies, or use or receive excessive criticism" (extracted from "Fifth Chakra at a Glance," pg 286. Emphasizing the importance of authentic communication, Ms. Judith states: "Communication binds culture together, as the primary means for sharing of information, values and relationships. It is through communication that we shape our future" pg 290.

348   League of Conservation Voters/San Francisco website Christine Fong. https://sflcv.org

349   Teens partnering with adult mentors in walking the walk for justice helps all civic partners to leverage moments of opportunity. The community-based organization Make the Road While Walking organizes and advocates for underserved in neighborhoods across New York City. Adults incorporated youth participation and counsel in their efforts to fight gentrification in Bushwick, Brooklyn. Neighborhoods that are undergoing gentrification have some landlords whose neglectful attention leads to the existence of multiple building code violations and deteriorating conditions. As existing tenants leave under untenable conditions, the landlord then fixes the apartments and charge higher rents to a more affluent constituency moving into the neighborhood for the first time. Make The Road invited youth though its Youth Power Project, where teen members learned skills in which they could assist families in standing up for their housing rights. Source: An article titled "Not Like It Used To Be: Teens Rally In The Hood" by Adam F. Hutton. Appeared in the City Limits Weekly (August 20, 2007). For more information on Make the Road, see https://maketheroadny.org/

350   Truth requires passion and discipline. This is a concept developed by Barry Lopez in his epic book, Arctic Dreams (First Vintage edition, 1986). In this book, Mr. Lopez asks the question, "How does the land shape the imaginations of the people who dwell in it?" (pg xxxvi). For people in neglected and underserved neighborhoods, living in chronically debilitated housing, the imagination can become shaped by despair because of receiving little government assistance in remedying terrible living conditions. As Mr. Lopez continues, "All of the land, the land that is, and that evolves is actual meaning…and is understood differently" (pg xxxvi) When people organize, fight back, and get remedied conditions, these results manifest because they

see their home as rightfully safe, healthy, and under good repair in their imagination first, and then because of their concerted action.

351   Literacy of survival...it is better to speak than to remain silent... In the book, Essays and Speeches of Audrey Lorde (Crossing Press, 2007), Ms. Lorde speaks to the challenge of being seen and heard by those who oppress the marginalized, and the necessity of the oppressed to speak up so that they remain healthy. In Ms. Lorde's essay "Sister Outsider: The Transformation of Silence and Action" (pp 40–44), she asks a question: "What are the tyrannies you swallow day by day and attempt to make your own" (pg 41). In other words, as you continue to choose to ingest that which debases and disqualifies you from just relations, you adopt these conditions as your legacy and future. It is when a person stands up by speaking up, that s/he takes ownership of the right for personal dignity and the rights due in lieu of unjust actions towards oneself by others. Once this decision is made, a person is no longer in "fear of the visibility without which we cannot truly live" (pg 42).

352   In an essay written by Virginia Satir, a founder of family therapy, she speaks to the need for ethical decisions and mutual respect between folk who do not see eye to eye. In her essay "Communication Congruence," she refers to her counseling experience with couples who are in marital distress or facing the prospect of separation or divorce. As Ms. Satir reflects on the verbal habits of those feeling offended, she states: "...so you don't understand me, and you make me up. When we are not really understanding each other, we hallucinate each other. Then we act as if our hallucination is fact." In my years of working for teen empowerment, I have found Ms. Satir's synopsis to be apropos to adult and teen dysfunctional relationships. When those exercising adult authority hallucinate about who a teen is, that adolescent feels divorced. This scenario repeatedly occurs, as perceptions and actions by parents, teachers, or other representatives of institutional authority. Ms. Satir's quote

cited from the book Thinking Allowed (Council Oak Books, 1992), pg 143, edited by Jeffrey Mishlow.

353   Opening the doors to inner wisdom, and following one's inner guidance, is a theme developed by the spiritual writer and activist Chris Saade in his book, Second Wave Spirituality: Passion for Peace, Passion for Justice (North Atlantic Books, 2014). In this book, Mr. Saade proudly proclaims: "The heart is the seat of nondual consciousness and fullness. We think with our hearts" (pg 236). The heart is the place of you-me relationship, where we give and receive generously, and think of the interests and needs of significant others as if they are our own.

354   Heart intelligence is a function of the mind, creating a mindscape of mutuality and shared interest. Daniel J. Siegel, in his book Mindsight: The Science of Personal Transformation (Bantam Books, 2011), explains the true nature of mind as "a mind sphere (a self-organizing process), addressing bodily regulation, emotional balance, and attuned communication…in its communication it (utilizes) responses of flexibility, empathy, moral awareness and intuition" (pg 26).

355   The harmony of inner traits with social goals is an insight shared about the early twentieth-century educator John Dewey by Laurel L. Tanner. Ms. Tanner, in her book, Dewey's Laboratory School: Lessons for Today (Teachers College Press, 1997), quotes John Dewey on the need for harmonizing inner work with desired social goals: "The need to harmonize individual traits with social goals is ever an ever-renewed problem, one which each generation has to solve, over and over again for itself" (pg 26).

356   Fear of teens or an adult's' internalized picture of teens or both. Mike Males refers to the fear of teens as "ephebiphobia—the fear and loathing of adolescents." (The Scapegoat Generation, Common Courage Press, 1995), pg 294, note 65). I have also heard Dr. Males

refer to "kourophobia—the fear of the stereotype about teens," although I have not been able to specifically identify the source of this definition.

357   Torched identities and lessons of diminishment. Teens in high school face lesson of diminishment from adults, but also from peers even while attending elite high schools with academically high performing students who have delayed social IQs.

     Source: "Being Black at Stuyvesant" by Gordon Banks and Maria Sarai Pudgen, NY Daily News, June 29, 2019). https://www,nydaily-news.com/opinion/ny-oped-being-black-at-stuyvesant-20190629

358   Torched identities and lessons of diminishment. Teens in high school face lesson of diminishment from adults, but also from peers even while attending elite high schools with academically high performing students who have delayed social IQs.

     Source: "Being Black at Stuyvesant" by Gordon Banks and Maria Sarai Pudgen, NY Daily News, June 29, 2019). See Daily News website story at: https://www.nydailynews.com/opinion/ny-oped-being-black-at-stuyvesant-20190629

359   Ibid NY Daily News Being Black at Stuyvesant "Those who don't know become creatures of our imaginations. They become assumptions, creatures of inference, based on faulty evidence if any at all." https://www.nydailynews.com/opinion/ny-oped-being-black-at-stuyvesant-20190629

360   Ibid NY Daily News Being Black at Stuyvesant Commentary by one student: "Our high school needs 'implicit bias training' to help build connections and break down stereotypes. An education in equity." https://www.nydailynews.com/opinion/oped-being-black-at-stuyvesant-20190629

361   The human heart is the first home of democracy. Terry Tempest Williams is quoted by Parker Palmer in his book, Healing the Heart of Democracy: The Courage to Create a Politics Worthy of the

Human Spirit (Jossey-Bass, 2011). As Ms. Williams is quoted: "The first home of democracy is not found in a century's old document, or in a distant city but in the human heart" (pg 49). She wrote this statement in an article titled "Engagement" for Orion Magazine (July/August 2004).

362   Using natural talents of doubt a finely calibrated shit-catcher...I lost my source for this quote, but have credited it to Dr. Marvin Hoffman, a Harvard University clinical psychologist who has also taught grades K -12 for the University of Chicago Urban Teacher Program. For a humorous review on Holden Caulfield's personality, taken from a variety of viewpoints, see The Catcher in the Rye and Philosophy: A Book for Bastards, Morons and Madmen (Open Court, 2012), edited by Keith Dromm and Heather Salter.

363   Fiercely focused attention and the need for eternal vigilance. This skill is addressed by the Latin American educator Paolo Freire in his book, Pedagogy of Indignation (Paradigm Publishers, 2004). Mr. Freire speaks to the valued activist role of students: "In the world of history, of politics, of culture, I apprehend not simply to adapt, but to change. By apprehending, we become able to intervene in reality...which implies decision, choice and intervention" (pg 60).

364   When do students feel that guided experiences are authentic? One measure of authenticity of guided experience is given by the "place-based" educator Sarah K. Anderson. Ms. Anderson proposes "an experiential, multi-disciplinary model" (pg 76) where (student and teacher) partnerships...start with a conversation and its participatory integration" (pg 109). See the book Bringing School to Life: Place-Based Education Across the Curriculum by Sarah K. Anderson (Rowman& Littlefield, 2017).

365   When do students feel that guided experiences are authentic? One measure of authenticity of guided experience is given by the "place-based" educator Sarah K. Anderson. Ms. Anderson proposes "an

experiential, multi-disciplinary model" (pg 76) where (student and teacher) partnerships...start with a conversation and its participatory integration" (pg 109). See the book Bringing School to Life: Place-Based Education Across the Curriculum by Sarah K. Anderson (Rowman& Littlefield, 2017).

366   When do students feel that guided experiences are authentic? One measure of authenticity of guided experience is given by the "place-based" educator Sarah K. Anderson. Ms. Anderson proposes "an experiential, multi-disciplinary model" (pg 76) where (student and teacher) partnerships...start with a conversation and its participatory integration" (pg 109). See the book Bringing School to Life: Place-Based Education Across the Curriculum by Sarah K. Anderson (Rowman& Littlefield, 2017).

367   When do students feel that guided experiences are authentic? One measure of authenticity of guided experience is given by the "place-based" educator Sarah K. Anderson. Ms. Anderson proposes "an experiential, multi-disciplinary model" (pg 76) where (student and teacher) partnerships...start with a conversation and its participatory integration" (pg 109). See the book Bringing School to Life: Place-Based Education Across the Curriculum by Sarah K. Anderson (Rowman& Littlefield, 2017).

368   Spark Action News (2010) website profiling accomplishments of projects led by teen activists: Spark Action Profile: Nebraska. https:// sparkaction.org

369   Spark Action News (2010) website profiling accomplishments of projects led by teen activists: Spark Action Profile: Colorado. https:// sparkaction.org

370   Information shown on the website of the San Francisco Youth Commission www.sfgov.org/yc.

371   These comments by Maurice Odelli were sent to me in an email from the Staten Island Voice program in 2014. Currently, Bobby Digi is

the President and CEO of Island Voice. Information and contact info can be found at: https://www.islandvoice.com

372 Balance and harmony with the soul… According to Taoist writers Harriet Beinfield and Efrem Korngold, they define "correspondence as a state of harmony, where in order for a larger system to be in balance as a whole, each smaller system within it must itself be balanced" (pg 35). In a society with record levels of inequality, I would say that from a Taoist perspective we still have balancing to do. Source: Between Heaven and Earth, A Guide to Chinese Medicine by Harriet Beinfield and Efrem Korngold (Ballantine Publishing Group, 1991). A corresponding thought is taken by a Western philosopher, Thomas Moore, in a chapter he wrote called "Educating for the Soul" (in the book Holistic Learning and Spirituality in Education, SUNY NY Press, 2005, John P. Miller et al, editors). In advocating for a balance between connecting to one's mind and one's soul, he suggests: "Our current focus on facts and science skills highlights a certain dimension of human reality but overlooks others. An emphasis on mind has generated neglect for the soul" (pg 9).

373 Being mindful of the soul does not preclude, but rather includes paying mind to the mind. An organization called the Icarus Project has constructed an approach they call mind-mapping. In a mind map, a person under chronic stress and performing poorly, who has been subject to trauma inducing social practices, needs to connect underlying conditions causing self-sabotage with external causes launched by unfair institutional policies and practices. In one of the zines posted by the Icarus Project, they outline this in a piece called "Mapping our Madness." Zine posted in April 2011. For the Icarus website, see www.nycicarus.org

374 Inequality with financial income and wealth does not cause adverse social outcomes but does have a strong correlation with them. Richard Wilkinson and Kate Pickett, in their book, The Spirit Level:

Why Greater Equality Make Societies Stronger (Bloomsbury Press, 2009), document dozens of scenarios which lead them to the conclusion that "almost all problems which are more common at the bottom of a socio/economic ladders are also more highly evidenced as amongst societies which have higher levels of inequality than others" (p 18). This pair of references has been included in the Introduction chapter, but we are still referring here to the correspondences and interactive influences of inside/out, and outside/in.

375   Ibid The Spirit Level Inequality with financial income and wealth does not cause adverse social outcomes but does have a strong correlation with them. Richard Wilkinson and Kate Pickett, in their book, The Spirit Level: Why Greater Equality Make Societies Stronger (Bloomsbury Press, 2009), document dozens of scenarios which lead them to the conclusion that "almost all problems which are more common at the bottom of a socio/economic ladders are also more highly evidenced as amongst societies which have higher levels of inequality than others" (p 18). This pair of references has been included in the Introduction chapter, but we are still referring here to the correspondences and interactive influences of inside/out, and outside/in. References to effects resulting in higher murder rates (pp 131 and 141).

376   Inequality with financial income and wealth does not cause adverse social outcomes but does have a strong correlation with them. Richard Wilkinson and Kate Pickett, in their book, The Spirit Level: Why Greater Equality Make Societies Stronger (Bloomsbury Press, 2009), document dozens of scenarios which lead them to the conclusion that "almost all problems which are more common at the bottom of a socio/economic ladders are also more highly evidenced as amongst societies which have higher levels of inequality than others" (p 18). This pair of references has been included in the Introduction chapter, but we are still referring here to the correspondences and

interactive influences of inside/out, and outside/in. References to stress (pg 75).

377   Ibid The Spirit Level Inequality with financial income and wealth does not cause adverse social outcomes but does have a strong correlation with them. Richard Wilkinson and Kate Pickett, in their book, The Spirit Level: Why Greater Equality Make Societies Stronger (Bloomsbury Press, 2009), document dozens of scenarios which lead them to the conclusion that "almost all problems which are more common at the bottom of a socio/economic ladders are also more highly evidenced as amongst societies which have higher levels of inequality than others" (p 18). This pair of references has been included in the Introduction chapter, but we are still referring here to the correspondences and interactive influences of inside/out, and outside/in. References to chronic disease (pg 75).

378   Standardized tests are not total measurements of assessment, but a major source of stress. The education and teacher preparation leader W. James Popham suggests that in our schools, assessment must also account for affective well-being. To generate transformative assessments, teachers need to consider all the dimensions of consciousness experienced by a student (that is, emotional factors as well as cognitive factors). In constructing what he calls transformative assessments, Mr. Popham recommends that this type of assessment "is a process, not just a test (pg 8). Transformative assessment considers the part of the student in the teaching and learning process. This inclusive assessment looks at decision-making by both teachers and students (pg 23); and teaches should administer affective inventories, garnering student perceptions of the classroom climate (pg 104). Transformative Assessment (ASCD Publications, 2008).

379   Peter Grey cites a thought by Albert Einstein had been noted in Mr. Einstein's autobiography. (Free to Learn Basic Books, 2013, pg 72)). Mr. Einstein's autobiography was written in 1949. Mr. Einstein had

this observation to make about American education: "It is nothing short of a miracle that the modern methods of instruction have not entirely strangled the holy curiosity of inquiry." (Mr. Grey cited this quote from Albert Einstein: Philosopher-scientist, Library of Living Philosophers, pg 19). In the book, Mr. Grey points out the democratic practice applied to the educational setting at the Sudbury Valley School in Massachusetts. According to Mr. Grey, the basic principle is: "Begin with the thought: Adults do not control children's education; children educate themselves" (pg 89). Great care is taken to structure the environment and put together a process where "the school is, first and foremost, a democratic community." (pg 89).

380   Ibid Free to Learn Peter Grey cites a thought by Albert Einstein noted in Mr. Einstein's autobiography. (Free to Learn Basic Books, 2013, pg 72)). Mr. Einstein's autobiography was written in 1949. Mr. Einstein had this observation to make about American education: "It is nothing short of a miracle that the modern methods of instruction have not entirely strangled the holy curiosity of inquiry." (Mr. Grey cited this quote from Albert Einstein: Philosopher-scientist, Library of Living Philosophers, pg 19). In the book, Mr. Grey points out the democratic practice applied to the educational setting at the Sudbury Valley School in Massachusetts. According to Mr. Grey, the basic principle is: "Begin with the thought: Adults do not control children's education; children educate themselves" (pg 89). Great care is taken to structure the environment and put together a process where "the school is, first and foremost, a democratic community." (pg 89).

381   Teachers implementing methods of persuasion and choice, and not demanding of students to 'do as I say'. Nikhil Goyal, in his book, Schools on Trial: How Freedom and Creativity Can Fix Our Educational Malpractice (Doubleday, 2016), seconds the democratic education philosophy of Mr. Grey as he describes the learning environment at the Brooklyn Free School: "One central feature that

separates free and democratic schools from other self-appointed alternative schools is the absence of coercion in learning" (pg 148).

382   Ibid Schools on Trial Learning how to function in a democratic classroom involves a detox process. Mr. Goyal refers to the concept of a detox process as the challenging adjustments that must be made when a student leaves a school where he or she is told almost everything they should do, and experiences challenges when engaged in open classrooms based on choice.

383   Ibid Schools on Trial As Mr. Goyal explains: "There is much difficulty in breaking a traditional school mindset that conditions students to resist having freedom and choice in their learning and in their own lives!" (pg 146). My question is how are students in traditional schools who have developed listen-to-and-follow-direction mindsets are suddenly ready to function as citizens in a democratic society once they graduate high school or turn eighteen? Ibid.

384   Ibid Schools on Trial As Mr. Goyal explains: "There is much difficulty in breaking a traditional school mindset that conditions students to resist having freedom and choice in their learning and in their own lives!" (pg 146). My question is how are students in traditional schools who have developed listen-to-and-follow-direction mindsets are suddenly ready to function as citizens in a democratic society once they graduate high school or turn eighteen? Ibid.

385   Stories help us to visualize possibilities. When we create a new story about ourselves, we enlist the inner ally of imagination in doing so. When we listen to and validate the stories of our friends and neighbors, we increase our understanding about "the other." As Bill Pfeiffer points out in his book, Wild Earth, Wild Soul (Moon Books, 2013), "The universe is an abundant place; there are many different stories and ways to live; the present moment is where life is lived" (pg 136).

386   Each of us is a unique operating system, alive and well within an operational system of friends. Penny Gil, who was a Mary Lyon Professor of Humanities at Holyoke College, believes that this process of living authentically and validating others assists in our thriving in the twenty-first century. As she points out in her book, What in the World Is Going On? (Balboa Press, 2015), Ms. Gil holds that we can escape our isolation, and celebrate our interdependence with all beings, heal our communities, dissolve our fears, and our natural compassion to flow out into the world. For Ms. Gil's commentary on moving beyond psychic roadblocks prohibiting ones recognition of interdependence, see pp 65-71.

387   Ibid Wild Earth, Wild Soul Are we meant to be bombarded with information and inflamed expressions of opinion, or to be guided in the art of open and sensitive listening? Bill Pfeiffer suggests that we develop the refined act of listening as an art: "A collective devotion to healthy relationship of which listening is always a nutrient… as with Native Siberian and Native American traditions (where) the act of listening has been elevated to an art form" (pg 65). Mr. Pfeiffer uses reiteration to emphasize the value of authentic stories and practicing active listening skills as part of an open process of communication that is reflected in the theme of this book. He holds a position that in cultivating and honoring uniqueness, we cultivate free choice. Mr. Pfeiffer quotes the author Muriel Rukeyser (The Speed of Darkness, Random House, 1968) when she wrote: "the universe is constructed not of atoms, but of stories." Mr. Pfeiffer points to examples of deep listening practice when he references the Leaver tribes in Russia. It is embedded in their belief systems that they are not just engaged in philosophizing, (as)…we don't just believe in things but experience them." pg 137. In another example, he cites the tribe's words: "Discover who we are, we can't fake it." pg 138 What this belief system points out is the importance of understanding "how the sacred path each of us is walking as individuals

corresponds with our collective destiny." pg 138. See the book Wild Earth, Wild Soul: A Manual for an Ecstatic Culture by Bill Pfeiffer (Moon Books, 2013).

388   Ibid Wild Earth, Wild Soul

Are we meant to be bombarded with information and inflamed expressions of opinion, or to be guided in the art of open and sensitive listening? Bill Pfeiffer suggests that we develop the refined act of listening as an art: "A collective devotion to healthy relationship of which listening is always a nutrient... as with Native Siberian and Native American traditions (where) the act of listening has been elevated to an art form" (pg 65). Mr. Pfeiffer uses reiteration to emphasize the value of authentic stories and practicing active listening skills as part of an open process of communication that is reflected in the theme of this book. He holds a position that in cultivating and honoring uniqueness, we cultivate free choice. Mr. Pfeiffer quotes the author Muriel Rukeyser (The Speed of Darkness, Random House, 1968) when she wrote: "the universe is constructed not of atoms, but of stories." Mr. Pfeiffer points to examples of deep listening practice when he references the Leaver tribes in Russia. It is embedded in their belief systems that they are not just engaged in philosophizing, (as)...we don't just believe in things but experience them." pg 137. In another example, he cites the tribe's words: "Discover who we are, we can't fake it." pg 138 What this belief system points out is the importance of understanding "how the sacred path each of us is walking as individuals corresponds with our collective destiny." pg 138. See the book Wild Earth, Wild Soul: A Manual for an Ecstatic Culture by Bill Pfeiffer (Moon Books, 2013).

389   Ibid Wild Earth, Wild Soul Are we meant to be bombarded with information and inflamed expressions of opinion, or to be guided in the art of open and sensitive listening? Bill Pfeiffer suggests that we develop the refined act of listening as an art: "A collective devotion

to healthy relationship of which listening is always a nutrient... as with Native Siberian and Native American traditions (where) the act of listening has been elevated to an art form" (pg 65). Mr. Pfeiffer uses reiteration to emphasize the value of authentic stories and practicing active listening skills as part of an open process of communication that is reflected in the theme of this book. He holds a position that in cultivating and honoring uniqueness, we cultivate free choice. Mr. Pfeiffer quotes the author Muriel Rukeyser (The Speed of Darkness, Random House, 1968) when she wrote: "the universe is constructed not of atoms, but of stories." Mr. Pfeiffer points to examples of deep listening practice when he references the Leaver tribes in Russia. It is embedded in their belief systems that they are not just engaged in philosophizing, (as)...we don't just believe in things but experience them." pg 137. In another example, he cites the tribe's words: "Discover who we are, we can't fake it." pg 138 What this belief system points out is the importance of understanding "how the sacred path each of us is walking as individuals corresponds with our collective destiny." pg 138. See the book Wild Earth, Wild Soul: A Manual for an Ecstatic Culture by Bill Pfeiffer (Moon Books, 2013).

390   Deference to social rank is surrender of autonomy and position. In our Teens on Board campaign and amongst the many teen-led social justice movements, we are joining a larger flow amongst the former and present organizers who discovered and are discovering the act of being heard. Robert W. Fuller, in his book, Somebodies and Nobodies: Overcoming the Abuse of Rank (New Society Publishers, 2014), paints a portrait of our historical and present-day allies: "As part of the Parade on Invisibles, whole categories of peoples have been treated as nobodies: racial, religious and national minorities; welfare mothers and the homeless; the downsized students and children, and always the poor. Until they organize and start marching, they find their voice, they become visible as human beings" (pg 57).

391   Teens flourish as wanderers who explore and experiment in their navigation of new territories (territories of place and ideas). The eco-philosopher Bill Plotkin, in his book, Nature and the Human Soul (New World Library, 2008), laments to absence of these opportunities in modern America. As Mr. Plotkin points out: "In mainstream America, there are virtually no remaining traditions of a genuine adolescent withdrawal from familiar social life. Preparation for soul initiation requires that you be separated from the ordinary life of the community so that you may cease to define yourself according to rules and norms" (pg 235).

392   For references addressing story and place, see Mortgaging the Earth by Bruce Rich (Beacon Press, 1994), pg 315, and "A Sort of Pope," Psychology Today (May 1972), pg 80.

393   What we need to find first is our inner light. This concept has been attributed to the social reform gospel of Nelson Mandela, the first Black President of South Africa. It was demonstrated in his life practice for social justice of demanding and extending to others a deep respect for being human.

394   Stories stimulate imagination and an attraction to alternative futures. The proponents of socially conscious shamanic practices, Linda Star Wolf and Nita Gage (Soul Whispering, Bear and Company, 2017), counsel that our animal brothers and sisters have stories of their own, expressed in their own language and life purposes. We can become more connected to them through storytelling in metaphoric ways. As Star Wolf and Gage state: "(Animals such as) the chipmunk teaches us the blessing that there are always spirit guides around and ready to help, but you must invite the assistance of their spirits" pg 250. As I write about in the later sections of this Introduction, as I raised a tribe of cats in my apartment, I would learn lessons about the joy of curiosity and exploration, suggesting that they served as my feline-wise mentors.

395   The life-enhancing contributions and evolutionary purpose of bacteria. One the role of evolving bacteria in freeing up oxygen, which is essential for higher forms of life, see the website article " Bacteria that changed the world". My point here is that when examining the process of evolution, adaptation and change, there are forces and processes at work in nature beyond the need to possess the attributes of what we refer to as higher life forms. See the website article posted in May of 2017 at: https://evolution.berkeley.edu/evolibrarynews The section of the article I am referencing addresses the bacteria called cyanobacteria.

396   See the chapter "Life Builds From the Bottom Up: The Influence of Small Things," in The Way Life Works (Three Rivers Press, 1995) by Mahon Hoagland and Bert Dodson. pp 2 and 3. I am making an analogy here about the process of creation in society – which I believe operates using natural principles of life purpose. For research demonstrating the need of adolescents to ask questions, and for adults to listen to their perspectives, see the research conducted by the Search Institute: https://www.search-institute.org/our-research/developmental .

397   See the chapter "Life Builds From the Bottom Up: The Influence of Small Things," in The Way Life Works (Three Rivers Press, 1995) by Mahon Hoagland and Bert Dodson. pp 2 and 3. I am making an analogy here about the process of creation in society – which I believe operates using natural principles of life purpose. For research demonstrating the need of adolescents to ask questions, and for adults to listen to their perspectives, see the research conducted by the Search Institute: https://www.search-institute.org/our-research/developmental .

398   See the chapter "Life Builds From the Bottom Up: The Influence of Small Things," in The Way Life Works (Three Rivers Press, 1995) by Mahon Hoagland and Bert Dodson. pp 2 and 3. I am making

an analogy here about the process of creation in society – which I believe operates using natural principles of life purpose. For research demonstrating the need of adolescents to ask questions, and for adults to listen to their perspectives, see the research conducted by the Search Institute: https://www.search-institute.org/our-research/ developmental .

399   See the chapter "Life Builds From the Bottom Up: The Influence of Small Things," in The Way Life Works (Three Rivers Press, 1995) by Mahon Hoagland and Bert Dodson. pp 2 and 3. I am making an analogy here about the process of creation in society – which I believe operates using natural principles of life purpose. For research demonstrating the need of adolescents to ask questions, and for adults to listen to their perspectives, see the research conducted by the Search Institute: https://www.search-institute.org/our-research/ developmental .

400   See the chapter "Life Builds From the Bottom Up: The Influence of Small Things," in The Way Life Works (Three Rivers Press, 1995) by Mahon Hoagland and Bert Dodson. pp 2 and 3. I am making an analogy here about the process of creation in society – which I believe operates using natural principles of life purpose. For research demonstrating the need of adolescents to ask questions, and for adults to listen to their perspectives, see the research conducted by the Search Institute: https://www.search-institute.org/our-research/ developmental .

401   Teen change-makers and their civic mentors suffer the diminishment of companionship- as outsiders. Yet as outsiders, they construct their own terms of teamwork and shared contributions.

    This orientation is aptly described by the futurist Marilyn Ferguson in her introduction to the book The Outsider by Colin Wilson (Jeremey Tarcher/Putnam, 1982). As I excerpt some of her points here: "The outsider wants to cease to be an outsider, he wants to be an integrated human being, achieving fusion between mind and heart, he wants to understand the soul and its workings, he sees his way out via intensity and extremes of experience" (pg xi).

402   Live the real or perish in superstition. The spiritual activist and writer Andrew Harvey quotes the Persian philosopher Rumi in his book, Radical Passion (North Atlantic Books, 2012). As Mr. Harvey cites Rumi: "Passion burns down every bridge of exhaustion; passion is the supreme elixir and renews all hope; run away, my friends, from all false solutions; let divine passion triumph and re-birth you in yourself" (pg xv).

403   Our bodies are universes within the universes, where "the other" helps us to survive and flourish. Ed Yong, an "award winning science writer for the Atlantic Magazine" (bio inside the jacket of the book, back cover) has a take another inside our bodies, enabling us to discover that what is inside is mostly not our body. In his book, I Contain Multitudes: The Microbes Within Us and a Grander View of Life (Harper Collins, 2016). As Mr. Young highlights in his book: "...your cells carry between 20,000 and 25,000 genes, but it is estimated that the microbes inside you wield five hundred times (more influence). This genetic wealth...helps us to digest our food, produce missing vitamins and minerals, and break down toxins and hazardous chemicals..." (pg 11).

404   For the emergent generation, the utopia of our parents is the nightmare of their lives. This is a re-occurring message in the magazine Adbusters. One example of their assertion about this thought is expressed through one of their "info-ads" called Break the Trance: "Advertising is the biggest psychological experiment ever carried out on the human race. It hypes and jolts us (with) info viruses and info toxins, fake news, and emotional blackmail. (These psychological invasions) have worked their way into the fabric of our lives.

Advertising is brain damage" (Adbusters Magazine, Jan/Feb 2019, Vol. 27, No. 1).

405   Ibid The Spirit Level (Bloomsbury, 2009) Page 77. The point of the authors here is that the social constructs developed through maintenance of inequalities becomes conflated with supposed traits possessed by those on the short end of economic and social outcomes.

406   Ibid The Spirit Level (Bloomsbury, 2009) Page 77. The point of the authors here is that the social constructs developed through maintenance of inequalities becomes conflated with supposed traits possessed by those on the short end of economic and social outcomes.

407   The social construction of 'patho-adolescence' is not the nature of adolescence. It is a compilation of ideas generated during the accelerated rise of the industrial revolution, and the demise of American ideals, propagated with the re-emergence of racialized and sexist narratives used to justify male, pale, and stale hegemony. It was during the period of the late 1800's that the toxin of adultism was added to the mix of socio/political diminishment of a newly identified 'other' – the adolescent. Bill Plotkin, in his book, Nature and the Human Soul (New World Library, 2008), speaks to the invasive imposition of a false nature that compromises and buries a teen's true nature: "The teen-ager has been sufficiently compromised—his innocence has been lost and his innate connection to nature severed, so that his alienation from self and the world is now independently self-sustained…consequently teenage life becomes one of the key battlegrounds on which ego-centric society wages its war against human nature" (pg 219). For a reference concerning the institutional battlegrounds resulting in delays for adults in their reaching full maturity, see "The Changing Nature of Maturity" in Arrested Adulthood: The Changing Nature of Maturity and Identity by James Cote (NY University Press, 2000), pp 11–44.

408   The social construction of 'patho-adolescence' is not the nature of adolescence. It is a compilation of ideas generated during the accelerated rise of the industrial revolution, and the demise of American ideals, propagated with the re-emergence of racialized and sexist narratives used to justify male, pale, and stale hegemony. It was during the period of the late 1800's that the toxin of adultism was added to the mix of socio/political diminishment of a newly identified 'other' – the adolescent. Bill Plotkin, in his book, Nature and the Human Soul (New World Library, 2008), speaks to the invasive imposition of a false nature that compromises and buries a teen's true nature: "The teen-ager has been sufficiently compromised—his innocence has been lost and his innate connection to nature severed, so that his alienation from self and the world is now independently self-sustained…consequently teenage life becomes one of the key battlegrounds on which ego-centric society wages its war against human nature" (pg 219). For a reference concerning the institutional battlegrounds resulting in delays for adults in their reaching full maturity, see "The Changing Nature of Maturity" in Arrested Adulthood: The Changing Nature of Maturity and Identity by James Cote (NY University Press, 2000), pp 11–44.

409   Ibid Nature and the Human Soul. A profile of pseudo-adolescence is also a portrait of adult narcissism. As further elaborated upon by Bill Plotkin, "In current western and westernized societies, in addition to the scarcity of true maturity, many people of adult age suffer from a variety of adolescent psychopathologies, (including) the incapacities of social insecurity, identity confusion, narcissism, relentless greed, arrested moral development, materialistic obsessions, substance addictions and emotional numbness" (Ibid, pg 9).

410   Respond through non-violent struggle and not regression into passivity. This is a theme repeated in the works and life of Dr. Martin Luther King, Jr. In an article he originally wrote for a publication called Presbyterian Outlook, and then reprinted for the New South

magazine (March 1958, pp 8–12), Dr. King called on those involved with the tactic of non-violent resistance not to confuse this strategy with passivity. As excerpted from his article, "Reject being victim of stagnant passivity and decode my complacency…while the method is passive physically, it is strongly active psychologically, and seeks not defeat of the opponent nor humiliation, but winning friendship and understanding in a restless determination to make brotherhood a reality." These passages are quoted from the book A Testament of Hope: The Essential Writings of Dr. Martin Luther King, Jr. edited by James M. Washington (Harper SF, 1986), pp 85, 87, and 89.

411   Ending self-sabotage through self-healing. These strategies for "overcoming persistent negative thoughts, triggering of manic episodes, and ending of obsessive disorders are addressed throughout the self-help guide Madness and Oppression – A Mind Map Guide by the Icarus Project (Mutual Aid Publication, 1st edition, 2015).

412   Madness and Oppression Ibid If we do not become proactive in exploring our personal and social responsibilities, we leave the diagnosis and cure of our toxic conditions in the hands of those managing the sources of oppressive authority. This is the overarching position suggested in the works of the Icarus Project (pg 42).

413   Teens and other targets of negative adult commentary learn to engage in an internal reconstruction of their fundamental assumptions about their identities. Compassionate and empathetic listening support is a key asset which is crucial to teens seeking to develop a new narrative about themselves. See Social and Developmental Assets, Support, Item #2 Positive Family Communication in the Search Institutes framework describing 40 forms of developmental assets for teens. For an overview of Search Institute's research and social/psychological framework on adolescent development needs, see their website at www.search-institute.org.

414   On the essential place of spiritual radicals as prophets. Rabbi Abraham Joshua Heschel was a rabbi who marched with Dr. Martin Luther King, Jr. and who also abhorred the violence inflicted on Americans and the Vietnamese as morally unacceptable. In his edited work of the works of Rabbi Heschel, Edward K. Kaplan shares with us some of the insights shared in Heschel's writings and public commentary (Spiritual Radical: Abraham Joshua Heschel in America, by Edward K. Kaplan (Yale University Press, 2007). Some of Heschel's counsel includes: "In times of prosperity, hidden persuaders are capable of leading people into selling their conscience for success" (pg 183); "If such sensitivity to evil is called hysterical, what name should be given to the deep callousness to evil which the prophet bewails?: (pg 186); and "America used to be a word of hope, of opportunity for the world—now the word America has become shame. Where are our Jews? We cannot limit the religious conscience. The Vietnamese are our Jews." Rabbi Heschel speaks to deficits from a spiritual and social responsibility perspective.

415   Aptitude, not just attitude. I suggest this perceptual adjustment for how we see the contributions of Greta Thunberg. Some press accounts would focus on her spoken tone, and not on the politically influential effect of her presence and messaging. The issue of Time magazine recognizing Greta as Person of the Year (2019) includes this observation: "…there is no magic solution. But she has succeeded in creating, a global attitudinal shift, transforming millions of vague, middle of the night anxieties into a worldwide movement calling for urgent change" (Cited from an article in Time magazine called "The Conscience" written by Charlotte Alter and S. Hayes, December 23–30, 2019, pp 50–65).

416   Ibid "The Storyteller Archetype" in Sacred Contracts by Carolyn Myss, pp 415–416.

417   In the All-Souls Church Tribute Journal for the Rev. Richard D. Leonard, the Rev. Galen Guengerich, Senior Minister, offered these warm words of praise: "I am deeply grateful that the Heart and Soul Charitable Fund has made Dick's life and ministry, and especially his witness to Selma the center of this year's auction. Dick is one of the best among us, and he amply illustrates our shared commitment to doing what we can do to heal this broken world." ("A Tribute to Richard D. Leonard" section of the journal).

418   In the All-Souls Church Tribute Journal for the Rev. Richard D. Leonard, the Rev. Galen Guengerich, Senior Minister, offered these warm words of praise: "I am deeply grateful that the Heart and Soul Charitable Fund has made Dick's life and ministry, and especially his witness to Selma the center of this year's auction. Dick is one of the best among us, and he amply illustrates our shared commitment to doing what we can do to heal this broken world." ("A Tribute to Richard D. Leonard" section of the journal).

419   In the All-Souls Church Tribute Journal for the Rev. Richard D. Leonard, the Rev. Galen Guengerich, Senior Minister, offered these warm words of praise: "I am deeply grateful that the Heart and Soul Charitable Fund has made Dick's life and ministry, and especially his witness to Selma the center of this year's auction. Dick is one of the best among us, and he amply illustrates our shared commitment to doing what we can do to heal this broken world." ("A Tribute to Richard D. Leonard" section of the journal).

420   My support for a few days became a life-changing event... Cited in Rev. Leonard's entry # 87: Call to Selma (1965). Wet Cement: Book One The Early Years 1927 – 1980 (Outskirts Press, 2017). There are no page numbers, only entry numbers.

421   Martin Luther King, Jr.'s national appeal to ministers to join the march. Dr. King included the following words in his appeal: "For never in Christian history have Christian churches been on the

receiving end of such brutality and violence..." Cited from the book A Testament of Hope: The Essential Writings and Speeches of Martin Luther King, Jr. edited by James M. Washington, (Harper/San Francisco, 1986), pg xi.

422   Martin Luther King, Jr.'s national appeal to ministers to join the march. Dr. King included the following words in his appeal: "For never in Christian history have Christian churches been on the receiving end of such brutality and violence..." Cited from the book A Testament of Hope: The Essential Writings and Speeches of Martin Luther King, Jr. edited by James M. Washington, (Harper/San Francisco, 1986), pg xi.

423   Martin Luther King's telegram on the extreme danger and intimidation fostered by officials in Selma. As stated in his telegram: "In the vicious maltreatment of defenseless citizens in Selma, old women and young children were gassed and clubbed at random. We have witnessed the eruption of a disease of racism which seeks to destroy all of America. No American is without responsibility." This quote is included in the All-Souls Church Tribute Journal to Richard D. Leonard.

424   Ibid All Souls Tribute Journal includes this quote by the Senator Robert F. Kennedy.

425   Ibid "From Assets to Agents of Change" is the title of a paper written by Shawn Ginwright and Taj James. New Directions for Youth Development (Wiley, No. 96, Winter of 2002). This paper develops a thesis that it is through the self-organizing led by young people that the path to a positive future is self-directed and bought in to by its practitioners.

426   Finding the magic to guide oneself toward an alternative future. Citation found in the Petra Foundation Twenty-Fifth Anniversary Journal: Biography sketch of Kurt Tofteland, pg 105. www.petrafoundation.org

427   Kurt Tofteland and his support for the quest for dignity. My point here is expressed by Robert Fuller in his book Somebodies and Nobodies: "Psychological change precedes an assault on the status quo." The collective energy of critique amassed by inmates managing to transcend the crushing impact by the prison system on people's souls is what is so impressive. Somebodies and Nobodies: Overcoming the Abuse of Rank by Robert W. Fuller (New Society Publishers, 2004), pg 61.

428   Ibid Petra Foundation Anniversary Journal www.petrafoundation. org

429   See Love and Will (Norton and Company, 1969) by Rollo May. Throughout this book Mr., May develops his theme on the necessity of developing the power of love to gain will power through developing one's life purpose.

430   The elements of "prison consciousness" were developed in a book named Global Awakening by Michael Schacker (Park Street Press, 2013). These elements are woven throughout the text of his book as organizing energies, process, and structures for what I refer to as the shadow of America. These elements include:

1.   Repressive practices which capture and control soul- purpose.

2.   Unconsciously and non-reflectively adopting self-destructive and aggressive codes of behavior.

3.   Habitual surrender and attachment/addiction to toxic materials and process.

4.   Abandonment of responsibilities and unconscious adoption of anxiety/fear driven tactics and social relations.

431   Ibid Global Awakening The elements of "prison consciousness" have been developed through expanding upon the themes developed in a book named Global Awakening by Michael Schacker (Park Street Press, 2013). These elements are woven throughout the text of his

book as organizing energies, process, and structures for what I refer to as the shadow of America. These elements include:

1. Repressive practices which capture and control soul- purpose.

2. Unconsciously and non-reflectively adopting self-destructive and aggressive codes of behavior.

3. Habitual surrender and attachment/addiction to toxic materials and process.

4. Abandonment of responsibilities and unconscious adoption of anxiety/fear driven tactics and social relations.

432   This is the Real was a theatric program operated by PAL in the early 2000s, which no longer exists. The text is extracted from an old program guide from one of the performances. www.palnyc.org

433   John Zeiler is a Board member of the Police Athletic League who introduced the theater project to PAL and oversaw its development as actors progressed in their performances. Mr. Zeiler's quote is included in the program guide for *This is The Real*. www.palnyc.org

434   How do we communicate. This reference is also from Anodea Judith's description of the Fifth Chakra. *Wheels of Life* by Anodea Judith. (Llewellyn Publications, 1996). See chapter "Chakra 5: Sound", on the nature of communication (pg 260).

435   The Asian Model Myth, that is, all Asians are comfortable, successful, and free from discriminatory harm. Source: NBC News broadcast by Victoria Nam Kuy (March 20, 2021). To see Ms. Kuy broadcast go to: https://www.nbcnews.com/news/asian-america/behind-the-minority-myth-why-studious-asian-stereotype-hurts-n792926

436   History and demographics of Chinese immigration to New York City. I used a source which delves into the histories and demographics of a variety of immigrant groups whose contributions became the backbone of New York City identity and progress. See City of

Dreams: The 400-year Epic History of Immigrant New York by Tyler Anbinder (Houghton-Mifflin, 2016), pp 521–539.

437   The Dennis Yu quote is taken from the ASAP program brochure used in its school year end closing ceremony in 2015.

438   The Asian Model Myth (the model minority myth). Students have learned to construct challenges to this myth, and to facilitate the nurturing of Asian-American student voice. See "Un-masking the Myth of the Model Minority" by Benji Chang and Wayne Au Rethinking Schools magazine (Winter 2007–2008), – pp 15–19; and "Taking A Chance With Words," by Carol A. Takeshi (pp 20–23).

439   This comment is included in the written program for the Asian Student Advocacy Project end of year celebration in 2015.

440   See Seven Constructivist Methods for the Secondary Classroom by Claire Gabler and Michael Schroeder (AP Press: Pearson, 2003) pg 4. As the authors also stress, "Learning from a constructivist perspective is best promoted through an active process emphasizing purposeful interaction and use of knowledge in real situations." pg 4.

441   Citation is from the book Open Minds to Equality by Nancy Schniedewind and Ellen Davidson (Rethinking Schools Publication, 3rd edition, 2006). pp 248- 249 and pg 360.

442   Forging congruence between practice and ideals in Social Studies. See the National Council on Social Studies Bulletin (September 2010) on the revised social studies standards (Bulletin 111, Introduction, comments on civic ideals and practice, pg 4).

443   Forging congruence between practice and ideals in Social Studies. See the National Council on Social Studies Bulletin (September 2010) on the revised social studies standards (Bulletin 111, Introduction, comments on civic ideals and practice, pg 4).

444   This quote, made by the student participant Anna Lu, is also taken from the Asian Student Advocacy Project written program for the end of semester ceremony in 2015.

445   City of Dreams, by Tyler Anbinder (Houghton-Mifflin, 2016) Ibid, pp 310–314 and pp 500–502.

446   Ibid City of Dreams, by Tyler Anbinder (Houghton-Mifflin, 2016) Ibid, pp 310–314 and pp 500–502.

447   Ibid City of Dreams, by Tyler Anbinder (Houghton-Mifflin, 2016) Ibid, pp 310–314 and pp 500–502.

448   Ibid City of Dreams, by Tyler Anbinder (Houghton-Mifflin, 2016) Ibid, pp 310–314 and pp 500–502.

449   Ibid City of Dreams, by Tyler Anbinder (Houghton-Mifflin, 2016) Ibid, pp 310–314 and pp 500–502.

450   Political conversations during the McCarthy period which I witnessed as a teen in the early 1960's.

I reference here conversations I overheard between my father and visiting friends of my parents. My parents could not afford an apartment in which I could have my own bedroom, or even share a bedroom until my high school years beginning in 1964. Up until that time, I slept in a foyer adjacent to the dining room, where my parents entertained close friends for dinner. In the late 1950s and early 1960s, my father's more progressive comments often clashed with those of his more conservative friends. My dad, tended to be sympathetic to social justice causes and policies supported by elected officials on the left-wing spectrum of politics. and some of his work colleagues and friends for whom anything closely resembling what they perceived to be a version of communist practices was hated and became a source of heated discussion even at dinner parties amongst friends. Joseph McCarthy was a US Senator who held hearings in which he outed people who at one time decades before his hearing were either affiliated with the Communist Party USA, or sympathetic to progressive causes. For commentary aligned with my father's perspective, see two references here: "Who is Loyal to America?" by Henry Steele Commager (an American historian), pp 370–377; and "TV Comment on Joseph McCarthy" by Edward R. Murrow, a muckraker from the 1950s, pp 377–379, both sourced in the book, 100 Key Documents in American Democracy (Praeger, 1994). A central lesson I learned during these years is to stand up for one's beliefs, even in the face of fierce rejection of your ideas.

451   I learned about Ms. Crenshaw's integrity through a conversation with Alan Shulman (2014) about the legacy of Dave Crenshaw's mother, Gwen Crenshaw, and how she remained independent and adhered to basic principles honoring an individual's right to basic dignity.

452   Ibid Conversation with Alan Shulman (2014) about the legacy of Dave Crenshaw's mother, Gwen Crenshaw, and how she remained independent and adhered to basic principles honoring an individual's right to basic dignity.

453   Conversations with Coach Dave Crenshaw about his experience as a student and organizer in the early 1980s at Hunter College High School. Dave has shared his Hunter High School memories numerous times during our three decades of youth service work together.

454   Conversation I had with Jackie Hurt, whom I re-connected with years after she was a participant with the Uptown Dreamer program. I met her at a reception at the Malcolm X Ballroom, hosted by Borough President Gale Brewer which was honoring civic heroes from the Muslim community (2014). https://www.manhattanbp.nyc.gov

455   Coach Dave's application of the golden rule—do unto others as you would have others do unto you—phrased using his own words. Be a best friend to yourself so that you could use the same habits and qualities to be a good friend to others. He peppered his motivational talks with his young participants with this phrase and used it in

describing his program philosophy to people who had come to visit his program.

456 Coach Dave conducted pep talks with his young program participants, which I witnessed dozens of times on the sidelines of basketball courts, classrooms, and even on subway train cars taking his players back from a game downtown. He continuously reminded his young participants not to resort to diminishing others, or thinking of oneself as a victim, when one of his players would become upset by a call of a referee which they viewed as unfair. Coach Dave would invariably try to have his upset player see temporary incidents in a larger frame, that of sharing the gym with friends, even those who had taken on the role of opponent for purposes of playing a basketball game.

457 Ibid "The Storyteller Archetype," Sacred Contracts by Carolyn Myss, pp 415–416. Ibid

458 Conversations with Carmen Guzman, a Dreamer Program alumnus who was a youth participant in the mid-1990s. Carmen would share her feelings with me in casual conversations and use this story to motivate students about the importance of community service to the Dreamers. She also shared this story in an interview with The Washington Heights and Inwood News local newspaper, but I have lost the copy of the article I had at the time. This local newspaper stopped publishing years ago.

459 Conversations with Carmen Guzman, a Dreamer Program alumnus who was a youth participant in the mid-1990s. Carmen would share her feelings with me in casual conversations and use this story to motivate students about the importance of community service to the Dreamers. She also shared this story in an interview with The Washington Heights and Inwood News local newspaper, but I have lost the copy of the article I had at the time. This local newspaper stopped publishing years ago.

460   Online profiles of two major women's organizations with which the Ivy League had partnered:

NY Women's Foundation: www.nywf.org ;Women's Sports Foundation: www.womensportsfoundtion.org

461   Online profiles of two major women's organizations with which the Ivy League had partnered:

NY Women's Foundation: www.nywf.org; Women's Sports Foundation: www.womensportsfoundtion.org

462   Open to new perspectives: developing trust for one's choices. "The pitch: talked up the right way, at the right time" is a phrase in the book. Coming of Age at the End of History by Camille de Toledo (Soft Skull Press, 2008), pg 89.

463   "Resentment is a degraded motive for social change." Jane Addams and the Dream of American Democracy by Jean Bethke Elshtain (Basic Books, 2002) pg 113

464   "Resentment is a degraded motive for social change." Jane Addams and the Dream of American Democracy by Jean Bethke Elshtain (Basic Books, 2002) pg 113

465   Minutes for the NY City Council Operations Committee Hearing on the resolution to support the amendment to Public Officers Law regulations in the state code, which, if approved, would lower the age of eligibility for members on community boards to age 16. To see the official transcript: City Council, City of New York, Transcript of the Minutes of the Committee on Governmental Operations (June 9, 2014; start 10:21 a.m., recess 11:39 a.m.). The session was held at 250 Broadway, committee room on the 16th floor. The Operation Committee members, in addition to the Chair Ben Kallos, included David C. Greenfield, Mark Levine, Richie J. Torres and Steven Matteo. Coach Dave Crenshaw's testimony is on page 22 of the transcript. https://council.nyc.gov

466   I wrote this obituary for a service honoring Ray Pagan, who had been the site supervisor for the Department of Parks and Recreation Center at what at the time was called the Carmine Recreation Center. As an additional note, I also mention the following:

Charles DeFino was the Youth Services Coordinator for Community Board #12, when I started my work with Southern Heights in 1984. The position was partially funded from the Community Board #12 budget, and partially from the NYC Department of Youth Services Budget. This position title was eliminated across the City in the 1990s. Mr. DeFino introduced me to the practice of establishing partnerships with the Southern Heights youth program. He would emphasize with me repeatedly, that a program such as mine, with such a small annual budget (initially $9,100 annually) needed the support of partners who were more established, and which could provide our participants with extra opportunities. Charlie DeFino introduced me to Ray Pagan, after which Ray and his center became a second, downtown home to the Dreamers.

467   Rabbi Lerner defined Chesed as "loving kindness, understanding of the complexities of others, recognizing the inner and outer obstacles we all face in giving and receiving love, recognition and care." This is experienced in the spontaneous and altruistic love for community and for humanity.

Jewish Renewal by Rabbi Michael Lerner (Putnam and Sons, 1994), pp 112–113.

468   On Agape, see A Spirituality Named Compassion by Matthew Fox (Harper & Row, 1979), pg 104.

On well-being and the interconnected nature of the whole mind, see Mindsight by Daniel J. Siegel, M.D. (Bantam, 2010), pg 259.

469   Sam Keen's poem on love: "Love without knowledge is sentiment without depth. To become a lover, one must become a private

investigator and a connoisseur of story." Hymns from An Unknown God by Sam Keen (Bantam, 1994).

470   Being superior to privilege barely exists today amongst elected officials. During the era in which our nation was founded, Dr. Johnson, a supporter of the colonies fights for independence, defined "disinterest" as when an elected representative "is superior to regard for private advantage, and not influencing public affairs for private profit." Revolutionary Characters by Gordon S. Wood (Penguin, 2006), pg 16.

471   Being superior to privilege barely exists today amongst elected officials. During the era in which our nation was founded, Dr. Johnson, a supporter of the colonies fights for independence, defined "disinterest" as when an elected representative "is superior to regard for private advantage, and not influencing public affairs for private profit." Revolutionary Characters by Gordon S. Wood (Penguin, 2006), pg 16.

472   Five intellectual habits to be instilled in students. These habits are "evidence, viewpoints, cause and effect, hypothesizing, and knowing who cares." The Power of Their Ideas by Deborah Meier (Beacon Press, 1995), pg 41.

473   Five intellectual habits to be instilled in students. These habits are "evidence, viewpoints, cause and effect, hypothesizing, and knowing who cares." The Power of Their Ideas by Deborah Meier (Beacon Press, 1995), pg 41.

474   "Do not excuse, but rebuke, the sins of our country" is a quote from a speech made by Frederick Douglas. 100 Key Documents in American Democracy, edited by Peter B. Levy (Praeger Press, 1994); Article: #41— "Address on the Anniversary of the Emancipation of Slaves in the District of Columbia (1888)" by Frederick Douglas, pp 176–183.

475   Commitment as a type of civic marriage (between a teen advocate and civic mentor) entails responsibility and devotion. See Socrates in Love by Christopher Phillips (Norton, 2007), pg 303.

476   "I slept and dreamed that life is joy; I awoke and saw that life is service; I acted, and behold, service is joy." Words from a poem by Rabindranath Tagore. Cited from the Brainy Quotes website.

477   Testimonials from Hull House alumni Ruby and Maria. "The great mother breasts of our common humanity must not be withdrawn from any of us" and "the settlement speaks to the broad and generous yearnings for a fuller life and use of the faculties." Jane Addams and the Dream of American Democracy by Jean Bethke Elshtain (Basic Books, 2002), pg 96 (both quotes appear on this page).

478   "White and Black does not matter, you and Dave are both our fathers." This was told to Dave and me in a casual conversation with Rose Chea and Catherine Payne, each of whom was an alumnus from the Dreamer programs in the 1980s.

479   "This not just a program, but a family." This thought was part of a conversation I had with an adult volunteer, Steve Ramos, in the late 1980s. He was temporarily boarding with the family of Johnny Rosario, who had been a teen volunteer supervisor at our PS 128M after school program. He told me that he appreciated that the Ramos family had given him a place to stay while he was looking for other permanent residence, and that he enjoyed volunteering and giving youth a chance to experience having a safe space to stay.

480   Using a multi-level approach of working in present time while keeping the future in mind. This is a type of message I heard frequently from fellow organizers in the 1960s: what you saw and experienced is real…it was nothing less than a glimpse from the future. I found this thought reiterated in spiritual books I started to read in the late 1990s and early 2000s. I use one reiteration which moved me in the book:

"Destiny" in The More Beautiful World Our Hearts Know is Possible by Charles Eisenstein (North Atlantic Books, 2013), pp 259 and 260.

481   For an overview of Generation Citizen programs and mission, find descriptions at their website In Generation Citizen school programs, young people are recruited not just to be helping hands, but to design and point the way forward for their projects. http://generationcitizen.org

482   For an overview of the Petra Foundation mission and biographical sketches of any of its 100 Petra Fellows, go to the site for Community Change: https://communitychange.org/real-people/petrafellows. or go to www.petrafoundation.org and click on download the journal.

483   Biography of Petra Fellow Ellen Baxter, pg 344. Soaring Spirits: Petra Fellows 1989–2015, page 24. Or see Community Change website listed in Note 482. Or go to www.petrafoundation.org

484   Biography of Petra Fellow Ellen Baxter, pg 344. Soaring Spirits: Petra Fellows 1989–2015, page 24. Or see Community Change website listed in Note 482. Or go to www.petrafoundation.org

485   Biography of Petra Fellow Ellen Baxter, pg 344. Soaring Spirits: Petra Fellows 1989–2015, page 24. Or see Community Change website listed in Note 482. Or go to www.petrafoundation.org

486   Ivy League impact on one player and one coach (IS 52 team). Player: Yanel Cordero. These Ivy League experiences inspired Yanel to also pursue leadership opportunities in other programs. Two examples are her participation in the Global Kids (an organization I refer to in the next footnote) and in the F.L.A.M.E. program, sponsored by the U.S. Olympic Committee. See the USA Today article, "Finding Leaders Everywhere," June 13, 1996, p 9C. Yanel's softball coach, Jean Marie Acunto, was a special education teacher at IS 52M. Ms. Acunto, who was affectionately referred to as "Ms. Jam" by her players, told a local newspaper reporter: "Most of the girls had never touched a mitt…some never participated in a group activity. It is so

important for them, at their age, to build self-esteem and to learn to work with others." Interview was with Lisa Stephenson of The Bridge Leader newspaper. August 1995, pg 4.

487   Ivy League impact on one player and one coach (IS 52 team). Player: Yanel Cordero. These Ivy League experiences inspired Yanel to also pursue leadership opportunities in other programs. Two examples are her participation in the Global Kids (an organization I refer to in the next footnote) and in the F.L.A.M.E. program, sponsored by the U.S. Olympic Committee. See the USA Today article, "Finding Leaders Everywhere," June 13, 1996, p 9C. Yanel's softball coach, Jean Marie Acunto, was a special education teacher at IS 52M. Ms. Acunto, who was affectionately referred to as "Ms. Jam" by her players, told a local newspaper reporter: "Most of the girls had never touched a mitt…some never participated in a group activity. It is so important for them, at their age, to build self-esteem and to learn to work with others." Interview was with Lisa Stephenson of The Bridge Leader newspaper. August 1995, pg 4. I made notes from each of these articles at the time they were published, but I cannot find these articles online.

488   Ivy League impact on one player and one coach (IS 52 team). Player: Yanel Cordero. These Ivy League experiences inspired Yanel to also pursue leadership opportunities in other programs. Two examples are her participation in the Global Kids (an organization I refer to in the next footnote) and in the F.L.A.M.E. program, sponsored by the U.S. Olympic Committee. See the USA Today article, "Finding Leaders Everywhere," June 13, 1996, pg 9C. Yanel's softball coach, Jean Marie Acunto, was a special education teacher at IS 52M. Ms. Acunto, who was affectionately referred to as "Ms. Jam" by her players, told a local newspaper reporter: "Most of the girls had never touched a mitt…some never participated in a group activity. It is so important for them, at their age, to build self-esteem and to learn to work with others." Interview was with Lisa Stephenson of The

Bridge Leader newspaper. August 1995, pg 4. I made notes from each of these articles at the time they were published, but I cannot find these articles online.

489   Global Kids: "99% high school graduation rate, and Global Kids alumni become campus leaders and advocates for global engagement and social action."

Global Kids aids its young civic actors to develop the spirit of agape.

An additional source for my developing an understanding for the spirit of agape…is developed by the Japanese concept of Ikigai, getting to know a "reason for being—whatever it is that gives your life meaning." The author and futurist, Rob Hopkins describes agape as "an intersection between what you love, what you are good at, what the world needs, and what you can be paid for." See From What Is to What If by Rob Hopkins (Chelsea Green, 2019), pg 92. An additional element I add in sections of this book is that participants who adopt the spirit of agape (participants from Global Kids as well as those from agencies teaching a like-minded frame of reference) choose careers promoting community service and contributions for the common good. A full description of the Global Kids program, including quotes by teen participants, are listed on the Global Kids website at https://globalkids.org.

490   Learning to care for the poor. An ashram for the poor in New Delhi, India, is listed on the website for the Reciprocity Foundation. To learn more of the work of Adam Bukko, a founder of the Reciprocity Foundation, and his program for homeless youth in downtown Manhattan, see: Occupy Spirituality by Adam Bukko and Matthew Fox (North Atlantic Books, 2013). This book contains an ongoing dialogue between the two authors. For information on Mr. Bukko's program, go to www.reciprocityfoundation.org

491   Learning to care for the poor. An ashram for the poor in New Delhi, India, is listed on the website for the Reciprocity Foundation. To learn more of the work of Adam Bukko, a founder of the Reciprocity Foundation, and his program for homeless youth in downtown Manhattan, see: Occupy Spirituality by Adam Bukko and Matthew Fox (North Atlantic Books, 2013). This book contains an ongoing dialogue between the two authors. For information on Mr. Bukko's program, go to www.reciprocityfoundation.org

492   For enchanting, and chanting testimony on the unique intelligence of the heart… See (or listen to) the CD, A Heart As Wide As the World by Krishna Das. Notone Music 2010 BMI 067703087827.

493   For enchanting, and chanting testimony on the unique intelligence of the heart… See (or listen to) the CD, A Heart As Wide As the World by Krishna Das. Notone Music 2010 BMI 067703087827.

494   Dorothy Day was a leader and organizer for the Catholic Workers organization who practiced giving love as a solution to the long loneliness felt by the poor and those ostracized from supportive community. For an inspiring reading about those who studied Ms. Day's approach, and practiced it, see a book about an organization that had been co-led by Petra Fellows Ed Loring and Murphy Davis on the Open-Door Community. In honor of that organization's twenty-fifth anniversary, Peter R. Gathje put together the book, Sharing the Bread of Life: Hospitality and Resistance at the Open-Door Community (Copyright Peter R. Gathje, 2006). Amongst its finer works, the Open-Door program offered solace and support for the homeless, the formerly incarcerated, and those on death row (in and around Atlanta, Georgia). To find out current information on the Open-Door Community programs, go to their website at: https://opendoorcommunity.org

495   Positive peer pressure, taking a leap into creative experience. See a study by Norma Trowbridge and Don C. Charles covered by Kaoru

Yamamoto in the Journal of Social Psychology, (Issue 64, 1964, pp 249–261). One of the findings was seeing a dramatic leap in creativity amongst those ages 15 to 18, as well as a dramatic drop in conformity. This study was cited in the book, Teen 2.0 by Robert Epstein, Ph.D. (Quill River Press, 2010), p 255.

496　A chart on the impact of international agreements with countries that had been dependent upon local economies. See Table 21-1 (Critical distinguishing features) on pg 343 in the book, The Great Turning: From Empire to Earth Community by David Korten (Barrett-Kohler, 2006).

497　A chart on the impact of international agreements with countries that had been dependent upon local economies. See Table 21-1 (Critical distinguishing features) on page 343 in the book, The Great Turning: From Empire to Earth Community by David Korten (Barrett-Kohler, 2006).

498　On the presence of consciousness "ever-present, unacknowledged, and invisible" … which "transmits messages from and to the spiritual universe." See the book, The Invisible Player Dr. Charles Johnson (Park Street Press, 1999), pg 1.

499　The Archetype of the Advocate (Attorney, Legislator and Lobbyist), in which the belief of "compassion in action" is linked to the spiritual activist Ram Dass. Also, see Sacred Contracts by Carolyn Myss (Three Rivers Press, 2002), pg 366, which mentions Ram Dass as a model of this archetype.

500　On experiencing the sorrow of the world as the blackness of hell, a thought expressed by Dorothy Day. See Original Blessing by Matthew Fox (Bear and Company, 1983), pg 143.

501　On the degrading effects of insensitivity and indifference. Rabbi Abraham Joshua Heschel addressed this as he "discovered that indifference to evil is worse than evil itself." See his essay "The Reasons for my Involvement in the Peace Movement" in the book, Moral

Grandeur and Spiritual Audacity, edited by Susannah Heschel (Farrar, Stauss and Giroux, 1996), –pp 224–226.

502 Imagination gives shape to the universe…observing animals at play. See Of Wolves and Men by Barry Lopez (Scribner and Sons, 1978), pg 285.

503 Migration Policy Journal website, Ron Hayduk and Michelle Wucker (November 11, 2004). Also see the book, Democracy For All Restoring Immigrant Rights in the United States by Ron Hayduk (Routledge, 2006), for a history of voting rights exercised in the United States, between 1793 and the early 1900s, which, at that time, had voting rights for legal residents phased out. For the journal article online, see https://www.migrationpolicy.org/article/immigrationvoting

504 Ibid Migration Policy Journal website, Ron Hayduk and Michelle Wucker (November 11, 2004). Also see the book, Democracy For All Restoring Immigrant Rights in the United States by Ron Hayduk (Routledge, 2006), for a history of voting rights exercised in the United States, between 1793 and the early 1900s, which, at that time, had voting rights for legal residents phased out. https://www.migrationpolicy.org/article/immigrationvoting

505 Immigrant Leaders Organize New Citizen's Right to Vote," article online at Voice of America, in the Student Union site. Written by Nico Zviovich (March 9, 2020).

506 Who are the Dreamers – White, Black and Asian" is an online article on Newsweek. Written by John Haltiwanger (September 17, 2017), https://www.newsweek.com.

507 Who are the Dreamers – White, Black and Asian" is an online article on Newsweek. Written by John Haltiwanger (September 17, 2017), https://www.newsweek.com.

508   Who are the Dreamers – White, Black and Asian" is an online article on Newsweek. Written by John Haltiwanger (September 17, 2017), https://www.newsweek.com.

509   Crossing Broadway by Robert W. Snyder (Cornell University Press, 2015), pp 229–230.

510   Practicing Social Inclusion (Routledge, 2014), Ibid, pp 29–31.

511   Sarah Andes representing the archetype of the architect (or engineer). Part of this profile states that the archetype of the engineer is "grounded and orderly and possesses strategic qualities of mind lending it disposed to convert creative energy into practical expression." Taken from the archetype descriptions offered by Carolyn Myss in her book Sacred Contracts (Three Rivers Press, 2002), pg 384.

512   The muscle of patience is developed through experience. Deborah Meier, who was a founder of the progressive Central Park East Academy, considers the notion that young people naturally have short attention spans is a cultural myth. As she states: "Think about how deeply we have accepted the notion that young children lack attention spans because they are immature, when in fact it is small children who have the longest attention spans and most tenacious attention spans." She comes to this observation after years of experience directly the school, at which her staff had activities which tweaked their curiosity and kept them engaged. See The Power of Their Ideas, by Deborah Meier, (Beacon Press, 1995), pg 47.

513   Texts, words, and phrases, although sometimes perceived as eternally relevant, are not set in time. Educators such as Matthew Fox have found that when these are "presented in changed contexts, or viewed over the passage of time, original words become inflected with new meaning." See A Spirituality Named Compassion by Matthew Fox (Harper and Row, 1979), pg 231.

514   Texts, words, and phrases, although sometimes perceived as eternally relevant, are not set in time. Educators such as Matthew Fox have found that when these are "presented in changed contexts, or viewed over the passage of time, original words become inflected with new meaning." See A Spirituality Named Compassion by Matthew Fox (Harper and Row, 1979), pg 231.

515   Texts, words, and phrases, although sometimes perceived as eternally relevant, are not set in time. Educators such as Matthew Fox have found that when these are "presented in changed contexts, or viewed over the passage of time, original words become inflected with new meaning." See A Spirituality Named Compassion by Matthew Fox (Harper and Row, 1979), p 231.

516   There is danger (and/or boredom) when a teacher adopts reliance upon "pre-emptive and prescriptive solutions" to questions. Rather, both questions and coming to conclusions should be constructed by students. See the book The Death of Why: The Decline of Questioning and the Future of Democracy by Andrea Schlesinger (Berrett-Kohler, 2009) on "question power" (pp 1–11) and coming to terms with "inquiry being risky, while resiliency is its reward" (pp 19–26).

517   For a comprehensive look at the civic research conducted in support of teen civic efficacy, see the website for CIRCLE at: http://www. civicyouth.org.

518   Sarah Andes was a geography major in college, and this field of study deeply influenced her relationship to place. The place occupied by students and teachers whom Sarah guided in her action civics training made significant difference to her guidance practice. Go to Getsmart.com to get some insight into the value of place-based education. In one article by Tom Vander Ark, he possesses three benefits by using placed-based education. A teacher "leverages the power of place to personalize learning; places students in local

heritage, cultures and landscapes, and gives them opportunities for experience; and "the connection to the environment for engaged learning by engaged citizens." See the article at getsmart.com: "Get Kids in the Community, Change the World" by Tom Vander Ark (May 14, 2018). https://www.getsmart.com

519   Generation Citizen's Hourglass approach incorporates principles of cooperative learning. Studies on cooperative learning and student acquisition of higher order learning skills. In one study by Johnson and Johnson, they found that "(Students participating in cooperative learning settings) showed strong effects on critical thinking, higher order thinking, and thinking more creatively in a group." Cited from the book, Enhanced Thinking Through Cooperative Learning, edited by Neil Davidson and Toni Worsham (Teachers College Press, 1992), pg 41.

520   Generation Citizen's Hourglass approach incorporates principles of cooperative learning. Studies on cooperative learning and student acquisition of higher order learning skills. In one study by Johnson and Johnson, they found that "(Students participating in cooperative learning settings) showed strong effects on critical thinking, higher order thinking, and thinking more creatively in a group." Cited from the book, Enhanced Thinking Through Cooperative Learning, edited by Neil Davidson and Toni Worsham (Teachers College Press, 1992), p 41.

521   In Generation Citizens approach for encouraging issue identification and problem solving, their research supported and practical experience in running Action Civic Clubs with youth have demonstrated the efficacy of using cooperative enterprise. Team-building and collaborative relationships amongst teens on civic projects have a meaningful impact on their roles in a project, and with their civic efficacy for creating change. In a white paper by the Annie Casey Foundation for the Center for the Study for Social Policy, the authors

cited the need for developing relationships among the goals chosen, the targets for change, and the tactics used by the advocacy group. One point the authors make is that it is important to "identify desired results… (and where) it is clear about what they want to accomplish (by considering) every young person has their own vision…and it is also important to align individual and shared goals through honest dialogue" (p 15). See "Engaging Youth in Community Decision Making" (2007). To find the article online go to:

522 In Generation Citizens approach for encouraging issue identification and problem solving, their research supported and practical experience in running Action Civic Clubs with youth have demonstrated the efficacy of using cooperative enterprise. Team-building and collaborative relationships amongst teens on civic projects have a meaningful impact on their roles in a project, and with their civic efficacy for creating change. In a white paper by the Annie Casey Foundation for the Center for the Study for Social Policy, the authors cited the need for developing relationships among the goals chosen, the targets for change, and the tactics used by the advocacy group. One point the authors make is that it is important to "identify desired results… (and where) it is clear about what they want to accomplish (by considering) every young person has their own vision…and it is also important to align individual and shared goals through honest dialogue" (p 15). See "Engaging Youth in Community Decision Making" (2007).

523 Generation Citizen also stresses, as they utilize their "hourglass approach", that when students collectively and interdependently work in seeking a common goal, students learn "a framework for action, where they think about an issue politically—and identify structural issues and causes of the problem." Their students practice identifying a community issue, focusing on a specific aspect of that issue, and the root cause of that specific issue. See the Generation Citizen website learn more about their successes with the hour-glass

approach and Action Civics programs. https://generationcitizen.org.

524   The organization Queens Community House began in 1976. The Forest Hills Beacon became one of its program sites. At the time of my visit, the director named Patrick and the Assistant Director named Marlena Starace were program leaders at the site closely supervising the middle-school students involved in civic programs. She is currently the Leadership Development Specialist at the IS190 Beacon in Forest Hills. The atmosphere which pleasingly struck me was one resembling a description offered by the biologist E.O. Wilson about healthy living environments: "(which are) a life-like process, promoting a proving ground for trust, optimism and mutuality." For more information on the history and programs offered by Queens Community House, go to: https://www.countyoffice.org/queenscommunity.

525   The Community Assistance Unit with the City of New York maintains a webpage giving detailed information about the structure, function, and history of community boards, as well as links to any one of the 59 community boards in New York City. https://www1.nyc.gov/cau/communityboards.page.

526   "To impose any faith on certain types of belief is to destroy understanding" is a quote from James Madison in his contribution to civic debate. See Nature's God by Matthew Stewart (Norton, 2014), pp 226–227. In the video shown to the students, Mr. Obama stressed the need, in a viable democracy, to exercise respectful listening to the differing viewpoints of others.

527   A major idea promoted by Mr. Stewart in his book, Nature's God, is constructed as an analogy between the functioning of the mind as an experimental laboratory, just as the process of nature is one of experimentation. He emphasizes again and again throughout his book, stressing the importance of experience, experimentation, and

observation. See page 89 for one reference to this idea as applied to nature: "…the eternal substance of the world expresses itself not as a set of inert material things whose properties we understand perfectly but an endless series of lawful transformations of a singular thing that we understand only imperfectly." On page 91, Mr. Stewart quotes a naturalist philosopher named Bruno: "Nature… as Bruno puts it…is nothing if not a force implanted in things and the law by which every being moves along its proper course." Ibid.

528   The three democratic dispositions, as defined by Jean Bethke Elshtain in her book, Democracy on Trial (Basic Books, 1995), p 2.

529   Generating hope and seeing the future. The founder of the Oxford Research Group, Scilla Elworthy, Ph.D., looks at hope not "as a strategy, but as a vision grounded in pragmatism and a humble receptivity to new ideas" (pp 17–18). At the same time, she believes that "the future belongs to those who can see it," and that this takes "a leap in consciousness to unlock the mysteries of the future pathways" (pp 17–18). See her book outlining her life's work as an international peacemaker and conflict resolution negotiator in her book, Pioneering the Possible: Awakened Leadership for A World That Works (North Atlantic Books, 2014).

530   Andrea Schlesinger raises the point that if working toward future-oriented goals, a person needs to be both nimble and flexible. As she states in her book, The Death of Why (Berrett Kohler, 2009), "The future is a moving target, and the ground is never still" (p 3). In addressing shifting grounds, she adds: "Absorbing and acting on today's answers is simply not enough. The only thing we can count on to see through an uncertain future is our ability to ask questions" (p 3).

531   Mary Parker Follett was an early twentieth-century organizer in the business world who also thought deeply about the nature of democracy. In her book, The Creative Experience (reprinted for

Martino Publishing, 2013), she talks about her belief that democracy is a self-creating process, and that one problem in democracy is to figure out how "to make our daily life creative" (p 230). As Ms. Follett reiterates, "Integration is both the keel and the rudder of life...the test of the vitality of any experience is its power to unite in a living generation of activity of self-yielding differences" (p 302).

532   "To be nobody but myself in the world. This is a line from a poet by E.E. Cummings titled A Poet's Advice to Students. https://www.goodreads.com.

533   Ken Wilbur, in his book, The Marriage of Sense and Soul (Broadway Books, 1998), proposed that science and spirituality need not be totally at odds, but rather could be seen as two realms which are complementary to each other, and shared some methodologies. One space shared in both realms is what Mr. Wilbur calls "instrumental injunction" or a practice paradigm where the observer is in a period of experimentation. Mr. Wilbur also shows how in each realm, "participants rely upon direct experience as a source for the apprehension of data, and that for each, there is a need for communal confirmation, where data is checked and shared with others." Source: Wikipedia: The Marriage of Sense and Soul: Part III Reconciliation. https://enwikipedia.org/wiki/The_Marriage_of_Sense_and_Soul For those interested in exploring the work of Wilbur further, a good start is his book, A Brief History of Everything (Shambhala Books, 1996). In the introduction to this book, he provides an overview of the scope of his book, including thoughts on human development, evolution of consciousness, and our relationship with nature. pp 1 – 13.

534   Sharing power rather than controlling others: The wisdom of patients. Dr. Richard Katz describes his therapeutic approach in his book, Indigenous Healing Psychology: Honoring the Wisdom of the First Peoples (Healing Arts Press, 2017). Dr. Katz practices with

the mandate of "establish a therapeutic alliance with patients" (p 27). Dr. Katz emphasizes the power of listening, where he carefully receives information and viewpoints from his patient and does not rely upon labels which marginalize them by discounting the validity of their knowledge.

535   Humans have an innate capacity to anticipate and choose our future. David Korten, in his book, The Great Turning (Berrett-Kohler, 2006), questions the assumption that humans prepare for the future based upon a system of random chance and survival of the fittest. As Dr. Korten elucidates: "The idea that evolution is nothing more than a playing out of a competitive struggle for domination seems hopelessly simplistic. More credible is that life is intelligent and purposeful, and that each living system embodies many levels of conscious intelligence" (p 280).

536   The "mind" is a connection between the head and the heart. This is a basic assumption from which Buddhist practice is developed by Robert Sachs. In his book, Becoming Buddha: Awakening Wisdom and the Compassion to Change (Watkins Publishing, 2010), he also states "that the master of the two (the head and the heart) is the heart" (p xxi). In addition to coordinating a vast complex of neurons and hormones in coordination with the body and the brain, the heart is also an intuitive gateway to the soul.

537   The Lasso of Truth. In her book, Our Superheroes, Ourselves (Oxford University Press, 2013), Robin Rosenberg profiles American super-heroes in fictional literature and speculates on how some of their attributes are shared with us. Wonder Woman who "was created to do battle with the Nazis" (p 87) has strength and impressive tools, allowing her to emerge triumphant in battle. What she also utilizes is "the Lasso of Truth." The Lasso is defined as a tool which "can extract in your world, truth, and erase memories" (p 80). What I found when engaging with Sarah was not a lasso, but a presence

which was felt by me to be optimistic and reassuring, leading me to erase doubts driven by my past mistakes, and to stay connected to the guidance of my inner wisdom.

538   The therapeutic benefit of facing reality. In their book, Wonder Woman: Lassoing the Truth (Sterling N.Y., 2017), the editors Travis Langley and Mara Wood point to the possibility that reality is what the psychologist Carl Rogers called an inherent condition: "People are naturally good, (and) want their actual selves to become like their ideal selves" (p 303).

539   The therapeutic benefit of facing reality. In their book, Wonder Woman: Lassoing the Truth (Sterling N.Y., 2017), the editors Travis Langley and Mara Wood point to the possibility that reality is what the psychologist Carl Rogers called an inherent condition: "People are naturally good, (and) want their actual selves to become like their ideal selves" (p 303).

540   Ellen J Langer is a professor of psychology at Harvard University who received an award from the American Psychological Association in 1988. In her book, The Power of Mindful Learning (Addison-Wesley, 1997), she draws a distinction between outer directed and inner guided values. As she states: "The capacity to achieve an outcome is different from the ability to explore the world and understand experience…the freedom to define the experience is more significant than achieving an outcome" (p 121).

541   Indeterminate potentiality is a concept developed by Jeffrey J Karpel, who has surveyed works of science fiction and linked some of its fictional vision with our obtaining capacities beyond what our traditional beliefs hold to be possible. In Mr. Karpel's book, Mutants and Mystics: Science Fiction, Superhero Comics and the Paranormal (University of Chicago Press, 2011), he elaborates on the concept of indeterminate potentiality: "Maybe creation goes both ways at the same time…maybe belief creates reality, and reality creates belief,

which creates new realities, and so on…this indeterminate reality 'collapses' and becomes determined through our individual beliefs and decisions…and through our collective culture and religions" (p 317). Mr. Karpel further speculates that "super-imposed para- doxes and psychical information are processed in the core of the brain near the site of the pineal gland" (p 325). In other words, the stories we make up about ourselves and others ultimately shape our perception and decisions. There is an old expression that science fiction precedes and predicts what we will learn through science. The relationship between the observer and the observed world is a subject of speculation amongst quantum theory scientists. See The Quantum Revelation: A Radical Synthesis of Science and Spirituality by Paul Levy (Select Books, 2018) pp xvii – xxxv.

542   The action stories of lived narrative assist with bringing on the improbable. Meira Levinson, in her book, No Citizen Left Behind (Harvard University Press, 2012) weaves a theme into her work through a theory that constructing of projects by those engaged in a living narrative "empower American history and identity from the building blocks of struggle." The ideals previously constrained by the visions of the future are entering a birth canal toward present-day possibility trying to be born.

543   The action stories of lived narrative assist with bringing on the improbable. Meira Levinson, in her book, No Citizen Left Behind (Harvard University Press, 2012) weaves a theme into her work through a theory that constructing of projects by those engaged in a living narrative "empower American history and identity from the building blocks of struggle." The ideals previously constrained by the visions of the future are entering a birth canal toward present-day possibility trying to be born.

544   "Position oneself at the edges of possibility, people in the center do not make change" (p 34). Krista Tippitt in her book, Becoming

Wise: An Inquiry into the Mystery and Art of Living (Penguin, 2017), speaks to a viewpoint that "(the) enduring question of what it means to be human has become indistinguishable from who we are to one another." In other words, when openly participating in the relationships of a multi-cultural world, the task is to redefine what had been seen as unacceptably foreign, and now, in new ways, become mysteriously and artfully attractive.

545   "Position oneself at the edges of possibility, people in the center do not make change" (p 34). Krista Tippitt in her book, Becoming Wise: An Inquiry into the Mystery and Art of Living (Penguin, 2017), speaks to a viewpoint that "(the) enduring question of what it means to be human has become indistinguishable from who we are to one another." In other words, when openly participating in the relationships of a multi-cultural world, the task is to redefine what had been seen as unacceptably foreign, and now, in new ways, become mysteriously and artfully attractive.

546   Idealistic writers, immersed in nature and spirit, express their devotion to the higher possibilities of democracy. In examining nine-teenth-century American literary work, the author David Reynolds sees them as agents describing transformative vision for a new way of living beyond the comfort zone of materialistic means. In Mr. Reynolds' book, Beneath the American Renaissance (Oxford University Press, 1988), he profiles these writers as "ardently devoted to the American ideals of democracy, allied with the hyperbolic reverence for our founding fathers, and at the same time (expressing) vitriolic bitterness toward perceived inequalities" (p 184).

547   Identify, observe, and practice from the heart of democracy, from which the celebration of transition arrives. Charles Eisenstein, in his book, The More Beautiful World Our Hearts Know is Possible (North Atlantic Books, 2013), criticizes our habits where "we take

for granted the very things that are at the root of our problems" (page 108).

548   To develop citizens later, start early with stories celebrating the practice. Albert J. Raboteau, in his book, American Prophets (Princeton University Press, 2016), shares the word of Dr. Martin Luther King, Jr for talking about the stories of social justice history-making as valuable for the young: "The civil rights movement exemplifies for us the faculty of empathy through the telling of and listening to each other's stories. Learning and protecting the virtues of citizenship and democratic process must happen from childhood on" (p 159).

549   Young activists are teachers about those teaching best practices for the new era. In an article written for Sierra, magazine (January/ February 2021) titled, "Teach Your Elders Well," Larshini Prakish, a co-founder of the Sunrise Movement, tells a story about how young activists are working the electoral system to elect proponents of renewable energy.

550   Adolescent hearts are powered through the guidance of the soul. Thomas Moore, in his book, Care Of The Soul (Harper Perennial, 1992), makes note of the subtlety of the soul's guidance: "The intellect works with reason and logic, the soul insinuates, offering fleeting impressions. Its effects are achieved more through magic than effort." (p 122). M. Scott Peck, author of A Different Drum (Simon & Schuster, 1987), speaks to the uniqueness of each person being an evolutionary need: "Psychologists...agree with theologians that the uniqueness of our individuality is called for. They envision it as a goal of human development that we should become fully ourselves." (p 53).

551   We sat at the center of an earthquake occurring along two intersecting fault lines. Rob Brezsny in his book, Pronoia, describes the meaning of apocalypse as being interpreted in ambiguous ways: "The apocalypse that we are living through can be described through

three meanings: an end to the world, a revelation, and an awakening. Disintegration and renewal are happening side by side" (p 108).

552   A transition from the mechanical to the ecological age. As pointed out by David Korten in his book, The Great Turning (Barrett-Kohler, 2006), this transition can be interpreted in two ways. The first take is as an "imperative," seeing "this troubled planet is a place of violent contrasts. Those who receive rewards are totally separated from those who shoulder the burdens. It is not wise leadership" (p 57). As the Chinese adage goes, every crisis can also be seen as an opportunity. Mr. Korten highlights this opportunity: "We are now experiencing a moment of significance beyond what any of us can imagine. The distorted realm of the industrial-technology paradigm is being replaced by the more viable realm of a mutually enhancing human presence within an ever-renewing, organic-based earth community" (p 74). The Time Magazine 20th anniversary commemorative special issue on the significance of 1968 was released in 1988. The title of that issue is "1968: The Year That Shaped A Generation". The website in which archived issues could be found is: www.timemagazine.content.time.com/timeararchive .

553   A transition from the mechanical to the ecological age. As pointed out by David Korten in his book, The Great Turning (Barrett-Kohler, 2006), this transition can be interpreted in two ways. The first take is as an "imperative," seeing "this troubled planet is a place of violent contrasts. Those who receive rewards are totally separated from those who shoulder the burdens. It is not wise leadership" (p 57). As the Chinese adage goes, every crisis can also be seen as an opportunity. Mr. Korten highlights this opportunity: "We are now experiencing a moment of significance beyond what any of us can imagine. The distorted realm of the industrial-technology paradigm is being replaced by the more viable realm of a mutually enhancing human presence within an ever-renewing, organic-based earth community" (p 74). The Time Magazine 20th anniversary commemorative special

issue on the significance of 1968 was released in 1988. The title of that issue is "1968: The Year That Shaped A Generation". The website in which archived issues could be found is: www.timemagazine. content.time.com/timearchive.

554   A critique of the existing paradigm about teen development, i.e., moving on from patho-adolescence to mature teens growing into mature adults. In his book, Wild Mind: A Field Guide to the Human Psyche (New World Library, 2013), Bill Plotkin anticipates what the holistic development of teens looks like: "...if what we want is a thriving planet, the most essential project is to raise children who have the capacity to grow into true adults and authentic elders—mature humans" (p 245).

555   Calling humans...a message from planet Earth. In his book, Nature and the Human Soul (New World Library, 2013), Bill Plotkin quotes the wilderness explorer Geneen Marie Haugen: "We might speculate that Earth is trying to imagine its own future through us" (page 17).

556   Calling humans...a message from planet Earth. In his book, Nature and the Human Soul (New World Library, 2013), Bill Plotkin quotes the wilderness explorer Geneen Marie Haugen: "We might speculate that Earth is trying to imagine its own future through us" (page 17).

557   "A distinctiveness of adolescence carrying gifts for others." Bill Plotkin elaborates on his theory of human development, specifically during the "period of late adolescence" which he describes as "the wanderer in the cocoon" (p 299). As Mr. Plotkin goes on to describe differences between adolescence and adulthood, he states: "The differences between adolescence and adulthood are radical indeed...the long progression...is a movement in and out of ordinary community life...where teenagers work to create authentic presence" (page 299).

558   "A distinctiveness of adolescence carrying gifts for others." Bill Plotkin elaborates on his theory of human development, specifically

during the "period of late adolescence" which he describes as "the wanderer in the cocoon" (p 299). As Mr. Plotkin goes on to describe differences between adolescence and adulthood, he states: "The differences between adolescence and adulthood are radical indeed… the long progression…is a movement in and out of ordinary community life…where teenagers work to create authentic presence" (page 299).

559   Summarizing the collective impact of teen movements. A white paper called "Youth-Led Social Change: Topics, Engagement Types, Organizational Types, Strategies and Impacts" (Futures, Vol. 67, March 2015, pp 52–62) analyzes the nuances of structure and process used by teen-led social change movements. In their findings, the authors of this paper, Elaine Ho, Amelia Clarke, and Ilona Dougherty, summarized findings of their research: "Youth (ages 15–24) can successfully create social change; results obtained show a strong relationship between the impact received and the approach used; and youth have had great impact participating in political action in political parties" (page 1). See https://www.sciencedirect.com/journal/futures/vol/67/suppl/C

560   The impact of "the 4 catastrophes" have hit teens in significant ways. The ways teen leaders have responded demonstrated their awareness of each type of catastrophe and the crucial need to address them before we see real change. I cite four examples here, one for each issue. Addressing materialism, Brower Youth Award recipient Chandler Payne created a project where neighbors could access food locally, by taking ownership over its production and distribution. See "Helping Marginalized Youth Grow Food," under New Leaders Initiative on the website www.broweryouthawards.org. For the issue of militarism, read about the work of the youth led Ya Ya Network, which trains teens to "unpack their identities, deconstruct implicit bias, and make space inside and outside of community." See Youth Activists, Youth Allies at the Ya Ya website, https://www.

yayanetwork.org. On the work of addressing racism, read about the work of teacher Fannie Davis in Oakland, California, with her students. As part of the classroom experience, students learned to use conferencing and counseling to achieve the end of making amends and not using retribution. See "Where Dignity is Part of the School Day" in YES! magazine, Spring 2014, Issue 69, p 32. In addressing the issue of poverty, a student named Maya Salcedo helped to lead a project called Roots in Community, which organized a summit on the topics of community gardening, food security, culinary training, social enterprise, and environmental justice work. Read about this project in the book, A Peoples Curriculum for the Earth, in an article titled "We Have the Right," starting on page 354.

What each of these diverse youth-led approaches share is in supporting holistically developed youth, but in transforming adverse conditions of teen development. As addressed by James Cote in his book, Arrested Adulthood (NY University Press, 2000), not addressing the problem of challenged adolescent development contributes toward seeing a society with an increased prevalence of "arrested adulthood," that is, delays in reaching full maturity or having many adults never actually maturing. He describes two conditions of arrested adulthood. The first is a process where "(teens are subject to a process of) default individualization—a life course dictated to by circumstance and folly, with little agentic assertion on the part of the person" (p 33). The second highlights the rewarding of passivity, where teens are kept in a period of "identity moratorium for community responsibility" (p 37).

561   The impact of "the 4 catastrophes" have hit teens in significant ways. The ways teen leaders have responded demonstrated their awareness of each type of catastrophe and the crucial need to address them before we see real change. I cite four examples here, one for each issue. Addressing materialism, Brower Youth Award recipient Chandler Payne created a project where neighbors could access food

locally, by taking ownership over its production and distribution. See "Helping Marginalized Youth Grow Food," under New Leaders Initiative on the website www.broweryouthawards.org. For the issue of militarism, read about the work of the youth led Ya Ya Network, which trains teens to "unpack their identities, deconstruct implicit bias, and make space inside and outside of community." See Youth Activists, Youth Allies at the Ya Ya website, https://www. yayanetwork.org. On the work of addressing racism, read about the work of teacher Fannie Davis in Oakland, California, with her students. As part of the classroom experience, students learned to use conferencing and counseling to achieve the end of making amends and not using retribution. See "Where Dignity is Part of the School Day" in YES! magazine, Spring 2014, Issue 69, p 32. In addressing the issue of poverty, a student named Maya Salcedo helped to lead a project called Roots in Community, which organized a summit on the topics of community gardening, food security, culinary training, social enterprise, and environmental justice work. Read about this project in the book, A Peoples Curriculum for the Earth, in an article titled "We Have the Right," starting on page 354.

What each of these diverse youth-led approaches share is in supporting holistically developed youth, but in transforming adverse conditions of teen development. As addressed by James Cote in his book, Arrested Adulthood (NY University Press, 2000), not addressing the problem of challenged adolescent development contributes toward seeing a society with an increased prevalence of "arrested adulthood," that is, delays in reaching full maturity or having many adults never actually maturing. He describes two conditions of arrested adulthood. The first is a process where "(teens are subject to a process of) default individualization—a life course dictated to by circumstance and folly, with little agentic assertion on the part of the person" (p 33). The second highlights the rewarding of passivity, where teens are kept in a period of "identity moratorium for community responsibility" (p 37).

562   The impact of "the 4 catastrophes" have hit teens in significant ways. The ways teen leaders have responded demonstrated their awareness of each type of catastrophe and the crucial need to address them before we see real change. I cite four examples here, one for each issue. Addressing materialism, Brower Youth Award recipient Chandler Payne created a project where neighbors could access food locally, by taking ownership over its production and distribution. See "Helping Marginalized Youth Grow Food," under New Leaders Initiative on the website www.broweryouthawards.org. For the issue of militarism, read about the work of the youth led Ya Ya Network, which trains teens to "unpack their identities, deconstruct implicit bias, and make space inside and outside of community." See Youth Activists, Youth Allies at the Ya Ya website, https://www. yayanetwork.org. On the work of addressing racism, read about the work of teacher Fannie Davis in Oakland, California, with her students. As part of the classroom experience, students learned to use conferencing and counseling to achieve the end of making amends and not using retribution. See "Where Dignity is Part of the School Day" in YES! magazine, Spring 2014, Issue 69, p 32. In addressing the issue of poverty, a student named Maya Salcedo helped to lead a project called Roots in Community, which organized a summit on the topics of community gardening, food security, culinary training, social enterprise, and environmental justice work. Read about this project in the book, A Peoples Curriculum for the Earth, in an article titled "We Have the Right," starting on page 354.

What each of these diverse youth-led approaches share is in supporting holistically developed youth, but in transforming adverse conditions of teen development. As addressed by James Cote in his book, Arrested Adulthood (NY University Press, 2000), not addressing the problem of challenged adolescent development contributes toward seeing a society with an increased prevalence of "arrested adulthood," that is, delays in reaching full maturity or having many adults never actually maturing. He describes two conditions of arrested adulthood. The first is a process where "(teens are subject to a process of) default individualization—a life course dictated to by circumstance and folly, with little agentic assertion on the part of the person" (p 33). The second highlights the rewarding of passivity, where teens are kept in a period of "identity moratorium for community responsibility" (p 37).

563　　The impact of "the 4 catastrophes" have hit teens in significant ways. The ways teen leaders have responded demonstrated their awareness of each type of catastrophe and the crucial need to address them before we see real change. I cite four examples here, one for each issue. Addressing materialism, Brower Youth Award recipient Chandler Payne created a project where neighbors could access food locally, by taking ownership over its production and distribution. See "Helping Marginalized Youth Grow Food," under New Leaders Initiative on the website www.broweryouthawards.org. For the issue of militarism, read about the work of the youth led Ya Ya Network, which trains teens to "unpack their identities, deconstruct implicit bias, and make space inside and outside of community." See Youth Activists, Youth Allies at the Ya Ya website, https://www. yayanetwork.org. On the work of addressing racism, read about the work of teacher Fannie Davis in Oakland, California, with her students. As part of the classroom experience, students learned to use conferencing and counseling to achieve the end of making amends and not using retribution. See "Where Dignity is Part of the School Day" in YES! magazine, Spring 2014, Issue 69, p 32. In addressing the issue of poverty, a student named Maya Salcedo helped to lead a project called Roots in Community, which organized a summit on the topics of community gardening, food security, culinary training, social enterprise, and environmental justice work. Read about this project in the book, A Peoples Curriculum for the Earth, in an article titled "We Have the Right," starting on page 354.

What each of these diverse youth-led approaches share is in supporting holistically developed youth, but in transforming adverse conditions of teen development. As addressed by James Cote in his book, Arrested Adulthood (NY University Press, 2000), not addressing the problem of challenged adolescent development contributes toward seeing a society with an increased prevalence of "arrested adulthood," that is, delays in reaching full maturity or having many adults never actually maturing. He describes two conditions of arrested adulthood. The first is a process where "(teens are subject to a process of) default individualization—a life course dictated to by circumstance and folly, with little agentic assertion on the part of the person" (p 33). The second highlights the rewarding of passivity, where teens are kept in a period of "identity moratorium for community responsibility" (p 37).

564   The impact of "the 4 catastrophes" have hit teens in significant ways. The ways teen leaders have responded demonstrated their awareness of each type of catastrophe and the crucial need to address them before we see real change. I cite four examples here, one for each issue. Addressing materialism, Brower Youth Award recipient Chandler Payne created a project where neighbors could access food locally, by taking ownership over its production and distribution. See "Helping Marginalized Youth Grow Food," under New Leaders Initiative on the website www.broweryouthawards.org. For the issue of militarism, read about the work of the youth led Ya Ya Network, which trains teens to "unpack their identities, deconstruct implicit bias, and make space inside and outside of community." See Youth Activists, Youth Allies at the Ya Ya website, https://www.yayanetwork.org. On the work of addressing racism, read about the work of teacher Fannie Davis in Oakland, California, with her students. As part of the classroom experience, students learned to use

conferencing and counseling to achieve the end of making amends and not using retribution. See "Where Dignity is Part of the School Day" in YES! magazine, Spring 2014, Issue 69, p 32. In addressing the issue of poverty, a student named Maya Salcedo helped to lead a project called Roots in Community, which organized a summit on the topics of community gardening, food security, culinary training, social enterprise, and environmental justice work. Read about this project in the book, A Peoples Curriculum for the Earth, in an article titled "We Have the Right," starting on page 354.

What each of these diverse youth-led approaches share is in supporting holistically developed youth, but in transforming adverse conditions of teen development. As addressed by James Cote in his book, Arrested Adulthood (NY University Press, 2000), not addressing the problem of challenged adolescent development contributes toward seeing a society with an increased prevalence of "arrested adulthood," that is, delays in reaching full maturity or having many adults never actually maturing. He describes two conditions of arrested adulthood. The first is a process where "(teens are subject to a process of) default individualization—a life course dictated to by circumstance and folly, with little agentic assertion on the part of the person" (p 33). The second highlights the rewarding of passivity, where teens are kept in a period of "identity moratorium for community responsibility" (p 37).

565   The impact of "the 4 catastrophes" have hit teens in significant ways. The ways teen leaders have responded demonstrated their awareness of each type of catastrophe and the crucial need to address them before we see real change. I cite four examples here, one for each issue. Addressing materialism, Brower Youth Award recipient Chandler Payne created a project where neighbors could access food locally, by taking ownership over its production and distribution. See "Helping Marginalized Youth Grow Food," under New Leaders Initiative on the website www.broweryouthawards.org. For the issue

of militarism, read about the work of the youth led Ya Ya Network, which trains teens to "unpack their identities, deconstruct implicit bias, and make space inside and outside of community." See Youth Activists, Youth Allies at the Ya Ya website, https://www. yayanet-work.org. On the work of addressing racism, read about the work of teacher Fannie Davis in Oakland, California, with her students. As part of the classroom experience, students learned to use conferencing and counseling to achieve the end of making amends and not using retribution. See "Where Dignity is Part of the School Day" in YES! magazine, Spring 2014, Issue 69, p 32. In addressing the issue of poverty, a student named Maya Salcedo helped to lead a project called Roots in Community, which organized a summit on the topics of community gardening, food security, culinary training, social enterprise, and environmental justice work. Read about this project in the book, A Peoples Curriculum for the Earth, in an article titled "We Have the Right," starting on page 354.

What each of these diverse youth-led approaches share is in supporting holistically developed youth, but in transforming adverse conditions of teen development. As addressed by James Cote in his book, Arrested Adulthood (NY University Press, 2000), not addressing the problem of challenged adolescent development contributes toward seeing a society with an increased prevalence of "arrested adulthood," that is, delays in reaching full maturity or having many adults never actually maturing. He describes two conditions of arrested adulthood. The first is a process where "(teens are subject to a process of) default individualization—a life course dictated to by circumstance and folly, with little agentic assertion on the part of the person" (p 33). The second highlights the rewarding of passivity, where teens are kept in a period of "identity moratorium for community responsibility" (pg 37).

566   On the purpose of public education. The purpose of education is to develop fully mature students who become capable of participating

in optimally functioning society. Neil Postman, in his book, The End of Education (1995) uses the word "end" with double entendre, suggesting that the goals of public education are not being addressed, and that if we continue this course, the institutions of education can no longer be called public. As Mr. Postman states, "The failure to provide this unifying narrative leaves the purpose of public education, and the future of public schools, wandering off course."

567   "When you walk away from yourself, you continue to walk in the dark." I reiterate this phrase here to suggest that it is not only who the individual walks in the dark. Society manufactures a darkness in which students do not find themselves, and its institutions remain lost. As proposed in his book, Ritual: Power, Healing and Community (Penguin, 1993), the shaman Malidoma Patrice Some proposes: "This means that the world of progress, with all of its consuming tendencies is an essentialist that feeds on anything that lives, turning the human into an indentured servant with things material, yet starved for everything else" (pg 22).

We best address the issues created in the dark by looking into the darkness. In her book, Hope in the Dark: Untold Histories, Wild Possibilities (Haymarket Books, 2016), the writer, historian, and activist Rebecca Solnit proposes action that bring light to the darkness. In her opening chapter called "Grounds for Hope," she quoted the philosopher Walter Bruggeman: "Memory produces hope in the same way that amnesia produces despair" (page xix). As we become more and more engaged with untold but powerful stories from marginalized peoples, we build an immunity against the loss of memory leading us toward a surrender of hope. As Ms. Solnit also proposes, engagement with stories generated from dispossessed and minimized people heightens the immunity response: "Changing the story isn't enough, but it has often been the foundation to real changes. Making an injury visible and public is often the first step to remedying it, and political change often follows culture, as what was long tolerated is seen to be intolerable, and what was overlooked becomes obvious" (p xvi).

568   Ancestral wisdom, on the fallacy of remaining in bondage to the past. In one of his classic texts called The Ambattha Sutta, the Buddha "denounced the principles of caste and the pretensions of the Brahmins." See Britannica at www.brittanica.com. Isabel Wilkerson, a Pulitzer Prize winner, denounces our continuing support, in conscious and unconscious ways, to the maintenance of an American caste system fueled by racism. In her book, Caste: The Origins of Our Discontents (Random House, 2020), Ms. Wilkerson posits the role of personal irresponsibility in maintaining the caste system: "A caste system persists in part because we, each and every one of us, allow it to exist—in large and small ways, in our everyday actions, in how we elevate or demean, embrace or exclude, on the basis of meaning attached to a person's physical traits. If enough people buy into the lie of natural hierarchy, then it becomes the truth, or is assumed to be" (p 380). I believe her amazingly astute analysis reveals the way that this exceedingly toxic and destructive social disease has affected the continuance of the defective adolescent archetype in terrible ways.

569   Break away from attachment to broken treaties of separation. This is developed in the book Soul Whispering by Linda Star-Wolf and Nita Gage (Bear and Company, 2017). In their sharing of narratives from people who have healed, they speak to making oneself more whole, and relationships more mutually affirming. They shared a thought expressed by Mariko Yamamoto, "(In) learning to be with people more authentically...(I) face my own darkest unconscious places in the company of compassionate people, (which) prepares (me) to do the same for others" (pp 24–25). We need to shine a light on the dark practices of societal institutions, and in the dark recesses of our consciousness, always supported in the empathetic company of friends.

570 "Every age and generation must be free to acts for itself" is a thought made by Thomas Paine. It is also true for each member of an emergent generation. Christopher Hitchens, in his book Thomas Paine's Rights of Man (Grove Press, 2006) shares a citation made by Thomas Paine on an insight made by the philosopher Thomas Hobbes in his work titled Leviathan: "…the right of nature, which writers commonly call Jus Naturale, is the liberty each man hath, to use his own power, as he will himself, for the preservation of his own nature" (p 104).

571 Methods of guiding wounded heroes against the unchallenged order of complacency or tyranny. One such method used is that of interactive theater participation. An anecdote by a person using interactive theater, "led by a facilitator using deep listening and thoughtful guidance connecting the individual with their personal archetypic dramas" is shared in the book Soul Whisperer (Ibid, p 44).

572 Linda Star-Wolf and Nita Gage (Soul Whispering, 2017) continue to develop the connection between exploring one's true self and constructing authentic story. They describe this connection as one which "assists people in bringing their authentic story to life" (p 44), and which "elicits powerful information that points to the longing of the soul that is seeking expression" (p 49).

573 "The habits of the heart inform the infrastructure of democracy" is a theme raised by Alexis de Tocqueville in his observations of American's social and political life in the nineteenth century. Isaac Kramnick, the editor of the book, Alexis De Tocqueville: Democracy in America (Penguin, 2003), includes the following two examples of De Tocqueville's observations about American character: "The acquisition of a materialist core of American individualism" (p xxxiii) and "the enthusiastic involvement in their private association

with using local self-government as checks upon the power of excessive individualism and the abuse of power" (pg xxxi).

574   The Community League of the Heights (CLOTH) is a multi-service community-based agency which provides and sponsors, amongst other projects, the Community League Health Clinic, and the Community Health Academy of the Heights (CHAH), grades 6–12. Find CLOTH online at www.communityleagueoftheheights.org. The Executive Director is Yvonne Stennett.

575   Expressive imagination is found in visual art as well as embedded within the nuances of language. Asian model myth and linguistic isolation are examples of shallow forms of art. These types of art forms produce toxic imagery for the sake of generating negative attention. I refer here to my previous mention of this myth, and the chasm in communication between the real needs of Asian youth, and the falsely constructed stereotype pasted on to these people. As stated by UC Berkley alumni Hua Hsu: "(The) needs and disadvantages of refugee communities and poor Asian-Americans have been obscured." Cited in the article "How the 'Model Minority Myth' Hurts Asian Americans" by Kim Girard, March 9, 2021 at https://newsroom.haas.berkeley.edu/thoughts—on-the-model-minority-myths-impact-on-asian-americans

576   Weaving the lessons of the past with the possibilities of the future.

Creative effort is nourished by the thoughts of our ancestral civic allies, and the whispers heard from the future. Rob Hopkins, author of the book, From What Is to What If (Chelsea Green, 2019), alludes to this partnership: "Imagination draws from the palette of options and possibilities we carry in and memories and uses unique combinations of experiences (that we may use to inform our approach toward constructing the future) (pg 57).

577   I have referenced the power of love previously in this book, a phrase I read about created by Anodea Judith in her book, Awakening the

Global Heart (Elite Books, 2006). An addition aspect of this power of love is as a source for navigation towards the future. As Ms. Judith proclaims: "If power is the capacity generated by our relationships... love is the most potent source of power" (p 247–248) As she continues: "We are entering a rite of passage into the future" (pg 19). It takes a village of those in close affinity to build a bridge to a more promising future.

578 History is composed of real people in living, breathing relationships. As stated by Gordon Wood, in his book Revolutionary Characters (Penguin Books, 2006), when advising on interpreting the character and intention of our nation's founders, "What we need is not more praise of the founders, but of them and their circumstances" (p 10). As Mr. Wood follows up: "...the revolutionary leaders... were...progenitors...of new circumstances. They helped to create the changes that eventually led to their own undoing" (p 11.) I believe these insights are food for thought for those of us who are quick to condemn the inconjunct between our founders' proposed ideals and their lifestyles (that is, owing slaves) which contradicted their stated ideals. Today, in our society, the average US person owns at least one computer, on which some people, social justice advocates, provide text upon text of testimony. As pointed out in the introduction to his book, Confessions of an Eco-Sinner: Tracking Down the Sources of My Stuff by Fred Pearce (Beacon Press, 2008), our complicity for contradiction remains alive and well today. Mr. Pearce uses a quote in the introduction to his book, called "Footprints," where he quotes a scientist he had conversed with about the outcomes of lifestyles in our nation: "...recently he told me he reckoned that the average household in Europe or North America has so many devices and such a variety of food and clothing that to produce the same lifestyle in Roman Times would have required six thousand slaves..." (p 3). Obviously, we do not live in Roman times, but we do live in a modern era in which we celebrate free trade, and the lowering of

consumer prices for those of us living with the benefits we hoard. As Mr. Pearce flushes out throughout his book, the living conditions, and life-diminishing consequences for peoples in less economically countries are severe. These include living under the rule of harsh dictators seeking profit and privilege at the expense of their own people, who work for poverty wages and suffer life-threatening disease due to the toxicity of the workplaces in which they labor for 12 hours a day or more. For a detailed breakout of one scenario, read the "Computing Power: Mice, Motherboards and the New Emperors of Suzhou" chapter (pp 117–125). I quote one line from that chapter on the severe level of economic inequality in Suzhou: "...a handful of senior Taiwanese managers earn a Western salary, (and) their more junior Chinese managers are on salaries of about $26,000 a year...five thousand or so production-line operators earn less than $2,000 a year" (pp 118–119). My question is: If the gold standard of moral judgment is that Thomas Jefferson was a hypocrite for not surrendering his slaves, who amongst us is willing to surrender their computers?

579   The urgency of making kin...co-evolution through friendship. adrienne marie brown, in an interview with Nick Montgomery and Carla Bergman, suggests this practice as one developed from "a circle of friends and family with whom I am radically vulnerable and trust deeply..." (p 81). My point here is that most of the co-generators of social justice movements come from tightly knit movements comprising vulnerable people. Trust for each other is the tool which promotes their resiliency. The quote is a citation from Joyful Militancy by Nick Montgomery and Carla Bergman (AK Press, 2017).

Those who are involved in this co-evolution do so not with undeveloped brains nor with supercharged hormones, which are two of the modern myths about adolescence. For a comprehensive review for myth-busting, see Teen 2.0 by Robert Epstein, Ph.D. (Quill Driver

Books, 2020). I quote from two chapters in the book. The first quote is from chapter 7, "Young People are Capable Thinkers": "Scientific research shows unequivocally that the cognitive abilities of teens, are, on average, superior to the cognitive abilities of adults" (p 163). In this chapter, he shows details from studies showing that cognitive ability declines throughout the adult years. Mr. Epstein also demonstrates that important behaviors, supposedly exhibited chiefly by teens, are based on forced choice laboratory studies, but do not reflect actual behaviors by adults such as record levels of creating unnecessary debt and ill-conceived violent intervention in the affairs of others. See the section in in Teen 2.0 called Teen Judgement: An Oxymoron? (in Quill Driver Books, 2020) (pp 185–190).

580   Professional providers teaching the skills of developing kinship with trauma-afflicted people. Until the sources and repercussions are uncovered, and safely brought to the surface, the power of trauma remains invisibly and destructive to both individuals and society. To see the unfolding guidance work of DYCD, go to one of their sources of education on trauma, the National Child Trauma Stress Network at https://www.samhsa.gov New York University has also been pioneering in the promotion of trauma-informed intervention. See their work at: https://steinhardt.nyu.edu/hdsci/on-the-ground-trauma-informed-intervention In his book, the Body Keeps the Score, Bessel Van Der Kolk, M.D. (Penguin Books, 2014) writes about the essential necessity of health providers connecting to real sources of a person's acute pain and trauma. As he states, before finding appropriate help, an trauma-afflicted person must " find support and acceptance before facing the engine of her distrust, shame and rage." pg 127. See the section of his book, " Terror and Numbness" pp 126 – 128.

581   Professional providers teaching the skills of developing kinship with trauma-afflicted people. Until the sources and repercussions are uncovered, and safely brought to the surface, the power of trauma

remains invisibly and destructive to both individuals and society. To see the unfolding guidance work of DYCD, go to one of their sources of education on trauma, the National Child Trauma Stress Network at https://www.samhsa.gov New York University has also been pioneering in the promotion of trauma-informed intervention. See their work at: https://steinhardt.nyu.edu/hdsci/on-the-ground-trauma-informed-intervention In his book, the Body Keeps the Score, Bessel Van Der Kolk, M.D. (Penguin Books, 2014) writes about the essential necessity of health providers connecting to real sources of a person's acute pain and trauma. As he states, before finding appropriate help, a trauma-afflicted person must " find support and acceptance before facing the engine of her distrust, shame and rage." pg 127. See the section of his book, " Terror and Numbness" pp 126 – 128.

582   Victims of alienation and despair became organizers for unity amongst "thugs and nerds" in addressing violence in the youth community. For a biographic overview of Mr. Bob DeSena's leadership with the Council for Unity, see the Petra Foundation's Soaring Spirits Journal: Petra Fellows 1989–2015 (pg 44). www.petrafounation.org

583   The contrast between patho-adolescence and mature adolescence. Bill Plotkin summarizes this contrast in his book, Nature and the Human Soul (New World Library, 2008) as he states: "The fabric of patho-adolescence within which western societies are mired is a way of life that emphasizes social acceptability, materialism, self-centered individualism and superficial security rather than authenticity, authentic relationships, soul-infused service, creative risk and adventure" (pg 224).

584   "You have a right to dream, and so do we" are the words used to describe our adult-led creations of dysfunctional social relations and their adverse consequences for the emergent generation. See the text of the speech, "How Dare You!" delivered by Greta Thunberg in her speech

to the United Nations. Edward Felsenthal, who contributed a piece to Time magazine called "The Choice,'" credited Greta with "marshaling 'Fridays for the Future' protests... (and cited her for becoming) the avatar of a broader generational shift in our culture..." See Time magazine, December 23–30, 2019. The article starts on page 48. https://time.com/person-of-the-year-2019-greta-thunberg-choice.

585   What is the nature of fractured space within our modern habitats we call cities? As described by Dr. Mindy Thompson-Fullilove in her book, Urban Alchemy (New Village Press, 2013), fractured spaces exist in neighborhoods that have been gutted out of prior safe spaces and cultural landmarks in the name of urban renewal. These spaces exist as under-resourced schools giving students only a partial experience in education. They exist in unexpressed frustration and remorse for citizens in need of basic services remaining unanswered in the petitions for help. These fractures are also experienced in the relationships between youth and adults. Dr. Thompson-Fullilove quotes one of her adult volunteers enrolled in a film-making project in Washington Heights called CLIMB, in which their volunteer, Molly, spoke to how she had discovered youth efficacy: "(Teens, in their) liminal space between childhood and adulthood, (understand) the whole lifespan as no one else could. This body of wisdom was crucial to society. It was a well spring of healing and fun...As Molly got to know the youth...she started to search for ways to liberate their insights" (p 185). To see Dr. Thompson-Fullilove's introduction to fractured space in the context of seeking urban restoration, see pp 38–39.

586   What is the nature of fractured space within our modern habitats we call cities? As described by Dr. Mindy Thompson-Fullilove in her book, Urban Alchemy (New Village Press, 2013), fractured spaces exist in neighborhoods that have been gutted out of prior safe spaces and cultural landmarks in the name of urban renewal. These spaces exist as under-resourced schools giving students only a partial

experience in education. They exist in unexpressed frustration and remorse for citizens in need of basic services remaining unanswered in the petitions for help. These fractures are also experienced in the relationships between youth and adults. Dr. Thompson-Fullilove quotes one of her adult volunteers enrolled in a film-making project in Washington Heights called CLIMB, in which their volunteer, Molly, spoke to how she had discovered youth efficacy: "(Teens, in their) liminal space between childhood and adulthood, (understand) the whole lifespan as no one else could. This body of wisdom was crucial to society. It was a well spring of healing and fun…As Molly got to know the youth…she started to search for ways to liberate their insights" (p 185). To see Dr. Thompson-Fullilove's introduction to fractured space in the context of seeking urban restoration, see pp 38–39.

587   Divisive adults do NOT get to choose who belongs in the youth coalition for equitable living and social change. In a book, Unsettled Belonging (University of Chicago Press, 2015), author Thea Renda Abu El-Haj quotes a youth activist named Yuval Davis who identifies a dynamic used by adults to divide people: "The politics of belonging involves not only construction of boundaries but also the inclusion or exclusion of particular people, social categories and groupings within these boundaries by those who have the power to do this" (p 5). The shadow side of America has frequently had tragic episodes in which this tactic was used (the genocidal policies created toward peoples native to North America; the internment of loyal Japanese Americans in World War II). A key tactic has been the socially constructed reflex of fear, which is still being used against targeted immigrant groups. It was also a key ingredient used for instilling fear about teens, such as in the Omnibus Crime Bill Debate of 1994.

588   Divisive adults do NOT get to choose who belongs in the youth coalition for equitable living and social change. In a book, Unsettled Belonging (University of Chicago Press, 2015), author Thea Renda

Abu El-Haj quotes a youth activist named Yuval Davis who identifies a dynamic used by adults to divide people: "The politics of belonging involves not only construction of boundaries but also the inclusion or exclusion of particular people, social categories and groupings within these boundaries by those who have the power to do this" (p 5). The shadow side of America has frequently had tragic episodes in which this tactic was used (the genocidal policies created toward peoples native to North America; the internment of loyal Japanese Americans in World War II). A key tactic has been the socially constructed reflex of fear, which is still being used against targeted immigrant groups. It was also a key ingredient used for instilling fear about teens, such as in the Omnibus Crime Bill Debate of 1994. For additional thoughts on how President Bill Clinton helped to create negative stereotypes about teens and crime, see the book, Framing Youth: 10 Myths about the Next Generation by Mike A. Males (Common Courage Press, 1999) pp 52 and 58.

589 "Put your body upon the gears" was a line used by the outspoken activist Mario Savio on the steps of Berkeley University in the 1960s. To see the speech, see "The 50th Anniversary of the speech at Sproul Hall" written by Michael Jackman. https://www.metrotimes.com/news-hits/archives/2014/12/01/mario-savios-bodies-upon-the-gears-speech-50-years-later

590 Un-fracture the space between our emotions and our positive thoughts… describe a place for using your passion, if in the service of healing oneself and relationships. Andrew Harvey is a mystic and spiritual searcher/teacher. He was born in India, and, after attending and the dropping out of Oxford, made his way to Santa Fe, New Mexico, and launched a movement called Sacred Activism. In Radical Passion: Sacred Love and Wisdom in Action (North Atlantic Books, 2012 by Andrew Harvey), he quotes the Middle Eastern mystic Rumi on the value of following one's passion (p 30).

591   Youth activists are willing to use their bodies in non-violent resistance and focus more closely than the Boomer generation did with
what the Catholic philosopher and activist Teilhard de Chardin
identified as the "problem of action." In his book, The Phenomenon
of Man (Harper Books, 1959), he identified the problem of action as
"(figuring out how is) our mindset to adjust itself to lines and horizons beyond measure...This obliges us at the outset to revise certain
absolute ideas...concerning the use of and values in our sciences in
explanation in terms of present causes" (p 97)/ Youth activists today
are heavily involved in deep ecology and social justice movements,
exposing the scientific and outdated institutional practices which
supported unjust and unsustainable policy practices.

592   A definitive rebuttal of racist application of IQ superbly presented
by a scientist. Most scientists do not feel comfortable in supporting
scientific research that had inadequately been designed and then
use to justify poor social policy. However, we have had periods of
history where a kind of herd psychology led scientists to fall into
the pit of misinformed research and studies. Two periods were
those of the late 1800s and early 1900s, which saw major scientific
support for the rise of Jim Crow, anti-immigrant legislation, and
squashing of the women's right to vote movement. See Are Racists
Crazy? by Sander L. Gilman and James M. Thomas (NY University
Press, 2016) for how this was conceived and applied against Blacks
and Jews. For a superb example of a work (against innate limits and
a biology of destiny—a description of this book on its back cover),
see The Mismeasure of Man by MacArthur Fellow and Harvard
University professor Stephen Jay Gould (Norton, 1996). In addition
to being a crucial account of racialized deforming of evidence, it
is a definitive model for separating well-constructed and poorly
engineered models of scientific research.

593   Unfounded assumptions and the governance of unsound policies.
Scilla Elworthy, in her book, Pioneering the Possible (North Atlantic

Books, 2014), summarizes the practice of applying poorly constructed social and cultural beliefs with her position: "What are essential historical constructs have come to be enshrined as perennial truths" (pg 375). Examination of undesirable social behaviors, and then blaming teens.

594   A professor named Mike Males has been producing rebuttals to established beliefs amongst adults, including policy makers, which pin inordinate responsibility for teens on the prevalence of problems such as crime, violence, unwanted pregnancies, and substance abuse. Two examples of his work in one of his books, Framing Youth: 10 Myths About the Next Generation (Common Courage Press, 1999), are a table he produces comparing serious crime committed by teens as compared to adults (Table 4 on p 35), and another comparison showing that teens are less likely to be admitted to emergency rooms than adults for drug-related overdoses (pg 110). Some recent research examining these studies have brought questions and criticism about the methodology of these earlier studies. However, the unjust blame put on teens for creating these problems is still an issue, as structures of racism and inequalities still show a socially constructed influence on social behaviors and outcomes—good and bad. In addition, I viewed Mike Males as a pioneer in challenging unwarranted bias and negative stereotyping of teens in the 1990s and early 2000s, and his evidence and arguments greatly influenced my work with teens during that time.

595   Dysfunctional teen behavior much less prevalent in "undeveloped nations" than in the US. Robert Epstein, who has had some concern with the methodology of earlier studies, still insists that problems identified as being due to the nature of adolescence do not occur at all or occur at negligible levels, when compared to the rate of occurrence in the US. He holds that the higher prevalence in the US is socially and culturally fostered, and not the result of innate teen nature. He forcefully states that he has never found a single

study that legitimately links dysfunctional teen behaviors as being caused by teen brains, teen hormones, or any other physiological structures. See The Myth of the Teen Brain online with his article for the Scientific American. https://drrobertepstein.com/pdf/-Epstein-the-Myth-Of-The-Teen-Mind/Scientific_American_Mind-4-07.pdf.

596   Accessing heart intelligence facilitates alignment amongst physical, emotional, and mental systems. According to research conducted by the Heart Math Institute, "accessing the heart's intuitive intelligence" bolsters our multi-system energies. See the Heart Math Institute work at www.heartmath.org.

597   Nineteenth-century humanist and transcendental writer Ralph Waldo Emerson spoke to the need to developing an edge (today we would call this an attitude) as critical to maintaining commitment to social change. In a journal entry Emerson wrote in 1852, he declared that it is "the street, the street", (which) is the school where the language is to be learned for the poet and the orator" (p 65). In his classic tome "Self-Reliance," he held that "man is his own star, and the soul can render an honest and perfect man" (pg 257). Cited from Selected Writings of Ralph Waldo Emerson (Signet, 1965), William Gilman, editor.

598   Cultural myths have been created to enshrine privilege and to jus-tify the actions of those who control institutions of power. In his book, Chants Democratic: The Rise of the American Working Class, 1788–1850 (Oxford University Press, 2004) Sean Wilentz cites how myths, manufactured, and controlled by elites' function to serve the interests of those in power. Mr. Wilentz describe one effect, where "(myths) flatten out a multitude of prejudices, hopes and motives for the sake of assimilation and graphic power" (pp 391–392). He also brings up a trap, that if these myths are "interpreted too literally,

they can disguise as much as reveal social perceptions and relations (pages 391–392).

599   School teachers intend to be educators but are governed by school systems which value speed of delivery over reflection made possible over time. John Taylor Gatto, a New York State Teacher of the Year recipient in 1989, wrote a book about the downside of the education system, which he described as "An Intimate Investigation of the Prison of Modern Schooling." The name of this book is The Underground History of American Education (Oxford Village Press, 2003). Coming from a Libertarian perspective, he connects the dots amongst statist orientation structures of power and influence which mitigate against the ideal of public education to encourage fully informed and pro-active citizens. Amongst the myriad of problems for teachers working in this system is the constraint of time and its diminishment of deep participation and thought. Mr. Gatto quotes one teacher in another book he wrote, The Exhausted School (Odysseus Group, 1993), who echoes a complaint I had heard continually made by teachers with whom I have partnered over the course of my youth services career: "I remember always being rushed in school. The teachers were rushed, the textbooks were impossible to cover in one semester, so classwork was always abbreviated. You couldn't ask too many questions, there was not enough time" (p 60).

600   Fannie Lou Hamer on the home of the brave, those who question "the fetters which lend them to the old." Ms. Hamer was an ardent civic rights activist, who gave powerful testimony to the Democratic National Convention in 1964. (That year, Lyndon Johnson was the Presidential nominee and Hubert Humphrey the Vice-Presidential candidate.) She had asked the powerful question, still left unresolved, "Is this America the land of the free, and home of the brave, where our lives (African-Americans) (are) threatened because we want to live as decent human beings in America? One hundred years after

the civil war, decency had been kept off the table by cultural and structural racism, practiced in governance, business, and White folks living their everyday lives infused with suspicion and intolerance for peoples of color. Ms. Hamer also had sage words of advice to the young: "The youthful elements…cannot submit themselves to rules of their own making, they must throw off the fetters which lend them to the old" (p 152) Source: 100 Key Documents in American Democracy by Peter B. Levy (Praeger, 1999), "Testimony before the credentials committee of the Democratic National Convention, 1964" by Fannie Lou Hamer (pp 402–404). Sage advice from the Black leadership of the civil rights movement would be adapted as sage wisdom and organizing tactics by those leading rights movements for women, Latinos, and youth.

601 The use of judicial and militarized methods for discipline and public safety became increasingly adopted beginning in the 1990s (when overall crime rates were dropping). Nikhil Goyal, in his book Schools on Trial (Doubleday, 2016), has decried the segregation of students from their communities, and the imposition of criminal sanctions in place of much-needed social and emotional counseling. As Mr. Goyal observed: "In both prisons and schools, you are cut off from the rest of society, stripped of your basic freedoms and rights…told what to do all day, and surveilled dragnet style" (p 19). The work of student activists working against these disabling and disempowering practices will be profiled in the section closing out this book titled Anecdotes Arising. To review the work of the Urban Youth Collaborative in advocating for reforms in school discipline policies, see their website at https://www.urbanyouthcollaborative.org To review the work of the New York Civil Liberties Union in training teen leaders to organize against unjust discipline policies and censorship, see the website page Your Rights As A Student Protester at https://www.nyclu.org/en/know-your-rights/your-rights-student-protester.

602   Traumatized and victimized...cited from "Getting on the Same
       Wavelength in The Body Keeps the Score by Bessel Van Der Kolk,
       M.D. (Penguin, 2014), (p 121). The Urban Youth Collaborative
       report finding (2013–2014): "There are 5,511 school safety person-
       nel citywide in the schools in New York City, and only 1,252 social
       workers to serve 1.1 million students" (p 2). The youth leadership
       arm of the New York Civil Liberties Union issued a mandate to "call
       out school officials and law enforcement partners who criminalize
       adolescence." Source: www.nyclu.org. This tragic atmosphere for
       criminalizing young men and women (predominantly Black and
       Latino targets) is not a description of Mississippi in 1880, but of
       New York City in the twenty-first century.

603   Coming from outside the establishment, fighting (old-school)
       entanglements and commitments. Bernard Bailyn, in his book, To
       Begin the World Anew (Vintage Books, 2003), spoke about a new
       generation of leadership being developed from outside the establish
       corridors of power, and in opposition to an old order favoring the
       previously privileged. On the perception of the British monarchy
       that the colonists were too provincial to govern themselves, see the
       quote on page 4. As Mr. Bailyn continues: "What conditioned and
       stimulated the founders' imagination, and hence their capacity to
       begin the world anew, was the fact that they came from outside the
       metropolitan establishment, with its age-old, deeply buried, arcane
       entanglements and commitments" (p 35). A comparative form of
       elitism and condescending attitudes is put on youth by adults who
       don't see them for their insights and capabilities. Beginning in the
       late 1800s adolescence became to be defined as a period of "mor-
       atorium", where responsibility for meaningful decisions should
       be delayed into adulthood, and "incessant interrogation" of teens
       became enshrined in school practice and government policies. For
       a historical review about the modern notions of adolescent, see
       the book Act Your Age: A Cultural Construction of Adolescence

by Nancy Lesko (Routledge Falmer, 2001). The introduction to the book provides an overview. (Pages 1 – 19) What is blossoming today is insurgent and engaged imagination from a plethora of well-informed and organized youth-led organizations, such as the Urban Youth Collaborative, Teens in Charge, Teens for Food Justice, as well as classroots (yes, I made up this word, classrooms with youth leadership developed at the grassroots) initiatives launched under the guidance of Generation Citizen. In New York City, there are dozens of others, which I will not cover in the Anecdotes Arising section of this book, as I will doing just brief profiling of a few as samples of youth impact changing unsound and outdated policies.

604   The inspirational work of youth-led groups, and my gratitude for civic co-mentors who see them. Adopting them into structures of co-leadership contributes to an initiation not just for teen leadership, but for an expansive, fully inclusive democracy yet to be born. It is high time that all adults, especially those in policy-making positions and leaders of municipal agencies, see the world of youth not as adults have seen them, but through the eyes of young people. It is time, as proposed by Bill Plotkin, that adults engage in an evolutionary transformation of their place in life when forming relationships with teens. As beautifully stated by Mr. Plotkin in Nature and the Human Soul (New World Library, 2008), this new era will be "a soul centric community; (where) the elders have their way of recognizing when your time of Confirmation is near…the elders see the signs that your paramount motivation in life has shifted from the further development of social identity to the primacy of spiritual adventure, or as Joseph Campbell puts it, from 'society to a zone unknown'" (p 237). The goal is not to develop a social identity of being a uselessly information-consumed consumer nor a manically militarized agent for the control and containment of suspiciously perceived others. It is to invite and manage the energy of the soul, which sees everyone,

and everything, as connected in webs of life-affirming meaning and purpose.

605   Generational adaptation (for Boomers and teens) …adventures in experimentation. As suggested by the study "From Assets to Agents of Change" (New Directions for Youth Development, No. 96, Winter 2002), in the construction of youth engagement (including the roles of adults who support them), we should be using "an ecological approach, (where) they examine how young people respond within oppressive social systems and identify the process of sociopolitical development" (pg 34). With these words fully acknowledged, I suggest that this be embedded in the wisdom of natural systems (organizing from the bottom up) and through the spiritual wealth of soul-inspired guidance (we are all connected for the purposes of personal development and for obtaining the fruits of supportive community).

606   Introducing a friend called "Entelechy" … the joining natural and spiritual systems.

As we induct ourselves in the doorway of a new eco/spiritual age, I highlight a concept called "entelechy" introduced to me by Jean Houston in her book, The Wizard of Us (Atria Books, 2012). Ms. Houston shares that this term is literally defined as "actuality, completion, the actualization of potential" (pg 36). As Ms. Houston further elaborates, engaging with this potential stimulates "a vitalism, the inherent force that directs the development of a human being" (pg 36). To this I respond, finally, a promise of progress and understanding that I agree, as a form of inherency is reflective of everyone's divine potential, capacity, and intelligence, and which serves the manifestation of beloved communities and a more beautiful world.

607 See the book by Anodea Judith, Ph.D., Waking the Global Heart (Elite Books, 2006), Chapter 14: Don't Agonize, Self-Organize. Pp 241 – 243.

608 See the book by Anodea Judith, Ph.D., Waking the Global Heart (Elite Books, 2006), Chapter 14: Don't Agonize, Self-Organize. pp 241 – 243.

609 Homogenized history: why is history taught like this?

In the book, Lies My Teacher Told Me (Touchtone, 2007), the author James W. Loewen offers a quote that in part explains homogenized history. As a representative of a book company once stated: "When you are publishing a book, if there is something controversial, it's better to take it out" (quoted in Joan Delatorre, What Johnny Shouldn't Read [New Haven, Yale University Press, 1992, p 120)]. This is an interesting comment from a book representative for textbooks covering American history. The American War for independence was controversial (about 1/3 of colonists supported the war, 1/3 was opposed, and 1/3 was neutral (many of whom were afraid to declare a position for fear of retaliation from one or the other side). Ending slavery was very controversial, resulting in a civil war. The fight for women's enfranchisement, initiated after the Civil War, did not achieve success until half a century later, with proponents having to have President Wilson drop his opposition. Up to 30 per cent of the US population reports in polls that the issue of climate change is a hoax. The suggestion made by this textbook rep, to deal with controversy by covering it up was put in place much of the time. When controversy was covered, it was done in ways to water down the intensity, or by remaking the personalities and/or altering positions of dissidents so as not to appear as controversial as they were. See, pages 301–339 in Lies My Teacher Told Me for fuller coverage of these tactics. In this section called Anecdotes Arising, I shall celebrate rabble-rousers who revel in controversy as a beacon bringing light to the shadow of American practices. Note 1a refers to the quote by Thomas Paine found in the appendix to his work titled Common Sense (January 1776). Earlier in this work, Paine writes: "Men who look upon themselves as born the reign, and others to obey, soon grow insolent. Selected from the rest of humankind, their minds are early poisoned by importance; and the world they act in differs so materially from the world at large, that they have but little opportunity of knowing its true interests, and when they succeed to the government are frequently the most ignorant and unfit of any throughout the dominions." This quote is found in the book The Life and Major Writings of Thomas Paine, edited and annotated by Philip S. Foner (The Citadel Press, 1974) pg 15.

610   Homogenized history: why is history taught like this?

In the book, Lies My Teacher Told Me (Touchtone, 2007), the author James W. Loewen offers a quote that in part explains homogenized history. As a representative of a book company once stated: "When you are publishing a book, if there is something controversial, it's better to take it out" (quoted in Joan Delatorre, What Johnny Shouldn't Read [New Haven, Yale University Press, 1992, p 120)]. This is an interesting comment from a book representative for textbooks covering American history. The American War for independence was controversial (about 1/3rd of colonists supported the war, 1/3rd was opposed, and 1/3rd was neutral (many of whom were afraid to declare a position for fear of retaliation from one or the other side). Ending slavery was very controversial, resulting in a civil war. The fight for women's enfranchisement, initiated after the Civil War, did not achieve success until half a century later, with proponents having to have President Wilson drop his opposition. Up to 30 per cent of the US population reports in polls that the issue of climate change is a hoax. The suggestion made by this textbook rep, to deal with controversy by covering it up was put in place much of the time. When controversy was covered, it was done in ways to water down the intensity, or by remaking the personalities and/or altering positions of dissidents so as not to appear as controversial as they were. See, pages 301–339 in Lies My Teacher Told Me for fuller coverage of these tactics. In this section called Anecdotes Arising, I shall celebrate rabble-rousers who revel in controversy as a beacon bringing light to the shadow of American practices. Note 1a refers to the quote by Thomas Paine found in the appendix to his work titled Common Sense (January 1776). Earlier in this work, Paine writes: "Men who look upon themselves as born the reign, and others to obey, soon grow insolent. Selected from the rest of mankind, their minds are early poisoned by importance; and the world they act in differs so materially from the world at large, that they have but little opportunity of knowing its true interests, and when they succeed to the government are frequently the most ignorant and unfit of any throughout the dominions." This quote is found in the book The Life and Major Writings of Thomas Paine, edited and annotated by Philip S. Foner (The Citadel Press, 1974) pg 15.

611   Beyond Psychology by Otto Rank (Dover, 1941), pg 14.

612   Students for A Democratic Society—Whittier College. My college years spent in resistance against compliance by force.

I was a student at Whittier College (Richard Nixon was an alumni of that school) in the years 1967–1969. The administration was conservative, as was a large sector of the student body. During that time, although college students were officially exempt from being drafted into the military, many others were drafted to serve in a war which gradually became unpopular. Young people could be drafted, serve, and be severely injured or die beginning at the age of 18. The minimum voting age was 21. President Johnson, who had run as a peace candidate in the 1964 presidential elections, began escalating the war beginning in the spring of 1965. As student protest activity increased the response of law enforcement became increasingly confrontational and violent. On college campuses, students also organized in protest about college administrations which they saw as complicit with the war effort. This included promoting military recruitment for graduating students and having Board of Director members who also served on companies profiting from the war.

Whittier College had a more conservative student population than universities in urban locations and those located in more liberal areas.

When I joined in anti-Vietnam War activity on campus, we rarely had more than 9 or 10 people join us in silent vigil. (The student body numbered about 2,000.) In my sophomore year, according to local reports, about 2/3rd of the campus body had strong reservations about the war or opposed it. Although the campus upheld conservative values, many supported the conservative movement's demands for fairness and accountability. When I helped to launch a chapter of Students for A Democratic Society in September of 1968, few opted to join, and with good reasons. Although the issues raised were important, such as an examination of the war machine, misuse of governmental power, and concerns for civil rights, the language we used was extreme, and our reliance upon rigid ideology, in hindsight, quite obnoxious. The Dean of Men, Charles D. Montgomery, was quoted in the Whittier College Yearbook titled Acropolis: "The challenge of involvement in the affairs at Whittier College is one of encouraging students to devote a portion of their time and talents to the essential task of redefining the goals and purposes of the institution." (Acropolis 68, p 28). Had I opened and listened, I might have exercised my protest with conservative values of respect for difference of opinion and more tolerance. What helped me to shift was a conversation I had with a student at a dorm party in the spring of 1969. He had just registered for the military, with the intention to fight in Vietnam. We had quite the difference of opinion on this subject. However, after a long discussion, he still disagreed with my tactics, but started to understand and examine the history of our government's decision-making about entering the war. I still disagreed with his going to Vietnam, but I no longer understood him as a thoughtless soldier, but rather as a patriot serving the cause of promoting democracy. I did not return to Whittier in the fall of 1969 but heard that the administration had embarked upon trying several experimental courses and open-education exercises. In the end, despite the heat of differences, a new light for those on all sides began to emerge. In the Anecdotes Arising section, I will be profiling student-led groups seeking big reform, under leadership seeking light beyond the heat. This notes are based upon my memories and reflections about my years as a student at Whittier College. (September 1967- June 1969)

613   Democracy's challenges inform democratic education technique. In a book titled On Democratic Education by Howard Zinn (Paradigm Publishers, 2005) (including dialogue with Donald Macedo), the author contests the traditional approach to education when teaching history as "indoctrination by willful blindness" (p 5). The result has been, as the authors lament "the construction of historical amnesia" (p 12). I remember attending a conversation about our invasion of Iraq in 2002, being led by Howard Zinn at the Quaker Friends House in the East Village. During the talk, he quipped that the USA could readily stand for the United States of Amnesia. In Anecdotes Arising, I will profile youth- ed organizations and their efforts to be the doctor in the house provoking us, and keeping us, "Awoke." Innovative schools are taking the lead in turning educational governance into laboratories of democratic participation by students. For a summary of deficits in traditional school process and governance, what Peter Gray calls the Seven Sins of Education, see his book, Free To Learn (Basic Books, 2013) Chapter 4, pages 66 -84, which describe the seven sins in detail. For a discussion on schools which

build student voice into their structures and processes, see Schools on Trial by Nikhil Goyal (Doubleday, 2016). Chapter 6 ' Schools Where Children Can Be Themselves' pages 135 – 183.

614   The Omnibus Crime Bill of 1994 resulted in paradox. Although rates of crime had been falling, the bill was drafted to contain a falsely perceived rise in crime. It imposed increasingly harsh prison terms (removing sentencing discretion from judges). It also led to municipal and state policies that were punitive, such as prohibiting parolees and those finishing their sentences to be eligible for college loans and public housing or having a reasonable chance for landing a job. See the article: "3 Ways the 1994 Crime Bill Continues to Hurt Communities of Color" by Rayna Shannon (May 10,2019) which is posted on the website for the Center for American Progress. https://www.ap-stage.devprogress.org/issues/race/news/2019/05/10/469642/3-ways-1994-crime-bill-continues-hurt-communities-color

In this chapter I call Anecdotes Arising, I will look at efforts to remedy the wrongs of the past and to reform the prison system. Some examples of agencies in this struggle include the Bay Area's Impact Justice (https://impactjustice.org), NYC Common Justice (https://www.commonjustice.org) , the American Friends Service Committee (https://wwwafsc.org) , the Innocence Project (https://innocenceproject.org) , and the Southern Poverty Law Center (https://www.splcenter.org) Teen-led organizations have collaborated with these organized movements including the Urban Youth Collaborative(https://www.urbanyouthcollaborative.org) , Teens Take Charge (https://www.facebook.com/teenstakecharg-enyc) and the youth arm of the NY Civil Liberties Union. (https://www.-nyclu.org).

615   The Declaration of Independence—the itemization of grievances. As this book has previously covered, these grievances detailing

deficiencies in governance stand relevant today, not against a monarchy holding on to its colonial privilege, but in protesting similar practices by remotely located and unresponsive leaders in our own government. The overarching term applicable to the movements organized by young people is that they seek to claim ownership as citizens, empowered to advise, participate in, and assess official decisions and governance practices affecting their lives and the course of their communities. To see the Grievances again, refer to 100 Key Documents in American Democracy by Peter B. Levy (editor) (Praeger, 1999), p 463–464. To view how the abuses and neglect imposed by educational governance mirrors closely with the Grievances put forth by our nation's founders, see the book titled Free to Learn by Peter Gray (Basic Books, 2013). I reference chapter 4: "The Seven Sins of our System of Forced Education," pp 66–84. (Two examples are "Sin 1: Denial of Liberty without just cause and due process" and Sin 2: "Interference with the development of personal responsibility and self-direction."

616 Peer courts, the American Probation and Parole Association, and restorative justice. There are many district attorneys and representatives in state and city government, who have come on board with an alternative to punishment in a movement known as restorative justice. In a guide developed by Tracy M. Godwin, with Steinhart and Fulton, an overview of peer courts is presented, which address fundamental issues, such as "why should we implement peer courts? (p 2); the value of capitalizing on peer influence (p 7); and empowering and involving your State Governments. see https://www.globalyouthjustice.org.

617 Dewey's teaching. The school as a community, and the community as a school. This is a paradigm that is increasingly being followed in our new era defined by the pursuit of social justice and environmental sustainability. Both communities and classrooms are being organized to include students in expressing voice for concerns

and remedies. The community has become an extension of the classroom, serving as a local reference for history and meaningful context, a laboratory of inter-generational cooperative change, and a supportive source of alliances with student-led initiatives. At the same time, more schools and classrooms are adopting democratic forms of governance. Models of student governance are arising now, in support of laying foundations for a more inclusive democracy later. For two sources here, see Generation Citizen at https://generationcitizen.org and the YMCA of Greater New York (Teens Take the City Curriculum) at https://www.ymca.net.

618   Paulo Freire had a major concept in constructing an approach to education. It is expressed by him as "before reading a book, read the world." In other words, experience provides the context, and books fill in some interesting and important details. One post on a website delineating the contrast between old school education, and education for liberation states: "Education either operates as an instrument which is used to facilitate the integration of the younger generation into the logic of the present system, and bring about conformity, OR, it becomes the practice of freedom, the means by which men and women deal critically and creatively with reality and discover how to participate in the transformation of the world." For an overview on this perspective, see The Civic Educator at https://learnciviced.org

619   Practices that have been tried in the past, and experimented with in the present, which aim to expand upon the quality of our democracy.

Jon Meacham, in his idealistic and practice overview of the promising qualities of elected leaders in the past, offers suggestion for best practices for prospects of evolved and deepened democracy to develop. He has so many valuable insights and suggestions in his book, The Soul of America. I recap three suggestions from his book, as well as reference two institutions which demonstrate his practices.

620   The first duty of an American citizen is to enter the arena (through voting, communicating with elected officials, and keeping friends and neighbors consistently involved). See Soul of America Enter the Arena, pages 266- 267.

621   See note 8 on the work of Generation Citizen for promoting student engagement with elected officials. https://www.generationcitizen.org

622   Ibid The Soul of America Resist Tribalism—pride in a tribe is great, pridefulness at the expense of another tribe is destructive of democracy. See Soul of America Resist Tribalism, pages 267-268.

623   Dr. Robert Fullilove trains his graduate students at Columbia University's Mailman School of Public Health to partner with community change agents in Washington Heights and Harlem. For a reading of his impressive work, see the biographical statement on Dr. Fullilove at : https://www.publichealth.columbia.edu/people/our-faculty/ref5

624   Ibid The Soul of America Strive for critical balance (between opposing viewpoints and proposals). Manufacture a workable consensus for a given time. See Soul of America Find A Critical Balance, pages 269-270. See The Soul of America: The Battle for our Better Angels by Jon Meacham (Random House, 2018).

625   I am reminded again about felines as fascinating educators. I bought the Joey Allgood print and accompanying text at an outdoor market in Union Square. Mr. Allgood gave a title to his work: A Cat and Existential Discovery- A ball of yarn. Over a period of 22 years, with the assistance of my goddaughter, Aida Ramos, I raised 12 cats who taught me continuously about these feline attributes. Feline models of enlightenment. Over the years my goddaughter and I have share good memories and laughs.

626   The Spell of the Sensuous by David Abram (Vintage Books, 1996), pp 74–75. Dr. Abram is an ecologist who graduated summa cum

laude from Wesleyan University. He earned his doctorate in philosophy from the State University of New York/Stony Brook. In this book he reminds us of the gifts benefiting indigenous peoples who maintain a worldview and deep connection to nature, and its spiritual connection to life. As I will share in later chapters, an important activity for my youth programs in Washington Heights was traveling with teens to camping locations in wooded areas, such as the Boy Scout reservation in New Jersey called Camp Alpine. Young people were afforded the rewarding experiences of strolling amongst trees and grass and escaping the confines of a world built in concrete and glass. Even the most anxious amongst our young participants would quickly relax and become comfortable with listening to the language of frogs and babbling streams. They got quality time feeling the natural world through their skin and their five senses.

627   Make the Road While Stalking. I post this attribute partially in jest, playing off the title of a grassroots social justice agency named Make The Road While Walking. I do so in admiration for their inducement for volunteer participation by both adults and teens. They organize on the ground in their own communities with projects such as the Youth Power Project. Participants develop a commitment to the cause, defy and overcome obstacles on their path, and keep a keen focus which they sustain over time. Make the Road has been a key partner with the NYC Department of Education in opening Community Schools and with the NYC Council in procuring passage of the School Safety Act. The latter legislation mandates that the Department of Education accurately tracks the number of school suspensions and expulsions of students daily. Make the Road has a board of directors which includes having youth amongst its membership. See https://maketheroadny.org

628   Compromise is an attitude which a prophet abhors is a phrase I lift from the work of Rabbi Abraham Heschel in one of his books,

Moral Grandeur, and the Spirit of Audacity. (Ferrer, Strauss, and Giroux, 1996) He criticizes one form of compromise, that of becoming compromised from your values. In his interpretation of Jewish doctrine, which influence his social justice engagement, he held that it is wrong to bring harm to others through the implementation of unjust wars. He stated in his book that "indifference to evil is worse than evil itself." He then follows up by asserting the need to encourage "the capacity to sense the depth of misery caused by our own moral failures." (These two quotes are found in the pages 224 – 229) He considers that his moral grandeur is constructed, in part, through his expression of unreserved audacity. During my times of working with teen activists struggling against unjust policies, some adults cited their passionately expressed traits as examples of bad attitude and insolence. When teens persist in correcting stubbornly held dismissive beliefs, they do so not with insolence, but with insistent rigor.

629   Admiring a girl with bad attitude. The negative label of bad attitude pinned on Greta Thunberg is a method of distractive targeting. Included in exercising this practice are business leaders leading companies which threaten the safety, good fortune, and health of the young. Some companies are accelerating climate change, and others fight to maintain rules still allowing the unrestricted use of automatic weapons by those who are mentally ill. Greta, in one speech (after which she was described as insolent) to the Economic World Forum (January 24, 2019) proclaimed, " I want you to feel the fear I feel every day. I want you to act…our house is still on fire, and you fan the flames…what you provide us are empty words and promises which give the impression that sufficient action is being taken." With deep passion, she was hammering away at hypocrisy. I have heard, over the years, the voices of adults insisting that teens are by nature a danger to themselves and others. If this were to be the case, how would we label the risk invoked by adults whose

companies are a danger to our society and the whole planet? See http://opentranscripts.org/presenters/greta-thunberg/.

630   The calling. This is a concept that the writers Linda Star-Wolfe and Nita Gage explore in their book called Soul Whispering. (Bear and Company, 2017) They share stories about shamans, who are people in search of become healers and thus fulfilling their life purpose. Shamans embark on a process of inner discovery and learn that the search begins deep within themselves. They also become attuned to a type of guidance in which they recognize that it is the path that is choosing them for the learning process. Both allies and folks who challenge them afford them teachable moments. See chapter 4 in their book, "Steps in the Journey", Pages 67 – 84.

631   A countless number of Police Athletic League Director are mentors that the young can count on both for their personal safety and with learning to accept life challenges. During my twenty-two years with the Police Athletic League, a few exemplary director/mentors have included Diane Shirley (Brownsville Beacon), Jenni Bonilla (Harlem Center), Jill Moore (Goldie Maple Beacon in Arverne, Miriam Pena (New South Bronx), Kobla Moats (the Wynn Center in Brooklyn), and Jennifer Tortora (Washington Heights Armory Center).m See www.palnyc.org for a current listing of PAL Centers and directors. www.palnyc.org

632   The Scholar Denied: W.E.B. DuBois and the Birth of Modern Sociology by Naomi Schneider (University of California Press, 2015), pg 95

633   Adopting the dogma of absolutism and chauvinist dreams. This describes a developing social disease becoming prevalent in American consciousness. Leaders, as well as their devoted followers, remain in bubbles of self-confirmational truth and wrapped in blankets of judgement about the identities of others. What is becoming lost in our national conversations and inter-group relationships is a

sense of the need for collective action amongst diverse people. We are losing sight of our responsibilities toward the whole human race and the planet. See Global Awakening by Michael Schacker (Park Street Press, 2013), pg 62.

634   A Theory about resiliency. Dr. Sven Hansen, in his book, Inside/Out: The Practice of Resiliency (The Resiliency Institute, 2015) has developed a series of exercises for individuals and for groups which aid in developing elements of resiliency. By incorporating these beliefs and behaviors, as folks become more resilient, they learn to "adjust to adversity, maintain calm and courage, cultivate emotions, mind and spirit, and better connect to others." Dr. Hansen flushes out four elements of resiliency – bounce, courage, creativity, and connection. For an overview of the four elements, see pages 13 -16. He follows this overview with a chapter devoted to each element. Dr. Hansen complements his suggestions for personal work with methods for working on collaborative relationships. When we also work on our collaborative needs, he states that we "open portals of empathy, increase our intuitive intelligence, and learn to work with the many." pg 245.

635   A Theory about resiliency. Dr. Sven Hansen, in his book, Inside/Out: The Practice of Resiliency (The Resiliency Institute, 2015) has developed a series of exercises for individuals and for groups which aid in developing elements of resiliency. By incorporating these beliefs and behaviors, as folks become more resilient, they learn to "adjust to adversity, maintain calm and courage, cultivate emotions, mind and spirit, and better connect to others." Dr. Hansen flushes out four elements of resiliency – bounce, courage, creativity, and connection. For an overview of the four elements, see pages 13 -16. He follows this overview with a chapter devoted to each element. Dr. Hansen complements his suggestions for personal work with methods for working on collaborative relationships. When we also work on our collaborative needs, he states that we "open portals of

empathy, increase our intuitive intelligence, and learn to work with the many." pg 245.

636   A Theory about resiliency. Dr. Sven Hansen, in his book, Inside/ Out: The Practice of Resiliency (The Resiliency Institute, 2015) has developed a series of exercises for individuals and for groups which aid in developing elements of resiliency. By incorporating these beliefs and behaviors, as folks become more resilient, they learn to "adjust to adversity, maintain calm and courage, cultivate emotions, mind and spirit, and better connect to others." Dr. Hansen flushes out four elements of resiliency – bounce, courage, creativity, and connection. For an overview of the four elements, see pages 13 -16. He follows this overview with a chapter devoted to each element. Dr. Hansen complements his suggestions for personal work with methods for working on collaborative relationships. When we also work on our collaborative needs, he states that we "open portals of empathy, increase our intuitive intelligence, and learn to work with the many." Pg 245.

637   A Theory about resiliency. Dr. Sven Hansen, in his book, Inside/ Out: The Practice of Resiliency (The Resiliency Institute, 2015) has developed a series of exercises for individuals and for groups which aid in developing elements of resiliency. By incorporating these beliefs and behaviors, as folks become more resilient, they learn to "adjust to adversity, maintain calm and courage, cultivate emotions, mind and spirit, and better connect to others." Dr. Hansen flushes out four elements of resiliency – bounce, courage, creativity, and connection. For an overview of the four elements, see pages 13 -16. He follows this overview with a chapter devoted to each element. Dr. Hansen complements his suggestions for personal work with methods for working on collaborative relationships. When we also work on our collaborative needs, he states that we "open portals of empathy, increase our intuitive intelligence, and learn to work with the many." pg 245.

638   A Theory about resiliency. Dr. Sven Hansen, in his book, Inside/
      Out: The Practice of Resiliency (The Resiliency Institute, 2015) has
      developed a series of exercises for individuals and for groups which
      aid in developing elements of resiliency. By incorporating these
      beliefs and behaviors, as folks become more resilient, they learn to
      "adjust to adversity, maintain calm and courage, cultivate emotions,
      mind and spirit, and better connect to others." Dr. Hansen flushes
      out four elements of resiliency – bounce, courage, creativity, and
      connection. For an overview of the four elements, see pages 13 -16.
      He follows this overview with a chapter devoted to each element.
      Dr. Hansen complements his suggestions for personal work with
      methods for working on collaborative relationships. When we also
      work on our collaborative needs, he states that we "open portals of
      empathy, increase our intuitive intelligence, and learn to work with
      the many." Page 245.

639   A Theory about resiliency. Dr. Sven Hansen, in his book, Inside/
      Out: The Practice of Resiliency (The Resiliency Institute, 2015) has
      developed a series of exercises for individuals and for groups which
      aid in developing elements of resiliency. By incorporating these
      beliefs and behaviors, as folks become more resilient, they learn to
      "adjust to adversity, maintain calm and courage, cultivate emotions,
      mind and spirit, and better connect to others." Dr. Hansen flushes
      out four elements of resiliency – bounce, courage, creativity, and
      connection. For an overview of the four elements, see pages 13 -16.
      He follows this overview with a chapter devoted to each element.
      Dr. Hansen complements his suggestions for personal work with
      methods for working on collaborative relationships. When we also
      work on our collaborative needs, he states that we "open portals of
      empathy, increase our intuitive intelligence, and learn to work with
      the many." Page 245.

640   How March for Our Lives Has Influenced State Legislatures and
      Congress. The teen led movement, some of whose leaders developed

at Parkland High School in Florida, successfully blocked deregulation of some gun safety laws. In their electoral work, they had some success in Democrats obtaining key pick-ups of seats in suburban districts, by candidates who are supportive of common-sense gun safety regulation. For coverage of their civic work, see the article in Slate by Daniel Politi (March 24, 2018) at: https://slate.com/news-and-politics/2018/03/march-for-our-lives-hundreds

641　　The Black Lives Matter (BLM) movement saves all lives as well as the life of our democracy. The leaders of BLM are leading a movement to ensure that disinherited and disenfranchised blacks take back what is rightfully owned by them, collect what is unjustly still owed to them. They organize to ensure that we reweave into the fabric of governance what is essential for safeguarding a just and balanced future for all. The magazine YES! which promotes "journalism for people building a better world" devoted their Fall 2020 issue to covering the crucial civic contributions of BLM and its affiliated organizations. A few articles in this issue include "Rebellion Works: We All Stand on the Shoulders of Those Who Came Before Us" by Jamon Jordon (pp 16 -25); "Black Lives Matters Founders: About This Uprising" (page 35); and "Toward A Cure: Cities Declare Racism a Public Health Crisis" (by Tamara E. Holmes, pp 44-48).

642　　The Voting Rights Coalition. Legal residents had the right to vote between 1787 and the early 20th Century, and then saw this right rescinded. These rights were removed during the same era in which we saw the rise of Jim Crow, and the force-feeding of women sent to prison for organizing for the right of women to vote. Nativism, racism, and sexism were dramatically on the rise. Since 2012, a coalition of voting rights partners, called the Voting Rights Coalition, has been organizing to have voting rights for green card residents restored in New York City. At the present time, voting rights legislation, introduced by Councilperson Ydanis Rodriquez, is pending in the City Council. For a comprehensive review of these campaign efforts, go on-line to MigrationPolicy.org. For a thorough historical record about voting rights for legal residents, see the book, Democracy For All: Restoring Immigrant Voting Rights in the United States, by Ron Hayduk (Routledge, 2006).

643   Dreamers – organizing for the right of the children of immigrants to remain in the USA and continue to contribute and thrive. In June of 2020, the Supreme Court rejected then President Trump's effort to bring an end to DACA. This policy has been enacted by the former President, Barack Obama, to ensure that those who had come to the USA while still children, and who are our valued neighbors, who attend and graduate from school, who pay their fair share of taxes, and who serve in the military will be treated honorably and be recognized to n https://www.theguardian.com.

644   Uncertainty and change, a recurring life experience in the United States. Since the dawn of our republic, when Thomas Paine spoke about the hurricane of the times resulting in people clutching at straws for answers, Americans have profiled their distrust for government. Today, this syndrome has surfaced again, as concern about failing institutions is on the rise. In the eyes of the alarmed, the fabric that used to unite all people appears to be unraveling. For some coverage on this, see an article in the Atlantic Magazine (October 5, 2020) by David Brooks called "America is Having a Moral Convulsion". In this article he cites statistics about the decline of trust, the explosion of psychological and social indicators reflecting rising levels on anxiety and stress, and the culture of isolation which has eroded a sense of individual responsibility for the commons. I suggest this piece, because even in such an atmosphere, the younger generation is increasing its level of civic participation and building movements that require solidarity and mutual trust. Young leaders are organizing uphill on this front and persisting despite a relative decline of positive indicators for their generation. One statistic revealed by Mr. Brooks in the article is that "... by

the time Boomers had hit the age of 35, their generation owned 21% of the nation's wealth. As of last year, Millennials who were due to hit the age of 35 within 3 years, owned just 3.2% of the nation's wealth." (pages 10-11 of the on-line article). See online article at: https://www.theatlantic.com/ideas/archive/2020/10/collapsing-levels-trust-are-devasting-america/616581

645   Building faith and trust in an age of uncertainty. Grace Lee Boggs, who passed away at the young age of 100, was a longtime activist and organizer from Detroit who counseled her peers about the need to build positive attitudes and relationships in the short term, for modest goals. One of her expressions was "The world is always being made, but never finished…activism isa journey rather than an arrival." See Good Reads, Grace Lee Boggs, quotes – online. For a more extended look at her work and philosophy, see her book, co-written with Scott Kurashige, called The Next American Revolution: Sustainable Activism for the Twenty-First Century (University of California Press, 2011).

646   Building faith and trust in an age of uncertainty. Grace Lee Boggs, who passed away at the young age of 100, was a longtime activist and organizer from Detroit who counseled her peers about the need to build positive attitudes and relationships in the short term, for modest goals. One of her expressions was "The world is always being made, but never finished…activism isa journey rather than an arrival." See Good Reads, Grace Lee Boggs, quotes – online. For a more extended look at her work and philosophy, see her book, co-written with Scott Kurashige, called The Next American Revolution: Sustainable Activism for the Twenty-First Century (University of California Press, 2011).

647   Dr. Susan Wilcox joined the leadership circle of Brotherhood Sol, and under her influence the organization expanded and was re-named Brotherhood – Sister Sol. Dr. Wilcox, in her lectures and public

speakers would often cite Native American quotes as influencing her social, cultural, and political beliefs. The quote "generations of ancestors within us" was one of the quotes she used often. There is a children's book called Brother Eagle, Sister Sky by Susan Jeffers (Random House, 1991) which attributes this quote to Chief Seattle. As beliefs and philosophical systems were passed down through oral tradition in Native America, I leave it to those who study its history and celebrate its truths so faithfully to verify the source. To find out more about the work of Brotherhood- Sister Sol, go to the website at https://brotherhood-sistersol.org

648 The modern state, in good faith, unable to govern. This quote is taken from a collection of New Republic essays in a book titled Insurrections of the Mind: 100 Years of Politics and Culture in America, edited by Franklyn Foer. (University of Chicago Books, 1958). One of the essays, from which quote is taken about the inability of the modern state to govern, is written by Hans J. Morgenthau, who at the time was a public policy analyst. Mr. Morgenthau's essay addressed the topics of power and powerlessness, and the decline of democratic government. The quote runs from pp 178 – 170 in the book.

649 Pew poll measuring trust in government. The poll measured levels of comparative trust for the years 1958, and 2021. The name of the poll, "Public Trust in Government: 1958 – 2021" was published online on May 17, 2021. See https://www.pewresearch.org .

650 "Globalization of the spirit…reconciliation of individual and social transformation" is a concept and clarion call to civic arms developed by the Rabbi Michael Lerner. In a movement he describes under the banner of Tikkun (to mend and heal the world), Rabbi Lerner includes the voices and programs of close allies seeking to build and develop a humanitarian consciousness guided by spiritual progressivism. Included in his book, The Tikkun Reader (Rowan

and Littlefield, 2007), he includes many articles by activists covering topics such as Judaism, Jewish identity, spiritual politics and earth democracy. See pages 269 and 305.

651   Crisis…disaster or opportunity? This is a question and a challenge posed by Charles M. Johnson in his book, Necessary Wisdom: Meeting the Challenge of Cultural Maturity (Celestial Arts Press, 1991). He sees our choices framed in "an age of ambiguously perceived promise…where we need to pose questions that are not either/or, but relational and evolutionary (by their nature)" (pg 172).

652   "Bootcamps" and the "project 118 initiative" were projected, conceived, and framed by the retired social studies teacher (and member of the National Council of Social Studies) Alan Shulman. He saw bootcamps as necessary to introduce teens to the experience of being a community board member by meeting current board members and practicing in mock committee exercises. He saw our campaign goal (after the legislation amending Public Officer Law had passed) as assisting elected officials in spreading the word about community board membership and working towards the goals of filling 118 seats (two 16- or 17-year-olds per board for each of 59 Boards citywide). For a reading of the legislation amending Public Officer Law, see the NY State government site: http://assembly.state.ny.us/leg (The legislation mandated lowering the official age for membership on boards to age 16 and limiting the number of seats available to 2 for each board).

653   Hosting bootcamps. Community organizations and elected officials did put together bootcamps across New York City. Amongst these efforts was a bootcamp hosted by Brooklyn Borough President Eric Adams (https://www.brooklyn-usa.org) and annual bootcamps hosted by Manhattan Borough President Gale Brewer both at program sites and at her Municipal Building Office (https://www.manhattanbp.nyc.gov).

654   There was a decline in interest and application by teens for applying for Board membership. I had a discussion with a representative from Manhattan Borough President Gale Brewer's office. She acknowledged that recruitment and placement for Board membership by teen had been challenging, and recently had become increasingly difficult. However, the Borough of Manhattan continued to place more teens that did other boroughs. In 2021, they had placed eight teens on Community Boards. By law, Community Boards are mandated to post a census of Board membership each year, including listing demographics about membership. When I looked online in early 2021 to look into 2020 Board listings, the Bronx had 0 teens appointed, and Manhattan had 8 teens appointed, as of the postings in March of 2021. The boroughs of Brooklyn, Queens and Staten Island had not yet posted their membership. The offices of Borough President are in charge of overseeing Community Boards in each of their own boroughs, I therefore provide links to each Borough President office: Manhattan – www.manhattanbp.nyc.gov; Brooklyn- www.brooklynusa.org; the Bronx- www.bronxboroughpres.nyc.gov; Staten Island- www.statenIslandusa.com/borough-board.html and Queens- www.queensbp.org

655   The thoughts about the value of generating the public good via genuine talk is taken from the book A Place for Us: How to Make Society Civil and Democracy Strong by Benjamin R. Barber (Hill and Wang, 1998) To see Mr. Barber's commentary on commonality, deliberation and inclusiveness, see pages 116-117.

656   Community boards do not capture the civic imagination or the commitment…of many New Yorkers.

       Some folks I had spoken to, and some written accounts, had shared viewpoints expressing disappointment and critique about the nature of community board culture. A typical concern was the relationships of local Boards (or lack thereof) with the community it represents, such as lack of concern or effectiveness for local issues. See "Urban Omnibus: Board to Death?" By Rebecca Amato, March 8, 2018, in publications of the Architectural League of New York.

New York State voter participation rates. As researched by PolitiFact, "New York State has a consistently low voter turnout." See https://www.politifact.com The article in which this data was cited was written by Andrea Stewart Cousins, who is now the Democratic Party leader in the New York State Senate. Also see "New York State's Registration and Turnout Continue to Lag" by Kimberly Gonzalez in City and State online. November 6, 2020. https://www.cityandstate.ny.com .

657 New York City is now the most unequal city in the most unequal state in the most unequal country in the developed world." Recently (1996–2007), "inequality grew three times as fast in New York State, and four times as fast in New York City… In NYC, the top 1% earn 44% of all income." Cited in: "14 Shocking Stats In The Rise Of Inequitable NY," by Gus Lubin, Business Insider, January 19, 2011). See Business Insider site at: https://muckrack.com/gus-lubin-and/articles

658 Ibid " 14 Shocking Facts" Business Insider (1/19/2011)

New York City is now the most unequal city in the most unequal state in the most unequal country in the developed world." Recently (1996–2007), "inequality grew three times as fast in New York State, and four times as fast in New York City… In NYC, the top 1% earn 44% of all income." Cited in: "14 Shocking Stats In The Rise Of Inequitable NY," by Gus Lubin, Business Insider, January 19, 2011). https://muckrack.com/gus-lubin-and/articles

659 Ibid " 14 Shocking Facts" Business Insider (1/19/2011) New York City is now the most unequal city in the most unequal state in the most unequal country in the developed world." Recently (1996–2007), "inequality grew three times as fast in New York State, and

four times as fast in New York City... In NYC, the top 1% earn 44% of all income." Cited in: "14 Shocking Stats In The Rise Of Inequitable NY," by Gus Lubin, Business Insider, January 19, 2011). https://muckrack.com/gus-lubin-and/articles

660   "Perpetual subordination results in childlike behavior" was a thought expressed by the late eighteenth-century commentator Mary Wollstonecraft in her arguments against keeping women away from the same rights enjoyed by men. As she wrote in her book, Vindication on the Rights of Women (Verso Books, 2019; introduced by Sheila Row Botham and annotated by Nina Power): "Would men but generously snap our chains and be content with a genuine fellowship instead of slavish obedience...they would find us, in a word, better citizens" (pp 203–204).

661   To be constantly prepared for" is a statement about being held by teens in a condition of always getting ready, but never quite included in decisions, made in a book by Dorothee Soelle, a spiritual writer who was a professor of theology at the Union Theological Seminary in New York City from 1975–1987. The Silent Cry: Mysticism and Resistance (Fortress Press, 2001). See her chapter called "Acting And Dreaming: Becoming Martha And Mary" (pp 199–203) and "Stepping From The Impotence Of Power To The Power Of The Weak" (p 205).

662   On the misrepresentation of women's contributions in history books. History books, mostly edited by men, and published by companies run by men, have omitted, and misrepresented the civic contributions of women such as Helen Keller. Most textbooks focused on her childhood tragedies of blindness and difficulty with speech, as well as her triumph in learning to manage these disabilities. What is often mentioned is that in her later work she focused on addressing the issue of blindness, especially amongst laborers and the poor. As covered in the book, Lies My Teacher Told Me by James W. Loewen

(Touchtone Press, 2007), Ms. Keller had stated: "…blindness is not distributed randomly in the population, but concentrated in the lower class" (pg 14). As Mr. Loewen elaborates on her later life work, "She helped to found the American Civil Liberties Union, the National Association for the Advancement of Colored People, and supported the socialist Eugene Debs for President" (pg 15). Her associations might have been seen as controversial by the textbook publishers, therefore, they deleted Ms. Keller's civic preferences in her adult life.

663   On the misrepresentation of women's contributions in history books. History books, mostly edited by men, and published by companies run by men, have omitted, and misrepresented the civic contributions of women such as Helen Keller. Most textbooks focused on her childhood tragedies of blindness and difficulty with speech, as well as her triumph in learning to manage these disabilities. What is often mentioned is that in her later work she focused on addressing the issue of blindness, especially amongst laborers and the poor. As covered in the book, Lies My Teacher Told Me by James W. Loewen (Touchtone Press, 2007), Ms. Keller had stated: "…blindness is not distributed randomly in the population, but concentrated in the lower class" (pg 14). As Mr. Loewen elaborates on her later life work, "She helped to found the American Civil Liberties Union, the National Association for the Advancement of Colored People, and supported the socialist Eugene Debs for President" (pg 15). Her associations might have been seen as controversial by the textbook publishers, therefore, they deleted Ms. Keller's civic preferences in her adult life.

664   Men are still "not seeing and hearing the disappearing girl." One study cites negligence by institutions, such as Boards of Education which are largely operated by men. In an article by Lisa Machoian, titled "Seeing and Hearing the Disappearing Girl: Risk and Resilience in Adolescent Girls: she cites a quote by a 14-year-old girl named

Olivia: "Girls have very few outlets for anger and negative emotions. And it's not a feminist thing. It's a cultural thing." (pg 95) This article is from a book titled Adolescents at School, edited by Michael Sadowski. (Harvard University Press, 2020).

665   Great health disparities examined in the context of racial inequalities and segregation. Providing preventative health services and equitably delivered treatment is a critically prominent issue in our economically imbalanced and severely segregated city of New York. In our so-called melting pot, if you are White and financially privileged, you are privy to the best of ingredients; if you are Black or Latinx, you get singed. As cited in an article analyzing the causes and conditions of racialized health disparities, "One of the characteristics of the elevated rates of disease for minorities compared to whites is the earlier onset of illness, the greater severity of the disease, and poorer survival" (p 71). This is cited from "Race, Socioeconomic Status and Health" by David Williams, et al. in the Annals of New York Academies of Science, 2010).

666   Great health disparities examined in the context of racial inequalities and segregation. Providing preventative health services and equitably delivered treatment is a critically important issue in our economically imbalanced and severely segregated city of New York. In our so-called melting pot, if you are White and financially privileged, you are privy to the best of ingredients; if you are Black or Latinx, you get singed. As cited in an article analyzing the causes and conditions of racialized health disparities, "One of the characteristics of the elevated rates of disease for minorities compared to whites is the earlier onset of illness, the greater severity of the disease, and poorer survival" (p 71). This is cited from "Race, Socioeconomic Status and Health" by David Williams, et al. in the Annals of New York Academies of Science, 2010). See his article at: https://pubmed. ncbi.inlm.nih.gov/10681897

667   Gotham Gazette article online featuring David Rogers and written by Seth Forum is titled "Community Boards". The page is not dated. See: https://www.gothamgazette.com/lessons/boards.shtml

668   Indypendent online article by Richmond, et al. Article with Liz Roberts. See https://indypendent.org/tag/communityboard11 November 24, 2015

669   Ibid Indypendent online article by Richmond, et al. Article with Liz Roberts. See https://indypendent.org/tag/communityboard11 November 24, 2015, https://indypendent.org/tag/communityboard11

670   Ibid Indypendent online article by Richmond, et al. Article with Liz Roberts. See https://indypendent.org/tag/communityboard11 November 24, 2015, https://indypendent.org/tag/communityboard11

671   Presencing (this is the author's intended spelling) or pre-sensing is practiced in the context of having conversation.

Otto Scharmer, in his book called Theory U (Berrett-Kohler, 2018), constructs a term he calls presencing, which in loose terms means staying present (not pre-occupied with the past or the future). Here, I refer to presensing in the context of group members staying present and receptive to others while in the act of discussing issues or planning. In this context, Mr. Scharmer describes presensing as "slowing down, space opening, widening, (a) sense of self-decentering. People no longer say 'This is my idea. Instead, the group engages in the art of thinking together" (p 46).

672   Presencing (this is the author's intended spelling) or pre-sensing is practiced in the context of having conversation.

Otto Scharmer, in his book called Theory U (Berrett-Kohler, 2018), constructs a term he calls presencing, which in loose terms means staying present (not pre-occupied with the past or the future). Here, I refer to presensing in the context of group members staying present and receptive to others while in the act of discussing issues or planning. In this context, Mr. Scharmer describes presensing as "slowing down, space opening, widening, (a) sense of self-decentering. People no longer say 'This is my idea. Instead, the group engages in the art of thinking together" (p 46).

673   Presencing (this is the author's intended spelling) or pre-sensing is practiced by counselors in the context of having conversation.

Otto Scharmer, in his book called Theory U (Berrett-Kohler, 2018), constructs a term he calls presencing, which in loose terms means staying present (not pre-occupied with the past or the future). Here, I refer to presensing in the context of group members staying present and receptive to others while in the act of discussing issues or planning. In this context, Mr. Scharmer describes presensing as "slowing down, space opening, widening, (a) sense of self-decentering. People no longer say 'This is my idea. Instead, the group engages in the art of thinking together" (p 46).

674   Steve Hansen, in his book, Inside/Out (Resilience Institute, 2015) suggests that it takes "practiced attention" across multiple levels of our consciousness to become disciplined with focus and sustained effort. (page198). Mr. Hansen also advises "cultivating and engaging the heart" (page 201) as well as "reframing the body-heart mind" (page 205) in order to optimize our efforts in life.

675   The idle gnawing of the mice, and Dorothy from The Wizard of Oz.

The phrase, the idle gnawing of the mice, was one used by Karl Marx when contrasting the evolved relevance of his ideas with those he considered to be outdated in a world of changed conditions and relationships.

In the book and film classic, The Wizard of Oz is interpreted for meaning by Salman Rushdie in his book with the same name (British Film Institute/Bloomsbury Publishing, 2012). Mr. Rushdie's take on the theme is summarized on the back cover of this book:

"The Wizard of Oz is more than a children's film, and more than a fantasy. It is a story whose driving force is the inadequacy of adults, in which the 'weakness of grown-ups forces children to take control of their own destinies.' Dorothy had to discard the assumptions held about her by her elders in Kansas and had to see through the misleading advice offered to her by the Wizard. Using the counsel of her three newly found allies (each of whom was learning to transcend the limits of self-diminishment), the subtle but sage guidance of her dog, Toto, and her internally discovered insights, Dorothy learns to make up her own mind, and follow her own counsel."

676   Arnstein's Ladder attributes needed for government accounting.

The points I reiterate here are those of the necessity for youth to move past being used by adult leaders as tokens, and the necessity of development of assertive relationship where youth gain control over input and outcomes. Practicing Social Inclusion (Taket, et al), Ibid.

677   "Constructing Arguments and Making Knowledgeable Claims," a social studies milestone as noted in "C-3 Framework: College, Career and Civic Life" (National Council of Social Studies, Silver Spring, Maryland). See developing claims and using evidence on pages 55 and 56.

678   Ibid "Constructing Arguments and Making Knowledgeable Claims," a social studies milestone as noted in "C-3 Framework: College, Career and Civic Life" (National Council of Social Studies, Silver Spring, Maryland). See developing claims and using evidence on pages 55 and 56.

679   Ibid "Constructing Arguments and Making Knowledgeable Claims," a social studies milestone as noted in "C-3 Framework: College, Career and Civic Life" (National Council of Social Studies, Silver Spring, Maryland). See developing claims and using evidence on pages 55 and 56.

680   Syllabus: Teaching Tolerance. This is a classroom syllabus developed by the Southern Poverty Law Center. (SPLC) The mission of this organization is to defend Black people and other vulnerable minorities from hate acts, discriminatory policies and alt-right groups. The SPLC has an education arm which has developed a classroom syllabus informing students about how to identify policies and actions which target minorities, and in the history and methods of the civil rights movement.

One of the measurable goals constructed in the civics syllabus for the organization called Teaching Tolerance is having students learn to recognize a thesis statement and use reason to assess it. In criticizing the practices of cable news, which resorts to interruption, shouting, and insults, the Teaching Tolerance lesson plan walks students through the methodology: look for supportive links presented with the evidence of statistics, testimony and credible historical examples" (p 205). Citation: "Teaching Civil Discourse in the Classroom," Teaching Tolerance syllabus. Available through the Southern Poverty Law Center. See https://www/frc.org/issuebrief/southern-poverty-law-centers-teaching-tolerance-project.

681   One example of exemplary civic contributions is that of the work by high school student leader with the Urban Youth Collaborative. Teen leaders advocate, meet with neighborhood partners, and negotiate with NYC officials in facilitating changes to agency practices and municipal policy. They have been successful in the areas of restorative justice, mental health services, and inducing great student policy input at local high schools. The innovative changes being made in New Jersey through Dr. Mindy Thompson- Fullilove's guidance are influenced by urging elected officials, policymakers, and leaders of local neighborhood agencies to look at neighborhoods as places of evolving cooperative enterprise rather than as fractured places overrun by problems. Those seeking change are learning to change the way they perceive local actors, including youth and

adults, seeing them as analytical people and creative change-makers. See Dr. Fullilove's book, Urban Alchemy: Restoring Joy in America's Sorted-Out Cities (New Village Press, 2013) by Mindy Thompson-Fullilove, M.D. To follow the work of the Urban Youth Collaborative, see their website at https://www.urbanyouthcollaborative.org

Significant teen-led change movements are admirably highlighted by Tina Rosenberg in the book, Join the Club: Peer Pressure Can Transform the World by Tina Rosenberg (Norton, 2011), pp 55–57 and 79–83). One of the stories shared in the book is about a campaign called Rage Against the Haze, about a teen organized campaign to lower the smoking rates amongst teens in Florida. It was extraordinarily successful after years of inadequate results obtained by adult led anti-smoking campaigns.

682   These quotes are by Ayesha, a student, who learned to become an advocate, to do some grant writing, and to set up educational classes, is found at the NYC Service websites at: https://www.nycservice.org.

On the west coast in our nation, successful teen municipal policy advocacy has been fostered by San Francisco's Board of Supervisors members have mentored teen leaders (called youth commissioners) since 1995. Training teens to engage in best civic practices is essential to personal and social development is a finding of mentors at the San Francisco Youth Commission. In its own way, they are saying that it is by learning civic responsibilities through advisement with city legislators which fosters social development. Traditional opposition to placing teens in these types of positions assumes that advanced social development having to be in place before a teen can effectively engage in civics. Social development and civic responsibility jointly enhance opportune development of the individual psyche and social responsibility. To see descriptions of their history, policy development and relationships between members of the San Francisco Board of Supervisors and the Youth Commission members, visit their website at: www.sfgov.org/yc.

683   These quotes are by Ayesha, a student, who learned to become an advocate, do to some grant writing, and to set up educational classes, is found at the NYC Service websites at: https://www.nycservice.org.

On the west coast in our nation, successful teen municipal policy advocacy has been fostered by San Francisco's Board of Supervisors members have mentored teen leaders (called youth commissioners) since 1995. Training teens to engage in best civic practices is essential to personal and social development is a finding of mentors at the San Francisco Youth Commission. In its own way, they are saying that it is by learning civic responsibilities through advisement with city legislators which fosters social development. Traditional opposition to placing teens in these types of positions assumes that advanced social development having to be in place before a teen can effectively engage in civics. Social development and civic responsibility jointly enhance opportune development of the individual psyche and social responsibility. To see descriptions of their history, policy development and relationships between members of the San Francisco Board of Supervisors and the Youth Commission members, visit their website at: www.sfgov.org/yc.

684   Developing interactive constellations of youth councils. Two borough presidents, Manhattan Borough President Bale Brewer, and Brooklyn Borough President Eric Adams have established avenues of teen participation through creating teen advisory councils. See https://www.manhattanbp.nyc.gov and https://www.brooklyn-usa.org.

685   For information on PAL programs serving disconnected youth (ages 16-24) which in the past had been called Youth Link programs, see the Police Athletic League website at www.palnyc.org

686   For information on PAL programs serving disconnected youth (ages 16 -24) which in the past had been called Youth Link programs, see the Police Athletic League website at www.palnyc.org

687   Establishing youth councils and creating networks amongst youth councils. Dr. Sarah Zeller-Berkman developed a syllabus and training tool she identified as an inter-generational change initiative. Her project was titled "Rolling Thunder: The Collective Impact of Intergenerational Youth Policy Making In NYC." In a nutshell, by having a reference library of successful initiatives from around the nation and the world, and by networking and sharing amongst NYC youth agencies and NYC municipal agencies, we would create a meta-marriage between idealism and wisdom, which would transform the nature and outcomes of policy making in New York City. For access to the Rolling Thunder curriculum, see: the Public Science Project at https://www.gc.cuny.edu

688   Ibid Public Science Project These notations include words on Dr. Zeller-Berkman's development of learning rubrics, publication of Rolling Thunder, the value of creating networks of youth networks, the history of teen led program in the United States, and references to teen led programs in Europe. During her early years of consulting with DYCD, and since, Dr. Berkman had also worked closely with the NYC Department of Youth and Community Development is establishing best practice for youth civic participation programs. In addition to her work, a dedicated staff at DYCD is continuously at work training their funded program leaders through what they call the Leadership Development Framework. This program and syllabus develop skill sets promoting SEL competencies, communication skills and methods for collaboration; interactive activities encouraging initiative for promoting change; and opportunities for reflection on connections and challenges, as well as for generating new opportunities for civic engagement. See the Public Science Project at: https://www.gc.cuny.edu

689 Ibid Public Science Project These notations include words on Dr. Zeller-Berkman's development of learning rubrics, publication of Rolling Thunder, the value of creating networks of youth networks, the history of teen led program in the United States, and references to teen led programs in Europe. During her early years of consulting with DYCD, and since, Dr. Berkman had also worked closely with the NYC Department of Youth and Community Development is establishing best practice for youth civic participation programs. In addition to her work, a resolute staff at DYCD is continuously at work training their funded program leaders through what they call the Leadership Development Framework. This program and syllabus develop skill sets promoting SEL competencies, communication skills and methods for collaboration; interactive activities encouraging initiative for promoting change; and opportunities for reflection on connections and challenges, as well as for generating new opportunities for civic engagement. See he Public Science Project at: https://www.gc.cuny.edu

690 Ibid Public Science Project These notations include words on Dr. Zeller-Berkman's development of learning rubrics, publication of Rolling Thunder, the value of creating networks of youth networks, the history of teen led program in the United States, and references to teen led programs in Europe. During her early years of consulting with DYCD, and since, Dr. Berkman had also worked closely with the NYC Department of Youth and Community Development is establishing best practice for youth civic participation programs. In addition to her work, a resolute staff at DYCD is continuously at work training their funded program leaders through what they call the Leadership Development Framework. This program and syllabus develop skill sets promoting SEL competencies, communication skills and methods for collaboration; interactive activities encouraging initiative for promoting change; and opportunities for reflection on connections and challenges, as well as for generating

new opportunities for civic engagement. See the Public Science Project at: https://www.gc.cuny.edu

691   Ibid Public Science Project These notations include words on Dr. Zeller-Berkman's development of learning rubrics, publication of Rolling Thunder, the value of creating networks of youth networks, the history of teen led program in the United States, and references to teen led programs in Europe. During her early years of consulting with DYCD, and since, Dr. Berkman had also worked closely with the NYC Department of Youth and Community Development is establishing best practice for youth civic participation programs. In addition to her work, a resolute staff at DYCD is continuously at work training their funded program leaders through what they call the Leadership Development Framework. This program and syllabus develop skill sets promoting SEL competencies, communication skills and methods for collaboration; interactive activities encouraging initiative for promoting change; and opportunities for reflection on connections and challenges, as well as for generating new opportunities for civic engagement. See the Public Science Project at: https://www.gc.cuny.edu

692   Ibid Public Science Project These notations include words on Dr. Zeller-Berkman's development of learning rubrics, publication of Rolling Thunder, the value of creating networks of youth networks, the history of teen led program in the United States, and references to teen led programs in Europe. During her early years of consulting with DYCD, and since, Dr. Berkman had also worked closely with the NYC Department of Youth and Community Development is establishing best practice for youth civic participation programs. In addition to her work, a resolute staff at DYCD is continuously at work training their funded program leaders through what they call the Leadership Development Framework. This program and syllabus develop skill sets promoting SEL competencies, communication skills and methods for collaboration; interactive activities

encouraging initiative for promoting change; and opportunities for reflection on connections and challenges, as well as for generating new opportunities for civic engagement. See the Public Science Project at: https://www.gc.cuny.edu

693   See the DYCD link: https://www1nyc.gov/site/dycd/index.page for descriptions of Middle School youth councils.

694   To see an overview of Dr. Zeller-Berkman's strategy of utilizing graduate students as partners in the teen enfranchisement movement, see the Public Science Project at https://www.gc.cuny.edu

695   The Teens Take Charge Leadership has successfully drawn attention to student needs and issues through their tireless and well-designed advocacy programs. Elected officials now actively consult with its leadership and participate in special events and annual conferences sponsored by Teens Take Charge. Find them online: https://www.facebook.com/teenstakecharge.nyc .

696   Teens for Food Justice, as is the case with Teens Take Charge, implement extensive training programs for their teen leaders in the skills of issue identification, advocacy, coordination with community partners, and assessing the efficacy of improvements by neighborhood and municipal agencies in meeting the needs of young people. Find them online at: https://www.teensforfoodjustice.org.

697   Constitution High School in Philadelphia, Pennsylvania. This school partners with former police commissioner Charles Romney. It also develops special initiatives of special import to teens, such as the Policing in a More Perfect Union Program. For information on this school, go to their website: www.constitutionhs.philasd.org.

698   Constitution High School in Philadelphia, Pennsylvania. This school partners with former police commissioner Charles Romney. It also develops special initiatives of special import to teens, such as the Policing in a More Perfect Union Program. For information on this school, go to their website: www.constitutionhs.philasd.org.

699   This quote is by a NYC Service teen leader named Nina Simmons. To see the fabulous work done by NYC Service is helping organizations establish and expand their teen councils, see their website at https://www.nycservice.org.

700   The Virgin Vote by Jon Grinspan (University of North Carolina, 2010).

701   Ibid The Virgin Vote See the Appendix on pg 163. There are two tables showing the comparative median age and percentage of Americans voting over the years, beginning in the late 1800s.

702   I have previously noted the impact of poor NY State Eligible Voter Turnout – which was the 2nd worst in the nation in 2016. Many of those with concern for declining interest and participation in the electoral process feel that by improving access to and quality of high school civics programs, this trend can begin to be reversed. New York state turnout declined from 58.5 per cent in 2008 to 53.2 per cent in 2012. The turnout improved for 2016, and we improved in national rankings to only the sixth worst state in the nation. For statistics on New York State, and to find analysis by the organization, Nonprofit VOTE, see the site: https://www.nonprofitvote.org/states/new-york

Michael Rebell was the lead council for the lawsuit on deficient civic education in Rhode Island. Mr. Rebell also was lead council for the NY State Campaign for Fiscal Equity, which, after 30 years and winning two lawsuits in court, finally saw the NY State Legislature implement equitable public-school funding for New York City. See coverage in The Washington Post from October 22, 2020, where the federal judge ruled against the student plaintiffs. However, the judge, while denying a constitutional right to civic education, praised the students for "not engaging in a wild-eyed effort…(but) rather issuing a cry for help from a generation, …and that American democracy is in peril amidst creeping authoritarianism." (Washington Post,

October 22, 2020, "Judge Rules Against..."). https://www.wash-ingtonpost.com/education/2020/10/22/federal-judge-rules-stu-dents-have-no-constitutional-right-civics-education

703   Yield to what his conscience demands in the moment...is a line from the Port Huron Statement, a statement of purpose drafted by the Students for A Democratic Society in 1962. In one line, they proclaimed: "Facing the fear of complexity over the emptiness of life, people are fearful of the thought that at any moment things might be thrust out of control...the fact that each individual sees apathy in his fellows perpetuates the common reluctance to organize for change" (page 415). Cited: 100 Key Documents in American Democracy (Praeger, 1999), Peter B. Levy (editor).

704   Bill Plotkin addresses the need for ritual and rites of passage which are missing in modern society. Mr. Plotkin speaks to function of this type of ritual and rite of passage as one of "induction", where a teen who has been defining the nature of the soul must now also look at "stepping up to a position of greater responsibility. This entails the need to "assume the full responsibility of cultural leadership, as well as the fulfillment and joy inherent in that status." See his words in the chapter "The Artisan and the Wild Orchard" in his book Nature and the Human Soul (New World Library, 2008, pages 353 and354) for the role of the adult mentor in this process.

705   It is the counterculture, which creates credible alternatives... In a book written by Theodore Roszak, titled The Making of A Counterculture (Anchor Books, 1969), he critiques the shortcom-ings of the adult culture being inherited by the young, and praises emergent leaders for seeing possibilities with new eyes and fervent determination: "It is the young, arriving with new eyes that can see the obvious, who must remake the lethal culture of their elders, and who must remake it in desperate haste" (p 47). When I re-read this passage, I also recalled a poster I saw in a Wall Street plaza that had

been temporarily appropriated by the youth of the Occupy Wall Street movement. The poster simply stated: Real Eyes see Real Lies.

706   It is the counterculture, which creates credible alternatives… In a book written by Theodore Roszak, titled The Making of A Counterculture (Anchor Books, 1969), he critiques the shortcomings of the adult culture being inherited by the young, and praises emergent leaders for seeing possibilities with new eyes and fervent determination: "It is the young, arriving with new eyes that can see the obvious, who must remake the lethal culture of their elders, and who must remake it in desperate haste" (p 47). When I re-read this passage, I also recalled a poster I saw in a Wall Street plaza that had been temporarily appropriated by the youth of the Occupy Wall Street movement. The poster simply stated: Real Eyes see Real Lies.

707   It is the counterculture, which creates credible alternatives… In a book written by Theodore Roszak, titled The Making of A Counterculture (Anchor Books, 1969), he critiques the shortcomings of the adult culture being inherited by the young, and praises emergent leaders for seeing possibilities with new eyes and fervent determination: "It is the young, arriving with new eyes that can see the obvious, who must remake the lethal culture of their elders, and who must remake it in desperate haste" (p 47). When I re-read this passage, I also recalled a poster I saw in a Wall Street plaza that had been temporarily appropriated by the youth of the Occupy Wall Street movement. The poster simply stated: Real Eyes see Real Lies.

708   It is the counterculture, which creates credible alternatives… In a book written by Theodore Roszak, titled The Making of A Counterculture (Anchor Books, 1969), he critiques the shortcomings of the adult culture being inherited by the young, and praises emergent leaders for seeing possibilities with new eyes and fervent determination: "It is the young, arriving with new eyes that can see the obvious, who must remake the lethal culture of their elders, and

who must remake it in desperate haste" (p 47). When I re-read this passage, I also recalled a poster I saw in a Wall Street plaza that had been temporarily appropriated by the youth of the Occupy Wall Street movement. The poster simply stated: Real Eyes see Real Lies.

709   Ancestral Counsel and justice for the Indigenous Peoples of North America. In the book, Original Instructions: Indigenous Teachings for a Sustainable Future edited by Melissa K. Nelson (Bear and Company, 2008), contributions from Native elders and wise people speak to one of the themes of my book, that is, in order to move forward with compassion and integrity, we need to join together the counsel of indigenous peoples who inhabited North America sustainably for 10,000 years, with those who plan on how we should move toward the future. As spoken to by Francisco X. Alarcon, a Chicano poet, this includes "the retrieval of...ecopoetics...to stress the deep sense of interconnection linking the poetic self and nature" (p 278) As Mr. Alarcon continues: "The main purpose of this ecopoetics is to reconcile and heal the internal split experienced by any Mestizo (also felt by most people currently living on the planet) which is the direct result of...conquering, colonizing and exploiting Indigenous Peoples" (p 279). Cited from the chapter with Mr. Alarcon's contribution to Original Instructions: "El Poder de la Palabra: The Power of the Word: Toward a Nahuatl/Mestizo Consciousness: (pp 265–287).

710   A mandate for the emergent generation – developing a practice reflecting the principles of "evolutionary convergence". See the book, Second Wave Spirituality: Passion for Peace, Passion for Justice by Chris Saade (North Atlantic Books, 2014) Mr. Saade also references our need to connect to and honor historical struggle. In a section of his book, he titles "Tenacious and Brave in the Struggle, he writes: "Hundreds and thousands of peaceful and courageous spirits preceded us...We are standing on the shoulders of spiritual

giants. Our task is to walk through the great opening toward the transformational opportunities ahead of us." Page 123.

711 Spiritual Principles for Creating a World That Works. Alan Seale, in his book Creating A World That Works (Weiser Books, 2011) weave four eco/spiritual principles into his book which dovetail with the practices of Indigenous peoples. These practices include engage your intuition, claim your power, practice collaboration and choose wisely for the common good.

712 Ibid Spiritual Principles for Creating a World That Works.

Alan Seale, in his book Creating A World That Works (Weiser Books, 2011) weave four eco/spiritual principles into his book which dovetail with the practices of Indigenous peoples. These practices include engage your intuition, claim your power, practice collaboration and choose wisely for the common good. See pp 80 – 83 on 3 intelligences.

713 Ibid Spiritual Principles for Creating a World That Works. Alan Seale, in his book Creating A World That Works (Weiser Books, 2011) weave four eco/spiritual principles into his book which dovetail with the practices of Indigenous peoples. These practices include engage your intuition, claim your power, practice collaboration and choose wisely for the common good. See pp 44 -49 on claiming your power with an ego-soul partnership.

714 Ibid Spiritual Principles for Creating a World That Works. Alan Seale, in his book Creating A World That Works (Weiser Books, 2011) weave four eco/spiritual principles into his book which dovetail with the practices of Indigenous peoples. These practices include engage your intuition, claim your power, practice collaboration and choose wisely for the common good. For thoughts on practicing collaboration and choosing for the common good, see the section in the book Exploration: High Heart and Low Heart, pp 157 – 161.

715   Vote 16 California's mixed returns. Generation Citizen's Vote 16 leaders and its allies organize for the right to vote. The mission statement of Generation Citizen's Vote 16 program can be found online at Vote16.org The data and quote is found in a link to an article in Teen Vogue on the Vote 16 site. The Teen Vogue issue is from March 26, 2018, and is written by Melissa Fike, with input from Melena Fike. See https://generationcitizen.org/policy-and-advocacy/vote16usa Go to Media Highlights on this site.

In 2020, San Francisco put an initiative on the ballot to lower the voting age to age 16. It lost by a margin of 51 per cent to 49 percent. In Oakland, right across the bay, a measure to allow 16-year-olds to serve on school boards passed.

716   Ibid Vote 16 California's mixed returns. Generation Citizen's Vote 16 leaders and its allies organize for the right to vote. The mission statement of Generation Citizen's Vote 16 program can be found online at Vote16.org The data and quote is found in a link to an article in Teen Vogue on the Vote 16 site. The Teen Vogue issue is from March 26, 2018, and is written by Melissa Fike, with input from Melena Fike. See: https://generationcitizen.org/policy-and-advocacy/vote16usa Go to Media Highlights on this site.

In 2020, San Francisco put an initiative on the ballot to lower the voting age to age 16. It lost by a margin of 51 per cent to 49 percent. In Oakland, right across the bay, a measure to allow 16-year-olds to serve on school boards passed.

717   Ibid Vote 16 California's mixed returns. Generation Citizen's Vote 16 leaders and its allies organize for the right to vote. The mission statement of Generation Citizen's Vote 16 program can be found online at Vote16.org The data and quote is found in a link to an article in Teen Vogue on the Vote 16 site. The Teen Vogue issue is from March 26, 2018, and is written by Melissa Fike, with input

from Melena Fike. See: https://generationcitizen.org/policy-and-advocacy/vote16usa Go to Media Highlights on this site.

In 2020, San Francisco put an initiative on the ballot to lower the voting age to age 16. It lost by a margin of 51 per cent to 49 percent. In Oakland, right across the bay, a measure to allow 16-year-olds to serve on school boards passed.

718 NY State Legislation to lower the voting age to age sixteen. Brad Hoylman, a State Senator, introduced legislation in Albany to lower the voting age to 16 in the 2019 session. It has been sitting in committee and was introduced for the 2020–2021 legislative session. Go to the State Senator site for Brad Hoylman at: https://www.nysenate. gov/senators/brad-hoylman and click on to legislation to find his lower the voting age to 16 bill.

719 Incorporates the lessons of the past with visions for the future…Paul Hawken, in his book, Blessed Unrest (Penguin, 2007), suggests the heart as a place of practice for this type of reconciliation: "To salve the world's wounds demands a response from the heart. There is a world of hurt out there, and to heal the past requires apologies, reconciliation, reparational and forgiveness. A viable future is not possible until the past is faced objectively, and communion is made with errant history" (pg188).

720 This is an expression I learned to bring into practice after being introduced to this term by my mentor Dr. Stephanie Marango during her The Doctor Is In mentoring session in 2013 and 2014. In subsequent mentoring sessions with Dr. Marango in which I have been engaged, she has continued to mentor me in staying in touch with my life purpose, accessing knowledge using heart intelligence, and staying connected to positive energies using spiritual practices.

721 The vision of the soul eclipses the reach even of the imagination is a concept I have referenced previously sourced in my reading of Jeffrey Krispel's book, Mutants and Mystics (University of Chicago

Press, 2011). He provides one example of using guidance from the invisible sources of intelligence when he quotes Alvin Schwartz, who wrote comic strips in the 1940s and 1950s featuring Batman and Superman: "... (when reflecting upon life) there are clumps of events that belong together...their connection having to do with value and meaning rather than the material event" (p 240).

722   The vision of the soul eclipses the reach even of the imagination is a concept I have referenced previously sourced in my reading of Jeffrey Krispel's book, Mutants and Mystics (University of Chicago Press, 2011). He provides one example of using guidance from the invisible sources of intelligence when he quotes Alvin Schwartz, who wrote comic strips in the 1940s and 1950s featuring Batman and Superman: "... (when reflecting upon life) there are clumps of events that belong together...their connection having to do with value and meaning rather than the material event" (p 240).

723   On metaphysical energies providing metaphoric guidance in our lives. Joy Michaud, an astrologer, in her biographic of the planets Uranus and Neptune, breaks down the distinction between physical objects and their representations of psychic energy. For instance, she states that we should look at planetary influence not as a function of their physical attributes or position in the solar system, but as "metaphorical images and energies which project images in the unconscious mind assisting (the observer) with (considering) one's place in the universe" (p 130). As I came to learn as I dabbled with astrological documents called solar charts, that map puts (the metaphoric) Uranus in what is called my ninth house. (A house is a metaphorical representation of the pieces of one's individual consciousness and the stages of experience one goes through in life). With this positioning, I am inclined to "do much questioning of the status quo" (p 141) and to be "engaged in an ongoing confrontation between myself and the world" (p 137). My high-school confrontation that I spoke about in the Prelude helped me to accelerate and

crystalize my opposition to imposed and misplaced adult authority. My work has advanced and is more complex, but is not finished, as I continue this quest in my advocacy for teen empowerment. Source of quotes: The Uranus-Neptune Influence by Joy Michaud (Weiser, 1994).

724   See the chapter "A Question of 'Faith': Adolescent Spirituality in the Schools by Eric Toshalis (page 195). This chapter appears in the book, Adolescents At School: Perspectives on Youth, Identity and Education, edited by Michael Sadowski (Harvard Education Press, 3rd Edition, 2020).

725   When engaged in community organizing, an activist shares a life script, and through engagement with others re-writes the script. When a person writes about these experiences, that person reflects on what happened in life, and lets his or her examination of that life lets life happen. Organizing influences writing, and writing can aid in re-organizing one's life. See the book, Fearless Writing by William Kenower (Writer's Digest Books, 2017) See Chapter 2, 'the Flow", for Mr. Kenower's elaboration on the connection between life experience and writing. Fearless writing also involves exercising faith.

726   When engaged in community organizing, an activist shares a life script, and through engagement with others re-writes the script. When a person writes about these experiences, that person reflects on what happened in life, and lets his or her examination of that life lets life happen. Organizing influences writing, and writing can aid in re-organizing one's life. See the book, Fearless Writing by William Kenower (Writer's Digest Books, 2017) See Chapter 2, 'the Flow", for Mr. Kenower's elaboration on the connection between life experience and writing. Fearless writing also involves exercising faith.

727   Sean Wilentz, in his labor history biographic titled Chants Democratic (Oxford University Press, 2004) presents a comprehensive labor history, focusing on the rise of the American working

class in New York City between 1788 and 1850. In this book, he cites a poem called Chants Democratic, which in one stanza speaks about the place of youth in the city: "...where outside authority enters always after the precedence of inner authority, where the citizen is always the head and the ideal...where children are taught from the jumpstart that they are to be the laws until themselves and to depend upon themselves...where equanimity is illustrated in public affairs...there the greatest city stands" (p 391).

728   I previously referenced Benjamin Barber from his book, A Place for Us (Hill and Wang, 1998), on the importance of civic participants feeling that they are in relationships of "uncoerced human association." Mr. Barber adds a word here about the nature of these civic participants who are: "democratic citizens (who) are active, responsible, and engaged members of groups and communities, that while having different values and conflicting interests are devoted to arbitrating their differences, exploring common ground, doing public work and pursuing common relations" (p 37).

729   A Place for Us Ibid Another political scientist, Michael Waltzer, is quoted by Mr. Barber on Page 37.

730   Extending one's scope of vision and recognizing common problems. I previously referenced the book by Robert Snyder titled Crossing Broadway (Cornell University Press, 2015) as he spoke to the issue of people living on different blocks in the Heights feeling they are seemingly in different universes in their daily lives. Mr. Snyder speaks to this again as he quotes another writer, Marshall Berman, who also studies history and subsequent changes in culture and politics: "As Marshall Berman observed of many corners of New York that emerged from the 'city of ruins' of the 1970s in Washington Heights, people who had faced disaster carried on, and in the midst of falling apart, found ways to rise" (p 225).

731   The U.N. charter and call for involving all members of a community to the maximum extent possible is better ensured if this engagement is embedded in democratic processes and governance structures: As noted by Gar Alperovitz et al. in their book, Making Place for Community in the Global Era (Routledge, 2002): "Nineteenth century theorists like Mill and Tocqueville pointed to the quality of democratic experience...and (educator) John Dewey held that fraternity, liberty and equality isolated from communal life is a hopeless abstraction" (p 312).

732   Civic participation practice and application is a civic ritual, and a rite of passage toward becoming a democratic citizen. For thoughts on the power and value of ritual, see Ritual: Power, Healing and Community by Malidoma Patrice Some (Penguin Classics, 1993), pp 49 and 53.

733   Civic participation practice and application is a civic ritual, and a rite of passage toward becoming a democratic citizen. For thoughts on the power and value of ritual, see Ritual: Power, Healing and Community by Malidoma Patrice Some (Penguin Classics, 1993), pp 49 and 53.

734   Civic participation practice and application is a civic ritual, and a rite of passage toward becoming a democratic citizen. For thoughts on the power and value of ritual, see Ritual: Power, Healing and Community by Malidoma Patrice Some (Penguin Classics, 1993), pp 49 and 53.

735   I previously looked at the process of ritual, as analyzed by Patrice Some. In the construction of civic ritual for the young, it is also crucial that developing activists are taught to resist what Aura Bogerdo, in a book review for YES! magazine, called "well-intentioned helpers practicing saviorism, led by charismatic (white) men leading marginalized people to freedom" (pp 55–56). As Ms. Bogerdo notes, young activists need to be trained by civic mentors to "decenter

privilege" (as do groups like Occupy Wall Street and Black Lives Matter), and to "ask questions as we walk" (that is, there are no pre-formed perfect solutions that apply to all situations; we have to re-construct as we build) (pp 55–56).

Cited from YES! magazine, Fall 2017 issue, pp 55–57, Aura Bogerdo, in her review of the book, No More Heroes.

736   Ritual: Power, Healing and Community Ibid Retrograde ritual or rituals of reform? In our society, we have retrograde rituals, some traditional and some subject to sanctions, such as proms and gang initiations. What they share are performative elements, such as dress code, ego-boosting etiquette, and the drama of rejection. As pointed out by Patrice Some, in the case of gang initiation, "when an initiated member of a community registers communication through pain (in these cases, feelings of worthlessness, and/or rage in cover of grief), it is a signal that the soul needs communion with its spiritual counterpart. To shut down the pain is a soul in longing" (p 22). In the case of proms, the rank order of being pretty or handsome, or being a talented dancer, reinforces the perception that to be recognized by adults as worthy of title (for example, Prom Queen), it is the superficial that counts. Our society is also experimenting with developing rituals of reform. In the arena of action-oriented civics, developing social justice actors is being given the chance to grow by civic mentors, who recognize both known and recently discovered skills and talents of teens providing service to a whole community. As written by Barbara Knight, in an article she wrote called "A Theory of Political Community": "Politics are to be structured to enhance the great unfolding of the universe, drawing forth the great interiority of the individual as well as the bonds of communion in many directions" (p 70). Cited from the book Transformational Politics (SUNY NY Press, 1998), Stephen Wolpert (editor).

737   See quotes from Dr. Elsworthy's book, Pioneering the Possible (North Atlantic Books, 2014) (p 87, p 255).

738   See quotes from Dr. Elsworthy's book, Pioneering the Possible (North Atlantic Books, 2014) (p 87, p 255).

739   See quotes from Dr. Elsworthy's book, Pioneering the Possible (North Atlantic Books, 2014) (p 87, p 255).

740   See introduction to the book, The Naked Voice (North Atlantic Books, 2015) by Chloe Goodchild. She uses her opening chapter to describe the pre-birth ritual where parents and community engage the spirit of a child.

741   See the book To Know As We Are Known: Education As A Spiritual Journey, by Parker J. Palmer (Harper San Francisco, 1993). One quote showing the dichotomy between what we should avoid in teaching style and what benefits both students and community speaks to the crucial importance of how we teach and learn. As Mr. Palmer states: "There is a simple reason why students resist thinking: they live in a world where relationships are quite fragile. They are desperate for more community, not less, so when thinking is presented to them as a way to disconnect themselves from the world, they want nothing of it. If we could represent knowing for what it is – a way of creating community, not destroying it – we would draw more young people into the great adventure of learning." Page xvi.

742   An article profiling Gale Brewer, Manhattan Borough President, in City and State magazine also posted online. See: www.cityandstateny.com/articles/politics/new-york-city/GaleBrewer-interns.html, November 28, 2018. Note 87a. City and State article on Gale Brewer Ibid.

743   City and State article on Gale Brewer Ibid.

744   I borrow the term American shadow from the work developed by Jeremiah Abrams, who edited this collection of essays. See The Shadow of America: Reclaiming the Soul of a Nation (Nataraj

Publishing, 1994) Mr. Abrams speaks to the effects of living contin-uously under the American shadow: "Unwittingly, those Americans who preceded us have bought themselves time by borrowing against our generation and those to follow us. Consequently, we are both the beneficiaries of their good intentions, and the bearers of their unre-deemed shadowy choices." pg 8. Today we bear the consequences as we see a retrograde resurgence in denial of basic choice and control over their bodies for women, institutional violence generated against innocent black people, and intolerance for immigrants who have always been the backbone of our economy and our communities. As Mr. Abrams further illustrates, by remaining fixed in the practice of the four catastrophes, our entire nation is suffering the conse-quences: "our cities are deteriorating...our schools are bankrupt, our government is inefficient, our politicians corrupt...our natural resources squandered... and our daily lives harried and rushed." pg 8.

The syndicate of the shadow is also promoted by language which demeans and diminishes targeted peoples amongst us.

I refer to the social/political/historical shadow of the US in parallel ways as the shadow is defined in humanistic psychol-ogy. In both scenarios, there is repressed resentment, projection of unwanted qualities onto a feared or rejected "other," compul-sive attachments and impulsive responses, and exploitative con-trol governed by the chaos, fear, and hatred shaped by our nation's practice with Dr. King's identified four catastrophes. The language of apartheid instigates the use of words and phrases that justify and reinforce negative perceptions and threatening action towards unwanted others. Examples that were in common use in the 1990s were the references to young Black men as "wolfpacks," and single Black mothers as "irresponsible and promiscuous."

745   When Thomas Paine expressed the thought that every generation must be free to act for itself, he was delivering a critique of inherited rights because one's position in a monarchy, as opposed to the inherent right to govern as self-evident in natural law. What we have seen since the post-World War II period is the rise of movements exercising citizenship in the spirit of Thomas Paine's words—from the freedom riders headed to the south to demand voting rights for Blacks, to young women occupying trees to prevent the overuse and diminishment of our forests, to the youth-led movements today such as the Dreamers, Black Lives Matter, March for Our Lives, and Teens Take Charge. By participating, raising their voice, and implementing change, they are successfully resisting and replacing relationships constructed with an understanding for the accepted place of "horizontal authority." In her book, Act Your Age: A Cultural Construction of Adolescence (Routledge Falmer, 2001), author Nancy Lasko defines "horizontal authority." She describes it as a toxic cocktail of superiority and authority, where adult leaders with official power dictate the terms for adolescent transition to adulthood. As Ms. Lasko elaborates: (The historical context stems from traditional leaders continuing their leadership from the roots of what was called The Great Chain of Being), where "the poetics of contagion justified a politics of exclusion and gave social sanction to the middle-class fixation with boundary order" (pp 3 and 10). Ms. Lasko validates Mr. Paine's call for the emergent generation to be validated and not violated.

746   When Thomas Paine expressed the thought that every generation must be free to act for itself, he was delivering a critique of inherited rights because one's position in a monarchy, as opposed to the inherent right to govern as self-evident in natural law. What we have seen since the post-World War II period is the rise of movements exercising citizenship in the spirit of Thomas Paine's words—from the freedom riders headed to the south to demand voting rights

for Blacks, to young women occupying trees to prevent the overuse and diminishment of our forests, to the youth-led movements today such as the Dreamers, Black Lives Matter, March for Our Lives, and Teens Take Charge. By participating, raising their voice, and implementing change, they are successfully resisting and replacing relationships constructed with an understanding for the accepted place of "horizontal authority." In her book, Act Your Age: A Cultural Construction of Adolescence (Routledge Falmer, 2001), author Nancy Lasko defines "horizontal authority." She describes it as a toxic cocktail of superiority and authority, where adult leaders with official power dictate the terms for adolescent transition to adult-hood. As Ms. Lasko elaborates: (The historical context stems from traditional leaders continuing their leadership from the roots of what was called The Great Chain of Being), where "the poetics of contagion justified a politics of exclusion and gave social sanction to the middle-class fixation with boundary order" (pp 3 and 10). Ms. Lasko validates Mr. Paine's call for the emergent generation to be validated and not violated.

747   Monsters in America by W. Scott Poole (Baylor University Press, 2011), Preface, p xiv.

748   Monsters in America by W. Scott Poole (Baylor University Press, 2011), Preface, p xiv.

749   Monsters in America Ibid, p 23.

750   Self-Evident, poem by Ani DiFranco, 2001 www.righteousbabe. com/ani_self-evident.html

751   Tattoos of the Heart by Gregory Boyle (Free Press, 2010), pg 190.

752   Tattoos of the Heart Ibid Back cover of the book.

753   Earth Island Journal, "Earth Island Reports—New Leaders Initiative," August 2020 pg 17.

754   Open Secrets of Rumi by John Moyne and Coleman Barks (Threshold Books, 1984), quatrain 91.

755   Hungry Ghosts: Close Encounters with Addiction by Dr. Gabor Mate, pg 18. Central Recovery Press 2011.

756   Hungry Ghosts Ibid pg 18.

757   See the book, America Dreamer: A Life of Henry A. Wallace by John C. Culver and John Hyde (W.W. Norton and Company, 2000) The first quote is on Page 328 and the second quote is on pg 342.

758   See the book, America Dreamer: A Life of Henry A. Wallace by John C. Culver and John Hyde (W.W. Norton and Company, 2000) The first quote is on Page 328 and the second quote is on pg 342.

759   See the book, the Cultural Creatives: How 50 Million People Are Changing the World by Paul H. Ray, Ph.D., and Sherry Ruth Anderson, Ph.D. (Harmony Books, 2000) pg 174.

760   See the book, the Cultural Creatives: How 50 Million People Are Changing the World by Paul H. Ray, Ph.D., and Sherry Ruth Anderson, Ph.D. (Harmony Books, 2000) pg 174.

761   See the book, the Cultural Creatives: How 50 Million People Are Changing the World by Paul H. Ray, Ph.D., and Sherry Ruth Anderson, Ph.D. (Harmony Books, 2000) pg 174.

762   See the book, Becoming Wise: An Inquiry Into the Mystery and Art of Living, by Krista Tippett (Penguin Books, 2016) pg 34.

763   See the book which is an anthology from the NY Times Learning Network. The title of the anthology is Student Voice: 100 Argument Essays by Teens on Issues That Matter to Them, which is compiled and edited by Katherine Schulten. (W.W. Norton and Company, 2020) I refer to an essay in the volume titled "A Generation Z'ers Take on the Social Media Age" by 17-year-old Elena Quartararo. pp 4 and 5.

764   The concepts of "emancipatory spirituality" and "spiritual progressive" are referred to by Rabbi Lerner in many of his public talks. An overview of these concepts is captured by Neale Donald Walsch in a chapter he wrote titled Millennial Possibilities. Find this chapter in a book edited by Rabbi Lerner titled Tikkun Reader: Twentieth Anniversary (Roman and Littlefield, 2007) Pages 343 – 345. There are many informative articles in this book. I mention one addition article called A Spirituality of Resistance by Roger S. Gottlieb. He notes the dual tasks, one internal, and one external, of finding a peaceful heart and protecting the earth. (Page 323) At the end of his article, Mr. Gottlieb notes: "If spirituality means, among other things, moving beyond my isolated ego… then resistance is that movement… I know that my kinship with the beings of this earth is essential to who I am; and that I will not allow them to be wantonly destroyed without some defiance." pg 332.

765   The concepts of "emancipatory spirituality" and "spiritual progressive" are referred to by Rabbi Lerner in many of his public talks. An overview of these concepts is captured by Neale Donald Walsch in a chapter he wrote titled Millennial Possibilities. Find this chapter in a book edited by Rabbi Lerner titled Tikkun Reader: Twentieth Anniversary (Roman and Littlefield, 2007) Pages 343 – 345. There are many informative articles in this book. I mention one addition article called A Spirituality of Resistance by Roger S. Gottlieb. He notes the dual tasks, one internal, and one external, of finding a peaceful heart and protecting the earth. (pg 323) At the end of his article, Mr. Gottlieb notes: "If spirituality means, among other things, moving beyond my isolated ego… then resistance is that movement… I know that my kinship with the beings of this earth is essential to who I am; and that I will not allow them to be wantonly destroyed without some defiance." pg 332.

766   The concepts of "emancipatory spirituality" and "spiritual progressive" are referred to by Rabbi Lerner in many of his public talks. An

overview of these concepts is captured by Neale Donald Walsch in a chapter he wrote titled Millennial Possibilities. Find this chapter in a book edited by Rabbi Lerner titled Tikkun Reader: Twentieth Anniversary (Roman and Littlefield, 2007) Pages 343 – 345. There are many informative articles in this book. I mention one addition article called A Spirituality of Resistance by Roger S. Gottlieb. He notes the dual tasks, one internal, and one external, of finding a peaceful heart and protecting the earth. (Page 323) At the end of his article, Mr. Gottlieb notes: "If spirituality means, among other things, moving beyond my isolated ego… then resistance is that movement… I know that my kinship with the beings of this earth is essential to who I am; and that I will not allow them to be wantonly destroyed without some defiance." pg 332.

767　These words are found in a recording by Steve Earle. See "Rich Man's War" in his recording The Revolution Starts Now, Artemis Records, 2004.

768　I bring up once again Jean Houston's reference to an old Greek concept called entelechy. One definition of this term is that entelechy is the inherent force which controls or directs all activities and development of a human being. Ms. Houston flushes out this concept on pp 32 – 36 of her book. The title of her book is The Wizard of Us: Transformational Lessons from Oz (Atria Books, 2012). I also hold to this concept, that when we are in touch and directed by our life purpose, we reach optimum human development and establish relationships which are aligned with our life path.

769　In our age of hyper individualism, Putnam and Feldstein look to the rebuilding and maintenance of community to restore collective mutually supportive ties amongst people. See the book: Better Together (Putnam, 2004) by Robert D. Putnam and Lewis M. Feldstein.

770   Professor West provides an overview of historical figures who were engaged in the practice of what he calls prophetic witness. See his book Democracy Matters (Penguin Books, 2004). pp 213 – 218.

771   To review the highlights of community building and issue identification activities launched by Teens Take Charge, see their webpage: https://www.facebook.com/teenstakechargenyc

772   See the Museum of the City of New York's companion book to its exhibit at the museum. The name of the book is Activist New York: A History of People, Protest and Politics by Steve H. Jaffe. (Washington Mew News: An Imprint of New York University Press, 2018). The Eric Foner quote appears on page 8.

773   Activist New York Ibid See the Weber quote in Foner's introduction to the book. pg 8.

774   See the book, Stories of the Courage to Teach: Honoring the Teacher's Heart edited by Sam M. Intrator (Jossey-Bass, 2002). I refer here to the chapter named "The Meaning of Life Assignment" by Robert Kunzman. The quote is on pg 89.

775   See the book, Sacred America, Sacred World by Stephen Dinan (Hampton Roads Publishing, 2016) In his book he distinguishes between the prior work of revolutionaries and the work of evolutionaries today who help us to transition to a new era constructively and peacefully.

776   See the book, Sacred America, Sacred World by Stephen Dinan (Hampton Roads Publishing, 2016) In his book he distinguishes between the prior work of revolutionaries and the work of evolutionaries today who help us to transition to a new era constructively and peacefully.

777   See the article on the Brower Youth Awards website at: www.broweryouthawards.org/winner/artemesio-romero-y-carver

778   See the Healthy Futures Texas website at: https://www.hf-tx.org/yac

779   See the NYC Participatory Voting website at: www.info@participa-
        torybudgeting.org

780   See the NYC Participatory Voting website at: www.info@participa-
        torybudgeting.org

781   See the Takoma Park website at: https://www.governing.com
See the Reddit website at: www.reddit.com

782   See the Takoma Park website at: https://www.governing.com
See the Reddit website at: www.reddit.com

783   See the Generation Citizen website at www.generationcitizen.com

784   See the website for the news outlet called the Hill: https://thehill.
        com/homenews/house/434115-pelosi

785   No Citizen Left Behind by Meira Levinson (Harvard University
        Press, 2012), pg 296.

BIBLIOGRAPHY AND NOTES:

INDUCTION

Apple, M. W., Educating *The Right Way: Markets, Standards, God, And Inequality* (2nd ed.). Routledge. 2013

> "Official knowledge" is the term used by dissenting historians and critics of tradition teaching history. It refers to the standardized use of concepts such as American exceptionalism, Manifest Destiny, the natural invisible hand of markets, and so forth.

Bly, R. *Iron John: A Book About Men* (1993 ed.). Harper Element.

> This is a work about finding the soul of being a man, using its inner guidance in order to find one's dignity and sense of personal purpose. I cite this here as I believe this principle applies to everyone simply because it is essential for human holistic development.

> Department of Youth & Community Development with NYU School of Health @ NY Law School. (n.d.). *Trauma Informed Intervention* [Conference session]. Trauma Informed Intervention, New York Law School.

Emerick, Y. *The Complete Idiot's Guide To Rumi Meditations*. Penguin. 2008

Emerson, R.W. 2010. *Self-Reliance, And Other Essays (Series One)*.

> Paul Hawken P. *Blessed Unrest: How The Largest Movement In The World Came Into Being, And Why No One Saw It Coming*. Penguin. 2007 Mr. Hawken describes the leadership and purposes of new

movements as being led by local leaders and spontaneously arising through collective effort at the local level.

Hopkins, R. *From What Is To What If: Unleashing The Power Of Imagination To Create The Future We Want*. Chelsea Green Publishing. 2019

International Council of Thirteen Indigenous Grandmothers. *Grandmother's Wisdom: Reverence For All Creation*. Ma Creative. 2019

Jung, C.G. *Memories, Dreams, Reflections*. Vintage. 2011

In this work, Mr. Jung emphasizes that we come into this world in a state of puzzlement, and that we also come in with a purpose, posed as a question, which, if we listen to it, leads us on a path true to our life purpose.

Loewen, J.W. *Teaching What Really Happened: How To Avoid The Tyranny Of Textbooks And Get Students Excited About Doing History*. Teachers College Press. 2009

Mr. Loewen critiques the repetitive use of cultural stories that have evolved in attempts to justify historical actions that today are seen as questionable, or which are used to manufacture a historical narrative to reinforce existing prejudice targeting marginalized peoples.

Lovric, M. *Women's Wicked Wisdom: From Mary Shelley To Courtney Love* (2004 ed.). Chicago Review Press. 2004

Maitri, S. *The Spiritual Dimension Of The Enneagram: Nine Faces Of The Soul* Putnam. 2000 edition

Ms. Maitri's work is an extension of a spiritual body of work introduced by Chilean psychiatrist Claudio Naranjo. She suggests that there is an architecture of souls, which fall into nine types of essences. Each has positive and problematic ramifications. The nine types are typically in the field of mediation and conflict resolution, which is good. But in their disposition for avoiding conflict, they can also neglect inner needs, which present to themselves as conflicting with their identities.

Marango, S., and Gordon, R. *Your Body And The Stars: The Zodiac As Your Wellness Guide.* Simon & Schuster. 2016

> The authors identify the heart as the center of an intelligence connected to one's inner purpose as well as to a larger community of souls.

Palmer, P.J. *Healing The Heart Of Democracy: The Courage To Create A Politics Worthy Of The Human Spirit.* John Wiley & Sons. 2014

> The point made here is the necessity for open community participation that is respectful of new people and cultures as opposed to closed communities ("self-protective enclaves," as attributed to Alexis de Tocqueville) in which people who feel threatened project an enemy status on to others.

Reeves, D.B. *Accountability For Learning: How Teachers And School Leaders Can Take Charge.* ASCD. 2004

> In this work the author critiques the standard use of worksheets, forced choice testing, and culturally standardized texts in shaping a one-size-fits-all understanding approach, which precludes the use of open-ended discussion, dialogue, and questioning unchallenged assumptions.

Shattuck, P.T., and Norgren, J. *Partial Justice.* Berg Publishers. 1991

Tick, E. 2012. *War And The Soul: Healing Our Nation's Veterans From Post-Traumatic Stress Disorder,* Quest Books. 2012 edition

> The author here discusses a person's confrontation with trauma and its aftereffects on the battlefield. At the height of the "war on drugs" in the 1980s and 1990s, the streets and even the homes of our families were like battlefields, given the high levels of gun violence and random episodes of violence faced by families and youth.

Tocqueville, A., and Goldhammer, A. *Democracy in America* (Library of America, 2004)

Unitarian Universalist Organizing Team. (n.d.). *Video conferencing, web conferencing, webinars, screen sharing.* (Conference session.) Zoom Video. https://zoom.us/webinar/tJUC.

Wilentz, S. *Chants Democratic: New York City And The Rise Of The American Working Class, 1788–1850.* Oxford University Press. 2004

Wilkinson, R., and Pickett, K. *The Spirit Level: Why Greater Equality Makes Societies Stronger* Bloomsbury Publishing USA. 2011 edition

The point I emphasize here is that in our culture, which promotes great focus on the individual responsibility for character flaws, we overlook the influence of social factors in shaping what has been previously identified as flaws in personality first.

BIBLIOGRAPHY AND NOTES:

FORWARD/BACKWARD
AND INSIDE OUT

Abrams, J. *The Shadow In America: Reclaiming The Soul Of A Nation*. Nataraj Pub. 2004

Agnes, M. *Webster's New World college dictionary*. Macmillan General Reference. 2000

Bucko, A., and Fox, M. *Occupy Spirituality: A Radical Vision For A New Generation*. North Atlantic Books. 2013

Cushman, K., and The students of What Kids Can Do. *Fires In The Mind: What Kids Can Tell Us About Motivation And Mastery*. John Wiley & Sons. 2012

Dewey, J. *Experience And Education*. Peter Smith Pub. 1983

Elworthy, S. *Pioneering The Possible: Awakened Leadership For A World That Works*. Sacred Activism. 2014

Fölsing, A. *Albert Einstein: A Biography*. Penguin Group USA. 1998

Freire, P. *Pedagogy Of The Oppressed*. Bloomsbury Press, 2000 (30th Anniversary edition)

Fullilove, M.T. *Urban Alchemy: Restoring Joy In America's Sorted-Out Cities*. NYU Press. 2013

Gilman, S.L., and Thomas, J.M. *Are Racists Crazy? How Prejudice, Racism, And Anti-Semitism Became Markers Of Insanity.* NYU Press. 2018

The authors document how early research and administration of the results of science studies based upon faulty models or misapplication of findings were often done in the early 1990s in order to reinforce and justify discriminatory policies against marginalized groups of people.

Goodman, P., and Blake, C. N. *Growing Up Absurd: Problems Of Youth In The Organized Society.* New York Review of Books. 2012

Gould, S.J. *The Mismeasure Of Man* (Revised and expanded ed.). W. W. Norton & Company. 2006

Mr. Gould's classic refutation of the racist tome promoted by the Bell Curve is a well-documented critique of how poorly constructed research or misinterpreted results can dovetail with belief systems in the United States, which dismiss, demean, and diminish whole categories of peoples.

Judith, A. *The Global Heart Awakens: Humanity's Rite Of Passage From The Love Of Power To The Power Of Love.* Red Wheel/Weiser. 2013

Kessler, S. *The Mysteries Sourcebook.* Crossroads School/Human Development Department. 1990

Kohn, A. *The Schools Our Children Deserve: Moving Beyond Traditional Classrooms And "Tougher Standards."* Houghton Mifflin Harcourt. 2000

The author documents that the average scores on SAT tests rise in correlation to a rise of family income among different socioeconomic categories.

Marango, S., and Gordon, R. *Your Body And The Stars: The Zodiac As Your Wellness Guide.* Simon & Schuster. 2016

Mead, M. *Culture And Commitment: A Study Of The Generation Gap.* American Museum of Natural History Special Members Edition. 1975 edition

Miller, A. *The Drama Of The Gifted Child: The Search For The True Self* (3rd ed.). Basic Books. 2008

Millman, D. *The Life You Were Born To Live: A Guide To Finding Your Life Purpose.* H J Kramer. 1993

Myss, C. *Anatomy Of The Spirit.* Random House. 2010

Palmer, P.J., and Linsey. *The Courage To Teach: Exploring The Inner Landscape Of A Teacher's Life.* Jossey-Bass. 1999

The authors speak about the need to welcome a student's soul into the classroom by being welcoming, attentive, respectful, and inclusive of viewpoints.

Phillips, C. *Six Questions Of Socrates: A Modern-Day Journey Of Discovery Through World Philosophy.* W.W. Norton & Company. 2011

The connection between individual development and wholeness was built into the web of governance by certain Native American tribes and is cited here as an element of virtue.

Robert Epstein. 2007, May/June. "Myth of the Teen Brain." *Scientific Mind.* 2007

Robert Epstein. 2007, April. "Myth of the Teen Brain." *Scientific Mind.* 2007

Roan, S. 1995, July 11. *Los Angeles Times.*

Sawyer, R.K., John-Steiner, V., Moran, S., Sternberg, R.J., Feldman, D.H., Gardner, H., Nakamura, J., and Csikszentmihalyi, M. 1996. *Creativity.* Harper/Perennial.

Siegel, D.J. *Mind: A Journey To The Heart Of Being Human* (Norton series on interpersonal neurobiology). W.W. Norton & Company. 2016

The point the author is making here is that there are positive attributes inherent to the adolescent period of life, which when kept alive by adults as their "inner adolescent" keep them vibrantly idealistic and creative.

Taket, A., Crisp, B.R., Graham, M., Hanna, L., Goldingay, S., and Wilson, L. 2 *Practising Social Inclusion*. Routledge. 2013

Wollstonecraft, M. 2012. *A Vindication Of The Rights Of Woman*. Courier Corporation.

BIBLIOGRAPHY AND NOTES:

INTRODUCTIONS

Abrams, J. 1994. *The Shadow In America: Reclaiming The Soul Of A Nation.* Nataraj Pub.

Agnes, M. 2000. *Webster's New World college dictionary.* Macmillan General Reference.

Bucko, A., and Fox, M. 2013. *Occupy Spirituality: A Radical Vision For A New Generation.* North Atlantic Books.

Cushman, K., and The students of What Kids Can Do. 2012. *Fires In The Mind: What Kids Can Tell Us About Motivation And Mastery.* John Wiley & Sons.

Dewey, J. 1983. *Experience And Education.* Peter Smith Pub.

Elworthy, S. 2014. *Pioneering The Possible: Awakened Leadership For A World That Works.* Sacred Activism.

Fölsing, A. 1998. *Albert Einstein: A Biography.* Penguin Group USA.

Freire, P. 1972. *Pedagogy Of The Oppressed.* Bloomsbury 2000 (30th Anniversary edition)

Fullilove, M.T. 2013. *Urban Alchemy: Restoring Joy In America's Sorted-Out Cities.* NYU Press.

Gilman, S. L., and Thomas, J.M. 2018. *Are Racists Crazy? How Prejudice, Racism, And Anti-Semitism Became Markers Of Insanity.* NYU Press.

The authors document how early research and administration of the results of science studies based upon faulty models or misapplication of findings were often done in the early 1990s to reinforce and justify discriminatory policies against marginalized groups of people.

Goodman, P., and Blake, C. N. *Growing Up Absurd: Problems Of Youth In The Organized Society*. Vintage Books (Random House) 1960

Gould, S.J. *The Mismeasure Of Man* (Revised and expanded ed.). W.W. Norton & Company. 2006

Mr. Gould's classic refutation of the racist tome promoted by the Bell Curve is a well-documented critique of how poorly constructed research or misinterpreted results can dovetail with belief systems in the United States, which dismiss, demean, and diminish whole categories of peoples.

Judith, A. 2013. *The Global Heart Awakens: Humanity's Rite Of Passage From The Love Of Power To The Power Of Love*. Red Wheel/Weiser.

Kessler, S. 1990. *The Mysteries Sourcebook*. Crossroads School/Human Development Department.

Kohn, A. 2000. *The Schools Our Children Deserve: Moving Beyond Traditional Classrooms And "Tougher Standards."* Houghton Mifflin Harcourt.

The author documents that the average scores on SAT tests rise in correlation to a rise of family income among different socioeconomic categories.

Marango, S., and Gordon, R. 2016. *Your Body And The Stars: The Zodiac As Your Wellness Guide*. Simon & Schuster.

Mead, M. 1970. *Culture And Commitment: A Study Of The Generation Gap* (1975 ed.). American Museum of Natural History Special Members Edition.

Miller, A. 2008. *The Drama Of The Gifted Child: The Search For The True Self* (3rd ed.). Basic Books.

Millman, D. 1993. *The Life You Were Born To Live: A Guide To Finding Your Life Purpose*. H J Kramer.

Myss, C. 2010. *Anatomy Of The Spirit*. Random House.

Palmer, P.J., and Linsey. 1999. *The Courage To Teach: Exploring The Inner Landscape Of A Teacher's Life*. Jossey-Bass.

> The authors speak about the need to welcome a student's soul into the classroom, by being welcoming, attentive, respectful, and inclusive of viewpoints.

Phillips, C. 2011. *Six Questions Of Socrates: A Modern-Day Journey Of Discovery Through World Philosophy*. W. W. Norton & Company.

> The connection between individual development and wholeness was built into the web of governance by certain Native American tribes and is cited here as an element of virtue.

Robert Epstein. 2007, May/June. "Myth of the Teen Brain." *Scientific Mind*.

Robert Epstein. 2007, April. "Myth of the Teen Brain." *Scientific Mind*.

Roan, S. 1995, July 11. *Los Angeles Times*.

Sawyer, R. K., John-Steiner, V., Moran, S., Sternberg, R. J., Feldman, D. H., Gardner, H., Nakamura, J., and Csikszentmihalyi, M. *Creativity*. Harper/Perennial. 2006iegel, D. J. 2016. *Mind: A Journey To The Heart Of Being Human* (Norton series on interpersonal neurobiology). W.W. Norton & Company.

> The point the author is making here is that there are positive attributes inherent to the adolescent period of life, which, when kept alive by adults as their "inner adolescent," keep them vibrantly idealistic and creative.

Taket, A., Crisp, B.R., Graham, M., Hanna, L., Goldingay, S., and Wilson, L. 2013. *Practising Social Inclusion*. Routledge.

Wollstonecraft, M. 2012. *A Vindication Of The Rights Of Woman*. Courier Corporation.

BIBLIOGRAPHY AND NOTES:
ANECDOTES ARISING

Bailyn, B. 2007. *To Begin The World Anew: The Genius And Ambiguities Of The American Founders*. Vintage.

Barber, B.R. 1998. *A Place For Us: How To Make Society Civil And Democracy Strong*. Hill and Wang.

Bayoumi, M. 2009. *How Does It Feel To Be A Problem? Being Young And Arab In America*. Penguin.

Bergman, C., and Montgomery, N. 2017. *Joyful Militancy: Building Thriving Resistance In Toxic Times*. AK Press.

Bly, R. 2013. *Iron John*. Random House.

Boggs, G.L., and Kurashige, S. 2012. *The Next American Revolution: Sustainable Activism For The Twenty-First Century*. University of California Press.

Bucko, A., and Fox, M. 2013. *Occupy Spirituality: A Radical Vision For A New Generation*. North Atlantic Books.

Campbell, J. 2003. *The Hero's Journey: Joseph Campbell On His Life And Work*. New World Library.

Chardin, P.T. 1970. *The Phenomenon Of Man; With An Introduction By Sir Julian Huxley*. Harper Collins.

Elshtain, J.B. 1993. *Democracy On Trial*. House of Anansi.

Elshtain, J.B., and Elshtain, J. 2002. *Jane Addams And The Dream Of American Democracy*. Basic Books.

Elworthy, S. 2014. *Pioneering The Possible: Awakened Leadership For A World That Works*. Sacred Activism.

Emerick, Y. 2008. *The Complete Idiot's Guide To Rumi Meditations*. Penguin.

Ferguson, M. 2005. *Aquarius Now: Radical Common Sense And Reclaiming Our Personal Sovereignty*. Weiser Books.

Follett, M.P. 1924. *Creative Experience*. Martino Publishing 2013

Freire, P. 2017. *Pedagogy Of The Oppressed*. Penguin Classics.

Fuller, R. W. 2004. *Somebodies And Nobodies: Overcoming The Abuse Of Rank*. New Society Pub.

Fullilove, M.T. 2013. *Urban Alchemy: Restoring Joy In America's Sorted-Out Cities*. NYU Press.

Goodchild, C. 2015. *The Naked Voice: Transforming Your Life Through The Power Of Sound*. North Atlantic Books.

Goodman, P., and Blake, C.N. 2012. *Growing Up Absurd: Problems Of Youth In The Organized Society*. New York Review of Books.

Gould, S.J. 2006. *The Mismeasure Of Man* (Revised and expanded ed.). W.W. Norton & Company.

Harvey, A. 2012. *Radical Passion: Sacred Love And Wisdom In Action*. North Atlantic Books.

Hawken, P. *Blessed Unrest: How The Largest Movement In The World Came Into Being, And Why No One Saw It Coming*. Penguin. 2007

Heschel, A.J. 2001. *The Prophets*. HarperCollins.

Hillman, J. 2013. *The Essential James Hillman: A Blue Fire*. Routledge.

Hoagland, M.B., and Dodson, B. 1999. *Patterns: Sixteen Things You Should Know About Life*. Jones & Bartlett Pub.

Hodge, D.W. 2010. *The Soul Of Hip Hop: Rims, Tombs And A Cultural Theology*. InterVarsity Press.

Hopkins, R. 2019. *From What Is To What If: Unleashing The Power Of Imagination To Create The Future We Want*. Chelsea Green Publishing.

Houston, J. 2016. *The Wizard Of Us: Transformational Lessons From Oz*. Simon & Schuster.

Judith, A. 2013. *The Global Heart Awakens: Humanity's Rite Of Passage From The Love Of Power To The Power Of Love*. Red Wheel/Weiser.

Jung, C.G. 1995. *Memories, Dreams, Reflections*. Harper Perennial.

Kenower, W. 2017. *Fearless Writing: How To Create Boldly And Write With Confidence*. Penguin.

Korten, D.C. 2007. *The Great Turning: From Empire To Earth Community*. Berrett-Koehler Publishers.

Kripal, J. J. 2011. *Mutants And Mystics: Science Fiction, Superhero Comics, And The Paranormal*. University of Chicago Press.

Lerner, M. 1994. *Jewish Renewal: A Path To Healing And Transformation*. Putnam Adult.

Levy, P.B. 1999. *100 Key Documents In American Democracy*. Praeger Pub Text.

Loeb, P. 2014. *The Impossible Will Take A Little While: A Citizen's Guide To Hope In A Time Of Fear*. Basic Books.

Loewen, J. W. 2008. *Lies My Teacher Told Me: Everything Your American History Textbook Got Wrong*. The New Press.

Loewen, J.W. 2009. *Teaching What Really Happened: How To Avoid The Tyranny Of Textbooks And Get Students Excited About Doing History*. Teachers College Press.

Lorde, A. 2012. *Sister Outsider: Essays And Speeches*. Crossing Press. Audre Lorde discusses the need to discard the tools that the masters used in order to oppress others, as these are inappropriate for those seeking to undo oppression.

Males, M.A. *Framing Youth: Ten Myths About The Next Generation*. Common Courage Press 1999

Malidoma Patrice Some, M. P. 2020. *Ritual: Power, Healing And Community*. Lulu Press.

May, R. 2007. *Love And Will*. W.W. Norton & Company.

Meacham, J. 2018. *The Soul Of America: The Battle For Our Better Angels*. Random House.

Millman, D. 1993. *The Life You Were Born To Live: A Guide To Finding Your Life Purpose*. H J Kramer.

Moore, T. *Care Of The Soul: Guide For Cultivating Depth And The Sacred*. HarperCollins. 2009

Myss, C. 2013. *Sacred Contracts: Awakening Your Divine Potential*. Harmony.

Needleman, J. 2003. *The American Soul: Rediscovering The Wisdom Of The Founders*. Penguin.

Neil Postman. 2011. *The End Of Education: Redefining The Value Of School*. Vintage.

Paine, T., and Foner, P.S. 1974. *The Complete Writings Of Thomas Paine, Collected And Edited By Philip S. Foner, Ph.D., With Biographical Essay, And Notes And Introductions Presenting The Historical Background Of Paine's Writings, Complete In Two Volumes* (2nd ed.). Citadel Press.

Palmer, P.J. 2010. *To Know As We Are Known: A Spirituality Of Education*. HarperCollins.

Payne, C.M., Strickland, C.S., Ayers, W., and Quinn, T. (2008). *Teach Freedom: Education For Liberation In The African American Tradition*.

Plotkin, B. 2010. *Nature And The Human Soul: Cultivating Wholeness And Community In A Fragmented World*. New World Library.

Plotkin, B. 2013. *Wild Mind: A Field Guide To The Human Psyche*. New World Library.

The Icarus Project: *Madness And Oppression: Paths To Personal Transformation And Collective Liberation*. Icarus Project Press 2015

Raboteau, A.J. 2018. *American Prophets: Seven Religious Radicals And Their Struggle For Social And Political Justice*. Princeton University Press.

Raphael, R. 2010. *Founding Myths: Stories That Hide Our Patriotic Past*. The New Press 2004

Roszak, T. 2009. *The Making Of An Elder Culture: Reflections On The Future Of America's Most Audacious Generation*. New Society Publishers.

Rushdie, S. 2012. *The Wizard Of Oz*. British Film Institute.

Schacker, M. 2012. *Global Awakening: New Science And The 21st-Century Enlightenment*. Simon & Schuster.

Schlesinger, A.B. 2009. *The Death Of "Why?": The Decline Of Questioning And The Future Of Democracy*. Berrett-Koehler Publishers.

Siegel, D.J. 2016. *Mind: A Journey To The Heart Of Being Human* (Norton series on interpersonal neurobiology). W.W. Norton & Company.

Smith, S.J. 2011. *The Young Activist's Guide To Building A Green Movement And Changing The World*. Random House Digital.

Snyder, R.W. 2014. *Crossing Broadway: Washington Heights And The Promise Of New York City*. Cornell University Press.

Sölle, D. 2001. *The Silent Cry: Mysticism And Resistance*. Fortress Press.

Stauffer, J. 2015. *Ethical Loneliness: The Injustice Of Not Being Heard*. Columbia University Press.

Stewart, M. 2014. *Nature's God: The Heretical Origins Of The American Republic*. W.W. Norton & Company.

Stout, J. 2012. *Blessed Are The Organized: Grassroots Democracy In America*. Princeton University Press.

Thompson, W.I. 1990. *At The Edge Of History And Passages About Earth: A Double Book*. Steiner Books.

Thurman, H. 2012. *Jesus And The Disinherited*. Beacon Press.

Toledo, C. D. 2008. *Coming Of Age At The End Of History*. Soft Skull Press 2008

Wallis, J. 1997. *Who Speaks For God? An Alternative To The Religious Right—A New Politics Of Compassion, Community, And Civility*. Delta.

Wilber, K. 2011. *The Marriage Of Sense And Soul: Integrating Science And Religion*. Random House.

Wilentz, S. 2004. *Chants Democratic: New York City And The Rise Of The American Working Class, 1788–1850*. Oxford University Press.

Wolf, L.S., and Gage, N. 2017. *Soul Whispering: The Art Of Awakening Shamanic Consciousness*. Simon & Schuster.

Wollstonecraft, M. 2014. *A Vindication Of The Rights Of Woman*. Yale University Press.

Yong, E. 2016. *I Contain Multitudes: The Microbes Within Us And A Grander View Of Life*. HarperCollins.

RESOURCES:

TEEN LEADERSHIP PROGRAMS AND SOURCES OF SUPPORT FOR TEENS

American Friends Service Committee: https://www.afsc.org

Center for Information and Research on Civic Learning and Engagement (CIRCLE) https://circletufts.org

Coalition for Asian-American Children and Families Asian Student Advocacy Project! cacf@cacf.org

Community Change Action https://communitychange.org

CUNY School for Professional Studies Advanced Certificate and master's degree in youth studies information@sps.cuny.edu

Department of Youth and Community Development https://www1.nyc.gov/site/dycd

Earth Island Institute https://www.earthisland.org

Generation Citizen Action Civics and Vote 16! https://generationcitizen.org

Global Kids https://globalkids.org

Hampton Youth Commission https://hampton.gov/2314

Harvard Graduate School of Education https://www.harvard.edu

National Council of Social Studies The C-3 Framework https://www.socialstudies.org

Petra Foundation www.petrafoundation.org

Police Athletic League, Inc. www.palnyc.org

Rethinking Schools www.rethinkingschools.org

Rockaway Youth Task Force http://rytf.org

San Francisco Youth Commission www.sfgov.org/yc

Spark Action Snapshots http://sparkaction.org

Team Dreamers teamdreamersuptown@gmail.com

Teens for Food Justice http://teensforfoodjustice.org

Teens Take Charge https://www.teenstakecharge.com/students

The Free Child Project https://freechild.org

UNHCR The Global Refugee's Youth Consultation Toolkit https://www.unhcr.org/youth-html

United Neighborhood Houses Summer Youth Jobs Program jfalcone@unhny.org

Ya Ya Network https://yayanetwork.org

YES! Magazine www.yesmagazine.org

YMCA of Greater New York Teens Take Charge Curriculum https://www.ymca.net

Elected Officials

Manhattan Borough President Gale Brewer gbrewer@manhattanbp.nyc.gov

Manhattan Borough President-elect Mark Levine mlevine@manhattanbp.nyc.gov

New York State Senator Brad Hoylman (lead sponsor of legislation (S 366) to lower the voting age in New York State to age 16. https://www.nysenate/legislation/bills/2021/S366

IN SUPPORT OF GETTING 16- AND 17-YEAR-OLD TEENS ON COMMUNITY BOARDS. SUBMITTED TO THE NY CITY COUNCIL IN JUNE 2014.

Ancestral Ally: Thomas Paine "Patriotic Presence" in his Age of Reason pamphlet

> "Every age and generation must be free to act for itself...the vanity and presumption of governing from beyond the grave is the most ridiculous and insolent of all tyrannies. Man has no property in man, neither has any generation on the generations which are to follow it. It is the living, and not the dead, that are to be accommodated."

> "At a time when we are struggling to combat youth disengagement and seeking to find programs that give our youth a place to grow...it would be unfortunate for us to turn away from those who want to serve their communities in a more official capacity...we urge the state legislature to enact this important bill and allow us to broaden the perspectives of our Community Boards and encourage civic involvement by our youth."